ARCTIC MIRRORS

ARCTIC MIRRORS

RUSSIA AND THE SMALL PEOPLES OF THE NORTH

Yuri Slezkine

CORNELL UNIVERSITY PRESS

ITHACA AND LONDON

First published 1994 by Cornell University Press.

Printed in the United States of America

⊗ The paper in this book meets the minimum requirements of the
American National Standard for Information Sciences—Permanence
of Paper for Printed Library Materials, ANSI Z39.48-1984.

Library of Congress Cataloging-in-Publication Data

Slezkine, Yuri, 1956–
    Arctic mirrors : Russia and the small peoples of the North / Yuri
Slezkine.
        p.   cm.
    Includes bibliographical references (p.   ) and index.
    ISBN 0-8014-2976-5 (alk. paper)
    1. Arctic peoples.   2. Arctic peoples—Russia, Northern—
History—20th century.   5. Russia, Northern—Ethnic relations.
    6. Russia, Northern—Politics and government.   I. Title.
GN673.S64   1994
947′.004971—dc20   93-48466

TO MY PARENTS

Resemblances are the shadows of differences. Different people see different similarities and similar differences.
—Vladimir Nabokov

Contents

Preface

Over the last one thousand years, East Slavic agrarian society with its increasingly elaborate social and legal institutions has expanded to include and partially absorb numerous hunting and pastoral groups. No longer "foreigners" but still alien insofar as they remained "unsettled," these peoples have repeatedly posed a challenge to government officials, Orthodox missionaries, and assorted intellectuals seeking to define Russianness and otherness to both Russians and others. The two flanks of the eastern frontier as delineated by the eventual victors have had very different fates: whereas the steppe nomads of the south have provided the Russian imagination, both popular and official, with some of its most enduring myths, the foragers of the "northern borderlands" have rarely threatened the settled/Christian/ civilized world and have remained invisible in most versions of its past. Yet of all the non-Russian subjects of the Russian state and of all the non-Russian objects of Russian concern, it is the circumpolar hunters and gatherers who have proved the most difficult to reform and conceptualize. From the birth of the irrational savage in the early eighteenth century to the repeated resurrection of the natural man at the end of the twentieth, they have been the most consistent antipodes of whatever it meant to be Russian. Seen as an extreme case of backwardness-as-beastliness or backwardness-as-innocence, they have provided a remote but crucial point of reference for speculations on human and Russian identity, while at the same time serving as a convenient testing ground for policies and images that grew out of those speculations. This book is a history of that relationship, a story of Russia's confrontation with its remotest "living ancestors," a study of the place of the "small peoples" in the Russian empire and in the Russian mind.

This approach has two important implications. First, both the empire and the mind discussed here are indeed Russian, and this means that I will present the native northerners indirectly through the eyes of the Russian protagonists. Second, the book's main focus is on the interaction of policies and perceptions (the empire and the mind), and this means that most of these protagonists are literate outsiders who had some claim to the "public" or bureaucratic ear. "Indirect" does not necessarily mean insular, however. A study of self's images of the other presupposes the existence of the other's images of self (in both senses) and allows for the possibility of a reciprocal—albeit unequal—relationship. I assume, in other words, that Russian "Hyperboreanism" may have been shaped, modified, and circumscribed by real-life northerners, both Russian and non-Russian.

Finally, the story that follows is based on the hypothesis that cross-cultural encounters cannot be fully described in terms of domination, that colonial representations cannot be wholly reduced to the "gross political fact" of colonialism; that there are meaningful differences between various colonial voices, and that it really matters to everyone concerned (including historians) whether a hunting band is to be "protected" or "developed," and whether one enters a tundra encampment expecting a demand for alcohol or an interest in world revolution. All the images traced in this book are in some ways informed by Russia's imperial ascendancy in northern Eurasia, but insofar as these images reflect a reality other than their own, it is important to distinguish among them and to explore their relationships with one another as well as with the world they confront, distort, and represent.

Portions of Chapter 7 have been published in *Current Anthropology* 32, no. 4 (August–October 1991): 476–84, © by the Wenner-Gren Foundation for Anthropological Research, all rights reserved; and in *Slavic Review* 51, no. 1 (Spring 1992): 52–76. I am grateful to the University of Chicago Press and the American Association for the Advancement of Slavic Studies for permission to reproduce them here.

I also thank the Social Science Research Council's Joint Committee on Soviet Studies, the Kennan Institute for Advanced Russian Studies,

Wake Forest University, and the University of Texas at Austin for financial support; Sheila Fitzpatrick, for generous help on countless occasions; Sidney Monas, for constant guidance; Caroline Boyd and Robert Fernea, for early encouragement; Marjorie Balzer, Bruce Grant, Igor Krupnik, Johanna Nichols, Aleksandr Pika, Nicholas V. Riasanovsky, Peter Rutland, and Reggie Zelnik, for useful suggestions; Kevin Doak, Michael Hughes, Alan Williams, the University of Chicago Human Sciences Workshop, and the Berkeley Colloquium on Theory and Method in Comparative Studies, for stimulating discussions; Konstantin Gurevich, Sarah Hepler, Brian Kassof, Molly Molloy, Patricia Polansky, Allan Urbanic, and the University of Illinois Slavic Reference Service, for bibliographic assistance; Michael Younger, for computer expertise; and Lisa Little, for all of the above. Whatever errors remain in the text are entirely her fault.

YURI SLEZKINE

Berkeley, California

Sources and
Abbreviations

Sources cited as "unpublished" in notes and bibliography are materials provided to me by their authors or by other persons who cooperated in my research. All such papers are in my possession.

AA	American Anthropologist
AI	Akty istoricheskie
ArA	Arctic Anthropology
DAI	Dopolneniia k aktam istoricheskim
E	Etnografiia
HRAF	Human Relations Area File
IG	Izvestiia GAIMK
IM	Istorik-marksist
IRGO	Imperatorskoe russkoe geograficheskoe obshchestvo
IV	Istoricheskii viestnik
MS	Morskoi sbornik
OPS	Okhotnik i pushnik Sibiri
ORS	Okhotnik i rybak Sibiri
OS	Okhotnik Sibiri
P	Pedologiia
PB	Pravoslavnyi blagoviestnik
PN	Prosveshchenie natsional'nostei
PS	Partiinoe stroitel'stvo
PSI	Pamiatniki sibirskoi istorii
PSRL	Polnoe sobranie russkikh letopisei, 1962–
PSZ	Polnoe sobranie zakonov Rossiiskoi imperii
RA	Russkii arkhiv
RIB	Russkaia istoricheskaia biblioteka
RN	Revoliutsiia i natsional'nosti
RV	Russkii viestnik

SA	Sovetskaia (Severnaia) Aziia
SAr	Sovetskaia Arktika
SE	Sovetskaia etnografiia
SEER	Slavonic and East European Review
SO	Sibirskie ogni
SP	Severnye prostory
SR	Slavic Review
SS	Sovetskii sever
SSb	Sibirskii sbornik
TsGAOR	Tsentral'nyi gosudarstvennyi arkhiv Oktiabr'skoi revoliutsii, Moscow, Russia
TT	Taiga i tundra
VK	Voprosy kolonizatsii
ZhMNP	Zhurnal Ministerstva narodnogo prosveshcheniia
ZhN	Zhizn' natsional'nostei
ZhS	Zhivaia starina

Languages of Northern Eurasia
in the Early Seventeenth Century

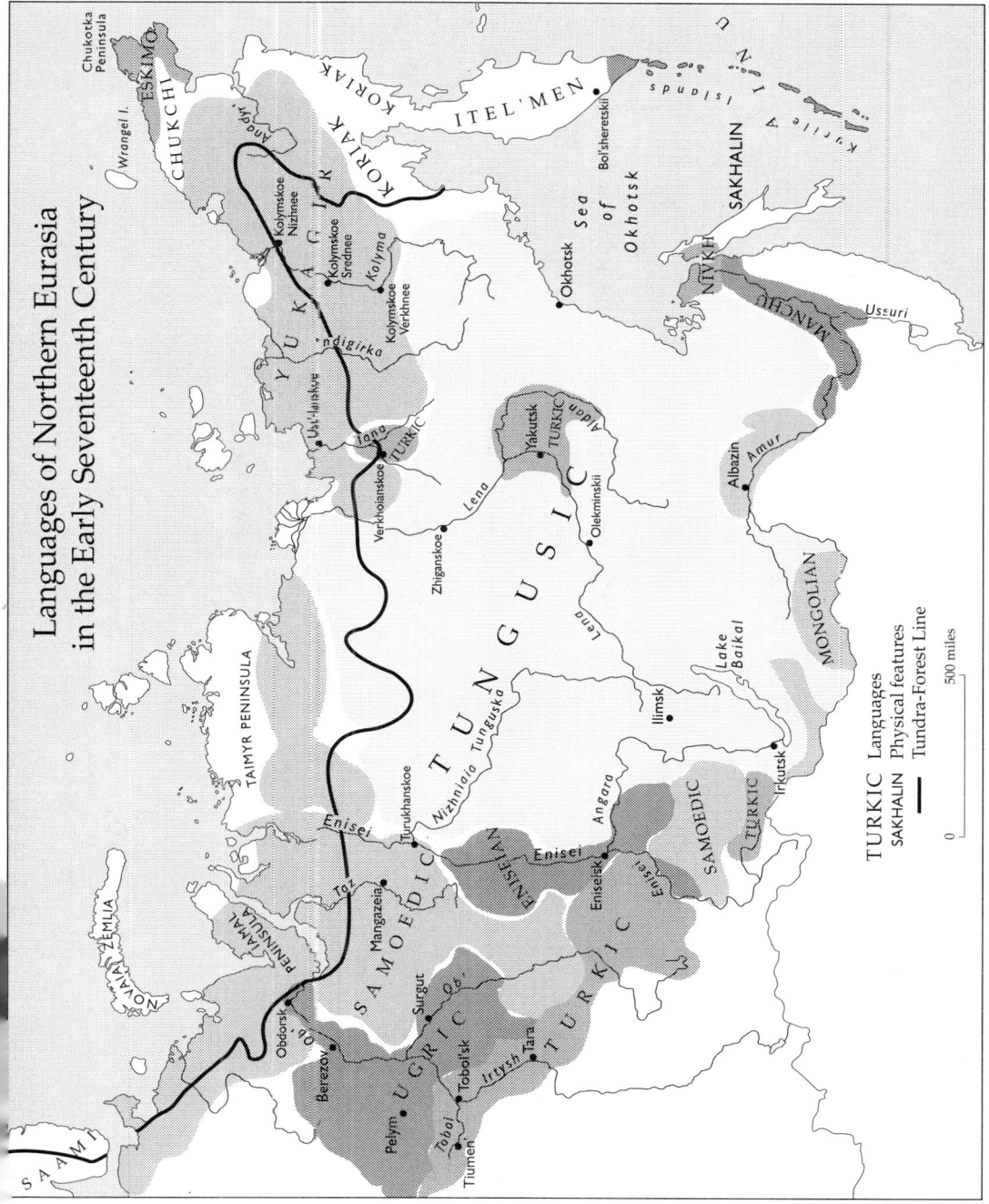

ESKIMO

Chukotka Peninsula

CHUKCHI

Wrangel I.

Anadyr

KORIAK

KORIAK

ITEL'MEN

Kurile Islands

Bol'sheretskii

SAKHALIN

Sea of Okhotsk

Okhotsk

NIVKH

MANCHU

Ussuri

Y U K A G I R

Kolymskoe Nizhnee

Kolymskoe Srednee

Kolyma

Kolymskoe Verkhnee

Indigirka

Ust'-Ianskoe

Iana

Verkhoianskoe

TURKIC

Yakutsk

TURKIC

Aldan

Albazin

Amur

Zhiganskoe

Lena

Olekminskii

TAIMYR PENINSULA

T U N G U S I C

Lake Baikal

Lena

Ilimsk

Nizhniaia Tunguska

Enisei

Turukhanskoe

ENISEIAN

Enisei

Angara

Irkutsk

Eniseisk

Enisei

SAMOEDIC

TURKIC

Toz

Mangazeia

S A M O E D I C

IAMAL PENINSULA

NOVAIA ZEMLIA

Obdorsk

Ob

Berezov

Surgut

U G R I C

Ob

Pelym

Tobol

Tobol'sk

Irtysh

Tara

T U R K I C

Tiumen

Tura

SAAMI

TURKIC Languages
SAKHALIN Physical features
—————— Tundra-Forest Line

MONGOLIAN

500 miles

0

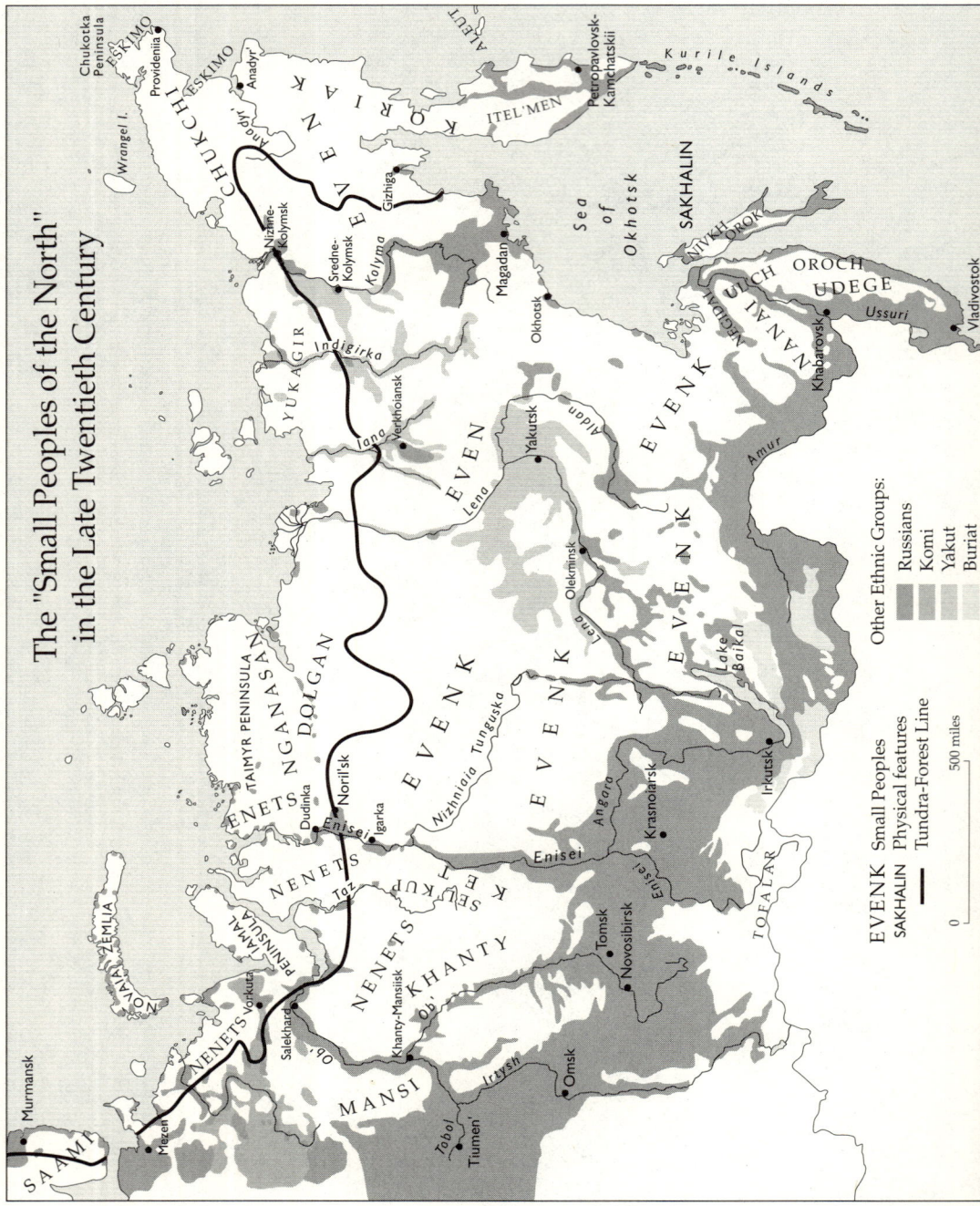

The "Small Peoples of the North" in the Late Twentieth Century

ARCTIC MIRRORS

The Small Peoples
of the North

In Russia, the "peoples of the north," "small peoples (of the north)," or "indigenous northerners" usually include twenty-six ethnic groups whose traditional occupations are hunting, trapping, fishing, and reindeer herding. They are the Saami (Lapps), Khanty (Ostiak), Mansi (Vogul), Nenets (Samoed, Iurak), Enets (Enisei Samoed), Sel'kup (Ostiako-Samoed), Nganasan (Tavgi Samoed), Dolgan, Ket (Enisei Ostiak), Evenk (Tungus), Even (Lamut), Yukagir, Chuvan, Chukchi, Koriak, Itel'men (Kamchadal), Eskimo, Aleut, Nivkh (Giliak), Negidal, Nanai (Gol'd), Ul'ch (Mangun), Oroch, Orok, Udege (Tazy), and Tofalar (Karagas).[1]

When the current classification was established in the 1920s, the "national affiliations" of the newly defined small peoples were determined by government agents on the basis of tradition, political exigencies, and contemporary linguistic and ethnographic data. None of these criteria was fully articulated or consistently applied, but the imperial practice of placing the circumpolar hunters and gatherers in a separate category was never questioned.[2] Whether they were characterized as "wanderers and foragers who move from one place to another," "primitive tribes," "native peoples of the northern borderlands," or "small peoples of the north," they were always seen as distinct from

---

[1] All names are Library of Congress transliterations of the contemporary Russian singular forms, with the exception of Chukchi, "Siberian Eskimo," Yukagir, and Yakut, for whom the traditional English names have been used (the most common old names are given in parentheses). For the earlier periods, when many of today's groups did not exist as such, I use broader geographic, economic, and linguistic descriptors or contemporary administrative designations.

[2] Reindeer breeders, as opposed to horse and cattle pastoralists, are invariably included in the hunter-gatherer, and therefore "small," category.

their more "developed" neighbors.[3] The Komi (Zyrian), the Sakha (Ya-kut), and the Russian "old settlers" might be both circumpolar and "indigenous" in strictly geographical terms, but according to the Russian scholars and officials who formulated and enforced such classifications, their "traditional" economies were not exclusively associated with foraging, their cultures were not fully associated with "tradition," and hence their societies did not always qualify as primitive, traditional, small, native, or indeed indigenous and circumpolar.[4]

Linguistically, the hunter-gatherers of northern Eurasia belong to the Uralic (Finno-Ugric and Samoedic) and Altaic (Turkic and Tungusic) families, as well as to smaller groupings usually subsumed under the nongenetic "Paleoasiatic" category.[5] The Saami of the Kola Peninsula speak a Finnic language (closest to Balto-Finnic but usually described as a separate branch) and are related to their namesakes in northern Scandinavia, whereas the Khanty and Mansi from the lower Ob' and northern Urals share the Ugrian subgroup with the Hungarians (Mansi is a cognate of Magyar.) The distant cousin of Finno-Ugric is Samoed, which is believed to have split off from Proto–Uralic around the fourth millennium B.C. Today's Samoed speakers include the Nenets, Enets, and Nganasan, who live along the Arctic coast between the Mezen' and the Khatanga, and the Sel'kup, who inhabit the Tym and the upper Taz. At the time of the Russian conquest, Samoedic languages were also spoken in the Saian area by the Kamasin, Mator, Koibal, and other now-extinct groups.

The Tungusic languages are spoken all over northern Asia. The Tungus proper (today's Evenk, Even, and Negidal) are widely dispersed throughout Siberia east of the Ob'-Irtysh watershed, whereas on the lower Amur and on Sakhalin the Nanai, Ul'ch, Oroch, Orok, and Udege

---

[3] See, for example, "Ustav ob upravlenii inorodtsev (1822)," in PSZ, vol. 38, no. 29.126, sec. 1; V. G. Bogoraz(-Tan), "O pervobytnykh plemenakh," ZhN, no. 1 (1922); and "Vremennoe polozhenie ob upravlenii tuzemnykh narodnostei i plemen Severnykh okrain RSFSR," SA, no. 2 (1927): 85–91.

[4] All "native northerners" except for certain Nenets groups and the Saami live in Asia, and are therefore "native Siberians." Not all native Siberians are either "small" or northern, however.

[5] Altaic is not universally accepted as a genetic family. Besides Turkic and Tungusic, it includes the Mongolian languages, which are not spoken in the circumpolar zone. For a general introduction to the languages of Northern Eurasia, see Bernard Comry, The Languages of the Soviet Union (Cambridge, 1981); Michael E. Krauss, "Many Tongues—Ancient Tales," in Crossroads of Continents: Cultures of Siberia and Alaska, ed. William W. Fitzhugh and Aron Crowell (Washington, D.C., 1988), pp. 145–50; N. A. Baskakov, Vvedenie v izuchenie tiurkskikh iazykov (Moscow, 1969); Peter Hajdu, Finno-Ugrian Languages and Peoples (London, 1975) and The Samoed Peoples and Languages

represent the closely related Manchu subgroup, which extends south of the Amur to include Solon, Juchen, and Manchu proper. Of the Turkic speakers, the Taimyr Dolgan are the descendants of four Tungus clans that adopted a Yakut dialect during the eighteenth century, and the Tofalar (Tofa) are usually distinguished from the Tuva pastoralists on cultural rather than linguistic grounds.

The speakers of the Siberian languages that predate Uralic and Altaic are known as Paleoasiatics or Paleosiberians. They include the Yukagir, Chukchi, Koriak, and Eskimo from the northeastern corner of the Asiatic mainland; the Aleut, transported from Atka and Attu to the Commander Islands in 1825 or 1826; the Kamchatka Itel'men; the Nivkh from the lower Amur and Sakhalin; and the Eniseians, who in the seventeenth century lived on the upper Enisei above the Elogui and of whom only the northernmost group, the Ket, have survived into the twentieth century.

Chukchi, Koriak, and Itel'men are genetically related members of the Chukotko-Kamchatkan family (with Chukchi and Koriak very close to one another). Eskimo and Aleut are representatives of a large family found mostly outside the Russian sphere of influence; Yukagir has been inconclusively linked to the Uralic languages; Nivkh is not clearly related to any known family; and Ket (Eniseian) is a linguistic isolate both genetically and typologically.

The area inhabited by the small peoples is divided into two principal ecozones, the Arctic tundra and the subarctic taiga. The tundra runs along the Arctic Ocean and is characterized by sparse ground cover of shrubs, lichens, and mosses and a low animal population density. The taiga consists of coniferous boreal forest dominated by pine, larch, and spruce. The border between the two is an important ecological and cultural divide known as the tree line or the "edge of the forest." Permafrost is continuous in the tundra and sporadic in the taiga. In addition to retarding the growth of vegetation, these layers of perennially frozen soil prevent the drainage of meltwater, in which enormous quantities of mosquitoes breed every summer.[6]

Modes of human subsistence vary according to the environment.[7]

(Bloomington, Ind., 1963), and V. Vs. Ivanov, V. N. Toporov, and B. A. Uspenskii, eds., *Ketskii sbornik* (Moscow, 1969), vol. 1 *(Lingvistika)*.

[6] Moira Dunbar, "The Arctic Setting," in *The Arctic Frontier*, ed. R. St. J. Macdonald (Toronto, 1966), pp. 3–25; Nelson H.H. Graburn and B. Stephen Strong, *Circumpolar Peoples: An Anthropological Perspective* (Pacific Palisades, Calif., 1973), pp. 1–4.

[7] For an introduction to circumpolar modes of subsistence, see Graburn and Strong, *Circumpolar Peoples*; Tim Ingold, *Hunters, Pastoralists, and Ranchers: Reindeer Econo-*

In the tundra the only mammal capable of supporting large predatory populations is the reindeer (known in North America as the caribou), and it is around reindeer—as prey and property—that most of the traditional economic activity of the Arctic is centered. At the time of the mass Russian invasion tundra populations tended to combine hunting and pastoralism. The reindeer wintered at the edge of the forest or in protected river valleys, and in the summer headed for the seashore or mountains to escape the gadflies and mosquitoes; humans followed their own animals or tried to intercept the migrating wild herds at river crossings. In the eighteenth century, as wild reindeer populations diminished, pastoralism became the prevalent form of inland tundra economy, and the majority of the Nenets, tundra Chukchi, Even, and tundra Koriak became full-time herders. The main economic unit was the camp, which usually consisted of several nuclear families, their dependents (including invalids, widows, and orphans from less successful camps), and the so-called assistants, who tended to be ruined herd masters or young men at the beginning of their herd-building careers. All animals were privately owned, and individual herders or households could attach themselves to other camps or start their own, always in pursuit of the "reindeer man's" overriding economic goal, the maximization of the herd.[8]

Another important source of subsistence was the sea, and in many coastal areas the native northerners hunted seal, whale, and walrus. Two groups in particular—the Eskimo and the "settled Chukchi"—lived almost exclusively off marine hunting. Their "boatfuls," or *baidaras*, were kinship units largely analogous to pastoral camps, but

mies and Their Transformations (Cambridge, 1980); and I. I. Krupnik, Arkticheskaia etnoekologiia (Moscow, 1989). For the most recent and most comprehensive "ethnic history" of most northern peoples (which, unfortunately, came out too late to be considered here), see James Forsyth, A History of the Peoples of Siberia: Russia's North Asian Colony, 1581–1990 (Cambridge, 1992).

[8] The most important general ethnographies of the tundra peoples are V. V. Antropova, Kul'tura i byt koriakov (Leningrad, 1971); Waldemar G. Bogoras, The Chukchee (New York, 1904); I. S. Gurvich, Etnicheskaia istoriia Severo-Vostoka Sibiri (Moscow, 1966); I. S. Gurvich and B. O. Dolgikh, eds., Obshchestvennyi stroi u narodov severnoi Sibiri XVII-nachala XX v. (Moscow, 1970); Peter Hajdu, The Samoed Peoples and Languages (Bloomington, 1963); Waldemar Jochelson, The Koryak (New York, 1913); idem, The Yukaghir and the Yukaghirized Tungus (New York, 1910); L. V. Khomich, Nentsy: Istoriko-etnograficheskie ocherki (Leningrad, 1966); A. A. Kiselev and T. A. Kiseleva, Sovetskie saamy: Istoriia, ekonomika, kul'tura (Murmansk, 1979); M. G. Levin and L. P. Potapov, eds., Narody Sibiri (Moscow, 1956); A. A. Popov, The Nganasan: The Material Culture of the Tavgi Samoeds (Bloomington, 1966); idem, Nganasany: Sotsial'noe ustroistvo i verovaniia (Leningrad, 1984); I. S. Vdovin, Ocherki istorii i etnografii chukchei (Moscow, 1965); idem, Ocherki etnicheskoi istorii koriakov (Leningrad, 1973).

varied in size according to the season and the task at hand: seal hunting was often done by individual hunters, whereas whaling expeditions required the labor of a large number of people. Farther south along the Pacific coast the settled Koriak complemented sea-mammal hunting with fishing, and the Itel'men relied almost exclusively on the annual salmon runs. Most peoples of the Pacific coast, including those of the Amur, used dogs for transportation.[9]

The foragers of the taiga zone (most Ob' Ugrians, the Forest Samoed, the Ket, Evenk, Tofalar, and the Amur peoples) engaged in various combinations of fishing and hunting.[10] In the summer most of them lived in temporary settlements along lakes and rivers; in the winter small bands or solitary hunters pursued bear, moose, wild reindeer, and fur-bearing animals.

None of the native northerners were "settled" in the Russian (agricultural) sense of the term. The nature of their subsistence activities required periodic movement, and even sea-mammal hunters and salmon fishermen had different summer and winter quarters. Economic associations were relatively unstable, fluctuating in size and composition according to the season, the availability of resources, and the political choices of individual conjugal pairs. Larger descent groups bound their members with mutual social and spiritual obligations but

[9] The most important general ethnographies of the Siberian sea-mammal hunters and coastal fishermen are Bogoras, *The Chukchee and The Eskimo of Siberia* (New York, 1913); Chester S. Chard, "Kamchadal Culture and Its Relationships in the Old and New Worlds," *Archives of Archaeology*, no. 15 (Madison, 1961); Gurvich, *Etnicheskaia istoriia*; Gurvich and Dolgikh, *Obshchestvennyi stroi*; *Istoriia i kul'tura itel'menov* (Leningrad, 1990); Jochelson, *The Koryak*; S. P. Krasheninnikov, *Opisanie zemli Kamchatki. S prilozheniem raportov, donesenii i drugikh neopublikovannykh materialov* (Moscow, 1949); Levin and Potapov, *Narody Sibiri*; R. G. Liapunova, *Ocherki po etnografii aleutov* (Leningrad, 1975); G. A. Menovshchikov, *Eskimosy* (Magadan, 1959); and Vdovin, *Ocherki etnicheskoi istorii koriakov*.

[10] The most important general ethnographies of the Siberian taiga foragers are E. A. Alekseenko, *Kety: Istoriko-etnograficheskie ocherki* (Leningrad, 1967); Lydia Black, "The Nivkh (Gilyak) of Sakhalin and the Lower Amur," *ArA*, no. 10 (1973): 1–110; Gurvich and Dolgikh, eds., *Obshchestvennyi stroi*; E. A. Kreinovich, *Nivkhgu: Zagadochnye obitateli Sakhalina i Amura* (Moscow, 1973); V. G. Lar'kin, *Orochi: Istoriko-etnograficheskii ocherk s serediny XIX v. do nashikh dnei* (Moscow, 1964); Levin and Potapov, *Narody Sibiri*; S. M. Shirokogoroff, *Social Organization of the Northern Tungus* (Shanghai, 1933); idem,, *Psychomental Complex of the Tungus* (London, 1935); L. Ia Shternberg, *Giliaki, orochi, gol'dy, negidal'tsy, ainy* (Khabarovsk, 1933); A. V. Smoliak *Traditsionnoe khoziaistvo i material'naia kul'tura narodov Nizhnego Amura i Sakhalina: Etnograficheskii aspekt* (Moscow, 1984); idem, *Ul'chi: Khoziaistvo, kul'tura i byt v proshlom i nastoiashchem* (Moscow, 1966); Ch. M. Taksami, *Nivkhi: Sovremennoe khoziastvo, kul'tura i byt* (Leningrad, 1967); G. M. Vasilevich, *Evenki. Istoriko-etnograficheskie ocherki (XVIII-nachalo XX)* (Leningrad, 1969).

rarely functioned as stable economic or military units. Among reindeer pastoralists in particular, constant herd accumulation and the concomitant tendency toward family autonomy resulted in minimal socialization outside the camp. Chukchi patrilineal lineages were rather loose (adoption was easy and multiform), consisted of few generations, did not have proper names, and were not exogamous, so that the authority of the "camp master" did not extend beyond his own camp. Moreover, as leadership status was based primarily on reindeer wealth, frequent epizootics and family realignments produced regular changes in the power structure.

Among less autonomous hunters and fishers, descent groups played a more significant role (particularly in the marriage politics of the taiga peoples), but communal prestige tended to be just as transient. Given the impossibility of accumulating wealth, the forager's insurance against the vicissitudes of a predatory economy was food sharing, so that political power depended on one's ability to distribute the kill and, eventually, on physical strength and "hunting luck" (understood as the favor of the spirits). The "strong men" were challenged, and sooner or later unseated, during races, wrestling matches, wars, or hunting expeditions.[11]

The division of labor was based on age and gender, with men generally responsible for food procurement, and women for processing, transportation, and household management. In the taiga zone most marriages represented long-term economic alliances between two exogamous lineages, whereby labor (and a source of future labor) was exchanged for property in the form of bridewealth; in case of divorce bridewealth had to be returned. In the tundra, particularly in the northeast, marriages were contracted by two individuals after the successful completion of bride-service by the groom.

Polygamy was both a sign of success and an investment for the future, but as few male northerners could afford more than one wife, raiding for women (as well as for children, dogs, and reindeer) was a frequent occurrence. Male captives were of little use and were put to death unless they forestalled defeat by killing their families and committing suicide. Some engagements, particularly those prompted by revenge, were carefully staged and regulated, with special representatives from both sides agreeing on the time, place, and strategy of the encounter.[12]

---

[11] Ingold, *Hunters, Pastoralists, and Ranchers*, pp. 264–81.

[12] S. V. Bakhrushin, "Ostiatskie i vogul'skie kniazhestva v XVI i XVII vv;" in *Nauchnye trudy* (Moscow, 1965), vol. 3, part 2, p. 95; V. V. Antropova, "Voprosy voennoi organizatsii

Another form of redistribution of property was barter, which usually involved exchange among the tundra, taiga, and coastal populations as well as tributary/commercial relations with southern and western merchants and tax collectors. Most of the trading was done by men in predetermined locations, although some transactions could be performed by deputations of female slaves or through "silent trade," whereby the two sides took turns leaving their goods in a particular spot until everyone was satisfied that the deal was fair.[13] Long-term commercial alliances commonly known as "friendships" were fairly widespread and involved rights of preferential (and sometimes exclusive) exchange as well as certain social privileges.

The idea of exchange lay at the very core of the traditional Arctic world: for life to continue, one had to give some of one's own and receive something else in return.[14] The Master of the Waters brought his riches and was fed the fruits of the Earth; the animals who came to be killed received food for their souls; and a lineage that married off a woman obtained bridewealth or labor. All things had their spiritual owners or counterparts who needed to be placated, propitiated, or bribed (usually by a shaman). Every successful kill or catch was a gift, and every slaughter a sacrifice.

By the late sixteenth century, when the Russians started arriving in northern Eurasia in large numbers and with serious intentions, some tundra and taiga dwellers had met humans whose terms of exchange were novel and sometimes confusing. The Chinese on the Amur, the Tatars and Mongols in southern Siberia, and the Novgorodians and then the Muscovites in the northwest insisted on regular deliveries of fur tribute in return for "protection." The trappers probably saw tribute as a kind of exchange, but one that involved new goods, new rules, and new obligations.

---

i voennogo dela u narodov krainego Severo-Vostoka Sibiri," in *Sibirskii etnograficheskii sbornik*, vol. 2 (Moscow. 1957); Khomich, *Nentsy*, pp. 145–46; Krasheninnikov, *Opisanie zemli Kamchatki*, p. 403; V. I. Ogorodnikov, *Ocherk Istorii Sibiri do nachala XIX stol.* (Irkutsk, 1920), 1:205; A. P. Okladnikov et al., eds., *Istoriia Sibiri s drevneishikh vremen do nashikh dnei* (Leningrad, 1968), 1:399.

[13] Antropova, "Voprosy," p. 168; Menovshchikov, *Eskimosy*, pp. 27–29; Bogoras, *The Chukchee*, p. 53.

[14] L. Black, "The Nivkh," pp. 49–50.

I

SUBJECTS OF

THE TSAR

"The delivery of iasak in Tiumen'," from S. U. Remizov, "Sluzhebnaia chertezh-naia kniga". Courtesy of Oregon Historical Society.

1

The Unbaptized

If on some nameless island Captain Schmidt
Sees a new animal and captures it,
And if, a little later, Captain Smith
Brings back a skin, that island is no myth.

—John Shade, *Pale Fire*

The Sovereign's Profit

One of the main reasons for the emergence of the Rus principalities was the fur trade, and some of the best furs came from the northern frontier. In an entry dated 1096, the Russian Primary Chronicle recounts a Novgorodian story about peculiar people who lived beyond high mountains "far in the midnight land" and spoke an unintelligible language. The annalist identifies them as belonging to one of the unclean tribes banished by Alexander the Great, but the Novgorodian scouts were probably more impressed by the fact that the captives "made gestures asking for iron . . . and gave furs in return."[1] Novgorod's wealth was based on the export of furs (to Bulgar, Kiev, and Byzantium, and later to the Hansa), and the most common way of obtaining them was through tribute. As the fur-bearing animals retreated, the Novgorodians moved from the Dvina to the Mezen' to the Pechora in search of new pelts and new trappers. By the late 1200s they routinely claimed the "Ugrian lands" of the northern Urals as their own.[2]

---

[1] *PSRL*, 1:235. The story of Alexander and the captive tribes dates back to the Arabic legends of Gog and Magog, known to the annalist in the Greek version attributed to St. Methodius of Patara. See M. P. Alekseev, *Sibir' v izvestiiakh zapadno-evropeiskikh puteshestvennikov i pisatelei, XIII–XVII vv.* (Irkutsk, 1941), vol. 1, part 2, p. 45, and Leonid S. Chekin, "The Godless Ishmaelites: Image of the Steppe in Pre-Muscovite Rus'" (Paper delivered at the International Conference on the Role of the Frontier in Rus' Russian History, 800–1800, University of Chicago, May 1992).

[2] Janet Martin, *Treasure of the Land of Darkness: The Fur Trade and Its Significance for Medieval Russia* (Cambridge, 1986), pp. 9–11, 44, 52, 54, 61–67, and "Russian Expan-

In the fourteenth century Novgorod's ascendancy along the Arctic seaboard was challenged by Moscow's grand princes, who had become important suppliers of furs to their southern neighbors, and by Moscow's monastic reformers, who sought solitude, "community life," new cloisters, and new converts in the forests of the northeast.[3] In 1383 Stefan, "the teacher of the Zyrian," was appointed the first bishop of Perm'; within the next century Novgorod was ousted from the Dvina; and in 1499 the forces of Ivan III founded the town of Pustozersk near the mouth of the Pechora and mounted a large expedition "into the Ugrian land and against the Gogul."[4]

The breakthrough came in the mid-sixteenth century. The capture of Smolensk resulted in increased trade with Poland-Lithuania and Leipzig; the English discovery of a northern route to Russia led to the founding of Arkhangel'sk; and the conquests of Kazan' (1552) and Astrakhan' (1555) opened up the markets of Central Asia and made vulnerable the Khanate of Sibir, a small remnant of the Golden Horde on the Tobol River and an important transit center for southbound Arctic pelts. The subsequent expansion of Moscow's trading interests coincided with the spread of fur fashions in Western Europe and at the Ottoman court. According to Giles Fletcher, "furres" were "transported out of the Countrey some yeers by the merchants of Turkie, Persia, Bougharia, Georgia, Armenia, and some other of Christendom, to the value of foure or five thousand rubbles."[5]

In the last quarter of the sixteenth century, access to the "treasure of the land of darkness" was being contested by the Chingiside Khan

---

sion in the Far North," in *Russian Colonial Expansion to 1917*, ed. Michael Rywkin (London, 1988), pp. 23–34; Raymond H. Fisher, *The Russian Fur Trade, 1550–1700* (Berkeley, Calif., 1943), pp. 3–7; *PSRL*, 10:22; S. V. Bakhrushin, "Ocherki po istorii kolonizatsii Sibiri v XVI i XVII vv.," in *Nauchnye trudy*, vol. 3, part 1, p. 138; A. V. Oksenov, "Snosheniia Novgoroda Velikago s Iugorskoi zemlei (istoriko-geograficheskii ocherk po drevneishei istorii Sibiri)," in *Literaturnyi sbornik "Vostochnago Obozreniia,"* ed. N. M. Iadrintsev (St. Petersburg, 1885), pp. 442–44.

[3] Martin, *Treasure*, pp. 90–92, 102; A. N. Murav'ev, *Russkaia Fivaida na Severe* (St. Petersburg, 1894).

[4] *PSRL*, 12:249; Janet Martin, "Muscovy's Northeastern Expansion: The Context and a Cause," *Cahiers du monde russe et soviétique* 24, no. 4 (1983): 459–70; R. G. Skrynnikov, *Sibirskaia ekspeditsiia Ermaka* (Novosibirsk, 1982), pp. 99–104; A. V. Oksenov, "Politicheskiia otnosheniia Moskovskogo gosudarstva k Iugorskoi zemle," *ZhMNP* 273 (1891): 257–64.

[5] Quotation from Richard Hakluyt, *The Principal Navigations Voyages Traffiques and Discoveries of the English Nation* (Glasgow, 1903), p. 365. See also Bakhrushin, "Ocherki," p. 140, Fisher, *The Russian Fur Trade*, p. 21; Mark Bassin, "Expansion and Colonialism on the Eastern Frontier: Views of Siberia and the Far East in the Pre-Petrine Russia," *Journal of Historical Geography*, 14, no. 1 (1988): 11; Martin, *Treasure*, 109.

Kuchum, who collected fur tribute from the hunters and fishermen of the lower Ob', and the merchant family of the Stroganovs, which had the tsar's charter to mine, trade, and tax the local trappers, as well as to make sure that "the Siberian Sultan" did not "prevent our Ostiaks and Voguls and Ugrians from sending tribute to our treasury".[6] Around 1581–1582, a Cossack army of several hundred men, hired by the Stroganovs, aided by local "volunteers," and led by a certain Ermak Timofeevich, crossed the Urals and after a year-long campaign sacked the capital of the khanate. The power of Cossack firearms and the lack of enthusiasm on the part of Kuchum's tribute-paying allies decided the matter, and "precious foxes, black sables, and beavers" were sent to Moscow.[7] Deprived of the center that had held together the complex structure of local alliances, the Siberian khanate quickly disintegrated. The gates to northern Asia were open, and hundreds and later thousands of the tsar's subjects rushed eastward in search of furs.

Independent trappers and traders led the way.[8] Then, "jealous for the sovereign's profit" and not forgetting their own, came soldiers, mercenaries, and Cossacks led by Moscow-appointed administrators (voevody).[9] Traveling along interconnected Siberian waterways, they found "new lands," built new forts (ostrogi), and imposed fur tribute (iasak) on the new "foreigners." When the fur resources were exhausted or the iasak-paying population became too large to be administered from one ostrog, a new one would be built and the whole process would be repeated.[10] About sixty years after Ermak's campaign, Ivan Moskvitin

[6] Quotation from G. F. Miller, Istoriia Sibiri (Moscow, 1937), 1:339. See also A. A Vvedenskii, Dom Stroganovykh v XVI-XVII vekakh (Moscow, 1962), p. 79; Skrynnikov, Sibirskaia ekspeditsiia Ermaka, pp. 113–18; Sibirskiia lietopisi, Russia, Arkheograficheskaia kommissiia (St. Petersburg, 1907), pp. 5–6, 53.

[7] Sibirskiia lietopisi, pp. 24, 70, 131, 201, 208, 331; Skrynnikov, Sibirskaia ekspeditsiia Ermaka, pp. 142–222; Miller, Istoriia Sibiri, 1:236.

[8] S. V. Bakhrushin, "Pokruta na sobolinykh promyslakh XVII v.," in Nauchnye trudy, vol. 3, part 1, pp. 200–210.

[9] The Cossacks received a salary or a plot of land and served the state when called on to do so. They were by far the most numerous group among Siberian servitors, and by the end of the seventeenth century most of the other units had been absorbed into their ranks. George V. Lantzeff, Siberia in the Seventeenth Century: A Study of the Colonial Administration (Berkeley, Calif., 1943), pp. 63–69; Terence Armstrong, Russian Settlement in the North (Cambridge, 1965), pp. 65–68; Basil Dmytryshin, "The Administrative Apparatus of the Russian Colony in Siberia and Northern Asia, 1581–1700," in The History of Siberia from Russian Conquest to Revolution, ed. Alan Wood (London, 1991), p. 22; F. G. Safronov, Russkie na severo-vostoke Azii v XVII-seredine XIX v: Upravlenie, sluzhilye liudi, krest'iane, gorodskoe naselenie (Moscow, 1978), p. 68; Fisher, The Russian Fur Trade, p. 32.

[10] On the Russian conquest of Siberia, see, in particular, V. A. Aleksandrov, Rossiia na dal'nevostochnykh rubezhakh (vtoraia polovina XVII v.) (Moscow, 1969); Bakhrushin,

reached the Sea of Okhotsk and Semen Dezhnev circled the cape that
now bears his name. Farther south, Moscow's advance into the southern Urals, the upper Enisei, and the Amur basin was blocked by the
steppe pastoralists and the frontier outposts of the Manchu empire.
It was the Northeast, therefore—with its thicker pelts and "smaller"
peoples—that attracted most of the Europeans.[11]

The instructions they received from the Siberian Chancellery in
Moscow were fairly consistent and unambiguous:

> The serving and the trading men should be ordered to bring under the
> sovereign's exalted hand the non-tribute-paying Yukagir and the Tungus
> and diverse foreigners of various tongues who live on those and other
> rivers in new and hostile lands. And the iasak for the sovereign should
> be taken with kindness and not with cruelty [laskoiu a ne zhestoch'iu],
> and the people of those lands should be placed, from now on, under
> the tsar's exalted hand in direct slavery [v priamom kholopstve] as iasak
> people for ever and ever.[12]

"Kindness" (trade) was preferable to "cruelty" (war) because it
seemed to assure a "steady and durable profit" for the sovereign (pri-
byl' prochna i stoiatel'na). According to one oral tradition, the Ket warriors were sapped of their courage by Russian bread.[13] For two heroes
of a Tungus tale, it was bread and sugar: "[One of them] chewed
some bread for a while—and liked it. He said in Evenk: 'Good.' Then
he took a cracker, ate it, and said: 'Delicious.' Then he ate some sugar.
'Don't even think about killing these good men,' he said [to the other].
So they threw away their bows and began to eat."[14] Other popular items
included knives, axes, cloth, tea, and colored beads, but it was tobacco
and alcohol that enjoyed the greatest and most consistent demand. Ac-

"Ocherki"; Fisher, The Russian Fur Trade; James R. Gibson, Feeding the Russian Fur
Trade: Provisionment of the Okhotsk Seaboard and the Kamchatka Peninsula, 1639–
1856 (Madison, 1969); Robert J. Kerner, The Urge to the Sea: The Course of Russian
History: The Role of Rivers, Portages, Ostrogs, Monasteries, and Furs (Berkeley, Calif.,
1946); Lantzeff, Siberia in the Seventeenth Century; George V. Lantzeff and Richard A.
Pierce, Eastward to Empire: Exploration and Conquest on the Russian Open Frontier to
1750 (Montreal, 1973); and Safronov, Russkie na severo-vostoke Azii.

[11] In seventeenth-century Russian vernacular, nebol'shie meant "few in number."
[12] N. S. Orlova, ed., Otkrytiia russkikh zemleprokhodtsev i poliarnykh morekhodov
XVII veka na severo-vostoke Azii: Sbornik dokumentov (Moscow, 1951), pp. 236–37. See
also pp. 135, 420, 423, and 426; and DAI, 2:263, 269, and 7:137.
[13] B. O. Dolgikh, Kety (Irkutsk, 1934), p. 14.
[14] G. M. Vasilevich, ed., Istoricheskii fol'klor evenkov: Skazaniia i predaniia (Moscow,
1966), p. 294.

cording to one Yukagir account, a small hunting band met a man with hair around his mouth and followed him to his house. There, the host offered them some food, which the Yukagir found to their liking, and some very special water, which the oldest of them, after serious deliberation, agreed to taste.

> He drank it and said: "Fellows, do not have any bad thoughts at all. In all my life, I have never tasted such water anywhere."
> Then he drank some water again and put it in front of us.
> Another old man drank it and said: "No, fellows, it seems that the old man has told us the truth—this water really is delicious."
> That old man drank some again and put it in front of us.
> "Now, young men," he said, "you taste it."
> We tasted it, too, and said:
> "Yes, our old men have told us the truth."
> Then one of the old men said:
> "I knew it right away and told you not to have any bad thoughts."
> Then we all got some more food and water. Our friends started telling us something, but we did not understand anything and pointed to our ears.
> They showed us something curved and shiny. We took it, looked at it, something was cut out in the middle. They put something in there, then brought some fire. Then they put that thing to our mouths. Then everyone took that thing and started sucking on it. We sat and talked by gestures. They told us:
> "Next summer come back again. We will bring you various things."
> Then we got up and started to leave. Our friends gave us some axes and knives and, in addition to that, gave us all kinds of clothes.[15]

If the hunters did come back the next summer, they would be asked for furs, and an attempt would be made to register them as fur suppliers "for ever and ever." If they accepted the deal as fair, they would become, in the eyes of the Russians, the tribute-paying "iasak people" (iasach-nye liudi). If they did not, the Cossacks were under strict instructions "to beat them a little bit" and, if that did not help, "to wage war and to capture their wives and children."[16]

Not that they needed instructions: war was their profession, and local women the only ones around. According to a Yakut tradition,

[15] L. N. Stebakova, ed., Tvorchestvo narodov Dal'nego Severa (Magadan, 1958), pp. 129–31.

[16] DAI, 3:310. See also DAI, 2:272–73 and 3:222; G. F. Miller, Istoriia Sibiri (Moscow, 1941), 2:176; and V. A. Kuleshov, Nakazy sibirskim voevodam v XVII veke: Istoricheskii ocherk (Bolgrad, 1894), p. 21.

The arriving Russians built high wooden towers . . . Marveling at that, both children and grown-ups approached the towers and started looking at them carefully. Then they saw that the Russians had scattered sweets, gingerbread cookies, and beads all around the houses. Many children, women, and men came and started picking them up. While they were picking them up, [the Russians] dropped logs that crushed and killed them. After that they started killing with flintlocks that shot powder fire.[17]

The Enets, too, have preserved an old account of the Russian arrival: "There is bad news. Somewhere people are on the march, killing people. They say that where there is the Pechora river, they have already crossed it. When they find people, they start beating them right away, and beat them all the time."[18]

Military resistance was common and occasionally successful, as various "foreigners" "brag[ged] that they would kill every single man and call the land and the rivers their own"; threatened to "destroy . . . the tsar's bread, and to kill the Russian people, and to make war on the town . . . , and to burn the town, and to kill the Russian people on the roads and in the fields"; or simply refused to pay iasak, claiming, as did one Chukchi encampment, that they had never paid tribute to the Russians, and "are not going to now." On the Ob', one Ugrian settlement fell to the Cossacks after a three-day assault, and another one capitulated only when cannon were used against it; in the northwestern tundra, according to Cossack reports, the reindeer hunters habitually raided Russian sled caravans and portage parties, "not letting [them] through and taking away [their] provisions;" and on the Pacific coast the fort of Okhotsk was continuously besieged for over thirty years, with about 230 Russians killed between 1662 and 1678.[19]

In the far northeastern portion of the continent, where tributary relations were unknown, Russian pacification campaigns lasted well into the eighteenth century. Most Kamchatka settlements were protected by ramparts, "and from those forts they fight, and throw stones from their

[17] G. U. Ergis, ed., *Istoricheskie predaniia i rasskazy iakutov* (Moscow, 1960), 2:9.

[18] B. O. Dolgikh, *Mifologicheskie skazki i istoricheskie predaniia entsev* (Moscow, 1961), p. 200. Cf. p. 206, and *RIB*, 2:854.

[19] *RIB*, 2:850; Miller, *Istoriia Sibiri*, 2:184; *PSI*, 1:457; *Sibirskiia lietopisi*, pp. 333–34; Miller, *Istoriia Sibiri*, 1:242, 287; N. S. Orlova, ed., *Otkrytiia*, p. 81; N. V. Sliunin, *Okhotsko-Kamchatskii krai: Estestvenno-istoricheskoe opisanie* (St. Petersburg, 1900), 2:12–13; N. N. Stepanov, "Prisoedinenie Vostochnoi Sibiri v XVII v. i tungusskie plemena," in *Russkoe naselenie Pomor'ia i Sibiri (Period feodalizma)*, ed. A. P. Okladnikov (Moscow, 1973).

slings, and big stones by hand, and hit with sharp stakes and sticks."[20] When they had no cannon, the Russians either starved the enemy or set fire to the settlements, killing those who tried to escape.[21] Sometimes the defenders themselves did the killing: "And when those dugouts were set on fire, some people started coming out of the dugouts . . . , and many of them killed each other, and stabbed their wives and children and, because of their cruelty, did not leave the dugouts, and all burned in the fire, to the last person."[22]

On the Chukotka peninsula, where sables were few and the trappers particularly unaccommodating, the fur rush ran out of steam. As the wild reindeer population diminished and traditional tundra hunting became less productive, the Chukchi increasingly turned to raiding.[23] In 1747 a large punitive force under Major Dmitrii Pavlutskii set out, according to the Senate's instruction, "not only to bring back what was unjustly taken from her imperial majesty's loyal subjects the Koriak, but to ruin the Chukchi themselves completely."[24] The expedition was defeated, and Major Pavlutskii, who had spent almost all of his military career trying to pacify the Koriak and the Chukchi, was killed in battle.[25] In 1769 the fort of Anadyrsk, founded over a century before by Dezhnev and used as a military base against the Chukchi, was abandoned by the Russians. It would take a century and a half of trade and two decades of collectivization to turn the Chukchi into Russian subjects.

Chukotka was uniquely inaccessible and undesirable. Elsewhere in northern Eurasia most of the tundra and taiga dwellers had become "iasak men" by the end of the seventeenth century. In the European tundra, in the Ob' basin, and in southern Siberia most people had known tribute before and were obliged simply to switch their allegiance to a new overlord, often within the same administrative unit.[26] The presumed "best men" (luchshie liudi) were offered tribute exemp-

[20] A. V. Efimov, Iz istorii velikikh russkikh geograficheskikh otkrytii (Moscow, 1949), p. 101.

[21] PSI, 2:44; Efimov, Iz istorii, p. 101.

[22] PSI, 2:513.

[23] Vdovin, Ocherki istorii i etnografii chukchei, pp. 18, 68; Gurvich, Etnicheskaia istoriia, p. 115. According to a nineteenth-century Cossack tradition, "in those days they were afraid of the very name of the Chukchee." See Bogoras, The Chukchee, p. 691.

[24] Vdovin, Ocherki istorii i etnografii chukchei, p. 119.

[25] Ia. P. Al'kor and A. K. Drezen, Kolonial'naia politika tsarizma na Kamchatke i Chukotke: Sbornik arkhivnykh materialov (Leningrad, 1935), pp. 170–71; Sliunin, Okhotsko-Kamchatskii krai, pp. 38–47.

[26] S. V. Bakhrushin, "Iasak v Sibiri v XVII v.," in Nauchnye trudy, vol. 3, part 2, pp. 52–54.

tion and military protection in exchange for the service of collecting iasak.[27] Successful "princes" were expected to move up in the Russian aristocratic hierarchy.[28]

Some Ugrian elders took advantage of the new opportunities. They caused "much violence and offense" in the exercise of their princely powers and called on the Russian servitors when in trouble. A few became Christians, built churches, and expressed a distaste for "pagan" practices.[29] Overall, however, the experiment in creating "Ostiak" and "Vogul" princedoms under baptized elites proved a failure. Lacking a comparable institution in their own societies, the hunters and fishermen of the Ob' basin showed little appreciation for an aristocracy imposed by Moscow. In 1636 the Koda Khanty rebelled against their ruler and begged the tsar to take them under his exalted hand. "It is impossible for us to pay iasak to prince Dmitrii Alachev," they declared, "and we do not want to do it."[30] Eventually, prince Dmitrii was packed off to Moscow to become a Russian nobleman, and within a few years the active search for local elites was abandoned. As one servitor pointed out in his report, the Tungus did have "princelings and elders," but "they listen to them when they want to, and if they find any fault with them, they depose and kill them."[31]

Whether directly or through Russian-approved representatives, all "newly tributized foreigners" (ob"iasachennye inozemtsy) were required to take a solemn oath of allegiance (shert'). Russian tribute-collectors assumed that every people had its own "faith" and that each faith had a sacred formula that was binding on all believers. Some Khanty trappers, for example, were forced to take their oaths in front of a bearskin, on which a knife, an axe, and other "frightening weapons" were laid out. While chewing on a piece of bread, they listened as an interpreter said: "If you do not take this oath in truth and do not serve loyally and do not bring the iasak dutifully, let this bear take vengeance on you and let him maul you to death. And let this bread and

[27] Lantzeff, *Siberia in the Seventeenth Century*, p. 92; Bakhrushin, "Ostiatskie i vogul'-skie kniazhestva," pp. 121, 134–35, 137; Miller, *Istoriia Sibiri*, 1:361.

[28] Some of the Ugrian elders and military leaders went on to found Russian noble dynasties. See Bakhrushin, "Ostiatskie i vogul'skie kniazhestva," pp. 132, 145, 149, 150–51.

[29] Bakhrushin, "Ostiatskie i vogul'skie kniazhestva," pp. 128–30.

[30] Ibid., p. 131.

[31] Stepanov, "Prisoedinenie Vostochnoi Sibiri," p. 112.

this knife kill you."[32] Few such pledges appear to have been effective, however, and the servitors were constantly encouraged to apply themselves to discovering the "real oath."[33] In the far northeast, where the Chukchi, Koriak, and Itel'men seemed to have "no faith at all,"[34] the tribute collectors "used the barrel of a gun . . . , declaring that whoever swears insincerely will not avoid the bullet."[35]

The "traitors" could be "besieged by many strong sieges"[36] and eventually beaten into submission, but the majority of the tribute payers were nomads who "wandered around every year, lived of their own free will, and beat the Russian people" before moving on to another jurisdiction or beyond the Russian reach altogether.[37] Chasing them in the tundra was a dangerous and generally thankless task. (On the Taz, for example, the servitors "[did] not follow them to collect the iasak . . . and [did] not dare leave their winter blockhouses, being scared of those foreigners.")[38] One possible solution was to recognize the reciprocal nature of the trapper-Cossack relationship and exchange sought-after commodities for tribute. The Tungus, for example, "ask for gifts—tin and beads, and food for themselves, and flour, and butter, and fat, and when they are given those gifts, tin and beads, and are fed, they give, in exchange for that and when asked, one sable from every one or two families. But without gifts they do not want to give anything. . . . And when they are told to . . . give the iasak . . . they kill [the iasak collectors]."[39] Some of the early transactions were carried out in accordance with local practices, with "tribute payers" leaving their furs on the snow while waiting at a distance in large armed bands to see what would be offered in exchange.[40] Another traditional procedure was gift-giving in return for hospitality. The Cossacks received their guests in full military formation, garbed in their best "colored" attire. Cannons (if available) and muskets were discharged, and bread and liquor

[32] Grigorii Novitskii, "Kratkoe opisanie o narode ostiatskom, sochinennoe Grigoriem Novitskim v 1715 godu," in Pamiatniki drevnei pis'mennosti i iskusstva (St. Petersburg, 1884), vol. 21, no. 53, p. 54.
[33] Bakhrushin, "Iasak v Sibiri," p. 66.
[34] Efimov, Iz istorii, p. 100.
[35] Krasheninnikov, Opisanie zemli Kamchatki, p. 457.
[36] PSI, vol. 1, p. 461.
[37] Ibid., p. 426.
[38] Bakhrushin, "Iasak v Sibiri," p. 62.
[39] Stepanov, "Prisoedinenie Vostochnoi Sibiri," p. 108.
[40] Bakhrushin, "Iasak v Sibiri," pp. 76–77.

were served.[41] "And without the sovereign's reward," complained one iasak collector, "the Tungus do not give the sovereign's iasak."[42] Clearly, however, what the Tungus saw as trade the Russians called tribute. Frightened and hard-pressed for merchandise as they were, the tsar's servitors referred to the furs as "iasak" and to the goods they gave in exchange, as "presents." One reason was a series of reminders to that effect emanating from Moscow ("Do not let those foreigners cheat— they give the iasak to the sovereign, not sell it"),[43] but it was probably the difference between the (Russian) market price of the furs and that of the gifts that made the distinction meaningful to the Cossacks.

In spite of the popularity of Russian goods, the behavior of the north-erners remained "fearless and willful" (besstrashnoe i samovol'noe) and the supply of furs unreliable. By far the most effective remedy was hostage taking, a method common on the southern frontier and prob-ably related to the old steppe practice of keeping captives for ransom. In most parts of northern Eurasia kinship ties were strong enough to be used as leverage over the prisoner's clansmen. Taken in battle or lured by food and drink and then overpowered, the hostages (amanaty) were locked inside Russian blockhouses and shown periodically to their relatives in exchange for iasak.[44] Occasionally they could be re-leased "home to their wives and their children" and replaced by volun-teers from among their kinsmen ("every year or half a year, or every month"), so that in some areas being a hostage became a sort of family obligation.[45]

Not all family members were worth the tribute. Effective hostages had to be lineage members in good standing (shamans, elders, or mili-tary leaders were preferred) and had to look well-fed and contented, "so that the iasak people did not have any doubts on account of [their treatment]."[46] Even if that was the case (and sometimes it was not),[47] the payment of tribute was not assured. As one Samoed hostage, aban-doned by his kinsmen, explained to the Russian tsar: "We, your or-

---

[41] Ibid., p. 73; DAI, 2:267–68, 4:219, 347, and 7:137; Miller, Istoriia Sibiri, 2:174; Lant-zeff, Siberia in the Seventeenth Century, p. 93; N. S. Orlova, ed., Otkrytiia, p. 426.

[42] Bakhrushin, "Iasak v Sibiri," p. 74.

[43] Ibid., p. 75.

[44] Ibid., p. 67; DAI, 2:270–73, and 7:138, 142; Lantzeff, Siberia in the Seventeenth Century, p. 96; Safronov, Russkie na severo-vostoke Azii, p. 87; N. S. Orlova, ed., Otkry-tiia, pp. 131–32; Kuleshov, Nakazy, p. 23.

[45] DAI, 2:270 and 4:21; Miller, Istoriia Sibiri, 1:399.

[46] DAI, 2:273. See also RIB, 2:856.

[47] Some hostages were fed on dog food or starved to death. See Lantzeff, Siberia in the Seventeenth Century, p. 96.

phans, sovereign, are wild and nomadic people, and it is impossible for us to live in one place."[48] In other words, the members of his encampment had migrated from the area and were, for the time being, unable to return. In such cases, the iasak collectors had to tour the tundra, showing the hostages around and demanding furs in exchange for their well-being.[49] Useless hostages (most of them Chukchi and Koriak "reindeer people") were hanged, starved, or tortured by their captors, but others escaped, "stabbed themselves to death," or served the Russians.[50] A young man named Apa chose the last course:

> In the last year of 156 [1647] I, Apa, was caught by the mouth of the Kolyma river by the boiar son of the Yakutsk fort, Vasilei Vlas'ev. And since then, sovereign, my father and my mother, and all my kinsmen have abandoned me, and do not pay your, sovereign, iasak for me. And now, sovereign, I, your orphan, want to serve you, the righteous sovereign, and be honest in everything, and bring my relatives the Chukchi under your, tsar, exalted hand.[51]

The proper registration of iasak-paying foreigners was relatively easy in the coastal settlements but proved exceedingly complicated in the case of the reindeer breeders and taiga foragers. One servitor, exasperated by the foreigners' "trickery," complained that "they change their names at the time of payment almost every year and cause great confusion in the books, and few people bring the iasak, and the collectors write down whatever names they tell them, but they do not tell them their real names." In the early stages, the accountant's nightmare was made worse by the sheer lack of familiarity with the foreigners: "Whether they paid or not is not known, because they, the iasak collectors, cannot tell them [the Samoed] apart."[52]

Problems and temporary reverses notwithstanding, the "tributizing" effort was clearly worth it as far as the Russian state was concerned. Between 1589 and 1605 (when most of western Siberia was brought under Russian control) the state's fur revenue tripled, and by the 1680s its value rose to about 125,000 rubles (as compared to about 15,000 in

---

[48] Bakhrushin, "Iasak v Sibiri," p. 67.

[49] DAI, 2:268 and 4:103–4.

[50] DAI, 7:139, 297–98; Gurvich, Etnicheskaia istoriia, p. 35; PSI, 2:525.

[51] N. S. Orlova, ed., Otkrytiia, pp. 254–55; see also Gurvich, Etnicheskaia istoriia, p. 49.

[52] Stepanov, "Prisoedinenie Vostochnoi Sibiri," p. 112; Bakhrushin, "Iasak v Sibiri," p. 64.

1589).[53] In the first years after the conquest the tribute was not fixed ("as much as can be gotten") and was usually levied on a territorial unit as a whole. Later, as the bookkeeping was deemed adequate, a set annual tax was imposed on every man between eighteen and fifty years old. The quotas were fixed according to number of pelts but in some areas cash equivalents were introduced in order to account for the differences in quality.[54] The value of the pelts brought by the hunters was to be determined by the local collectors. Policies toward slaves, dependents, and adolescents varied over the years, but "the poor, the sick, and the maimed" were exempt.[55]

Such was Moscow's official policy. In practice, it was hardly possible for the servitors to combine "kindness" with the "sovereign's profit." On the one hand, the success of a voevoda was measured by the number of furs he procured—and so, naturally, was his personal fortune. On the other hand, the size of the iasak that the native northerners delivered depended on their hunting luck, need for Russian goods, and migration routes. This divergence of interests did not augur well for a fixed or uniform tax, let alone kindness. Year after year, the collectors forged the books, undervalued the furs, and demanded "gifts" (pominki) from the iasak people, while the latter paid "for last year" and for their dead relatives.[56] Every voevoda had to deliver at least as much iasak as his predecessor. If somebody in his district died or fled, he was supposed to report it to Moscow. An investigation was held, and if the voevoda's claim was found to be correct, the tsar issued a special ukaz relieving his iasak people of excess obligations. (In the meantime, the hunters had to pay for the dead and the missing.)[57] Perhaps most important, the treasury demanded a guaranteed profit: that is, the Moscow price of every pelt had to be higher than the Siberian price. If this was not the case, the voevoda paid the difference—something that clearly did not happen very often.[58]

Sometimes the tribute payers and tribute collectors joined forces in sabotaging the official policy. The individual tax on all adult males

[53] Fisher, The Russian Fur Trade, pp. 114, 119; Bassin, "Expansion and Colonialism," p. 11; James R. Gibson, "The Significance of Siberia to Tsarist Russia," Canadian Slavonic Papers 14, no. 3 (1972): 443.

[54] P. N. Butsinskii, Zaselenie Sibiri i byt pervykh ee nasel'nikov (Khar'kov, 1889), p. 313; Bakhrushin, "Iasak v Sibiri," p. 58.

[55] Miller, Istoriia Sibiri, 2:170.

[56] Butsinskii, Zaselenie Sibiri, pp. 314–18; Lantzeff, Siberia in the Seventeenth Century, pp. 105–6; Bakhrushin, "Iasak v Sibiri," p. 83.

[57] Butsinskii, Zaselenie Sibiri, p. 315.

[58] Ibid., p. 316; Kuleshov, Nakazy, pp. 26, 46.

remained largely a fiction until the second half of the eighteenth century, when it was officially abolished. After the first census in the Tomsk *uezd* in 1720, for example, it was discovered that in all the previous years the iasak had been levied from whole districts (*volost'*), often through a local representative. It was also discovered that the state treasury had been receiving only one half of all the iasak. The person found responsible was sentenced to the galleys but received royal clemency and was "beaten unmercifully with a knout" instead.[59] Soon afterward, the practice of taxing whole settlements or encampments was legitimized.

Iasak was not the only obligation of the iasak men. Having been brought under the sovereign's exalted hand, they had to take part in Moscow's campaigns against the "non-iasak men" ("unpeaceful foreigners"). From the White Sea to the Pacific, Russian conquest was made possible through the assistance of local warriors, many of whom were eager to take a hand in destroying their rivals. The Koda Khanty, for example, could boast a very impressive service record: "Like our fathers and our brothers, we built towns and forts all over Siberia and, together with the Tobol'sk and Berezov Cossacks, we fought against your, sovereign, traitors and rebels, the Kalmyk people and the Tatars, and the Ostiak, and the Samoed, and the Tungus and the Buliash people, and all kinds of rebels."[60] In the process, they "killed disobedient foreign people and captured their wives and children and shared those prisoners among themselves."[61] Farther east, Russian reliance on local allies was even greater. The Koriak and Chukchi wars were as much a Yukagir and Evenk effort as they were a Russian conquest. Some of the Cossacks' allies did not have to pay iasak and were allowed to keep their prisoners.[62]

Other colonial obligations included serving as guides and interpreters, building forts, and providing transportation. Cart duty (*podvodnaia povinnost'*) was especially onerous and provoked numerous complaints. Waiting in one place for Russian officials and then leading them about on unpredictable errands interfered greatly with the hunting and herding routine. Some of the drivers were willing to pay three

---

[59] A. N. Kopylov, "K voprosu o printsipe iasachnogo oblozheniia i poriadke sbora iasaka v Sibiri," *Izvestiia Sibirskogo otdeleniia Akademii nauk SSSR: Seriia obshchestvennykh nauk*, no. 1 (1969): 64–65.

[60] Bakhrushin, "Ostiatskie i vogul'skie kniazhestva," pp. 122–23. The Buliash people are the Eniseiars.

[61] Ibid., p. 119.

[62] Al'kor and Drezen, *Kolonial'naia politika tsarizma*, p. 114.

times the usual tribute quota in order to avoid the disruption.[63] They were rarely successful, however: the needs of imperial administrators and the sorry state of the transportation system in the north ensured the survival of cart duty well into the twentieth century.

No less unpopular but much less persistent was the government attempt to use native labor in agriculture. Through the years, one of the main concerns of the Siberian administration was the provision of new forts, and later towns and mines, with food. Importing grain from Russia was very expensive, and the creation, where possible, of local agriculture was constantly and vigorously encouraged. Russian peasants were forced or lured into Siberia, and Siberian vagrants and exiles were declared peasants and settled on the land.[64] In the early years some Ob' Ugrians were also attached to the "sovereign's field" (gosudareva pashnia), with dire consequences for both.[65] "And from now on, sovereign," reported a group of Mansi in 1598, "it is impossible for us, your orphans, to plough your, sovereign, field, because, sovereign, we have lost all our property, sold our wives and children, and are now starving to death."[66] Moscow tended to be responsive to such pleas, less perhaps from any sense of compassion than from a continuing interest in the fur tribute. The same Mansi, for example, offered to pay as much sable iasak as the tsar "would see fit to exact from his orphans."[67] Skillful trappers were much more profitable than unproductive peasants, and given the presumed alternative of Russian colonization, the policy of employing forced native labor never took root in the north.

The continuation of the fur trade required more peasant settlement, but the spread of peasant settlement undermined the fur trade. The arriving peasants ploughed, hunted, and fished on land that was being used by the "tributized" trappers. More significant, they cleared the fields by burning down the forest, which drove away the animals. Some servitors, settlers, and monasteries leased the land from the local hunters, who claimed to agree to such deals "for our own needs and to be able to pay iasak and to pay back our old debts, and not because of any dishonest intention." Dishonest or not, the government strongly

[63] Lantzeff, Siberia in the Seventeenth Century, p. 105; RIB, 2:146–47; Miller, Istoriia Sibiri, 1:307, 380, and 2:152; Gurvich, Etnicheskaia istoriia, p. 21.

[64] James R. Gibson, "Russia on the Pacific: The Role of the Amur," Canadian Geographer 12, no. 1 (1968): 17; idem, Feeding the Russian Fur Trade, pp. 46–47; Safronov, Russkie na severo-vostoke Azii, pp. 107–9; V. I. Shunkov, Ocherki po istorii kolonizatsii Sibiri v XVII-nachale XVIII vekov (Moscow, 1946), pp. 11–56.

[65] Butsinskii, Zaselenie Sibiri, pp. 311–12.

[66] Miller, Istoriia Sibiri, 2:512; RIB, 2:146–48.

[67] RIB, 2:146–48.

disapproved of any alienation of "iasak lands" and often demanded their return, as well as the punishment of those involved. The founding of new peasant settlements had to be preceded by a determination "whether it is an empty place or whether it belongs to the iasak people." In the latter case, permission was not given, and "the people who ravage the land of the iasak people [were] . . . , for such thievery . . . , to be beaten unmercifully with a knout, so that others would not get the idea to . . . cause ruin to the iasak people in their hunting." Caught between the demands for more furs and the insistence that the Siberians feed themselves, the voevody tried their best to do both—a task made easier by the fact that one voevoda's peasants often lived among another voevoda's iasak people. The resulting conflicts caused much animosity among different uezdy, much complaint writing on the part of the voevody, and ultimately the creeping takeover of the local hunting and fishing grounds by the Russian settlers.[68]

Even where Russians did not settle permanently (and that meant most of circumpolar Eurasia outside of a few areas along the great rivers), they seriously affected the local economic life. In the early years Cossacks and traders in search of food and women often raided the encampments of the iasak people and "tortured them with various tortures and took great gifts of furs from them, and robbed them, and took from them by force their foxes and dogs, and fish and oil, and whatever they needed to eat."[69]

> In the last year of 164 [1654] a boiar son Kirilo Vaniukov, having assembled on the Indigirka river many serving and trading and hunting men from all the blockhouses for the sake of his own idle self-interest, accused the iasak Yukagir of betrayal and, after the iasak collection, sent against them more than one hundred serving and trading and hunting men . . . with orders to rout them. And according to his, Kirilo's, order, the serving, trading, and hunting men routed those Indigirka iasak people, taking, during that rout, their wives and children and about three hundred reindeer and various other Yukagir possessions. And because of that rout the Indigirka Yukagir became poor.[70]

As the frontier moved on, raiding stopped, but the relentless demand for furs continued to clash with the other economic pursuits. The win-

---

[68] Ibid., pp. 330, 766; Shunkov, Ocherki, pp. 64–75; Butsinskii, Zaselenie Sibiri, pp. 331–32.

[69] RIB, 2:182.

[70] Gurvich, Etnicheskaia istoriia, p. 18. See also DAI, 4:18, 20.

ter tracks of the best polar foxes lay far north of the reindeer migration routes; the taiga sable took many fishermen away from their rivers; and the settled sea hunters had to exchange much of their catch for the furs brought by their inland "friends." "We, the walking and the settled little Tungus [Tungusishka]," complained the iasak men of the Okhotsk coast, "are not used to hunting sable, and we do not know how to do it. . . . We live by the sea . . . and we catch fish for the reindeer Tungus, and for those fish we buy, from those reindeer Tungus, sable for the . . . iasak." Some taiga hunters had to buy furs from the Russians for elk and reindeer skins, pay 10 percent tax to the treasury, and then take the same furs to the same treasury as iasak (the tithe was designed as a tax on Russian traders).[71]

In the second half of the seventeenth century, the supply of fur-bearing animals began to drop.[72] (Some of the goods that the native trappers received in exchange for pelts—particularly firearms and metal traps—greatly contributed to this decline.) As the iasak quotas changed much more slowly, the native economy found itself under severe strain. Constant arrears in iasak payments and the growing dependence on iron tools, clothing, flour, tea, and liquor led to the deterioration of the tribute payers' economic and social position vis-à-vis the Russians. In the words of the Pelym Mansi, "In our heathen faith, sovereign, we do not have any artisans, so that we do not have anything, sovereign, with which to cut our wood; and without an axe, sovereign, it is impossible to make traps for animals; and to make shoes without knives is also impossible. So that we, your orphans, sovereign, are going to die from hunger, from cold, and from barefootedness [s bosoty]."[73]

The economic changes, however, were neither the most immediate nor the most dramatic effects of the Russian conquest. In 1633, the servitors from Mangazeia failed to collect iasak at Khantaiskii and Inbatskii blockhouses because "the foreigners who used to pay the sovereign's iasak in those two blockhouses had died in the last year of 140 [1632], and the others, who had survived, had migrated it is not known where, also fearing death."[74] According to one calculation, about one

[71] M. A. Sergeev, *Nekapitalisticheskii put' razvitiia malykh narodov Severa* (Moscow, 1955), p. 33; N. N. Stepanov, "Peshie Tungusy Okhotskogo poberezh'ia v XVI–XIX vv.," in *Ekonomika, upravlenie i kul'tura Sibiri XVI–XIX vv.*, ed. V. I. Shunkov (Novosibirsk, 1965), p. 133; Butsinskii, *Zaselenie Sibiri*, pp. 317–18.

[72] Fisher, *The Russian Fur Trade*, pp. 94–107; *DAI*, 3:214 and 7:193–94.

[73] Miller, *Istoriia Sibiri*, 2:152.

[74] Ibid., p. 403; see also p. 387.

half of the Inbak Ket and more than two-thirds of the Khantaika Enets had died of smallpox in the previous two years.[75] Especially hard hit were the Yukagir: in 1694, the Omolon collection point was closed permanently because the local iasak people "by God's will, all died in the smallpox pestilence. And from now on there are no great sovereign's Omolon Yukagir from whom to take iasak, and the said Omolon winter blockhouse has been taken off the lists."[76] In the first century of Russian rule the overall Yukagir population dropped from around 4,500 to 1,450. Although smallpox was probably the main cause, it was not the only one: in the 1670s and 1680s at least 10 per cent of all Yukagir women were living outside of the Yukagir settlements (as wives, slaves, or concubines), and at any one time about 6 percent of all adult males were being kept as hostages by the Russians. Many died in the Russian raids and in the wars with the Chukchi, Koriak, and Tungus, and some starved as a result of bartering their staple foods for furs (the Yukagir tundra was poor in sable).[77]

The unequal distribution of Russian forces, goods, and diseases altered the local balance of power. Closeness to the Cossacks could be a military advantage, as in the case of the Koda Khanty, or it could lead to economic and demographic catastrophe, as in the case of the Yukagir. One thing was fairly constant, however: the presence of the Russians invariably resulted in severe clashes between the "iasak foreigners" and the as yet "unpeaceful" ones. Thus, while the Koda Khanty (Ostiak) bragged about "killing disobedient foreign people and capturing their wives and children and sharing those prisoners among themselves," their neighbors the "thievish" Evenk wanted "to beat the sovereign's iasak Ostiak . . . so that they would not give iasak to the sovereign."[78] Moved by revenge and new military opportunities, driven away by Russian competitors and their native allies, fleeing from raiders and tribute collectors, or looking for more and better furs, the iasak men often encroached on their neighbors' territory.[79] "In this year of 196 [1688]," related the Okhotsk Tungus, "we went to the Koriak land

[75] Dolgikh, Rodovoi i plemennoi sostav, pp. 128–29, 143–44. See also pp. 88, 92–93, 141, 155, 158, 169, 187, 306, 451–521, 561, and 571, and Stepanov, "Prisoedinenie Vostochnoi Sibiri," p. 115.

[76] Dolgikh, Rodovoi i plemennoi sostav, p. 410.

[77] Gurvich, Etnicheskaia istoriia, pp. 69, 19–23; Dolgikh, Rodovoi i plemennoi sostav, p. 440.

[78] Bakhrushin, "Ostiatskie i vogul'skie kniazhestva," p. 119; Miller, Istoriia Sibiri, 2:215.

[79] Gurvich, Etnicheskaia istoriia, p. 43; Lantzeff, Siberia in the Sevententh Century, pp. 89–90.

to hunt for sable, but the Koriak did not let us hunt sable on their hunting grounds and drove us away, and they, the Koriak, beat our kinsmen the best men and killed six people, but around here there is no place besides the Koriak land to hunt the sable."[80] The Russians, of course, proceeded to wage war against the Koriak, who were then raided by the Chukchi, who were then attacked by the Russians. Such developments caused major population shifts all over the north. Following in the footsteps of the Cossacks, the reindeer-herding Nenets continued their march eastward along the Arctic coast. In southern Siberia, the expansion of the Turkic-speaking population led to the disappearance of the Saian-Altai branches of the Samoedic and the Eniseian languages, as well as the migration of the Ket (northern Eniseians) deeper into the taiga. On the Lena the Yakut pastoralists continued their expansion, pressuring the Evenk in the west and the Yukagir in the east.[81] And in the northeast, as one Chukchi detachment explained, the Chukchi "searched for the reindeer Koriak in order to ruin them, kill them to death, and take their reindeer herds away from them."[82] By the 1770s, when the Russians admitted their defeat at the hands of the Chukchi, over 50 percent of the Koriak had been killed and 240,000 head of Koriak reindeer had been captured by the Chukchi. The Chukchi, meanwhile, had expanded far beyond their seventeenth-century borders, moving to the Omolon and the Aniui in Yukagir territory and reaching the Penzhina and Oliutora Koriak lands in the south.[83]

Most serious clashes were over tribute, and the most frequent targets were the tribute collectors. In 1607, about two thousand "foreigners" besieged the Russian fort of Berezov for two months. After their defeat the body of the Obdorsk "prince" Vasilii hung for three years on the Berezov gallows, "so that there would be no stealing in the future and for the others to see."[84] The others saw but did not listen: in 1609 Vasilii's son attempted to attack Tobol'sk, and half a century later Vasilii's grandson was hanged for inciting "treachery."[85] Such treachery, or attempts to renegotiate the terms of tribute payment by force of arms, were fairly frequent in the first hundred years of Russian rule. In 1649

[80] Stepanov, "Peshie Tungusy," p. 135. See also DAI, 4:22; N. S. Orlova, ed., Otkrytiia, p. 130.

[81] Okladnikov, et al., eds., Istoriia Sibiri, 2:56–58.

[82] Vdovin, Ocherki istorii i etnografii chukchei, p. 68.

[83] Gurvich, Etnicheskaia istoriia, pp. 108, 112; Dolgikh, Rodovoi i plemennoi sostav, p. 561. The almost certainly exaggerated estimate of reindeer losses was made by the Anadyr' authorities. See Vdovin, Ocherki istorii i etnografii chukchei, p. 65.

[84] Miller, Istoriia Sibiri, 2:202–5.

[85] Ibid., p. 212; Bakhrushin, "Ostiatskie i vogul'skie kniazhestva," p. 136.

the kinsmen of a murdered Tungus hostage embarked on a war that lasted until the end of the century and led to the sacking of the fort of Okhotsk; in 1679 a Samoed band made an unsuccessful attempt to capture the town of Obdorsk; and in 1714 a large group of Yukagir mercenaries rebelled against the Cossacks, killing fifty-seven and imprisoning fifty.[86] The tribute payers of the fur-rich Kamchatka "were in an almost constant state of treason," and in 1730 they succeeded in taking over most of the peninsula. It took the Russians over two years to suppress the uprising, and in Nizhnekamchatsk "the Cossacks, saddened by the violence done to their wives and by the loss of their property, killed them all to the last man."[87]

There were many more uprisings, as well as mass suicides and mass destruction of furs,[88] but the superiority of the tsar's arms and the allure of his merchandise made accommodation inevitable. As foreigners became the sovereign's, they had to recognize the authority of the Russian state over tribute payment, trade, war, and all social interaction with the Orthodox Christians. Submission implied protection, however, and the new Russian subjects routinely petitioned the tsar for "mercy" and assistance. Sometimes they skillfully took advantage of the tensions within the Russian administration, as in the case of a Tungus hostage who justified his escape by the fact that his captor

> moved along hesitantly and spent much time in one place because of his own idle profit. And I appealed to him that it was time to proceed with the sovereign's business and that he should move faster, because the blockhouse was far away. But he told me that Russian holidays were many and did not apply himself to the business of the sovereign's iasak, and I had the fear of God and of the sovereign and . . . ran away.[89]

Such petitions were translated, written down, and perhaps inspired by Russian "profit-seekers," but the obligations of tribute and tradition became so intertwined that eventually most of the "sovereign's for-

---

[86] DAI, 3:176 and 7:277–304; Lantzeff, Siberia in the Seventeenth Century, p. 113; PSI, 2:92–93.

[87] Krasheninnikov, Opisanie zemli Kamchatki, pp. 479, 796. The job begun by the Cossacks was all but completed by smallpox, and by the 1780s the overall Itel'men population had fallen to about 3,000 (compared to almost 13,000 at the turn of the century). See Gurvich, Etnicheskaia istoriia, pp. 101–3; Dolgikh, Rodovoi i plemennoi sostav, p. 571.

[88] See, for example, Dolgikh, Kety, p. 14; DAI, 3:322; Lantzeff, Siberia in the Seventeenth Century, p. 110; S. B. Okun', Ocherki po istorii kolonial'noi politiki tsarizma v Kamchatskom krae (Leningrad, 1935), p. 39; and Stepanov, "Prisoedinenie Vostochnoi Sibiri," p. 115.

[89] Bakhrushin, "Iasak v Sibiri," p. 69.

eigners" were forced to master some bureaucratic procedures and learn how to manipulate them in a variety of settings (including the most traditional and apparently unrelated to tribute). It was extremely important, for instance, to prove to the voevoda that a certain kinsman was murdered by outsiders and that the missing pelts should be supplied by the offending family (and not by the petitioner). Conversely, a promise to pay more iasak could ensure Russian help in resolving a family dispute, preventing a blood feud, or repossessing an unlawfully abducted wife.[90]

All of these cases were based on the understanding that the Russians would uphold the local customs. And they did. As long as the iasak kept coming in, the voevody were willing to enforce levirate, bride-wealth, and other norms that were taboo in their own society but were recognized as legitimate among the "foreigners." Except for the cases involving murder and large sums of money, all native disputes brought to the attention of the Russians were to be resolved jointly by the iasak collectors and the local elders ("And without them and in small matters do not try them, lest [they] suffer losses and offences and taxes from you").[91] The great majority of conflicts, however, were taken care of by the native "foreigners" themselves—to the perfect satisfaction of the conquerors.

Thus, although providing an alternative source of authority, the seventeenth-century Russian administrators did not establish an alternative law. A Tungus iasak man could expect a sympathetic reaction when he complained that an ill-intentioned shaman had caused disease and death in his family.[92] Even in mixed cases, decisions were often justified with reference to traditional law. When another Tungus family demanded the extradition of the Russian hunter Feodulka who had murdered their father, the Yakutsk authorities refused, but only after the killer repeated under torture that he had done it by accident, whereupon he was "beaten unmercifully with a knout" in the presence of the plaintiffs. "And let the foreigners not get offended that the said Feodulka was not given to them . . . , because among them, the Tungus, involuntary deadly killings also take place, and they do not send such killers from one clan to another, do they?"[93] An important exception

---

[90] Lantzeff, *Siberia in the Seventeenth Century*, p. 100; *RIB*, 2:157; Butsinskii, *Zaselenie Sibiri*, p 306; Stepanov, "Prisoedinenie Vostochnoi Sibiri," p. 122.

[91] *DAI*, 7:147, 154.

[92] A. P. Okladnikov, "Kureiskie tungusy v XVIII v.," in *Osvoenie Sibiri v epokhu feodalizma*, ed. V. I. Shunkov (Novosibirsk, 1968), p. 109.

[93] *DAI*, 3:176.

was the deliberate effort by Moscow to suppress blood-feuding, for "those internecine battles of theirs and the deadly killing will cause ruin and great shortages in the great sovereign's iasak collection."[94] If there was no fighting and no iasak shortages, the Siberian Chancellery urged the voevody to

> favor them in everything [vo vsem l'gotit'] . . . so that they, the Siberian people, will not suffer any hardship in anything and so that all kinds of people of the Siberian land can live in our royal favor in complete relief, peace, and quiet, without any doubt, and so that they can engage in all kinds of hunting and bring their children, and brothers, and uncles, and nephews, and friends to our royal mercy.[95]

In short, the iasak people were to be protected from Russian "thievery" (violation of the tsar's decrees) and corrupting vices. No tobacco or liquor were to be sold; no gambling was to be allowed; and no "insults" [obidy] of any kind were to be tolerated. The Russian peasants were to stay away from the iasak people; the traders could not buy furs before tribute-collection time; and the servitors were not allowed to impose too much tribute, "so as not to overburden them [chtob im bylo ne v tiagost']."[96]

The sovereign's profit was neither "steady" nor "durable," however. By the end of the century traders and servitors had overrun most of Siberia, and the Siberian fur revenue had begun to decline.[97] The government tried more protection measures—some hunting grounds could not be entered by any Russians under any pretext, and in some areas the serving men lost their right to punish the iasak people[98]—but the trend continued. The iasak collectors knew that, for all the decrees, delivering this year's tribute without "ruin and shortages" was their most important duty They also knew that Moscow was far away; that next year they could be transfered elsewhere; and that a few extra pelts could make a man rich. By about 1680,

[94] Stepanov, "Prisoedinenie Vostochnoi Sibiri," p. 120.

[95] Miller, Istoriia Sibiri, 2:169–70.

[96] DAI, 2:263. See also 2:270, 274, 4:362–63, and 7:347; PSZ, 3:545, 574; RIB, 2:70, 176, 766, 831, and 8:494; Shunkov, Ocherki po istorii kolonizatsii Sibiri, pp. 65–66; Butsinskii, Zaselenie Sibiri, pp. 331–32; Miller, Istoriia Sibiri, 1:381 and 2:169–70, 174, 176, 191; and N. S. Orlova ed., Otkrytiia, p. 237.

[97] Fisher, The Russian Fur Trade, pp. 34, 114; James R. Gibson, "Sables to Sea Otters: Russia Enters the Pacific," Alaska Review 111 (Fall/Winter 1968): 204, 207.

[98] Lantzeff, Siberia in the Seventeenth Century, p. 98; Stepanov, "Prisoedinenie Vostochnoi Sibiri," p. 119.

many hunting people had left those faraway foreign rivers . . . because sable hunting had become bad, and as for your, great sovereign, faraway two-year service, there are sometimes sixty or thirty or twenty or ten foreign hostages in forts and winter blockhouses, and in those forts and winter blockhouses there are sixty or thirty or twenty or ten serving men who, because of their small number, have to stay there to guard those hostages and to catch fish for those hostages and to guard against their kinsmen, and, because of this small number of people, there is great hardship from the foreigners, and life is frightening, and there is nobody to guard the hostages.[99]

It was the consistent violation of the government's "noninterference" policy that eventually brought about relative noninterference. Fortunately for the "peace and quiet" of the native northerners and unfortunately for the satisfaction of their consumer needs, fewer pelts meant fewer Russians. Except for the vigorous and largely agricultural communities in the upper Ob' and Enisei basins and a few important towns such as Berezov and Yakutsk, the Russian Arctic at the turn of the eighteenth century was a land of isolated forts manned by ill-equipped but increasingly well-adapted Cossacks.

The Sovereign's Foreigners

The Russians who followed the sables to the Pacific did not chance on a *terra incognita*, sought no forgotten Christian king, and did not "discover Siberia." They knew that the "Eastern land" was rich in furs and that they could obtain those furs from "the people called Samoeds." They had probably also heard that the Samoeds ate each other as well as fish and reindeer meat, slaughtered their children to feed their guests, rode on dogs and reindeer, excelled at marksmanship, wore skins, had flat faces and small noses, and sold sables. "In the same country," reportedly, there were Samoeds who spent the summer months in the sea lest their skin split; Samoeds who died every winter when water came out of their noses and froze them to the ground; Samoeds with mouths on top of their heads who ate by placing their food under their hats and moving their shoulders up and down; Samoeds with no heads at all who had mouths between their shoulders and eyes in their chests, could not speak, and ate raw reindeer heads;

---

[99] *DAI*, 7:365.

Samoeds who wandered underground, and Samoeds who drank human "and other kinds of blood."[1]

The fifteenth-century tale that contains this intelligence was a compilation of Russian travelers' accounts and translated literary sources, particularly the famous romance known in Russia as the *Aleksandriia*.[2] Most of these "Samoeds"—as well as the ever-popular Dogheads and other creatures frequently mentioned as denizens of the midnight country—had long been commonplaces in Eurasian oral traditions and the stock-in-trade of ancient and medieval cosmographies.[3] Herodotus (who placed the men who slept six months a year beyond the impassable mountains north of the bald-headed Argippaei),[4] Pliny, Pomponius Mela, Solinus, Isidore of Seville and their students and imitators peopled the edges of the known world with headless Blemmyae, one-eyed Arimaspi (also frequently located in northern Scythia), and countless other monsters whose presence distinguished wilderness from civilization.[5] In the thirteenth century, traders, missionaries, and spies who passed through "Tartary" on their way to the Great Khan confirmed the existence of such people by questioning their native informants. John de Plano Carpini learned about a people beyond the Samoed who had dog faces and whose every third word was a bark; Marco Polo, who placed the Cynocephali on the Andaman Islands, referred to the fur trappers of the "Land of Darkness" as people who live "like brute beasts in subjection to none."[6] Sixteenth-century ambassadors to Muscovy gave further—though not always eager—support to this theory by incorporating the local lore (some of it derived from the

[1] "Skazanie o chelovetsekh neznaemykh v vostochnei strane," in A. V. Oksenov, "Slukhi i viesti o Sibiri do Ermaka," SSb, no. 4 (1887): 113–14. Also in D. N. Anuchin, "K istorii oznakomleniia s Sibir'iu do Ermaka," *Trudy Imperatorskago moskovskago arkheologicheskago obshchestva* 14 (1890): 230–36; A. A. Titov, ed., *Sibir' v XVII veke. Sbornik starinnykh russkikh statei o Sibiri i prilezhashchikh k nei zemliakh* (Moscow, 1890), pp. 4–5; and A. N. Pypin, *Istoriia russkoi etnografii* (St. Petersburg, 1892), 4:187.

[2] Alekseev, *Sibir'*, pp. 122–23. For mostly "oral" interpretations, see Anuchin, "K istorii," and Oksenov, "Slukhi i viesti." For an interesting new explication, see A. I. Pliguzov, "Skazanie o chelovetsekh neznaemykh v Vostochnei strane," forthcoming in *Russian History/Histoire russe*.

[3] Alekseev, *Sibir'*, p. 12; David Gordon White, *Myths of the Dog-Men* (Chicago, 1991).

[4] He strongly doubted their existence, however. See Herodotus, 4.25–27.

[5] Margaret T. Hodgen, *Early Anthropology in the Sixteenth and Seventeenth Centuries* (Philadelphia, 1971), pp. 17–77; Richard Bernheimer, *Wild Men in the Middle Ages: A Study in Art, Sentiment, and Demonology* (New York, 1970), pp. 85–93; White, *Myths*, pp. 47–70; Alekseev, *Sibir'*, pp. 19–20.

[6] C. Raymond Beazley, *The Texts and Versions of John de Plano Carpini and William de Rubruquis* (London, 1903), pp. 122–23; Marco Polo, *The Travels of Marco Polo* (Harmondsworth, U.K., 1988), p. 331.

same written tradition) into their travelogues. Sigismund Herberstein cited a Russian source about the northern dog-heads, chest-heads, fish-men, and people who die each winter; Richard Johnson quoted verbatim the passage from *Skazanie o chelovetsekh neznaemykh v vostochnei strane* about Samoed cannibalism; Raffaello Barberini attributed the sightings of fish-men, frozen mucus, and human hibernation to two Tatar witnesses; and Daniel Printz summed up the prevailing view by calling all inhabitants of "Permia," "Sibiria," and "Ustyusia" "wild men and even total barbarians."[7]

Not all barbarians were brutes and not all wildness was an abomination. Ever since the Fall—however construed—humans had yearned for the lost innocence of the Golden Age and envied those who were untouched by civilization (or at least better equipped to deal with its burdens). After most nymphs and satyrs had been confined to specific geographical locations, the universe beyond the *oikumene* came to consist of peoples who were in some way the antipodes of "real" ("cooked," "civil"-ized, orthodox) humanity. They could be defined by their association with the woods and the beasts (savages, from *silva*, forest); their inability to speak, or muteness (*barbaroi*, or "babblers," the Russian *nemtsy*, or "mutes"); their irrationality (a person without *logos* is also without *logic*); or their paganism ("pagan" meant "rustic" before it came to mean "unbeliever").[8] Invariably, however, they manifested their otherness by breaking the dietary and sexual taboos that bound human societies together and made them "normal."[9] Savages were people who ate uncooked flesh ("Eskimo" means "raw-eater" in the Algonquian languages), ate one another ("self-eater" is the folk etymology of "Samoed" in Russian), shared their women indiscriminately (like the mythical Garamantes), and otherwise did violence to the fundamental rules of survival and procreation. Depravity, however, is also freedom, and beastly savages had always been opposed by noble ones. Few histories and cosmographies of antiquity and the Middle Ages could be complete without virtuous Ethiopians, wise "Brahmans,"

[7] Sigismund Herberstein, *Zapiski o moskovitskikh dielakh* (St. Petersburg, 1908), pp. 129–33; Alekseev, *Sibir'*, pp. 105–6, 127, 134–35, 150.

[8] Anthony Pagden, *The Fall of Natural Man: The American Indian and the Origins of Comparative Mythology* (Cambridge, 1982), pp. 16–19, 203; Todorov, *The Conquest of America*, p. 76; Bernheimer, *Wild Men*, p. 20.

[9] Hayden White, "The Forms of Wildness: Archaeology of an Idea," in *The Wild Man Within: An Image in Western Thought from the Renaissance to Romanticism*, ed. Edward Dudley and Maximilian E. Novak (Pittsburgh, 1972), pp. 19–22.

manly Scythians, and gentle Hyperboreans.[10] A preference for the virile enemy of decadence or the gentle opponent of violence depended on what one bemoaned in one's own society, but until humanity attained—or returned to—total perfection (and as long as there were alternative ways of being human), there would be demand for savages, good as well as bad.[11] Julius Pomponius Laetus pointed out that the "ancient Ugrians" had no tsars and were very happy in spite of the cold weather; Francesco Da Collo wrote that they were completely devoid of any *politia, humanita et commertio* and had no roofs over their heads, yet considered themselves happy and could not think of a better life; and Adam Olearius compared the Samoed to Ulysses, who preferred his austere homeland to the many pleasures of Calypso's island.[12]

Well into the Age of Discovery, most Europeans continued to fit new peoples into familiar landscapes. Vasco da Gama carried letters to Prester John, and Columbus was accompanied by an interpreter who spoke Hebrew, Arabic, and Chaldaic. Discovery meant recognition, and the New World could only make sense in terms of the Old. Oviedo called pumas "lions" and jaguars "tigers"; Cortés compared Aztec temples to mosques, and the market place of Tenochtitlan to that of Salamanca. The natives, too, were like natives elsewhere, so that Columbus had no trouble distinguishing the gentle Arcadians of Hispaniola from the ferocious dogheads of Caniba.[13] But things were changing, and just as some people back home were increasingly wondering how old and familiar the Old World really was, some people on the frontier were beginning to say that perhaps the New World was indeed new and unfamiliar. The metaphors of similitude were wearing thin, and the differences seemed more and more glaring.[14] "Everything is very different," wrote Fray Tomás de Mercado, "the talent of the natives, the disposi-

[10] George Boas and Arthur O. Lovejoy, eds., *A Documentary History of Primitivism and Related Ideas in Antiquity* (Baltimore, 1935); Bernheimer, Wild Men, pp. 102–19; Henri Baudet, *Paradise on Earth: Some Thoughts on European Images of Non-European Man* (New Haven, 1965), pp. 10–22; Hoxie Neale Fairchild, *The Noble Savage: A Study in Romantic Naturalism* (New York, 1928), pp. 2–8.

[11] H. White, "The Forms of Wildness," p. 28; Boas and Lovejoy, A Documentary History, pp. 1–22.

[12] Alekseev, Sibir', pp. 69, 88–89, 297.

[13] J. H. Elliott, *The Old World and the New: 1492–1650* (Cambridge, 1970), pp. 18–22; Pagden, *The Fall of Natural Man*, pp. 10–12; Baudet, Paradise on Earth, pp. 18, 20, 26–28; Stephen Greenblatt, *Marvelous Possessions: The Wonder of the New World* (Chicago, 1991), pp. 88–89.

[14] Pagden, *The Fall of Natural Man*, p. 5; Michel Foucault, *The Order of Things: An Archaeology of the Human Sciences* (New York, 1973), p. 51.

tion of the republic, the method of government and even the capacity to
be governed."[15] So different, in fact, that reducing the newly discovered
variety of objects to the species known in Europe was, in the words of
José de Acosta, "like calling an egg a chestnut."[16] When words failed,
pictures were drawn, and if both proved inadequate ("for such things,"
according to Alonso de Zuazo, "cannot be understood without the
three senses"), the least one could do was to invite one's audience to
come and see these things "in their country."[17] As this was rarely possible, a common solution was to send the anonymous animals, minerals, and savages back home to be named, classified, observed, touched,
and smelled. By the late sixteenth century, isolated exhibits of Indians
and iguanas had been largely replaced throughout Western Europe by
permanent cabinets de curiosités, Kunstkammern, closets, and reposi-
tories.[18] In the Baconian scheme of things, "nature" could be natural,
"erring and varying" ("Marvels"), or "altered or wrought" ("Arts"), and
it was fairly clear to most collectors that savages belonged in the second
category beside the abnormal and the deformed.[19] But what about "the
disposition of the republic" and "the method of government," which
one could not touch or smell? What about "customs, manners, and
rites"? Colonial administrators needed to understand the native systems of land tenure, marriage, and inheritance; merchants wanted to
know what the natives produced and how they traded; and missionaries soon discovered that, in the words of Diego Durán, pagans could
not be converted "unless we are informed about all the kinds of religion which they practice."[20] Accordingly, there appeared countless
collections of customs and costumes; "instructions for gentlemen,
merchants, students, soldiers, and mariners"; and dictionaries, grammars, and government questionnaires.[21] Even more important, the current concepts of time and space, humanity and wildness, reason and
passion had to accommodate the newly discovered and newly invented
peoples and words. Where did barbarians (pagans) come from? Were
they truly human (receptive to divine grace)? What was the reason for
their plight (punishment)? What accounted for the diversity of their
customs (religions)?

[15] Elliott, The Old World and the New, p. 21.
[16] Ibid., p. 41; Pagden, The Fall of Natural Man, p. 12.
[17] Elliott, The Old World and the New, p. 22; Pagden, The Fall of Natural Man, p. 12.
[18] Hodgen, Early Anthropology, pp. 111–61.
[19] Ibid., p. 129.
[20] Elliott, The Old World and the New, p. 33.
[21] Ibid., pp. 36–37; Hodgen, Early Anthropology, pp. 131–206.

In the seventeenth century, some of the answers to these questions came from "Northern Tartary," a portion of the Old World that had long been separated from *politia, humanita et commertio* by "snowy deserts and impassable mountain ranges" but had been made increasingly more transparent through conquest and the redrawing of maps. Combined with the Russian advance into Siberia, English and Dutch exploration of the Northeastern Passage, German interest in Oriental trade via Muscovy, and Jesuit attempts to find the shortest land route to China, the new efforts to classify humanity in general and barbarians in particular had resulted in detailed descriptions of Samoed and Tungus physical appearance, garments, dwellings, diet, religious practices, and economic pursuits.[22] None of these descriptions was written by a Russian, however, and as Isaac Massa complained in 1612, the Enisei Tungus religion was still totally unknown because, "thanks to the carelessness of the Muscovites, hardly anything is enquired into."[23] The tsar's servitors traveled to a most "beautiful country," and they "saw many curious plants, flowers, fruits, and rare trees, animals, and strange birds. But as the Muscovites themselves are not inquisitive folks they care nothing for such things, seeking only profit everywhere, for they are a rude and negligent people."[24] Indeed, neither the clerks who directed the fur-procurement effort from Moscow nor the Cossacks who "gathered" the local population under the sovereign's exalted hand had any interest in things that Massa called curious and beautiful. In their world, chasing "strange birds" was ludicrous and perhaps dangerous behavior, and "inquisitiveness," however translated, was a bad word.

Unlike the Spanish royal instructions to colonial officials, which demanded detailed information on local religions, writing systems, and government ("and whether they have kings and whether they are elected or rule by hereditary right, or whether they are governed as a republic or by lineages"),[25] the orders sent to Siberian servitors rarely

---

[22] See, in particular, Isaac Massa, Adam Olearius, Philippe Avril, and Isbrand Ides in Alekseev, *Sibir'*; John Harris *A Compleat Collection of Voyages and Travels* (London, 1705), 2:19–20, 253–57; Cornelis de Bruyn, *Travels into Muscovy, Persia, and Part of the East-Indies* (London, 1737), 1:6–14, 98–138; and John F. Baddeley, *Russia, Mongolia, China* (New York, 1964 [1919]), 2:3–12. See also Nikolai Milescu Spafarii [Spathary], *Sibir' i Kitai* (Kishinev, 1960), and Iurii Krizhanich [Križanić], "Historia de Sibiria," in Titov, ed., *Sibir' v XVII v.*, pp. 115–216.

[23] Baddeley, *Russia*, p. 8.

[24] Ibid., p. 10.

[25] "Ordenanzas de Su Magestad hechas para los nuevos descubrimientos, conquistas y pacificaciones, Julio de 1573," in *Coleccion de documentos inéditos relativos al descu-*

strayed from the immediate tasks of iasak collection. There was no indication that the tsar and his men had any interest in claiming any
land or people the way Columbus "took possession" of the New World
"for their Highnesses, by proclamation made and with the royal standard unfurled." The Cossacks were to find out if a "new river" had any
potential as a source of "profit for the sovereign," and if it did, to secure
it by imposing tribute on the local "foreigners."

> And he, Vasilii, should order the serving men to inquire, and should
> himself question the traders about that island in the sea opposite the
> Kalyma river on the New Land, and find out if on that island there is the
> sea animal the walrus. And if there is, then find out if the Chiukhchi
> foreigners go to that island in the winter to hunt that animal and if they
> kill that sea animal. And if they go there and kill that walrus, then he,
> Vasilii, should send his men to those foreigners the Chiukhchi and call
> them under the sovereign tsar's exalted hand and, having convinced
> them, take some good best people as hostages as many as would be appro-
> priate, and order them to deliver those walrus tusks as the sovereign's
> iasak.[26]

The implication seemed to be that if there were no tusks, or if the Chukchi could not deliver them, the servitors should go elsewhere and try
to find richer shores and better foreigners. Indeed, in order to receive
authorization and payment for new expeditions, servitors had to prove
that "on those rivers of the unpeaceful lands there are lots of Tungus
people of various clans as well as different kinds of animals, and the
sables are good and black," and that therefore, with some provisions
and reinforcements, "it will be possible to gather those Tungus under
the sovereign Tsar's exalted hand, and the sovereign will have great
profit."[27]

If profit was the only reason for annexing new lands (and whatever
Massa and other "inquisitive foreigners" might say, no one concerned
seemed in the least defensive about it), and if profit meant tribute, then
some "ethnographic" information was in order. First of all, one needed

---

brimiento, conquista y organizacion de las antiguas posesiones españolas de América
y Oceania sacados de los archivos del Reino (Madrid, 1871), 16:147.

[26] N. S. Orlova, ed., Otkrytiia, pp. 238–39.

[27] V. A. Divin, ed., Russkaia tikhookeanskaia epopeia (Khabarovsk, 1979), p. 70; N. S.
Orlova, ed., Otkrytiia, p. 216. Similarly, when it turned out that the Amur valley would
not be able to serve as a source of bread for the northern fur trade and that the local
trappers were duly paying tribute to a "powerful khan," all Russian claims to the area
were ceded to the Chinese. See Bassin, "Expansion and Colonialism," p. 15.

to know if the foreigners in question possessed anything of value—
mostly furs, but also "whether there is silver, and copper and lead ore,
and blue paint that is used for cotton and silk cloth," and "whether
there is agricultural land right there or somewhere else not far from
there, and if there is a lot of it, and what kind" (and if there is none,
whether servitors "could live well on fish and meat without bread").[28]
Having established that the tsar might have an interest in the "new
land," the Cossacks needed to find out if there were any competing
claims to the area ("Do those people pay iasak to anybody?"); what was
the best route to take ("How far is that river from the upper Indigirka?");
whether the foreigners were well-armed ("They shoot with bows and
arrows, and arrowheads and spears are all made out of bone"); and how
numerous they were ("If they are not numerous, then ask for God's help
and the sovereign's luck and attack those people").[29] In addition, both
tactical and fiscal concerns required some knowledge of clan division,
linguistic differences, and local status hierarchy. "And, sovereign, having captured that shaman in battle, we asked him: what kind of man
are you and do you have kinsmen? And he said: I am the best man of
the Shoromboiskii clan and I have four sons. And so we kept that shaman Iuliada as a hostage."[30] There were also occasional references to
the local dwellings ("and they live in earth dugouts"), religious practices ("and they feed bears"), clothing ("and on those Tungus . . . he
saw silver rings"), and physical appearance ("because they drive two
large bones through their lips"), but such mentions were very infrequent and served as pieces of military and commercial intelligence
rather than examples of peculiar customs.[31] The categories considered
basic and used almost universally were those of "settled" versus "nomadic" (sidiachie and kochevye, or kochevnye) and, as subgroups,
"pastoral or agricultural" (skotnye or pashennye) and "walking, horse-
riding, and reindeer-riding" (peshie, konnye, and olennye). Attached
to proper names, these qualifiers contained much useful information
relative to the natives' ability to defend themselves, feed the newcomers, and deliver certain types of tribute.

Remarkably, however, the proper names themselves were never
changed. Unlike the discoverers of New Spain, New England, and New
France, the seventeenth-century Russian Cossacks did not endeavor to

---

[28] DAI, 3:52 and 2:266; N. S. Orlova, ed., Otkrytiia, pp. 100–101.
[29] DAI, 3:52, 55, N. S. Orlova, ed., Otkrytiia, p. 139 and passim; DAI, 2:262, and passim.
[30] N. S. Orlova, ed., Otkrytiia, p. 131.
[31] Ibid., pp. 125, 140; Divin, ed., Russkaia tikhookeanskaia epopeia, p. 90; DAI, 4:21.

dissolve this new world into the old by renaming, destroying, or converting it.[32] They knew themselves to be on foreign rivers among foreign peoples, and they duly reported the various "real names" and "real oaths" to the tsar in Moscow. For his part, the tsar acquired new tribute payers without acquiring new Russians. Foreigners remained foreigners whether they paid iasak or not: there was to be no New Russia—no attempt at total appropriation—until well into the eighteenth century. Indeed, Russian attitudes toward their Northeastern possessions might well be described by contemporary Western Europeans in terms traditionally reserved for wild men and savages, or rather, in terms of what they were not (as Massa, among others, suggested). The Cossacks did not expect to find much besides furs; they were not particularly surprised or perturbed by the natives; they did not talk of "foreign faith" as inferior to their own; they did not refer to the natives as savages, barbarians, or pagans; they sought nothing but tribute and did not know of any other form of conquest; and they never doubted the "foreigners'" humanity or cared where they came from.

This concentration on "profit" was of course not peculiar to the Russians. According to Sebastian Munster's Universal Cosmography, the Spaniards, "who sought for gold and spices, and not for monsters," refused to waste their time on an island "in which were a kind of men not only with hanging ears, but also with ears of such breadth and length, that with one of them they might cover their whole head."[33] Still, wherever Europeans went, an earthly paradise or yet another fabulous island was always around the corner, and various natives were mostly intelligible in terms of biblical or classical traditions, or perhaps in relation to the pagans and barbarians of one's own time. If the Aztecs were not like the dogheads or Hebrews, they might be similar to the Scythians or Ethiopians.[34] On the other hand, the taiga and tundra peoples of northern Eurasia were simply foreigners, some of whom rode horses, some of whom fished for salmon, and some of whom hunted on foot. If they were ever compared to anybody, it was either to Russians back home ("and those Lamut men have permanent settlements like big Russian suburbs, . . . and they have large [fish] stockpiles like Russian granaries")[35] or to other foreigners who also rode horses, fished for salmon, or hunted on foot ("the Chiukhchi" for

---

[32] Cf. Greenblatt, Marvelous Possessions, pp. 82–83; Bernard McGrane, Beyond Anthropology: Society and the Other (New York, 1989), pp. 19–20.

[33] Quoted in McGrane, Beyond Anthropology, pp. 24–25.

[34] Pagden, The Fall of Natural Man, pp. 24–25; Todorov, The Conquest of America, pp. 108–9; Elliott, The Old World and the New, pp. 19, 21.

[35] N. S. Orlova, ed., Otkrytiia, p. 142.

one, were "nomads after the fashion of the reindeer Samoed").[36] The
tales about the self-devouring monsters from the midnight lands were
fairly popular in sixteenth and seventeenth-century Russia, yet none of
the Cossacks ever associated them with the actual "reindeer Samoed"
whom they were expected to "tributize." To some extent this was because there were no "wide seas," high mountains, or other symbolically significant divides between the Russians and the northerners (the
Europe-Asia border along the Tanais had no meaning outside the small
readership of translated Western cosmographies and the Urals were
not yet an important landmark).[37] Unlike the Spanish or the Portuguese, who crossed oceans to discover new islands, most of the Cossack
pioneers moved gradually across the Eurasian landmass, encountering
an endless and obviously interconnected chain of foreigners.

Yet proximity did not necessarily preclude wonder or revulsion, as
many Greek and Christian travelers had proved. According to William
of Rubruck, "among [the Tatars] being entered, me thought I was come
into a new world."[38] The Cossacks, however, never entered a new world
because, unlike William, they had not been sent to a new world and
because they had no "public" that wanted to hear about new worlds.
Most important, however, the Cossacks' own world was not as starkly
divided into the Christian and non-Christian spheres as was William's.
Rather, it consisted of an apparently limitless number of peoples, all of
whom were assumed to have their own faiths and languages. This was
not a temporary aberration to be overcome through conversion or revelation—this was a normal state of affairs whereby foreigners were expected to remain foreigners. Some local warriors and women could
join the Cossacks, and some Cossacks could ask local spirits for protection, but no one on the frontier seemed to assume that gods were mutually exclusive and that the Russian one(s) would or should prevail any
time soon.

Not all Russians saw it that way, of course. Soon after its establishment in 1621, the archbishopric of Tobol'sk had set about the task of
incorporating the Siberian peoples, landscapes, and past into the Russian—and thus universal Christian—literary and religious tradition.
Followed by annalists working for the house of Stroganov and the Siberian Chancellery, who had their agendas but generally cooperated with
the Church in the symbolic christening and Christianizing of the "new

---

[36] Ibid., p. 233.
[37] Bassin, "Russia between Europe and Asia," pp. 4–7.
[38] Quotation from Beazley, The Texts and Versions, p. 188. See also Greenblatt, Marvelous Possessions, p. 54.

lands," the Tobol'sk scribes radically reinterpreted the Cossacks' reports and recollections. Ermak's campaign was transformed into a crusade for Orthodoxy, an act of revenge against evil foes (*suprotivnye supostaty*), and a quest for eternal glory (*vechnaia slava*) by brave Cossack warriors, whereas the various foreigners became "godless Hagarenes, "accursed infidels," and "filthy barbarians" led by the "proud sultan Kuchum" and punished by the Russian messengers of the Christian God.[39] In other words, if some of the savages discovered by Western European travelers had no religion and most of the foreigners "gathered" by the Cossacks had neutral "faiths," the infidels anathematized by learned Siberian churchmen and administrators were all aggressive and uniformly impious (*zlochestivye*) anti-Christians. There were two general ways of being heathen: one was associated with haughtiness, arrogance, and pride; the other with filth, impurity, and darkness. The former drew on the images of Oriental "perfidy, flattery, and cunning" (*kovarstvo, lest' i lukavstvo*); the latter relied on the oral as well as literary vocabulary of savagery and beastliness. [They live] "like animals in wild forests,"[40]

> Indeed these people are worse than animals, for even dumb animals [*skot bezslovesen*] do not eat beasts, fowl, or grass that God forbade them to eat, while these people, not knowing God who dwells in heaven and refusing to accept His law from those who bring it to them, are raw-eaters [*syroiadtsy*] who eat the meat of beasts and vermin, drink animal filth and blood like water, and eat grass and roots.[41]

Accordingly, the true meaning and the inevitable outcome of Russia's eastward movement was "to carry the Gospel across Siberia to the end of the universe,"[42] eradicating godlessness and thus all foreignness, because in the discourse of Tobol'sk chronicles the opposite of "heathen" was "Russian."

The traders and servitors on the frontier did not seem interested in this outcome, did not preach the Gospel, and did not use words like "heathen." They did, however, use the word "Russian" and they did agree that religion lay at the heart of the difference between them and foreigners (as well as among various foreigners). The term *inozemets*

---

[39] *Sibirskiia lietopisi*, passim. The most common modifiers used to describe "Kuchum's host" are *bezbozhnye, busormenskie, nechestivye, nevernye, okaiannye,* and *poganye.*

[40] *Sibirskiia lietopisi*, p. 331.

[41] Ibid., p. 112.

[42] Ibid., p. 312.

(a person from a different land) could be replaced by the term *inoverets* (a person of different faith) and sometimes by *inoiazychnik* (a person of different language].[43] In any case, the status of being foreign had nothing to do with being the subject of the tsar. The natives who agreed to pay iasak received royal protection and the title of "peaceful," but they did not become Russian. The payment of tribute was, in fact, an exclusively foreign obligation—the Russians paid taxes to or served their sovereign.[44]

Legally, the only way to stop being a foreigner was to become a Christian. Once baptized, a iasak man acquired full rights of "citizenship," ceased to pay tribute, and as a state servitor, received his wages in food or cash. Baptized women were to be married to servitors.[45] The most likely candidates for voluntary conversions were hostages abandoned by their relatives, "criminals" who hoped to escape punishment, slaves who did not want to stay with their masters (Christians could not serve non-Christians), and starving iasak men anxious to be released from tribute and to receive food wages.[46] Generally, however, very few northerners showed any interest in this opportunity—at least to some extent because all "new Christians" (*novokreshchenye*) had to break with their kinsmen and move in with the Russians.[47] As fewer foreigners meant fewer pelts in the treasury, the government in Moscow seemed quite happy with this state of affairs, constantly urging the local authorities "not to baptize any foreigners by force" and not to offend their religious feelings, "so that the Siberian land of the Lena flourish and not become deserted."[48]

For their part, the traders and servitors on the frontier did not normally evince any desire to engage in missionary work, but there was one category of the native population whose souls they were determined to save—the women. In the first half of the seventeenth century most of the Russians in Siberia were single males, "with nobody to bake and to cook for them."[49] By the eighteenth century many of the

---

[43] See, for example, Titov, ed., *Sibir' v XVII v.*, p. 85, and L. A. Gol'denberg, *Semen Ul'ianovich Remezov: Sibirskii kartograf i geograf* (Moscow, 1965), p. 138.

[44] There were a few exceptions; see Shunkov, *Ocherki*, p. 92.

[45] *DAI*, 2:273, 3:223, 4:360; N. S. Orlova, ed., *Otkrytiia*, pp. 531–34; Butsinskii, *Zaselenie Sibiri*, pp. 309–10.

[46] N. S. Orlova, ed., *Otkrytiia*, pp. 254–55; I. I. Ogryzko, *Khristianizatsiia narodov Tobol'skogo Severa v XVIII v.* (Leningrad, 1941), pp. 22–23.

[47] "And the foreigners said that since they had abandoned their faith they would not be allowed back on their land." *RIB*, 2:184. See also Ogryzko, *Khristianizatsiia*, pp. 16–17.

[48] *PSZ*, 2:662–63; *DAI*, 4:360. See also *DAI*, 4:360; Ogryzko, *Khristianizatsiia*, pp. 7–10; *RIB*, 2:215; Miller, *Istoriia Sibiri*, 1:416.

[49] V. A. Aleksandrov, *Russkoe naselenie Sibiri XVII–nachala XVIII v.* (Moscow, 1964), p. 122.

settlers had been allowed to bring their families, but the lack of women remained a serious problem, especially for the traders and Cossacks who lived in faraway forts.[50] Over and over again, they begged the tsar to send them women, for "it is quite impossible for us to be without wives."[51] As few were forthcoming, the Russians "obtained the wives and children of the foreigners for lecherous business"[52] and, in the words of the patriarch Philaret, "mix[ed] with the Tatar, and the Ostiak, and the Vogul heathen women and [did] filthy things, and some of them live[d] with unbaptized Tatar women as with their wives, and [had] children by them."[53] The solution that proved satisfactory to most of the Russians concerned was to baptize the women (and children). Like children but unlike men, the women were not registered tribute payers, so that their removal from the taiga and tundra did not result in any immediate loss of state revenue while at the same time placating the priests and legitimizing some of the children born on the frontier.[54] As far as the Muscovite state was concerned, the Siberian foreigners were to remain iasak men—that is, they were to remain *inozemtsy (inovertsy)* and they were to remain men (tribute payers). The sporadic baptism of foreign women and children added to the number of Russians without subtracting from the number of foreigners.

Converts who were not properly married or adopted could be legally kept as slaves *(kholopy)* provided they came from non-iasak, "unpeaceful" foreigners.[55] Domestic slavery was a common institution in northern Eurasia, and the enemy women were considered legitimate prizes of war. Many circumpolar groups, however, could not cope with the Russian demand, and some settlements and encampments lost almost all of their women.[56] Also, such traditional economic transactions as the payment of bridewealth or adoption of camp "assistants" were obviously perceived by the Russians as the selling of people. This added to the number of slaves, as well as the number of petitions that the iasak people wrote to Moscow, complaining that, in their ruin, they had to "sell and lease" their wives and children.

Slaves, wives, or state servitors, the new Christians seem to have

[50] Ibid., pp. 123–29.

[51] N. N. Ogloblin, "'Zhenskii vopros' v Sibiri v XVII veke," *IV* 41 (1890): 197.

[52] *DAI*, 7:303.

[53] Miller, *Istoriia Sibiri*, 2:276.

[54] Ogryzko, *Khristianizatsiia*, pp. 11, 14; S. S. Shashkov, "Rabstvo v Sibiri," in *Istoricheskie etiudy* (St. Petersburg, 1872), p. 113; Lantzeff, *Siberia in the Seventeenth Century*, pp. 102–3.

[55] *DAI*, 7:143–44; Ogryzko, *Khristianizatsiia*, pp. 11–12.

[56] Butsinskii, *Zaselenie Sibiri*, p. 325.

been accepted as Christians and Russians. Few in number, isolated from their former kinsmen, and integrated into particular Russian estates, they did not remain new for very long, if only because there was no alternative to intermarriage. The term "new Christian" was rarely used, and Cossacks of native origin were never singled out as such in official reports and directives. What did it mean to be Christian (Russian), then? In a land with few churchmen and almost no churches one tended to fall back on the most basic distinctions between human and beastly, godly and godless, us and them: those having to do with dietary and sexual prohibitions. Foul food and fornication, *skarednaia iad'* and *skvernaia pokhot'*, "eating raw food" and sleeping with idolaters, were the most important concerns of frontier priests.[57] Some Cossacks seemed to agree, at least in part. Although they did not attach great importance to the formal baptism of their local concubines and seldom ran the risk of breaking incest taboos because Russian women were not available, they seemed to accept that nothing "defiled one's soul" as much as eating dogs and other "unclean food" (*dushi svoi oskvernili, sobaki eli*).[58] As far as they were concerned—and after the matter of allegiance to the tsar had been taken care of—the difference among various peoples in general and between Russians and foreigners in particular consisted in their "language," "faith," and "customs," not clearly differentiated among themselves and comprising diet, (probably) marriage arrangements, symbols of religious devotion (icons, idols, and temples), and all those practices that made people settled or nomadic, agricultural or pastoral, horse- or reindeer-riding. As the Yakutsk servitor Nekhoroshko Kolobov reported in 1646, the Amur Daurs were less foreign than other foreigners because they "live in households [*dvorami*] and have bread, and horses, and cattle, and pigs, and chickens, and also make wine, and weave, and spin, all according to the Russian custom [*so vsego obychaia s russkogo*]."[59]

Thus, through most of the seventeenth century, the tribute-paying foreigners who wished to remain foreigners were welcome to stay in the woods and pay tribute, whereas those who were convinced or compelled to become Russian could do so if they played by the rules. Unless the rules changed, of course.

[57] See, in particular, Miller, *Istoriia Sibiri*, 2:276; *Sibirskiia lietopisi*, p. 112.
[58] N. S. Orlova, ed., *Otkrytiia*, pp. 83, 98.
[59] Ibid., p. 140; Divin, ed., *Russkaia tikhookeanskaia epopeia*, p. 69.

"Chukchi women," from S. P. Krasheninnikov, *Opisanie zemli Kamchatki. S prilozheniem raportov, donesenii i drugikh neopublikovannykh materialov* (Moscow, 1949)

2

The Unenlightened

The whole World, without Art, and Dress,
Would be but one great Wilderness
And Mankind but a savage Heard
For all that Nature has Conferd
         —Samuel Butler, "The Ladies Answer to the Knight"

The State and the Savages

The rules began to change at the turn of the eighteenth century. When Peter the Great decided that Russia was to catch up with "Europe," it seemed only natural that Russia's non-European foreigners had some catching up of their own to do. According to one of the ideologues of Peter's new elite, V. N. Tatishchev, the history of the world was a steady progression from infancy to maturity, with every new stage brought about by an advance in knowledge. "And so it appears that we can conveniently compare the time before the introduction of writing and the law of Moses with the infancy of man."[1] The concept of world history (universal chronology) and the unqualified support for the "moderns" over the "ancients" were recent imports from Germany, both crucial to Russia's state-sponsored "growing-up" project.[2] The chain of being had become temporal, and just as many of Russia's idiosyncrasies as seen from Europe were now a matter of age difference, the *inozemtsy* were not only "from a different land" but also from a different time. Infants must be baptized and taught how to write, and if the Russians were to become like Swedes, the Russian

---

[1] V. N. Tatishchev, "Razgovor dvu [sic] priiatelei o pol'ze nauki i uchilishchakh," in *Izbrannye proizvedeniia* (Leningrad, 1979), p. 70.

[2] McGrane, *Beyond Anthropology*, pp. 57–61. Most of Tatishchev's "Razgovor" was a translation of Johann Georg Walch's *Philosophisches Lexicon* (Leipzig, 1726). See P. N. Miliukov, *Glavnyia techeniia russkoi istoricheskoi mysli* (St. Petersburg, 1913), pp. 20–21.

47

iasak-payers were to become like the Swedish Lapps. "The Swedes," Tatishchev reported, "have the same Laplanders that we do, and much wilder than the Mordva, Chuvasha, Cheremisa, Votiak, Tungus, etc., but through untiring spiritual labor a large number of them have been baptized, and books in their languages have been printed for them."[3] In addition, according to Peter, converted Asians "would become agreeable to the people of the Russian nation who every year take their caravans for trade and other foreign business."[4] Thus, secularization efforts seemed to require a missionary crusade. Belonging to the new bureaucratic state presupposed a certain degree of civilization, and the pursuit of civilization had to begin with baptism.

There was no question who should introduce the northern foreigners to Christianity. If practical goals and skills were to be borrowed from northern Europe, the mentors of the Russians in matters spiritual came from the Ukraine. Most of the new church hierarchs recruited by Peter had graduated from the Kiev Academy, which had been greatly influenced by the Jesuit colleges in Poland. In Poland, meanwhile—as an anonymous well-wisher reported to Peter in 1700—"they say that the Jesuits, without pay, go to all the faraway and unknown lands to preach the word of God and convert the unfaithful to the Orthodox [sic] faith—like the apostles of old."[5] Coincidentally or not, less than two months after receiving this letter Peter ordered the metropolitan of Kiev to find some good people for missionary work in China and Siberia, and in 1701 the first Ukrainian churchman arrived in Tobol'sk to head one of the largest dioceses in the world.[6]

Missionary activity began almost immediately. The Russian Siberians were ordered to shave their beards and wear German dress;[7] the natives were to be baptized and rewarded with Russian clothes. (In this way, each group was expected to move one step higher.) Special missions were sent to Peking, Kamchatka, Irkutsk, and later to Kolyma, Alazeia, and Anadyr',[8] but it was the Ob' Ugrians who were singled out as the main beneficiaries. In 1702 the new Siberian metropolitan,

[3] Tatishchev, "Razgovor," p. 104.

[4] PSZ, ser. 1, vol. 4, no. 1800, p. 60.

[5] K. V. Kharlampovich, Malorossiiskoe vliianie na velikorusskuiu tserkovnuiu zhizn' (Kazan', 1914), 1:848.

[6] PSZ, ser. 1, vol. 4, no. 1800, p. 60; Kharlampovich, Malorossiiskoe vliianie, pp. 851–52. From 1701 to 1762, all Siberian metropolitans were Ukrainians.

[7] PSI, 1:271–76.

[8] N. A. Abramov, "Materialy dlia istorii khristianskogo prosveshcheniia Sibiri," ZhMNP 81, no. 5 (1854): 41, 44; Kharlampovich, Malorossiiskoe vliianie, pp. 852–56.

Filofei Leshchinskii, received Peter's permission to convert the iasak people without lifting their tribute obligations, and in 1706 he was urged to go down the Ob', "burn the idols," and baptize the "Ostiaks big and small." Force, however, was not to be used, and the first missionary expedition, unsupported by the secular authorities, was driven away by the Mansi.[9] Greatly annoyed, Peter ordered Filofei to "find their seductive false gods-idols and burn them with fire and ax them, and destroy their heathen temples, and build chapels instead of those temples, and put up the holy icons, and baptize these Ostiaks [ikh ostiakov]. . . . And if some Ostiaks show themselves contrary to our great sovereign's decree, they will be punished by death."[10] At the same time, Siberia was made a centralized gubernia, and its first governor, Prince M. P. Gagarin, arrived in Tobol'sk in 1711 with instructions to lend the missionaries a hand. A year later, the metropolitan had a ship, soldiers, interpreters, and gifts for the converts, and as he set out on his first large expedition, the future Christians were being rounded up, "so that these Ostiaks do not run away."[11]

In the course of the next decade Filofei Leshchinskii repeatedly "[tore] down the foundations of their idolatry, ruin[ed] their heathen temples, and demolish[ed] their idols."[12] On reaching an Ugrian settlement a party of several monks and a dozen soldiers would go ashore, and "the teacher" would address the assembled villagers with a sermon on the advantages of Christianity over paganism. An interpreter would translate his words, and the missionaries would proceed to burn "the idols and the heathen temples." Having accomplished this, they would herd the villagers into the river for baptism, whereupon the "new Christians" would receive tin crosses, shirts, pants, bread, and other presents.[13] Some Ugrians tried to flee, refused to leave their houses, or "covered their ears with their hands, like deaf vipers."[14] Others attempted to bargain, anxious to keep their "many wives" and to place the images of their spirits "between the icons." A few attacked the missionaries "with a deadly hand."[15] (According to Filofei's

---

[9] Ogryzko, Khristianizatsiia, p. 26.

[10] PSI, 1:413–14.

[11] Ibid., 2:180. See also Ogryzko, Khristianizatsiia, pp. 33–34.

[12] Novitskii, "Kratkoe opisanie," p. 70.

[13] Ibid., pp. 70–109; PSZ, ser. 1, vol. 5, No. 2863, p. 133; Ogryzko, Khristianizatsiia, p. 34.

[14] Novitskii, "Kratkoe opisanie," pp. 88, 92, 93, 106.

[15] Ibid., pp. 71–72, 75, 100–103.

chronicler, the "teacher" himself was hit "in the belly" [*chrevo*] but escaped unhurt thanks to divine intervention.)[16] In the long run, however, the threat of "punishment by death," the generous distribution of valuable gifts, and a number of special baptism benefits such as three-year iasak waivers and pardons for minor criminals combined to ensure the apparent success of the enterprise, and in 1720 Peter congratulated Filofei on having baptized more than forty thousand pagans.[17]

Another area of mass conversion was Kamchatka. The first of Filofei's envoys, Archimandrite Martinian, arrived there in 1705,[18] but his interests lay elsewhere. In 1711 he took part in a Cossack rebellion and earned himself "a sable overcoat and Petr Chirikov's stolen unbaptized house serfs of the Kamchadal breed, by the foreign names of Shchochka and Chistiak, as well as Volodimer Otlasov's unbaptized house serf girl Nastas'ia."[19] Soon afterward Martinian was strangled by his Itel'men slaves, and his work was inherited by another rebel, Ignatii Kozyrevskii, who founded a monastery before being arrested by the authorities.[20] Finally, in 1745 a special mission consisting of nineteen preachers and led by Archmandrite Ioasaf Khotuntsevskii arrived in Kamchatka to baptize the local population, found schools, and straighten out the priorities of the iasak-centered administration.[21] Five years later, Ioasaf reported to the government that

> all the Kamchadal, except for the Koriak who move from one place to another far away from Kamchatka, have been, by God's grace, baptized by holy baptism, taught, and brought into the faith according to Christ's grace, and for that reason the cause of the preaching of the word of God has ended and there is no one left to be converted from paganism to the Christian Faith.[22]

By then, however, nobody in St. Petersburg seemed to care. Fur revenues were declining rapidly, and Peter's heirs of the mid-eighteenth

---

[16] Ibid., pp. 94.

[17] *PSZ*, ser. 1, vol. 5, no. 2863, p. 133; M. M. Fedorov, *Pravovoe polozhenie narodov Vostochnoi Sibiri, XVII–nachalo XIX v.* (Iakutsk, 1978), pp. 86–88; Ogryzko, *Khristianizatsiia*, pp. 39, 54–57. In fact, the total number of Ob' Ugrians was approximately 13,400. See Ogryzko, *Khristianizatsiia*, p. 49.

[18] Abramov, "Materialy," p. 41.

[19] *PSI*, 2:538.

[20] Okun', *Ocherki*, p. 98; Gurvich, *Etnicheskaia istoriia*, p. 98.

[21] Al'kor and Drezen, eds., *Kolonial'naia politika tsarizma*, pp. 139–49.

[22] Abramov, "Materialy," p. 50.

century were not particularly interested in iasak men, heathen or Orthodox. Churches were still being built; new seminaries were being opened; large groups of people (particularly in the Irkutsk diocese) were being baptized; and concern over the quality of conversions was being voiced,[23] but the central government was no longer willing to commit large sums of money or "good people," let alone military detachments. Banished to the "snowy desert" for various infractions of church discipline and largely forgotten by their superiors, the priests stationed in the north were faced with the formidable task of serving the Christian needs of people who did not seem to have any. Most of the new converts continued to deal with the old spirits and were, as a rule, unable to remember their Christian names and unwilling to follow the prescribed rituals. Under the circumstances, the function of the priests consisted in uncovering and eradicating pagan practices, particularly those relating to marriage. Polygamy and incest (defined according to Russian consanguinity rules) were banned and fitfully prosecuted, whereas the use of bridewealth and the marriage of minors were bemoaned but widely tolerated as ineradicable.[24] Otherwise, the vigor of the routine enforcement of Christianity depended on the local priests. In 1747, for example, Father Pykhov gave the following account of his activities:

In the last year of 1747, in the months of April and May, I beat the new Christian, Ostiak Fedor Senkin, with a whip, because he married his daughter off at the said time and celebrated the wedding feast during the first week of Lent. I also beat his . . . son-in-law with a whip, because he buried his deceased son himself, outside of the church and without the knowledge of the priest. . . . Semen Kornilov Kortyshin was beaten with a whip because he never went to the holy church. . . . I also beat the widow Marfa and her son Kozma with a whip . . . because . . . they kept in their tent a small stone idol, to whom they brought sacrifices, . . . and I broke the said idol with an ax in front of an Ostiak gathering and threw the pieces in all directions.[25]

The broken idols were replaced by icons, some of which made their way into the religious pantheon of the new Christians. In 1754, for ex-

[23] Fedorov, *Pravovoe polozhenie*, pp. 89–95; *Etnicheskaia istoriia narodov Severa* (Moscow, 1982), pp. 125; *Istoriia Iakutskoi ASSR* (Moscow, 1957), 2:208.

[24] Fedorov, *Pravovoe polozhenie*, pp. 95–99.

[25] Ogryzko, *Khristianizatsiia*, p. 91.

ample, Pykhov uncovered a major case of "iconoclasm": seven Khanty, upset about a poor catch, "threw the holy images to the floor and trampled upon them."[26] The most obstinate apostates, especially "magicians," were sent to prison in Tobol'sk where they were interrogated by the consistory and beaten some more. While in detention, many of them died or committed suicide, and at least one shaman was burned at the stake.[27]

As far as most parish priests were concerned, however, a good native was a live native, for the fees for administering Christian rites and the fines for "idolatry" constituted the priests' main source of income. According to the complaints of the iasak people, Father Pykhov charged one ruble for each Christian burial and five rubles in hush money for each traditional one (he seemed to prefer the latter).[28] The other priests who worked among the newly converted "foreigners" were accused of similar practices, and in some areas it was "impossible for them to go to the iasak *volosti* because of great hostility on the part of the new Christians."[29] (One of the leaders of the Itel'men uprising of 1746 admitted to a desire "to kill the father archimandrite Iosaf Khotuntsevskii . . . and to exterminate the Christian faith.")[30]

Not all "pagans" objected to Christianity and its agents. Some were attracted by the economic benefits granted to new converts; others were anxious to enlist the support of the demonstrably powerful Russian spirits. Moreover, the official disapproval of traditional marriage practices provided those dissatisfied with such practices with a new vocabulary and a forceful new protector. By the early nineteenth century the flight of native women from their husbands into the custody of churches had become so widespread that the secular authorites of the Irkutsk province felt it necessary to defend the integrity of the iasak man's family (and thus safeguard their source of fur tribute, because a motherless family was rarely self-sufficient and the traditional requirement that the woman's father or new husband return the bridewealth could not be enforced against the Church). In 1807, the Irkutsk provin-

---

[26] Ibid., pp. 79–80.

[27] Ibid., pp. 94–95; N. A. Minenko, *Severo-zapadnaia Sibir' v XVIII–pervoi polovine XIX v.* (Novosibirsk, 1975), p. 280.

[28] Ogryzko, *Khristianizatsiia*, pp. 106–13.

[29] PSZ, ser. 1, vol. 12, no. 9528, p. 889; V. K. Andrievich, *Istoricheskii ocherk Sibiri po dannym predstavliaemym polnym sobraniem zakonov* (St. Petersburg, 1886–89), 3:215–16.

[30] Al'kor and Drezen, eds., *Kolonial'naia politika tsarizma*, p. 101.

cial administration issued a special decree in which it proclaimed that baptism was fully compatible with the maintenance of all traditional marriage customs except polygamy and incest. Converts to Christianity were not allowed to use their new status to renege on their obligations toward non-Christian spouses.[31]

Wholesale conversions unaccompanied by immediate changes in common law resulted in the creation of a substantial group of Christians who were indistinguishable from pagans. Unlike the individual converts of the seventeenth century (who were freed from iasak insofar as they freed themselves from foreignness), the new mass-produced Christians continued to pay tribute and to violate—with relative impunity—the sacred rules of diet, settlement, and procreation. Official religious affiliation became divorced from both the formal tax status and the traditional meaning of faith. Some subjects of the tsar were different from others in ways that were legally recognized but had no legal justification. By the early nineteenth century "foreigners" (inozemtsy—people from a different land) had become "aliens" (inorodtsy—people of a different birth). Outsiders who used to be redeemable by baptism had become congenital and apparently perennial outsiders. A Khanty Orthodox Christian, a Yakut merchant, and a Tungus cart driver were all inorodtsy; a Polish Catholic noble, a Baltic farmer, and a German landowner usually were not.[32]

The solution to this mystery lies in the innovative and apparently fruitful concept of backwardness. And again, it was Peter who initiated the change. Something of a Renaissance man himself, he inherited the sixteenth and seventeenth-century West European passion for cabinets de curiosités, Kunstkammern, and "fardles of fashions." In Peter's domain, Siberia was the most likely source of things monstrous and fabulous, and, in various impatient decrees, the tsar demanded to see rare birds, animals, stones, "all sorts of antiquities," and pagan idols "that are a marvel to men."[33] The pagans themselves belonged on the same list, especially the more extraordinary specimens like the "foreigners

---

[31] Fedorov, Pravovoe polozhenie, pp. 97–99.

[32] Colloquially, by the early twentieth century any non-Russian could be referred to as an alien, but the use of the term in the sense of "particularly backward non-Russian" remained prevalent in informal speech and obligatory in legal documents. See L. Ia. Shternberg, "Inorodtsy," in Formy natsional'nogo dvizheniia v sovremennykh gosudarstvakh, ed. A. I. Kastelianskii (St. Petersburg, 1910), pp. 531–32.

[33] PSI, 2:292–93, 418–20. See also Andrievich, Istoricheskii ocherk Sibiri, pp. 113, 309–10.

known as sewn faces" and the shamans, "who talk to their idols about all sorts of things and ask them questions, and, in their shamanery . . . throw themselves into the fire and engage in other fantasies."[34] Such requests puzzled low-level Russian administrators, who did not see anything interesting about shamans. The Berezov voevoda, for example, did not send Samoed shamans to Moscow because, in his opinion, they could do nothing special except "beat on the tambourine and scream." It was not up to him to decide, however, and the next decree threatened punishment for using such "excuses."[35]

But even as "wild rams with great horns" and the Tungus with sewn faces were on their way to zoos and exhibits, the eclectic collections of curios were being replaced by orderly classifications based on rigorous hierarchies. In 1719 Peter sent a German scientist, Daniel Messerschmidt, to Siberia to study the country's geography, natural history, medicine and medicinal plants, peoples and their philology, old monuments and antiquities, and "everything noteworthy."[36] Messerschmidt was followed by several large expeditions, most of them led by learned Germans, who, with the assistance of their Russian students and local Swedish prisoners, were expected to determine prospects for mining, food provisioning, and commerce; discover whether Asia was connected with America; prove Russian claims to various Asian territories; "and generally find out everything that has scientific interest," from "grasses, animals, fish, birds, and minerals" to "astronomical observations."[37] At the same time, local officials received specially prepared questionnaires about all aspects of life in their districts.[38]

The peoples were second in importance to the birds and minerals—let alone the "great wealth and loud fame . . . of our merchantry"—but they, too, were to be described and classified (categories of humanity were part of the "system of Nature," as Linnaeus made clear in 1735). An important reason for this interest was "curiosity" (liubopytstvo) and "entertainment" (uveselenie), new virtues brought to Russia by

[34] PSI, 1:242. See also 1:240–41 and 2:365–67 and 437–42.

[35] Ibid., 1:241–42.

[36] Pypin, Istoriia, 1:83.

[37] Miller, Istoriia Sibiri, 1:8–13; M. V. Lomonosov, Polnoe sobranie sochinenii (Moscow, 1952), 6:422, 534; Russkie ekspeditsii po izucheniiu severnoi chasti Tikhogo okeana (Moscow, 1984), 1:21, 30, 35, 116, and passim; J. Lawrence Black, "Opening Up Siberia: Russia's 'Window on the East'," in Wood, ed., The History of Siberia, pp. 57–68.

[38] A. I. Andreev, ed., "Opisaniia o zhizni i uprazhnenii obitaiushchikh v Turukhanskoi i Berezovskoi okrugakh raznogo roda iasachnykh inovertsev," SE, no. 1 (1947): 84–103; V. N. Tatishchev, Izbrannye proizvedeniia (Leningrad, 1979), pp. 8–11.

Western Europeans and seen as an important prerequisite to enlightenment. Gerhard Friedrich Müller exulted at the "multicolored paradise of unknown grasses," "the zoo of rare Asian animals," and "the cabinet of antiquities containing pagan burial sites" that he found in Siberia and did his best to recreate in St. Petersburg.[39] Yet in the new world of St. Petersburg curiosity and entertainment were always accompanied by "profit"—not the "sovereign's profit" (vygoda) of the seventeenth-century Cossacks, which stood solely for material gain, but general pol'za (benefit, practical use), which implied a certain educational utility and was ultimately based on natural law.[40] Müller and his colleagues knew that the scientific pol'za of their endeavors consisted in establishing scientific regularities among the various "multicolored" objects. If the frontiersmen identified different groups of iasak men with their ways of life (settled or nomadic, traveling by horse or on foot), and the annalists traced all "tongues" to certain biblical ancestors or prototypes, the professional academics of the eighteenth century searched for "scientific"—mostly historical and philological—connections and regularities among the multicolored peoples that they discovered. Relying on Leibniz (via Schlözer and Stralenberg), they all agreed that the true basis for ethnic classification was "not mores and customs, not food and economic pursuits, and not religion, for all these may be the same in peoples of different tribes and different in peoples of the same tribe. The only foolproof standard is language: where languages are similar, there are no differences among peoples."[41] Indeed, in Schlözer's words, "just as Linnaeus divides animals according to their teeth, and plants, according to their stamens, the historian must classify peoples according to language."[42]

Having done this (by the end of the century most circumpolar peoples had been placed in their current "families"), the historian or government official proceeded to describe his subjects as fully as possible, in an effort to render them totally and permanently transparent. Such portraits of nations—and ultimately definitions of what constituted human life—usually described the origins, territory, physical appear-

---

[39] V. G. Mirzoev, Istoriografiia Sibiri: Domarksistskii period (Moscow, 1970), p. 78; Miller, Istoriia Sibiri, 1:30.

[40] The first Russian monthly, published by the Academy and edited by Müller, was titled "Monthly essays serving to instruct and to entertain" (Ezhemesiachnye sochineniia, k pol'ze i uveseleniiu sluzhashchie).

[41] Miller, Istoriia Sibiri, 1:31.

[42] Quoted in Miliukov, Glavnye techeniia, p. 89.

ance, clothes, temperament, intellectual and economic life, dwellings, food, religion, writing systems, methods of time reckoning, marriage and burial practices, child-rearing, health, and festivals.[43] Within this framework, all nations were comparable; all belonged to the same hierarchy, which in the eighteenth century was increasingly represented as temporal in nature. The editor of *Opisanie vsekh obitaiushchikh v Rossiiskom gosudarstve narodov* (A description of all the peoples inhabiting the Russian state) noted that the ethnic variety of the Russian empire mirrored "the World in all the stages of transition to the modern World, refined and enriched by needs." The lowest stage was represented by the "crude and warlike . . . peoples who wander without any laws, live off hunting and fishing, and wear only animal skins and bird feathers;" the middle one, by the pastoralists; and the third, by the "agricultural estate," which stretches "from early cultivation to complete perfection."[44]

In other words, the second encounter between the Russians and the native northerners was that between perfection and crudity. Eighteenth-century Russian travelers to Siberia were acutely conscious of this, all the more so because their own perfection was fairly recent. Fresh converts to the cause of scientific progress, they judged the northerners by the loftiest standards of reason and civility and found them severely wanting. The gloomy picture that they drew was approved and corroborated by their German teachers, most of whom were scornful of the French flirtation with primitivism, and to some extent picked up by the Cossacks and merchants of the frontier.[45]

The most striking feature of aboriginal life was dirt. According to Krasheninnikov, the Kamchadal "do not keep themselves clean at all, do not wash their hands and faces, do not cut their fingernails, eat off the same plates as dogs and never wash them, all smell like fish, . . . do not comb their hair."[46] V. F. Zuev, who was sent by Peter Simon Pallas to study the Samoed and the Ugrians, was at a loss for words to

[43] See, for example, Andreev, ed., "Opisaniia"; Iogann Gottlib [Iohann Gottlieb] Georgi, *Opisanie vsekh obitaiushchikh v Rossiiskom gosudarstve narodov* (St. Petersburg, 1799); Krasheninnikov, *Opisanie zemli Kamchatki*; Novitskii, *Kratkoe opisanie*; *Russkie ekspeditsii*, 1:155, 2:67–68, 130–31; V. N. Tatishchev, *Izbrannye trudy po geografii Rossii* (Moscow, 1950), pp. 37–40; V. F. Zuev, *Materialy po etnografii Sibiri XVIII veka (1771–1772)* (Moscow, 1947).

[44] Georgi, *Opisanie*, pp. vii–x.

[45] Eugene E. Reed, "The Ignoble Savage," *Modern Language Review* 59 (1964): 53–64; Al'kor and Drezen, eds., *Kolonial'naia politika tsarizma*, pp. 29–33; *Russkie ekspeditsii*, 2:93.

[46] Krasheninnikov, *Opisanie zemli Kamchatki*, p. 367.

describe their "swinish living": "All the dogs usually eat in the same tents, and some sleep there, as well, and relieve themselves without any subsequent cleaning, for which reason the smell in those tents is so revolting that probably no one would agree to sit there for a long time."[47]

This "incredible foulness," manifested primarily but not exclusively in revolting smells and filthy (gnusnaia) food, was compounded by very bad manners. For Russian students brought up on the moralistic literature of the Enlightenment (much of it translated—via French or German—from Addison and Steele's instructions on how to be a "true fine gentleman"),[48] the native lack of social graces was truly appalling. "Their actions are exceedingly rude," wrote S. P. Krasheninnikov. "There is no civility in speech and no courtesy whatsoever. They do not take off their hats and do not bow to each other."[49] (It must be noted that Russian settlers were found to be almost as bad. Krasheninnikov, for one, could see little difference between them and the Itel'men.)[50] Among the many social improprieties, however, the one that struck the "true fine gentlemen" as the most despicable was the aboriginal treatment of women. Zuev called it "barbaric" and compared the position of the "lovely sex" to that of slaves and animals. He saw the native division of labor as grossly unfair and interpreted the various rules of avoidance as rudeness: "Although one cannot argue with them about it because of their wildness, one wishes that, under the circumstances, [the men] would at least speak nicely to them."[51]

The travelers' scorn and indignation were moderated by the utter ridiculousness of many of the things they saw. Just as all the sciences could be ranked according to their usefulness, from "useful" (poleznye) to "stupid" (glupye),[52] so could customs and religions. Indeed, the main function of the numerous and influential eighteenth-century

[47] Zuev, Materialy, p. 29. See also Peter Simon Pallas, Puteshestvie po raznym mestam Rossiiskago gosudarstva po poveleniiu sanktpeterburgskoi imperatorskoi Akademii nauk (St. Petersburg, 1788), 3:58. Bad smell also figured prominently in the first Siberian impressions of Russians. According to a Nanai tradition, "the newcomers smelled so much of soap and rancid fat that some people fainted." V. K. Arsen'ev, Izbrannye proizvedeniia v 2kh tomakh (Moscow, 1986), 2:33.

[48] Iu. D. Levin, "Angliiskaia prosvetitel'skaia zhurnalistika v russkoi literature XVIII veka," in Epokha Prosveshcheniia. Iz istorii mezhdunarodnykh sviazei russkoi literatury (Leningrad, 1967), p. 27.

[49] Krasheninnikov, Opisanie zemli Kamchatki, p. 369.

[50] Ibid., p. 505.

[51] Zuev, Materialy, pp. 31, 59. See also G. A. Sarychev, Puteshestvie po severo-vostochnoi chasti Sibiri i Ledovitomu moriu i Vostochnomu okeanu (Moscow, 1952), p. 244.

[52] Tatishchev, "Razgovor," p. 93.

satirical journals was to demonstrate how ludicrous and preposterous various superstitions (that is, practices "not regulated by virtue and disciplined by reason")[53] were. Accordingly, many of the northern customs and traditions were found to be stupid (silly, foolish) or funny. According to Zuev, "Although they follow the example of their ancestors, the stupidity [*glupost'*] of the old ways is not diminishing but, on the contrary, foolishness is constantly increasing [*umnozhaetsia durachestvo*]."[54] The farther from the "true fine gentleman," the greater the foolishness: Zuev, for example, ranked the mental abilities of the Ugrians above those of the Samoed because they lived closer to the Russians.[55]

Even more numerous were the customs and traditions that the indigenous northerners did not have at all. If history was perceived as a triumphal march of reason based on the development of the arts and sciences, it was only reasonable to measure the new peoples against the "complete perfection" of the eighteenth century. The result was the negative mode of description used by Hobbes to represent the state of nature, or rather, an enumeration of traits and institutions that the people in question did not possess.[56] Thus, "They do not have any idea about divinity and the duty of man to his creator and his neighbor; they do not see virtue in anything; . . . they do not understand anything about the afterlife or the soul; [and] they do not have any holidays."[57] Also, they "do not keep themselves clean," "do not follow any rules in marriage," and generally "do not have any good customs."[58] Even their laws, according to Zuev, were so stupid and few in number that, "to put it simply, they do not have any law at all."[59]

This state of not having civilization was known as wildness or savagery, and in the course of the eighteenth century the corresponding Russian term *dikii* became a descriptive synonym of "alien." Moreover, if not having European traits made an alien savage, then sharing certain

[53] Quoted from Addison in Rudolf Neuhäuser, *Towards the Romantic Age: Essays on Sentimental and Preromantic Literature in Russia* (The Hague, 1974), p. 47.

[54] Zuev, *Materialy*, p. 40. See also Andreev, ed., "Opisaniia," pp. 96, 101; A. N. Radishchev, *Polnoe sobranie sochinenii* (Moscow, 1952), 3:135; G. I. Shelikhov, *Rossiiskogo kuptsa Georgiia Shelikhova stranstvovaniia iz Okhotska po Vostochnomu okeanu k Amerikanskim beregam* (Khabarovsk, 1971), p. 45.

[55] Zuev, *Materialy*, p. 23.

[56] Cf. Hodgen, *Early Anthropology*, pp. 196–201.

[57] Andreev, ed., "Opisaniia," p. 90. See also *Russkie ekspeditsii*, 1:93, 130.

[58] Krasheninnikov, *Opisanie zemli Komchatki*, p. 367; Andreev, ed., "Opisaniia," p. 97; Divin, ed, *Russkaia tikhookeanskaia epopeia*, p. 144.

[59] Zuev, *Materialy*, p. 40.

traits with an alien could be very embarassing for a European. In 1783 a Berezov official was asked about the average child-bearing age among native women. "Women," he reported, "start having babies and become fruitful, and then stop having babies in the same way as Russian and other women." This sentence—the only one out of a long questionnaire with numerous explicit descriptions—was deleted by the censor.[60]

An almost unrelieved picture of foulness and savagery persisted through most of the eighteenth century—in spite of the popularity in Russia of French primitivist literature. Where in France, however, the wise Huron was useful as a detached critic of the state, in Russia—in an atmosphere of universal enthusiasm for the achievements and the potential of science and bureaucracy—he was largely irrelevant. Most Russian travelers seemed well aware that the absence of civilization and enlightenment (ignorance) could also be interpreted as the absence of pride and affectation (innocence),[61] but it was the ignorance that struck them the most. Until the last quarter of the century, there were no noble Tungus or perspicacious Buriat, and Rousseau's first *Discours* met with stern rebuke from all quarters.[62]

Ignorance, foolishness, and other forms of immaturity could be overcome through education. Theoretically, conversion to Christianity remained an important goal, but both the logic of Tatishchev's argument and the results of Filofei's crusade seemed to indicate that Christianization was only the beginning of a much larger process. To be truly enlightened, one had to fill the remaining absences in one's life and identity (of intelligence, laws, manners, clothes, and so on) and thus move from infancy to maturity, that is, to grow up. In the case of the Arctic foragers, by far the "wildest" and most infantile inhabitants of the Russian empire, growing up involved adopting the "better buildings, more profitable lifestyles, more convenient hunting and fishing tools," and the "easier ways of satisfying one's needs" that the Russians had brought to them.[63] In other words, enlightenment meant Russification, just as baptism had a century before. And once again, the door was theoretically open to all: the native who adopted the Russian ways

[60] Andreev, ed., "Opisaniia," p. 97.

[61] See, for example, Krasheninnikov, *Opisanie zemli Komchatki*, p. 368, and Zuev, *Materialy*, p. 52.

[62] Iu. M. Lotman, "Russo i russkaia kul'tura XVIII veka," in *Epokha prosveshcheniia*, pp. 223–28; Neuhäuser, *Towards the Romantic Age*, p. 91.

[63] Ivan Boltin, *Primechaniia na Istoriiu drevniia i nyneshniia Rossii g. Leklerka* (St. Petersburg, 1788), 2:146.

of satisfying his needs was expected to become Russian. As Ivan Boltin saw it, many of the intrepid Siberian frontiersmen were natives who had "become like Russians, accepted their law, adopted their customs and traditions, and intermarried with them."[64] Some authors believed that this transformation involved nothing but the schooling of rational individuals,[65] whereas others expected a relatively lengthy struggle against environmental handicaps,[66] but all agreed that eventual success was assured. This seemed to be the consensus of Russia's European mentors and the crucial assumption behind Russia's own quest for perfection.

The State and the Tribute Payers

Whatever the place of "the wild men" in the chain of being, it was their place in the structure of the state that mattered the most. In the words of Krasheninnikov, the newly acquired scientific knowledge was "mostly needed by the great men who, because of their highest power, have charge of the successful governance of the state and of the increase in the state's profit."[1] The state's profit, or rather, the good of the state—pol'za rather than vygoda—was now the main reason for the aliens' existence, the true goal of enlightenment, and, retroactively, the main cause of Russian eastward expansion. The "usefulness" of Siberia, according to Müller, consisted in the "peopling of those parts by Russian citizens [Rossiiskimi zhiteliami], in order to ensure the obedience of the conquered peoples and to add an ever greater number thereof to the Russian state [k Rossiiskoi derzhave]."[2] As the Russian state became a European empire and Siberia became a Russian colony, the existence of obedient conquered peoples was seen as an important source of international prestige.[3] Russia had its own legitimate savages

---

[64] Ibid.

[65] Krasheninnikov, Opisanie zemli Kamchatki, p. 411; Mirzoev, Istoriografiia Sibiri, p. 107.

[66] Boltin, Primechaniia; Andreev, ed., Opisaniia, pp. 94, 99; Radishchev, Polnoe sobranie, 2:64–67.

[1] Krasheninnikov, Opisanie zemli Kamchatki, p. 87.

[2] G. F. Miller [Gerhard-Friedrich Müller], Opisanie sibirskago tsarstva i vsekh proisshedshikh v nem diel, ot nachala, a osoblivo ot pokoreniia ego Rossiiskoi derzhavie po sii vremena (St. Petersburg, 1750), chap. 4, sec. 24. See also Boltin, Primechaniia, 2:143, and Johann Eberhard Fischer, Sibirskaia istoriia s samago otkrytiia Sibiri do zavoevaniia sei zemli Rossiiskim oruzhiem (St. Petersburg, 1774), pp. 111–12.

[3] Bassin, "Russia between Europe and Asia," pp. 5–6, and "Inventing Siberia," pp. 768–70.

because "the similarity between the way of life, customs, and traits of our crude peoples and of the numerous savages from other parts of the World is . . . obvious."[4] Indeed, if one measured greatness by the number and variety of conquered peoples, there was no other "State or Power" in the world that could compare to Russia.[5] The Russian empire was the greatest ever because neither Greece nor Rome, neither the old World nor the New—"however much they may brag about their heroes . . . would have been able to conquer one-eighth of the globe in eighty years." And not just any one-eighth, but "the roughest and most dangerous part of all, where hunger and cold have their eternal abode."[6] Paradoxically, it could also be the richest—provided its wealth, its location, and its natives could be rendered "useful."[7]

The usefulness of the natives continued to be equal to the amount of iasak that they delivered, but throughout the eighteenth century the quantity and the quality of the latter continued to decline.[8] The characteristic reaction of Peter and his followers was to streamline the bureaucracy. The first governor of Siberia, Prince Gagarin, was executed in 1721, the voevoda of Irkutsk in 1722, and the vice-governor of Irkutsk in 1736.[9] Scores of minor officials were hanged, "beaten unmercifully with a knout," or had their nostrils ripped out; and in 1730 the Siberian Chancellery, abolished in the heady days of the early Petrine reforms, was reestablished in the interests of closer supervision.

The first change in tribute policy occurred in 1727–28, when the government abolished the state monopoly on sable trade, raised tariffs, authorized payment of iasak in cash, and recommended the transfer of iasak collection from the Russian officials to the native elders.[10] The reform backfired, however: the iasak people circumvented low official estimates by selling their pelts to merchants and then paying state collectors in cash; the merchants continued to be fairly successful at evading taxation; and the state collectors made up their losses by more energetic "stealing." Unable to keep up, the government promptly re-

---

[4] Georgi, *Opisanie*, p. x.

[5] Ibid., p. vi.

[6] Fischer, *Sibirskaia istoriia*, p. 630. See also Boltin, *Primechaniia*, 2:145, and Miller, *Opisanie*, chap. 2, sec. 1.

[7] Boltin, *Primechaniia*, 2:144, 149; Lomonosov, *Polnoe sobranie sochinenii*, 6:422.

[8] Fedorov, *Pravovoe polozhenie*, p. 48.

[9] L. S. Rafienko, "Sledstvennye kommissii v Sibiri v 30kh–60kh godakh XVIII veka," in Shunkov, ed., *Osvoenie Sibiri*, p. 161.

[10] E. M. Zalkind, "Iasachnaia politika tsarizma v Buriatii v XVIII–pervoi polovine XIX vv.," in Shunkov, ed., *Ekonomika, upravlenie*, p. 237; Fedorov, *Pravovoe polozhenie*, pp. 49–50, 107; Marc Raeff, *Siberia and the Reforms of 1822* (Seattle, 1956), p. 93.

established the state monopoly on furs and forbade private traders to enter the iasak districts.[11] Judging by the relentless ferocity of official merchant-bashing, however, the policy of separation could not be enforced. The population of the north, both Russian and native, had become too dependent on trade to heed any admonitions from St. Petersburg.

Intoxicants (liquor, tobacco, tea), metal utensils (particularly kettles and axes), weapons (including traps), and some foodstuffs (especially flour, butter, and sugar) had become indispensable elements of aboriginal culture. According to a Chukchi tradition, for example, some of their neighbors included people who cut themselves in half and gave large fish and otters in exchange for tobacco; dwarfs not larger than a forearm who paid for tobacco with lynx and muskrat skins; and shaggy creatures with human faces and polar-bear bodies who gave a whole marten for a small piece of the black deposit from a pipe. "And all men of that land covet tobacco throughout their lives."[12]

The strong dependence on trade was not confined to tribute payers and Arctic centaurs. With the decline in fur trade and the transformation of foreigners into aliens, most Russian settlements in the taiga and tundra lost their commercial and military importance. Between 1700 and 1782, only eight new families moved into Berezov, which was praised by Müller as the richest town of the north.[13] Smaller forts and blockhouses became very small indeed: in 1731, Okhotsk had about thirty Cossacks who lived on fish and roots behind delapidated walls, and by the middle of the century, only about thirty permanent townsmen survived in Olekminsk and sixty, in Srednekolymsk.[14] Most of the children and grandchildren of the original settlers were poorly-paid *mestizo* foragers who relied on local goods and spirits and "[did] not know how to use . . . harquebuses and bows, . . . so that in battle the enemy, seeing their simplicity and inexperience, behave[d] with bravery."[15] It took Peter only a year to reverse his order concerning the intro-

[11] Zalkind, "Iasachnaia politika," p. 238; Fedorov, *Pravovoe polozhenie*, p. 52.

[12] Bogoras, *The Chukchee*, pp. 59–60.

[13] Minenko, *Severo-zapadnaia Sibir'*, pp. 37–48. See also Safronov, *Russkie na severo-vostoke Azii*, pp. 182–84.

[14] Safronov, *Russkie na severo-vostoke Azii*, pp. 187, 204, 210. Russian settlements in the still-turbulent Kamchatka, Anadyrsk, and later Gizhiga were somewhat more populous. See Gurvich, *Etnicheskaia istoriia*, pp. 123–32.

[15] *PSI*, 1:406. See also Sarychev, Puteshestvie, p. 40; Gurvich, *Etnicheskaia istoriia*, pp. 125, 127; N. S. Shchukin, *Poezdka v Iakutsk* (St. Petersburg, 1844), pp. 228–29; Peter Dobell, *Travels in Kamchatka and Siberia* (London, 1830), 1:153; and S. S. Hill, *Travels in Siberia* (1854; reprint, New York, 1970), 2:197–99.

duction of German dress in Siberia, and in the early nineteenth century the Cossacks were allowed to wear parkas on official business.[16]

Cossack life in Kamchatka is almost no different from that of the Kamchadal, for both live on roots and fish and toil in the same occupations: in the summer they catch fish and store it for the winter, in the fall they dig up roots and pick nettles, and in the winter they weave nets from them. The only difference is (1) that the Cossacks live in cabins, and the Kamchadal, for the most part, in earth dugouts; (2) that the Cossacks eat more boiled fish, and the Kamchadal prefer it dry; (3) that the Cossacks prepare various other dishes from fish.[17]

After the hunting grounds open to most Russian settlers had been exhausted, the furs, skins, fish, and mammoth tusks that they obtained from the natives became the only goods they could offer the southern merchants in exchange for bread, tools, and clothes. By the end of the eighteenth century, a fairly large number of the former Cossacks and peasants had become full-time trading middlemen between the iasak people and the rest of the empire.[18]

The growth in trade led to the establishment of permanent commercial networks that linked the settler communities with the inhabitants of the tundra and the taiga. Most iasak people had special "friends" to whom they would bring their goods and from whom they would receive fresh supplies. "Friendship" had been a common way of formalizing exchange relationships in the precolonial north, and, in the absence of cash, the Russians were quickly incorporated into the system. In market terms, this arrangement amounted to full individual monopolies: each merchant had exclusive rights to all of his friend's produce (sometimes including the iasak). The trapper's ability to fulfill the contract was, however, greatly impaired by the depredations of iasak collectors, the extermination of fur-bearing animals, and the effects of the very commodity they desired most—alcohol. As one official put it, "many of those iasak Tungus live in . . . villages and work for the peasants, and get drunk on beer and tobacco and do not hunt for ia-

---

[16] Andrievich, *Istoricheskii ocherk Sibiri*, 2:108; Minenko, *Severo-zapadnaia Sibir'*, p. 106.

[17] Krasheninnikov, *Opisanie zemli Kamchatki*, p. 505.

[18] Gurvich, *Etnicheskaia istoriia*, p. 129; Minenko, *Severo-zapadnaia Sibir'*, pp. 68–78.

sak."[19] Thus, the monopoly of "friendship" worked both ways: if the iasak man failed to deliver, the trader, who usually had little capital, was forced to borrow from his southern supplier in much the same way as the "alien" borrowed from him.[20] The exchange relationship was still far from equal, however; the Russian traders functioned in two economic systems and did their best to profit from their intermediate status.[21]

Another source of income for the Cossacks was tribute collection. According to an Itel'men "rebel,"

> We plotted because of the intolerable offence of the collectors and servitors who come to us for collections. Namely in the year of 1730 Commissar Ivan Novgorodov sent his brother Matvei to the Elovka to collect iasak from me, and he took double iasak for my kinsmen, and besides the iasak he took five sable or fox pelts from every man as gifts, and those who did not have anything had to give clothes, of the male and female sex. And with him, Novgorodov, there was a clerk, Ekim Mukhoplev, who, during iasak collection, raped my wedded wife in lecherous sin.[22]

Kamchatka and Chukotka were still relatively "unpacified," but the iasak collector's job remained the same all over the north: he bore the ultimate responsibility for, and provided all the information on, the numbers of iasak people and the quantity and price of the furs that they delivered. This combination proved lethal for the state treasury, as well as for the tribute payers. In the 1720s, the officials of the Tomsk uezd failed to mention 83 percent of their iasak people; and between 1752 and 1762, 1500 cases of "pilfering the state's interest" were under investigation in Yakutsk (there were only half as many servitors in the city).[23] In some areas the decline in iasak deliveries was compounded

[19] Quoted in Okladnikov, "Kureiskie tungusy," p. 118. There were few peasants in northern Siberia, however; most people belonging to that estate were actually traders, hunters, fishermen, or cart drivers.

[20] Minenko, Severo-zapadnaia Sibir', p. 69.

[21] Ibid., p. 70.

[22] Al'kor and Drezen, eds., Kolonial'naia politika tsarizma, p. 70. The next year the collectors were different, but the results were the same, and when the rebels caught a third Novgorodov brother, they killed him together with his wife and four children (Ivan was executed by the Russian authorities and Matvei and Mukhoplev were beaten with a knout). See Krasheninnikov, Opisanie zemli Kamchatki, p. 497.

[23] Kopylov, "K voprosu o printsipe iasachnogo oblozheniia," p. 64; Rafienko, "Sledstvennye kommissii v Sibiri," p. 146; V. M. Kabuzan and S. M. Troitskii, "Chislennost' i sostav gorodskogo naseleniia Sibiri v 40–80-kh godakh XVIIIv.," in Shunkov, ed., Osvoenie Sibiri, p. 173.

by a decline in the iasak-paying population. Although the economically diversified, cattle-owning Yakut and Buriat communities continued to grow and expand, most hunting and gathering groups grew very
slowly or did not grow at all. By the nineteenth century the numbers
of Yukagir, Koriak, Eniseians, and Itel'men fell very substantially (in
the case of the Yukagir, to a few hundred).[24]

Seeing such constant "loss of interest," the government issued
countless decrees aimed at protecting the iasak people and sent numerous "investigative commissions," which resulted in beatings and be-
headings of local officials.[25] Russians of all estates were to stay away
from the native areas unless they were "on her imperial majesty's business or on a matter of utmost urgency"; no trade was to take place outside of specially indicated fairs "for pain of severe fines and physical
torture"; and as many court cases as possible were to be tried by the
iasak people themselves, "on regular [as opposed to sealed] paper" or
even "out loud."[26] In an attempt to stop the undervaluing of furs, the
government declared in 1738 that iasak collectors were not responsible
for price shortfalls on the Moscow market. Relieved, the collectors began to sell the best pelts on the side and send the low-quality ones to
the treasury. Four years later the new law was scrapped—to be reintro-
duced in 1754, along with an exhortation not to accept cash, if at all
possible.[27]

As the administrative and legal reshuffling continued, more and
more high officials, special investigators, and exiled well-wishers arrived at the conclusion that the iasak man's only salvation lay in his
separation from the Russians.[28] A logical continuation of a long-
standing policy, this view acquired an important moral dimension in
the 1760s, when the influence of the French encyclopedists began to
replace that of the staunchly antiprimitivist Germans; Russian senti-
mentalism made its appearance in Kheraskov's early journals; and V.

[24] V. M. Kabuzan and S. M. Troitskii, "Chislennost' i sostav naseleniia Sibiri v pervoi
polovine XIX veka," in Russkoe naselenie Pomor'ia i Sibiri (Period feodalizma), ed. A. P.
Okladnikov (Moscow, 1973), pp. 271–77.

[25] PSZ, ser. 1, vol. 9, nos. 6407 and 7009, pp. 131–32, 876–79; G. P. Basharin, Istoriia
agrarnykh otnoshenii v Iakutii: 60e gody XVIII–seredina XIX v. (Moscow, 1956), p. 47;
Fedorov, Pravovoe polozhenie, pp. 52–53; Rafienko, "Sledstvennye kommissii," pp.
143–46; Istoriia Sibiri s drevneishikh vremen do nashikh dnei, Okladnikov et al., eds.,
(Leningrad, 1968), 2:311.

[26] Al'kor and Drezen, eds., Kolonial'naia politika tsarizma, p. 85; Minenko, Severo-
zapadnaia Sibir', pp. 239–40.

[27] Minenko, Severo-zapadnaia Sibir', pp. 234–35; Basharin, Istoriia, pp. 47–48.

[28] Rafienko, "Sledstvennye kommissii," pp. 143–46; Minenko, Severo-zapadnaia
Sibir', p. 242.

K. Trediakovskii published his famous translation of Fénelon's *Aventures de Télémaque* (there were about thirty different versions in all).[29] With Catherine's ascension to the throne, the Russian monarchy became enlightened; the Russian Muslims became well-regarded; Siberia became a "tsardom"; and its savage subjects became noble—or at least not entirely beastly. As such, they needed to be protected not only for the sake of Her Majesty's "interest" but also for their own sake, in order to preserve some of their original purity. In her instruction to Captain Billings, Catherine recommended kindness for the usual reason that it had "always enjoyed the best success with unenlightened peoples and that conquest achieved by such kind methods was always the firmest," but went on to explain that the "poor creatures" lived "in the darkness of ignorance rather than ferocity" and that whatever "vengefulness" they exhibited had been provoked by the Europeans.[30] As certain aliens became poor creatures, the scorn and revulsion of educated travelers was partly replaced by pity and a certain (qualified) admiration. A. N. Radishchev, the first exiled martyr of the Russian revolutionary tradition, found the native Siberians stupid and not very different from animals, but pointed out that, "if not reasonable," they were definitely "sensitive and suffering."[31] Captain Sarychev, Billings's second-in-command and a man not usually given to philosophizing, had this to say about the Tungus: "No matter how poor the state of these people might seem, they are much happier in it than enlightened rich people who have their pleasures all the time. They do not know any troubles or worries; their needs are limited; and their whole welfare consists in the abundance of fish."[32] The much more self-consciously literary Martin Sauer, Billings's English secretary, was totally "enchanted with [the Tungus] manly activity" and, quoting Dryden, pronounced them to be "as free as Nature first form'd man."[33]

Both Sarychev and Sauer wrote in the 1780s, when the sentimentalist canon had become common in Russia, but the vocabulary of royal decrees began to change from the first days of Catherine's reign. In 1763 she ordered Major Shcherbachev to go to Siberia, to punish those responsible for the ruin of the "timid and helpless iasak people," and to

[29] Neuhäuser, *Towards the Romantic Age*, pp. 37, 45–46; Reed, "The Ignoble Savage."

[30] Sarychev, *Puteshestvie*, pp. 289–90.

[31] Radishchev, *Polnoe sobranie sochinenii*, 3:135, 424–25.

[32] Sarychev, *Puteshestvie*, p. 60.

[33] Martin Sauer, *An Account of a Geographical and Astronomical Expedition to the Northern Parts of Russia* (London, 1802; reprint, Richmond, England, 1972), p. 46.

come up with a plan for improving their lot and raising the fur revenue, for "without our special motherly condolence, we cannot even imagine the disorder and popular burden that are going on in the remote parts of Our Empire and that our loyal subjects have to endure with utmost offence, all because of the robbery and the oppression of the iasak collectors and their assistants."[34]

Thus the old tribute problem and the new intellectual fashion came together in favor of reform—all the more opportunely as Catherine was busy restructuring her empire in accordance with reason. Under the circumstances, as she pointed out to her governors, the promotion of the welfare of her subjects would show "the indisputable truth that a whole could never be perfect if the parts remained in disorder and disarray."[35] The northern tribute payers, among others, were to be protected in such a way "as to assure their peaceful residence in Our Empire, not forgetting the interest of the treasury."[36]

The solution suggested by Catherine and spelled out in detail by the Shcherbachev commission (First Iasak Commission) consisted in the maximum isolation of the "timid and helpless iasak people," or rather, in establishing as direct a link as possible between the Arctic furs and the crown. Individual tribute was officially replaced by group tribute from entire volosti; hostage-taking was banned; and the Siberian Chancellery was abolished (from then on, all pelts were received by the Royal Cabinet, the empress's personal treasury). Each native unit was assigned a particular form of tribute that was to be collected by the local "elders and princelings" and handed over to the Russian officials at special reception points. Iasak rates were fixed, but, if the prices were too low or the catch poor, the assigned furs could be replaced by payments in cash or kind. Trading was allowed only at annual fairs; the priests were to stay away from their flock before iasak collection time; and the iasak people were not to be summoned to town, whatever their debt.[37]

Much of the reform was, of course, the legitimation of existing prac-

[34] PSZ, ser. 1, 16:154.

[35] Ibid., p. 716.

[36] Catherine's "Instruction to Second Major Shcherbachev of the Semenovskii regiment of the Royal Guards," in Ivan T. Bulychev, Puteshestvie po Vostochnoi Sibiri. Chast' 1: Iakutskaia oblast', Okhotskii krai (St. Petersburg, 1856), p. 254.

[37] Ibid., pp. 251–68; Zalkind, "Iasachnaia politika," pp. 239–40; Minenko, Severozapadnaia Sibir', pp. 242–43; Ogryzko, Khristianizatsiia, pp. 128–30; Fedorov, Pravovoe polozhenie, pp. 58–59, 116–18.

tices, but the abolition of roving iasak collectors did deprive the settlers of an important advantage over the tribute payers. The constraints imposed on church activities were also fairly effective: the local administrators had long fought against the missionaries' demands for subsidies and fur payments; with St. Petersburg definitely on their side, they could completely shut out the competitor. Metropolitan Pavel, who refused to admit defeat for three years, was defrocked in 1767, and in 1791 the commander of the fort of Petropavlovsk, Vasilii Shmalev, did not allow a missionary to go to the Kurile islands, declaring that "it is a great burden for the Kamchadal, and for that reason our Lord, merciful lover of humanity that He is, cannot be pleased with such a manner of spreading the word of God."[38]

For the new system to work, however, "the elders and the princelings" had to be found, strengthened, and rendered cooperative. The local administration supervised the "elections," paying special attention to whether all the families in the volost' were represented (this way, it was believed, a "real" chief would be chosen). On taking the oath of office, the newly elected elder or princeling (the name depended on the local tradition or the existence of old title charters) would receive detailed instructions about iasak collection and judicial procedures, as well as tobacco, beads, medals, and other signs of distinction. Some "clan commanders" were made salaried servitors and released from tribute obligations.[39] The success of "elite-building" varied from one area to another. Among the Yakut, for example, the transfer of important administrative duties to the chiefs seriously worried the local Russian officials, who complained of ruin and pointed to the danger of leaving "the loyal iasak men" at the mercy of their elders.[40] Among most hunters and gatherers, on the other hand, even the "best" of men had difficulty becoming taxmen. Already before 1763, some iasak collectors had been forced to issue special receipts, labels, or notched sticks to the local elders, but the idea did not bear fruit because of

[38] A. Sgibnev, "Istoricheskii sbornik glavneishikh sobytii v Kamchatke," in Morskoi sbornik 7 (1869): 42. See also Ogryzko, Khristianizatsiia, pp. 129–30 and Andrievich, Istoricheskii ocherk sibiri, vol. 5, part 2, p. 98.

[39] V. V. Rabtsevich, "K voprusu ob upravlenii aborigennym naseleniem Sibiri v 80-kh godakh XVIII–pervykh desiatiletiiakh XIX stoletiia," in Voprosy istorii Sibiri dosovetskogo perioda, ed. A. P. Okladnikov (Novosibirsk, 1973), pp. 237–40; Fedorov, Pravovoe polozhenie, pp. 106–9.

[40] Basharin, Istoriia, pp. 69, 71–74. See also Fedorov, Pravovoe polozhenie, pp. 118–22.

continuing disagreements over what constituted comparable value.[41] After the reform the basic relationship remained the same, with the low-level Russian administrators largely uncontrollable and many of the native elders totally ineffective outside of their extended families. The creation of the title of "main Samoed commander," for example, brought nothing but confusion and was soon abolished in favor of the old system whereby the Berezov Nenets paid tribute to Khanty princelings.[42]

Another serious problem was the fact that, in order to prevent speculation, the commission fixed the form and the value of iasak once and for all. As the market price continued to rise, it made less and less sense to pay tribute in "assigned pelts" if one could sell them at a much higher price to private traders and leave low-quality furs or cash for the state. In an attempt to ignore or reinterpret the law, many local officials demanded the best furs and refused to accept cash, but they had a very hard time competing against the merchants who could (illegally) travel all the way to the native's tent and offer a better price.[43]

The conflict between the merchants and the administrators was at the center of northern politics (as Russians understood it). Bitter enough in the seventeenth and eighteenth century, it became an all-out war between 1805 and 1819, when Siberia was ruled by governor-general Ivan Pestel and the civilian governor of Irkutsk N. I. Treskin. Both were physiocrats keen on promoting free trade and peasant agriculture, and both saw merchant monopolies as the greatest obstacle to economic development. The merchants, for their part, showed little appreciation for laissez-faire economics and continued to pursue monopolies in grain purchases, native barter, and China trade (legalized by Catherine a year before the creation of the Shcherbachev commission).[44] Inevitably, Treskin's promotion of trade turned into a war against traders—a war described in numerous merchants' complaints and immortalized by nineteenth-century historians as a struggle of society against bureaucracy.[45]

[41] Basharin, Istoriia, pp. 51–52; Minenko, Severo-zapadnaia Sibir', pp. 235–36.

[42] Minenko, Severo-zapadnaia Sibir', pp. 179–81.

[43] Zalkind, "Iasachnaia politika," pp. 240–41.

[44] Raeff, Siberia, pp. 21–38.

[45] See, for example, V. I. Vagin, Istoricheskie svedeniia o deiatel'nosti grafa M. M. Speranskogo v Sibiri s 1819 po 1822 god (St. Petersburg, 1872), 1:6–42; N. M. Iadrintsev, Sibir' kak koloniia (St. Petersburg, 1882), pp. 299–321; S. S. Shashkov, "Sibirskie inorodtsy v XIX stoletii," in Istoricheskie etiudy (St. Petersburg, 1872), pp. 170–75. For a dissenting view, see A. P. Shchapov, "Sibirskoe obshchestvo do Speranskogo," in A. P. Shchapov, Sochineniia (St. Petersburg, 1905–8), vol. 3.

As far as the iasak people were concerned, trade without the traders meant more "protection" and thus less vodka, tobacco, flour, and ammunition. Some settled communities were encouraged to engage in agriculture, but the taiga and tundra foragers were to continue their traditional pursuits under the watchful eye of local administrators, "so that no one, under any pretext, dared distract them from their occupations."[46] Accordingly, the watchful administrators chased the merchants out of the iasak volosti and launched trading networks of their own.[47] In 1815 Treskin concluded that this "love of travel" had "utterly ruined the inhabitants of Kamchatka" because "almost throughout the year, the Kamchadal and other inhabitants did nothing but transport everybody around, from the commander down to the last Cossack and merchant who, under various pretexts of official business, constantly traveled around in order to trade."[48]

The governor's solution was to ban almost all contact "so that . . . not only rank-and-file military personnel, but none of the officials nor even the commander himself traveled in Kamchatka."[49] Priests were also to stay away from the native districts: one project suggested that they be allowed to visit the Olekma Tungus once every three years.[50] Similar policies—not all quite as uncompromising, however—were followed in other iasak areas, and although illegal trade continued, many circumpolar groups saw their markets drastically reduced and asked repeatedly for the repeal of the trade restrictions.[51] At the same time, in contradiction to the government's native policies but in full accord with its renewed attempts at the economic development of Russian Siberia, the iasak men's other (non-tribute) responsibilities had grown substantially by the end of the century. Coupled with unfavorable terms of trade, the obligation to maintain the roads, provide transportation, heat up military barracks, and man border outposts further un-

[46] Sgibnev, "Istoricheskii sbornik," no. 7, p. 96.

[47] John Dundas Cochrane, A Pedestrian Journey through Russia and Siberian Tartary from the Frontiers of China to the Frozen Sea and Kamchatka, performed during the years 1820, 1821, 1822, and 1823 (London, 1824), pp. 405–11; S. M. Prutchenko, Sibirskie okrainy (St. Petersburg, 1899), pp. 109, 112–13; Vagin, Istoricheskie svedeniia, 1:89; Okun', Ocherki, pp. 110–11; Bogoras, The Chukchee, pp. 703–5.

[48] Sgibnev, "Istoricheskii sbornik," no. 7, p. 105. Also p. 37.

[49] Ibid., p. 101.

[50] Vagin, Istoricheskie svedeniia, 2:113–17; Cochrane, A Pedestrian Journey, pp. 409, 416–17.

[51] Minenko, Severo-zapadnaia Sibir', pp. 249–50.

dermined their economic position.[52] Iasak payers with little iasak to offer, savages with few chances for speedy enlightenment, and poor creatures who seemed to suffer equally from autonomy and protection, the circumpolar people had become a challenge for the ruling rationalists.

[52] Ibid., p. 248; Fedorov, *Pravovoe polozhenie*, pp. 36–48, 70; Vagin, *Istoricheskie svedeniia*, 1:486, 2:27; *Istoriia Iakutskoi ASSR*, 2:207–8; Okun', *Ocherki*, p. 109.

"A shaman," from F. I. Beliavskii, *Poezdka k Ledovitomu moriu* (Moscow, 1833)

3

The Uncorrupted

I am as free as Nature first made man,
Ere the base laws of servitude began,
When wild in woods the noble savage ran.
                    —John Dryden, *The Conquest of Granada*

High Culture and the Children of Nature

Land that was sufficiently virgin to house pagans and savages was not entirely fit for Christians and Europeans. The "snowy desert" of the north (usually called "Siberia" irrespective of the Europe-Asia divide)[1] was a place of exile, a prison where metaphorical savages (criminals) could join the real savages (aliens), and where disgraced courtiers could be entombed without being executed. With the arrival of romanticism in Russia, however, and particularly with the arrival of romantic exiles in Siberia, this image began to change. Even before "December," the Decembrist Ryleev had placed some of his Byronic characters in the appropriately awesome Siberian surroundings, but when the actual noble outcasts, acutely conscious of their poetic antecedents, found themselves "in the depths of the Siberian mines," the erstwhile repository of things useful and despicable was transformed into a realm of wild Nature, the more alive for being desolate.[2] Untamed Nature produced untamed children, and before long the Siberian literary landscape was populated with proud natives who

[1] Alexander Herzen referred to his Viatka days as "Siberian exile" in the same way that twentieth-century Vorkuta camps are often considered to be "in Siberia."
[2] See, in particular, Bassin, "Inventing Siberia," pp. 773–74, 776; Harriet Murav, "'Vo glubine sibirskikh rud': Siberia and the Myth of Exile," in Galya Diment and Yuri Slezkine, eds., *Between Heaven and Hell: The Myth of Siberia in Russian Culture* (New York, 1993), pp. 95–111; and Iu. M. Lotman, "The Decembrist in Everyday Life: Everyday Behavior as Historical-Psychological Category," in *The Semiotics of Russian Culture*, ed. Ann Shukman (Ann Arbor, 1984), pp. 71–123.

"wandered fearlessly around the shamans' graves," valued nothing above freedom, and confidently enjoyed the simple pleasures of a care-free nomadic existence.[3] Soon the exiled poets were joined by budding Siberian *littérateurs*, and in the 1830s a number of tales about half-savage but fair Tungus girls touched the hearts of St. Petersburg reviewers.[4] Russian Siberia had acquired "its own James Fenimore Cooper" (in the person of Ivan Kalashnikov),[5] and the native Siberians had acquired some of the features of the Mohicans.

The romantic recasting of former savages as children of nature involved a complete reconsideration of both nature and childhood. As Tatishchev's infancy-to-maturity scheme was expanded to include old age and death, infancy became a great deal more attractive, particularly because Russia's own youth was increasingly being perceived as an asset. Unfortunate rather than repulsive savages had been around since Catherine, but in the early nineteenth century some authors began to claim that perhaps Europeans were the real savages, that European beauties were "sickly bodies" compared to "Oriental Asians," that "every nation is to some degree a victim of superstitions" (except that the Tofalar superstitions are "innocent"), that European armies would be just as frightened of superior weapons as were the natives, that the northern aliens were generally "kinder and simpler than the Russians," and that therefore education was probably "more harmful than useful."[6]

But beside the Indians, Albanians, and Scottish Highlanders celebrated by romantic travelers in this fashion, the native northerners were not particularly visible or remarkable. In the Byronic age of "dread and splendor," the taiga and the tundra could not compete with

[3] See A. A. Bestuzhev-Marlinskii's "Saatyr'," in *Dekabristy*, ed. Vladimir Orlov (Moscow, 1951), pp. 160–62, and Nikolai Chizhov's "Nucha," in ibid., pp. 192–93. Also see Iu. S. Postnov, *Russkaia literatura Sibiri pervoi poloviny XIX v.* (Novosibirsk, 1970), pp. 115–38.

[4] A. P. Okladnikov, ed., *Ocherki russkoi literatury Sibiri* (Novosibirsk, 1982), 1:236, 244, 258–62; Iu. S. Postnov, "Literatura Sibiri v russkoi kritike pervoi poloviny XIX veka," in *Ocherki literatury i kritiki Sibiri* (Novosibirsk, 1976), pp. 100–102; Iu. S. Postnov, "Poeziia romantizma v literature Sibiri," in *Voprosy russkoi i sovetskoi literatury Sibiri* (Novosibirsk, 1971), pp. 122–23; Postnov, *Russkaia literatura Sibiri*.

[5] See I. T. Kalashnikov, *Doch' kuptsa Zholobova* (St. Petersburg, 1831), and *Kamchadalka* (St. Petersburg, 1833). On Kalashnikov, see Galya Diment, "Exiled from Siberia: The Construction of Siberian Experience by Early-Nineteenth-Century Irkutsk Writers," in Diment and Slezkine, *Between Heaven and Hell*, pp. 54–59.

[6] See A. V. Gurevich, ed., *Vostochnaia Sibir' v rannei khudozhestvennoi proze* (Irkutsk, 1938), p. 48; Aleksei Martos, *Pis'ma o vostochnoi Sibiri* (Moscow, 1827), pp. 16–17; V. N. Golovnin, *Sochineniia* (Moscow-Leningrad, 1949), p. 381; and M. M. Gedenshtrom, *Otryvki o Sibiri* (St. Petersburg, 1830), pp. 9, 94.

the glorious peaks, lush valleys, and mutinous streams of the Caucasus, just as the relatively peaceful pursuits of the northerners seemed "timid" compared to the implacable ferocity of the fictional Circassians.[7] Marlinskii, one of the first writers to introduce the Arctic dwellers into high literature, was obviously relieved to be transferred from the north and its fish-like, "half-melted" inhabitants to the magnificent mountains of the south.[8] More important, by the late 1840s both Siberians and Circassians—as well as Lord Byron, Sir Walter Scott, and numerous aliens and exotic sons of nature—had become largely irrelevant to the world as conceived by the Russian intelligentsia. The increasingly alienated cultural elite of Moscow and St. Petersburg had discovered a noble savage with whom it would concern itself to the exclusion of most others: the Russian peasant. He was to be admired, studied, or rescued; he was the repository of pure values, the core of the intellectuals' elusive identity, and the savior of Russia and perhaps of the whole world. Most of the writers descended from the mountains to the Great Russian Plain, as did most of the scholars. By 1850 the academic "Germans" had been completely routed by the academic "Patriots," and the Russian Geographic Society formally defined its goal as "the study of the *Russian* land and the *Russian* people."[9] According to historian Gavriil Uspenskii, stories about unenlightened peoples should be abandoned in favor of a "description of the old customs, traditions, and institutions of the people that, in our days, has reached the highest degree of its greatness, power, and glory."[10] In the north, too, it was now the *Russian* rebels and *Russian* warriors who populated the "frozen deserts" and "the virgin taiga." As Ermak exclaims in the last lines of Khomiakov's romantic play, "There is no Siberia any more: from now on this is Russia!"[11]

The north was still perceived as distinct, except that now "Siberia" was associated—both spatially and temporally—with "Russian Northern Asia" and not with the "Tsardom of Kuchum" or the exotic tundra tribes. The nineteenth century had returned to the seventeenth-

---

[7] See Susan Layton, "The Creation of an Imaginative Caucasian Geography," *SR*, no. 3 (1986): 470–85.

[8] A. A. Bestuzhev-Marlinskii, *Sochineniia v dvukh tomakh* (Moscow, 1958), 2:294ff.

[9] Mark Bassin, "The Russian Geographical Society, the 'Amur Epoch,' and the Great Siberian Expedition 1855–1863," *Annals of the Association of American Geographers* 73, no. 2 (1983): 242–43; ' Piatidesiatiletie Imperatorskogo russkogo geograficheskogo obshchestva," in *IV*, 63 (1896): 279–90.

[10] S. A. Tokarev, *Istoriia russkoi etnografii. Dooktiabr'skii period* (Moscow, 1966), p. 180.

[11] A. S. Khomiakov, *Stikhotvoreniia i dramy* (Leningrad, 1969), p. 277.

century annalists' view that Siberia had no history before Ermak, or, as
P. A. Slovtsov now put it, "Siberia did not emerge from the diapers of
oblivion [*iz pelen samozabveniia*] until the Khan's turban fell from
Kuchum's head."[12] Gone was Tatishchev's and Müller's preoccupation
with native antiquities and tribal origins: Siberia began with the arrival of the Russians.

Who were these Russians and what did their arrival signify? The
concepts of orthodoxy and state interest (increasingly reinterpreted as
the mystique of autocracy) remained popular in some quarters, but the
magic of nationality had begun to eclipse them both.[13] Whether joined
with the other two in the "official" and Slavophile versions of Russian
messianism or pitted against them in various opposition creeds, "nationality" referred to the Russian people and their *Volksgeist*.
"Carrying in their souls this lofty gift of nature, Ermak set out to conquer a whole tsardom; Khabarov with 150 people rushed to acquire the
Amur; Dezhnev dared to challenge the storms and ice-floes of the Arctic Ocean"; and one fictional merchant "moved by his restless genius"
resolved to undertake a voyage "that even the government, with all its
countless possibilities, had not been able to accomplish."[14] They were
all "simple Russian folk," and their most enduring contribution to the
new lands was to share their simple Russian ways: to "cook Russian
kasha on the icy tundras of the Chukchi peninsula and the Aliutor
shore, [and to] sing the Russian songs . . . on the mouth of the famed
and fabulous Amur."[15] The glory of these "national discoveries" may
have been stolen by "von Bering" and other Germans, but

> it was the Russian people, strangers to the oppressive policies of the in-
> habitants of the West, who had established friendly relations with the
> conquered tribes; who had unself-consciously imparted to them their
> customs and beliefs; who had suppressed their nationality quietly and
> without violence—if the savage tribes to whom even the word "nation"
> was not applicable could have nationality—and who, by raising them, to
> the extent possible, to their own level, had changed them to the point
> where, with the exception of the extreme north and south, Siberia had
> become almost completely Russified.[16]

[12] P. A. Slovtsov, *Istoricheskoe obozrenie Sibiri* (1838; St. Petersburg, 1886), p. xx.
[13] Nicholas V. Riasanovsky, *Nicholas I and Official Nationality in Russia, 1825–1855*
(Berkeley, Calif., 1959), pp. 124–67.
[14] Ivan Kalashnikov, "Izgnanniki," in Gurevich, ed., *Vostochnaia Sibir'*, pp. 11–12, 29.
[15] M. Aleksandrov, "Vozdushnyi tarantas ili vospominaniia o poezdkakh po vostochnoi Sibiri," in Gurevich, ed., *Vostochnaia Sibir'*, p. 97.
[16] P. I. Nebol'sin, *Pokorenie Sibiri: Istoricheskoe issledovanie* (St. Petersburg, 1849),
p. 113. Cf. Bassin, "The Russian Geographical Society," p. 244, and David N. Collins,

Indeed, so thorough had this process been; so unimpeded in its natural unfolding; and so remote from St. Petersburg's Germans that, if Russia stood for *kasha*, folk songs, and other attributes of unpolluted nationality, then Siberia had become more Russian than Russia itself.[17]

Whatever the effect of conquest on new lands and native tribes, everyone agreed that its impact on Russia as a whole had been profound and largely salutary. After 1812 most educated Russians agreed that their country was a "great European power" and that size was an excellent proof of both greatness and Europeanness. Already N. M. Karamzin had called Ermak "the Russian Pizarro ("no less terrifying for savage peoples than the Spanish one but less terrible for humanity"), who

> had discovered for Europe a second new world . . . . , where in desert silence navigable rivers, large lakes rich in fish, and fruitful blossoming valleys shaded by tall lindens are awaiting industrious inhabitants, in order to see centuries upon centuries of new civic accomplishments, give room to peoples overcrowding Europe, and offer generous hospitality to the excess of their overflowing population.[18]

Karamzin's goal in writing his history had been to prove that Russia possessed its own Charles the Great (Vladimir), its own Louis XI (Ivan III), and its own Cromwell (Godunov)—as well as Peter the Great, of course, who had no earthly prototype;[19] a Russian New World and a Russian Pizarro were relatively minor parts of the same project. In the 1830s and 1840s, however, when the "Russian people" seriously challenged the "Russian state" for the loyalty of the elite and when territorial expansion was often seen as a measure of the expansive, untrammeled, and freedom-loving spirit of "simple Russians," Ermak and other lowly born "land-surface Vasco da Gamas" emerged as major national icons.[20]

"Russia's Conquest of Siberia: Evolving Russian and Soviet Historical Interpretations," *European Studies Review* 12, no. 1 (1982): 20–21.

[17] Bassin, "Inventing Siberia," pp. 782–90; Diment, "Exiled from Siberia," pp. 47–65.

[18] N. M. Karamzin, *Istoriia gosudarstva Rossiiskogo* (1843; reprint, Moscow, 1989), vol. 9, chap. 6, pp. 226, 218–19. For background and analysis, see Seymour Becker, "Contributions to a Nationalist Ideology: Histories of Russia in the First Half of the Nineteenth Century," *Russian History/Histoire russe* 13, no. 4 (1986): 331–53.

[19] Miliukov, *Glavnye techeniia*, pp. 143–44.

[20] Nebol'sin, *Pokorenie Sibiri*, p. 2; Aleksandrov, "Vozdushnyi tarantas, p. 97; V. P. Parshin, *Poezdka v Zabaikal'skii krai* (Moscow, 1844), vol. 1, p. ix and vol. 2; N. A. Polevoi, *Ermak Timofeevich ili Volga i Sibir'* (St. Petersburg, 1845); A. S. Khomiakov, "Ermak," in *Stikhotvoreniia i dramy*; Slovtsov, *Istoricheskoe obozrenie Sibiri*, p. xiii. For analysis and bibliography see Bassin, "Inventing Siberia," pp. 780–81.

In this context, the role of the circumpolar peoples was very modest indeed. Their past consisted of a feeble resistance to the Cossacks and an eager acceptance of Russian guidance; their future promised total Russification; and their mostly irrelevant present was lost somewhere between the inferno of "brutes and savage cannibals" and "the happiest state of harmony and perfect equality."[21] Indeed, the real "brutes and savage cannibals" were now the Russian bureaucrats, and the true "state of harmony and perfect equality" was now the exclusive possession of the Russian peasants. In the age of romantic nationalism the natives were not eligible simply because they were not Russian in terms of language, faith, kasha, and songs: because, as Polevoi's Ermak says to a Siberian shaman, there was no Russian heart beating in their chests.[22] The more specific and more easily remedied failings had changed little since the mid-eighteenth century: the division of humanity into infants and adults continued to be important, and even the most enthusiastic champions of simplicity were self-conscious "adults" who did not totally abandon the standards that made their own enlightenment meaningful. The most basic of such standards still included a degree of cleanliness, the proper treatment of women, and the existence of a coherent religion or higher purpose in life, with the natives invariably failing in all three.[23] The only important additions were the concepts of spirituality and "poetic sense," which promoted the image of the "beautifully, even elegantly dressed" Tungus and even partially rehabilitated the much derided shaman ("not a cool and ordinary deceiver but a psychological phenomenon deserving attention"), but it did not help most other northerners: music was not in evidence, folklore remained unknown because of the language barrier, and dancing ("wild, funny, and often obscene") usually offended European sensibilities.[24] "Crude, materialistic minds" replaced "stupidity" as the

---

[21] Those were the terms Kruzenshtern used to characterize the Marquesas islanders and the Ainu. See Ivan F. Kruzenshtern, *Voyage round the World in the Years 1803, 1804, 1805, and 1806 by Order of His Imperial Majesty Alexander the First on Board the Ships Nadeshda and Neva* (London, 1813), part 1, pp. 180–82, and part 2, pp. 75–76.

[22] Polevoi, *Ermak Timofeich*, p. 110.

[23] N. A. Abramov, "Opisanie Berezovskogo kraia," *Zapiski IRGO*, no. 12 (1857): 331; F. I. Beliavskii, *Poezdka k Ledovitomu moriu* (Moscow, 1833), pp. 69, 74; Kalashnikov, *Doch' kuptsa Zholobova*, part 2, pp. 90, 93, and *Kamchadalka*, part 1, pp. 48, 86, 89–94, 98–99; Fedor Shemelin, *Zhurnal pervogo puteshestviia rossiian vokrug zemnogo shara* (St. Petersburg, 1816), p. 167; A. P. Stepanov, *Eniseiskaia guberniia* (St. Petersburg, 1835), 1:64–65; Slovtsov, *Istoricheskoe obozrenie Sibiri*, pp. 5, 139.

[24] Karl Ditmar, *Poezdki i prebyvanie v Kamchatke v 1851–1855* (St. Petersburg, 1901), pp. 435, 541; Ferdinand von Wrangell [Vrangel'], *Narrative of an Expedition to the Polar Sea in the Years 1820, 1821, 1822, and 1823* (London, 1844), p. 120; Beliavskii, *Poezdka,*

usual explanation for the various inadequacies of native life, and when the exiled Herzen visited the Votiak and the Cheremis he found everything about them—their songs, language, religion—"purely materialistic."[25] Later, N. M. Przheval'skii would draw the extreme conclusion and find an Oroch hunter not very different from his dogs: "Living like a beast in a lair, . . . he forgets all human aspirations and, like a beast, thinks only about filling his stomach. . . . Nothing spiritual, nothing human exists for him."[26]

And yet romantic primitivism would not go away. The native might be rebuked for eating rotten fish, abusing his wife, and killing his elderly parents, but he absolutely had to be praised for his simplicity, generosity, and stoicism. This combination of the contemptible and the admirable became canonical early in the century and remained a commonplace for over a hundred years. Even the sternest of critics (of whom the majority were Russian-Siberian intellectuals) felt compelled to wax sentimental about the "artless scions of nature" (prostodushnye chada prirody) who "do not think about wealth, honor, or glory, and do not care about what tomorrow may bring."[27] In effect, this was the old negative mode of description turned upside down. The natives were still being represented in terms of what they were not or what they did not care about, but the meaning of certain absences was reversed. The Samoed, who for Radishchev and Zuev had been by far "the most stupid" people in western Siberia, were now preferred to their neighbors the Ostiak;[28] the "free" and carefree nomadic natives were seen as morally superior to the settled ones; and of the

---

pp. 78–79, 111–12; M. A. Kastren [Castrén], "Puteshestvie Aleksandra Kastrena po Laplandii, severnoi Rossii i Sibiri," Magazin zemlevedeniia i puteshestvii 6, no. 2 (1860): 188.

[25] A. I. Gertsen, Sobranie sochinenii v 30 tomakh (Moscow, 1954), 1:369–71. The Votiak (Udmurt) and the Cheremis (Mari) did not live in the circumpolar zone, but Herzen's attitude was typical as well as influential. Cf. Abramov, "Opisanie," p. 338; Beliavskii, Poezdka, p. 68.

[26] N. M. Przheval'skii, Puteshestviia v Ussuriiskim krae, 1867–1869 (St. Petersburg, 1870), p. 104.

[27] A. M. Kornilov, Zamechaniia o Sibiri senatora Kornilova (St. Petersburg, 1828), p. 56; Kalashnikov, Doch' kuptsa Zholobova, part 4, p. 139. See also Abramov, Opisanie, pp. 335, 353; Beliavskii, Poezdka, pp. 73–74; Bulychev, Puteshestvie, pp. 79, 184, 240; Stepanov, Eniseiskaiia guberniia, 2:61.

[28] Radishchev, Polnoe sobranie sochinenii, 3:135, and Zuev, Materialy, p. 23. Cf. Abramov, "Opisanie," p. 355; Kastren, "Puteshestvie," p. 265; Beliavskii, Poezdka, pp. 165–66; Slovtsov, Istoricheskoe obozrenie Sibiri, p. 5. Among the Samoed, pagans were more "natural" than Christians. See, for example, Vladimir Islavin, Samoiedy v domashnem i obshchestvennom bytu (St. Petersburg, 1847), p. 108.

nomads, the "cheerful" and proud Tungus (Evenk) remained every-one's favorites.[29]

The ambiguity in the image of the native northerners was best summed up by their most famous and most dedicated student, a Finn-ish linguist Matthias Alexander Castrén. A highly romantic figure him-self, Castrén traveled all over Siberia in search of his people's past until the northern climate killed him at the age of forty. He lived among his "distant relatives" the Samoed and tirelessly studied their language and culture, but he was constantly offended by their treatment of women, their drinking, their diet, their rudeness, their gloom, their "self-centered" religion, and their general inability to distinguish be-tween good and evil:[30] "Sometimes it even occurred to me that the pure instinct, the innocent simplicity, and the geniality of these so-called children of nature could, in many ways, put European wisdom to shame, but all in all, in the course of my travels through the deserts, I regretfully noticed, beside such good traits, so much that was repulsive, crude, and beastly, that I pitied rather than loved them."[31]

The Empire and the Aliens

The ennoblement of the northerners as savages coincided with their near demise as tribute payers. By the 1800s wars, epidemics, and the dramatic expansion of the Chukchi herds had led to a change in the migration routes of the wild reindeer. As a result, the first quarter of the nineteenth century saw repeated and severe famines among the Yukagir, the Lamut, the Evenk, and the Koriak.[1] Thousands starved to death, moved to different areas, or joined more prosperous communi-ties.[2] Meanwhile, the clan-based rates of tribute, set by the Iasak Com-mission, remained unchanged and caused great distress both in tundra and in St. Petersburg. As one local official put it, "Because some clans have fewer people and other clans have more, and because of a change in the manner of living and hunting, the current method of tribute pay-

[29] Bulychev, Puteshestvie, pp. 79, 240; Ditmar, Poezdki, pp. 435, 440; Wrangell, Narra-tive of an Expedition, p. 208; Stepanov, Eniseiskaia guberniia, 2:61, 73.

[30] Kastren, "Puteshestvie," pp. 134–35, 139, 142, 146, 148–49, 188, 191, 228–31, 307, 335, 345.

[31] Ibid., p. 178.

[1] Gurvich, Etnicheskaia istoriia, pp. 136–37, 151, 104–5, 183–84; Vagin, Istoricheskie svedeniia, 1:380–87, 402–3, and 2:27–30, 53, 416–21.

[2] Gurvich, Etnicheskaia istoriia, pp. 138–42, 155, 185–86.

ment has become extremely unequal for the iasak people, and for some of them completely ruinous."[3]

Complaints of this sort, as well as desperate pleas for mercy from Siberian merchants, were routinely ignored in the capital for as long as Governor Pestel enjoyed the favor of the all-powerful Count Arakcheev.[4] As soon as he lost it, however, he lost his job as well, and in 1819 Alexander I brought his ablest bureaucrat, Mikhail Speranskii, back from exile and sent him to Siberia to "decide on the spot on the most appropriate organization and government of that remote region."[5] As state secretary to the young tsar, Count Speranskii had greatly excited Russian "society" by writing a project for far-reaching administrative reform. The reform had never been implemented, and its author had eventually been dismissed, but now both were brought back to life for the benefit of the long-suffering Siberians. The inhabitants of "that remote region" (no one could really decide if it was part of Russia or not) were to receive something that so many young Russian nobles had been vainly hoping for—a completely new administrative arrangement. The land of the prodigal sons and "scions of nature" had overtaken the mother country. "Having been taught by experience to submit to Providence," Speranskii wrote to Arakcheev, "it is, of course, not without grief that I embark on this journey."[6]

The romantic universe that Speranskii shared with many of his contemporaries consisted of organic nations, each having its own spirit, its own life cycle, and its own unique contribution to the whole. The crucial first step was to determine which groups of people possessed these qualities and hence qualified as truly "historic nations." Most educated Russians assumed that their uneducated countrymen ("the people") constituted a nation of which they, the intelligentsia, were either the traitors or the vanguard. Moreover, given the persistence of the old "state principle," Russians were usually seen as the only historic nation in the Russian empire. This meant that, with the possible exception of the Poles, all other subjects of the tsar would sooner or later become Russified—either immediately, as suggested by the "offi-

[3] Zalkind, "Iasachnaia politika," p. 244. It should be noted that some clans disappeared only on paper as local officials wrote off famine survivors or transferred them to other iasak volosti. See Prutchenko, *Sibirskie okrainy*, p. 119, and Vagin, *Istoricheskie svedeniia*, 1:89.

[4] Modest A. Korf, *Zhizn' grafa Speranskogo* (St. Petersburg, 1861), 2:171–73.

[5] Ibid., p. 176. See also M. M. Speranskii, "Pis'ma k docheri," *RA*, vol. 6 (1868): 1201.

[6] Korf, *Zhizn' grafa Speranskogo*, p. 183.

cial nationalist" M. P. Pogodin, or eventually, as envisaged by the Decembrist Pestel.[7]

The case of the childlike foragers "to whom even the word 'nation' was not applicable" seemed particularly clear-cut. They had "no nationality" because they "found themselves at the lowest stage of civic consciousness" and were not "linked by common interests or bound to a single, common, deeply-felt idea of independence."[8] And yet their very "wildness" seemed to require special legislative provisions that other nonhistoric peoples did not need. This was a result of the particular needs of taxation and Christianization in the "northern deserts," but for a romantic legislator it was also a matter of principle. A follower of Schelling, Fichte, and Herder, Speranskii believed that laws should reflect the spiritual and intellectual needs of the people, as defined by national history and tradition.[9] All societies go through childhood, maturity, and old age, and "the legislator cannot and should not change this age, but he should know it exactly and govern each according to its own character."[10] One instructive example of a total disregard for this rule was Spain's colonial fiasco—such at least was the argument of Dominique de Pradt's popular treatise *Des colonies*, which Speranskii had read soon after his appointment.[11] "The Europeans," wrote de Pradt, "had never given their colonies anything that would . . . merit the honor of being called organization."[12] They had persisted in imposing on their remote subjects laws that did not fit the local conditions, and now both Spain and France were paying the price.[13]

Speranskii was determined to avoid such mistakes. Shortly after his arrival in Siberia he ascertained that Siberian Russians were different from European Russians, and that Siberian aborigines were different from anything he had ever seen before. "There is nothing more repulsive than wild nature," he wrote to his daughter after seeing a Kirgiz (Kazakh) feast outside of Omsk—"if it is, indeed, nature and not its

[7] Riasanovsky, *Nicholas I*, pp. 144, 159; M. V. Nechkina, ed., *"Russkaia Pravda" P. I. Pestelia i sochineniia, ei predshestvuiushchie* (Moscow), p. 149.

[8] Nebol'sin, Pokorenie Sibiri, p. 112.

[9] Marc Raeff, *Michael Speranskii: Statesman of Imperial Russia, 1772–1839* (The Hague, 1957), pp. 217–18.

[10] Ibid., p. 222.

[11] Raeff, *Siberia*, p. 45.

[12] Dominique de Pradt, *Des colonies, et de la révolution actuelle de l'Amérique* (Paris, 1817), 2:2.

[13] Ibid., pp. 13–14.

creation gone wild."[14] One thing was clear: Siberian Russians were to be ruled differently from European Russians, and Siberian aborigines differently yet.

Before legislating for a nation, however, one needed to determine "its age" and to study its life and traditions. For this task the governor general chose Gavrila Stepanovich Baten'kov, a native of Tobol'sk, a veteran of the 1812–1813 campaigns, and an enthusiastic reformer who was now a communications engineer in charge of a nonexistent district in Siberia. Together with Speranskii, Baten'kov believed that Russian imperial laws "failed to take history, ethnography, or climatology into account and did not have any basis in fact."[15] Accordingly, he set out to examine the facts and, over the course of 1819–1820, compiled statistical data on the native population of Siberia. Having divided the country into three climatic zones—the northern, the middle, and the southern—Baten'kov found that social and economic conditions varied significantly from one to the other. In the north, "aliens" constituted 91 percent of the population and engaged almost exclusively in fishing and hunting; in the middle zone, they made up 17 percent and were either agriculturalists (mostly Tatars) or foragers (the Ostiak, Tungus, Yakut, and Iurak): finally, in the south native Siberians comprised 26 percent of the total population and devoted themselves primarily to agriculture and cattle breeding, with 20 percent (mostly Tungus) still living the lives of nomadic hunters and fishers.[16] In other words—and allowing for some inevitable overlapping—three distinct geographic zones supported three different types of economic organization (three "ages"). True to his principles ("A constitution is nothing but mores"),[17] Baten'kov proceeded to describe this situation in a special project, which was revised by Speranskii and in 1822 became law as the Statute of Alien Administration in Siberia. The only comprehensive official statement of its kind, the statute codified some of the existing practices and fixed the status of the native Siberians for the next one hundred years.[18]

[14] Speranskii, "Pis'ma," p. 1689.
[15] V. G. Kartsov, Dekabris: G. S. Baten'kov (Novosibirsk, 1965), p. 93.
[16] Ibid., pp. 93–99.
[17] Ibid., p. 93.
[18] In 1835, the Samoed of the European North received their own statute, modeled very closely on the Statute of Alien Administration in Siberia. For its text, see Alexander Gustav Schrenk, Reise nach dem Nordosten des europäischen Russlands, durch die Tundren der Samojeden, zum arktischen Uralgebirge (Dorpat, 1854) pp. 141–61 [HRAF RU4, no. 16], and Archimandrite Veniamin, "Samoiedy mezenskie," in Viestnik IRGO part 14 (1855), pp. 130–40 [HRAF RU4, no. 5].

First, all Siberian aborigines were formally classified as aliens (*ino-rodtsy*) and, "according to the different levels of their civic education and present way of life," divided into three categories: "settled, that is, those who live in towns and settlements; nomadic, those who occupy definite places depending on the season; and wandering or foragers [*brodiachie ili lovtsy*], those who move from one place to another."[19] The settled aliens were legally equated with Russians of the same estate (mostly merchants or state peasants) and were to have the same rights and obligations, with one exception: they could not be drafted into the army. The nomads were to carry on as before: separate clans owned their own territories, from which the Russians were barred, and paid fur tribute as well as local (*zemskie*) taxes. The wandering aliens were freed from all exactions except for iasak, kept their lands en bloc (without subdivisions), and had the right of unrestricted movement from one district or province to another.[20] Finally, the Chukchi were singled out as aliens "not fully dependent" who paid tribute "as they saw fit, with respect to both quality and quantity."[21]

The authors of the statute did not include precise guidelines for distinguishing among the categories, but limited themselves to a few examples and left this decision to the local officials. The criteria they gave were vague and sometimes contradictory: belonging to a particular class depended on the main economic activity (*glavnyi promysel*), "civic education" or "way of life" in general, relative "simplicity" and "peculiarity" of customs, difficulty of communication, ability to sell produce, availability of cash, or even place of residence, as in the case of those aliens who lived among Russians or worked for them as hired laborers (these latter were classified as settled).[22] Besides a certain ignorance—neither Speranskii nor Baten'kov had ever traveled in northern Siberia or seen any wandering aliens—the reason for this was an apparent desire to make alien classes open-ended and flexible. The basic assumption was that eventually the wanderers would become nomadic and that the nomads would sooner or later settle down—and that it was up to the local administrators to follow their progress. The emphasis was certainly on later rather than sooner: the statute repeatedly cautioned against haste and against the forced transfer of

[19] PSZ, ser. 1, vol. 38, no. 29.126, p. 394, sec. 1. For a detailed analysis of the statute, see Raeff, *Siberia*, pp. 112–28, and Watrous, "Russia's 'Land of the Future'," pp. 26–43.

[20] PSZ, ser. 1, vol. 38, no. 29.126, pp. 395–97, secs. 12–62.

[21] Ibid., p. 399, secs. 75–80.

[22] Ibid., p. 394, secs. 1 and 7; p. 395, sec. 10; p. 404, sec. 170.

aliens from one category to another.[23] Given this expectation of gradual but inevitable development, it is curious that there was no provision for settled aliens to become Russians. The settled category seemed closed. Even those who were in every other way equal to peasants were still known as aliens unfit for military service, and no indication was given by the statute of how—if ever—this gap could be bridged. This reticence was probably due to the old religious and the new cultural standards of nationality, sometimes supplemented with the vague requirement that a true Russian have Russian blood "boiling" in his veins.[24] Coupled with Speranskii's distaste for wholesale proselytizing and with the common assumption that many Russians were of non-Russian origin, this meant that Russification was expected to take place through *individual* education, conversion, and possibly intermarriage. The term "alien" was not legally defined: the statute applied to all "alien tribes who hitherto have been known as iasak people,"[25] including those who were not to pay iasak anymore and, presumably, those among them who spoke only Russian and considered themselves Russian and Christian. The term "iasak" was dropped altogether.

The circumpolar hunters, gatherers, and reindeer herders were all indisputably "alien" and belonged to either the nomadic or the wandering category.[26] The main principle of their administration was indirect rule with as little Russian interference as possible. Every encampment or settlement of fifteen or more families was to have a permanent name and its own clan administration (*rodovoe upravlenie*) that would consist of an elder, either elected or hereditary, and, in nomadic clans, two assistants. Smaller units were attached to neighboring clan administrations, and respected clansmen who were not part of the administration were to be prevented from exercising their influence (that is, even in theory—and somewhat surprising given Speranskii's and Baten'kov's views—the official clans did not have to coincide with the actual kinship groups and the clan administration did not have to replicate the existing power structure).[27] Among wandering aliens one-man clan administrations were the only official organs of government; the nomads also had a "native administration" (*inorodnaia uprava*), which was responsible for several neighboring

[23] Ibid., p. 395, secs. 9–11; p. 396, sec. 25.
[24] Polevoi, *Ermak Timofeich*, p. 110.
[25] PSZ, ser. 1, vol. 38, no. 29.126, p. 394, sec. 1.
[26] So did the Samoed of the European north. See Schrenk, *Journey to the Northeast*, p. 141.
[27] PSZ, ser. 1, vol. 38, no. 29.126, p. 100, secs. 94–99; p. 398, sec. 66.

clans and was made up of a head elder, two assistants, and, where possible, a permanent clerk. Particularly well-educated, numerous, and centrally organized peoples, of which only the Transbaikal Buriat were specifically identified, were to have a Steppe Duma, a sort of supreme council that represented the whole nation before the Russian provincial administration.[28] All elders were to be confirmed and supervised by the local Russian officials, but they were expected to rule and mete out justice in accordance with traditional "steppe laws and customs." These laws had eventually to be collected, codified, freed of everything "savage and cruel," and published in Russian and, if possible, in the original language.[29] The aliens were to be tried in the Russian courts only for major crimes, such as rebellion, premeditated murder, robbery, rape, counterfeiting, and the pilfering of state or public property.[30] All other cases were considered civil and placed within tribal jurisdiction.[31]

Apart from maintaining internal order and conveying superior orders to their kinsmen, the elders were responsible for the distribution, collection, and delivery of tribute and local taxes, with every clan counting "as one indivisible unit."[32] The Russian officials were to facilitate their task as much as possible, receiving payment at fairs or sending special agents to faraway encampments. The statute was particularly adamant about the obligatory issue of receipts and even suggested specific symbols to be used by illiterate aliens. All contact between Russian and native officials was to be limited to an absolute minimum, and every visitor was to make do with as few carts or sleds as possible; wandering aliens were not to be inspected more than once a year. Russian administrators were prohibited from trading with the aliens of their province, and tribute-collecting trips were allowed only if it was inconvenient for the elders to travel to the courthouse or if a clan owed more than two years' worth of tribute.[33]

[28] Ibid., pp. 400–401, secs. 114–21; p. 406, secs. 202 and 213; p. 409, sec. 267. The Transbaikal Buriat were the only native Siberians among whom Speranskii lived and in whose life and beliefs he was personally interested. See Vagin, Istoricheskie svedeniia, 1:269–70.

[29] PSZ, ser. 1, vol. 38, no. 29.126, p. 398, secs. 68–72; pp. 403–4, secs. 170 and 174. Some of these laws were indeed collected but never adopted as legally binding. They were accidentally found and published half a century later in D. Ia. Samokvasov, Sbornik obychnogo prava sibirskikh inorodtsev (Warsaw, 1876).

[30] PSZ, ser. 1, vol. 38, no. 29.126, p. 396, sec. 37; p. 408, secs. 244–55.

[31] Ibid., p. 396, secs. 33, 37; p. 401, secs. 122–32.

[32] Ibid., p. 404, sec. 177, pp. 411–14, secs. 296–339.

[33] Ibid., p. 397, secs. 48 and 49; pp. 407–8, secs. 236–45.

Traders, on the other hand, were to be given a free hand. With the exception of liquor, all goods required by the aliens could be sold to them at any time and without any restrictions, preferably at regular fairs.[34] (Foreign trade was not included: the profitable Pacific commerce was banned in 1820 under pressure from the Russian-American company and the Kiakhta merchants.)[35] All possible abuses were to be prevented by the local police, who were also relied on to check their own abuses.[36] As Speranskii had written before the publication of the statute,

As far as trade with aliens is concerned, before 1819 two systems existed in Siberia. One of them may be called prohibitive, the other one, free. The prohibitive system was introduced and, where possible, promoted by various officials of the police department. The free system was always requested . . . by the merchants, all traders in general, and the aliens themselves. The police submitted that the traders cheated the aliens, taking advantage of their ignorance of prices . . . ; that the aliens could not defend themselves against the abuses of private persons; that with free trade it was impossible to determine whether the legal prohibition of the liquor trade was being followed, impossible to expect the timely payment of iasak with the assigned animals of the best quality, and, finally, impossible to sell bread at a profit for the treasury. . . . To these excuses of the local police the merchants and traders submitted that the restrictions on trade with aliens could be tolerated in the past but not now, when the number of traders was greater and, consequently, there was competition; that the reason that moved the police officials to insist on prohibitions was their own profit and not that of the state . . . ; and that, finally, the . . . system of granting . . . trade permits to private persons by police officials served no other purpose but their own self-interest. The aliens, for their part, complained of the ruin that resulted from trade with the officials, of having to buy necessities at exorbitant prices, of the unfairness of police reports about iasak payments, and so on.[37]

Speranskii did not trust either side but had infinite faith in the free market, "which makes any interference by local officials unnecessary and useless."[38] Thus the only obligation on the part of the police was to ensure "that commercial traffic and barter . . . be completely free;

[34] Ibid., p. 397, secs. 45–47; p. 401, secs. 133–34.
[35] Vagin, *Istoricheskie svedeniia*, 2:1–80.
[36] PSZ, ser. 1, vol. 38, no. 29.126, p. 407, secs. 221, 237–43.
[37] Vagin, *Istoricheskie svedeniia*, 1:321–22.
[38] PSZ, ser. 1, vol. 38, no. 29.126, p. 412, sec. 317.

that the number of buyers be as large as possible; and that the collection of dues not take place at the very beginning of the fair."[39] In case the free market or hunter's luck failed the aliens, there were state stores, whose function was to keep prices at a minimum and to provide emergency reserves of bread, salt, powder, and shot.[40] Finally, the aliens were granted complete freedom of religion. The Russian clergy was enjoined to spread Christianity "by persuasion only, without any force" and not to persecute those native Christians "who, through ignorance, lapsed in their observance of church rites."[41]

The emphasis on gradual and voluntary change was the most important feature of the document. The authors expected progress and enlightenment in various spheres, but their goal as legislators was to be faithful to the particular age at which they had found the native peoples. All violations of the natural balance were seen as counterproductive, with the introduction of free trade clearly perceived as a return to the natural state, in which the market would take care of itself. For the peoples covered by the statute this meant almost total cultural and administrative autonomy: the Orthodox clergy, which was to ensure their future salvation, and the local state officials, to whom all native elders were ultimately responsible, were instructed to exercise the most general guidance and to refrain from interfering in clan affairs.

Before they could begin to carry out their duties, however, the local state officials had to set up the basic administrative framework as required by the statute. The greatest difficulty was in deciding which native group belonged to which category. Most aliens were extremely reluctant to move up in the hierarchy and bitterly disagreed with Baten'kov and Speranskii concerning the degree of their "backwardness." The "settled" groups, in particular, greatly resented their promotion to full-fledged taxpayers and wrote numerous petitions to that effect.[42] The Obdora Khanty, too, became very agitated when they found out that as "nomads," they would have to pay local taxes whereas their "wandering" Samoed neighbors and fellow reindeer herders would be exempt. Worried, Governor Bantysh-Kamenskii went to Obdorsk, ordered a halt to the tax collection, and recommended that the Obdora Khanty be classified as "wandering." St. Petersburg had rea-

[39] Ibid., p. 412, sec. 318.
[40] Ibid., pp. 409–10, 270–85.
[41] Ibid., p. 410, secs. 286–92.
[42] Shashkov, "Sibirskie inorodtsy," in *Istoricheskie etiudy*, 191–96.

sons to question the wisdom of dividing the "Ostiak" and, faced with a choice between peace and (insignificant) revenue, opted for the former: in 1827 all the Khanty, Mansi, and Nenets of the Northern Ob' basin were assigned to "wandering" category.[43]

Not all financial matters could be resolved with such ease. The transfer of a large group of aliens to quasi-peasant status apparently meant an increase of revenue for the state treasury at the expense of the Royal Cabinet, which was the sole recipient of iasak. The statute was silent on this issue, and the local administrators had to guess whether the Cabinet would calmly accept this loss or demand its full share from the remaining iasak-payers, the new peasants, or both. In 1824, Governor-General of Eastern Siberia Lavinskii, unable to postpone the decision any longer and anxious for the "state's interest" (and, presumably, his job), ordered the settled aliens to pay iasak in addition to the new taxes. Soon afterward he conceded that "the measure, as extremely burdensome to the aliens, cannot be put into effect" and pleaded with the government to resolve the matter. Finally, a royal decree of 1827 announced that settled aliens were, indeed, exempt from iasak but that the obrok (quit rent) part of their taxes was to be handed over to the Cabinet.[44]

The decree solved the problem for Governor Lavinskii but did not raise more revenue. The amount of tribute had fallen dramatically; the "clans" refused to act as stable administrative units; the new peasants were unable to pay their dues; and the nomads either preferred to sell all their furs to private merchants or else insisted on paying in hard-to-get furs rather than in cash for fear of being promoted to the next "age."[45] In 1827 two iasak commissions were sent to Siberia to make sense of the situation. Known collectively as the Second Iasak Commission, they spent almost eight years counting the aliens, clarifying their status, and establishing new rates of tribute—all "in the spirit" of Speranskii's statute. Because of the latter constraint, they could not do the one thing that most of those concerned seemed to be demanding—abolish the settled category. They did, however, pardon all pre-1832 arrears, permit some groups to remain nomadic "until such time when their situation is sufficiently improved so as to make it possible for them to pay peasant dues," and allow several others to pay only two-thirds of their taxes for a period of ten years.[46]

[43] Minenko, Severo-zapadnaia Sibir', pp. 256–57.
[44] Zalkind, "Iasachnaia politika," pp. 245–46. See also Basharin, Istoriia, pp. 236–37.
[45] Iadrintsev, Sibir' kak koloniia, pp. 110–11; Shashkov, "Sibirskie inorodtsy," in Istoricheskie etiudy, pp. 191–205.
[46] Shashkov, "Sibirskie inorodtsy," in Istoricheskie etiudy, pp. 208–11.

As for the future small peoples of the north, all of them—except for
a few Evenk groups—were classified as wandering aliens and declared
tax-exempt. Otherwise, little had changed in their dealings with the
administration: the rates of iasak had been raised two- or even three-
fold, but more realistic fur prices had annulled most of the increase.
The method of iasak-collecting had also remained the same: shortly
before payment time, the elder asked a literate Cossack to record the
number of pelts being brought in, whereupon both went into town to
hand them over to the local authorities (usually the okruzhnoe upravlenie) for evaluation. The actual process of evaluation varied from
place to place but, in any case, remained a mystery to the treasury officials, who continued to complain of shortfalls and the deteriorating
quality of the pelts.[47] Sometimes, in accordance with the statute, the
tribute was delivered at fairs. Andrei Argentov, the Nizhnekolymsk
missionary who visited Aniui in 1843, thus describes the proceedings:

> Dressed in their best attire, with daggers attached to their bright belts,
> the alien [Even and Yukagir] elders and headmen solemnly appear be-
> fore the policeman [ispravnik]. Without sitting down, they explain that
> they had a bad year, that they did not have enough shot, that there was
> no powder left, and that the hunting season was generally unsuccessful.
> Also, that some people have left for Gizhiga, have not been seen in three
> years, and do not send the tsar's tribute; and that this one, that one, or
> the other one have been sick the whole time.
>   The compassionate policeman expresses great sympathy for their mis-
> fortune but demands tribute all the same.
>   "Would it be possible for your Honor to accept cash?"
>   The policeman accedes to the request of the mountain diplomats, col-
> lects the full amount, and hands out the receipts. They are not supposed
> to receive gifts [i.e., unlike the Chukchi], but they are offered tea—with
> all the appurtenances [so vsemi prinadlezhnostiami] called for by the
> occasion, as far as I can tell.[48]

No less daunting was the task of setting up and maintaining new
organs of native self-government. In 1865 the Tomsk provincial council
(gubernskii sovet) looked into the voluminous documentation relating
to the matter and resolved "to stop this correspondence, which has

[47] Minenko, Severo-zapadnaia Sibir', pp. 258–60; Basharin, Istoriia agrarnykh otnoshenii v Iakutii, p. 250.
[48] Andrei Argentov, Putevye zametki sviashchennika missionera Andreia Argentova.
Vostochnaia Sibir' (Nizhnii Novgorod, 1886), p. 26.

dragged on fruitlessly for forty years, as cumbersome for the state officials and totally useless for the aliens, and start it all over again."[49]

Meanwhile G. S. Baten'kov—the man who had set all of this activity
in motion—had spent half of these forty years in solitary confinement
for his participation in the Decembrist movement. Tried with him and
later executed was the leader of the conspiracy Pavel Ivanovich Pestel.
Son of the governor general of Siberia, Pestel had given the native Siberians some thought and had discussed their fate in his project for a
Russian constitution. Although in basic agreement with Baten'kov and
Speranskii (he almost certainly had read the statute),[50] Pestel was
much blunter in spelling out their common assumptions. All peoples,
he declared, could be divided into two categories: those that had the
right to independent existence and those that did not.[51] It was history,
tradition, and the degree of power and civilization that determined the
status of various nations. Siberians, for example, "have never enjoyed
and will never be able to enjoy full independence, and have always
belonged to some strong State . . . , for which reason . . . they must renounce forever their right to separate nationhood."[52] Eventually, all
such peoples "should be fused into one mass, so that the inhabitants
of the whole territory of the Russian State would *all be Russians*,"[53]
but for the time being the Provisional Supreme Government was to pay
"profound attention" to the nomadic peoples (divided, as in the statute,
into two classes).

> They are half-savage people, and some of them are complete savages; peo-
> ple who do not know their own good and find themselves in ignorance
> and humiliation. Consequently, out of a sheer sense of Christian duty, it
> is necessary to make an effort to improve their situation, all the more so
> because they happen to live in our State, our fatherland. So let them be-
> come our brothers and not languish any more in their miserable state.[54]

The only way to achieve this end was for the nomads and the wanderers to settle down and take up agriculture. The method suggested
by Pestel—the creation of native administrative units, missions, and

[49] Shashkov, "Sibirskie inorodtsy," in *Istoricheskie etiudy,* p. 219.
[50] Kartsov, *Dekabrist G. S. Baten'kov,* pp. 98–100.
[51] Cf. E. J. Hobsbawm, *Nations and Nationalism since 1870: Programme, Myth, Reality* (Cambridge, 1990), pp. 31–38.
[52] Nechkina, ed., "Russkaia Pravda," pp. 121–22.
[53] Ibid., p. 149.
[54] Ibid., p. 142.

bread supplies[55]—differed little from that of the statute. Indeed, given the same general goal, the main difference between the two documents was precisely Speranskii's and Baten'kov's emphasis on "indirectness" and their belief that sooner or later history itself would guide the natives toward a union with the Russian people.[56]

[55] Ibid., pp. 143, 146.
[56] Cf. Raeff, *Siberia*, p. 134.

II

SUBJECTS OF CONCERN

"Ostiak musicians," from *Sibirskii sbornik*, vol. 1 (1886)

4

The Oppressed

And pity melts the sympathizing breast.
Ah! fatal virtue! for the brave distress'd.
—Thomas Day, "The Dying Negro"

Aliens as Neighbors and Tribute Payers as Debtors

In the late 1850s the Russian empire added to the number of its wandering subjects by acquiring the formerly Chinese Amur and Ussuri territories. Indeed, theoretically the empire acquired the Amur and Ussuri territories *because* they contained some of its wandering subjects. According to A. F. Middendorf, who had led an Academy expedition to Siberia in 1842–1845, many of the Tungus living on the Chinese side of the border were paying tribute to the Russian Cossacks, which made them de facto Russian subjects and their hunting grounds de facto Russian territory.[1] This discovery had been warmly received by Governor-General N. N. Murav'ev of Eastern Siberia, who was worried about the British penetration of East Asia; by Captain N. G. Nevel'-skoi of the Imperial Navy, who was keen on proving that the mouth of the Amur was navigable; by the Irkutsk merchants, who were anxious to take part in the partition of China; and by a motley group of Russian patriots—from the Great Prince Konstantin to Murav'ev's exiled charges—who dreamed of Russia as an Asian superpower. The Amur was to provide Russia with a new El Dorado, a bottomless breadbasket, and an easy access to the Pacific, while the Amur natives (about 15,600 in all, including 11,700 Tungus-Manchu and Nivkh foragers)[2] were to

---

[1] A. F. Middendorf, *Puteshestvie na sever i vostok Sibiri* (St. Petersburg; 1860), part 1, pp. 159–68.

[2] Four thousand Gol'd (Nanai); 1,700 Orok, Oroch, and Udege; 2,100 Tungus; and 3,900 Giliak (Nivkh). The other 3,900 were Chinese, Manchu, and Daur. See V. M. Kabuzan, *Dal'nevostochnyi krai v XVII–nachale XX vv., 1640–1917: Istoriko-demografi-cheskii ocherk* (Moscow, 1985), pp. 81–85.

supply the legal justification and the White Man's Burden.[3] The "point man" of Russian imperialism on the Amur, N. G. Nevel'skoi, recorded as symbolically significant his speech to a small group of Nivkh fishermen and Manchu traders on Russia's historic rights to the Amur, used the presence of Tungus migrants on Sakhalin to claim permanent occupation of the island by "Russian subjects," and tried hard "to instill in the aliens the notions of right and seniority."[4]

Once the annexation had been completed, however, the local aliens diminished in importance to the point of total invisibility. Even Richard Maack, whose *Travels on the Amur* contains detailed and sympathetic descriptions of the native population, called the newly acquired land "almost completely empty" when he spoke about it in terms of the imperial economy and administration.[5] For the Amur territory to be the Promised Land, it had to be virgin today and Russian tomorrow. Immediately after the transfer of the left bank of the Amur to Russia, a special Amur Cossack Regiment was created, large groups of exiles were forcibly moved, and thousands of peasant settlers received state land, government loans, and various draft and tax exemptions. Ten years later, there were three times as many Russians as there were "Amur peoples" on the Amur.[6] As peasant "resettlement" (both state-sponsored and illegal) increased toward the end of the century, the "Far Eastern" foragers were too few to be included in various land-allotment schemes and generally regarded as too "wandering" to need any land anyway.[7] As a result, many were driven out of their settlements, died of

[3] See Mark Bassin's excellent "A Russian Mississippi?" Also see G. I. Nevel'skoi, *Podvigi russkikh morskikh ofitserov na krainem vostoke Rossii, 1849–1855* (St. Petersburg, 1878; reprint, 1947); Ivan Barsukov, *Graf Nikolai Nikolaevich Murav'ev-Amurskii po ego pis'mam, offitsial'nym dokumentam, rasskazam sovremennikov i pechatnym istochnikam: Materialy dlia biografii* (Moscow, 1891); and Yuri Semyonov, *Siberia: Its Conquest and Development* (Baltimore, 1963).

[4] Nevel'skoi, *Podvigi*, pp. 121–22, 134, 265. On the annexation of Sakhalin, see John Stephan, *Sakhalin: A History* (Oxford, 1971), pp. 42–64.

[5] R. Maak [Richard Maack], *Puteshestvie na Amur, sovershennoe po rasporiazheniiu Sibirskago otdela Imperatorskogo russkogo geograficheskogo obshchestva, v 1855 godu* (St. Petersburg, 1859), p. v.

[6] Kabuzan, *Dal'nevostochnyi krai*, pp. 56–86.

[7] "Polozhenie o pozemel'nom ustroistve krest'ian i inorodtsev na kazennykh zemliakh sibirskikh gubernii i oblastei," *VK*, no. 8 (1910): 458. Between 1897 and 1916 the native population of the Amur fell from about 17,900 to about 15,900. See Kabuzan, *Dal'nevostochnyi krai*, pp. 154–55. For peasant colonization of southern Siberia, see *Aziatskaia Rossiia* (St. Petersburg, 1914), 1:446–66; François-Xavier Coquin, "Aperçus sur le peuplement de la Sibérie au XIX siècle," *Cahiers du monde russe et soviétique* 7, no. 4 (1966): 564–81; Okladnikov et al., eds., *Istoriia Sibiri*, 3:27, 308; Steven G. Marks, *Road to Power: The Trans-Siberian Railroad and the Colonization of Asian Russia, 1850–1917* (Ithaca, N.Y., 1991), pp. 153–69; Donald W. Treadgold, *The Great Siberian*

smallpox, or moved across the border without creating a bureaucratic "problem."[8] Even the "yellow peril" slogan, popular at the turn of the century, did not refer to the Amur natives but to the Chinese and Koreans.[9]

Outside the Amur territory, the efforts of the Russian state to modernize, colonize, and expand were much less apparent to the wandering population. The zone of new settlement never reached the sixtieth parallel; in fact, the official resettlement department defined ninetenths of Siberia as "completely uninhabited and badly explored."[10] In the peak migration period of 1897–1911, the Russian population of the huge Yakutsk province actually fell from 30,007 to 18,035 (to about 7 percent of the total).[11] Agriculture was, for the most part, impossible; fur supplies continued to drop; and after the sale of Alaska in 1867 the region lost a great deal of its strategic and commercial importance. Most circumpolar areas were administered at a considerable loss. The diminishing fur tribute remained the property of the Imperial household, and the taxes collected by the state treasury could not cover the costs of maintaining local priests, Cossacks, and administrators. The payment of salaries to its employees was, in effect, the only form of government investment in the area, and, left to their own devices, the inhabitants of the north were speedily proceeding along the path of mutual adaptation.

The Russian "old settlers" (starozhily) of the Arctic coast—registered as peasants, townsmen, Cossacks, or merchants—were primarily hunters, fishermen, and petty traders. Depending on where they lived, they adopted the Yukagir, Ugrian, Koriak, or Yakut subsistence patterns, tools, diet, clothing, spirits, and shamans. Many went hungry

Migration: Government and Peasant in Resettlement from Emancipation to the First World War (Princeton, N.J. 1957), pp. 13–80.

[8] Kabuzan, Dal'nevostochnyi krai, p. 155; Ch. M. Taksami, "Vliianie khristianstva na traditsionnye verovaniia nivkhov," in I. S. Vdovin, ed., Khristianstvo i lamaizm u korennogo naseleniia Sibiri (Leningrad, 1979), p. 117; Aziatskaia Rossiia, 1:78; Arsen'ev, Izbrannye proizvedeniia, 2:34, 300; Otto Genest, "Kapitän Jakobsen's Reisen im Gebiete der Giljaken und auf der Insel Sachalin," Globus 52 (1887): 382 [HRAF RX2, no. 19].

[9] A. Grigor'ev, "Nizhnee techenie Amura v kolonizatsionnom otnoshenii," VK, no. 5 (1909): 347; A. Panov, "Zheltyi vopros v Priamur'e," VK, no. 7 (1910): 53–117; A. Tatishchev, "Amurskaia oblast' v kolonizatsionnom otnoshenii," VK, no. 5 (1909): 210; N. K. Kolin, "Zheltyi vopros na russkom Vostoke," RV 252 (January 1898): 310–20. Some Amur aliens were seen as pro-foreign and considered "an unreliable anti-state force" by association. See Kolin, "Zheltyi vopros na russkom Vostoke," p. 312.

[10] Aziatskaia Rossiia, 1:60.

[11] Ibid., pp. 70, 82. See also maps following p. 490; Armstrong, Russian Settlement in the North, pp. 41–59.

every spring, and some remembered Ermak as an enemy invader. Many spoke local languages, and some did not speak any Russian.[12] Indeed, not all "old settlers" considered themselves Russian, and not all travelers recognized them as such. During the 1897 census the members of a Yakut-speaking Ust' Olenek community gave "peasant" as their nationality. Apparently, their peasant rank and form of taxation was the only thing that distinguished them from their neighbors (the neighbors, meanwhile, regarded them as a Yakut clan with special magic powers).[13] One Russian taxpayer from Nizhnekolymsk petitioned the administration to be allowed to become a Chukchi. To him, the only difference was the number and quantity of exactions.[14] In parts of western Siberia the term "iasak man" had come to mean any hunter,[15] and most members of the old-settler communities in the northeast defined themselves by the name of their settlement: the "Markovo people," the "Gizhiga people," and so on. They included taxpayers of various ranks as well as former Yukagir or Koriak who were still registered as aliens but were now full-fledged "Markovo people" or "Gizhiga people." In Kamchatka, the term "Kamchadal" (Kamchatka people), formerly used to refer to the native Itel'men, was now applied to the whole forager population of the peninsula. Legal status and kinship ties continued to be important for self-identification within the group, but to the outside world they were all "Kamchatka people."[16] The outside world consisted primarily of the "Russians"—usually officials, merchants, priests, and exiles—and the surrounding nomads or "wanderers," whom the old-settlers knew not as generic aliens, for some of them were aliens, that is, tribute-payers, themselves, but as the "little" Chukchi, "little" Tungus, and so on.[17] In parts of the lower Enisei all native males were referred to as Vasilii Ivanovich.[18]

[12] Vladimir Zenzinov, with Isaac Don Levine, The Road to Oblivion (New York, 1933); Ditmar, Poezdki, pp. 434–35; Gurvich, Etnicheskaia istoriia, pp. 196–211; Minenko, Severo-zapadnaia Sibir', pp. 32–132; Safronov, Russkie na severo-vostoke Azii, pp. 215–19; Iadrintsev, Sibir' kak koloniia, pp. 13–63, esp. pp. 61 and 63; Shchapov, Sochineniia, 3: 634, and 4: 97–99, 106–50; P. Riabkov, "Poliarnye strany Sibiri," SSb, no. 1 (1887): 6–25; I. A. Khudiakov, Kratkoe opisanie Verkhoianskogo okruga (Leningrad, 1969), pp. 92–98; Kastren, "Puteshestvie," p. 179; "Puteshestvie ital'iantsa Som'e po Sibiri," SSb, no. 1 (1886): 187; Wrangell, Narrative of an Expedition, pp. 53–70; P. Tret'iakov, "Turukhanskii krai," Zapiski IRGO po obshchei geografii 2 (1869): 367–68.
[13] Gurvich, Etnicheskaia istoriia, p. 196.
[14] Bogoras, The Chukchee, p. 721.
[15] D. N. Mamin-Sibiriak, Sobranie sochinenii v 10 tomakh (Moscow, 1958), 4:339.
[16] Gurvich, Etnicheskaia istoriia, p. 209; Ditmar, Poezdki, p. 159.
[17] It is unclear to what extent the nomads distinguished among various categories of Russians, old and new.
[18] V. V. Peredol'skii, Po Eniseiu. Byt eniseiskikh ostiakov (St. Petersburg, 1908), p. 25.

The most important connection among the three groups was trade, with the old settlers serving as intermediaries between the Russian world of towns and villages and the nomads' world of taiga and tundra. The methods of these transactions had changed little since the eighteenth century. The old-settler traders (to a greater or lesser extent, almost all old settlers were traders) purchased liquor, tobacco, tea, flour, ammunition, cloth, needles, beads, hatchets, kettles, knives, and other goods from the visiting Irkutsk, Eniseisk, Tobol'sk, or Arkhangel'sk merchants. Then they traveled to the native encampments, awaited the arrival of the nomads in their own settlements, or attended regular fairs such as the ones at Olekminsk, Aniui, or Obdorsk. Every trader had his own native "friends" who owed him all of their produce (mostly furs, fish, mammoth tusks, and reindeer skins) and relied on his credit during the rest of the year.[19] According to Castrén, for example, at the Obdorsk fair "the sons and daughters of the tundra . . . seemed like idle visitors because they did not bring any goods. I was told, however, that under their bulging fur coats they were hiding silver and red foxes, among other things. But not everybody could see the merchandise: the seller surreptitiously made his way towards his friend and, after receiving appropriate refreshment, showed him his riches."[20]

The appropriate refreshment was, of course, vodka, without which no commercial transaction could ever take place—at the passionate insistence of the trappers and as a result of sober calculation by the merchants. The liquor trade was theoretically illegal but practically universal, and even Innokenty P. Tolmachev, the head of an official Academy of Sciences expedition to Chukotka, was instructed by the governor of the Yakutsk province to take along a good load of alcohol: Without it, the governor said, they would be "unable to travel among the Chukchi."[21] According to I. S. Poliakov, the usual procedure on the lower Ob' was "first of all, to give each Ostiak a cup of good vodka, free of charge; then sell the first bottle for one ruble; two more bottles— mixed half-and-half with water—for one and a half rubles; and then

[19] Abramov, "Opisanie," p. 365; Riabkov, "Poliarnye strany Sibiri," pp. 28–32; Wrangell, Narrative of an Expedition, pp. 16, 114; Safronov, Russkie na severo-vostoke Azii, p. 222; Okun', Ocherki, pp. 111, 139–40; Iadrintsev, "Osuzhdennye na smert' plemena," SSb, no. 1 (1904): 19–20. For an interesting case of an amicable "friendship" relationship surviving into the 1930s, see Ethel John Lindgren, "An Example of Culture Contact without Conflict: Reindeer Tungus and Cossacks of Northwestern Manchuria." AA 40 (October–December 1938): 605–21.

[20] Kastren, "Puteshestvie," p. 180. Cf. Kai Donner, Among the Samoyed in Siberia (New Haven, Conn., 1954), p. 43; Beliavskii, Poezdka, pp. 40–41.

[21] Innokenty P. Tolmacheff, Siberian Passage: An Explorer's Search into the Russian Arctic (New Brunswick, N.J., 1949), p. 61.

three bottles of pure water for three rubles each, so that the Ostiak left completely drunk."[22]

The exchange itself often took place indoors, in the merchant's house or in the hunter's hut. "The Ostiak with the pelts comes to the salesman, agrees on the price of each one of them, and puts them down on the floor; the buyer puts the agreed amount on top of each pelt; the Ostiak collects the money, and the buyer, the pelts. When the Ostiak has sold all of his pelts, he begins to buy the salesman's goods in exactly the same way."[23]

Usually all the merchandise was bartered directly, but as time went on, more and more trappers became involved in the money economy. Because of the difference between the prices fixed by the state and those offered by the merchants, it was more advantageous for the aliens to sell their furs, fish, or labor to the merchants and then to pay tribute in cash (with the growth of a large-scale fishing industry in the north there was more cash to go around).[24] Very rarely, however, did they actually sell their goods for a particular price. Almost all native hunters, fishermen, and reindeer breeders were heavily in debt, so that every transaction constituted a loan payment, a new advance, or a part of regular labor service.[25] The old settlers of the village of Sherkalinskoe, for example, owned all the native labor between Kondinsk and Berezov on the Lower Ob'. In exchange for providing their "friends" with food, clothes, tools, and weapons (as well as paying their tribute), they had exclusive right to all their produce and leased most of their fishing sites.[26] On the Enisei a certain Kobachev formally asked the government to legalize a similar situation and grant him an exclusive charter to the whole of the Turukhansk region.[27]

State antimonopoly measures did not seem to help. According to V. K. Brazhnikov, the head of the government fishing agency on the Amur,

[22] I. S. Poliakov, Pis'ma i otchety o puteshestvii v dolinu reki Obi (St. Petersburg, 1877), pp. 151–52.

[23] Ezhegodnik Tobol'skogo gubernskogo muzeia, 19: 112; quoted in V. G. Kartsov, Ocherk istorii narodov severo-zapadnoi Sibiri (Moscow, 1937), p. 88. See also Donner, Among the Samoyed in Siberia, p. 43.

[24] Minenko, Severo-zapadnaia Sibir', pp. 261.

[25] Shashkov, "Sibirskie inorodtsy," in Istoricheskie etiudy, pp. 259–61; Donner, Among the Samoyed in Siberia, p. 26; Okun', Ocherki, pp. 11, 139–40.

[26] Poliakov, Pis'ma i otchety, pp. 75–76; Iadrintsev, "Osuzhdennye na smert' plemena," p. 11. All of these settlers bore the name of Novitskii and traced their descent to Filofei Leshchinskii's chronicler.

[27] M. F. Krivoshapkin, Eniseiskii okrug i ego zhizn' (St. Petersburg, 1865), 1:15–17.

In order to feed his family and his dogs, the Giliak has to go to his friend
the merchant and borrow his shoddy goods at inflated prices, although
at a nearby store he could buy better and much cheaper products; but
who, besides the fish merchant, would be willing to accept payment in
fish and, moreover, trust a Giliak who lives several dozen versts away? As
for the merchant, he is happy to get a deal in advance, so he loans whatever is needed, not forgetting to offer some vodka, so that the Giliak does
not go to his rival.[28]

Although sleepy in comparison to the rapidly changing south, the
circumpolar regions of the Russian empire were not entirely insulated
from new economic and political developments. The wandering aliens
were leasing their fishing sites to large shipowners; losing their hunting
grounds to the Lena, Enisei, and Baikal gold diggers; and changing
their migration routes to avoid new settlements.[29] Where Russian subjects could not or would not go, there were others to take their place.
The swelling Chinese population of northern Manchuria dominated
the Amur trade; the American whalers and merchants became the
main trading partners of the Chukchi; and the Portsmouth treaty of
1905 resulted in the formal Japanese takeover of southern Sakhalin and
the de facto Japanese control of the Okhotsk Sea fishing.[30]

Not all change was due to the Russians and their great-power competitors. In the northwest, the Nenets reindeer breeders had many of
their herds taken away by the Komi; in the northeast, a growing number
of Tungus and Yukagir groups adopted the Yakut language; and on the

[28] V. K. Brazhnikov, *Rybnye promysly Dal'nego Vostoka*, vol. 1, *Osennii promysel v
nizov'iakh r. Amura* (St. Petersburg, 1900), pp. 50–51.

[29] See Henry Johnson, *The Life and Voyages of Joseph Wiggins, F.R.G.S., Modern Discoverer of the Kara Sea Route to Siberia, Based on His Journals and Letters* (New York,
1907); Tret'iakov, "Turukhanskii krai," pp. 502–17; Krivoshapkin, *Eniseiskii okrug*,
2:39; Poliakov, *Pis'ma i otchety*, pp. 81–99; Donner, *Among the Samoyed in Siberia*,
p. 32; Iadrintsev, *Sibir' kak koloniia*, p. 277, and "Osuzhdennye na smert' plemena,"
pp. 9–12; Abramov, "Opisanie," pp. 409–12; Shashkov, "Sibirskie inorodtsy," in *Istoricheskie etiudy*, p. 249; *Etnicheskaia istoriia*, p. 145; and Okun', *Ocherki*, pp. 135–36.

[30] Grigor'ev, "Nizhnee techenie Amura," p. 347; Panov, "Zheltyi vopros," p. 96; Andrew Malozemoff, *Russian Far Eastern Policy 1881–1904* (Berkeley, Calif., 1958), pp. 22–
23; Przheval'skii, *Puteshestvie*, p. 105; Kolin, "Zheltyi vopros," p. 312; V. K. Arsen'ev, *Po
Ussuriiskomu kraiu* (Moscow, 1955), pp. 75–76, 107, 187, 237; and *Izbrannye proizvedeniia*, 1:358–62, 407, 409, 525–26; Liakhotskii, "Iz dnevnika missionera Dole-Troitskogo
stana Kamchatskoi missii," *PB*, no. 19 (1897): 122; S. N. Brailovskii, "Tazy ili udikhe,"
ZhS, no. 3–4 (1901): 327–31; Vdovin, *Ocherki istorii i etnografii chukchei*, pp. 245–46,
258–62; Bogoras, *The Chukchee*, pp. 61–64, 731–32; Waldemar Jochelson, *The Koryak*
(New York, 1918), p. 808; I. I. Gapanovich, *Rossiia v Severo-vostochnoi Azii* (Beijing,
1933), pp. 122–48; Okun', *Ocherki*, pp. 131–32; N. K. Kolin, "Inostrantsy v Sibiri," *RV*
252 (December 1897): 419–22.

Taimyr peninsula Russian officials singled out four Yakut-speaking Tungus clans as a separate people, the Dolgan (the people in question had apparently retained clan-based self-identification and did not have a common name for themselves).[31] Still, it was non-native influence that had the most profound economic and social effect. Disease, the introduction of new technology, the destruction of forests, the extermination of animals, and various administrative pressures forced large numbers of people to migrate to new areas or modify their economic activities.[32] Some tribute payers were forcibly moved to service mail routes; some taiga hunters had to switch to reindeer breeding; some foragers had to become cart drivers, guides, or traders; and certain traditional methods of fishing and hunting had to be abandoned because Russian officials considered them barbaric.[33] To varying degrees, all former "foreigners" were learning new skills and acquiring new houses, tools, and clothes. Social status was increasingly associated with the ownership of imported manufactured goods; hunting luck depended on the availability of guns (as well as help from the icon of St. Nicholas); and Russian medicine was widely acknowledged to have great magic powers.[34] ("The Russian god is stronger than the Giliak god, so the Russian shaman must also be stronger than the Giliak shaman," said Shternberg's Giliak friends about medical doctors.)[35]

Migrations, epidemics, and new occupations affected the size and the composition of native communities. Koriak groups stricken by syphilis were shunned and not accepted into marriage alliances; Ugrian villages began to coopt Russians as members, and some Tungus hunting parties could now consist of members of different clans.[36] The largely fictitious clans instituted by the Russian authorities for fiscal

[31] Etnicheskaia istoriia, pp. 36, 64, 67–68, 110–11, 142, 151, 223–32; Islavin, Samoiedy, pp. 11–20, 70–74; Shashkov, "Sibirskie inorodtsy," in Istoricheskie etiudy, p. 256; Kastren, "Puteshestvie," pp. 170–72; Levin and Potapov, Narody Sibiri, p. 655. These are only a few random examples of ethnic and economic change among circumpolar peoples in the nineteenth century. The best general sources are Etnicheskaia istoriia; Gurvich, Etnicheskaia istoriia; and A. V. Smoliak, Etnicheskie protsessy u narodov Nizhnego Amura i Sakhalina: Seredina XIX–nachalo XX v. (Moscow, 1975).

[32] Ditmar, Poezdki, pp. 345–46, 373, 385; Arsen'ev, Izbrannye proizvedeniia, 1:34, 300, 556; Kabuzan, Dal'nevostochnyi krai, pp. 82–83, 155; Minenko, Severo-zapadnaia Sibir', p. 172.

[33] Smoliak, Etnicheskie protsessy, p. 209.

[34] M. A. Czaplicka, My Siberian Year (London, n. d.), p. 69; Donner, Among the Samoyed in Siberia, p. 31.

[35] Shternberg, Giliaki, p. 76.

[36] Ditmar, Poezdki, pp. 177, 373; Sliunin, Okhotsko-Kamchatskii krai, 1:522; Kartsov, Ocherk, pp. 92–93; Istoriia Iakutskoi ASSR, 2:327.

purposes could gradually become meaningful as their members regularly paid tribute, built roads, and carried mail together. Similarly, the
bemedaled "princelings" sponsored by the administration and ridiculed by the travelers who preferred their natives "unspoiled" might
use the much valued Russian connections to become effective political
brokers.[37] Knowledge of Russian could be an important test of com-
mon-law competence, and an appeal to the Russian police, an important factor in the resolution of local disputes.[38]

When the government urged the aliens to remain in possession of
their land, the concept of land and the character of possession were
bound to be interpreted differently, but it was the government that
made the final decision, and some taiga communities were paying attention. On the Amur, for example, large Nanai clans began to put up
special signs to demarcate "their land" in areas where before the 1880s
anyone could hunt.[39] A much more forceful (though much less debated) government policy consisted in the granting of "alien" rights
and obligations to only one-half of the indigenous population. Since
first contact, most Russian travelers had been appalled by what they
saw as the inferior position of women in native societies, yet for just as
long the imperial tribute system had continued to create new reasons
for indignation. Only native men paid tribute, so only native men had
a legal existence in the Russian state: if a native man and a native
woman were murdered, the administration would naturally be upset
in the first case and might very well ignore the second.[40] Even in the
areas where women worked for cash (in fish-salting, tanning, or prostitution) or were encouraged by the missionaries to go to school, nothing
could compare with the universal and vigorously enforced obligation
to pay tribute.

Once again, however, it was in trade that the changes were most apparent to outside observers. As N. M. Iadrintsev, the greatest champion

---

[37] See, for example, William Hulme Hooper, *Ten Months among the Tents of the Tuski,
with Incidents of an Arctic Boat Expedition in Search of Sir John Franklin, as Far as the
Mackenzie River and Cape Bathurst* (London, 1853), pp. 59–61 [HRAF RY2, no. 6]; A. E.
Nordenskiöld, *The Voyage of the Vega round Asia and Europe, with a Historical Review
of Previous Journeys along the North Coast of the Old World* (New York, 1882), p. 373;
Ditmar, *Poezdki*, p. 40; Kastren, "Puteshestvie," p. 333; Charles H. Hawes, *In the Uttermost East* (New York, 1903), p. 261 [HRAF, RX2, no. 9]; *Istoriia Iakutskoi ASSR*,
2:326–27, 332–33; *Etnicheskaia istoriia*, p. 69; and Czaplicka, *My Siberian Year*, p. 169.
[38] B. O. Dolgikh, ed., *Bytovye rasskazy entsev* (Moscow, 1962), pp. 82–88. See also
Czaplicka, *My Siberian Year*, pp. 164–86, and Zenzinov, *The Road to Oblivion*, p. 175.
[39] Smoliak, *Etnicheskie protsessy*, pp. 164–65.
[40] Minenko, *Severo-zapadnaia Sibir'*, p. 194.

of "alien rights," put it, "the alien yielded to the temptation. . . . Traditional notions have changed, old honesty and trust have disappeared. . . . The tribes that used to be remarkable for their ingenuous, irreproachable morality, have lost their childlike purity and are now demoralized."[41]

Many native northerners had indeed adapted to the new trade practices and modified their traditional rules of exchange. The reindeer pastoralists often refused to show their herds to the Russians. (P. Tret'-iakov, for one, observed that the Avam Samoed [Nganasan] were terrible "misers" toward the Russians but not toward each other).[42] Some hunters began to accept credit from other people's "friends," and one Udege group allegedly "tried to accumulate as much credit as possible so that the creditor, fearful of losing the debt completely, would agree to better terms."[43] Occasionally such tactics worked, and, according to N. Gondatti, "Some traders, seeing that hunting was less and less productive and that the aliens had learned to cheat as much as they used to be cheated, were ready to stop all trade relationships with them and devote themselves exclusively to commercial fishing, but the fear of losing all their debts prevents them from doing it and forces them to . . . continue being the guardians of the local population."[44]

Some native northerners could actually dictate their own terms to the Russian traders and travelers. The Koriak, for instance, were usually the only source of food and transportation at the entrance to Kamchatka, and many of them seemed to know how to take advantage of their monopoly, prompting Peter Dobell to call them "treacherous rascals," "villains," and "the most rapacious barbarians I ever saw."[45] "Indeed, . . . they always pretend to be in want of food, in order to impose on travelers, and make them pay the dearer for what they want. Should any one object to their terms, they quarrel with him, and either beat him, or cut him with their knives, if he be unarmed and unable to de-

---

[41] Iadrintsev, "Osuzhdennye na smert' plemena," p. 21. Cf. K. D. Nosilov, "Voguly desiat' let nazad i teper'," *PB*, no. 19 (1897): 130–36.

[42] Tret'iakov, "Turukhanskii krai," pp. 401–2. See also N. V. Latkin, *Eniseiskaia guberniia, ee proshloe i nastoiashchee* (St. Petersburg, 1892), pp. 136.

[43] Quotation from Arsen'ev, *Izbrannye proizvedeniia*, 1:470. See also Vagin, *Istoricheskie svedeniia*, 1:292; Krivoshapkin, *Eniseiskii okrug*, 2:35–36, 136–37; Iadrintsev, "Osuzhdennye na smert' plemena," p. 20; Arsen'ev, *Izbrannye proizvedeniia*, 1:470; Brazhnikov, *Rybnye promysly*, p. 52; Latkin, *Eniseiskaia guberniia*, pp. 180–81.

[44] Quoted in Iadrintsev, "Osuzhdennye na smert' plemena," pp. 21–22.

[45] Dobell, *Travels in Kamchatka and Siberia*, 1:146, 148, 152.

fend himself."⁴⁶ Others joined the already established commercial routes or launched profitable networks of their own, as those Tungus who got involved in the Aian-Yakutsk trade (bringing goods from foreign ships to the capital of the northeast) or those who traveled from Aian to the Uda to sell their furs to the Daurs.⁴⁷ Finally, there appeared people who would buy merchandise from the Russians and resell it at a profit to their kinsmen.⁴⁸

Yet no one was as successful at dealing with the outsiders as were the Chukchi. Based on Speranskii's statute, the 1857 Legal Code of the Russian Empire classified them as "aliens not fully conquered" who "pay iasak to the amount and of the quality that they themselves desire,"⁴⁹ and although subsequent editions of the code dropped this category, the Chukchi remained fully independent until well after the collapse of the Russian empire. Several attempts were made to organize them into administrative units and make them pay tribute, but there was practically no Russian presence in Chukotka and all such attempts ended in failure. In the 1860s Baron Maydell (Maidel'), a Kolyma official "with special powers," capitalized on the Chukchi interest in the Aniui trade and banned the "Chukchi presents," that is, goods that were given to the Chukchi in exchange for tribute. In effect, iasak was transformed from an item of trade into a tax for the right to trade: those who did not come to the fair did not pay anything. At the same time, Maydell introduced the rank of "The Highest Chief of All the Chukchi," sometimes referred to as the Chukchi tsar, and tried to boost the authority of the "clans chiefs."⁵⁰ These reforms, intended to "try and bring [the Chukchi] under Russian sovereignty,"⁵¹ did not survive their initiator. The clans existed on paper only, and the chiefs were usually influential reindeer herders who could easily lose their reindeer as well as their influence and their "clansmen." As one of them told V. G. Bogoraz, "Now I am a chief, and I have this dagger and a package of paper as signs of my dignity. Still where in the world are my people? I

⁴⁶ Ibid., p. 141. See also George Kennan, *Tent Life in Siberia and Adventures among the Koraks and Other Tribes in Kamtchatka and Northern Asia* (New York, 1872), pp. 232–33, and Cochrane, *A Pedestrian Journey*, p. 371.

⁴⁷ *Etnicheskaia istoriia*, p. 146; Vasilevich, *Evenki*, p. 180.

⁴⁸ Poliakov, *Pis'ma i otchety*, pp. 99–100; Minenko, *Severo-zapadnaia Sibir'*, p. 185; Vasilevich, *Evenki*, p. 181; Smoliak, *Etnicheskie protsessy*, p. 174.

⁴⁹ PSZ, ser. 1, vol. 38, no. 29.126, sec. 78; *Istoriia Iakutskoi ASSR*, 2:335; Vdovin, *Ocherki istorii i etnografii chukchei*, p. 251.

⁵⁰ Bogoras, *The Chukchee*, pp. 543, 706–8.

⁵¹ Vdovin, *Ocherki istorii i etnografii chukchei*, p. 232. See also pp. 230–36.

am unable to find any."[52] The heir to the Chukchi throne inherited his father's crimson robe and medals but did not inherit his prestige, so that Maydell's successors dropped the use of the title and forgot the incumbent. By 1910 the local officials had decided that "the Chukchi do not form communes and do not have chiefs, so that all attempts by the Russian administration to create elders among them have ended in failure."[53]

No communes and no chiefs meant no tribute. After the sale of Alaska American ships became frequent guests on the Chukotka coast, and the Chukchi began to lose interest in the more expensive Russian wares. In exchange for whalebone, reindeer skins, and walrus tusks, the U.S. merchants brought rum, powder, and Winchester rifles, as well as flour, biscuits, sugar, black molasses, beads, hardware, and cutlery.[54] Except for brick tea and strong "Cherkasskii" tobacco, few Russian goods (many of which were actually American imports via Vladivostok) could compete in the new market. On the other hand, the American pelts that used to be brought to Kolyma by the Chukchi traders were now sent from Alaska to the continental United States. As a result, more and more gifts were needed to lure the maritime Chukchi to the Kolyma fairs.[55] In 1892 Vladimir Iokhel'son witnessed the following scene at the Aniui fair:

> Ten or so Chukchee from various localities came to the official cabin, and in the presence of the district chief were entertained by the Cossacks with tea, sugar, and biscuits. After a speech suitable to the occasion had been made by the chief through an interpreter, to the effect that the Czar loved the Chukchee and was sending them presents, each of the natives made a small contribution to the tribute with a red or an arctic fox. Then the imperial presents were inspected and additions begged for, which were generally granted by the chief, who was anxious to get rid of his tiresome guests. The results of the barter were very favorable to the Chukchee. They had received presents which in value greatly exceeded their tribute; the hides meanwhile were ceremoniously stamped with the official seal and dispatched to the Court Treasury in St. Petersburg as a token of Chukchee submissiveness.[56]

[52] Bogoras, The Chukchee, p. 706.
[53] Vdovin, Ocherki istorii i etnografii chukchei, p. 247. See also pp. 248—49 and Tolmacheff, Siberian Passage, pp. 15—16, 169.
[54] Bogoras, The Chukchee, p. 61.
[55] Ibid., pp. 62—64, 708; Vdovin, Ocherki istorii i etnografii chukchei, pp. 236—37.
[56] Jochelson, The Koryak, pp. 802—3. See also Argentov, Putevye zamietki, pp. 23—25; and Vdovin, Ocherki istorii i etnografii chukchei, p. 252.

There was no more talk of "free" tribute or supreme chiefs—in fact, there was very little talking going on between the Russians and their "not fully conquered" neighbors. Very few Chukchi had ever spoken Russian, and by the turn of the century English had definitely become the language of international commerce in eastern Chukotka, particularly since some coastal Chukchi worked on American whaling ships.[57] In 1902 Colonel Vonliarliarskii's Eastern Siberian charter company was granted exclusive rights to Chukotka. Most shares in the new company were owned by American traders, and soon their commercial outposts mushroomed all over the peninsula.[58] The routes of the Chukchi traders became shorter, often not reaching the Russian settlements on the Kolyma, and some Eskimo agents on the coast accumulated considerable wealth.[59] So important had they become and so "enigmatic" had they remained that many Russians perceived the Chukchi as a considerable military threat. According to Lieutenant-Colonel Kozik, "In 1877 there were rumors in Petropavlovsk that the Chukchi were fighting among themselves and approaching Kamchatka, that they were well armed with rifles and even cannons, and that they were being equipped by American whalers."[60]

Seven years later, a trader from Nizhne-Kolymsk was accused by the Chukchi of cheating and had his purchase confiscated. Enraged, the trader threatened the Chukchi with Russian military retribution. When the incident became known to the officials, the trader was put in jail, and the police commander of the Kolyma district wrote that, "for fear of military tribunal, the Russian population of Nizhne-Kolymsk should not irritate the Chukchi in any way." In case this statement did not prove satisfactory to the Chukchi, the commander was willing to meet their "chiefs" personally.[61]

Far removed from the main centers of Russian influence and elusive in their almost inaccessible territory, the Chukchi were in a unique position. Most other wandering aliens were quite "fully conquered" and, when not ignored completely, were rarely seen as either a danger

[57] See, for example, George W. Melville, *In the Lena Delta: A Narrative of the Search for Lieut.-Commander DeLong and His Companions* (Boston, 1892), p. 4, and Nordenskiöld, *The Voyage of the Vega*, pp. 324–25, 340–41.

[58] Tolmacheff, *Siberian Passage*, pp. 18–19, 209; Izaak V. Shklovsky, *In Far North-East Siberia* (London, 1916), p. 134 [HRAF RY2, no. 11]; Okun', *Ocherki*, pp. 145–47; Vdovin, *Ocherki istorii i etnografii chuckchei*, pp. 245–46.

[59] Bogoras, *The Chukchi*, pp. 57, 64–67, 708.

[60] Quoted in Okun', *Ocherki*, p. 143. See also Tolmacheff, *Siberian Passage*, pp. 132, 172.

[61] Okun', *Ocherki*, pp. 143–44; Bogoras, *The Chukchee*, p. 709.

or an asset. Though often pitied and sometimes admired by occasional visitors from Central Russia, they remained a separate class due to their "backwardness" and—with the significant exception of the Chukchi warriors and some successful traders—tended to occupy the lowest rung in the status hierarchy.[62] In an old-settler village or frontier town, an alien, often drunk and disoriented, was fair game for practical jokers and rock-throwing boys. Many native northerners saw every Russian as a boss and acted accordingly; most native elders considered Russian scribes their superiors and took orders from them.[63]

No matter how fast the circumpolar peoples adapted to their changing economic circumstances, for most of them it was not fast enough. On the Ob' and the Amur, in particular, they could not keep up with the speed at which the fish were being exterminated and the fishing sites were being leased.[64] The continuing epidemics and, on the Amur, the loss of women compounded the problem. Perhaps most significant, the needs of the tribute payers continued to grow faster than their ability to pay for them. Some of the imported goods, such as guns, nets, traps, and household utensils were invested in the native economies (although with potentially destabilizing effect); some, such as bright cloth, beads, and rings, acquired an important symbolic value but were of no economic consequence outside the native societies; whereas others, particularly vodka, actually undermined the alien's position vis-à-vis his trading partner.[65] Some native northerners became totally insolvent as hunters, fishermen, or reindeer herders and hired themselves out to Russian merchants or peasants. Some starved,

[62] In some old-settler areas mutually advantageous "friendship" agreements could probably result in status equality. See Lindgren, "An Example."

[63] Iadrintsev, "Osuzhdennye na smert' plemena," p. 26; Riabkov, "Poliarnye strany Sibiri," p. 27; Richard J. Bush, Reindeer, Dogs, and Snow-shoes: A Journal of Siberian Travel and Exploration Made in the Years 1865, 1866, and 1867 (New York, 1871), pp. 202–3; Bogoras, The Chukchee, p. 723; Khudiakov, Kratkoe opisanie, pp. 82–86; A. A. Dunin-Gorkavich, Tobol'skii sever: Geograficheskoe i statistiko-ekonomicheskoe opisanie strany po otdel'nym geograficheskim raionam (Tobol'sk, 1910), pp. 59–62.

[64] Erman, Travels in Siberia (1848; reprint; New York, 1970), 2:94; Abramov, "Opisanie," p. 412; Shashkov, "Sibirskie inorodtsy," in Istoricheskie etiudy, pp. 250–53; Iadrintsev, Sibir' kak koloniia, pp. 99–100, and "Osuzhdennye na smert' plemena," pp. 9–12; Donner, Among the Samoyed in Siberia, pp. 22–23; Minenko, Severo-zapadnaia Sibir', p. 159; Smoliak, Etnicheskie protsessy, p. 160; Brazhnikov, Rybnye promysly, pp. 45–52.

[65] Erman, Travels in Siberia, 1:415–16; Abramov, "Opisanie," p. 416; Kastren, Puteshestvie, pp. 141, 182; Tret'iakov, "Turukhanskii krai," p. 409; Poliakov, Pis'ma i otchety, pp. 69–70; Minenko, Severo-zapadnaia Sibir', p. 171; Etnicheskaia istoriia, p. 146.

some hung around piers waiting for an occasional boat to load, and some begged at tavern entrances.[66]

Every once in a while, the government tried to interfere. In the course of his fight against merchant monopolies, Treskin introduced state bread stores and encouraged the "improvident" natives to store fish in the expectation of spring famines. Speranskii made it easier for wandering aliens to obtain food at state stores: in case of starvation, bread could be loaned to anyone on demand and debts were to be collected sparingly.[67] Very soon, however, it became obvious that the measure was largely counterproductive. The debts grew with such speed that the local officials, pressured by their budget-minded superiors, found it increasingly difficult to pardon them. Sometimes the debtors had their produce confiscated and auctioned off, and sometimes they were rounded up for work, but even such policies did not help cover the expenses or prevent further borrowing. Many of the native consumers regarded state bread as a gift; others felt that buying bread from the government was their duty as Russian subjects. This last conviction might have been prompted by the Cossacks in charge of the bread stores (vakhtera), who stood to profit by diverting the native trade from the private traders. There were other ways of making profit. The Cossacks and traders could agree on the prices beforehand, or else the traders could buy state goods and then resell them to the aliens. None of this, of course, was necessary when the government clerks and the local merchants were the same people, as was the case in some areas.[68]

Along with exacerbating the chronic indebtedness of the local population, the state stores greatly contributed to their dependence on outside sources of food. Before the winter season, some hunters routinely

[66] Iadrintsev, Sibir' kak koloniia, pp. 96–98, and "Osuzhdennye na smert' plemena," p. 12; G. N. Potanin, Zametki o Zapadnoi Sibiri, (N.p., n.d.), pp. 200, 213–14; Shashkov, "Sibirskie inorodtsy," in Istoricheskie etiudy, pp. 263–65; Donner, Among the Samoyed in Siberia, pp. 22–23, 25; Smoliak, Etnicheskie protsessy, pp. 174–75; Kastren, "Puteshestvie," p. 194; Latkin, Eniseiskaia guberniia, pp. 126, 131–32; Czaplicka, My Siberian Year, pp. 38–40; Edward Rae, The Land of the North Wind, or Travels among the Laplanders and the Samoyeds (London, 1875), pp. 205–6; Islavin, Samoiedy, pp. 59–70; Alexander Platonovich Engelhardt, A Russian Province of the North (Westminster, 1899), pp. 291–92.

[67] PSZ, ser. 1, vol. 38, no. 29.126, secs. 270–85; Shashkov, "Sibirskie inorodtsy," in Istoricheskie etiudy, pp. 266–67; Vagin, Istoricheskie svedeniia, 1:334–408.

[68] Dunun-Gorkavich, Tobol'skii sever, pp. 56–64; Shashkov, "Sibirskie inorodtsy," in Istoricheskie etiudy, pp. 267–70; Tret'iakov, "Turukhanskii krai," pp. 445–47; Krivoshapkin, Eniseiskii okrug, 2:125; Okun', Ocherki, pp. 139–40; Vdovin, Ocherki istorii, pp. 263–64.

demanded flour products to take with them to the taiga. If they were too heavily in debt, the *vakhter* could refuse, in which case they would sometimes not leave at all. If they stayed by the store, no debts could be paid, and the Cossack might very well be forced to feed them anyway.[69] In the mid-nineteenth century the government set a limit on the amount of bread that could be loaned to aliens and instructed the officials to seek a guarantee from the applicant's community that he was indeed in desperate straits. This did not prove very useful: as always with the nomadic foragers, the information they provided was impossible to verify and the "community" was usually nowhere to be found.[70] According to A. F. Middendorf,

> The treasury, which for many years supported them altogether too generously through its stores, has now demoralized them. There is no question of the debts ever being returned. . . . When the distribution of food to the poor creatures, who were getting deeper and deeper in debt . . . , was finally stopped, they began to die of starvation. I noted in my diary that, given this situation, one could not, in my opinion, demand from the government any other help except the distribution of their children among Russian settlers.[71]

In fact, government help was effectively limited to maintaining the bread stores. There was neither time nor money for the aliens; regular health care was unfeasible; and the few attempts to launch state-run schools ended in failure because of a lack of funds and the protests of the population.[72] As for the local administrators, most of them had been banished to remote northern districts for various crimes and indiscretions, and grappling with the perennial "alien problem" was not the best way to get back to the "mainland." According to Bogoraz, who lived in the Kolyma district,

[69] Tret'iakov, "Turukhanskii krai," pp. 447–48.

[70] Ibid.

[71] Quoted from Iadrintsev, "Osuzhdennye na smert' plemena," p. 14.

[72] Vdovin, *Ocherki istorii i etnografii chukchei*, pp. 256–58; P. F. Unterberger, *Primorskaia oblast' 1856–1898* (St. Petersburg, 1900), pp. 20–32; Tret'iakov, "Turukhanskii krai," pp. 342, 525; Iadrintsev, *Sibir' kak koloniia*, pp. 117–21; Shashkov, "Sibirskie inorodtsy," in *Istoricheskie etiudy*, pp. 243–44; Bogoras, *The Chukchee*, pp. 718–20; Okun', *Ocherki*, pp. 137–38; *Istoriia Iakutskoi ASSR*, 2:328, Sliunin, *Okhotsko-Kamchatskii krai*, pp. 513–32.

The inquiries for all persons wanted by the courts or police throughout
the immense empire are sent, as a rule, to every district, however remote.
Thus the mail . . . would bring piles of such orders, and all local archives
are full of them: as, for example, the order of the chief secretary of military affairs inquiring for the dismissed Lieut-Col. von Stempel and his
step-daughter Eugenie Krumones, in reference to their petition for the
acceptance of the said Eugenie Krumones into the Institution for the
Education of Gentle-born Girls; another order inquiring for a banker,
Matthias Leibion, from the Hague in Holland; and many more; not to
speak of the political refugees who fled abroad, and none of whom of
course might wish to go to the Kolyma of their own free will.[73]

The Kolyma foragers were reported to have contributed 3.35 rubles
for the monument to Count A. A. Bobrinskii, 1.50 rubles for the monument to the composer Glinka in Smolensk, and undisclosed amounts
for a hospital in Constantinople and the Volunteer Fleet. While they
were at it, the district officials duly filled out lengthy government
forms:

Asses and mules	000
Camels and buffaloes	000
Catholics	000
Protestants	000
Corn sowed	000, and so on.[74]

Some local administrators went further and produced their own statistics. One kept a detailed account of all sexual intercourse on the
Lower Kolyma in the hope of establishing the source of a syphilis epidemic; another filed the following report:

Petr Rybin	52 years old.
Semen Berezkin	43 years old, and so on.
Total for the whole village	2236 years old.[75]

[73] Bogoras, *The Chukchee*, pp. 713–14. In 1913 the chief of police of Verkhoiansk received an official letter instructing him to increase surveillance over the Socialist Revolutionary Vladimir Zenzinov, exiled to Russkoe Ust'e, "in view of the proposed trip in
August of His Imperial Majesty to the Crimea." Russkoe Ust'e is a month (by reindeer)
away from Verkhoiansk. The letter arrived in September. See Zenzinov, *The Road to
Oblivion*, p. 229.
[74] Bogoras, *The Chukchee*, p. 714.
[75] Ibid.

Some officials did launch far-reaching reforms, such as prohibitions on catching spawning fish or the replacement of all team-dogs by reindeer. Both would have led to famine, and both failed.[76] Other projects could not be put to the test. In Petropavlovsk, one district commander was declared insane and deported from the peninsula after he banned the liquor trade, made traders pay for their transportation, and allowed foreign merchants to take part in a fur auction. Shortly afterward he reemerged in Khabarovsk as the editor of the provincial newspaper.[77]

Such anecdotes were relished and perhaps blown out of proportion by amused and indignant outsiders, many of whom were unwilling guests from Central Russia. But even if most northern officials had been as solicitous about their alien charges as Gondatti and V. K. Brazhnikov were, the fact remains that they had no money and no long-term policy guidelines. In the whole of the Russian empire there was not a single agency or permanent administrative position that would deal specifically with the alien population. Provincial governors were responsible for all aspects of local administration, and the tax-paying and food-producing Russians occupied all of their time. "I am sure," wrote one traveler, "that many local administrators do not even know that under their 'enlightened' rule there live 'some' wandering savages who occupy the lowest stage of intellectual development."[78]

As the century progressed, however, more and more travelers and more and more readers assumed that the administrators—local or otherwise—were generally incapable of enlightening anyone and that helping savages advance was the special mission of special people who were the sole legitimate representatives of the highest stage of intellectual development (the "intelligentsia"). According to Petr Lavrov, most Europeans in positions of power were passive participants in European civilization who could not help reducing its achievements to a few words and mannerisms ("mi Deus instead of Mumbo-Jumbo" and a cover for one's nakedness). The real job of civilizing the savages—wandering or settled, naked or dressed, Giliak or Russian—was to be undertaken by the "people of ideas" who "know the defects, needs, and possibilities of a given society better than the natives, and so will be

---

[76] Ibid., pp. 711, 716.

[77] A. Sil'nitskii, "14 mesiatsev sluzhby na Kamchatke," *IV* 11 (1909): 507–41; Okun', *Ocherki*, p. 141.

[78] A. M. Maksimov, "Nashi zadachi na Dal'nem Vostoke," *Sankt-Peterburgskie viedomosti*, no. 177–78 (1880); quoted in Brailovski, "Tazy ili udikhe," p. 324.

better than the natives at using the possibilities in order to correct the defects."[79]

The Russian Indians and the
Populist Intellectuals

Among the hundreds of young provincials who arrived in St. Petersburg University in the exhilarating years between 1858 and 1861 was a small group of Russian Siberians. They grew beards and long hair, chain-smoked, demanded the emancipation of the peasants, defied the authorities, talked about revolution, took part in demonstrations, made speeches at martyrs' funerals, worshiped Herzen and N. G. Chernyshevskii, and were generally indistinguishable from most other students.[1] They faced unusual challenges, however. Siberia had no serfdom, almost no industry, not much in the way of state interference, and thus little room for revolutionary self-sacrifice as defined elsewhere. To remain patriots and "people of ideas" at the same time, the Young Siberians[2] needed a cause entirely their own, a crusade that would tie their "remote region" to the immediate tasks of liberation.[3] They did not have to wait very long. Both Herzen and Chernyshevskii were chastizing the centralized bureacracy as the enemy of the people; Polish separatism, supported by *The Bell*, was an important part of student agitation; and the popular professor N. I. Kostomarov was preaching Pan-Slav "tribal federalism" and Ukrainian autonomy.[4] In 1861, the St. Petersburg Siberians were further inspired by the arrival from Kazan' of their fellow-country man and influential historian, Afanasii Shchapov. As he declared to his students, "It is not with the idea of the state and not with the idea of centralization, but with the idea of

[79] P. L. Lavrov, "Tsivilizatsiia i dikie plemena," *Otechestvennyia zapiski* 184, no. 8 (1869): 292–93; no. 9 (1869): 95, 101.

[1] For a description of student life at the time, see Abbott Gleason, *Young Russia: The Genesis of Russian Radicalism in the 1860s* (New York, 1980), pp. 114–60.

[2] They did not call themselves Young Siberians, but the term conveniently describes both their age at the time and, by analogy with various Young Europeans, their ideological inclinations in the early 1860s.

[3] For an excellent history of Siberian regionalism, see Watrous, "Russia's 'Land of the Future.'" A convenient summary is Stephen Watrous, "The Regionalist Conception of Siberia, 1860–1920," in Diment and Slezkine, eds., *Between Heaven and Hell*, pp. 113–32.

[4] S. G. Svatikov, *Rossiia i Sibir' (K istorii sibirskogo oblastnichestva v XIX v.)* (Prague, 1929), pp. 40–53; M. K. Lemke, *Nikolai Mikhailovich Iadrintsev: Biograficheskii ocherk* (St. Petersburg, 1904), pp. 33–41; Watrous, *Russia's 'Land of the Future,'"* pp. 200–236.

nationality [*narodnost'*] and regionalism that I am entering this university as a professor of Russian history."[5] If the concept of nationality or "folkhood" had long been the mainstay of radical thought, its "regionalist" aspect was both novel and strikingly obvious, for when "truly popular" customs and institutions were compared, "did the Little Russian, Belorussian, and Siberian population have much in common? Did Poland and Kamchatka have much in common?"[6] Finally, and again through the good services of Herzen and Chernyshevskii, the young Siberians discovered America—that "young and vigorous" land that, just like their own, "was a part of Europe . . . without castles, without the Middle Ages."[7]

The conclusion seemed inescapable. On the one hand, Siberia was a long-abused colony, exploited for its resources, despised for its backwardness, and polluted with Russia's rejects. On the other hand, it was a young and vigorous land settled by freedom-loving pioneers who had by now formed a separate nation, just as the English had done in America and Australia. They had their own history, defined by "free and popular" colonizaton according to Shchapov; their own social institutions, remarkable for the strong peasant commune and the absence of serfdom; and their own national spirit, characterized by independence and egalitarianism. What they needed to fulfill their potential (and to emulate the United States) was development, both economic and cultural. The former called for the abolition of the exile system and—most important—mass peasant immigration from Russia; the latter consisted in the launching of a university and a vigorous press, so that Siberia could acquire its own "Jeffersons and Franklins."[8]

In other words, Siberia was to Russia what Russia was to the "West": underdeveloped and therefore unspoiled, uncultured and therefore unadulterated—a land of absences as drawbacks and absences as

[5] Shchapov, *Sochineniia*, 4: iv; Watrous, *Russia's 'Land of the Future,'"* pp. 236–58.
[6] Ibid., p. vii.
[7] N. M. Iadrintsev, "K moei avtobiografii," *Russkaia mysl'* (June 1904): 156; A. I. Herzen [Gertsen], *Sobranie sochinenii v tridtsati tomakh* (Moscow, 1957), 12:339–40, 349. For Herzen's and Chernyshevskii's views on the United States, see Bassin, "Inventing Siberia," pp. 788–92, David Hecht, *Russian Radicals Look to America, 1825–1894* (Cambridge, Mass. 1947), pp. 16–39, 122–24.
[8] See in particular the programmatic statement of Siberian regionalism, N. M. Iadrintsev's *Sibir' kak koloniia*. The quotation is from G. N. Potanin's letter to N. S. Shchukin, cited in Okladnikov, ed., *Ocherki russkoi literatury Sibiri*, 1:343. For a detailed analysis, see Watrous, *Russia's 'Land of the Future,'"* pp. 272–95, 392–420.

assets.[9] Nostalgic for the putative purity of their homeland yet jealous of Russian technological and intellectual superiority, the Siberian regionalists inherited Herzen's predicament, and nowhere was their ambivalence more obvious than in the so-called alien problem. On the one hand, the original population of the country constituted its roots, its distinctiveness, "a means to humanize Siberian society."[10] On the other hand, it epitomized the colony's backwardness, provincialism, and underdevelopment. "The moral life of the aliens," wrote S. S. Shashkov, "is a bizarre mixture of repulsive vices and patriarchal virtues."[11]

The most repulsive vices remained the same throughout the century: virtually all travelers without exception were struck by the "filthy living" of the aliens, as well as by the fact that alien women were "slaves who could be bought like things."[12] It was no longer stupidity and rarely crudeness, however, that accounted for these peculiar practices: in the age of Bazarov, it was disease. As Dr. M. F. Krivoshapkin put it, "medicine deserves the greatest credit" for putting an end to persecutions stirred by ignorance and for "transferring to disease" what used to be known as crimes and deviations.[13] Moreover, as a result of the popularity of biological and environmental determinism the actual list of deviations was much reduced. Just as shamanism and "Arctic hysteria" could be traced to body chemistry—and thus eventually cured, nomadism and an unappetizing diet could be attributed to the physical conditions of the Arctic—and thus considered normal (for those conditions). Attacking the most common complaint about the natives and specifically citing the passage from the Siberian chronicle on the beastliness of the northern "raw-eaters," Krivoshapkin explained to his readers that raw fish was nature's remedy against scurvy and that "Western" oysters were "filthier" (gazhe) anyway; Iadrintsev argued

[9] Cf. Bassin, "Inventing Siberia," pp. 787–88; Watrous, "The Regionalist Conception." For Herzen's influential statements on the subject, see Sobranie sochinenii, 8:256–57, and 21:45, Cf. N. V. Basargin, Zapiski (Petrograd, 1917), pp. 189–90.

[10] G. N. Potanin, Oblastricheskaia tendentsiia v. Sibiri (Tomsk, 1907), p. 18.

[11] Shashkov, "Sibirskie inorodtsy," in Istoricheskie etiudy, p. 246.

[12] Tret'iakov, "Turukhanskii krai," pp. 365, 372, 386. See also A. P. Chekhov, Polnoe sobranie sochinenii i pisem (Moscow, 1978), 14–15:174, 178; Khudiakov, Kratkoe opisanie, pp. 179–81. Poliakov, Pis'ma i otchety, pp. 53–57, 71, 73; Latkin, Eniseiskaia guberniia, pp. 132, 136; Sliunin Okhotsko-Kamchatskii krai, 1:379, 392, 455.

[13] Krivoshapkin, Eniseiskii okrug, 1:319.

that *given their environment* the northerners were highly advanced and demonstrated remarkable adaptability and ingenuity.[14]

For most travelers who saw salvation in the organic unity of the peasant commune, the virtues were more apparent than the vices. The aliens "amazed travelers with their phenomenal honesty and the heavenly [*raiskie*] rules of their social life":[15] they lived in close-knit collectives and held everything in common; they never stole; they valued equality and independence. Unfortunately, the influence of Russian officials, merchants, and prospectors was beginning to corrupt these rules: some natives "were seduced,"[16] and even the popular Tungus were not as attractive as they used to be. According to N. V. Latkin, "drunkenness, knavery, laziness, apathy, and a kind of feebleness caused by various sicknesses, smallpox, and especially venereal diseases . . . have changed the character of this people, which used to be known for its courage, valor, agility, kindness, and truthfulness."[17]

Lamented but apparently irreversible, the passing of "heavenly" communalism among aliens was not the main aspect of the "alien problem" (Russian communalism was of much greater concern). The Siberian regionalists had discovered that the aliens were in such desperate straits both physically and economically that only the most urgent intervention could save them from total extinction. N. M. Iadrintsev, the leader of the regionalists and the greatest champion of the "native cause," appealed to the moral sense of his readers as he described the sick, hungry, naked, drunk, cheated, and neglected inhabitants of the tundra and taiga.[18] Following the overall change in radical elite attitudes toward "the people," the regionalists redefined savagery as poverty. The evolutionary scheme remained firmly in place, but the main symptom of backwardness was now indigence, attributed largely to social injustice (exploitation) and government neglect. For most regionalists and indeed populists in general, environmental determinism

---

[14] Ibid., 1:320–24, and 2:130–33; N. M. Iadrintsev, *Sibirskie inorodtsy, ikh byt i sovremennoe polozhenie* (St. Petersburg, 1891), pp. 159–66.

[15] Potanin, *Oblastnicheskaia tendentsiia*, p. 49.

[16] Iadrintsev, "Osuzhdennye na smert' plemena," p. 21; Iadrintsev, *Sibirskie inorodtsy*, pp. 148–49.

[17] Latkin, *Eniseiskaia guberniia*, p. 124. See also Tret'iakov, "Turukhanskii krai," p. 377.

[18] Iadrintsev, *Sibir' kak koloniia*, chaps. 3 and 4, and "Osuzhdennye na smert' plemena." For fictional representations, see N. I. Naumov, *Sobranie sochinenii* (Novosibirsk, 1940), 2:18–63, and *Rasskazy o staroi Sibiri* (Tomsk, 1960), pp. 169–85; and I. V. Fedorov (Omulevskii), *Polnoe sobranie sochinenii Omulevskogo (I. V. Fedorova)* (St. Petersburg, 1906), 2:302–3.

coexisted with a faith in the limitless possibilities of directed social change, and given the tsarist state's inability and unwillingness to effect this change, the guilt-stricken beneficiaries of intellectual progress would have to do it themselves. Just as the Russian intelligentsia had assumed moral responsibility for the suffering of the peasant, the Siberian patriots, according to Iadrintsev and his followers, should take charge of the native. After all, it was the Russian conquest, Russian administrative abuse, and Russian trade practices that had reduced the original inhabitants of the country to near extinction. "Every time we hear about their predicament," wrote Iadrintsev, "we should experience pangs of conscience."[19] It was not just a matter of guilt, however—it was a matter of pride. Russians had proved themselves to be good colonizers—as good as the Spaniards or the English. Now they needed to show that they could be more caring and more humane. What had happened to the American Indians or the Tasmanians would not happen to the aboriginal Siberians.[20]

The first step was to educate the Russians. Before they could civilize the natives, they had to be civilized themselves, and most Siberian regionalists considered this their principal task (Russian old settlers might be morally healthy, but in Lavrov's popular formulation implicitly shared even by N. K. Mikhailovskii, spontaneous "culture" was still inferior to the thinking man's "civilization").[21] Next came the practical work of saving and civilizing: progressive administrators would rationalize and humanize the government; merchants and peasants would stop all unfair practices; and missionaries would devote themselves to educational work. Education and Christianization—gradual, sensitive, and based on the natives' languages and experiences—should, indeed, go hand in hand. All of these things were "the obligation of the superior race engaged in spreading civilization,"[22] that is, they were something that civilization owed the aboriginal Siberians. For the first time since colonization, the aliens were regarded as having "rights"—not legal rights as citizens but rights as members of the human family. As Iadrintsev put it, "the preservation of alien tribes, the spread of education among them, as well as their involvement in civic and intellectual life, is as much the historic right of aliens for human existence as it is the historic duty of the Russian people in the East."[23]

---

[19] Iadrintsev, "Osuzhdennye na smert' plemena," p. 29.

[20] Iadrintsev, *Sibir' kak koloniia*, pp. 95, 157.

[21] Ibid., p. 124; Shashkov, "Sibirskie inorodtsy," in *Istoricheskie etiudy*, p. 292.

[22] Iadrintsev, *Sibir' kak koloniia*, p. 119.

[23] Ibid., p. 124.

Were they capable of such advances? Iadrintsev definitely thought so,[24] but others were not so sure. Shchapov, exiled back to Siberia shortly after his conversion to the Pisarev-inspired "socio-anthropological theory," discovered that the aliens could not fully assimilate "the lofty ideas and feelings of the truth of the Gospel and the love of one's neighbor." This, he claimed, was due to the insufficient development of their "nerve and brain capabilities"—a conclusion all the more extraordinary because Shchapov's mother was a Buriat; because he found the Buriat *ulus* to be much closer to the "truth" of collectivism than the Russian commune; and because the advance of collectivism was in turn caused by the development of the "higher nerve cells of the large brain centers of the human nervous system."[25] Shashkov, too, was sceptical about the aliens' ability to evolve in the right direction. Those with some education, he warned, "despised their fellow countrymen, bragged about their titles, and acted in such a silly and pompous fashion that they could not be tolerated in any halfway decent society," and the only two truly enlightened aliens (Dorzhi Banzarov and Chokan Valikhanov) had allegedly reverted to the old ways and drunk themselves to death.[26]

Still, neither Shashkov nor Shchapov completely precluded the possibility of progress for the native northerners: their journey might be very slow and not pleasing to the eye, but it was possible. As one conservative critic pointed out with disapproval, the radical intellectuals were desperately trying to reconcile biological heredity and the struggle for existence with a faith in equality.[27] Indeed, Varfolomei Zaitsev was quite lonely in his "scientific" racism:[28] Chernyshevskii's "rational egoists" selflessly worked for universal brotherhood; Lavrov's "thinking people" had the obligation to civilize the savage tribes; and even Pisarev's "realists" grudgingly conceded that their individualism would ultimately serve the "common good." Even those who regarded the northern aliens as victims of natural selection believed that education could and should reverse that process. Thus I. S. Poliakov saw "the Ostiak selection of spouses" as "most unnatural, weakening the tribal

[24] Iadrintsev, *Sibirskie inorodtsy,* pp. 147–59.
[25] Shchapov, *Sochineniia,* 3:607–8, 640; vol. 4, "Buriatskaia ulusnaia rodovaia obshchina."
[26] Shashkov, "Sibirskie inorodtsy," in *Istoricheskie etiudy,* p. 243.
[27] M. A. Miropiev, *O polozhenii russkikh inorodtsev* (St. Petersburg, 1901), p. 346.
[28] V. A. Zaitsev, "Otvet moim obviniteliam po povodu moego mneniia o tsvetnykh plemenakh," *Russkoe slovo,* no. 12 (1864): "Bibliograficheskii listok," pp. 20–24, 81–82; James H. Billington, *Mikhailovsky and Russian Populism* (Oxford, 1958), pp. 28–29.

strength of the Ostiak and leading to their regress" but was convinced that correct government policies would prevent their extinction.[29] The view that progress was not inevitable if it was immoral was central to the philosophy of Russian populism.[30] As G. N. Potanin put it, the law of the survival of the fittest was correct but not obligatory. "The undeveloped tribes do disappear after contact with civilization," he admitted, "but it does not mean that this fact is impossible to prevent."[31]

Whatever the future state of the "alien tribes of Siberia," everyone agreed that at present it was extremely low—so low, in fact, that it had caused the degeneracy and corruption of the Russian settlers. Iadrintsev, Shchapov, and numerous European travelers pointed repeatedly to the deplorable "nativization" of Russian Siberians, and Iadrintsev used this fact as a major argument in his campaign for increased immigration from European Russia. "Where the number of aliens exceeds that of Russians, we see the weakening and the degeneracy of the Russians," he declared. But "where the Russian population in Siberia predominates, we see the absorption, the assimilation of the aliens."[32] In other words—and in a manner common to romantic nationalists in countries perceived as backward—the Siberian regionalists were bemoaning the extinction of the "underdeveloped tribes" while advocating the kind of development that resulted in their extinction. The solution, as suggested by Lavrov and especially Mikhailovskii, lay in the distinction between collective and individual progress. As Potanin put it,

> If the Russian element completely absorbs the Finns, still the close proximity, population density, and the increased sophistication of life will make sure that, even though the nation will disappear, at least each individual Finnish family will live its life in happiness, quietly, and without privation. It is better than . . . to deprive the Ostiak of the benefits of Russian settlement and have them starve to death.[33]

The few government officials who took an interest in the northerners proceeded from the same assumption. Vladimir Islavin left native

[29] Poliakov, Pis'ma i otchety, pp. 54, 102–3.
[30] See in particular N. K. Mikhailovskii's exposition of his "subjective method," in Poslednie sochineniia (St. Petersburg, 1905), vol. 1, and Billington, Mikhailovsky, pp. 27–36.
[31] Potanin, Zametki, p. 204.
[32] Iadrintsev, Sibir' kak koloniia, p. 162.
[33] Potanin, Zametki, p. 206. A "Finn" was a common Russian term for all Finno-Ugric and Samoedic-speaking peoples.

administration out of his report on the European Samoed (Nenets) because he considered their assimilation by "stronger peoples" inevitable.[34] Fifty years later Governor Engel'gardt concluded that various protective measures based on "the exaggerated pretensions of a relatively small group of Samoyede race" had all failed, and that it was both economically sound and historically inevitable to allow the Russians and the Komi to do their civilizing work.[35] Finally, M. A. Miropiev, an extreme conservative and a passionate foe of all unrepentant aliens, wrote that the Russification of Siberia was not only desirable and inevitable—it was the same phenomenon that Iadrintsev and others mistook for extinction. "The so-called extinction of the aliens," he argued, "is to a significant extent their fusion with Russians," and reflects nothing but "the beneficent and educational impact of Russian culture on savage and half-savage aliens."[36] In other words, antigovernment intellectuals, government administrators, and Orthodox ideologues were in fundamental agreement when it came to the "savage and half-savage aliens." Progress, citizenship, and salvation in the Russian empire were all bound up with Russification. Even the physical survival of the northern aliens—as well as extinction understood as survival—meant a "fusion with the Russians."

The oldest and most consistent member of this unacknowledged alliance was the Orthodox Church.[37] Unlike the marriage of progress with Russian messianism, which was announced by Herzen after 1848, or the equation of the Russian state with the Russian nationality, which became official policy under Alexander III, the near total overlap of Russian Orthodoxy and Russianness had been assumed by the Church since the first encounter between the Cossacks and the foreigners-as-pagans. As far as most priests were concerned, a "baptized alien" was an oxymoron as long as the alien practiced "savage, frightening, disgusting rituals"[38] and persevered in his "natural backwardness, crudeness of manners, and frivolity in matters of faith"[39]—that is, for as long as he remained alien. A convert to Russian Orthodoxy was expected to become as thoroughly Russian as any convert to progress and civiliza-

---

[34] Islavin, *Samoiedy*, pp. 140–41.
[35] Engelhardt, *A Russian Province of the North*, pp. 270–71, 295–98.
[36] Miropiev, *O polozhenii russkikh inorodtsev*, pp. 318–19.
[37] See Yuri Slezkine, "Savage Christians or Unorthodox Russians? The Missionary Dilemma in Siberia," in Diment and Slezkine, eds., *Between Heaven and Hell*, pp. 15–31.
[38] *Trudy pravoslavnykh missii Vostochnoi Sibiri* (Irkutsk, 1883), 1:370.
[39] "Amurskie inorodtsy i religiozno-nravstvennoe sostoianie ikh," *PB*, no. 8 (1896): 358.

tion. According to Archbishop Veniamin of Irkutsk and Nerchinsk, "Orthodoxy should struggle not only against an alien faith, but also against an alien nationality—against the mores, customs, and the whole of the domestic arrangement of alien life; it should convince the aliens of the superiority of the Russian way of life, so that they will become Russian not only in faith, but also in nationality."[40]

Even Church tactics increasingly resembled those advocated by Iadrintsev and his teachers. In the early 1860s Lavrov's "missionary" approach to progress was met by a newly "progressive" approach to missionary work when the scholar and Church official N. I. Il'minskii proposed a radically new conversion policy.[41] According to Il'minskii, aliens persisted in their alienness because they had never had a chance to hear the Christian message in their own language. With that artificial obstacle out of the way, the message would take care of itself and "truly, rather than only superficially, set the people on the path of Christianity" (and hence eventual Russification).[42] As one of Il'minskii's followers explained, "the native language speaks directly to the mind and the heart. As soon as Christian concepts and rules have taken root in the hearts of aliens, the love of the Russian people arises by itself."[43] The language was not quite enough, however, for even if the "messenger of Grace" (blagoviestnik) knew what to say, learned how to say it, and reached the people he needed to say it to (by joining one of the newly proposed "traveling missions," for example),[44] his success would only be lasting if he directed his greatest efforts at winning over the women. Only the women, linguistically and culturally conservative yet vitally important as educators, could truly open the door to "the hearts of aliens."[45]

The "Il'minskii system" struck some missionaries as defeatist, but government dissatisfaction with "formal conversions" led to its official

[40] Veniamin, Arkhiepiskop Irkutskii i Nerchinskii, Zhiznennye voprosy pravoslavnoi missii v Sibiri (St. Petersburg, 1885), p. 7. See Slezkine, "Savage Christians," pp. 23–24.

[41] Isabelle Teitz Kreindler, "Educational Policies toward the Eastern Nationalities in Tsarist Russia: A Study of Il'minskii System" (Ph.D. diss., Columbia University, 1969).

[42] Ibid., p. 132.

[43] A. I. Iakobii, O missionerskom stane v strane Nadyma i o vozmozhnoi postanovke khristianskoi missii v stranakh russkogo inorodcheskogo Severa (Tobol'sk, 1895), p. 36.

[44] K. D. Nosilov, "K proektu luchshei postanovki Obdorskoi missii," PB, no. 9 (1895): 27–37; Iakobii, O missionerskom stane.

[45] M. Mashanov, Obzor deiatel'nosti Bratstva Sv. Guriia za 25 let ego sushchestvovaniia (Kazan', 1892), p. 32 See also Trudy pravoslavnykh missii, 1:337; A. G. Bazanov, Ocherki po istorii missionerskikh shkol na Krainem Severe (Leningrad, 1936), pp. 57, 74; Iu. A. Sem, "Khristianizatsiia nanaitsev, ee metody i resul'taty," in Vdovin, ed., Khristianstvo i lamaizm, p. 203.

adoption in 1870.[46] The chief procurators of the Synod and foremost advocates of Russification D. A. Tolstoi and K. P. Pobedonostsev agreed with Il'minskii's view that the lingering nonconformity of "eastern pagans" was due "to the inertia of their way of life, habits, and ideas," and not to deliberate national self-assertion, of which they were incapable.[47] Accordingly, the Orthodox Missionary Society received more money and more missionaries; some missionaries received language training; and newly created schools for aliens received primers and Christian literature in the local languages.[48] Few of these initiatives reached the polar circle, however. Unlike the Muslims and the Lamaists, the northerners did not seem interested in proselytizing and thus were not considered a threat; traveling missions proved too expensive; native schools had trouble recruiting students (boys or girls); and very few missionaries wanted to go to the Arctic.[49] Most diocesan reports were vain calls for volunteers and never-ending complaints that there was nobody to minister to the aliens, and most missionary diaries consisted of hair-raising descriptions of impassable swamps, fierce snowstorms, revolting local food, and the hostility of traders, aided and abetted by local officials.[50]

[46] Kreindler, "Educational Policies," pp. 79–87; "Postanovleniia Soveta Ministra Narodnogo Prosveshcheniia," ZhMNP 148 (April 1870): "Pravitel'stvennye rasporiazheniia," pp. 47–63; Kreindler, "Educational Policies," pp. 84–87.

[47] Kreindler, "Educational Policies," p. 97 (quotation), 6–7, 95–96, 127; Frank T. McCarthy, "The Kazan' Missionary Congress," Cahiers du monde russe et soviétique 14, no. 3 (1973): 317.

[48] "Pravoslavnoe missionerskoe obshchestvo," PB, no. 1 (1893): 10–2, no. 2 (1893): 12–19; "Ustav Pravoslavnogo missionerskogo obshchestva," PB, no. 1 (1893): 12–20; Eugene Smirnoff, A Short Account of the Historical Development and Present Position of Russian Orthodox Missions (London, 1903), pp. 24–25; Bazanov, Ocherki, pp. 67–97; E. A. Alekseenko, "Khristianizatsiia na Turukhanskom Severe i ee vliianie na mirovozzrenie i religioznye kul'ty ketov," in Vdovin, ed., Khristianstvo i lamaizm, pp. 56–59; Sem, "Khristianizatsiia nanaitsev," pp. 206–9; I. S. Vdovin, "Vliianie khristianstva na religioznye verovaniia chukchei i koriakov," in Vdovin, ed., Khristianstvo i lamaizm, p. 97; "Perevodcheskaia Kommissiia pri Bratstve Sv. Guriia v Kazani i eia deiatel'nost'," PB, no. 12 (1893): 18–35; I. Iastrebov, "Vopros ob ustroistve i organizatsii obrazovatel'nykh zavedenii dlia prigotovleniia pravoslavnykh blagoviestnikov (missionerov)," PB, no. 4 (1895): 181.

[49] Bazanov, Ocherki, pp. 82–83, 94–95, 98; G. N. Gracheva, "K voprosu o vliianii khristianizatsii na religioznye predstavleniia nganasan," in Vdovin, ed., Khristianstvo i lamaizm, p. 36; Alekseenko, "Khristianizatsiia na Turukhanskom Severe," p. 59; Iastrebov, "Vopros ob ustroistve," pp. 181–83.

[50] See, for example, "Otchet Zabaikal'skoi dukhovnoi missii," PB, no. 6 (1893): 98; "Otchet iakutskogo Eparkhial'nogo komiteta pravoslavnogo missionerskogo obshchestva za 1892 g.," PB, no. 24 (1893): 120; "Kratkii ocherk missionerstva v Tobol'skoi eparkhii," PB, no. 15 (1893): 12–14; "Otchet o sostoianii missii i missionerskoi deiatel'nosti v Eniseiskoi eparkhii," PB, no. 12 (1894): 127–28; "Kratkii obzor deiatel'nosti Eniseiskogo

The involvement of the Siberian intelligentsia in the affairs of the "near-extinct tribes" of the north proved just as short-lived as that of the government officials and the government-sponsored missionaries. The first Siberian university was opened in Tomsk in 1888, and mass Russian colonization became a huge flood in the 1890s, but as regionalist goals were being achieved, regional identity—and with it the "alien question"—was being undermined.[51] New industries and new arrivals brought new concerns, and the seventy-two-year-old Potanin complained that Iadrintsev's favorite child, the journal Vostochnoe obozrenie, was now more interested in the Belgian proletariat than in Siberian autonomy. 'There is not a single patriotic newspaper any more," he wrote, "but there are newspapers of the Social Democrats, the Party of People's Freedom, the Union of 17 October, etc."[52] Even in 1905, when the regionalist movement made something of a comeback, the issues discussed were a Siberian Duma, the introduction of zemstva (elective district councils), and the relation of (Russian) Siberia to the rest of the empire; the aliens were effectively off the agenda.[53]

Ironically, it was the very inaccessibility, "stagnation," and irrelevance of the circumpolar zone that ultimately led to its rediscovery and remapping. With southern Siberia coming "alive" (that is, becoming more Russian), the Far North and parts of the Far East remained the only true House of the Dead (that is, ideal for political outcasts).[54] Increasing numbers of Polish nationalists (after 1863) and Russian revolutionaries (especially from the 1870s on) found themselves among the taiga and tundra foragers. Few of them had ever heard of the Koriak or the Giliak before, but most of them were well prepared for the encounter.

In the 1860s folkloric studies were very popular with the would-be liberators of the Russian peasant (Ivan Khudiakov, a terrorist and a collector of riddles and fairy tales, could easily switch to the study of Yakut folklore when he was exiled to Verkhoiansk), but it was in the 1870s and 1880s that the intelligentsia's interest in folk culture became particularly intense and not entirely Russo-centered. The replacement

komiteta Pravoslavnogo missionerskogo obshchestva za poslednee 25-letie," PB, no. 16 (1896): 358; Venedikt. Ieromonakh, "U chukchei," PB, no. 5 (1895): 248–54.

[51] Watrous, "The Regionalist Conception," pp. 123–30.

[52] Potanin, Oblastnicheskaia tendentsiia, p. 35.

[53] S. G. Svatikov, Rossiia i Sibir' (K istorii sibirskogo oblastnichestva v XIX v.) (Prague, 1929), pp. 111–15; Gary Hanson, "Grigory Potanin, Siberian Regionalism and the Russian Revolution of 1905" (Paper delivered at the Nineteenth National Convention of the American Association for the Advancement of Slavic Studies, Boston, November 1987).

[54] Okladnikov et al., eds , Istoriia Sibiri, 3:114.

of the mythological school by V. V. Stasov and A. N. Veselovskii's "historical method" awakened some curiosity about Russia's Mongol and Turkic neighbors but, more important, folklore as such was largely replaced in the public mind by an interest in common law. Post-emancipation administrative and judicial authorities launched numerous studies of peasant communities; urban populists dedicated themselves to the sociological, economic, and ethnographic study of rural life; provincial teachers, historians, and museum curators mined their districts for treasures of folk traditions; the Russian Geographic Society and the Academy of Sciences continued to explore the lands that the government annexed; and writers of all persuasions took to the road in search of the perfect travelogue ("live pictures of popular existence").[55] Some of this activity extended to the wandering aliens of the north,[56] but it was the revolutionary exiles who made a virtue of necessity by turning their involuntary hosts into the privileged subjects of a new science. Avid readers of Comte, Spencer, Engels, Tylor, and Morgan, the radicals of the 1880s and 1890s were almost all ethnographers and evolutionists.[57] The direction of human progress—and hence the future of the peasant commune and hence the future of socialism—could be determined through the study of "our living ancestors." The ancestors that most readily came to mind were the natives of America, Africa, and Australia, but when young intellectuals arrived in their places of exile, they had a noble and challenging task ahead of them: here were Russia's own Indians, unspoiled and unstudied, worthy of both scrutiny as remote ancestors and admiration as consistent communalists.

Their scrutiny and their admiration pulled them in different directions. In order to reconstruct the grand design of human evolution, the exiles-turned-anthropologists were always on the lookout for the most ancient social forms and the most primitive savages. Thus Lev Shternberg read Engels's *Origins of the Family* while he was in prison awaiting trial for membership in the People's Will. In Sakhalin among the Nivkh, he found correspondences with the Iroquois and Punaluan

---

[55] Tokarev, *Istoriia russkoi etnografii*, pp. 287–97; Mirzoev, *Istoriografiia Sibiri*, pp. 230–37, 260–61; Bassin, "The Russian Geographical Society," p. 252.

[56] See, for example, Brazhnikov, *Rybnye promysly*; Dunin-Gorkavich, *Tobol'skii Sever*; P. M. Golovachev, *Sibir': Priroda, liudi, zhizn'* (Moscow, 1905); Krivoshapkin, *Eniseiskii okrug*; Latkin, *Eniseiskaia guberniia*; Sergei Maksimov, *Na vostoke. Poezdka na Amur* (St. Petersburg, 1964); Poliakov, *Pis'ma i otchety*; L. I. Shrenk [Leopold von Schrenck], *Ob inorodtsakh Amurskogo kraia* (St. Petersburg, 1883–1903); Sliunin, *Okhotsko-Kamchatskii krai*; and Tret'iakov, *Turukhanskii krai*.

[57] Tokarev, *Istoriia russkoi etnografii*, pp. 357–61.

kinship terminology and promptly discovered some survivals of group marriage, that "original type of family and clan organization."[58] Similarly, Shternberg's fellow-revolutionaries Vladimir Bogoraz and Vladimir Iokhel'son were exiled in northeastern Siberia and found some of the earliest forms of religion, marriage, and pastoralism.[59] Early meant primitive, and primitive meant incomplete or backward. Both Western evolutionists and their Russian disciples assumed—not always explicitly—that social and technological progress was accompanied by an expansion, and perhaps structural perfection, of human mental abilities.[60] Thus, the survivals of group marriage had serious "psychic" consequences among the Nivkh; the Chukchi were not at all quick-witted; and the Koriak were not very intelligent and had "no standard for the expression of relations of space."[61] All these things were ultimately caused by the environment and hence were in some sense relative (Bogoraz was careful to point out that the Chukchi were dirty only "from a civilized point of view"),[62] but everyone agreed that although a primitive man was not responsible for his condition, he was decidedly inferior to the people who had the ability to study him scientifically.[63]

And yet evolution was not identical to progress, certainly not for the Russian populists. The more primitive, they assumed, the more communist—and therefore the more admirable. According to the most influential Russian publicist of the 1880s and 1890s, N. K. Mikhailovskii, the inexorable movement from simplicity toward complexity à la Spencer was true enough for society as a whole but totally false in the case of individual human beings. The greatest possible division of labor among men resulted in the least possible division of labor among man's organs, or rather, in the loss of the wholeness, versatility, and independence typical of the primitive hunter.[64] Accordingly, the Nivkh elder as portrayed by Shternberg was "a whole human being in its highest expression of individuality. [His] influence [was] therefore truly factual

[58] Shternberg, Giliaki, pp. xiii, 36, 223–46.

[59] Bogoraz's and Iokhel'son's main works were commissioned by the Jessup North Pacific Expedition and published in the United States. See Bogoras, The Chukchee and The Eskimo of Siberia (New York, 1913), and Jochelson, The Koryak and The Yukaghir and the Yukaghirized Tungus.

[60] George W. Stocking, Jr., Race, Culture, and Evolution: Essays in the History of Anthropology (New York, 1968), pp. 115–20.

[61] Shternberg, Giliaki, pp. 182–90; Bogoras, The Chukchee, p. 50; Jochelson, The Koryak, pp. 426, 428.

[62] Bogoras, The Chukchee, p. 40. See also Jochelson, The Koryak, p. 733.

[63] Cf. Stocking, Race, Culture, and Evolution, pp. 129–30.

[64] N. K. Mikhailovskii, Sochineniia (St. Petersburg, 1896), 1:2–150, esp. 78–91.

and moral; he [was] not yet separated from his kinsmen either mentally or economically, and everything [was] subsumed in the fraternal union of the religious and social alliance of the clan."[65] Even Bogoraz, who tried to "follow the facts" and "stay away from generalizations"[66] in his Boas-inspired academic writings, followed a very different American model in his "Chukchi stories":

> They were hunters who attacked huge polar bears with spears in their hands; seafarers who bravely navigated the inhospitable expanses of the northern ocean in their frail leather boats; people for whom cold was one of the elements, the ocean—a field to be harvested, and the icy plain—a home where they lived and struggled. They were the indomitable fighters against nature whose bodies were tempered like steel.[67]

They did not just fight against nature—they were "natural" themselves, unencumbered by petty conventions and proudly following the unsentimental law of survival.[68] "This is the way it always is in the taiga," explains one of I. G. Gol'dberg's Tungus: "A bear attacks a moose, and the moose fights back with all the strength it has. A wolf chases its prey, which, to save its life, does not stop at anything."[69] This conception of nature remained relatively unpopular, however, and those turn-of-the-century "modernists" who attempted to revive it were a small minority among the exiles and the travelers. For most authors, being natural still meant being artless, generous, collectivist—and thus easily seduced and exploited. Building on regionalist literature and adapting populist themes to northern settings, Garin-Mikhailovskii, D. N. Mamin-Sibiriak, V. M. Mikheev, S. Ia. Elpat'evskii, V. V. Peredol'skii, and V. Ia. Shishkov lamented the extinction of the "trusting savage" and pitied his oppressed and benighted condition.[70] "Yes, he was pushed around all his life! By the elders and clerks who demanded dues; by the priests who demanded fees; by poverty and

---

[65] Shternberg, *Giliaki*, p. 120.

[66] Quoted in D. K. Zelenin, "V. G. Bogoraz—etnograf i fol'klorist," in *Pamiati Bogoraza (1865–1936). Sbornik statei* (Moscow-Leningrad, 1937), p. xii.

[67] V. G. Bogoraz, *Sochineniia* (Moscow, 1929), 1:98.

[68] I. G. Gol'dberg, *Izbrannye proizvedeniia* (Moscow, 1972), pp. 1–94; Waclaw Sieroszewski (V. Seroshevskii), *Sochineniia* (St. Petersburg, 1908–9), especially 1:259–96.

[69] Gol'dberg, *Izbrannye proizvedeniia*, p. 24.

[70] N. G. Mikhailovskii [Garin-Mikhailovskii], *Sobranie sochinenii v 5 tomakh* (Moscow, 1957), 3:480–81, 5:81–82; Mamin-Sibiriak, *Sobranie sochinenii v 10 tomakh*, 4:21, 5:311–29; V. M. Mikheev, *Pesni o Sibiri* (Moscow, 1884), pp. 22–37; S. Ia. Elpat'evskii, *Ocherki Sibiri* (Moscow, 1893), pp. 5–6; Peredol'skii, *Po Eniseiu*; V. Ia. Shishkov, *Sobranie sochinenii* (Moscow, 1960), 1:29, 193–217, 242–95, 382–409.

hunger; by the cold and the heat; by rains and droughts; by the frozen earth and the cruel taiga!"[71]

An interesting and ultimately productive compromise between Bogoraz's Chukchi-as-Apache and Shishkov's natives-as-serfs was V. K. Arsen'ev's Dersu Uzala, a Nanai hunter who was both independent and loyal, clairvoyant and defenseless, eternal and doomed. Serving as a guide to a party of Russian explorers, Dersu introduces his charges to "primitive communism" and to a "special taiga morality"—the only morality "completely free of the vices that urban civilization brings with it."[72] Revealing the secrets of primitive communism, he exposes it to the polluting vices and, in a Christlike fashion, sacrifices himself in order to redeem the gleeful world "of usury, slavery, plunder, murder, and, finally, war."[73]

Arsen'ev never dwelt on the irony that he, and his literary alter ego, were army officers leading the assault. He could not "forgive himself" for bringing Dersu to the city, but he seemed at ease with bringing the city to Dersu. Like Iadrintsev, the new friends of the native wanted good administration and no administration at the same time. In any case, most of them—like Iadrintsev—had other causes that they considered much more important. Dersu's plight never became a matter of political choice in the capitals: as the exiles came back, they returned to the urgent issues of world war and world revolution. Even those who would never forget their savages had other priorities at the time. In his 1910 article on aliens Lev Shternberg excluded the northern foragers from consideration because the focus of the collection—and the focus of the debate throughout the country—was not on nationalities but on national movements. As for the wandering aliens, they did not have movements:

> They are so small, so widely scattered over huge territories, so low on the scale of culture, and, finally, due to geographical conditions, find themselves in circumstances so unfavorable to interaction both among themselves and with more cultured populations that, in spite of their

---

[71] Vladimir Korolenko, Ocherki i rasskazy (Petrograd, 1915), 1:126–27. Korolenko's hero was a Yakutized Russian peasant, thus providing a link between the old anti-serfdom texts and the newly popular taiga travelogues.

[72] Arsen'ev, Izbrannye proizvedeniia, 1:23, 41.

[73] Ibid., p. 554. For a fascinating analysis of assumptions underlying Arsen'ev's portrayal of Dersu, see Johanna Nichols, "Stereotyping Interethnic Communication: The Siberian Native in Soviet Literature," in Diment and Slezkine, eds., Between Heaven and Hell, pp. 185–98.

originality, they cannot rise to national consciousness and will hardly ever do so.[74]

Even at a time when the indigenous northerners were better known than ever before, they hardly mattered as part of the empire and seemed irrelevant in terms of the "accursed questions" that the politicians and the intellectuals were grappling with. They were not even history: as far as most people were concerned, the conquest of Siberia had ended with "Ermak's rout of Kuchum," which had been followed by the dark ages of exile and the dramatic epic of resettlement. (M. I. Veniukov complained that the educated public knew the names of Spanish and Portuguese conquistadors but had never heard of the great Russian pioneers.)[75] Even Dersu Uzala was not really "the last of the Gol'd"; he symbolized the demise of a higher morality, not the extinction of a native tribe (the tribe as such is not present in the book). The one concerted effort at Arctic myth-building ended in failure: no sooner had the emergent Siberian intelligentsia discovered the glory of "free popular colonization" and formulated the native problem than it was almost completely absorbed by the world of Russian exiles—just as the erstwhile "free colonists" were being displaced by the wave of new Russian immigration. When they were not in exile and not scouting the tundra in search of the ultimate Russian peasant, most Russian intellectuals lived in a world that consisted of Russia and the West, and even those who posed as Scythians or Turanians did so to threaten or punish the West—not to impress the "Asiatics."[76] Within Russia, they saw themselves tragically and sometimes triumphantly positioned between the eternally polarized state and the "people." Their role, their guilt, and their responsibilities were conceived with regard to this Russian—not imperial—opposition. Whatever grievances they had against the regime, it almost never was colonialism or imperialism. The long and bloody war in the Caucasus, the conquest of Central Asia, the Russification of the Ukraine, or the "extinction of the northern tribes" never became widely debated moral issues.[77] As Iadrintsev put it, "cen-

[74] Shternberg, "Inorodtsy," p. 533.
[75] M. I. Veniukov, Rossiia i Vostok: Sobranie geograficheskikh i politicheskikh statei M. Veniukova (St. Petersburg, 1877), p. 72.
[76] Riasanovsky, "Asia through Russian Eyes," in Vucinich, ed., Russia and Asia, p. 17.
[77] They were not even sufficient causes for celebration. There was talk about Russia's civilizing mission in the East and the empire's territorial needs; there was glee over apparent limits to England's might; and there was pride that Russia had joined the European powers in their worldwide expansion; but there was nothing like the colonial fever—or subsequent colonialist's guilt—that captured England, France, and Germany. See

tralist bureaucrats are replaced by centralist Kulturträgers, by centralists going to the people, by centralist Jacobins, etc."[78] By the early twentieth century, however, the virtues of the periphery and non-Russian nationalism were being loudly proclaimed by increasingly self-assertive ethnic elites. The northern aliens remained unrepresented—until the new revolutionary regime called on the former exiles to perform that task.

Dietrich Geyer, Russian Imperialism: The Interaction of Domestic and Foreign Policy, 1860–1914 (New Haven, Conn., 1987), pp. 93–94; Louise McReynolds, The News under Russia's Old Regime: The Development of a Mass-Circulation Press (Princeton, 1991), pp. 168–97, esp. pp. 170–71, 196–97; Malozemoff, Russian Far Eastern Policy, 1881–1904, pp. 41–44; Riasanovsky, "Asia through Russian Eyes," pp. 3–29, and "Russia and Asia," California Slavic Studies, no. 1 (1960): 170–81.

[78] Iadrintsev, "K moei avtobiografii," pp. 165–66.

"The first Ostiak district conference," from *Istoriia Sibiri*, vol. 4 (Leningrad, 1968)

5

The Liberated

All changes, even the most longed for, have their
melancholy.
> —Anatole France, *The Crime of Sylvestre Bonnard*

The Commissariat of Nationalities and the Tribes
of the Northern Borderlands

The wandering aliens could claim no exemption from the
Russian Revolution. The Amur peoples found themselves in the midst
of a full-scale war that dragged on long after Vrangel' left the Crimea;
the Cossack ataman Semenov announced a total mobilization of the
Tungus; the White commander Bochkarev drafted the dog-sled drivers
of the Okhotsk coast; and the Red partisans active among the Nanai
"obtained" 670 rifles, 779 kilos of powder, 571 kilos of shot, 1518 boats,
1188 horses, and 1489 dog teams.[1] Even after the reimposition of government authority, Siberian and central officials continued to receive
reports "about murders, robberies, and other crimes committed by the
militia and military units in alien teritories."[2] In the absence of en-
forceable legal barriers, thousands of land-hungry and just plain hungry Russian peasants moved into traditional native territories, hunting
throughout the year, pillaging hunters' stockpiles of food, stealing fur
animals from traps, and killing wild and domestic reindeer indiscrimi-

---

[1] M. A., "Sibirskie inoroctsy i Kolchak," *ZhN*, no. 24 (1919); U. G. Popova, *Eveny Magadanskoi oblasti: Ocherki istorii, khoziaistva i kul'tury evenov Okhotskogo poberezh'ia,
1917–1977* (Moscow, 1981). p. 52; V. A. Zibarev, *Sovetskoe stroitel'stvo u malykh narodnostei Severa, 1917–1932* (Tomsk, 1969), p. 37. See also TsGAOR, f. 1318, op. 1, d. 845,
ll. 7, 12; G. Afanas'ev, "Zaniatiia i zhizn' Sakhalinskikh Evenkov," *TT*, no. 1 (1928): 40;
and Bogdan Khodzher, "Kak ia partizanil," *TT*, no. 2 (1930): 142.
[2] TsGAOR, f. 1318, op. 1, d. 845, l. 12, and d. 992, l. 7.

131

nately. On the Chunia River, even setting fire to the forest did not save the local Evenk from the invading Angara peasants.[3]

Trade broke down completely in most areas. The Arctic and subarctic areas were isolated from the rest of the country, and various native groups were isolated from one another. There were no guns, powder, shot, nets, kettles, flour, oil, or sugar.[4] There were no more fairs: the nomads withdrew into distant tundras and lived off their reindeer. There was no strychnine to be used against predators, so that the reindeer not slaughtered or requisitioned were killed off by wolves. As a result, herds belonging to the Kanin Nenets, Chukchi, Koriak, and northeastern Even were reduced by 50 percent; the Saami and the Kamchatka Even, by 70–75 percent; and some groups of the Enisei Evenk, by 90–95 percent. In the Amur province, ravaged by particularly heavy fighting, one half of the Evenk population lost all their reindeer.[5] In the absence of their trading partners, many northerners were left without food or clothing. In the absence of guns and ammunition, many hunters were forced to reinvent the bow and arrow, as well as various weirs, nooses, and snares. It was not enough. As one Khanty put it, "without powder, shot, and percussion caps it is impossible for an alien to live."[6] Between 1918 and 1920, the production of squirrel furs in the Turukhansk region dropped from 200 thousand to 50 thousand pelts.[7] In many places starvation and migrations were followed by severe smallpox and typhoid epidemics.[8]

The establishment of the new Soviet regime meant that all provincial-level and a few district-level administrative positions were taken

---

[3] N. I. Leonov, "Tuzemnye sovety v taige i tundrakh," in *Sovetskii sever. Pervyi sbornik statei* (Moscow, 1929), p. 222. See also TsGAOR, f. 1318, op. 1, d. 845, l. 13, and d. 969, l. 4, E. D. Rinchenko, "Inorodcheskii vopros v Sibiri," *ZhN*, no. 6 (1921); D., "Iz doklada o deiatel'nosti Tomskogo gubnatsa," *ZhN*, no. 9 (1922); V. V. Nikiforov, "Sever Iakutii," *SA*, no. 1–2 (1925): 91–94; Vl. I. Mel'nikov, "K voprosu o pomoshchi brodiachim i kochevym narodnostiam," *SA*, no. 5–6 (1925): 162; and M. A. Sergeev, *Nekapitalisticheskii put'*, p. 209.

[4] The import and production of hunting rifles in Russia stopped in 1914. See Sergeev, *Nekapitalisticheskii put'*, p. 210. See also TsGAOR, f. 1318, op. 1, d. 969, l. 4.

[5] Zibarev, *Sovetskoe stroitel'stvo*, p. 51.

[6] Ibid., p. 52.

[7] V. N. Uvachan, *Put' narodov Severa k sotsializmu: Opyt sotsialisticheskogo stroitel'stva na Eniseiskom Severe* (Moscow, 1971), pp. 87–88.

[8] TsGAOR, f. 1318, op. 1, d. 965, ll. 2, 20; B. Z., "Sredi tuzemtsev DVR," *ZhN*, no. 15 (1922): 13; G. Lebedev, "Iakutskaia avtonomnaia respublika," *ZhN*, no. 1 (1923): 137; D. T. Ianovich, "Severnye tuzemtsy," *ZhN*, no. 1 (1923): 251–54; Anatolii Skachko, "Piat' let raboty Komiteta Severa," *SS*, no. 2 (1930): 22; Popova, *Eveny*, pp. 49–53. An exception to this bleak picture were areas dominated by other imperial powers: the Chukotka and Kamchatka coasts and parts of the Ussuri taiga.

over by Communist outsiders from southern Siberia or European Russia, most of them former Red Army commanders. Their first encounter with the native northerners was a terrible shock over what they saw as appalling backwardness and wretched living conditions. "It is impossible to talk about any culture, even of the most elementary type, among the Turukhansk natives."[9] In the recollection of one of the two Vladivostok sailors who represented the revolution in Chukotka between 1920 and 1922, "we were, of course, first of all struck by the backwardness of the population."[10] Indeed, the Chukchi epitomized the ignorance and poverty of the "old world" that the two sailors and their comrades had set out to destroy.[11] The following appeal of the Kamchatka revolutionary committee, although fashioned specifically for the "childlike" natives, is a fair representation of the world according to the Communist plenipotentiaries:

> This appeal of the Kamchatka revolutionary committee is addressed to you, the inhabitants of the taiga and tundra. There used to be bad people in Russia. They wanted to get rich, and so they killed and robbed many other people. We in Kamchatka also had people like that.

> Then the poor people got together, grabbed their guns, and decided to drive the bad people away. A terrible war started. The people suffered. There was little flour, tea, tobacco, guns, and powder. Ships with goods stopped coming. A lot of blood was spilled during that time. But the poor people beat the bad people. The common people put an end to the war right away. All working people got together and set up a strong Soviet republic.[12]

In a world divided into poor people and bad people there was no doubt where the Chukchi and other wandering aliens belonged. Not only were they all poor—every one of them—they were the most exploited and the most downtrodden of the poor. It was equally obvious that the bad people were represented by the traders—old-settler, new-settler, American, Chinese, and Japanese. The solution was clear, and

[9] "O sibirskikh tuzemtsakh," ZhN, no. 14 (1921).

[10] B. I. Mukhachev, Bortsy za vlast' sovetov na Kamchatke (Petropavlovsk-Kamchatskii, 1977), p. 62.

[11] Ibid.; B. I. Mukhachev, Bor'ba za vlast' sovetov na Chukotke (1919–1923). Sbornik dokumentov i materialov (Magadan, 1967), p. 133; Grazhdanskaia voina na Dal'nem Vostoke (1918–1922). Vospominaniia veteranov (Moscow, 1978), pp. 223–24.

[12] Revkomy Severo-vostoka SSSR (1922–1928 gg.). Sbornik dokumentov i materialov (Magadan, 1973), p. 180.

most provincial revolutionary committees, executive committees, and extraordinary conferences issued decrees introducing full legal equality (no more old-settlers, Cossacks, or aliens), nationalizing large merchants, and drastically limiting the activities of small traders.[13] The same Kamchatka revolutionary committee, for example, pardoned all debts and forbade all trade "in spirits, vodka, cologne, fly agaric (mushroom) and other strong and intoxicating substances." Also prohibited was trade in "various trinkets such as beads, bells, accordions, etc." All traders had to obtain special permits and have their price lists approved by the police or revolutionary committees. Once in a native settlement, they were supposed to show the local officials their permits and price lists, and, on receiving authorization, engage in honest and orderly trade.[14]

There were some very serious problems with this approach. First of all, in many areas no one could take the place of the local merchants. In the extreme northeast, for example, the property of the largest American company in the region was solemnly confiscated and then, for lack of a better alternative, promptly returned to the owners.[15] Most important, the new policy presupposed the existence of an army of like-minded and "conscious" officials who would expose the cheating, educate the nomads, and generally protect poor people from bad people.[16] Such officials were nowhere to be found. The few revolutionaries who pioneered Soviet power among the northerners were not very keen on staying there.[17] As the senior of the two Chukotka sailors wrote to his superiors, "My request for a replacement is due to the difficult climatic conditions of the district and the poor quality of our quarters, where we have to spend the severe winter, which lasts almost all year long. You can't even imagine what the Chukotka peninsula is like! . . . Next year be sure to send a replacement. I'm not staying, come what may."[18] The replacement did not arrive, and he did not stay.

The officials who did remain had been there all along. They were old

[13] P. N. Ivanov, "Pervye meropriiatiia partiinykh i sovetskikh organizatsii Sibiri po likvidatsii ekonomicheskoi otstalosti nerusskikh narodov (1920–1925)," in *Sibir' v period strotel'stva sotsializma i perekhoda k kommunizmu* (Novosibirsk, 1966), pp. 7–9; I. P. Kleshchenok, *Narody Severa i leninskaia natsional'naia politika v deistvii* (Moscow, 1968), p. 74.

[14] *Revkomy*, pp. 94–96.

[15] Mukhachev, *Bor'ba za vlast' sovetov na Chukotke*, pp. 44, 59.

[16] To achieve that, they were expected to learn the local languages—an "easy task" given their "relative simplicity and limited vocabulary." See *Revkomy*, p. 132.

[17] TsGAOR, f. 1318, op. 1, d. 994.

[18] Mukhachev, *Bor'ba za vlast' sovetov na Chukotke*, p. 124.

settlers/traders whose elders now chaired soviets and sat in revolutionary committees.[19] The new regime, based in the capitals and large provincial centers, had a problem with these people. On the one hand,
they were undeniably bad when compared to the natives; on the other
hand, they were just as undeniably poor by any Tomsk, Krasnoiarsk, or
Vladivostok standards. They were the "working people" of the north,
and it was their representatives who spoke on behalf of the northern
districts at provincial congresses and conferences. In any case, if the
natives could not take care of themselves (and everyone seemed to
agree on that), any policy toward them had to be carried out by the
local Russians. As low-level officials of the newly created cooperative,
trading, and—increasingly—Party organizations, the settlers regained
their role as the only link between the state and the former wandering
aliens.

For most of them, this role remained an important source of livelihood, and soon after the end of the war the native trade, including trade
in liquor, began to recover.[20] The improvement in the economic position of the Russian settlers was made easier by the de facto cancellation
of the Speranskii statute, which had provided for autonomous native
administration, and by the liquidation of "alien" as a separate legal
category. Most village soviets in the taiga and tundra were supposed to
include the neighboring nomads. This allowed the settlers to make legal decisions concerning native rights, particularly on the annexation
of land and the distribution of taxes.[21]

Those provincial bosses who did not like this arrangement were
powerless to do anything about it. There was no radio and there were
no roads. Transportation (dogs, boats, and reindeer) and native drivers
were rarely available. "Instructors" willing to brave the elements were
hard to come by. The few directives that reached the polar circle arrived up to a year late and the local officials to whom they were addressed could not read or found it convenient to "play the fool" when
questioned about them. According to the Enisei provincial executive
committee, "the remoteness of the [Turukhansk] region and the lack of
a means of communication result in the virtual independence of the

[19] Sten Bergman, *Through Kamchatka by Dog-sled and Skis* (London, 1927), p. 108;
Popova, *Eveny*, pp. 205–7.
[20] Kleshchenok, *Narody Severa*, pp. 68–70; Ia. Khodam., "O deiatel'nosti organov Narkomnatsa na mestakh," *ZhN*, no. 15 (1922).
[21] TsGAOR, f. 1318, op. 1, d. 993, ll. 4–5, and d. 994, l. 151; Kleshchenok, *Narody
Severa*, p. 74; "O sibirskikh tuzemtsakh," *ZhN*, no. 14 (1921); D. "Iz doklada"; V. G. Bogoraz (-Tan), "Ob izuchenii i okhrane okrainnykh narodov," *ZhN*, no. 3–4 (1923): 172.

[Turukhansk] regional executive committee."[22] At the same time, any suggestion that this independence be legalized and made to reflect (or rather, protect) the interests of the indigenous population met with fierce resistance. In 1922 Petr Sosunov, the head of the Polar Subcommittee of the Commissariat of Nationalities, was sent to the Tiumen' province to organize a conference of the national minorities of the lower Ob' region ("the Tobol'sk north," as the area was known at the time). The conference adopted a resolution asking for the creation, within the Tiumen' province, of a new administrative unit of the Tobol'sk north.[23] As some native delegates put it, the long history of their exploitation by the Russians could only be "undone through the creation of our independent government which would defend its own nation and attempt to direct at the dark masses a ray of enlightenment and to cultivate their lifestyles [kul'tivirovat' ikh byt zhizni]."[24] Sosunov, who was formally asked to lobby the authorities on the issue and who believed that "the natives' desire for national independence" was an expression of their "resistance to oppression,"[25] was arrested on his arrival in Tiumen' and put in jail "for attempting to transform the extreme north into an autonomous region"[26] (that, of course, at a time when the formation of autonomous regions for national minorities was an official Party policy).

The most commonly cited objection to native self-rule was the alleged inability of the "northern tribes" to manage their own affairs. Another, and increasingly popular, view appealed to the urgent national need for large-scale economic development. According to the Tomsk province executive committee, "State policy in the Narym area should encourage colonization by the Russian population. Only settlement is capable of bringing the area back to life. Separation as an alien autonomous province would condemn it to remaining uninhabited and to living off the state for many years to come."[27]

There was a more immediate reason, too. The taiga and tundra not only fed the settler population—they had become an important source of revenue for many Siberian towns ruined by the war, as well as for

---

[22] Anatolii Skachko, "Desiat' let raboty Komiteta Severa," SS, no. 2 (1934): 10.
[23] TsGAOR, f. 1318, op. 1, d. 994, ll. 120f.
[24] Ibid., l. 100.
[25] Ibid., ll. 99, 146.
[26] Skachko, "Desiat' let," pp. 10–11.
[27] TsGAOR, f. 1318, op. 1, d. 969, l. 58. The local representatives of the Peoples' Commissariat of Nationalities warned the Tomsk province executive committee about the dangers of massive Russian settlement but agreed that autonomy was impossible "because of the natives' low cultural level" (l. 59).

the Soviet state desperate for exportable assets. Even in the Far Eastern Province, the most heavily colonized of the northern areas, the native hunters provided 86.5 percent of all the furs.[28] Various provincial administrations may have been unable to control their local agents politically, but they had to rely on them to extract fish, furs, and reindeer meat from the indigenous peoples. Moscow, while showing occasional concern for the natives, added to the incentive by promoting food requisitioning and, later, a tax in kind. These policies were primarily directed against Russian peasants (they were designed in European Russia), but in the north it was the aboriginal peoples who had all the reindeer, produced the majority of the valuable pelts, and caught a considerable portion of the fish. As a result, in many areas native settlements and encampments were regularly looted by traveling groups of government officials.[29] The situation was complicated by the new bosses' ignorance about the native economy and unwillingness to resume the traditional practices of providing long-term credit to the hunters.[30] Instead, they experimented with various systems of rationing and fixed norms, often borrowing them whole from agricultural areas.[31] In 1921 and 1922 the indigenous peoples of the Surgut district were expected to pay butter, meat, wool, hide, fur, and hay taxes, perform cart duty, pay for the upkeep of the (Russian) township executive committees and (Russian) schools, make obligatory contributions to the victims of starvation in the Volga region, and turn over 10 percent of their fish to the state as "lease payments."[32] As calculated by one local official, even without the so-called general state tax, the amount of which was not clear, a native fisherman would have to work twenty-eight months a year to discharge all his obligations[33]—provided, of course, that the "food inspectors" agreed to accept his catch in lieu of butter and wool. If they did not agree, the fisherman might have his property confiscated, because, in the words of one witness, "when you ask an Ostiak for butter, he asks in puzzlement what it is

[28] Na novom puti. Zhizn' i khoziaistvo Dal'nevostochnoi oblasti v 1923–1924 gg. (Vladivostok, 1925), p. 560.

[29] Bogoraz (-Tan), "O pervobytnykh plemenakh"; Ivan Evsenin, "Karagassy," ZhN, no. 6 (1922); P. Ostrovskikh, "Sredi tuzemtsev Sibiri," ZhN, no. 18 (1922): 12; Bogoraz (-Tan), "Ob izuchenii i okhrane," p. 172.

[30] TsGAOR, f. 1318, op. 1, d. 969, ll. 4, 11–12.

[31] Ibid., d. 993, ll. 4–5.

[32] Ibid., d. 992, ll. 6–7.

[33] Ibid.

and how to make it."[34] If they did agree, he and his family might starve—because there were only twelve months in a year and the food inspectors did not have anything to give in return.[35] As the Obdorsk delegate put it in his report to a conference of northern peoples in Moscow in July 1922, "the alien is no longer dependent on the free market, but he is much more dependent on . . . state economic policies. . . . If before he used to be totally beholden to the trader, now the state has become the trader."[36] Or rather, the trader had become the state.

By 1921, an increasing number of reports on the plight of the northern peoples began reaching the one organ in Moscow that could claim jurisdiction in the matter—the People's Commissariat of Nationalities (Narkomnats). With the continuing unrest in Central Asia, the growing discontent in Transcaucasia and the Ukraine, and the potentially dangerous anticolonialist rhetoric by Sultan Galiev, People's Commissar Stalin and his staff were busy enough without the northerners; however, the urgent and sometimes panicky reports from Siberia demanded attention. The authors of the reports (many of them ethnographers) insisted that in spite of their small size and apparent political irrelevance, the native peoples of Siberia held the key to the economic development of almost one-third of the country's territory. Taking their cue from the turn-of-the-century missionaries of the Il'minskii school, the scholars and the local activists assured the bureaucrats that protecting the "backward tribes of the north" was not an act of charity—or even class solidarity. In fact, they argued, it was a matter of the utmost urgency and of paramount national importance. The north possessed enormous animal and mineral wealth; only the well-adapted natives could exploit that wealth; hence, the disappearance of the natives would turn a potentially rich country into a frozen wasteland; hence, a failure to help them would be an economic crime of gigantic proportions.[37]

The case seemed compelling enough. Nobody questioned the validity of the argument. But what could and should be done? The informa-

---

[34] Ibid., d. 969, l. 6. See also D., "Iz doklada"; "O sibirskikh tuzemtsakh"; and Bogoraz (-Tan), "Ob izuchenii i okhrane," p. 172.

[35] TsGAOR, f. 1318, op. 1, d. 969, l. 9.

[36] Ibid., d. 993, ll. 8–9.

[37] G. Lebedev, "Vymiraiushchie brat'ia," ZhN, no. 19 (1920); V. D. Vilenskii-Sibiriakov, "Inorodcheskii vopros v Sibiri," ZhN, no. 30 (1920); Bogoraz (-Tan), "O pervobytnykh plemenakh"; Evsenin, "Karagassy"; P. E. Ostrovskikh, "K sanitarnomu polozheniiu severnykh tuzemtsev," ZhN, no. 3 (1922): 7; Bogoraz (-Tan), "Ob izuchenii i okhrane," p. 169.

tion about the northern regions was scanty and unreliable.[38] As one of the most influential officials in the Commissariat of Nationalities, S. M. Dimanshtein, wrote in 1919, "the wilds of the Transbaikal region are populated by the Buriat and the Enisei Tunguz, about whom we in Russia do not hear very much. The only thing we know is that they are Mongols, Lamaists, and quite wild, and that is about it."[39]

A year later Narkomnats statistics on the population of the north appeared as follows: Hyperboreans, Yukagir, Chukchi, Koriak, Kamchadal, Ainu, Teleut—67,606 persons; others—545,999 persons.[40] A chart published in 1922 included 106 "Chunantsy" and 800 "Yukashir."[41]

Even if better information had existed, there were no cadres through whom a central policy could be effected. The Siberian Revolutionary Committee's Nationalities Affairs Section (Sibnats), which was formed in 1920 and had branches (gubnatsy) in several Siberian provinces, was mostly concerned with the immediate problem of growing and largely unsupervised immigration (it had special German, Jewish, Latvian, and Estonian subsections).[42] More important, it was desperately short of funds, people, office space, and even paper to write on, while its local branches were in constant danger of being taken over by the executive committees who could always think of a better use for money and personnel.[43]

After about a year of such precarious existence Sibnats was closed down and replaced by the Siberian Office of the Peoples' Commissariat of Nationalities, affiliated with Sibrevkom as a nonvoting agency but responsible directly to Moscow.[44] Presumably, the idea was to obtain an independent source of funding, although one angry and unwilling employee of the Office claimed that the former head of Sibnats, a comrade Plich, had designed the whole reshuffle in order to flee from Siberia and deal with Siberian nationalities in the more congenial environment of the capital.[45] In any case, Plich went on to become the chief of the new National Minorities section of the Commissariat, his Siberian successor soon followed him to Moscow, and the successor's

[38] TsGAOR, f. 1318, op. 1, d. 856, l. 6.
[39] S. M. Dimanshtein, "Sovetskaia vlast' i melkie natsional'nosti," ZhN, no. 46 (1919). The Tungus were, of course, neither Mongol nor Lamaist.
[40] Skachko, "Desiat' let," p. 10.
[41] "Iz deiatel'nosti predstavitel'stva Narkomnatsa v Sibiri," ZhN, no. 14 (1922).
[42] TsGAOR, f. 1318, op. 1, d. 856, ll. 21, 23, and d. 958, ll. 2–4.
[43] Ibid., d. 958, ll. 17, 23.
[44] Ibid., d. 958, ll. 37–41.
[45] Ibid., d. 965, l. 22.

successor spent his short term of office pleading for funds and being accused by his deputy of showing much greater dedication to the female sex than to national minoritites.[46] Meanwhile, funds were still unavailable, and the beleaguered representatives of the Siberian Office continued at the mercy of the local administrators, who "[saw] the nationality issue as totally irrelevant and thus practically nonexistent," "an unnecessary drag" (volynka), and "an expendable luxury."[47] After Orosin, the Office's only specialist on the aboriginal peoples, died of typhoid, the remaining three employees survived a "nightmarish" move from Tomsk to Novo-Nikolaevsk in the spring of 1922 and devoted their flagging energies to procuring food, writing denunciations, and urging the Commissariat to send them money and generally "pay particular attention to the work of its local institutions, know where things are located, and not confuse Azerbaijan with Siberia, and Siberia with the Ukraine."[48] Plich, who did not have any money and did not always know who he was writing to, countered by accusing the Siberians of idleness, empty talk, and plagiarism.[49] In the meantime, the forgotten agents of the Siberian Office's provincial branches (gubnatsy) were being harassed, ignored, starved, and occasionally "mobilized for some other work without the chief's authorization."[50]

Finally, in November 1922 all but two of the gubnatsy and all nationalities offices in Siberian Party committees and education boards were abolished.[51] Their former staffers became the Office's local "plenipotentiaries," and when the Commissariat of Nationalities failed in its attempts to get funding for them, the Office sent a telegram to Moscow saying that it "refuses all responsibility for local work." The unsalaried plenipotentiaries survived a while longer on food parcels before they moved on to more promising pursuits.[52] The Office itself issued a few desperate warnings about the predicament of the natives and the need to "exploit the untold wealth of Siberia,"[53] and then expired quietly and without a trace. In April 1923 the head of the Administration Department of the Siberian Revolutionary Committee wrote to the head of the National Minorities Section of the Peoples' Commissariat of Na-

---

[46] Cf. ibid., d. 965, ll. 23, 26–27, and d. 901, ll. 47–55.
[47] Ibid., d. 901, l. 10, and d. 965, ll. 23–24.
[48] Ibid., d. 965, l. 24, and d. 901, ll. 5–7.
[49] Ibid., d. 901, ll. 16–17, and d. 902, l. 5.
[50] Ibid., d. 901, ll. 2, 7, and d. 958, ll. 2–4.
[51] Ibid., d. 901, ll. 18, 52.
[52] Ibid., d. 901, ll. 18, 24, 29, 52, 54, 55.
[53] Ibid., d. 901, l. 53, and d. 965, l. 20–21.

tionalities: "I would like to report that because the Office of Narkomnats does not have a single employee left, there is no one to reply to
your inquiries Nos. 211 and 314."[54] On May 24, 1923, the Commissariat of Nationalities announced the "temporary liquidation" of its Siberian branch,[55] and the new and very energetic head of the National
Minorities Section, Anatolii Skachko, had to turn his undivided attention to Moscow-based lobbying and theorizing.

Theorizing about the circumpolar peoples was hardly easier than
trying to administer them through the Commissariat's Siberian Office.
The term "aliens" (inorodtsy) was replaced by various combinations
usually including the word "native" (tuzemtsy, tuzemnyi), but the effort to integrate them into the conceptual framework of the "nationality
question" proved extraordinarily difficult.

In classical Marxism, the only meaningful differences were those of
class. Capitalists would disregard national boundaries in pursuit of
profit, and proletarians of all countries would unite in opposition to
capitalism. Even the "classics of Marxism," however, talked about "the
Irish" and "the Poles" as real historical agents, and by the time of the
Russian Revolution capitalism had turned into "imperialism" and nationality had become a "question."[56] The Bolsheviks' answer to this
question was to recognize nationalities as "objective" entities and to
enlist them as allies in the common struggle against oppression. In
Stalin's words, "A nation can organize its life as it sees fit. It has the
right to organize its life on the basis of autonomy. It has the right to
enter into federal relations with other nations. It has the right to complete secession. Nations are sovereign and all nations are equal."[57]
Nations were real, all real nations were sovereign, and all sovereign
nations had the right to political self-determination on "their own"
territory. Nations without territories were not real; all territorial
boundaries could be divided into artificial and natural ("those based

[54] Ibid., d. 965, l. 40.

[55] Ibid., d. 965, l. 44.

[56] For Marxist debates on nationalism, see Walker Connor, The National Question in
Marxist-Leninist Theory and Strategy (Princeton, N.J., 1984); Hélène Carrère-
D'Encausse, The Great Challenge: Nationalities and the Bolshevik State, 1917–1930
(New York, 1992); Helmut Konrad, "Between 'Little International' and Great Power Politics: Austro-Marxism and Stalinism on the National Question," in Nationalism and Empire: The Habsburg Empire and the Soviet Union, ed. Richard L. Rudolph and David F.
Good (New York, 1992); Richard Pipes, The Formation of the Soviet Union: Communism
and Nationalism, 1917–1923 (Cambridge, Mass., 1964); and Roman Szporluk, Communism and Nationalism: Karl Marx versus Friedrich List (New York, 1988).

[57] I. V. Stalin, Marksizm i natsional'nyi vopros (Moscow, 1950), p. 51.

on popular sympathies"); and the natural result of popular sympathies was, in Lenin's words, "the greatest possible homogeneity in the national composition of the population."[58] If this required the creation of countless "autonomous national districts," then the world-wide proletarian society would consist of countless "autonomous national districts"—however small and however nonproletarian.[59]

Why these concessions to what was after all a "philistine ideal" that slowed down the transformation of "somnolent peasants" into "mobile proletarians"?[60] First, because neither somnolent peasants nor even mobile proletarians would become communists without special guidance from a special communist party. And if they happened to speak a wide variety of languages, the party proselytizers would have to "reach them" by "preaching . . . in all languages and 'adapting' themselves to all local and national requirements."[61] For Lenin, as for the Kazan' missionary reformers of his youth, language was a totally transparent conduit: Marxist schools would have the same Marxist curriculum irrespective of the linguistic medium.[62] Nationality was "form." "National form" was acceptable because there was no such thing as national content.

Another reason for Lenin and Stalin's insistence on national self-determination was the distinction that they drew between oppressor-nation nationalism ("great-power chauvinism") and oppressed-nation nationalism (nationalism proper). The first one was a bad habit that could be kicked through an effort of proletarian will and an act of "intelligentsia-like" introspection; the second was an understandable (over)reaction to oppression that could only be assuaged through sensitivity and tact.[63] The gift of national self-determination was a gesture of repentance that would eventually lead to national forgiveness and therefore to the end of nationalist paranoia and therefore to the end of national differences.

> Having transformed capitalism into socialism, the proletariat will create an *opportunity* for the total elimination of national oppression; this opportunity will become a *reality* "only"—"only"!—after a total democra-

---

[58] V. I. Lenin, *Voprosy natsional'noi politiki i proletarskogo internatsionalizma* (Moscow, 1965), pp. 32–33.

[59] Ibid., pp. 26, 33–34.

[60] Ibid., pp. 15, 16, 81, 107.

[61] Ibid., p. 9.

[62] Ibid., p. 27.

[63] Ibid., pp. 41, 61–62, 102, 113–14.

tization of all spheres, including the establishment of state borders according to the "sympathies" of the population, and including complete freedom of secession. This, in turn, will lead in practice to a total abolition of all national tensions and all national distrust, to an accelerated drawing together and merger of nations which will result in the withering away of the state.[64]

When the proletarian revolution finally arrived, it was as much national as it was proletarian. The first Bolshevik decrees described the victorious masses as "peoples" and "nations" endowed with "rights"; proclaimed all peoples to be equal and sovereign; guaranteed their sovereignty through an ethnoterritorial federation and a right to secession; endorsed "the free development of national minorities and ethnic groups"; and pledged to respect national beliefs, customs, and institutions.[65] By the end of the war the need for local allies and the recognition of existing national entities combined with principle to produce an assortment of legally recognized and ethnically defined Soviet republics, autonomous republics, autonomous regions, and toilers' communes. Some "internationalist" Left Communists were not amused, but Lenin beat them at the Eighth Party Congress by insisting that nations existed in nature and that "not to recognize something that is out there is impossible: it will force us to recognize it."[66] In addition to being out there, the various nationalities had suffered from such relentless national oppression and were full of such "bitter hatred" for the Russians that anything short of linguistic and territorial autonomy would be seen as an attempt to preserve the Russian empire.[67] What followed was a wild scramble for ethnoterritorial recognition based on claims of being out there and having been oppressed. National intellectuals, regional bureaucrats, Commissariat of Nationalities officials, "native conferences," and sympathetic Petrograd scholars all demanded institutional autonomy, offices, and funding (for themselves or their proteges).[68] Funding was scarce, but autonomous areas and offices

---

[64] Ibid., p. 129.

[65] Dekrety sovetskoi vlasti (Moscow, 1957), 1:39–41, 113–15, 168–70, 195–96, 340–44, 351, 367.

[66] "Vos'moi s"ezd RKP(b)," ZhN, no. 11, 30 March 1919.

[67] Ibid., no. 13, 13 April 1919.

[68] See, for example, Fedor Kriuchkov, "O Krashenakh," ZhN, no. 27 (84), 2 September 1920; R. El'mets, "K voprosu o vydelenii chuvash v osobuiu administrativnuiu edinitsu," ZhN, no. 2 (59), 11 January 1920; V. D. Vilenskii-Sibiriakov, "Samoopredelenie iakutov," ZhN, no. 3 (101), 2 February 1921; "Chetyre goda raboty sredi estontsev Sovetskoi Rossii," ZhN, no. 24 (122), 5 November 1921.

became particularly plentiful after the Tenth Party Congress equated (non-Russian) nationality with backwardness and thus legitimized the policy of institutionalized ethnicity. In Stalin's formulation, "the essence of the nationality question in the USSR consists of the need to eliminate the backwardness (economic, political, and cultural) that the nationalities have inherited from the past, to allow the backward peoples to catch up with central Russia."[69] To accomplish this goal, the Party was to help them

> (a) develop and strengthen their own Soviet statehood in the form that would correspond to the national physiognomy of these peoples; (b) introduce their own courts and organs of government that would function in the native languages and consist of local people familiar with the life and mentality of the local population; (c) develop their own press, schools, theaters, local clubs, and other cultural and educational institutions in the native languages.[70]

Nationality equaled backwardness, but backwardness did not equal nationality. In the world according to Bolshevism, it was much larger, much older, and much more central. It provided the (unacknowledged) difference between Marxism and Leninism, described Russia outside the party, and defined "East" as opposed to "West"—as well as representing the fifth column of the past in the midst of the future-bound present. Yet some kinds of backwardness were more backward than others. The "somnolent" Russian peasant "glued to his pile of manure"[71] was obdurate and obtuse but ultimately reformable (that was the premise behind the revolution, of course), but what about those areas that had been asleep for most of human history and knew nothing of slash-and-burn agriculture, let alone piles of manure? In Lenin's words, "To the north of Vologda, to the southeast of Rostov-on-Don and Saratov, to the south of Orenburg and Omsk, and to the north of Tomsk lie the vastest expanses with enough room for dozens of huge cultured states. And in all those expanses there reigns backwardness, semi-savagery, and outright savagery."[72]

Even outright savagery had its uses, however, for if imperialism stood for global capitalism, then the "backward masses of the Orient" repre-

[69] *Desiatyi s"ezd Rossiiskoi Kommunisticheskoi partii. Stenograficheskii otchet* (Moscow, 1921), p. 101.

[70] Ibid., p. 371.

[71] Lenin, *Voprosy,* p. 81n.

[72] Lenin, *Polnoe sobranie,* 43:228.

sented the new global proletarians. As such, according to Lenin, they were the natural allies of the revolutionary proletarians of the West. "We will spare no efforts in order to get together and form a union with the Mongols, Persians, Indians, and Egyptians; we consider it our duty and in our interest to do so, for otherwise socialism in Europe will not be secure."[73] For this union to be firm, the Europeans were to provide their backward brothers with "disinterested cultural assistance" and extend to them the promise of national self-determination (in the "Orient," backwardness seemed to equal nationality).[74]

When the Revolution transformed "Asia" into an immediate tactical concern, the great revolutionary tactician convinced his followers to exempt it from the familiar class approach. In the special case of backwardness, he argued, a special policy was required:

> What can we do with regard to such peoples as the Kirgiz and the Sart,[75] who are still under the influence of their mullahs? Can we go to the Sart and say: "We will get rid of your exploiters"? No, we cannot do this, because they are completely dependent on their mullahs. We must wait for the development of each nation and for the differentiation of the proletariat from bourgeois elements.[76]

These were the frightening days of March 1919, when the Bolsheviks needed every friend they could get. Sixteen months later, after decisive victories over Denikin and Kolchak, Lenin changed his mind. One did not have to wait for development and class differentiation, after all.

> Can we consider as correct the statement that the capitalist stage of economic development is inevitable for those backward peoples who are now liberating themselves and among whom—now, after the war—one notices a tendency toward progress? We have answered this question in the negative. If the victorious revolutionary proletariat engages in systematic propaganda in their midst, and the soviet governments come to their assistance using all the means at their disposal, then it is incorrect to suggest that the capitalist stage of development is inevitable for backward peoples.[77]

If Russia could be pulled out of the "idiocy of rural life," then, with

[73] Ibid., 30:120.
[74] Ibid.
[75] The modern Kazakh and Uzbek, respectively.
[76] "Vos'moi s"ezd RKP (b)." ZhN, no. 10 (1919).
[77] Lenin, Polnoe sobranie, 41:245–46.

some extra effort, the savages could also be saved from savagery. To achieve this aim, the Tenth Party Congress prescribed industrial development, class differentiation from above, and, in the case of natives threatened by extinction, protection from Russian colonialism.[78] The Party's main task was to overcome economic backwardness by "transferring factories to the sources of raw materials" and to overcome social backwardness by "depriving all native exploiters of their influence on the masses."[79] In other words, the Party should go to the Sarts and get rid of their exploiters. They may have depended on their mullahs yesterday, but they would not depend on them tomorrow.

Such was the ideological framework within which the Commissariat of Nationalities operated. The problem of nationality was to be solved by autonomization, and the problem of backwardness, by direct central intervention. If the two coincided (as they did in all the non-Russian areas of the former Russian empire, according to the Tenth Congress), then perhaps one of them should prevail, but no one knew which one. The new spirit of the New Economic Policy seemed to favor national autonomy, but some nations seemed so hopelessly influenced by their mullahs that they required immediate rescue.

And then there were the "outright savages" of the northern borderlands. Their nationality seemed extremely underdeveloped, and their underdevelopment seemed extreme. Hence, there was not much talk of national autonomy any time soon.[80] To the Narkomnats officials, people with no "national" consciousness, no national demands, no intelligentsia, and no "culture" were not really nationalities, all the more so because their names, their languages, and their very existence were often in doubt. This left backwardness pure and simple, or rather class without nationality—which meant that the "outright savages" were in fact "the poorest of peasants" or even "the real and most authentic proletarians."[81] Then came the usual dilemma: should the "missionaries of communism" attempt to "instill culture in them" and thus transform them into real and potentially equal nationalities, or should they take advantage of their total oppression to create total proletarians?[82] For,

[78] KPSS v rezoliutsiiakh i resheniiakh s"ezdov, konferentsii i plenumov TsK (Moscow, 1983), 2:365–69.

[79] Ibid., p. 367.

[80] See, for example, TsGAOR, f. 1318, op. 1, d. 856, l. 22.

[81] Dimanshtein, "Sovetskaia vlast'"; Lebedev, "Vymiraiushchie brat'ia."

[82] S. Pestkovskii, "Partiinaia agitatsiia sredi kochevnikov," ZhN, no. 47 (1919), and "Natsional'naia kul'tura," ZhN, no. 21 (1919); Dimanshtein, "Sovetskaia vlast'"; A. V. Lunacharskii, "Problemy obrazovaniia v avtonomnykh respublikakh i oblastiakh," ZhN, no. 1 (1924): 32.

in the Bolshevik scheme of things, the other side of outright savagery was primitive communism, which meant that the outright savages could be expected to become excellent students of scientific communism and eventually "the propagandists of the ideas of sovietization and communism in the eastern part of the country."[83] If it did not turn out that way, there was always the possibility of grasping at what they called the "embryos of class struggle" and attempting to promote true class differentiation.[84] This was an unpopular view, however. Until the dissolution of Narkomnats in 1924 most of its officials involved in northern affairs believed that the circumpolar peoples presented a special case of a classless communistic society, which in effect meant a society consisting of one exploited class.

Such an attitude on the part of Communist administrators was due to the influence of professional ethnographers, who served as the only source of information about the northern peoples. Most of them former revolutionaries and exiles, the polar ethnographers were not "bourgeois experts" needed for their expertise but distrusted for their political views. On the contrary, many of them believed that now something could finally be done about what they saw as a long-neglected human tragedy. In April 1922 the National Minorities Section of Narkomnats formed a Subsection of the Polar North, and six months later the anthropologist D. T. Ianovich succeeded in creating a one-man Ethnographic Bureau. Before formulating policy guidelines, he was saying, the new regime should consult the few people who knew the subject, for otherwise "the most valuable material, which [had] enormous scientific, social, and administrative importance, [would] be irretrievably lost."[85] Accordingly, Ianovich proclaimed scholarly work to be the main purpose of his bureau and dedicated himself to promoting debate on professional policy and to procuring means of existence for his underemployed and underfed colleagues (while never ceasing to wage his own desperate struggle against a student dormitory, which had taken away his bathroom and was trying to deprive him of the rest of his apartment).[86]

As far as the ethnographers were concerned, the most urgent task was to protect the circumpolar peoples from Russian traders, peasants, and administrators. The motives for concern were, of course, primarily

---

[83] TsGAOR, f. 1318, op. 1, d. 856, l. 5, and f. 1377, op. 1, d. 45, ll. 34, 54. See also Rinchenko, "Inorodcheskii vopros v Sibiri."

[84] F. Ia., "K voprosu ob agitatsii sredi kochevnikov," ZhN, no. 48 (1919).

[85] TsGAOR, f. 1318, op. 1, d. 755, l. 10, and d. 772, ll. 1–5.

[86] Ibid., d. 772, l. 1, and d. 991, ll. 4–15, 25.

couched in terms of state interest, but just as important were the continuing martyrdom of the natives, the unique value of their culture,
and human compassion "for these children of nature, naive, pure, and
honest."[87] As the local Russian settlers were the main enemies, the
only solution was to deprive them of all administrative responsibility
for native territories and to create a completely centralized and independent system of native government. In the opinion of many ethno-
grapers (and their allies, colleagues, and fellow exiles from among
provincial teachers, historians, and museum curators), the best way to
do this was to form tribal reservations.[88]

V. G. Bogoraz, the author of the most carefully thought-out and
talked-about project for the future of the "primitive tribes," suggested
that the recent experience in the United States, Canada, Brazil, Argen-
tina, and Greenland had proved the need for a physical separation between "stronger" and "weaker" cultures. In Siberia, too, "coexistence
with the Russians meant—with no exceptions whatsoever—death for
the aliens."[89] The U.S. model seemed particularly worthy of imitation.
In Bogoraz's opinion, the Bureau of Indian Affairs had been singularly
successful in protecting its charges from trade in alcohol, assisting the
needy with gifts and loans, and promoting education and health care.[90]
What Russia needed was a similar government body responsible for
the welfare of its own Indians. It would study the native way of life
and, based on such a study, carry out enlightened policies aimed at
protecting the natives, rationalizing their subsistence practices, preserving the environment, and, generally, "improving the overall economic life of the natives and introducing new elements that would
ensure painless progress." Bogoraz was rather vague on what exactly
those elements would be, but they were sure to include health and vet-

---

[87] Bruno Adler, "Eniseiskie ostiaki," *ZhN*, no. 31 (1921). See also TsGAOR, f. 1318, op.
1, d. 856, l. 19; Bogoraz (-Tan), "O pervobytnykh plemenakh" and "Ob izuchenii i
okhrane"; D. T. Ianovich, "Zapovedniki dlia gibnushchikh tuzemnykh plemen," *ZhN*,
no. 4 (1922).

[88] Bogoraz (-Tan), "O pervobytnykh plemenakh" and "Ob izuchenii i okhrane"; Ianovich, "Zapovedniki dlia gibnushchikh tuzemnykh plemen," *ZhN*, no. 4 (1922); TsGAOR,
f. 1377, op. 1, d. 8, ll. 126–27, and d. 45, l. 53, 77, 81.

[89] Bogoraz, "O pervobytnykh plemenakh." Aliens were renamed "borderland peoples" in the second edition of the project. See his "O pervobytnykh plemenakh" and "Ob
izuchenii i okhrane."

[90] Ironically, just as Bogoraz was speaking, John Collier was embarking on his campaign against the interventionist and assimilationist policies of the "Indian Bureau" in
the name of the absolute worth of Indian cultures and tribal self-rule. See Francis Paul
Prucha, *The Great Father: The United States Government and the American Indians*
(Lincoln, Nebr., 1984), pp. 273–74.

erinary care, education, technological assistance, and an (eventual) state monopoly on trade.

The exact relationship between reservations and central native administration was open to debate, but most participants agreed that aboriginal life was to be governed by traditional law; that the funding for most future programs should be based on a certain fixed deduction from the income of the state enterprises active in the north (or else on leasing native territories to such enterprises); and that the new U.S.-style Indian agents were to be absolutely and unequivocally independent from any local control.[91]

Who were the people qualified to serve as agents, inspectors, and supervisors? The ethnographers had no doubts on that score: they, the ethnographers, were such people, for only they were "competent to form judgments on the peculiarities of native domestic and spiritual life and, due to the nature of their profession, accustomed to regard the natives with thoughtfulness and affection."[92] Thus, the first step should be to invest in the teaching of ethnography and the organization of field trips, ensuring growing availability of competent cadres.[93]

Bogoraz and most of his colleagues did not have any doubts about getting involved in government work. In the tradition of the Russian liberal intelligentsia, moral and political activism was regarded as a sacred duty of science, and "armchair scholar" (kabinetnyi uchenyi) was a term of abuse. Whatever one thought of Lenin's political platform, the new government seemed to offer a unique opportunity to effect some meaningful changes, particularly because, in the early years, the Bolshevik attitude to the nationality question seemed relatively flexible (especially when compared to the nationality policies of other parties). Another reason for such optimism was the dramatic increase in the prestige and role of anthropology in the West. The world war had sent many future scholars on protracted field trips and brought about a much greater involvement of the imperial powers in the management and economic exploitation of their colonies. Anthropology asserted it-

[91] TsGAOR, f. 1377, op. 1, d. 45, ll. 36–42, 51–54, and 60–84, and d. 63, ll. 11–14.

[92] Bogoraz (-Tan), "O pervobytnykh plemenakh." See also P. E. Ostrovskikh, "Okhrana pervobytnykh plemen v sviazi s podniatiem ekonomicheskoi zhizni okrain,'" ZhN, no. 6 (1922). Ostrovskikh questioned the state's ability to compete with private traders and considered the reservation idea utopian, but he, too, believed that the natives' survival could only be ensured by ethnographers. Later he came out in support of Bogoraz, although with some reservations. See his "Addenda" to the second version of Bogoraz's project in ZhN, no. 3–4 (1923): 180–81.

[93] Bogoraz (-Tan), "Ob izuchenii i okhrane," pp. 176–77; TsGAOR, f. 1377, op. 1, d. 14, l. 2, and d. 45, l. 39.

self as a science of considerable practical importance, and anthropologists, particularly in the British Empire, were being used as advisors or responsible administrators. Many people felt that anthropology could, indeed, make a difference.[94]

In Russia, too, Soviet bureaucrats tended to be impressed by the ethnographers' enthusiasm, their claims to competence, and their obviously passionate interest in the matter. In fact, the positions of the two groups were remarkably close. The Bolshevik politicians-turned-ethnographers recognized the need for protecting the natives and training future officials in northern languages and anthropology, while the populist ethnographers-turned-politicians subscribed to the idea of progressive change brought from the outside. Many of them had shared the same Siberian exile, and most of them shared the same intellectual roots. Both distrusted local officials and, in slightly different terms, agreed about the backwardness and helplessness of the "native tribes." Both believed in evolution, progress, and the role of conscious intelligentsia in helping them along. As far as the role of the intelligentsia was concerned, Lenin's brand of Marxism was a dramatic return to the Russian intellectual tradition, and in the very special case of the "primitive tribes of the north," the Bolsheviks and the populists tended to agree on what that role should be. Said one old Bolshevik later accused of populism: "Raising the tribes of almost Neolithic reindeer breeders and hunters to the level of world civilization—what a difficult and yet fascinating task it was!"[95]

The Committee of the North: The Committee

After the formation of the Union of Soviet Socialist Republics the management of nationality matters was transferred to the new federal parliament. The Commissariat of Nationalities ceased to exist. So, legally speaking, did the "tribes of the northern borderlands." They were not properly constituted natonalities, did not have their own autonomy, and were not represented in any government bodies. Still, the ethnographers and some northern officials continued to speak on their behalf. Anatolii Skachko, a former exile, commander of the Second

---

[94] L. Ia. Shternberg, "Sovremennaia etnologiia. Noveishie uspekhi, nauchnye techeniia i metody," *E*, no. 1–2 (1926): 15–22; G. M. Foster, *Applied Anthropology* (Boston, 1969), pp. 184–94.

[95] P. G. Smidovich, "Sovetizatsiia Severa," *SS*, no. 1 (1930): 5.

Ukraininan Army during the Civil War, and the last head of the Narkomnats's Section of National Minorities, bombarded his Commissariat and Central Committee bosses with dire predictions that, "if things [did] not change, within ten years the peoples of Siberia [would] be totally extinct, and the immense tundra [would] turn into an uninhabited desert."[1] To drive the point home, Skachko dramatized the familiar "economic" argument by claiming that, not counting the already autonomous Buriat and Yakut, there were about five million natives in Siberia (in fact they were approximately 150,000), and that never in three hundred years had their exploitation "reached the shameless heights and forms that it did under the Soviet government."[2] The state had in effect granted full monopoly to the old Siberian merchants alias Soviet officials, who had "always been ruthless colonizers" and continued to treat the natives as "animals destined for exploitation by nature itself."[3] In other words, the new government was encouraging the very people who were undermining the government by "killing the hen [that is, the natives] which laid the golden eggs [that is, "precious metals, coal, graphite, . . . fur, . . . fish, valuable timber"]." More ominous, if the Whites were to attempt an invasion of the lower Ob' and Enisei, the hen could not be blamed for switching allegiances, because "the starving natives would take the side of anybody who would offer them a half-way decent exchange rate."[4] The solution sounded familiar: a national, Moscow-based organization should run northern affairs "directly through its own people, independent of Siberian authorities." Even the secret police would not have the right to arrest the agents of the new organization and the agents themselves would have limited terms of office because in the north "even the most honest workers end up as drunkards or thieves in a few years."[5] In the absence of such an autonomous central body, Skachko concluded, the north would lose its natives, and the Russian Republic would lose the north.[6]

The government of the Russian Republic could not ignore such arguments. "Taking into consideration the enormous political and economic importance of the northern borderlands," as well as the ne-

[1] TsGAOR, f. 3977, op. 1, d. 2, l. 2; TsGAOR, f. 1318, op. 1, d. 1001, l. 54; Skachko, "Piat' let," pp. 5–6.

[2] TsGAOR, f. 3977, op. 1, d. 2, l. 2.

[3] Ibid., l. 5.

[4] Ibid., ll. 3–4.

[5] Ibid., ll. 7–8.

[6] For similar arguments, see TsGAOR, f. 1377, op. 1, d. 45, ll. 42, 51–84, and d. 63. ll. 11–14.

cessity to "awaken the creativity of the tribes that inhabit the said borderlands" and to "protect their interests," on June 29, 1924, the Presidium of the All-Russian Central Executive Committee announced the creation of the Committee for the Assistance to the Peoples of the Northern Borderlands (the Committee of the North, for short).[7] The new body was headed by an old Bolshevik, assistant chairman of the Presidium of VtsIK, Petr Smidovich, and included several high-ranking Party officials: S. M. Dimanshtein, A. S. Enukidze, Emel'ian Iaroslavskii, P. A. Krasikov, L. B. Krasin, F. Ia. Kon, A. V. Lunacharskii, S. I. Mitskevich, and N. A. Semashko. As in the case of many other committees created in the mid-1920s, the big names were expected to compensate for the lack of a budget. The real work was to be done by the activists who had asked for it in the first place, most notably the Narkomnats's Anatolii Skachko and a group of scholars led by Bogoraz.[8]

The concensus that these people had reached in the early 1920s became the basis for the Committee's policies. The peoples of the northern borderlands (or the "small peoples of the north," as they were sometimes called to distinguish them from the administratively autonomous and politically self-assertive Yakut, Buriat, and Komi) did not have social classes and were all without exception victims of poverty and oppression. The prevailing view was expressed by P. I. Sosunov (the one arrested by the Tiumen' authorities for "separatist" activities on behalf of the aliens):

A hunter and fisherman with no reindeer . . . and an owner of a dozen thousand heads of reindeer, a master and his worker live in the same conditions, eat from the same trough, and even share the work of tending and protecting the reindeer in a relatively equal fashion. . . .

Although every Samoed dreams of owning his own herd and never stops collecting reindeer, he does not treat his herd as capital, as a means of obtaining profit and exploiting others (he has no notion of rational

---

[7] "Komitet sodeistviia narodnostiam severnykh okrain pri Prezidiume VTsIK," *SA*, no. 1–2 (1925): 136. The term *narodnost'* refers to small, usually preindustrial, ethnic groups. With the elaboration of Soviet theory of ethnic evolution, *narodnost'* came to denote a community situated above the tribe (primitive communism) but below the nation (formed under capitalism). In the 1920s and 1930s the term was used loosely in its colloquial meaning.

[8] The most prominent Russian ethnographer, L. Ia. Shternberg, was also a member, but he gave all of his time and energy to academic and pedagogical work and took no part in the Committee's activities.

economy). On the contrary, he gives the impression of collecting his reindeer especially for the next epizootic, which will inevitably ravage his household in one, two, or five years—certainly no later than in ten years. The nomad's reindeer herd is his guarantee against hunger and the elements.[9]

If that guarantee was no longer there, he could always count on the disinterested help of his more fortunate neighbors. The idea of class and exploitation was totally alien to the native way of life.[10] Even shamans did not constitute a separate caste. As N. Galkin explains, "They are not clergy needed for officiating religious rites. The shamans are the keepers of tradition and prejudice. They cure the sick, find out the will of the spirits, and stand guard against the machinations of the evil forces."[11] They were, in other words, no more exploiters than the lucky herdsman between the two epizootics and should by no means be equated with Orthodox or Catholic priests.[12] "Small" meant primitive, and primitive meant classless. All small peoples were equally primitive and classless.

From the time of Captain Sarychev and especially after Iadrintsev, these images had always contained a great deal of moral approbation. During NEP, they were music to the ears of the frightened and alienated urbanite. In Novitskii's words, "The native life is characterized by honesty, hospitality, and a lack of homeless children. Among the non-Russified ones, prostitution is completely unknown."[13] When this picture was challenged by a provincial radical who had detected class exploitation among the lower Ob' natives, the Committee leaders sternly reminded everyone concerned that "it would be totally incorrect to equate such economic differences with the classes of more developed countries. . . . The herdsman who happens to be rich today may easily lose all his reindeer tomorrow and become a pauper,

[9] P. I. Sosunov, "Tobol'skii Sever," SA, no. 4 (1925): 79. See also D. Dmitriev, "Severnce olenevodstvo i ego ekonomika," SA, no. 5–6 (1925): 105–6.

[10] Sosunov, "Tobol'skii Sever,' p. 79; G. M. Vasilevich, "Na Nizhnei Tunguske," SA, no. 5–6 (1926): 152.

[11] N. Galkin, V zemle polunochnogo solntsa (Moscow, 1929), p. 43.

[12] Leonov, "Tuzemnye sovety," p. 226.

[13] V. M. Novitskii, "Tuzemtsy Tobol'skogo Severa i ocherednye voprosy po ustroeniiu ikh zhizni," SA, no. 5–6 (1928): 69. To many middle-class city dwellers, importunate prostitutes and marauding gangs of teenage orphans were the most menacing symbols of the troubled times.

whereas a poor man may chance to catch a black fox . . . and easily obtain some reindeer."[14]

According to the official view, the only exploiters in the north were the Russians, so that the first task of the Committee was to "determine and reserve the territory necessary for the habitation and cultural development of every ethnic group in accordance with its way of life" and to ensure the protection of these territories from "predators" and "exploiters."[15] Due to the universal enthusiasm for the colonization and economic development of Asiatic Russia, however,[16] the idea of U.S.-style reservations had to be abandoned in favor of *natsional'noe raionirovanie*, or rather, the demarcation of ethnic boundaries (literally, "national districtization"). This was a standard element of the "Leninist nationality policy," which assumed that the Soviet federation consisted of ethnic groups, that all ethnic groups were entitled to their own duly demarcated territories, that all national territories should have political and cultural autonomy, and that the vigorous development of such autonomy was the only precondition for future unity. In theory, none of this applied to the small peoples because they were too classless and "cultureless" to be real nationalities, yet theory was not a serious obstacle when it came to protecting the small peoples from predators.[17] With large-scale industrialization still a slogan for the distant future, the fugitives from the overpopulated villages of European Russia continued to travel northward and eastward in search of land. In 1925, eighty percent, and in 1926, fifty percent of all new immigrants to Siberia arrived there illegally. Government resettlement offices could not and would not accommodate everybody, and most new settlers dealt with the native population as they saw fit.[18] As far as the Committee was concerned, however, the situation became even worse when the government began to take charge of the process and to

[14] See the editorial note to M. Nepriakhin, "Sotsial'naia podpochva pushnogo i rybnogo promyslov Tobol'skogo Severa," *SA*, no. 2 (1926): 40–50.

[15] TsGAOR, f. 1377, op. 1, d. 4, l. 13; "Komitet sodeistviia," pp. 136–37.

[16] See, for example, V. D. Vilenskii-Sibiriakov, "Zadachi izucheniia Severnoi Azii," *SA*, no. 1–2 (1925): 7–14; A. I. Notkin, "Severnyi morskoi put'," *SA*, no. 1–2 (1925): 28–43, and no. 4 (1925): 53–57, and V. I. Rubinskii, "Perspektivy kolonizatsii Sibiri," *SA*, no. 1–2 (1925): 132–33.

[17] TsGAOR, f. 1377, op. 1, d. 195, ll. 7–17, and d. 198, ll. 6–9, 47; P. G. Smidovich, "Soprovoditel'noe pis'mo mestnym komitetam severa," *SA*, no. 1–2 (1925): 130; "Soveshchanie sibirskikh komitetov sodeistviia malym narodnostiam," *SA*, no. 4 (1925): 88.

[18] V. I. Rubinskii, "Sovremennaia postanovka pereselencheskogo dela v Sibiri," *SA*, no. 3 (1927): 43–50, and "Pereselenie v Sibiri i na Dal'nem Vostoke," *SA*, no. 1 (1928): 13–26.

draw up ambitious plans for the orderly transfer of millions of new colonists to Siberia and the Far East.[19] Coping with official state-sponsored colonization proved much more difficult than complaining about illegal settlers. Unable to campaign against the ever bolder programs of economic development, the Committee urged the speediest possible completion of the demarcation work and demanded a significant supervising role for itself.[20] The need for such supervision continued to hinge on the assumption that only the well-adapted natives could successfully exploit the great natural wealth of the north. The Russian peasants-turned-polar-hunters were guilty of deserting the all-important front of grain production and disturbing the subtle balance of northern foraging patterns, whereas the Russians who had always been polar hunters were guilty of commercial exploitation.[21] Private trade was to be drastically curtailed and the sale of liquor and "trinkets" banned.[22] Local officials were, if possible, to be replaced by special instructors answering directly to the Committee, and all taxation was to be suspended.[23] Finally and most urgently, the Committee had to make sure that the small peoples receive food, guns, and ammunition. The policies of long-term credit and state "bread stores" were formally revived, and all Arctic "toilers" were encouraged to enter cooperatives, which the Committee regarded as the correct Soviet way of doing things as well as the best training ground for native self-government and self-defense.[24]

Protecting the helpless natives and keeping their body and soul together were necessarily the most pressing tasks of the moment, but the Committee's true and sacred vocation was to assist the small peoples

[19] TsGAOR, f. 1377, op. 1, d. 198, l. 47.

[20] TsGAOR, f. 1377, op. 1, d. 277, ll. 84–101; "Rasshirennyi [4th] plenum Komiteta Severa pri Prezidiume VTsIK," SA, no. 3 (1927): 77; N. I. Leonov, "Na fronte Krainego Severa," SA, no. 3 (1928): 96, 101–2; "Protokol zasedaniia rasshirennogo [5th] plenuma Komiteta Severa pri Prezidiume VTsIK," SA, no. 4 (1928): 120.

[21] N. Sushilin, "K voprosu o novoi granitse mezhdu Priangarskim kraem Kanskogo okruga i raionom Podkamennoi Tunguski," SA, no. 3 (1929): 120–21. See also V. D. Vilenskii-Sibiriakov, "Zadachi izucheniia malykh narodnostei Severa," E, no. 1 (1926): 55; Leonov, "Na fronte Krainego Severa," p. 92; and "Protokol zasedaniia rasshirennogo [5th] plenuma," pp. 121–22.

[22] TsGAOR, f. 1377, op. 1, d. 99; "Soveshchanie sibirskikh komitetov," p. 92; M. E Zinger, Osnovnye zakony po Krainemu Severu (Leningrad, 1935), pp. 91–94.

[23] TsGAOR, f. 1377, op. 1, d. 15, ll. 4, 19; "Rasshirennyi [2d] plenum Komuteta Severa," SA, no. 3 (1925): 121; "O nalogovykh l'gotakh plemenam, naseliaiushchim severnye okrainy SSSR," SA, no. 2 (1926): 86; Zinger, Osnovnye zakony, pp. 94–95.

[24] "Rasshirenyi [2d] plenum," pp. 114–15; "Soveshchanie sibirskikh komitetov," p. 92; "Itogi raboty Komiteta sodeistviia narodnostiam severnykh okrain pri Prezidiume VTsIK," SA, no. 3 (1926): 81.

in their difficult climb up the evolutionary ladder. Cultural progress meant getting rid of backwardness, and backwardness, in the very traditional view of the committee members, consisted of dirt, ignorance, alcoholism, and the oppression of women.

> The conditions in which the natives live seem to have been deliberately designed to make sure that they get sick and, having gotten sick, never recover. First of all, it is impassable dirt; bodies that are never washed; clothes that, once put on, are worn until they disintegrate from sweat and dirt; parasites; dishes that are not cleaned for years; smoked-filled tents; abrupt changes in temperature. Their food consists of half-raw unleavened flat rye bread, as well as meat and fish that even infants eat raw. And, of course, everyone without exception smokes tobacco.[25]

The author of this description advocated the old missionary method, which would again become popular in 1930: convert women first, for it is women who are the homemakers, the housekeepers, and the educators. In the 1920s, however, reaching women seemed almost impossible: the only native representatves were males, and the remote "smoke-filled tents" were rarely accessible because of the difficult terrain, ignorance of the language, and lack of emissaries. Hence the fight for hygiene was to be conducted by traveling medical detachments,[26] and the position of women was to be improved by the increasingly conscious men. An example was set by the resolution written on behalf of the natives at the First Native Congress of the Far Eastern Province:

> Having heard the report on the position of women under Soviet power we, the natives, have for the first time learned about the rights that the Soviet government has given to women. Only now do we understand just how hard the life of our women is. We approve of all the measures taken by the Soviet government in the sphere of women's emancipation and defense of women's rights and consider it inadmissible to continue keeping women in conditions of slavery, as has been the case until now.[27]

Back in the capital, few members of the Committee of the North believed in such a swift and thorough conversion. In their view, the way to the internalization of progressive notions lay through long-term education—eventually by native teachers in the local languages but for the

[25] L. Dobrova-Iadrintseva, "Puti k novomu bytu," OPS, no. 9 (1928): 49.

[26] "Rasshirennyi [2d] plenum," pp. 114–15; "Itogi raboty," p. 82.

[27] Dal'revkom, Pervyi etap mirnogo stroitel'stva na Dal'nem Vostoke, 1922–1926. Sbornik dokumentov (Khabarovsk, 1957), p. 203.

time being by Russian volunteers familiar with "local peculiarities." Elsewhere in the country, school-as-a-reflection-of-life was a popular revolutionary concept born in opposition to the formal education system prevalent under the old regime; in the north, it was an expression of the ethnographers' long-standing concern about the fragility of native culture. According to the plan, school activities should not disrupt the seasonal economic cycle, take children out of their environment, or promote hostility to traditional lifestyles. Their civilizing work must be gradual and ever so careful because an overly hasty assault on backwardness could result in the depopulation of a strategically important area (and, as many an ethnographer must have said to himself, the destruction of a unique way of life). There was a significant exception, however. Everyone agreed that to ensure correct progress through education, every ethnic group needed its own intelligentsia, and that meant that some children had to be trained faster and more thoroughly than others.[28]

Until then, however, someone had to lay the groundwork, spread the word, found the schools, recruit the students, and select the future elite. It was clear that given the constraints of budget, climate, and personnel, the Committee's traveling instructors could not even begin to perform so formidable a task, and the local officials could not be counted on to do anything for the "Asians." The creation of a sufficiently large network of independent stationary schools was altogether out of the question. The solution, as in so many other cases, was to be found in missionary practice, both foreign and domestic. Every important region and, ideally, every small people was to have its own "cultural station" (kul'tbaza)—a communist mission that would house a hospital, a veterinary center, a school, a museum, scientific laboratories, and a House of the Native, where local folks could relax with a cup of tea and a newspaper.[29] This way, a cold and hungry teacher or doctor would not have to chase the nomads all over the tundra; on the contrary, attracted by the useful services the station had to offer, the natives would come by themselves. Few in number, the stations might

[28] "Rasshirennyi [2d] plenum," pp. 113–14; Sosunov, "Tobol'skii Sever," p. 82; "Soveshchanie sibirskikh komitetov," p. 88; S. Gruzdev, "Novaia shkola dlia narodnostei Severa," SA, no. 5–6 (1925): 101–4; "Itogi raboty," p. 83; Leonov, "Na fronte Krainego Severa," p. 99; A. G. Bazanov and N. G. Kazanskii, Shkola na Krainem Severe (Leningrad, 1939), p. 75.

[29] TsGAOR, f. 1377, op. 1, d. 14, l. 3, 6; d. 19, ll. 11–12, 25–28; and d. 95, l. 28. Rasshirennyi [2d] plenum," pp. 105, 112–13; A. K. L'vov, "Kul'turnye bazy na Severe," SA, no. 3 (1926): 28–36.

not cover large areas right away—they would serve as examples, as magnets, as focal points of spreading civilization. "In the course of their everyday activities, they would create a local culture and train native Kulturträger."[30]

Finally, the Committee of the North—the first central organ of native administration in the history of the Russian empire—had to design an overall legal framework for its activities. The first attempt to codify new principles of native administration was made in the Far Eastern province in August 1924.[31] Over the next two years the central Committee of the North debated two versions of its own regulations,[32] and in October 1926 the Central Executive Committee and the Council of Peoples' Commissars of the Russian Republic ratified the final draft of *The Provisional Statute of the Administration of the Native Peoples and Tribes of the Northern Borderlands of the RSFSR.*[33]

It is remarkable (although given the Committee members' protectionism, not entirely surprising) to what extent this document, intended to ensure the smooth transition of the northern natives to Communism, was modeled after Speranskii's Statute of 1822. Intended for hunters, fishermen, and reindeer pastoralists who had no autonomous units of their own, it was based on the clan principle and allowed plenty of time for "catching up." General clan meetings were to elect clan soviets (*rodovye sovety,* formerly *rodovye upravleniia*) consisting of three members. The clan soviets' main function was to gather the statistical information requested by their superiors and maintain internal law and order. The primary units of native government kept their jurisdiction in all civil matters (except litigation over formally notarized acts and cases involving state interest and abuse of power by government officials) and in minor criminal cases. In all their judicial activity, the clan soviets were to follow their traditional customs unless such customs directly contradicted the Constitution of the Russian Republic (particularly singled out as unacceptable were punishments involving torture and humiliation). Such tolerance toward common law is worthy of note because at the very same time the government's legal

---

[30] Vilenskii-Sibiriakov, "Zadachi izucheniia malykh narodnostei Severa," p. 58.

[31] "Vremennoe polozhenie ob upravlenii tuzemnykh plemen, prozhivaiushchikh na territorii Dal'nevostochnoi oblasti," in Dal'revkom, *Pervyi etap,* pp. 175–80, and TsGAOR, f. 1377, op. 1, d. 45, ll. 56–59.

[32] SA, no. 1–2 (1925): 123–30; no. 3 (1926): 94–101.

[33] SA, no. 2 (1927): 85–91. For native judicial arrangements, see "Postanovlenie VTsIK i SNK RSFSR o vypolnenii sudebnykh funktsii organami tuzemnogo upravleniia narodnostei i plemen severnykh okrain RSFSR," SA, no. 1 (1928): 79–81.

assault on both the tribal and Islamic courts of Central Asia intensified dramatically.[34] As late as 1928, when the Soviet state declared an all-out war against tradition, the Committee of the North requested that the new law on "crimes constituting survivals of the tribal way of life" not be applied to the circumpolar peoples. According to the Committee's Fifth Plenum, in the north there were no vendettas, almost no murders, no abduction of women, no forced marriages, and no buying and selling of women (for the bridewealth was usually equal to the dowry).[35]

All clan soviets of a given district were to send their representatives to the district native congress, which was to elect the district native executive committee (tuzemnyi raionnyi ispolnitel'nyi komitet, abbreviated tuzrik). Roughly equivalent to the prerevolutionary inorodnye upravy, the tuzriki were directly responsible to the non-native district executive committees and were entrusted with supervising clan activities, passing on government orders, serving as courts of appeal, and fighting against illegal trade, exploitation, gambling, and alcoholism.

Thus, after almost ten years of debate and uncertainty the peoples of the north got back a slightly reshaped version of their old administrative system. Wandering aliens became natives, nomadic and settled aliens were on their own, and upravleniia became soviets, but the underlying principle of unhurried progress through cultural borrowing remained the same. The only revolutionary provision was the denial of the vote to former exploiters and members of the clergy, but this passage was copied whole from the RSFSR Constitution and, in its almost comic irrelevance to native life (no vote for monks, gendarmes, and rentiers), did not seem to apply.

Nor was administrative innovation one of the Committee's important goals. The key to progress lay in the hands of the well-trained and incorruptible new missionaries. As Bogoraz put it,

We must send to the North not scholars but missionaries, missionaries of the new culture and new Soviet statehood. Not the old ones but the young ones, not the experienced professors but the recent graduates, brought up in the new Soviet environment and ready to take to the North the burning fire of their enthusiasm born of the Revolution, as well as the practical skills perfected by revolutionary work. Before they begin their

[34] Gregory J. Massell, The Surrogate Proletariat: Moslem Women and Revolutionary Strategies in Soviet Central Asia, 1919–1929 (Princeton, N.J., 1974), pp. 204–6.
[35] "Protokol zasedaniia rasshirennogo plenuma Komiteta sodeistviia narodnostiam severnykh okrain pri Prezidiume VTsIK," SA, no. 4 (1928): 122.

work, these young agents of the Committee of the North must receive complete and thorough academic instruction—primarily in ethnography—but in the North their main work will be practical, not academic, in nature.[36]

By the time the *Provisional Statute* was ratified, the first detachment was already out there, ready for selfless work. They were the first of Shternberg's and Bogoraz's students, the first professionally trained field ethnographers in the history of the USSR, and the first missionaries of socialism to the primitive peoples of the north. They were fully aware of the great responsibility and, in the words of one of them, felt themselves fully prepared to "bring the sun" into the lives of the natives.[37]

The formal teaching of anthropology in Russia had begun at the University of Moscow in 1884 (under D. N. Anuchin). It concentrated on physical anthropology, geography, and archaeology and was administered by the Chair of Natural Sciences at the Department of Physics and Mathematics.[38] It was not until the turn of the century, when Shternberg returned from the Far East and organized a series of lectures at the St. Petersburg Museum of Ethnography, that ethnography as an autonomous "science of culture" made its appearance. The series was not officially recognized, but by 1915 Shternberg's untiring efforts on the academic and bureaucratic fronts bore fruit, and he became an instructor of ethnography at the newly created School for the Advanced Study of Geography. The school offered a new and very broad approach to education, but it offered no career (there were no diplomas or certificates of any kind), and a great majority of the students were women. The teachers were men and received no pay for their work.[39]

After the revolution the new education officials showed more understanding toward the exiles' science, and the school became a duly constituted Institute of Geography, divided into the Geography and Ethnography departments. Shternberg chaired the Ethnography department and, until his death in 1927, remained at the head of his field

[36] V. G. Bogoraz (-Tan), "Podgotovitel'nye mery k organizatsii malykh narodnostei," *SA*, no. 3 (1925): 48.

[37] Kreinovich, *Nivkhgu*, p. 13.

[38] K. I. Kozlova and N. N. Cheboksarov, "Etnografiia v Moskovskom universitete," *SE*, no. 2 (1955): 104–7. V. V. Bunak, who took over from Anuchin in 1923, retained the emphasis on physical anthropology.

[39] S. A. Ratner-Shternberg, "L. Ia. Shternberg i leningradskaia etnograficheskaia shkola 1904–1927 gg.," *SE*, no. 2 (1935): 134–38; N. I. Gagen-Torn, *Lev Iakovlevich Shternberg* (Moscow, 1975), pp. 120–53; TsGAOR, f. 1377, op. 1, d. 279, ll. 110–11.

both in rank and by professional acclaim. He was a frail but very intense man, a discoverer and crusader. He felt that the new science, which introduced meaning and reason into the history of mankind, had to be taught to every child in every school. "He who knows but one people does not know any; he who knows but one religion and one culture, does not know any."[40] Those who chose ethnography as their vocation should serve it faithfully and "never stray away from that path," for ethnography was not one subject among many: in a world of relative values and institutions it was the only science that had a global view of cultural evolution. "Ethnography is the crown jewel of the humanities"[41] because

> The science of culture is by its nature universal. It should include the full range of man's creativity, both in time and in space. In other words, it should include the culture of all the peoples of the world and of all stages of development, from the earliest periods to the present time. History should have been such a universal science, but up to now it has been studying only the top layer of mankind—the so-called historical peoples who have left literary texts and attained a relatively high degree of social development. Outside its scope is the huge portion of humanity which, due to certain conditions, has remained at a lower stage of cultural history.[42]

The goal of ethnography was to study culture in general and the nonliterate peoples in particular. It both included and was a part of history, sociology, archaeology, philosophy, folklore, linguistics, and the study of religion. Accordingly, along with various ethnology courses, the curriculum of Shternberg's department included all of the above disciplines plus traditional Sinology, Egyptology, and Oriental studies. A convinced evolutionist and a believer in the "psychic unity of mankind," Shternberg attributed backwardness to the environment. It was only natural, therefore, that his students were required to master the basics of physics, chemistry, anatomy, physiology, biology, and geology.[43] Finally Shternberg never waivered in his commitment to Mikhailovskian populism and the "subjective method." Culture may be affected by environment, but it is created by individuals. "Creativity is

---

[40] Quoted in N. I. Gagen-Torn, "Leningradskaia etnograficheskaia shkola v dvadtsatye gody. (U istokov sovetskoi etnografii)" SE, no. 2 (1971): 142.

[41] Ibid., pp. 142–43.

[42] Ratner-Shternberg, "L. Ia. Shternberg," p. 149.

[43] Ibid., pp. 140–41; Gagen-Torn, "Leningradskaia etnograficheskaia shkola," pp. 138–39.

unthinkable without intellect, and only individuals possess intellect."[44] Hence, another indispensable subject was psychology, an important course at the Institute and a prominent theme in Shternberg's own writings.[45]

In addition to receiving an encyclopedic education, the future missionaries were expected to acquire various practical skills that might be needed in the course of their travels. In 1922 Shternberg invited his colleague Bogoraz to join the faculty and take charge of this side of the curriculum (thus making even stronger the northern complexion of Russian ethnography). Temperamentally the direct opposite of Shternberg, Bogoraz was a big and jolly man greatly interested in matters practical and political. His main concerns as a teacher were linguistic competence and field experience, and he showed prodigious imagination as a fund-raiser, particularly for the many student expeditions that he organized. One of his more spectacular triumphs was the acquisition of scarlet liveries worn by former Winter Palace guards, to be used as gifts to native informants.[46]

The new science and its two charismatic champions proved popular. Between 1918 and 1922 the number of students grew from 577 to 1,530, the majority of them women.[47] There were also many young Jews who had flocked to the capitals from the former Pale. The story of Erukhim Kreinovich, the future expert on the Nivkh, is fairly typical. After the revolution he went to the N. G. Chernyshevskii School for Teenage Workers in Vitebsk, where in the course of his Marxist education, he became fascinated with Morgan's and Engels's theories of evolution. That led him to Shternberg, and Shternberg persuaded him that there was no higher calling than that of researcher and protector of the helpless and unspoiled people hitherto ignored by science. At the time of his graduation Kreinovich knew that obstacles and distances notwithstanding, he would follow in the footsteps of his deeply revered teacher, "the infinitely dear and beloved Lev Iakovlevich."[48] He would go to Sakhalin, "take any job available, and . . . study the life of the Nivkh."[49] In a similar spirit, Vladimir Ivanchikov wrote to Bogoraz, whose writings he had obviously found inspirational, that he would

---

[44] Ratner-Shternberg, "L. Ia. Shternberg," p. 150.
[45] See, for example, his late work, "Izbrannichestvo v religii," in E, no. 1 (1927): 3–56.
[46] Ratner-Shternberg, "L. Ia. Shternberg," pp. 141–43; Gagen-Torn, "Leningradskaia etnograficheskaia shkola," p. 140, and Lev Iakovlevich Shternberg, p. 169.
[47] Ratner-Shternberg, "L. Ia. Shternberg," p. 144.
[48] Kreinovich, Nivkhgu, p. 12.
[49] Ibid., p. 9.

learn the Chukchi language "and then go work long and hard in the 'country of those born of the White Sea Woman', continuing the work that [Bogoraz] started on the Kolyma in 1894."[50] The atmosphere at the institute was one of intense personal and professional loyalty, as well as the traditional populist blend of enthusiasm and preparation for martyrdom. The seminars were held in cold rooms by the light of kerosene lamps, and the students knew that they were, in the words of Kreinovich's father, "sending themselves into exile."[51]

Of the 1,530 students enrolled in 1922, only twelve were Bolsheviks.[52] As a result of the admission quotas introduced in 1923 that ratio changed very quickly, but the first cohorts that graduated in 1925–26 had been brought up on values far removed from Leninism, "proletarian" iconoclasm, or leather-jacket-and-revolver Civil War radicalism. The "Ten Commandments of an Ethnographer," formulated by Shternberg, enjoined the students to love science, be faithful to it, and protect its purity from plagiarism, careerism, and hasty conclusions. Old-fashioned to a fault, they concluded in the following manner:

Do not bear false witness to your neighbor or to other peoples and their character, rituals, customs, and mores. Love your neighbor more than you love yourself.

Do not impose your culture on the people you study. Approach them carefully and cautiously, with love and attention, whatever their stage of development, and they themselves will aspire to reach the level of higher cultures.[53]

The Committee of the North: The North

When the Committee's new agents (young and old) arrived in the north, they found that the situation was every bit as bad as they had been told. There were not enough guns, ammunition, fishing nets, cloth, flour, tobacco, or kettles. Reindeer herds had not recovered, and

---

[50] V. V. Antropova, "Uchastie etnografov v prakticheskom osushchestvlenii leninskoi natsional'noi politiki na Krainem Severe (1920–1930 gg.)," SE, no. 6 (1972): 24; Gagen-Torn, Lev Iakovlevich Shternberg, pp. 207–9.

[51] Kreinovich, Nivkhgu, p. 10. See also Gagen-Torn, Lev Iakovlevich Shternberg, pp. 172–88.

[52] Ratner-Shternberg, "L. Ia. Shternberg," p. 144.

[53] Gagen-Torn, "Leningradskaia etnograficheskaia shkola," p. 143, and Lev Iakovlevich Shternberg, p. 175.

the supply of fur-bearing animals continued to diminish. Many people were starving, and some were looking for work outside the traditional economy.[1]

In accordance with the Committee's policies and the ethnographers' assumptions, most emissaries saw the Russians as the greatest menace to the life and well-being of the native peoples. They reported on the continuing advance of the peasants, burning of forests, disappearance of animals, and indiscriminate year-round hunting.[2] Peasant settlers had been followed by an army of fortune-seekers, uprooted by the Civil War and encouraged by NEP. Gold prospectors had driven the Evenk from the Aldan area; Far Eastern officials were terrorizing the population along the Okhotsk coast as part of their border dispute with Yakutia; and in Kamchatka thousands of seasonal workers hired by Japanese-run fisheries were giving the natives liquor for furs—when they weren't stealing them outright.[3] In 1925 a large Evenk rebellion had to be put down by force.[4]

Most native trade was still in the hands of the old "friends," who used the usual methods and some of the old connections as they competed under the banners of various state and cooperative agencies.[5] Only now the staple colonial merchandise was not always available because of bans and shortages, and the "friends'" monopoly was no longer complete because some large companies tried to go over their

[1] TsGAOR, f. 1377, op. 1, d. 175, l. 54; A. Bonch-Osmolovskii, "Kamchatsko-Chukotskii krai," SA, no. 1–2 (1925): 86; S. A. Buturlin, "Polozhenie tuzemtsev Chukotsko-Anadyrskogo kraia," SA, no. 2 (1926): 90–91; "Itogi raboty," p. 81; "Etnograficheskie raboty Komiteta Severa," SA, no. 2 (1926): 98; Vasilevich, "Na Nizhnei Tunguske," p. 152; Leonov, "Na fronte Krainego Severa," p. 95; "Protokol zasedaniia rasshirennogo [5th] plenuma," p. 118; V. Egorov, "Bol'nye storony olenevodstva v Turukhanskom krae," OPS, no. 10 (1928): 46.

[2] See TsGAOR, f. 1377, op. 1, d. 150, ll. 22–30; "Etnograficheskie raboty," pp. 98–100; Vasilevich, "Na Nizhnei Tunguske," pp. 150–51; N. Amyl'skii, "Kogda zatsvetaiut zharkie tsvety," SA, no. 3 (1928): 55; T. Rastvorov, "Dva suglana," OPS, no. 10 (1928): 50–51; V. P. Zisser, "Brodiachie tungusy Charinskogo nagor'ia," ORS, no. 3 (1929): 52; Z. Gaisin, "Karagasskoe bol'shoe zimnee sobranie," ORS, no. 4 (1929): 10–11; and Sushilin, "K voprosu o novoi granitse," pp. 114–22.

[3] TsGAOR, f. 1377, op. 1, d. 64, l. 11; T. Akimova, "Poezdka na Aldanzoloto," SA, no. 2 (1927); G. G. Kolesov and S. G. Potapov, eds., Sovetskaia Iakutiia (Moscow, 1937), p. 138; V. I. Kantorovich, Po Sovetskoi Kamchatke: Kniga putevykh ocherkov (Moscow, 1931), pp. 24–30, 79, 131; B. M. Lapin, Tikhookeanskii dnevnik (Moscow, 1933), pp. 19, 98–122; Galkin, V zemle polunochnogo solntsa, p. 28; E. P. Orlova, "Koriaki poluostrova Kamchatki," SA, no. 3 (1929): 96.

[4] TsGAOR, f. 1377, op. 1, d. 65, ll. 1–2; TsGAOR, f. 5408, op. 1, d. 43, ll. 7, 6–8.

[5] D. Verbov, "Okolo samoedov," SA, no. 5–6 (1925): 165; "Plenum [3d] Komiteta Severa," SA, no. 3 (1926): 89; Akimova, "Poezdka na Aldanzoloto," p. 104; V. Shipikhin, "K sozdaniiu natsional'nykh tuzemnykh okrugov," SA, no. 5–6 (1929): 107–26.

heads and send their own representatives and cheaper goods far into the tundra. Still, the old settlers could be counted on to deliver the furs, and as long as that was the case, the provincial administrators did not mind the liquor trade, the collection of prerevolutionary debts, and illegal taxation.[6] Local officials were, of course, old settlers themselves.

One way to bypass the "predators" was to rely as much as possible on those large companies (such as Gostorg or AKO and OKARO in the Far East) which could afford to recruit their own nonlocal personnel; however, native trade with its enormous transportation costs proved unprofitable for the unwieldy and overextended operations based further south (with the possible exception of fishing, for which there was no local commercial market).[7] Part of the problem was the unwillingness of the imported agents to play by the local rules: they avoided traditional "friendship" arrangements, broke the laws of hospitality, and refused to provide their clients with long-term loans.

Indeed, why would the most diligent employee . . . get up in the middle of the night and open the gates for a freezing alien? Why would he wake up his wife, put the samovars on, warm up the soup, and give the alien food and shelter—just because he brought some furs? Let him wait outside. If he did not freeze during the three days and three nights that he has been on the road, surely he won't freeze now. If he could go without food for three days, surely he can wait one more day. After all, he [the agent] can't work day and night without a break.[8]

Next time, the trapper would probably stay away from the new agent, and before long the agent's employers would give up on the tundra as a serious source of income. As a result, the north was increasingly becoming the dumping ground for shoddy goods that could not be sold elsewhere. Trading posts were filled with scissors that did not cut, wicks that did not fit lamps, and binoculars through which nothing could be seen, as well as goods of less than vital importance in the tundra such as high-heeled shoes or mirrors decorated with pictures of naked women.[9] Furthermore, some basic necessities were not avail-

[6] Sosunov, "Tobol'skii Sever," p. 79; "Etnograficheskie raboty," pp. 98–100; T. Marin, "O sklokakh i travle spetsialistov na Severe," SS, no. 1 (1931): 53.

[7] Leonov, "Na fronte Krainego Severa," p. 95.

[8] TsGAOR, f. 1377, op. 1, d. 35, l. 11.

[9] TsGAOR, f. 1377, op. 1, d. 35, l. 7; d. 108, ll. 1–15; d. 170, l. 25; and d. 192, ll. 136–56. Also, Buturlin, "Polozhenie tuzemtsev," p. 92; "Itogi raboty," p. 81; Leonov, "Na fronte Krainego Severa," p. 96; "Protokol zasedaniia rasshirennogo [5th] plenuma," pp. 114, 118; E. P. Orlova, "Khoziastvennyi byt lamutov Kamchatki," SA, no. 5–6 (1928): 99.

able or arrived in the north in various stages of decomposition. "Even the bosses of [Russian] cooperatives, who had always smoked cigarettes of the highest quality, had to make do with the cheapest kinds of tobacco, sinking so low as to buy it from the 'friends' of the natives."[10] The natives, for their part, often had no tobacco and sometimes no food at all.[11] As one Chukchi said to a Russian contract agent, "It's not such a terrible thing that you have to drink your tea without sugar for one year, but we, who live here all our lives—we want our tea sweet."[12]

Another way to bypass the local dealers was to encourage the creation of native cooperatives, but they had little money and a very different approach to trade.[13] According to a Russian who was sent on an urgent mission to salvage one such operation, "If you've got your own store full of goods, no one should be left wanting. . . . Why ask the salesman if it's so much more fun to walk behind the counter, examine the merchandise, touch everything, dip your fingers in butter casks, and then suck your greasy fingers. Meanwhile, the salesman, full of dignity and self-importance, is sitting solemnly in his chair, pencil behind his ear, writing down who takes what."[14]

As various economic and administrative measures continued to fail, most native peoples continued to be worse off than they had been before the revolution (or so many of them claimed). In the words of some Kamchatka Even, "We'd gotten used to bread, and tea, and tobacco, and to wearing shirts, too, so it's kind of embarassing without all that, and we get sad and upset when there's nothing to buy."[15] Also, according to the Even's neighbors the Koriak, "We're real scared of taxes. In 1923 they ruined us completely: we had to sell our last *kukhliankas* to pay the taxes. We sold our boots and all our clothes; and there are almost no reindeer left; and we ourselves have become so skinny—we have no bellies any more, and our cheeks are sunken like this. . . . We're mighty scared of taxes."[16]

The Committee was anxious to help but had no resources to do so.[17]

[10] Gaisin, "Karagasskoe bol'shoe zimnee sobranie," p. 8.
[11] Leonov, "Na fronte Krainego Severa," p. 96; "Protokol zasedaniia rasshirennogo [5th] Plenuma," pp. 114, 118; Orlova, "Khoziastvennyi byt lamutov Kamchatki," p. 99.
[12] Galkin, *V zemle polunochnogo solntsa*, p. 191.
[13] "Rasshirennyi [2d] plenum," p. 104; "Protokol zasedaniia rasshirennogo [5th] plenuma," p. 120.
[14] Vesnovskii, "Mashel-Pel'tesh," *ORS*, no. 6 (1929): 25.
[15] Orlova, "Khoziastvennyi byt lamutov Kamchatki," p. 99.
[16] Orlova, "Koriaki poluostrova Kamchatki," p. 87.
[17] TsGAOR, f. 1377, op. 1, d. 19, l. 8, and d. 34, l. 4; "Protokol zasedaniia rasshirennogo [5th] plenuma," p. 111; Skachko, "Piat' let," pp. 6–10.

It had been conceived as a "consultative body," but consulting did not amount to much when it came to putting pressure on trading companies or giving financial assistance to native cooperatives. Most of the Committee's resolutions expressed a desire to ask the Central Executive Committee to prevail on various people's commissariats to invest more in the native areas, or else to ask local committees of the north to try and convince provincial officials to respect the *Provisional Statute*.[18] Most of these pleas were ignored. With no power to enforce its decisions and no marketable assets to offer, the Committee of the North had little clout as a lobbying institution. The agencies it appealed to had either no interest in the native northerners or, indeed, a very strong interest in trying to absorb or remove them. One needed a great deal more influence than the Committee of the North could muster in order to convince the Resettlement Agency to compensate the natives it had dispossessed; the provincial executive committees, to finance the clan soviets they considered irrelevant; and the Commissariat of Enlightenment, to build enormously expensive schools for elusive nomads who refused to attend them.[19] The idea of taxing northern enterprises (based as it was on some unarticulated notion of indigenous sovereignty) had become almost ludicrous, and the talk about taxing the northern peoples themselves seemed to undermine the whole project as well as being "extraordinarily difficult to explain to the natives."[20]

Under these conditions, the "missionaries of the new culture" became the Committee's only real hope. The teachers, historians (*kraevedy*), and other Committee employees and sympathizers persevered in the face of Moscow's impotence and surrounding hostility,[21] and the young graduates thought of themselves as both apostles and pioneers. According to one admiring report, Bogoraz's students A. S. and K. M. Forshtein "are prepared to live in a Chukchi *iaranga*, in the

[18] See, for example, TsGAOR, f. 1377, op. 1, d. 192, ll. 19–31; "Otchet o deiatel'nosti Komiteta Severa pri Prezidiume VTsIK za aprel'–oktiabr' 1926 g.," SA, no. 1 (1927): 119; "Protokol zasedaniia rasshirennogo [5th] plenuma," pp. 112–13; and Skachko, "Piat' let," pp. 6–10.

[19] "Rasshirennyi [4th] plenum," pp. 78–80; "Protokol zasedaniia rasshirennogo [5th] plenuma," pp. 112–13.

[20] TsGAOR, f. 1377, op. 1, d. 277, ll. 48–60.

[21] Particularly active among them were I. M. Suslov (university-trained ethnographer, amateur composer, Shternberg's disciple, army officer, Red commander, opera conductor, museum director, fur trader, and Committee member), D. E. Lappo (People's Will member, Siberian exile, judge, Krasnoiarsk Duma member, fiction writer, professor, Soviet prisoner, and Eniseisk soviet legal consultant), Iukhnevich (economist, former exile, and Tomsk regional museum employee), and Dvorakovskii (former officer and teacher). TsGAOR, f. 1377, op. 1, d. 147, ll. 8–22, and d. 175, ll. 30–31.

same way as do the Chukchi. They are not deterred by the fact that, for three years, they may not see a single European face."[22] Another graduate, N. B. Shnakenburg, declared: "I will go to the most remote wilderness, to the Vankarem river. I have full confidence in myself and in my work."[23] Over a year later, he wrote from his temporary winter quarters in Korf bay: "I am still unable to get to my place of work. Looks like we are going very far indeed. The steamer *Kolyma* may not stop at Cape Severnyi, but I will jump off anywhere in Chukotka and get there somehow. I am not the kind to go back."[24] He got there all right, and so did most of his classmates. They became teachers, interpreters, or census takers, and they took their responsibilities as protectors of the natives very seriously.[25] They taught them the mysteries of civilization, tried to organize them politically, and reported to the Committee on settler activities. One young researcher gave a special talk in which he explained to the local officials that the criminal code was not applicable to the natives if it contradicted their common law (the *Provisional Statute* held the reverse to be true).[26]

Trained professionals were to be the wave of the future. For the time being, however, the government, the Committee of the North, and various ministries and trading organizations active in the north tried their best to lure volunteers by offering them lucrative contracts, high salaries, and pension benefits.[27] Others were drawn by exotic visions of distant lands and savage tribes; some hoped to profit from native trade; and yet others were cheated by recruiting agents who were paid according to the number of people they hired.[28] A few people volunteered for the Far East in order to escape to America: two of Chukotka's young teachers were such would-be refugees who had decided that the high northern salaries were a surer way to success (and a college education) than the hazardous trip to Alaska.[29] Another teacher confessed: "Leaving for the North, I wanted to do a lot of duck and goose hunting, as well

[22] "K organizatsii pervykh tuzemnykh shkol na severnom poberezh'e Chukotskogo poluostrova," SS, no. 1 (1931): 51; Skachko, "Piat' let," pp. 6–10.

[23] Antropova, "Uchastie etnografov," p. 24.

[24] "K organizatsii pervykh tuzemnykh," p. 51.

[25] Antropova, "Uchastie etnografov," pp. 21–23; "Etnograficheskie raboty," pp. 96–100; Gagen-Torn, *Lev Iakovlevich Shternberg*, pp. 199–209; TsGAOR, f. 1377, op. 1, d. 32, ll. 61–62; d. 306, ll. 77–82.

[26] "Etnograficheskie raboty."

[27] TsGAOR, f. 1377, op. 1, d. 192, ll. 54–55, and d. 213, ll. 5–6; "Protokol zasedaniia VI rasshirennogo plenuma Komiteta Severa," SA, no. 3 (1929): annex, p. 7.

[28] Kantorovich, *Po Sovetskoi Kamchatke*, pp. 14–28; Lapin, *Tikhookeanskii dnevnik*, pp. 19, 21.

[29] Lapin, *Tikhookeanskii dnevnik*, pp. 47–48.

as sturgeon and sterlet fishing because I considered myself an expert sportsman."[30]

Most of these volunteers did not know what they were in for. (The hunting expert "did not kill a single duck, not to mention a goose.")[31] None of them received personal instructions from Professor Bogoraz, and few of them had ever heard either his name or those of the peoples among whom they were supposed to work. Their encounter with the north was a shock. "The [Chukotka] coast presented a most depressing sight: bare tundra, black mountains in the distance, no signs of life. . . . The employees whom the ship left at the trading point looked gloomy, especially the wives. It seemed a desert island."[32] For some of them, it never got better. According to one eloquent statement,

> It is a fallacy to think that work in the north is nothing but heroism and romanticism. . . . Try to spend a whole year as a nomad—for that is how the doctors and veterinarians of traveling detachments live. A whole year in a chum or a iaranga, in fifty below zero weather; endless blizzards that for days on end prevent you from venturing outside; inescapable smoke from the fire; inescapable dirt; no chance to wash yourself; and long weeks without taking off your coat, filled with lice. Just try to do research or treat patients when medicine freezes solid and instruments fall out of your numb fingers. . . . In the winter you shiver from the cold and cannot breathe because of the smoke, and in the summer you cannot breathe because of the mosquito nets or else you walk around in a dense cloud of bugs and mosquitoes, which get into your nose, eyes, and ears, and will not let you open your mouth. The only salvation is once again the dense smoke from the fire. All this has very little of heroism and a great deal of discomfort.[33]

Doctors had no hospitals and teachers had no school buildings. The few existing ones had no roofs, windows, or furniture.[34] In some places even the employees of state trade organizations survived on tea and bread alone and suffered from scurvy.[35] The diary of one such employee recorded a truly desperate question: "Will there ever be an end

[30] Bazanov and Kazanskii, Shkola na Krainem Severe, p. 120.

[31] Ibid.

[32] Galkin, V zemle polunochnogo solntsa, p. 33. Cf. T. Z. Semushkin, Chukotka (Moscow, 1941), p. 8.

[33] Marin, "O sklokakh i travle," p. 52.

[34] T. Sinitsyn, Pod voi purgi. Zapiski o shkole za poliarnym krugom (Moscow-Leningrad, 1929), pp. 13–20; Bazanov and Kazanskii, Shkola na Krainem Severe, p. 70.

[35] D. Kytmanov, "Tuzemtsy Turukhanskogo kraia," SA, no. 3 (1927): 39.

to the biting frost, cold nights, endless white haze, sleds, and dogs?"[36]
The local agents of the Committee of the North were even worse off.
Their salary was one-third of the salary of state trading officials, and
those of them who ventured out of the towns did so at their own risk
and expense.[37] Of the relatively small first group of young ethnographers, Georgii Kaminskii died of typhoid on the Lower Ob', Vladimir
Ivanchikov (the one who wanted to continue Bogoraz's work) drowned
in Chukotka, Pavel Moll succumbed to tuberculosis, and Natal'ia Kotovshchikova died of cold and starvation somewhere on the Iamal peninsula.[38]

In these conditions, not only the ethnographers but many of the new
cadres had no choice but to sleep, eat, and work in the "smoke-filled
tents" of the native peoples. Unwarned and unprepared, they resented
the "unbelievable filth" of their surroundings and watched in total con-
sternation as the Chukchi, for example, ate lice or used the same bowls
to relieve themselves and to serve food.[39] Even the most earnest, curious, and romantically inclined of the untrained volunteers did not last
long in what seemed like the worst kind of prison. As agent Galkin
put it, "I've had enough of these *iarangas*. Let somebody else look for
excitement and get to know the way of life of the Chukchi people."[40]

And yet the cold and the dirt were "not the hardest or the most unpleasant things."[41] According to both ethnographers and laymen, that
distinction belonged to the local Russian officials. Absolute rulers over
tens of thousands of miles of sparsely populated territory, the old-
settler chairmen of district executive committees did all they could to
harrass the unwelcome outsiders.

The reasons were many. First of all, the new emissaries tended to
dislike and despise their fellow countrymen who had "gone native."
What may have been understandable or even fascinating in "Asians"
and yesterday's aliens was an affront to civilization when coming from
a Russian. In fact, the old settlers were not true Russians. They talked
funny, dressed funny, and lived in a dark world of superstition, cruelty,
promiscuity, and drunkenness. The same beliefs and practices seemed

[36] Galkin, *V zemle polunochnogo solntsa*, p. 175. See also pp. 66–67 and Lapin, *Tik-hookeanskii dnevnik*, pp. 97–98.
[37] Skachko, "Piat' let," p. 9.
[38] V. G. Bogoraz (-Tan), *Voskresshee plemia* (Moscow, 1935), p. 178; Kreinovich, *Nivkhgu*, p. 460.
[39] Galkin, *V zemle polunochnogo solntsa*, pp. 80–83, 113–14.
[40] Ibid., p. 172. See also TsGAOR, f. 1377, op. 1, d. 192, l. 56.
[41] Marin, "O sklokakh i travle," p. 52. See also Skachko, "Piat' let," p. 21.

"natural" (albeit backward) in a smoke-filled tent but totally out of place—if not disloyal—in a Russian hut (or tent). In addition, most old settlers lived off native trade and were, therefore, exploiters. The Committee of the North, always mindful of the uniqueness and adaptive resourcefulness of native cultures, described the old-settler way of life as "unbearable, predatory, and uncultured."[42]

Such an attitude did not bode well for fruitful collaboration. The central agencies made it quite clear that they wanted as little dependence on the old settlers as possible. The medical detachments and the cultural stations were supposed to have their own budgets and were not to be subordinated to the local authorities. For their part, the old settlers had a long-standing tradition of mistrusting "Russians" of every description. Thus, Aleksandr Forshtein, the intrepid ethnographer who, together with his wife, was prepared to spend three years "without seeing a single European face," was universally hated by the local "Europeans" who assumed that "this red-haired, long-nosed rat was probably writing a denunciation."[43] According to another report, an "unbalanced and illiterate revolutionary committee chairman was chasing his literate secretary. . . . all over Gizhiga with a revolver, accusing him of counterrevolution." Allegedly, the secretary had maliciously submitted a written statement for "final editing."[44]

Particularly annoying was the newcomers' preoccupation with the natives. It seemed unreasonable under any circumstances, but at that time of economic crisis wasting money on native schools, hospitals, or tea rooms was obviously seen by many as a deliberate provocation.[45] The jealously guarded administrative and financial independence of these institutions was an obvious challenge to the people used to being masters of "their own" districts. Finally, the very appearance in the tundra of relatively large sums of money and medical supplies, including alcohol, was often a temptation impossible to resist.[46]

All over the north, the "old" officials declared war on the new ones. In one district, between the summer of 1927 and the summer of 1928 five doctors in a row were driven out of their jobs amid accusations of illegal fur trade, embezzlement, stealing of alcohol, incorrect personnel

---

[42] "Rasshirennyi [2d] plenum," p. 111. See also TsGAOR, f. 3977, op. 1, d. 301, ll. 67–75.

[43] Lapin, Tikhookeanskii dnevnik, p. 80.

[44] TsGAOR, f. 1377, op. 1, d. 306, l. 146.

[45] Leonov, "Tuzemnye sovety," pp. 247–48, and "Tuzemnye shkoly na Severe," in Sovetskii sever, p. 204.

[46] Ibid., p. 70; "Rasshirennyi [2d] plenum," p. 111; Marin, "O sklokakh i travle."

policies, faulty accounting, and unnecessary trips into town, among other things. Three of the doctors left (one was officially exonerated by the Health Commissariat); a fourth committed suicide; and, at the time of the investigation, a fifth was writing desperate letters from prison asking to be allowed to go to the provincial center and prove his innocence.[47] In another district a certain Doctor Mukharshev refused to share hospital alcohol with the local officials. He was accused of seducing a nurse (with the help of a half-gallon bottle of potent aphrodisiac), fired, thrown out of his apartment and eventually sentenced to two years in prison (the alcohol was duly consumed by the arresting officers). When Mukharshev's complaint reached the attorney general's office via the Committee of the North, the case was dropped and the "nearly demented" doctor was freed.[48]

Charges of sexual misconduct had always been popular with provincial officials trying to get rid of troublesome outsiders. In the far north of the Tobol'sk province School Principal Bobrov was also accused of harrassing a local female. In his telegram addressed to two people's commissariats, the Committee of the North, and the attorney general he compared the area's "spiritual climate" to the "climate of the polar tundra" and begged for urgent help and protection. In the Taz district, Doctor Norkina was charged with prostitution, performing illegal abortions, and bribing the natives because she insisted on sticking to the central policy of recruiting native trainees rather than hiring the relatives of the local Party boss. She was severely beaten and forced to move to a Nenets dugout. Her native protégés were kicked out of the hospital.[49]

Some missionaries of the new culture fought and won their battles. Erukhim Kreinovich was driven out of western Sakhalin but did not quit and even organized a school on the east coast.[50] Many more fled, despaired, or started drinking.[51] In the words of one veterinarian from Karagassia, "I can't stand this any more. . . . I'm simply scared. My health is poor, and my nerves are completely shot."[52]

All these difficulties—the climate, the diet, and the "spiritual cli-

---

[47] Marin, "O sklokakh i travle," pp. 54–56.

[48] Ibid., pp. 57–58. See also TsGAOR, f. 3977, op. 1, d. 301, l. 56.

[49] Marin, "O sklokakh i travle," pp. 59–61.

[50] Bogoraz (-Tan), *Voskresshee plemia*, p. 207; Gagen-Torn, *Lev Iakovlevich Shternberg*, pp. 220–21.

[51] "Rasshirennyi [2d] plenum," p. 111; Bazanov and Kazanskii, *Shkola na Krainem Severe*, p. 120; TsGAOR, f. 3977, op. 1, d. 300, l. 99.

[52] Marin, "O sklokakh i travle." See also TsGAOR, f. 3977, op. 1, d. 301, l. 56.

mate"—were usually referred to as the "conditions of existence." But there was also the "work among the natives"—the ostensible and some-times real reason for being in the North and the high purpose that made the suffering worthwhile. To those few who could overcome the diffi-cult conditions, this work presented some very formidable challenges.

First of all, the implementation of the *Provisional Statute*, or rather, the reintroduction of order into the system of native administration, proved much more difficult than expected. Most local Russians op-posed or ignored native self-government, and district executive com-mittees refused to spend their limited resources on clan soviets.[53] Provincial bodies, which were supposed to supervise the work in the districts, were either too far away or had more important things to do. After the publication of the Far Eastern Statute the Khabarovsk execu-tive committee refused to organize clan soviets because it would spoil the election campaign statistics.[54]

The universal application of the clan principle was just as impos-sible now as it had been under Speranskii. Inspectors working with the Nenets in the Arkhangel'sk province and the Even of the Okhotsk coast discovered that members of the same clan had different migration routes. Accordingly, clan soviets were replaced by territorial ones (known as tundra or island soviets among the Nenets and nomadic soviets among the Even).[55] On examining the Amur peoples scat-tered among the growing number of Russian settlements, the local au-thorities decided to organize "native soviets" subordinated directly to Russian districts.[56] In Narym, another area of peasant migration, no one even bothered with native self-government. There the only ad-ministrative organs were village soviets and Russian-dominated "mixed soviets," which leased native fishing sites and lifted hunting prohibitions.[57]

As usual, the Chukchi and Koriak presented special problems. The local authorities were reconciled to the absence of clans, but they

[53] "Protokol zasedaniia rasshirennogo [5th] plenuma," p. 112; Leonov, "Tuzemnye so-vety," pp. 247–48.

[54] Dal'revkom, *Pervyi etap*, p. 190.

[55] Leonov, "Tuzemnye sovety," pp. 225, 230; V. A. Zibarev, "Sovetskoe stroitel'stvo u malykh narodnostei Severa (1927–1930)," in *Sibir' v period stroitel'stva sotsializma i perekhoda k kommunizmu* (Novosibirsk, 1966), 6:41; Popova, *Eveny*, pp. 224–25.

[56] Ch. M. Taksami, "Ustanovlenie sovetskoi vlasti i organizatsiia sovetov sredi niv-khov," in *Velikii Oktiabr' i malye narody Krainego Severa* 353 (1967): 39–40; Leonov, "Tuzemnye sovety," p. 235.

[57] Leonov, "Tuzemnye sovety," pp. 231, 247. Cf. A. Voronin, "Zhizn' evenkov-murchenov," *TT*, no. 1 (1928): 23–24; Zibarev, *Sovetskoe stroitel'stvo*, pp. 157–60.

hoped to introduce some form of administrative control by organizing the so-called encampment committees *(lagerkomy)*. [58] As one such organizer wrote in 1927, success was very limited: "Upon my arrival in the encampment, I invited the whole population to Rishchip's *iaranga* and declared that they ought to elect their representatives to the encampment committee. To this they replied that they did not need any committee because they had always lived without a representative, and that if they elected one, the number of walruses would not grow."[59]

Another organizer of the Chukchi reported that would-be representatives or soviet chairmen refused the honor because "people will laugh." "We are all equal," they would say, "and there can be no bosses among us." The organizer concluded that the sovietization of the nomads would have to remain minimal because of "the absolute lack of any form of self-government."[60]

Even in those areas where the clan principle seemed to fit, the introduction of the soviet system ran into difficulties. Among the Avam Nganasan, "the change from clan administration to clan soviets" meant the arrival of a meddlesome district instructor, unneeded trips to faraway meeting places, and a partial redistribution of the much-resented cart duty. At a subsequent council, the Nganasan declared: "we have resolved to go on without the clan soviet because it was imposed on us by force."[61] As for the native executive committee, they said, "We do not understand why it is being created and fear that it will become a tool in the hands of the Dolgan and the Yakut to put pressure on us, the Samoed. That is why we are asking if we owe the instructor the same kind of unquestioning obedience that we used to give the police."[62]

Assured that they did not, the Nganasan refused to have an executive committee, saying that they would like to wait and see how things developed.

> We spoke like that because the instructor had told us that now we were free and could say what we thought. We asked him to explain once again what an executive committee was, so that we could later explain it to our kinsmen. While we were saying all this, the instructor interrupted us, yelling "here they go again," and when we were through, he told us: "You

---

[58] One group of officials did decide that to introduce clan soviets among the Koriak they had to start by organizing clans. See TsGAOR, f. 1377, op. 1, d. 123, l. 2.

[59] Lapin, *Tikhookeanskii dnevnik*, p. 36.

[60] *Revkomy*, pp. 196–97. See also TsGAOR, f. 1377, op. 1, d. 170, ll. 22–23.

[61] Leonov, "Tuzemnye sovety," pp. 238–39.

[62] Ibid., p. 234.

old men are sticking to the old law, believe in god, and go against the soviet regime. If you continue in this way, soldiers from Krasnoiarsk will come here with guns and lock you up in an iron box." We got scared and stopped talking, so that the meeting ended in silence."[63]

One way or another, on paper and sometimes in reality, most native northerners ended up with some sort of local soviet.[64] The usefulness of these local soviets as defenders of native interests against the old settlers and as enforcers of government policies was minimal. Indeed, there was no reason why the clan soviets should have been any more successful in this regard than their prerevolutionary predecessors were. The balance of power between the settlers and the natives had not changed, central support was slow to materialize, and even when the political skills of native representatives were deemed improved, there was no money for bargaining (several attempts to introduce native "self-taxation" had failed).[65]

Native groups themselves had no reason to believe that their relationship with the state was any different. Accordingly, clan soviets consisted of the same elders who had served as chiefs under the old regime.[66] Russians responsible for carrying out the reform were continually frustrated by the natives' "lack of understanding" of the new democratic principles of local government. The "toilers of the tundra" applied the new cumbersome names to familiar realities, and phrases like "I am the clan soviet" or "The executive committee is out fishing" were just as common as they were exasperating to the reformers.[67] The activities of such soviets were quite traditional, as witnessed by the following report of the Taz Nenets soviet for 1927:

After the elections Comrades Iamkin and Lyrmin became members of the clan soviet; after which we, namely Iamkin, received from the old clan soviet the box with documents, the old stamp, and the badge of the chairman of the clan soviet. During the whole time we had three meet-

[63] Ibid., p. 240.

[64] Zibarev, Sovetskoe stroitel'stvo, pp. 133–53.

[65] Leonov, "Tuzemnye sovety," p. 248; "Protokol zasedaniia rasshirennogo [5th] plenuma," p. 112.

[66] Sosunov, "Tobol'skii Sever," p. 81; P. Tyvlianto, "Rabota kochevykh sovetov v Chukotskom natsional'nom okruge," TT, no. 4 (1932): 6; Popova, Eveny, pp. 221–22, 226; Zibarev, Sovetsoe stroitel'stvo, pp. 163–64.

[67] TsGAOR, f. 1377, op. 1, d. 224, ll. 8, 32; Amyl'skii, "Kogda zatsvetaiut zharkie tsvety," p. 58; Leonov, "Tuzemnye sovety," p. 242; Popova, Eveny, p. 223; P. G. Smidovich, "Sovetizatsiia Severa," SS, no. 1 (1930): 6; Zibarev, Sovetskoe stroitel'stvo, pp. 174–76.

ings and five trials. There were no diseases among the people, and the reindeer were well, too. Hunting was good and continues to be just fine. Everybody is okay. In the summer somebody set the tundra on fire and we were in danger. I had to get the people together to put the fire out. There were no trips to the district executive committee due to its remoteness. I carried out only the spoken orders of the executive committee, while the written ones have remained unread because there is no secretary and no literate people. Children have not been sent to school because the parents refused. Apart from that, I didn't go anywhere and didn't do anything.[68]

The only way to ensure that the native soviets acted on government instructions and kept up with the required paperwork was to provide them with Russian secretaries. This was an old practice legitimated by the *Provisional Statute*, and it had the obvious—and long-proven—disadvantage of banishing all hope of "genuine self-government" and handing the soviets over to the old settlers (new cadres were still too few to be seriously considered).[69]

With or without secretaries, most native groups heard the government's message only during rare (usually election-time) visits by district instructors. Even then what they heard was not necessarily what the instructor had to say. In the recollection of one Leningrad-educated Chukchi,

During an election campaign there comes an instructor who does not know a word of Chukchi and speaks through an interpreter who, not knowing scientific terms, says something completely different. . . . After that the instructor leaves a whole pile of directives and instructions, which the chairman of the soviet receives and puts in a sack, and there they remain until a year later somebody else comes from the district executive committee. And if, for example, the executive committee sends in directives in envelopes, nobody opens them because they are inside the envelopes and the chairman is afraid to open them.[70]

Many instructors were content to limit their activities to such visits and occasional one-way correspondence. Some obviously assumed that there was no alternative: "Because of the living conditions of the

[68] Zibarev, *Sovetskoe stroitel'stvo*, p. 169.

[69] Amyl'skii, "Kogda zatsvetaiut zharkie tsvety," pp. 57–58; Leonov, "Tuzemnye sovety," pp. 241, 246, 248.

[70] Tyvlianto, "Rabota kochevykh sovetov," p. 16. See also Popova, *Eveny*, pp. 218–20.

population, the election campaign had to be limited. All I could do was inform the population through several influential groups."[71]

Particularly vexing was the statute's only revolutionary innovation, the disenfranchisement of exploiters. In the words of the same Kamchatka instructor,

> According to the general instruction on the election campaign, the disenfranchised category among the nomadic natives was to consist primarily of shamans, but due to the fact that the problem of shamanism among the peoples of the North has not yet been sufficiently studied, the classification of shamans as opposed to regular natives who know how to beat on the tambourine is no easy task. There is no question that native shamanism represents a cult with some quackish tendencies, but that shamanism is a source of livelihood for a certain category of people is a question that requires detailed study. For the above reasons I had to abstain from disenfranchising the said category. In any case, it would have been impossible to do because in every tent you can find one or two tambourines that serve cult purposes and that the owner of the place beats on in his free time.[72]

Other officials would not relent and insisted on compliance, some because they had a different temperament, and others because they dealt with peoples like the Evenk or the Tofalar who seemed to have professional shamans. This and other forms of uncompromising assault on traditional ways resulted in silence, flight, or resistance. Orders to register civil status were ignored; shamans refused to surrender their regalia; and women were not allowed to attend meetings.[73] One newly appointed manager of a state trading post decided to put an end to the customary and, from a townsman's point of view, economically unsound practice of providing indefinite long-term credits. His Eskimo clients tied him up and helped themselves to the goods.[74] Elsewhere, the Avam Nganasan declared that if the instructor who had threatened them with an iron box kept his job, there would be no more soviet meetings.[75]

[71] Revkomy, p. 194. See also Popova, Eveny, pp. 221, 222.
[72] Revkomy, p. 194.
[73] TsGAOR, f. 1377, op. 1, d. 150, l. 32; I. M. Suslov, "Sotsial'naia kul'tura u tungusov basseina Podkamennoi Tunguski i verkhov'ev r. Taimury," SA, no. 1 (1928): 60; Amyl'-skii, "Kogda zatsvetaiut zharkie tsvety," pp. 54, 58–59; Leonov, "Tuzemnye sovety," pp. 234, 239–41; Galkin, V zemle polunochnogo solntsa, p. 131; Gaisin, "Karagasskoe bol'shoe zimnee sobranie," p. 10.
[74] Galkin, V zemle polunochnogo solntsa, p. 31.
[75] Leonov, "Tuzemnye sovety," p. 239.

Attempts to hasten progress through the courts led to similar results. The native northerners continued to use Russian legal institutions (now represented in the north by people's courts) when they considered their elders' decisions unfair or when they had no power to enforce them; however, they accepted Russian help only if it made sense in terms of common law. Thus, when a Pur Nenets woman was abducted and her husband received only half of the original bridewealth (one reindeer instead of two), he formally sued the offender. The Russian court announced that bridewealth was illegal and ordered the plaintiff to return the one reindeer that he still had. On leaving the court the two men agreed that the decision was ridiculous and that taking the case to court had been a mistake.[76]

The Committee of the North had every reason to worry about such attitudes.[77] As one Chukchi put it, "The Chukchi never see big bosses. If good people are sent here, then the big boss must be a good man; if bad people come here, the big boss may very well be bad, too."[78]

In spite of the Committee's best efforts, the reputation of the new regime was low and did not show signs of improving. The circumpolar peoples complained about the government's continuing inability or unwillingness to curb Russian settlement and improve the quality of imported goods.[79] One frustrated group of Oliutora Koriak issued a truly desperate threat: "We'll stop smoking, drinking tea, and putting tobacco behind our cheeks, and we'll live by ourselves; and then let them laugh at us all they want."[80] Furthermore, most native groups disliked the few reforms that the regime was trying to push through: the administrative reshuffling, the arrival of new bosses, the equality of women, the prohibition of liquor, and, in particular, the creation of schools.[81] As the People's Commissar of Enlightenment put it, "the small nomadic peoples of the north are scared of Russian culture to the point of hating it."[82] In the northeast, where the remaining American

[76] Ibid., pp. 255–56.

[77] Ibid.

[78] Galkin, V zemle polunochnogo solntsa, p. 57.

[79] "Etnograficheskie raboty," pp. 98–99; Amyl'skii, "Kogda zatsvetaiut zharkie tsvety," p. 55; Rastvorov, "Dva suglana," pp. 50–51; Nikolai Nikolaevich, "Samoedskaia iarmarka," ORS, no. 3 (1929): 47; TsGAOR, f. 3977, op. 1, d. 528, l. 81.

[80] Zibarev, Sovetskoe stroitel'stvo, p. 111.

[81] TsGAOR, f. 1377, op. 1, d. 23, l. 35 and d. 123, l. 11; Kytmanov, "Tuzemtsy Turukhanskogo kraia," p. 44; Suslov, "Sotsial'naia kul'tura," p. 60; P. N. Orlovskii, "God Anadyrsko-Chukotskogo olenevoda," SA, no. 2 (1928): 61; Gaisin, "Karagasskoe bol'shoe zimnee sobranie," pp. 10–11; Leonov, "Tuzemnye sovety," pp. 234, 239–41, and "Tuzemnye shkoly," pp. 200–201.

[82] A. V. Lunacharskii, "Zadachi Narkomprosa na Dal'nem Severe," SA, no. 3 (1927): 18.

traders provided an alternative, the local people definitely preferred them to the Russians.[83]

Of course, all of that could be temporary. The Committee expected more funding as the Soviet state grew stronger and better understanding as the small peoples saw the usefulness of the innovations. (After all, many of them did appreciate the arrival of doctors and even asked for more.)[84] The most serious disappointment was that the cadres continued to be conspicuous by their absence. One detachment after another (to use the military terminology popular at the time) was defeated by the cold, hunger, local hostility, and, most of all, by the natives' refusal to cooperate. The great sacrifice had been rejected.

Many years later, one Mansi student remembered her first teacher, a young girl who did not speak the local language and did not know how to deal with the resentful children: "She tried to persuade us, Maria Andreevna did; she asked us and asked us again, and then suddenly she sat down and started crying." A few days later she got sick and left the settlement.[85]

In late 1928 P. G. Smidovich wrote about his committee's charges:

> Over the centuries, their beliefs and their relationships have been molded by the struggle for existence. Their shamanism; homes and families; methods of hunting for polar foxes, walruses, seals, and whales; primitive communism, dogs, and deer—all that is still the way it was in remotest antiquity. Little has been changed by whatever the new culture has brought. . . . The last few years have not altered this basic situation. The natives still depend on the elements, still starve after a bad season, and are still decimated by epidemics in the absence of medical help.[86]

There was a certain disappointment but no dejection in these words. Progress beyond the polar circle demanded more time and more sacrifice than had been expected but it was by no means impossible. After all, no one had thought that the natives' "dependence on the elements"

[83] Bonch-Osmolovskii, "Kamchatko-Chukotskii krai," p. 84; Buturlin, "Polozhenie tuzemtsev," p. 92; Galkin, V zemle polunochnogo solntsa, pp. 117, 190–91, 194–95; Kantorovich, Po Sovetskoi Kamchatke, p. 46; Lapin, Tikhookeanskii dnevnik, pp. 74, 87–93.

[84] Kytmanov, ' Tuzemtsy Turukhanskogo kraia," pp. 40–41; Orlovskii, "God Anadyrsko-Chukotskogo olenevoda," p. 61; Gaisin, "Karagasskoe bol'shoe zimnee sobranie," p. 10. Midwives were an important exception. Lapin heard the Chukchi complain: "Have Russians nothing better to do than teach us how to have babies? Don't we know how to do it ourselves?" See Lapin, Tikhookeanskii dnevnik, p. 80.

[85] M. Vakhrusheva, "Na beregu Maloi Iukondy," in My—liudi Severa (Leningrad, 1949), p. 85.

[86] P. G. Smidovich, introduction to Galkin, V zemle polunochnogo solntsa, pp. 5–6.

would stop in four years. In 1928 the tone of the Committee's reports was gloomy but not panicky. The situation was bad, it is true; the advance detachments were scattered; but the war was not lost. The main reason for this optimism was the belief that sooner or later the well-trained professional cadres would take their places in the taiga and tundra. Colleges continued to produce more graduates, and, perhaps most important of all, the first group of future native doctors, teachers, journalists, and Party secretaries was in Leningrad, learning about the "civilized world" and how to join it.[87]

The Committee theoreticians believed that the circumpolar peoples would be able to shed backwardness and become full and equal members of the multinational family only if they were led by their own "conscious" vanguard (the same applied to all peoples anxious to catch up with history). Thus the creation of a native elite was one of the most important goals of the Committee and, as it turned out, the most realistic one. Underfunded and understaffed, the Committee may not have been able to accomplish much in the "remote borderlands," but it surely could take care of a few youngsters sent to Leningrad.

The promotion of workers to managerial positions through education was a prominent and repeatedly emphasized policy of the Soviet regime. It was, therefore, perfectly natural that the school for future native leaders was modeled after the "workers' departments" (rabfaki), where future Russian officials were being trained. In 1925–26, a native rabfak was created within Leningrad University, and a year later it was transferred to the rabfak of the Leningrad Institute of Oriental Languages (as its Northern section).

Recruitment posed some problems. The local officials could not understand why anybody would want a savage in college and insisted on sending Zyrians, Yakuts, or Russians. Some took advantage of this once-in-a-lifetime opportunity and sent their own children.[88] Of the "real minorities," many candidates refused to go or got sick and could not make the trip.[89] The trip itself was a monumental experience. Bewildered, frightened, and often speechless, the students took weeks

---

[87] There was one more reason for this emphasis on elite-building. At the Committee's fourth plenum in 1927, when Smidovich was accused by a Yakut delegate of "culture-mongering" (i.e., kul'turnichestvo, or concern with culture at the expense of the economic base), he agreed, saying that it was easier to get funding for schools and hospitals than for economic innovations. TsGAOR, f. 1377, op. 1, d. 192, l. 81.

[88] Bogoraz (-Tan), Voskresshee plemia, pp. 133, 137; TsGAOR, f. 1377, op. 1, d. 32, ll. 21–38.

[89] V. G. Bogoraz (-Tan), "Severnyi rabfak (Severnoe otdelenie rabfaka Leningradskogo instituta zhivykh vostochnykh iazykov)," SA, no. 2 (1927): 54–55.

and sometimes months to get to Leningrad, discovering crowds, cities, and trains and being discovered by other passengers. When a group of Nanai travelers stopped the train because one of their number had been left behind, the railway authorities did not fine them "out of respect for such rare representatives of national minorities and their future activity."[90] One Ket student remembers:

> We arrived in Leningrad during the day. As we were leaving the train, I grabbed an Evenk boy by the hand so we would not get lost in the crowd. In this manner, we came to a square. On the square, we jumped on a cart. On the cart, I sat facing backwards. I looked at the square, and there, on a big rock, there was a big horse, and on the big horse there was a big man. I thought to myself: it must be the chief policeman, who is keeping order.[91]

Perhaps appropriately, the big man was Peter the Great, the initiator of the only other attempt by the state to force the small peoples of the North toward progress.

The arrival at the institute was followed by a trip to the bathhouse, a ritual that marked the beginning of the struggle against backwardness in all native schools across the country. Next there was a quarantine, until finally the students, dressed in austere black uniforms, were ready to tackle European culture.[92] The transition was difficult. Many came down with venereal diseases, tuberculosis, trachoma, flu, or food poisoning and had to be sent back home. Some were taken to the hospital straight from the train and never got a chance to see the institute.[93] The dormitory rooms were cold, damp, and crowded; the city outside was threatening.[94] As one Koriak put it, "The tall buildings crowd in on you—you feel like seeing farther away."[95] Many students were robbed and beaten up by local teenage gangs. Some became alcoholics and ended up in jail, some never returned from vacations, and some refused to go back home.[96]

The institute authorities tried to combat adaptation problems with

---

[90] Ibid., p. 59.

[91] Ivanov, Toporov, and Uspenskii, eds., *Ketskii sbornik*, 2:225.

[92] Bogoraz (-Tan), "Severnyi rabfak," p. 57.

[93] TsGAOR, f. 3977, op. 1, d. 340, ll. 202–9; Bogoraz (-Tan), *Voskresshee plemia*, p. 135. 209–10, and "Severnyi rabfak," p. 54.

[94] Bogoraz (-Tan), "Severnyi rabfak," p. 53; TsGAOR, f. 1377, op. 1, d. 81, ll. 115–16.

[95] N. Noianov, 'S Kamchatki v Leningrad," TT, no. 4 (1932): 49.

[96] Bogoraz (-Tan), *Voskresshee plemia*, pp. 131, 179; TsGAOR, f. 3977, op. 1, d. 277 l. 10, and d. 340, l. 73.

discipline and a very intensive program of work. The students got up at eight, drank their morning tea, and had classes until dinner at four. Then there were club meetings, organized excursions, and various rehearsals. Everyone had to do volunteer work.

The problems continued in the classroom. The students were of different ages and spoke different languages. Some had had some training, whereas others had been plucked up from "smoke-filled tents" and knew no Russian at all. Primary readers were full of unfamiliar realities, and Chukchi women absolutely refused to speak "the man's language."[97] The constant invention and reinvention of native terms for "bourgeoisie," "proletariat," and "poor peasant," was as difficult for the students as it was fascinating for their teachers. Still, they kept learning—mostly Russian, math, government, northern linguistics, and geography, but also drawing, physical education, and even English.[98] In 1927 the first thirty students were joined by fifty-two more. Those who survived the shock and disease were being successfully converted to a new way of looking at the world and themselves. A few years later, a Koriak graduate would say:

> Before I left home I did not believe that people lived anywhere outside of Kamchatka. And when the district executive committee sent me off to study I thought that an ignorant Koriak like me would not ever amount to anything. One question kept bothering me: what if they take me to the wrong place? The thing is, on the sea you cannot see land or forest anywhere, and so I had all kinds of doubts: will they take me to the sea where the seals will eat me, or will they hire me to work on a steamer? . . .

> This is how I imagined things when I did not know anything, did not understand Russian, and was ignorant. But now, thanks to the correct nationalities policy of the Soviet government and the Party with regard to the small peoples of the north, the other students and I have gradually come to understand a great deal and will now be able to tell our people about it. I study at the Institute of the Peoples of the North, and I have found out what makes a steamer move and what a radio is, and it is funny to me now how incorrectly I understood everything before. [99]

The Committee members felt that with people like this they had reason for optimism. The struggle would be long and hard, but the army

---

[97] In Chukchi, the pronunciation of some consonants varies according to the sex of the speaker. The newly created literary standard was based on the "male variant."

[98] Bogoraz (-Tan), "Severnyi rabfak," pp. 59–62, and *Voskresshee plemia*, pp. 188–96.

[99] Noianov, "S Kamchatki v Leningrad," p. 49.

was growing. The ethnographers would train more and more people at cultural stations; the best of them would come to Leningrad and then go back, to train even more people; and so it would develop, until, several generations later, all native northerners would turn their back on the old ways and start marching in step with the rest of the country.

III

CONQUERORS OF

BACKWARDNESS

"A Chukchi kulak on trial," from Nikolai Shundik, *Na Severe Dal'nem* (Moscow, 1952)

6

The Conscious Collectivists

His style was considered brilliant but his main thesis
mistaken.

—V. Erofeev, *Moskva-Petushki*

Class Struggles in a Classless Society

All plans of gradual development had to be revised or discarded after the spring of 1928, when Stalin and his men plunged the
country into another revolution. The NEP was over, and so were "sensitivity," protection, and gradualism. No economic plan was too ambitious, no ethnic group too backward, and no climate too severe for a
cohesive army of determined revolutionaries. The "Great Transformation" was to be the last war against the past, and the battle cry was
heard by all those whose future was not yet present: the Red Army men
upset by the regeneration of the defeated enemy; young Komsomol
radicals cheated out of their revolution; Communist visionaries unhappy about the death of a dream; and those blue-collar workers to
whom revolution did not make sense if they remained blue-collar
workers. The goal was to conjure modernity as industrialization-cum-
classlessness; the means was to exorcise backwardness through a total
class war. All identifiable phenomena contained some vestiges of the
past; all vestiges of the past were ultimately anthropomorphic ("enemies of the revolution"); and all enemies of the revolution were to be
defined in class terms and then destroyed. Industrialization required
the unmasking of wreckers; collectivization required the liquidation
of kulaks; administrative streamlining required Party purges; and
popular unity required the destruction of the enemies of the people.
All people(s) had enemies because the road to classlessness lay
through the abolition of deliberate backwardness.

187

But what about people too backward to have classes? What about the "primitive communists"? The "offensive of socialism all along the front" reached the Committee offices in March 1929, when several guest speakers at its sixth annual "plenum" accused the organizers of either misunderstanding socialism or deliberately not applying it to the northern borderlands. V. M. Tarantaeva, a representative of the women's section of the Party's Central Committee, attacked the Committee of the North for not following the example of Central Asian activists in combatting the inferior position of women in backward societies. The Committee's "scientific secretary" S. A. Buturlin, she charged, did not even consider bridewealth an absolute evil.[1] Tarantaeva was backed by the delegate from the Central Union of Consumer Cooperatives (Tsentrosoiuz), S. I. Kozlov. Defensive about the Tsentrosoiuz's inability to guarantee the normal functioning of native cooperatives, annoyed by the Committee's constant criticism on that score, and nervous about the apparent need to collectivize the "primitive communists," Kozlov attempted to turn the tables and shift the blame for whatever might follow onto the leaders of the Committee. Their policies on cooperatives and collectives had been contradictory and confused, he claimed; their interference in the work of others had been unhelpful; and their reports on native hostility to soviets should never have been published. Moreover, one Committee member (Koshkin) had suggested that northern shamans might not be total parasites, and the other (Buturlin) had gone so far as to deny the existence of class conflict in the tundra and to maintain that there existed some kind of primitive communism among the native peoples. In fact, to be primitive was the opposite of being a Communist, and to be nomadic was incompatible with being truly collectivized.[2]

The next, and the most vicious, attack came from a predictable source. For over a year, the Northern Section of the Leningrad Institute of Oriental Languages had been the scene of intense rivalry between the "northerners," who wanted administrative autonomy, and the "orientalists," who were trying to retain control. At the beginning of the Stalin revolution, the orientalists proclaimed their cause to be a part of the "Great Transformation," quickly adopted new slogans, and went on

---

[1] TsGAOR, f. 3977, op. 1, d. 391, ll. 2–7. S. A. Buturlin was a leading Russian zoologist specializing in circumpolar fauna and an active "protectionist" member of the Committee of the North.

[2] Ibid., ll. 60–69.

the offensive. They were in the majority in the administration as well as in the Institute's Party and Komsomol cells, and they had much more experience in Soviet politics: while the northern students were trying to cope with disease and the unusual surroundings, most "orientalist" activists were Russian *rabfak* students, veterans of many a battle and keen on participating in the nationwide search for class enemies. Before long, an obscure institutional intrigue had become a campaign to discredit the founding father of the northern section, V. G. Bogoraz (Shternberg having died in 1927).[3] At various meetings, the old revolutionary had been accused of turning the institute into a scientific laboratory; of trying to split the institute and gain personal power; of "populist culture-mongering [as opposed to Marxist socio-economic revolutionism] and of a sentimental approach to the peoples of the north"; of denying the existence of classes among the natives and, "as a result . . . , protecting them from the (supposedly harmful) influence of economic development."[4] At the same time, Bogoraz's students and institute allies Ia. P. Koshkin (Al'kor) and E. A. Kreinovich were exposed as his spineless Communist clones and urged to "publicly and categorically disassociate themselves from [his] anti-Marxist views."[5] More ambitiously, the "orientalists" charged the Committee of the North with not exercising proper political control and publishing "anti-Party and anti-Marxist" materials in their official organ *Sovetskii Sever.* [6]

Now, at the Committee's sixth plenum, the delegate from the Leningrad Institute of Oriental Languages, an "orientalist" student by the name of E. T. Potapov, took the floor to make what he called a "nonparliamentry" speech (this was in response to Skachko's admonitions that Kozlov refrain from rudeness). Having introduced himself as a new man who had never been to the north, Potapov proceeded to accuse the Committee leaders of that major Bogoraz sin: concentrating on "social welfare programs" at the expense of "real work." Defining indigenous societies as "primitive," he pointed out, the Committee had denied the obvious fact of class differentiation in their midst, failed to put an end

[3] TsGAOR, f. 3977, op. 1, d. 340, ll. 81–105. For a broader perspective on the "class war" in academe see Chapter 7, second section.

[4] TsGAOR, f. 3977, op. 1, d. 340, ll. 102–5.

[5] Ibid., d. 340, ll. 102–4.

[6] Ibid., d. 340, U. 102–4.

to the buying and selling of women, and generally persisted in "keeping the natives at their present stage of development." "Both the local and central bureaucracies of the Committee of the North must be rejuvenated [nado osvezhit'])," he concluded.[7]

A few other delegates expressed themselves in similar vein, but none of the radicals, including the initiators of the debate, could match the anger and the intensity of the presumed victims of rejuvenation as they rose to defend their policies and their philosophy. Buturlin maintained that northern shamans were not by nature exploiters; that polygamous marriages constituted only about six percent of all indigenous marriages; that the position of women in the north was better than (and very different from) the position of women in Muslim Central Asia; and that in any case he had been talking about realities, not personal preferences. Speaking of class differentiation and collectivization, Bogoraz asked what should be done with the Lamut [Even] who believed that large debts made a person wealthy, and whether his critics were prepared to disenfranchise all Chukchi and Eskimo heads of families because of their shamanistic activities. Kudriavtsev accused Kozlov's Tsentrosoiuz of not doing its own work and of being abysmally ignorant of northern conditions. Finally, S. I. Mitskevich, a veteran Bolshevik, a Kolyma doctor/exile, a leading authority on polar medicine, and at the time a prominent Soviet health administrator as well as the director of the Museum of the Revolution, showed some of the spirit that had led him to form the underground "Workers' Union" in 1893. He said that Potapov knew nothing about the Committee of the North and what he did know, he did not understand, "perhaps because he had not quite mastered written Russian." (Voice from the audience: "He is Russian." Mitskevich: "Not all Russians are literate.") Referring to his own field of expertise, he asserted that shamanism was a kind of culture-specific "psychoneurosis" that sometimes affected large groups of people. "I had the occasion to observe such an epidemic of shamanism in one Yukagir clan. Whom are you going to disenfranchise? Surely not those people." As for women, he continued, "I spent six years in the north, traveled beyond the polar circle, slept in Tungus tents and saw that the position of women there, while not ideal, was better than in Central Russia, at least with regard to battery." Ultimately, however, these were but specific cases of a much broader—and potentially very frightening—disagreement. Addressing all Stalin

[7] Ibid., d. 391, ll. 72–78.

revolutionaries wherever they might be, the chief guardian of the relics of the Lenin revolution declared that there were natural limits to coercion. Did not Krupskaia, the First Widow of the Revolution, say the other day "that according to Vladimir Il'ich revolutionary violence and dictatorship were good things when used properly, but that it was incorrect to substitute violence for the questions of organization and education?" Was it not obvious that an immediate forced settlement of tundra dwellers was a dangerous illusion, a case of "crackpot bureaucratic scheming that [had been] laughable enough under the tsarist regime and [was] . . . a complete waste of time nowadays?"[8] In the opinion of most Committee members, the native northerners possessed unique cultural traits, peculiar social and economic arrangements, ancient age-and-gender-based division of labor, and mysterious collective psychoneuroses, all of which needed to be seriously dealt with for the sake of future progress—not willed out of existence in the name of today's political expediency. As Buturlin summed up the old-guard view, "these are the facts, and whether comrade Tarantaeva likes them or not, she cannot change them."[9]

This was, of course, the real source of the problem, for changing these facts was exactly what comrade Tarantaeva and her fellow revolutionaries proposed to do. The new revolution was already raging outside, and though the Committee had succeeded in beating off the first frontal assault, it apparently was not going to fight an open war, as P. G. Smidovich made clear in his concluding remarks. Furious and defensive at the same time, the chairman of the Committee of the North charged that Kozlov and Potapov could not have been in possession of their mental faculties when they said what they said, and that comrade Tarantaeva did not need to teach them what they already knew. His line of argument, however (and it was soon to become the Committee's official line of argument) was greatly at variance with what the other members had said. In effect, what Smidovich offered was a kind of defiant capitulation. No, the Committee had not divided all indigenous peoples into the exploiters and the exploited, but it was not because it did not believe in their existence—rather, it was because one needed to form Soviet government bodies first. Now that it had been done, the Committee would certainly "draw the class line across the natives." The same was true of the shaman question. Certainly they had to be

[8] Ibid., d. 392, ll. 27–33.
[9] Ibid., l. 127.

disenfranchised—now that the time was right. Work among women ought to proceed with the same vigor, for the Committee had always thought it important, with due attention to local differences. And what could be more ridiculous than to assert that the Committee was trying to preserve the native peoples in their present state? Comrade Potapov should have thought a little bit before saying something that absurd.[10]

In other words, Smidovich was protecting his Committee and his less savvy colleagues by reversing their goals and distorting their positions. It may or may not have been the case before, but from now on native women would become the proletarians of the north, and the native shamans would become priests.[11] Most urgent, however, someone would have to become an exploiter. At the time of the "intensification of the class struggle" one had to find class enemies or face the risk of becoming one.[12]

At the conclusion of the sixth plenum the Committee renounced its main article of faith and declared a policy of class differentiation and a "laying of the groundwork for collectivization." The wording was deliberately vague, and the gradual character of the process strongly emphasized.[13] Several months later collectivization became a reality, and the Committee's leaders had to scramble for new formulas and for some very specific definitions. One had to devise precise criteria for identifying the class enemy, a task notoriously difficult even in the much more familiar Russian villages. As Smidovich complained, things were further complicated by "the primitive character of native life, the strength of kinship ties, and the relatively widespread 'charity' which often confounds all calculations."[14]

The Committee's ideologue and a de facto new leader A. E. Skachko came up with a compromise solution. There was no point in looking for exploiters among hunters and fishermen, he announced. No reliable measure of wealth could be found, and there was no capital to be accumulated. Boat leaders, for example, received a larger share of the catch because of their skill and experience, not because they owned the

---

[10] Ibid., d. 394, ll. 20–29.

[11] See Chapter 7, first section.

[12] Smidovich himself recoiled from dealing with the practical consequences of the turnaround. After his speech at the sixth plenum all major policy pronouncements were made by Skachko; Smidovich himself performed mostly ceremonial functions. Buturlin retired "due to illness."

[13] "Protokol zasedaniia VI rasshirennogo plenuma," pp. 4, 14.

[14] Smidovich, "Sovetizatsiia Severa," p. 8.

means of production. In all areas of non-native settlement social oppression coincided with national oppression. The Committee need not reverse its policy: whatever kulaks existed in the taiga were all Russians, Yakut, or Chinese. The situation of the reindeer pastoralists was quite different. Some people's herds were much larger than others'. Wolves, hard freezes, and epidemics could alter the situation, but provident herders divided their herds and were often in a position to transfer their wealth to their sons. Some of these herders used "hired labor," leased reindeer, or took part in trading operations, and could thus be classified as kulaks.[15]

The beauty of Skachko's scheme was that it defended the Committee's record and saved the majority of the northerners while at the same time providing the expropriators with an easily identifiable target. Skachko himself would not put it this way, but it followed from his analysis that all one needed to do in order to find an exploiter was to count the reindeer. Accordingly, the scientific-looking easy-to-use tables of reindeer/owner ratios became the most popular form of social analysis.[16]

It is doubtful, however, that any of these tables were ever used as practical guides by local authorities. By the time the Committee adopted Skachko's theses in the spring of 1930, collectivization had snowballed into "the last and decisive battle" against the countryside. As elsewhere in the country, northern officials received vague but threatening orders to obtain more produce, collectivize the "poor and middle peasants," and "squeeze out the kulaks." In some areas collectivization was to be total and the exploiters were to be "liquidated as a class," or "dekulakized."[17] What exactly it all meant and how much of it applied to the native peoples was not clear. The Committee of the North urged caution and suggested class-based taxation and fixed production assignments as the best means to smash the power of the ku-

[15] TsGAOR, f. 3977, op. 1, d. 496, ll. 8–18, and d. 503, ll. 8–31. Anatolii Skachko, "Klassovoe rassloenie, merv bor'by s kulachestvom i kollektivizatsiia," SS, no. 2 (1930): 38–49; "Protokol sed'mogo rasshirennogo plenuma Komiteta," SS, no. 4 (1930): 127–32.
[16] Smidovich, "Sovetizatsiia Severa," p. 9; Skachko, "Klassovoe rassloenie," p. 40, and "Imushchestvennye pokazateli sotsial'nykh grupp u malykh narodnostei Severa," SS, no. 3 (1930): 5–14; I. M. Suslov, "Raschet minimal'nogo kolichestva olenei, potrebnykh dlia tuzemnogo khoziaistva " SS, no. 3 (1930): 29–35; Iu. A. Kudriavtsev, "Na putiakh rekonstruktsii olenevodstva v sovetskoi Azii, SA, no. 1–2 (1931): 36.
[17] TsGAOR, f. 3977, op. 1, d. 499, l. 54, 64.

laks and boost the new cooperatives.[18] As Skachko warned, "a hasty and badly implemented 'total' collectivization involving the liquidation of kulaks as a class may destroy the very foundation of the native economy, ruin reindeer breeding, and turn all natives into dependents of the state."[19] However, the Committee could not fire or arrest anyone, and it was ignored (if indeed it had ever been noticed) by local administrators bombarded with Party appeals for unspecified urgent action. One such administrator expressed the prevailing unease when he wondered about the implications of yet another bloodthirsty article by a provincial boss: "In his article he depicted the utter dependence of the native poor and hired hands on the tundra kulaks, which undoubtedly still takes place in some borderlands of our enormous northern territories. But comrade Egorov does not indicate what should be done in order to put an end to this centuries-old intolerable situation."[20]

The solution seemed frightening but inescapable. The air resounded with frontline rhetoric and demands to do more, faster, now or never. Plan targets were being constantly raised; more and more regions proclaimed themselves "areas of total collectivization;" and big-city volunteers brought far-fetched plans of revolutionary action. With no specific instructions, local officials preferred to err on the side of "more" and "faster," and the apprehensive Siberian administrator arrived at the following conclusion: "At first glance, the peculiarities of the North require extreme caution in dealing with the causes of this problem. Still, it must be stated that the struggle against tundra kulaks can be pursued along the general lines of liquidation of the kulaks as a class."[21] Accordingly, district officials of the Tobol'sk north dekulakized fishing-net owners, and in relatively accessible Karagassiia the entire native population (439 persons) was forcibly settled in collective houses. All reindeer and all private possessions, including smoking pipes, were collectivized.[22] The Main Hunting Administration promised to complete the whole campaign by the end of the five-year plan.[23]

[18] Skachko, "Klassovoe rassloenie," p. 44; TsGAOR, f. 3977, op. 1, d. 496, ll. 14–16; "Protokol sed'mogo rasshirennogo plenuma Komiteta," p. 145.

[19] TsGAOR, f. 3977, op. 1, d. 496, l. 17; Skachko, "Klassovoe rassloenie," p. 44.

[20] Pervukhin, "Na bor'bu s tundrovym kulachestvom," ORS, no. 2 (1930): 25.

[21] Ibid.

[22] B. E. Petri, "Karagasiia stroitsia," ORS, no. 6 (1929): 8–10; Skachko, "Imushchestvennye pokazateli," p. 14; I. Tobolaev, "V Tofalarskom raione," SS, no. 2 (1933): 94; Murnik, "V Tofalarskom raione," SS, no. 2 (1934): 95–98.

[23] P. N. Orlovskii, "Kollektivizatsiia na Severe," SS, no. 1 (1930): 49. See also TsGAOR, f. 3977, op. 1, d. 496, l. 25; d. 500, ll. 2–6; and d. 526, ll. 2–3.

The majority of the native northerners, however, were not affected by the first and, as far as Russia proper was concerned, the strongest wave of anti-rural violence of the winter of 1929–30. By the time local officials received word of the new policy and got around to doing their share, the Party leadership in Moscow ordered a halt to the campaign. Apparently frightened by the chaos he had unleashed, Stalin declared that coercion and wholesale socialization were deviations from the central policy and blamed local officials ("dizzy with success") for all the "excesses." In the ensuing finger-pointing much attention was paid to the "total disregard for the local peculiarities" in the "national regions of the Soviet East"—meaning primarily Central Asia but also Yakutia and Buriatia.[24] The Central Committee issued a special resolution to that effect, and *Pravda* declared that the "culturally and economically backward" areas were not ready for total collectivization.[25] Still, the immediate tasks of procurement remained the number one priority, and coercion remained Stalin's primary means to accomplish those tasks. In the fall of 1930 the assault on the countryside was resumed, and non-Russians—no matter how "Eastern"—were not going to get special treatment. Dimanshtein, the Central Executive Committee spokesman on nationality policies and the main advocate of caution in dealing with the Asian peoples, recanted and "admitted his mistakes."[26] The Party and soviet bosses of the Nenets region were dismissed for "protecting the kulaks."[27] For the same offense, the leaders of the Koriak region and Penzhinsk district were executed by the firing squad.[28]

This time both the local northern officials and the central organizations active in the north were ready for the race that was to continue for several years. Not that there was a great and urgent demand for reindeer meat. Collectivization first emerged as an answer to the grain procurement problems, but as the hysteria grew and the tempos increased it became one of the regime's ideological cornerstones and the crucial test of loyalty, political reliability, and professional ability for all rural officials. Wheat, cotton, and walruses were to be procured in the same

[24] See, in particular, *RN*, nos. 1, 2, 3 (1930).

[25] *Pravda*, 27 February 1930, p. 1.

[26] S. M. Dimanshtein, "Natsional'nye momenty na XVI s"ezde," *RN*, no. 3 (1930): 3–13 and "Predvaritel'nyi otvet tov. Tobolovu," *RN*, no. 4–5 (1930): 140–41; "Postanovlenie biuro redaktsii zhurnala 'Revoliutsiia i natsional'nosti,'" *RN*, no. 8–9 (1930): 3.

[27] TsGAOR, f. 3977, op. 1 d. 743, l. 3.

[28] Ibid., d. 758, l. 207.

way. The Hunting Administration pledged to complete the five-year plan by collectivizing 46.7 percent of the fur production in the Far East; 50 percent in western Siberia; and 64.4 percent in eastern Siberia. The RSFSR Commissariat of Agriculture decided to transfer half a million reindeer to the kolkhozy. The Katanga, Taimyr, Evenk and northern Komi regions promised to achieve total collectivization by 1932; Berezov, Konda, and Tigil' decided on 1931.[29]

In a characteristic move, the Tobol'sk province Party committee revived the grand plans for the procurement of reindeer meat which had been pronounced fantastic in the spring of 1930. The Obdorsk delegation to the provincial plenum was told to go back and correct the rightist deviations, or rather, to go to the tundra and obtain as many reindeer as possible. Presently the agents of the state trading organization (Gostorg), the northern cooperative administration (Integralsoiuz), the local kolkhozy, and occasionally the secret police (OGPU) loaded their guns and went to work.[30] There was no mistaking their intentions. As one clan soviet chairman put it: "The Russian has arrived. He will take away our reindeer."[31] In exchange the herders received "contract receipts," which stated that they had undertaken the obligation to provide a certain number of animals to the state. Some agents paid in cash, some gave only signed receipts. (Elsewhere, the provincial executive committee of Eastern Siberia formally allowed procurement without payment, promising to honor the receipts in 1937. In fact, the receipts were annulled as part of taxation.)[32] Every organization had its own plan, and the competition was fierce. According to the Obdorsk Integralsoiuz agent, dealing with the Gostorg representative made no sense because state stores did not have any merchandise and because "the state would take away all the reindeer anyway."[33] Indeed, the state took the reindeer and other native produce not only as part of procurement

[29] Anatolii Skachko, "Resheniia XVII partkonferentsii v ikh primenenii k Severu," SS, no. 1–2 (1932): 14; "O rabote v natsional'nykh raionakh Krainego Severa," PS, no. 13 (1932): 53; Anatolii Skachko, "Postanovleniia TsK partii i SNK v ikh primenenii k Severu," SS, no. 3 (1932): 8, 10; Sergeev, Nekapitalisticheskii put', pp. 345–46.

[30] TsGAOR, f. 3977, op. 1, d. 497, l. 3; d. 641, ll. 37–38; d. 949, l. 20; and d. 989, ll. 136–37. Also "Za leninskuiu natsional'nuiu politiku (po materialam KK RKI Tobol'-skogo okruga)" SS, no. 9 (1931): 144–46.

[31] "Za leninskuiu natsional'nuiu politiku," pp. 144–46.

[32] A. Kruglov, "O revoliutsionnoi zakonnosti na mestakh," SS, no. 1 (1933): 98.

[33] "Za leninskuiu natsional'nuiu politiku," p. 145.

but also as taxes. In spite of the legal prohibition, which was never officially repealed, the income tax and the agricultural tax were extended to all the "small peoples."[34]

As far as some local agents were concerned, the seizure of reindeer, fish, and furs was what collectivization was all about. As one district representative told the Kamenskoe Koriak, their settlement owed the state a certain amount of salmon. In order to fulfill the plan, the fishermen had to form a kolkhoz. By working collectively, they proved that they already had a kind of kolkhoz. Consequently, the representative could report on the success of his mission and leave the place without delay.[35] Such an attitude became increasingly unusual as more administrators realized that the numbers of new collectives and newly expropriated exploiters were just as crucial for their survival as the quantity of produce that they extracted. In this they were helped by the new breed of theoreticians—the first-generation Soviet intellectuals whose sense of mission and reason for existence depended on the availability of class enemies. In 1923 class-based entrance quotas were introduced in Shternberg's ethnography department, and by 1925 the combined pressure from the new students and the government had produced a curriculum completely free of natural sciences but replete with such subjects as the history of the revolution; historical materialism; the nationality policies of the era of imperialism and proletarian revolution; the methodology of social work in the villages; the history of the class struggle; the history of the Communist Party; and the foundations of Leninism.[36] In 1925 the ethnography department had been transferred from the Institute of Geography to the much more tightly controlled Leningrad University. When the call for class war came, some of the products of the new system were already in the field, ready to act. As one such revolutionary put it, "We are sick of . . . hearing speeches by learned gentlemen who reject all practical initiatives with the argument that we have not criss-crossed a given stretch of territory ten or twenty or a hundred times with all the necessary instruments."[37] The Committee's official definitions lost all meaning as new types of kulaks were discovered among fishermen, sea hunters, and small taiga herd-

[34] Ibid.
[35] N. N. Bilibin, "Sredi koriakov," SS, no. 3 (1933): 93–94.
[36] Ratner-Shternberg, "L. Ia. Shternberg," pp. 144–47.
[37] TsGAOR, f. 3977, op. 1, d. 853, l. 111.

ers.[38] Grooms working for their brides, widows living with relatives, and poorer kinsmen provided with temporary reindeer herds became "hired labor," and many heads of households became exploiters for being heads of households.[39] One emissary from Moscow observed a group of Nivkh fishermen in action and confirmed that the catch was divided equally plus one extra share for the owner of the boat and the net. He also noticed, however, that the group included five members of the owner's immediate family, meaning that the fellow actually received seven shares. He was therefore a kulak whose property (presumably the boat and the net) could be confiscated.[40] Not far from there, a young Komsomol member pursued class differentiation "according to the bear principle: anyone who had a bear was considered a kulak and expelled."[41] At the opposite end of Siberia, a Communist organizer among the Nenets complained about "various forms of cohabitation among kinsmen which, given a rather poor knowledge of the language, were almost impossible to figure out."[42] Still, he made the effort based on his class instinct and produced the following report about a man who lived with his wife and seven children and owned fifty-one reindeer:

> As far as the means of production are concerned, he can be classified as a solid middle herder. I classify him as a kulak on the strength of the available information about his involvement in petty speculation. He provides food to neighboring families, including his brother who does not own any reindeer. He sells and leases reindeer. He delivers goods from the trading center to poor herders.[43]

When another collectivizer found fewer hired laborers than he had expected, he ascribed it to the shrewdness of the class enemy:

[38] P. E. Terletskii, "Osnovnye cherty khoziaistva Severa," SS, no. 9–12 (1930): 72–81, 85; Anatolii Skachko, "Sotsial'no-proizvodstvennye otnosheniia v okhotnich'em khoziaistve severa," SS, no. 11–12 (1931): 28–33; M. A. Bol'shakov, "Naselenie Kamchatki i ego khoziaistvo," SS, no. 11–12 (1931): 78; A. F. Anisimov, "O sotsial'nykh otnosheniiakh v okhotkhoziaistve evenkov," SS, no. 5 (1935): 41–43.
[39] TsGAOR, f. 3977, op. 1, d. 646, ll. 52, 57; V. N. Skalon, "V tundre Verkhnego Taza," SSb, no. 3 (1930): 136; Terletskii, "Osnovnye cherty," p. 53; S. Kozin, "Dal'nevostochnaia kompleksnaia ekspeditsiia," SE, no. 3–4 (1931): 202–4; N. Firsov, "Rabota sredi malykh narodov Severa v Iakutskoi ASSR," SS, no. 11–12 (1931): 20; V. G. Bogoraz (-Tan), "Klassovoe rassloenie u chukoch-olenevodov," SE, no. 1–2 (1931): 93–116.
[40] Kozin, "Dal'nevostochnaia kompleksnaia ekspeditsiia," pp. 202–4.
[41] TsGAOR, f. 3977, op. 1, d. 739, l. 25.
[42] Skalon, "V tundre Verkhnego Taza," p. 132.
[43] Ibid., p. 137.

An indirect but fairly convincing proof of that can be found in the very odd fact of free transfer of reindeer among nomadic households. Sometimes this free transfer involves up to sixty reindeer per household. What would be the economic rationale for this original form of gift-giving found nowhere else in the world? It probably would not be a mistake to suggest that this "free transfer," disguised by declarations of brotherhood and mutual aid among kin, is in fact nothing more than hidden payment to poor households for using their labor.[44]

In Yakutia the Workers' and Peasants' Inspection used the tested method of counting reindeer and ended up with the discovery that 73 percent of the Kolyma nomads were kulaks or feudal lords.[45] Almost overnight "the poorest and most exploited" people of the Soviet Union were unmasked as mainly exploiters hopelessly attached to private property. According to N. N. Bilibin, who worked among the Koriak, "The whole system of traditional attitudes and popular beliefs prevalent in the tundra; the system that is encountered by everyone who attempts to carry out any kind of work in the tundra; the system that impresses the superficial and usually naive observer as a national peculiarity—all of this turns out to be a system of ideological defense of private property."[46]

In other words, the whole culture of native northerners was hostile to revolution and progress. Consequently, it had to be smashed and revamped according to the principles of Marxism-Leninism.

[The kulaks'] direct ideological domination often limits our work to rather timid culture-mongering [kul'turnichestvo] and all sorts of concessions to the false idol of national peculiarity, which in fact end up helping the insolent kulak autonomy. The institutions of Soviet culture do not fit into the existing relations of production in the tundra, and for that reason our task consists in bringing about a radical change in those relations, so that they cease to serve as a basis for kulak domination.[47]

As another Okhotsk coast collectivizer explained, it was necessary to "break up the national and tribal unity cultivated by the kulaks."[48]

[44] Bol'shakov, "Naselenie Kamchatki," p. 73.

[45] Skachko, "Imushchestvennye pokazateli," p. 17. See also N. K. Karger, "Ocherednye zadachi etnografii na Severe," SA, no. 3–4 (1931): 237; TsGAOR, f. 3977, op. 1, d. 499, l. 64; A. I. Pika, "Malye narody Severa: Iz pervobytnogo kommunizma v 'real'nyi sotsializm'," in V chelovecheskom izmerenii, ed., A. G. Vishnevskii (Moscow, 1989), p. 320.

[46] N. N. Bilibin, "U zapadnykh koriakov," SS, no. 1–2 (1932): 207.

[47] Ibid., p. 208.

[48] Ivan Bagmut, "Kochevoi sovet na Okhotskom poberezh'i," SS, no. 4 (1934): 19.

In practical terms, it meant that one or several officials accompanied by an interpreter would descend on a native settlement or encampment, determine who was a kulak, and demand that these people be expelled from the soviets, deprived of the vote, and then "limited" and "neutralized" economically. The first difficulty was getting the message across. Sometimes there were no interpreters; some interpreters were bad; and most of the new policies and new terms did not make any sense to the native northerners: "We the Tungus met by ourselves in the winter and started talking about the laws of the Soviet system and the party, saying that we did not understand anything although Russian workers, instructors, representatives . . . , and so forth came to us all the time, and that we could not agree on anything and did not understand their language."[49]

The degree of bewilderment can be illustrated by some of the questions put by Kirensk Evenk to their instructor: "Who are the bourgeois elements? What is the October Revolution? What is 'religion-induced daze' [religioznyi durman]? Who are the petit bourgeois elements? What is industry? What is technology?"[50]

When future collective farmers understood what was wanted of them, they did not like the idea. Some claimed that there were no rich and poor among them ("all natives are poor");[51] and although the majority agreed that some people were more prosperous than others they refused to equate wealth with badness. "What kind of kulak is he?" asked a group of Nenets about their kinsman singled out as an exploiter. "He's a good man and not a kulak at all!" "This kulak gave us a lot, and you didn't give us anything."[52] A Koriak "hired laborer" expressed a popular view when he declared: "We don't have people who don't help the poor; if they see that you're hungry, they feed you."[53] In fact, heads of households who could "feed" others were often the group's only security. They enjoyed the greatest prestige and represented their people before the Russians. (Vasilevich wrote that one "obviously poor" Tungus asked to be promoted to the "middle"

---

[49] Petr Ustiugov, "Samokritika na suglanakh," SS, no. 7–8 (1930): 43. See also I. M. Suslov, "Shamanstvo i bor'ba s nim," SS, no. 3–4 (1931): 140.

[50] TsGAOR, f. 3977, op. 1, d. 530, l. 2.

[51] Ustiugov, "Samokritika," p. 51; TsGAOR, f. 3977, op. 1, d. 528, l. 30.

[52] Petr Ustiugov, "Tuzemnye sovety i zadachi ikh ukrepleniia," SS, no. 9–12 (1930): 31.

[53] Bilibin, "U zapadnykh koriakov," p. 199. See also TsGAOR, f. 3977, op. 1, d. 528, l. 30.

category.)[54] Two propagandists who tried to reason with the reindeer Koriak reported thus on their fiasco:

> The poor people say that, from what they hear, the new soviet power is for their good but that they do not want to do things the new way. We have our bosses, they say, and however they will live, that's the way we'll live, too. We don't want to have meetings by ourselves. Talk to our masters and bosses, and as for us, we've never had meetings before and we don't want to have them now. . . . Why change the old boss, he's a good man. We won't elect anybody else anyway.[55]

For their part, the elders and the "strong men" often defended themselves by saying that they never failed to discharge their obligations before the community. "If somebody is really poor, we invite him and say: go ahead and eat, drink, and work."[56] This, of course, only confirmed the collectivizers' worst suspicions.

Whether they had any suspicions or not, the officials needed to deliver their quotas, and so they pressed on relentlessly, fully aware that "the poor masses all over the tundra . . . believe that they are being fed by the rich."[57] Various combinations of threats, direct coercion, economic blackmail, and bribes tended to produce the needed results.[58] The "toilers" of one Koriak encampment refused to talk, refused to give their names, even refused tea, but were finally cornered and, having left their fingerprints on the anti-kulak resolution, "ran in embarassment out of the tent where the committee was sitting."[59] In Ugur the collectivizers stripped unwilling kolkhozniks naked and staged mock executions.[60] Eventually—at least as far as most Russian administrators

[54] G. M. Vasilevich, "Symskie tungusy," SS, no. 2 (1931): 146. See also TsGAOR, f. 3977, op. 1, d. 300, ll. 68–69

[55] Bilibin, "U zapadnykh koriakov," p. 200. Cf. I. Pervukhin, "Na Tobol'skom severe," SS, no. 1 (1930): 82.

[56] Kantorovich, Po Sovetskoi Kamchatke, p. 157. See also TsGAOR, f. 3977, op. 1, d. 646, l. 52.

[57] Bilibin, "U zapadnykh koriakov," p. 197.

[58] TsGAOR, f. 3977, op. 1, d. 737, ll. 14–17, and d. 757, l. 98; D. F. Medvedev, "O rabote sredi tuzemnoi bednoty i batrachestva na Tobol'skom severe," SS, no. 1 (1931): 49; Anatolii Skachko, "Vos'moi plenum Komiteta Severa," SS, no. 5 (1931): 7; "Za leninskuiu natsional'nuiu politiku," pp. 144–45; Kruglov, "O revoliutsionnoi zakonnosti," pp. 98–99; N. Gerasimovich, "V Taimyrskom okruge," SS, no. 6 (1933): 61–62. Also see Gail A. Fondahl, "Native Economy and Northern Development: Reindeer Husbandry in Transbaykalia" (Ph.D. diss., University of California, Berkeley, 1989), pp. 189–91.

[59] Bilibin, "U zapadnykh koriakov," p. 199.

[60] TsGAOR, f. 3977, op. 1, d. 737, l. 14.

were concerned—the old native power structure was discovered and dislodged, to be replaced by representatives of the "toiling natives." This "revolution" did not, however, result in a speedy awakening of class consciousness, as a few young ideologists seem to have hoped. According to one newly elected soviet member, "we can't live without rich people. And we don't need their reindeer. Now that I am the boss, I'm going to help both rich and poor."[61] Even when they boasted about the successful execution of official class policies, the new "native cadres" tended to interpret their tasks in the old familiar ways: "I told the herders: live in peace; and I told the masters: don't forget to give your herders tea; and I myself gave the herders the last piece of brick tea or tobacco. The masters give their herders meat and fur to make clothes, and when the herders leave, they give them some steers."[62] In any case, the bosses imposed by the Russians were bosses only as long as the Russians were around. As some Nenets who had secretly elected a "prince" told their instructor, "You Russians need the clan soviet, and we need our prince."[63]

"Defeated" politically, the kulaks needed to be "squeezed" economically. They were given elevated "fixed [work] assignments" and fined for noncompliance; assigned increased transportation duty; denied credit; forced to buy state bonds; fined for "social and economic crimes"; and charged special double prices at the stores. All debts owed to them were canceled.[64] The Penzhinsk herders gave up almost one-third of their reindeer over the course of one week; their neighbors the Even were expected to pay fines of up to thirty-thousand rubles for nonfulfillment of fixed assignments; and nine Eseisk Tungus households had to pay 34,995 rubles between March 1 and April 1 of 1931.[65] In these and other such cases it meant the total ruin of the punished households, particularly because the most forceful collectivizers were outsiders who had a very vague notion of the "various forms of cohabi-

[61] Ibid., p. 197. See also N. P. Nikul'shin, Pervobytnye proizvodstvennye ob"edineniia i sotsialisticheskoe stroitel'stvo u evenkov (Leningrad, 1939), p. 79.

[62] Bilibin, "U zapadnykh koriakov," p. 209.

[63] Suslov, "Shamanstvo i bor'ba s nim," p. 140. See also Zibarev, Sovetskoe stroitel'-stvo, pp. 185–86.

[64] TsGAOR, f. 3977, op. 1, d. 757, ll. 77–79; I. Barakhov, "V Evenkiiskom natsional'nom okruge Vostsibkraia," SS, no. 3 (1933): 52; Gerasimovich, "V Taimyrskom okruge," pp. 61–62; Kruglov, "O revoliutsionnoi zakonnosti," pp. 98–99; Anatolii Skachko, "Osnovnye voprosy sotsialisticheskogo stroitel'stva na Krainem Severe," SS, no. 3 (1934): 16; Ustiugov, "Samokritika na suglanakh," pp. 52–53; Nikul'shin, Pervobytnye proizvodstvennye ob"edineniia, pp. 78–79.

[65] V. Krylov, "V Penzhinskom raione," SS, no. 1 (1935): 94–95; Popova, Eveny, p. 241; Nikul'shin, Pervobytnye proizvodstvennye ob"edineniia, pp. 78–79.

tation among kinsmen" and tended to be outraged by the unreasonably large size of reindeer herds. Not only were they under pressure to obtain meat but they had no idea that an Even family of six could barely subsist on a herd of 400 head of reindeer.[66]

The native response took traditional forms: they asked for more time, withdrew into silence, or tried to placate the Russians by passing resolutions such as "The 'five-year plan in four years' is a very good initiative of the Soviet government."[67] Those who could do so moved away or changed their migration routes.[68] When confronted directly, they often refused to pay new taxes and part with their animals, as the Penzhinsk "kulak" Khachikeev, who said: "We're not going to sell our does. If poor people need reindeer, we'll give them reindeer."[69] (Obligatory state bonds were seen as another tax and caused enough irritation to make one official suggest that maybe some natives should be able to redeem them.[70]) The pastoralists classified as middle or poor had to go slow on what was the main goal of their economic activity—increasing their herds.[71] The "kulaks" divided their herds among kinsmen or divided their families in order to get rid of "hired labor" (at least while the Russians were watching).[72] Both exploiters and their alleged victims worked together to fulfill fixed assignments and pay fines. As one collectivizer remarked sarcastically, "They thought that it was quite normal to help 'their own people' persecuted by the Soviet regime."[73] When there were no more people, ploys, and arguments left and no more pastures to go to, the herders slaughtered their animals ("The reindeer will be taken away anyway . . . , so it's better if we eat them ourselves") or killed the collectivizers.[74]

Finally, there was the ultimate and most traditional act of resist-

[66] Popova, Eveny, p. 241.

[67] Ustiugov, "Samokritika na suglanakh," pp. 44, 53; Bilibin, "U zapadnykh koriakov," pp. 196, 198.

[68] TsGAOR, f. 3977, op. 1, d. 646, l. 7; d. 739, l. 31; d. 756, l. 62; and d. 936, ll. 4–5. Also, "Za leninskuiu natsional'nuiu politiku," p. 145; Nikul'shin, Pervobytnye proizvodstvennye ob"edineniia, p. 78; Popova, Eveny, p. 244.

[69] Kantorovich, Po Sovetskoi Kamchatke, p. 157. See also "Za leninskuiu natsional'nuiu politiku," p. 145; Orlovskii, "Kollektivizatsiia na severe," p. 51; and D. F. Medvedev, "O rabote s bednotoi i batrachestvom na Krainem Severe," SS, no. 6 (1932): 74–75.

[70] S. Kertselli, "Gozaimy i nash Sever," SS, no. 7–8 (1931): 61–62.

[71] Ustiugov, "Samokritika na suglanakh," p. 45.

[72] Orlovskii, "Kollektivizatsiia na severe," p. 52; Skalon, "V tundre Verkhnego Taza," p. 136; Ustiugov, "Tuzemnye sovety," p. 30.

[73] Bagmut, "Kochevoi sovet," p. 19.

[74] TsGAOR, f. 3977, op. 1, d. 646, ll. 7, 48–49, and d. 833, ll. 27–28, 121; "V Taimyrskom okruge," SS, no. 3 (1934): 84. See also "Postanovlenie VTsIK i SNK RSFSR o merakh protiv khishchnicheskogo uboia olenei," SS, no. 5 (1931): 146; Fondahl, "Native

ance—suicide. Aleksei Sokorgin, an Evenk, was forced to fish for the state, to buy state bonds ("for the fourth and final year of the five-year plan"), to cut wood, and to give his reindeer away as "salary." When he was fined sixty reindeer for disobedience, "he cut his throat on the same day. At first this suicide attempt, which turned out to be unsuccessful, caused great confusion among the whole population of Viliga. Nervous breakdowns and fainting fits among women aggravated the already tense situation."[75] But Ivan Bagmut, the sarcastic collectivizer, kept his cool and came out on top. The general meeting that he chaired condemned the attempted suicide as a "political demonstration aimed at forcing the soviet to renounce the policy of limiting kulak influence," and Aleksei Sokorgin had to give up five hundred more head of reindeer as well as undertake some more transportation duty.[76]

A kulak remained a kulak even when there was nothing left to expropriate. In 1933 in the Ostiak-Vogul region all indigent exploiters received a "fixed assignment" to gather 300 kilos of berries and 150 kilos of mushrooms. As Skachko put it, "all that was left were the bare hands of a former kulak."[77]

Hunting and Gathering under Socialism

Theoretically, all this dekulakizing activity was designed to facilitate the real aim of the campaign, collectivization. The theory was, of course, not of long standing. Before 1928 the small peoples of the north had been presumed to lead a collective existence, perhaps even too collective for their own good. When collectivization became an urgent government policy, the Committee of the North wasted no time erecting a solid theoretical foundation. According to Skachko, the problem of native economy consisted in the contradictions between reindeer breeding and hunting in the tundra, and reindeer breeding and fishing in the taiga. In other words, different types of economic activity required the presence of northern foragers in two places at the same time: what was good for reindeer breeding was not good for fishing or hunting. Integration into larger cooperative units would take care of the problem by allowing specialized "brigades" to devote them-

---

Economy," pp. 211–17; Medvedev, O rabote s bednotoi," p. 75; Pika, "Malye narody Severa," pp. 321–22.

[75] Bagmut, "Kochevoi sovet," p. 20.

[76] Ibid., pp. 20–21.

[77] TsGAOR, f. 3977, op. 1, d. 990, l. 174.

selves entirely and profitably to only one type of economic pursuit. Meanwhile, the wives and other auxiliary personnel could remain at the central base, saved from the discomfort of nomadic life.[1] And that, of course, would open the way for eventual settlement. "Correctly organized hunting requires the presence of the hunter in hunting areas only during specific seasons, so he does not need to wander all year long, dragging his wife, tent, and household possessions behind him."[2] Nevertheless, although Skachko, Smidovich, and other Committee leaders argued that there was "nothing shameful in being a nomad in the twentieth century" and foresaw settlement as a distant result of global economic change, many young activists of the Stalin revolution could not be reconciled to what they saw as total economic irrationality and technological backwardness. In the absence of funds and permanent building materials immediate settlement was rarely a practical proposition, but collectivization seemed to require nothing but strength and determination on the part of the "scientifically" oriented enthusiasts who were appalled by "the total unfamiliarity of the majority of the natives with the most elementary rules of reindeer breeding."[3] Most traditional techniques struck the collectivizers as "utterly backward" and "economically irrational": the natives slaughtered young reindeer because "their meat was tastier," raised useless bears instead of cows, and wasted precious time during hunting season on ludicrous religious rituals.[4] Collectivization would make it easier to teach common sense to the natives and to introduce modern technology into their work.

To collectivize people who lived and worked communally, one needed to define one's attitude toward traditional native groups. Should such groups be used as a basis for future kolkhozy or were they sources of hidden exploitation that needed to be destroyed? Were they "some of the best preconditions for collectivization" or was their role "purely reactionary"? Finally, were they genuine social and economic communities or was it only "in opposition to the class solidarity of the

[1] Anatolii Skachko, "Problemy Severa," SS, no. 1 (1930): 29–30. See also Anisimov, "O sotsial'nykh otnosheniiakh," p. 45.

[2] Petri, "Karagasiia stroitsia," p. 9.

[3] Skalon, "V tundre Verkhnego Taza," p. 135.

[4] M. A. Sergeev, "Rekonstruktsiia byta narodov Severa," RN, no. 3 (1934): 90; N. I. Leonov, "Kul'tbaza v taige," PN, no. 9–10 (1930): 90; K. E., "Kolkhoznye zametki," SS, no. 3–4 (1935): 187; E. Kantor, "Liudi i fakty. Staroe i novoe," SS, no. 3–4 (1935): 189; Kertselli, "Olenevodstvo v SSSR i ego perspektivy," SA, no. 1–2 (1931): 134.

toiling northerners" that "the class enemy put forward the slogan of
clan solidarity and blood relationship"?[5]

The debate on all these questions did take place, but it took place
after the main collectivization drive.[6] In the heat of the campaign, the
northern instructors were guided by plan targets and their own understanding of Party policy. Between late 1930 and late 1932 that sometimes meant collectivizing everything that could be collectivized: all
reindeer, tents, household utensils, guns, sleds, dogs, and traps.[7] Such
measures could not be very popular. As one Evenk hunter tried to explain to his Russian instructor, "We don't hunt together, we hunt in
different places. I know and like my place, and Pavel Mikhailovich
knows his. Everybody hunts separately. I don't want some other
kolkhoz member to check my traps."[8] Similarly, fishermen refused to
fish "not for themselves," and reindeer herders took care only of "their"
part of the collectivized herd.[9]

When 20 to 25 percent of all northern households were considered
collectivized and about 200,000 head of reindeer were reported missing, Moscow intervened—on behalf of its furs, reindeer, and natives.[10]
In a special resolution of June 1932 the Central Committee of the Party
demanded an immediate stop to the "mechanical and crude application of the experience of the advanced regions of the Union to backward native regions."[11] As in 1930, the local officials were blamed for
collectivizing and dekulakizing the people whose level of development
had not prepared them for such undertakings. Personal property
should not have been collectivized; the kulaks should have been limited and squeezed out—not liquidated; and the speed of reform should
have been adjusted to local conditions. The way to correct all these

[5] Krylov, "V Penzhinskom raione," p. 93; Pavel Maslov, "Kochevye ob"edineniia edinolichnykh khoziaistv v tundre Severnogo kraia," SS, no. 5 (1934): 34; Anisimov, "O
sotsial'nykh otnosheniiakh," p. 47.
   [6] For a discussion of the debate, see Chapter 7.
   [7] N. Saprygin, "Olenevodcheskii sovkhoz i olenkolkhozy v Nenetskom okruge," SS,
no. 9 (1931): 37; "O rabote v natsional'nykh raionakh Krainego Severa," p. 53; Skachko,
"Resheniia XVII pertkonferentsii," p. 14; "Postanovleniia TsK partii," pp. 3–4; Tobolaev,
"V Tofalarskom raione," p. 95; A. Andreev, "Iz opyta kollektivizatsii," SS, no. 4 (1934):
97; I. Vyucheiskii, "Slet rabotnikov olenevodstva," SS, no. 2 (1934): 92.
   [8] Nikul'shin, Pervobytnye proizvodstvennye ob"edineniia, p. 101; TsGAOR, f. 3977,
op. 1, d. 1070, l. 42.
   [9] Nikul'shin, Pervobytnye proizvodstvennye ob"edineniia, pp. 98–99; Bilibin, "Sredi
koriakov," p. 94.
   [10] "Postanovlenie TsK VKP(b) ot 22 iunia 1932 goda," PS, no. 13 (1932): 56; "O rabote
v natsional'nykh raionakh Krainego Severa," pp. 53–54; P. G. Smidovich, "Nashi zadachi
na Severnykh okrainakh," SS, no. 3 (1932): 21; Sergeev, Nekapitalisticheskii put', p. 342.
   [11] "O rabote v natsional'nykh raionakh Krainego Severa," p. 53.

"deviations" was "to supervise the leading cadres . . . in national regions with a view to their consolidation."[12]

The Committee of the North came alive again. Skachko pointed out triumphantly (and truthfully) that "the Committee of the North had never even hinted at any total collectivization in reindeer breeding regions under existing conditions" and told the local officials that, had they listened to him all along, they would be in much better shape now.[13] The Party leadership was not impressed. A Central Executive Committee secretary, A. S. Kiselev, addressed the Ninth Plenum of the Committee of the North with a question all the more devastating because it was unfair: "Did the number of animals increase or diminish after collectivization?"[14] The numbers had most certainly diminished, and Kiselev made it clear who would be held responsible if the trend continued: "In order to avoid any further excesses in the regions of the Far North, I would ask you, comrades, to give very careful thought to all the latest initiatives of our Party and government."[15]

Chastened but obviously relieved, the leaders of the Committee of the North resurrected their old appeals for maximum caution, attention to local peculiarities, and support for traditional northern economy.[16] At the same time, some of the more thorough collectivizers were fired or arrested, and the two regions specifically mentioned in the resolution all but stopped collectivization: Taimyr "abandoned the fight against the kulaks almost completely," and in the European north, according to one Nenets, "the kolkhozniki got back their tents and sleds and some of their reindeer, so our life got better."[17] The main emphasis was on transforming native kolkhozy into so-called simple productive units in which members were supposed to pool their resources for specific tasks while keeping their property ownership. To some local organizers that was no different from the traditional bands or encampments, and many "simple producers" were allowed simply to retrieve their

[12] Ibid., p. 54.

[13] Skachko, "Postanovleniia TsK partii," pp. 3–13.

[14] A. S. Kiselev, "Ocherednye zadachi sovetov na Krainem Severe," SS, no. 4 (1932): 14. Also see TsGAOR, f. 3977, op. 1, d. 738, ll. 19–21.

[15] Kiselev, "Ocherednye zadachi," p. 14.

[16] TsGAOR, f. 3977, op. 1, dd. 738–39; "Rezoliutsii Deviatogo rasshirennogo plenuma Komiteta Severa pri Prezidiume VTsIK," SS, no. 4 (1932): annex, 1–32; E. Kantor, "Sever zovet," RN, no. 10–11 (1932): 133–38; Anatolii Skachko, "Deviatyi Plenum Komiteta Severa," SS, no. 5 (1932): 14–22.

[17] Gerasimovich, "V Taimyrskom okruge," p. 62; Vyucheiskii, "Slet udarnikov olenevodstva," p. 92. See also Murnik, "V Tofalarskom raione," p. 96; Skachko, "Osnovnye voprosy," p. 9; TsGAOR, f. 3977, op. 1, d. 737, ll. 14–5.

property and resume the old ways.[18] Even the kulaks were to remain kulaks for the time being. The Iamal district executive committee announced that "the imposition of the 6000 ruble fine on the household of Khudia Nanui, who owns no more than 150 head of reindeer, is to be considered a leftist deviation bordering on outright dekulakization."[19] In Lovozero, "Kanev Grigorii Gavrilovich hired a day laborer for a number of years, but having a family of eight and a herd of 480 reindeer is an extenuating circumstance. The household of Kanev Grigorii Gavrilovich is to be placed in the solid middle category. The confiscated living quarters are to be returned; the fixed assignment is to be lifted."[20]

In most northern areas, however, the Party resolution and the Committee's appeals fell on deaf ears. A year had passed before the Ostiako-Vogul regional bosses responded to the campaign with a perfunctory decree of their own, and in northern Yakutia the kolkhozes did not hear about the change in policy until the winter of 1933–34.[21] The collectivization of household items and domestic activities was reversed, but there was a definite reluctance to return the "basic means of production."[22] The plan remained the number-one priority, and officials at every level, although condemning deviations, continued to press their subordinates for more furs, fish, and reindeer. And at least in the short run—with no funds and no merchandise to offer in exchange—forced labor in the kolkhoz and the expropriation of the kulaks seemed to be the only reliable means of obtaining native produce. Both local administrators and central procurement organizations continued the policy of high taxation, fixed assignments, and fines. Even the government decree of June 1932 against violations of "revolutionary legality," widely advertised by the Committee of the North as a direct order to curb these practices, seems to have made almost no impression.[23] The

[18] P. Beskorsyi, "Nekotorye itogi (Materialy o sostoianii kollektivizatsii na Krainem Severe)," SS, no. 2 (1934): 58–60.
[19] E. K., "V Iamal'skom (Nenetskom) natsional'nom okruge Ob'-Irtyshskoi oblasti," SS, no. 5 (1934): 77. See also TsGAOR, f. 3977, op. 1, d. 757, ll. 167–70.
[20] TsGAOR, f. 3977, op. 1, d. 757, l. 167.
[21] "Za liniiu partii v kolkhoznom stroitel'stve na Krainem Severe," SS, no. 4 (1933): 6; Skachko, "Osnovnye voprosy," p. 9.
[22] "Za liniiu partii," p. 7; Beskorsyi, "Nekotorye itogi," pp. 57–61; "Rezoliutsiia Pervogo Vsesoiuznogo s"ezda integral'noi kooperatsii o rabote na Krainem Severe," SS, no. 5 (1934): 68.
[23] Kruglov, "O revoliutsionnoi zakonnosti," pp. 98–99; "V Komitete Severa pri Prezidiume VTsIK," SS, no. 1 (1933): 126–27; "V natsional'nykh okrugakh," SS, no. 6 (1933): 80. Cf. L. Rabinkov, "Za vnimatel'noe otnoshenie k zhalobam trudiashchikhsia," RN, no. 8 (1934): 20–23.

Committee was as powerless as ever, and the few non-local government prosecutors who ventured that far north were completely at the mercy of the people they were supposed to restrain. As Skachko pointed out, "In terms of financial support, food provisions, living arrangements, and means of transportation, the judicial personnel is totally dependent on various economic agencies. . . . After all that, try and ask the judge to be objective and disinterested when dealing with the employees of the institution that feeds him and provides his accommodation."[24]

Indeed, many judges tried very hard to help their hosts deal with the procurement problem—and have some old-fashioned fun in the process. In the Ostiako-Vogul region a certain judge Kurdiukov, accompanied by his "kulak' friends, set out for the taiga to investigate the underfulfillment of the plan by a group of Khanty fishermen.

> Approaching the settlement by boat at night, the judge and the kulaks decided to scare the population and started spraying the water with small shot, creating the impression of machine-gun fire. They also fired several salvos at the bank. Once on land, they spread out in battle formation. The native population decided they were being attacked by some gang, got frightened, and retreated deep into the tundra.[25]

Unprotected from various "violations of revolutionary legality" but spared the rigors of collective sleeping and eating, the native kolkhozy were little more than a form of mobilizing native labor for the fulfillment of the plan. Just as before, "the plan grew like a snowball as it passed from the center to the periphery, and reached its immediate executor—a kolkhoz or a single fisherman—as an absolutely impossible task."[26] In 1932 the Narym region received a plan target for 80,000 centners of fish and passed it on as a plan target for 110,000; the Ostiako-Vogul region added 10,000 centners to its plan for 1934. Even when there was no demand for native produce (as in the case of sea mammal skins and blubber in Chukotka) and thus no pressure from the center, the local officials earned their bread by coming up with impossible plans of their own.[27]

---

[24] Skachko, "Osnovnye voprosy," p. 8.

[25] N. Firsov and Petrova, "Organy iustitsii v otdel'nykh raionakh Krainego Severa," SS, no. 2 (1934): 84. Cf. "Nam pishut," SS, no. 1 (1935): 104.

[26] A. Sevrunov, "O nekotorykh nedochetakh v rybozagotovitel'noi rabote," SS, no. 3 (1934): 27.

[27] TsGAOR, f. 3977, op. 1, d. 990, ll. 157–64; Skachko, "Osnovnye voprosy," p. 13.

Where the pressure was strong, as in fishing, the annual plans exceeded performance by about 50 percent, so that when armed Russian agents came to receive what belonged to the state, they took everything.[28] For many native fishermen, arguments against this kind of collectivization were arguments against starvation. According to the Koriak from Malaia Itkana, "If we all work in the kolkhoz, who'll catch seals and fish for us?" Their neighbors from Talovka were even more blunt: "There's no way we can form a kolkhoz here because we all have children."[29] As settled groups had no choice in the matter, it became common practice to delegate some fishermen to do corvée for the kolkhoz, with the rest working for the community.[30] Those who combined fishing with reindeer breeding could either try to abandon the more collectivized fishing or simply regard it as the part of the season devoted to the Russians.[31] In such circumstances, the catch continued to fall in direct ratio to the pressure applied. Between 1931 and 1933, the amount of fish taken in the Ob'-Irtysh basin dropped from 24,000 tons to 16,500, and in Kamchatka the catch fell by over a half to a disastrous 2,000 tons.[32]

Most large reindeer herders remained on their own. Outside the relatively accessible territory of the European Nenets, the proportion of collectivized households among tundra dwellers remained very low. All in all, about 10 percent of the reindeer were owned by the kolkhozy, and 8.8 percent by the sovkhozy.[33] Of these, many existed on paper only, and occasional visits by collectivizers could not lead to much more than "dekulakization without collectivization."[34] According to one such collectivizer, "They criticize us, they demand information, but we don't get to see nomadic kolkhozy for three or four months, and when they finally come, we need to draw up a balance, but they are illiterate and don't speak any Russian."[35] Most native collectives had

[28] Skachko, "Osnovnye voprosy," pp. 6, 12–14; "Rezoliutsiia Pervogo Vserossiiskogo s"ezda," p. 68.

[29] Bilibin, "Sredi koriakov," p. 94.

[30] Ibid., pp. 94–95.

[31] Bagmut, "Kochevoi sovet," p. 19.

[32] Skachko, "Osnovnye voprosy," pp. 12–13.

[33] Sergeev, Nekapitalisticheskii put', pp. 342, 353.

[34] P. E. Terletskii, "K voprosu o stroitel'stve olenevodcheskikh kollektivnykh khoziaistv," SS, no. 11–12 (1931): 47.

[35] Ispravnikov, "Kolkhoznoe stroitel'stvo na Iamale," SS, no. 2 (1933): 91.

no accounts, no accountants, and no permanent non-native supervisors. It was not always clear just what made them kolkhozy.[36]

The most promising kolkhozniki were to be found among those pastoralists who had lost their reindeer.[37] They could not flee, depended
on Russian goods, and were relatively easy to threaten. Some even welcomed the idea, apparently because they understood collectivization
as keeping what was theirs and also receiving free gifts from the Russians.[38] Most of those who had anything substantial to contribute had
been expropriated as kulaks, so that the new kokhozy consisted almost
exclusively of paupers who had little to lose. Such kolkhozy, which
Skachko called "feeble, dwarf little things," could survive only on state
credits (obtained, in turn, from the "kulaks").[39] The members saw these
new assets as gifts or nobody's property, and dealt with them accordingly. Everyone took care of his own animals, whereas "the 'government' reindeer loaned to the kolkhoz were neglected or eaten in the
most shameless way, and, what was more . . . , the kolkhoz members
absolutely refused to consider the slaughtered reindeer as part of their
pay."[40] District officials contributed to the depletion of livestock by
selling large numbers of animals for meat and using does to transport
heavy loads. Large reindeer herds that formerly belonged to the kulaks
went wild and roamed the tundra unattended.[41] There was a shortage
of humans, as well. One kolkhoz ceased to exist because all herders
were in jail, and another could not fulfill its plan because "the remaining members [were] being sent to attend various courses."[42] The
desperate pleas for help by the kolkhoz chairmen who took their responsibilities seriously were either ignored or answered by people

[36] Ustiugov, "Samokritika na suglanakh," pp. 55–56; Mikhalev, "Uspekhi i tormozy
kolkhoznogo stroitel'stva," SS, no. 3–4 (1931): 170; D. Chudinov, "V Tomponskom raione," SS, no. 1 (1934): 109.

[37] P. Lebedev, "Na perelome," SS, no. 5 (1934): 20; A. Mikhalev, "Sovetskaia torgovlia
na Krainem Severe," SS, no. 6 (1933): 18.

[38] Nikul'shin, Pervobytnye proizvodstvennye ob"edineniia, pp. 96–98.

[39] Skachko, "Sotsial'no-proizvodstvennye otnosheniia," p. 29. See also Skachko, "Resheniia XVII partkonferentsii," p. 14; P. N. Orlovskii, "Beseda s predsedatelem PNOKa,"
SS, no. 5 (1931): 135; Saprygin, "Olenevodcheskii sovkhoz," p. 38; TsGAOR, f. 3977,
op. 1, d. 645, l. 24.

[40] Skachko, "Resheniia XVII partkonferentsii," p. 14; See also TsGAOR, f. 3977, op. 1,
d. 738, ll. 43–62, and d. 833, l. 58; Skachko, "Sotsial'no-proizvodstvennye otnosheniia,"
p. 29; Medvedev, "O rabote s bednotoi," p. 75; "Sostoianie kolkhoznogo stroitel'stva v
Iamal'skom okruge Uraloblasti," SS, no. 3 (1933): 108; and TsGAOR, f. 3977, op. 1,
d. 710, l. 42, and d. 737, ll. 15–17.

[41] "Nam pishut," p. 104.

[42] TsGAOR, f. 3977, op 1, d. 738, l. 19, and d. 757, l. 79.

with very vague notions of how a kolkhoz was supposed to be run. According to one such chairman,

> The district kolkhoz management has some instructors, but they are children themselves. They come to the koklhoz, fool around with the Komsomol members, play games with the adolescents, dance, but offer no help as far as the organization of work is concerned. One time three instructors—Zviagin, Simukhin, and Silaev—came to check up on the kolkhoz. Each one of them was smart in his own way. Whenever they would start arguing, one would say one thing; the other would say another thing; and the third would say something different. They argued so much that I asked if I could go eat. They turned all the files upside down, and finally left everything as it was—except that they lost one document. It took me a whole day to find it.[43]

Disgusted with the kolkhozy, the Commissariat of Agriculture invested most of its northern resources into reindeer sovkhozy, that is, state-owned enterprises run by appointed officials and salaried employees.[44] The officials, however, tended to be outsiders unfamiliar with reindeer breeding; the employees, dekulakized natives who slaughtered the animals when they were hungry and not when the plan called for it; and the district administrators, old settlers who could not care less about "Moscow's reindeer."[45] Of the 346,000 reindeer acquired by the state 170,000 (51 percent) perished.[46]

All in all, as a result of the continuing collectivization and dekulakization—and to the great apprehension of those administrators who had heard Kiselev's threat—the number of reindeer continued to fall. Between 1930 and 1934 the total herd diminished by about 35 percent (including in Evenkia, by 40 percent; in the Koriak region, by 48 percent; and in Komi, by 67 percent).[47] In Skachko's bitter summary, "we have paid for the transferral of 20 percent of the herd into the socialist sector by destroying 35 percent of the reindeer."[48]

The fur industry was in much better shape. Pastoralists and fish-

---

[43] Pakin, "Kolkhoz 'Krasnaia zvezda' Ostiako-Vogul'skogo okruga," SS, no. 1 (1933): 107.

[44] Skachko, "Vos'moi Plenum Komiteta Severa," p. 13, and "Sotsial'no-proizvodstvennye otnosheniia," p. 29; Terletskii, "K voprosu," pp. 45–50.

[45] TsGAOR, f. 3977, op. 1, d. 737, ll. 19–20; Ia. Koshelev, "V Iamal'skikh tundrakh," SS, no. 5 (1934): 79–82; "Rezoliutsii Deviatogo rasshirennogo plenuma," annex, p. 15; Ia. K-ev, "Po olenevodcheskim sovkhozam Severnogo kraia," SS, no. 5 (1933): 78–84.

[46] Skachko, "Osnovnye voprosy," p. 17.

[47] Ibid. (The data for Komi is for the period between 1927 and 1934.)

[48] Ibid.

ermen could not stop producing that which was the source of their livelihood, and the state could always reach for what they intended for themselves. Trappers, on the other hand, had the choice of switching to a subsistence economy if pelts could not be exchanged on terms that they regarded as fair. There were reports of natives arriving at trading stations, finding nothing they needed, and going back into the taiga, pelt in hand.[49] Introducing kolkhozy and forced labor among hunters and trappers was very difficult, and in many cases economic incentive was the only way to keep furs coming in. And as furs, unlike other native produce, generated hard currency, such incentive could often be found. On one occasion, having received reports that trappers refused to sell their pelts, the Commissariat of Foreign Trade ordered that a cargo of alcohol be sent to the native areas of the north.[50] In 1933 the fur procurement plan was reportedly fulfilled by 95.5 percent.[51]

Just as in reindeer breeding, however, the state fur-trading agency (Soiuzpushnina) found that it was sometimes easier and cheaper to bypass the natives and get the furs through its own means. One such means was to open game reserves, forbid the local hunters from entering, and hunt relentlessly throughout the year. When all the animals had been exterminated, the "reserve" would be closed.[52] Such tactics jeopardized not only the native economy but also the long-term state interests, and the whole management of Soiuzpushnina was fired in 1934. The correct and much heralded way to raise productivity was to form the so-called machine-tractor stations (MTS), the outposts of state-run industrialization in the midst of rural backwardness. The central argument for collectivization was that only by pooling their resources would the peasants—instructed by their elder brothers the proletarians—be able to take full advantage of tractors and other machinery of the future. The role of the MTS was to spearhead the change and provide the new kolkhozy with both new equipment and political guidance.

In the north these economic equivalents of kul'tbazy emerged in the shape of hunting stations (POS) and motor-boat stations (MRS). The former were supposed to promote "rational" methods of hunting and combat wasteful practices; the latter were to rent motorboats to collectivized teams of native fishermen and sea hunters. Once again, how-

---

[49] Anatolii Skachko, "Ocherednye zadachi sovetskoi raboty sredi malykh narodov Severa," SS, no. 2 (1931): 16.
[50] Ibid.
[51] "Rezoliutsiia Pervogo Vserossiiskogo s"ezda," p. 68.
[52] TsGAOR, f. 3977, op. 1, d. 990, l. 152; Skachko, "Osnovnye voprosy," p. 10.

ever, the managers of these stations were primarily responsible for the fulfillment of the plan, and that meant that the POS and MRS became new and rather powerful procurement centers. The POS tended to use the "reserve" system, employing hired volunteers in "their own" areas and seeking to assert themselves as the sole agents of the natives who hunted nearby (theoretically, the much weaker kolkhoz administration was supposed to have independent channels for fur sales). The MRS, on the other hand, relied on labor dues from the native kolkhozy. They found it more efficient to have the kolhoz come to them than go out and engage in the unpredictable business of organizing the natives.[53]

The state organizations had little or no economic incentive to offer. The central Commissariat of Supplies was supposed to determine the quantity of merchandise to be sent to the north on the basis of the number of inhabitants (classified as "workers" and "others"); the amount of goods procured from every given area; the purchasing power of the population; and the availability of goods locally.[54] Any such information about the native areas had to be very approximate at best, but even if the information did exist, there was little use for it. The chain of command and the transportation routes were very long indeed, and just as the plans grew on their way down, the quantity of supplies diminished. A certain percentage never got shipped because of various bureaucratic delays and the short navigation time in the north. In 1932 20 percent of all goods intended for the north were stopped in various bottlenecks along the way.[55] An increasing portion of the supplies had to be diverted for new categories of local population: exiled Russian peasants and contract laborers.[56] Finally—and not surprising in an atmosphere of chronic shortages—a great deal was stolen by officials, transportation workers, and sales agents.[57] By the time a given shipment arrived at the end of the line (that is, at a native trading center) there was often little left besides spoiled and unwanted goods rejected

[53] Skachko, "Osnovnye voprosy," p. 10; M. A. Sergeev, "Zadachi vtoroi piatiletki na Severe," RN, no. 7 (1934): 47.

[54] Ia. Klimushev, "Tselevoe naznachenie v tovarosnabzhenii Krainego Severa," SS, no. 6 (1933): 23.

[55] A. Mikhalev, "Grimasy snabzheniia i torgovli na Krainem Severe," SS, no. 2 (1934): 51–52.

[56] Pakin, "Kolkhoz," p. 107; Mikhalev, "Grimasy," p. 54; Klimushev, "Tselevoe naznachenie," pp. 23–24.

[57] A. Mikhalev, "Sovetskaia torgovlia na Krainem Severe," SS, no. 6 (1933): 14–15; Gerasimovich, "V Taimyrskom okruge," pp. 64–65; Firsov and Petrova, "Organy iustitsii," p. 86.

elsewhere.[58] (Most trading centers in the taiga and tundra were over-flowing with rubber boots, makeup kits, and toothbrushes but had no hunting rifles, needles, or cooking utensils.)[59] The local agents disposed of the remaining merchandise in ways that made sense to them as former traders. In the Narym region fifty percent of the flour reached the natives in the form of home brew.[60] As N. N. Bilibin put it, "When it comes to the supply situation, kulaks have an easy time finding arguments to discredit us."[61]

After the hardest collectivization season of 1931–32 the destruction of the native economy and the shortages of southern merchandise combined to make the situation very difficult indeed. The Committee of the North, unable to do anything on its own, vowed "to inform the government about the grave supply problems in 1932–33 in remote areas of the north and to request that urgent measures be taken to solve them."[62] The government responded by creating a special commission chaired by the Commissar of Supplies A. I. Mikoian and by issuing a special decree on this "extraordinarily difficult situation."[63] In 1933 the commission announced its solution. The (presumably untrustworthy) local officials lost the right to distribute the goods that they received. The central plan was to cover the whole operation from Moscow to the remotest tundra encampment, establishing precise norms for all kinds of merchandise and all groups of the population. Thus for every ruble of reindeer meat delivered to the state, the kolkhoz members of the Ostiako-Vogul region received 400 grams of flour, 40 grams of groats, 15 grams of sugar, and 2.3 grams of tea; individual (noncollectivized) herders received 350 grams of flour, 35 grams of groats, 18 grams of sugar, and 2.1 grams of tea; and "kulaks" received 150 grams of flour, 15 grams of groats, 0.3 grams of sugar, and 1 gram of tea.[64]

This system presupposed the smooth working of the supply mechanism, the availability of precise information, and an ability to forecast the native production down to the last pelt. It also ignored the difficulty of endlessly dividing goods among the consumers. Thus sales clerks

[58] "Vos'moi rasshirennyi plenum Komiteta Severa," SS, no. 6 (1931): 132; Aksenov, "Khatangskaia tundra," SS, no. 7–8 (1931): 213; Mikhalev, "Grimasy," pp. 46–55.

[59] Skachko, "Ocherednye zadachi," p. 15; N. Firsov, "O severnom assortimente tovarov," SS, no. 3 (1932): 89–93; Mikhalev, "Grimasy," pp. 49–50.

[60] D'Amov, "Grammofon i varshavskaia krovat' (Narymskie ocherki)," ORS, no. 6 (1930): 56.

[61] Bilibin, "U zapadnykh koriakov," p. 211.

[62] "Rezoliutsii Deviatogo rasshirennogo plenuma," annex, p. 11.

[63] "Postanovlenie Kommissii ispolneniia pri SNK SSSR," SS, no. 5 (1932): 149.

[64] Klimushev, "Tselevoe naznachenie," p. 30.

were not allowed to sell to any one customer more than 1.66 rubles worth of textiles even though the cheapest baby shirt cost 3.5 rubles.[65] While the clerks amused themselves by inviting the natives to "touch the boots for the amount of one ruble fifteen kopeks," the exchange situation continued to deteriorate.[66]

"What is it, stupidity or sabotage?" was the usual question.[67] In the spirit of the times, the Committee of the North and everyone interested blamed the low-level cadres. "There is no doubt that in the Extreme North, where it is particularly easy to conceal one's past, the trade organizations are infested with hostile and alien elements."[68] That, of course, was the official policy applicable to all spheres of life. In Stalin's new world failure was always the result of stupidity or sabotage on the part of the executors, and that, in turn, could only result from a wrong social background or insufficient ideological training. The Party purge of 1933 marked the beginning of a concerted effort to rid the apparatus of all the fools, wreckers, and "has-beens" who had "sneaked in" under false pretenses during the great migration of peoples caused by the First Five-Year Plan. The other bureaucracies were expected to follow suit.

Yet the Committee of the North was not merely echoing the official pronouncements. As far as the cadre policy was concerned, the "Party Line" fit in nicely with the Committee's long-standing belief that the source of most of the evil in the north was the corruption, ignorance, backwardness, and just plain meanness of the local Russians. No wonder kolkhozy were falling apart, sovkhozy were inefficient, and material incentives were nonexistent—after all, the people immediately in charge were the same old "predators" plus a few confused young fools.[69] Speaking at the Committee's tenth (and last) plenum, Skachko cited as typical the case of a Yakutia district boss who had been arrested by the OGPU for "shooting at the portrait of Lenin and sending out to local cells memoranda with pictures of genitals."[70] By 1934 the Com-

[65] Mikhalev, "Grimasy," p. 46.
[66] Skachko, "Osnovnye voprosy," pp. 13–15.
[67] Firsov, "O severnom assortimente," p. 92.
[68] Mikhalev, "Sovetskaia torgovlia," p. 14.
[69] E. Kavelin, "Kolymskii krai," SS, no. 2 (1931): 171; D. F. Medvedev, "Sostoianie i zadachi partiinogo stroitel'stva na Krainem Severe," RN, no. 2 (1933): 34–35; Kruglov, "O revoliutsionnoi zakonnosti," p. 99; Pakin, "Kolkhoz," p. 107; G. Aronshtam, "K chistke natsional'nykh partorganizatsii," pp. 9–15.
[70] TsGAOR, f. 3977, op. 1, d. 990, l. 143.

mittee of the North all but declared the total failure of collectivization among the native peoples and pointed to its erstwile enemy (the Russian settlers-turned-kulak) as the main culprit.[71]

[71] Skachko, "Osnovnye voprosy," pp. 3–18; "Rezoliutsii Desiatogo rasshirennogo plenuma Komiteta Severa," SS, no. 3 (1934): 138–56.

"The first picture show," from M. G. Levin and L. P. Potapov, eds., *Narody Sibiri* (Moscow, 1956)

7

The Cultural Revolutionaries

I'm the Great and Mighty Bathtub,
I'm the Chief of Clean Latrines,
I'm the Boss of Baths and Soap Suds,
I'm the Dreaded Scrub-'em-clean!

If I call my troops to battle,
Hordes of tubs will fill this place.
They will scream, and screech, and rattle
Till you've washed your dirty face!
—K. Chukovskii, *Moidodyr*

The War against Backwardness

Collectivization was only one aspect of the Great Transformation. The "socialist offensive" was to involve a wholesale cultural revolution that would replace all antiquated customs, beliefs, and practices with civilized norms of behavior and the new scientific ideology.

> In such a case the arriving correspondents would hopefully not be regaled with the spectacle of the amazing dance of the nomadic reindeer breeders, in which men and women imitate the love between a buck and a doe; the Lamut would stop calling themselves . . . reindeer people; the Chukchi would stop calling themselves . . . reindeer riders; and the nomads would stop intoxicating themselves with their favorite drink—human urine with fly agaric.[1]

The leaders of the Committee of the North and the older generation

[1] Kantorovich *Po Sovetskoi Kamchatke*, p. 159.

219

of northern ethnographers would have had no problem subscribing to this aim, if not in all particulars. Their revulsion may have been more tempered, but they had always assumed that the "backward" elements of the native culture would have to go. The difference was in the speed and the willingness to use force. To the young soldiers of the Stalin offensive all this bride grabbing and urine drinking was totally incompatible with the kind of society they were building.

Recent graduates from the school of "progressive culture," the newly trained ethnographers, teachers, and administrators were absolutely intolerant of the backwardness they, with the help of the Party, had just managed to escape. Any lack of enthusiasm for the modernity they served was a deliberate personal insult, a pointed refusal to recognize their achievement and their sacrifice. More than that, it was a direct threat to the viability of that achievement because, in the official rhetoric, one drop of backwardness was enough to poison a barrelful of modernity. The vanguard's grasp on civilization seemed very tenuous, and the ultimate fate of the revolution depended on the speed with which they would "instill real culture" in the wide masses of the formerly exploited and benighted. Backwardness was "a swamp": if the enlightened ones did not pull out the ignorant, everyone would be swallowed up.

The greater the backwardness, the greater the speed needed. In Dimanshtein's words, "The advanced peoples are tearing along on the fast locomotive of history. . . . At the same time, the backward peoples have to 'race like the wind' . . . in order to catch up." As Skachko explained,

> This means that if the whole of the USSR, in the words of comrade Stalin, needs ten years to run the course of development that took Western Europe fifty to a hundred years, then the small peoples of the north, in order to catch up with the advanced nations of the USSR, must, during the same ten years, cover the road of development that took the Russian people one thousand years to cover, for even one thousand years ago the cultural level of Kievan Rus' was higher than that of the present-day small peoples of the north.[2]

In the most general sense, the means remained the same: backwardness was to be fought at its roots (in people's huts, tents, and minds) and through the promotion of a loyal group of future leaders. Only now every year had to include a whole century's worth of work. Persuasion was replaced by a determined frontal attack, and the experimental edu-

---

[2] S. M. Dimanshtein, "Rekonstruktivnyi period i rabota sredi natsional'nostei SSSR," *RN*, no. 1 (1930): 14; Skachko, "Ocherednye zadachi," p. 20.

cation of a handful of orphans became an all-embracing and methodi-
cal policy.

Throughout the Soviet Union the destruction of the old intelligentsia
went hand in hand with the creation of a new one, and that meant
upward mobility for working-class Party members. Yet what was class
in Russia was nationality elsewhere. According to the Tenth Party Congress, the non-Russian ethnic groups had been oppressed as ethnic
groups, were collectively backward as ethnic groups, and were therefore entitled to special assistance as ethnic groups. Besides autonomization, the officially prescribed way to deal with the situation was
"indigenization" (korenizatsiia), which entailed granting non-
Russians preferential treatment in education and employment. A Russian could benefit from government-sponsored quotas because he was
a proletarian; a Nenets could claim privilege because he was a Nenets.[3]
During the Stalin Revolution indigenization was redefined to exclude
native exploiters (the Nenets also had to be proletarian), but the practice of granting preferential treatment to members of particular ethnic
groups was greatly intensified.[4] The idea was "to create national proletarian cadres on whom the Soviet government could rely wholly and
unequivocally in its grandiose work of constructing socialism," and
the method consisted in the massive recruitment of non-Russians into
educational institutions and key management positions.[5] In the "extreme north," the continuing shortage of non-native volunteers provided an additional incentive.[6]

In 1930 the northern rabfak became a separate Institute of the Peoples of the North—with a new management and a new curriculum. The
fate of the Committee had been replicated in its favorite creation. The
"northerners," vigorously supported by Smidovich and led by Ia. P.
Koshkin (who was himself a young Civil War veteran who wore his
trenchcoat to class and knew how to use class-war rhetoric)[7] had prevailed in their struggle for administrative autonomy but lost the war
for the soul of the institution. There would be no more education for

[3] Desiatyi s"ezd Rossiisskoi Kommunisticheskoi partii," p. 101; See Gerhard Simon,
Nationalism and Policy toward the Nationalities in the Soviet Union: From Totalitarian
Dictatorship to Post-Stalinist Society (Boulder, Col., 1991).

[4] See, for example, M. Amosov, "Problema natskadrov v period sotsialisticheskoi rekonstruktsii," RN, no. 1 (1930): 20–28; A. Bogdanov, "Kolkhoznoe stroitel'stvo v natsional'nykh raionakh," RN, no. 3 (1930): 41; E. Mostovaia, "Sovety v natsional'nykh
respublikakh i oblastiakh," RN, no. 4–5 (1930): 47–57; A. Oshirov, "Korenizatsiia v sovetskom stroitel'stve," RN, no. 4–5 (1930): 110–15.

[5] A. A. Takho-Godi, "Podgotovka vuzovskikh kadrov natsmen," RN, no. 6 (1930): 83.

[6] "Protokol sed'mogo rasshirennogo plenuma Komiteta," p. 147.

[7] Gagen-Torn, Lev Iakovlevich Shternberg, pp. 162–63.

the sake of education and no more English language classes. The emphasis was on practical skills and ideological correctness. New departments of kolkhoz administration, foraging techniques, and industrial education were added to the existing departments of Party/soviet administration and pedagogy. Every student was expected to learn how to fix a motorboat or a radio receiver, as well as how to interpret Party policy. According to stringent new class requirements, only certified children of poor parents could be accepted.[8] Overall, the goal of the Institute's activity was to teach the students how to detect backwardness in economic, social, domestic, and spiritual life; purge one's own mind and body; and then go back home and pull their kinsmen out of the proverbial swamp. As one Nanai student described his conversion,

> I had always lived in a remote, dark little village in the heart of the taiga. I never thought that I would some day live the way I live now. Life here is very strange to me, for I had never seen anything like it before, living as I did in complete ignorance and without any idea of culture and the successes of our socialist construction. When I arrived in Leningrad, a new and unknown world opened before me. When I saw the May First demonstration for the first time, I became frightened because I could not understand where all those people were going. But then I asked other students, and they told me that it was a demonstration of the toilers of the Soviet Union celebrating Labor Day. All plants grow. We, too, will grow in the direction of the new life—all of us, toilers of the Soviet Union. We will march in step with our Young Communist League and we will all participate in our socialist construction.[9]

Many of them did participate, and as later, "postrevolutionary" complaints implied, did march in step with the Young Communist League, "carrying out collectivization through intimidation and so forth."[10] The Evenk student Putugir did not mince words when he found out that his parents had been condemned as kulaks (which meant he would have to be expelled from the Institute): "As soon as I heard about it I immediately broke all relations with them because I consider it unnecessary to deal with kulaks and nonproletarian elements. I had corresponded with them as middle peasants, but they turned out to

[8] TsGAOR, f. 3977, op. 1, d. 340, ll. 1–19, 69, 76–107, 126–56, 187, 224–27; "Protokol zasedaniia VI rasshirennogo plenuma Komiteta," p. 13; K. Ia. Luks, "Institut narodov Severa, ego mesto i zadachi," SS, no. 1 (1930): 130–36; "Protokol sed'mogo rasshirennogo plenuma Komiteta," pp. 151–53; "V Institute narodov Severa," SS, no. 5 (1931): 130–34.

[9] Ia. Samar, "Vpechatlenie o demonstratsii," TT, no. 4 (1932): 49.

[10] "V Komitete Severa pri Prezidiume VTsIK," p. 126.

be different. On the same day I wrote to the Katun native executive committee about my separation from them."[11]

Yet even if all the students internalized all of the progressive notions, the Institute's success was only a drop in the ocean (swamp). After the dramatic expansion of the cultural revolution, the number of graduates rose from sixteen in 1931 to fifty in 1935,[12] and that could barely produce ripples. According to a 1930 report, 85 percent of all students were sick, and all were underfed. Some wrote desperate letters to their local sponsors complaining of cold and hunger and asking for money. "I guess you have succeeded in 'training' me . . . for the grave," wrote N. Spiridonov to I. M. Suslov. "Farewell, we will probably never see each other again."[13]

Meanwhile, the campaign to recruit native students to provincial technical schools was not very successful because the local authorities and the Russian students were, understandably, indifferent or hostile to indigenization. The schools were intended for Russians; instruction was in Russian; and native students ("culturally and politically undeveloped and having difficulties with Russian") rarely felt welcome.[14] Besides, during the Stalin revolution many such schools were practically run by local Komsomol cells that terrorized the teachers, the "bureaucracy," and—why not?—the natives. Such, for instance, was the case at the Tsipikan mining apprenticeship school (FZU), where a group of Evenk were sent to study.

We wanted to study, so we walked all the way to Tsipikan and arrived on time. There we were told that classes would begin in fifteen days. We were housed in an attic. Nobody gave us any food. Then they postponed the classes again and sent us to fell trees fifteen kilometers from Tsipikan. When the time came to return, they would not let us go back to Tsipikan and would not give us any horses. Then classes started. The conditions for studying were bad. Everybody laughed at us and made fun of us, and nobody helped us. Finally, it became impossible to go on studying and we left the mining school.[15]

The solution was to create a network of separate native departments or even special native technical schools—with the result that whole

[11] TsGAOR, f. 3977, op. 1, d. 532, ll. 209–10.

[12] "Gotovim spetsialistov-ratsionalov," SAr, no. 5 (1935): 56.

[13] TsGAOR, f. 3977, op. 1, d. 532, l. 8. See also ll. 46–47.

[14] See "Vos'moi rasshirennyi plenum Komiteta Severa," SS, no. 6 (1931): 154–58; TsGAOR, f. 3977, op. 1, d. 933, ll. 9–10; D. F. Medvedev, "Za podgotovku kadrov i vydvizhenie tuzemnykh sovetskikh rabotnikov," SS, no. 10 (1931): 12–13.

[15] A. Gilev, "Zapiski o Bauntovskom raione," SS, no. 4 (1934): 92–93.

institutions rather than individual students were ignored or persecuted. There were no textbooks, no teachers, and often no roofs
overhead, and the "polytechnic system of education" was either not
possible due to lack of equipment or was used as a form of organizing
native labor, with very little education involved.[16] When the Executive
Committee of the Far Eastern province received some funds intended
for the native technical school, it kept the money, took over the school
building, and had the students and all their possessions thrown out
into the street.[17] At their new home in Nikolaevsk-on-Amur, the students were not allowed to fish for subsistence.[18] In the course of a
month, the starving students of the Evenk regional course for soviet
and kolkhoz administration had six teachers of math, three teachers of
kolkhoz administration, two teachers of Russian, and three directors.
After they "spat into the salty soup, threw down the raw bread, and
demonstratively left the cafeteria," the ringleaders were sentenced to
carrying boards with the inscription "Underminer [razlagatel'] of the
work of the course."[19]

In 1934, one way or another, 148 representatives of the small peoples
of the north were graduated from various professional schools.[20] Many
more attended short-term literacy courses, usually organized by the
Komsomol "cultural armies." Once again, however, whatever "cultural
headquarters" existed in the north dealt exclusively with the Russians,
and it took special "raids" by non-local volunteers to reach the native
peoples. The most successful such raid on record was a visit by a "brigade" of three Leningrad students to the Far Eastern province. The
Chukotka, Okhotsk, Koriak, and Sakhalin regions could not be reached
due to their remoteness, and the brigade concentrated on the area
around Khabarovsk. Having overcome the indifference of the local
administration and mobilized some teachers and students from the local schools, the Leningraders spent three months during the fishing
season organizing courses for "literate and semiliterate" natives. The
graduates became official "soldiers of the cultural army" responsible
for spreading education farther afield. To overcome considerable resistance, attendance was made compulsory and the "soldiers" were promised special certificates which allowed them to shop at trading centers

[16] Davydov, "Ocherednye zadachi kul'turnogo stroitel'stva na Krainem Severe," SS,
no. 4 (1932): 96–99.
[17] Ibid., p. 96.
[18] Skachko, "Osnovnye voprosy," p. 12.
[19] TsGAOR, f. 3977, op. 1, d. 933, ll. 9–10.
[20] E. D. Kantor, "Kadry na Krainem Severe," SAr, no. 2 (1935): 29.

without waiting in line. At the end of the raid the native cultural army of the Far Eastern province numbered 227 recruits.[21]

The value of these people as cultural revolutionaries is difficult to gauge. One unusually enthusiastic Evenk "liquidator of illiteracy" had the following career record:

> When our achievements at the courses were tested, I demonstrated good results in my reading. I can read fluently and loudly, and understand what I read. I can tell all my kinsmen what I have read in a book. I have already performed on stage one time, when classes ended. I read the story "The Red Army" from the Tungus primer. Once again, I read it very well. Now I will go home to the kolkhoz to liquidate illiteracy in the Tungus language among the kolkhozniki.[22]

To facilitate his task, the authorities forced the native soviets to subscribe to a wide gamut of the periodical press. Even before the Evenk liquidator could start working, his Katanga national region was receiving an astonishing thirty different newspapers and fifty-six magazines (presumably, in Russian).[23] At the same time, the native areas began receiving the first books printed in their languages: *What Is a Kolkhoz?*; *What Is a Soviet?*; *What Is a Court Trial?*; *The Party Is Guiding Us*; *What the October Revolution Gave to the Toilers of the North*; *The Threat of War and Our Tasks*; and *How to Treat a Sick Person*.[24]

The prospect of somebody reading these books loudly and fluently by a fireside did not impress the Russians who worked in the north. The goals of the cultural revolution were too ambitious to wait for the Leningrad graduates to arrive or for the local cadres to become "sufficiently literate both politically and technologically."[25] If the great transformation of native culture could not be carried out by the natives, the Russian "missionaries" would have to do it themselves. The most determined detachment were young ethnographers; the rest (and the majority) were the volunteers in search of adventure and retirement benefits. Finally, there were the old settlers, who as state employees and collectivizers were expected to carry out the directives on cultural work as well. Few of these people could define backwardess, but all of them knew it when they saw it. Dirt, economic irrationality, "wild

---

[21] P. Skorik, "Kul'turnyi shturm taigi i tundry," PN, no. 10 (1932): 32–39, and "Kul'-turnyi shturm taigi i tundry," SS, no. 1–2 (1932): 158–67.

[22] Il'ia Markov, "Kul'tpokhod v deistvii," SS, no. 4 (1933): 89.

[23] Ibid., p. 91.

[24] "Vseobuch na Krainem Severe," SS, no. 5 (1933): 95.

[25] D. F. Medvedev, "Ukrepim sovety na Krainem Severe i ozhivim ikh rabotu," SS, no. 1 (1933): 6 (quotation), 7–8. See also "V natsional'nykh okrugakh i raionakh," SS, no. 1

superstitions," and bizarre customs offended the senses and contradicted the official (and sometimes deeply felt) ideology. In fact, cultural work consisted in nothing less than the destruction of a whole way of life and its replacement by a new, "progressive" civilization. How does one approach such a task? Where does one begin?

For the central government, the most obvious route was to simply make backwardness illegal. In the spring of 1928 the Central Executive Committee expanded the Criminal Code of the RSFSR to include a new chapter, "Crimes That Constitute Survivals of Tribalism." Highest on the list were various forms of blood feud and those aspects of family organization that struck the legislators as based on inequality, particularly bridewealth and polygamy. A year later the Supreme Court recommended in a special decree that the criminality of survivals be judged from a class point of view. Both bridewealth and polygamy became a matter of kulak exploitation pure and simple.[26]

Yet ideologically reliable courts were nonexistent in the far north (native judges started referring to bridewealth as fines),[27] and in any case legalism was an uncongenial method of cultural engineering as far as the new revolutionaries were concerned. In the civil war according to Stalin, every evil had to be personified, socially defined, and then, by some method or other, neutralized. The kulaks were obviously responsible for most of the economic and social problems, but who was to blame for the overall cultural backwardness, ignorance, and "darkness"? The answer came easily: the shamans were to blame. They were the immediately identifiable and self-confessed guardians of tradition, the intermediaries between their communities and a world that the officials considered both nonexistent and powerfully pernicious. Just as obviously, they were the northern equivalents of that old and familiar enemy—the priest. The new missionaries assumed, and the Committee members obligingly (albeit belatedly) discovered, that shamanism was a religion like any other, and as such "supported and reinforced the relations of oppression and exploitation by sanctifying them with the authority of religious ideology."[28] Moreover, the odd rituals of

---

(1933): 127; "O sostoianii korenizatsii apparata po Iamal'skomu (Nenetskomu) okrugu," SS, no. 2 (1933): 112–14.

[26] Sobranie uzakonenii i rasporiazhenii raboche-krest'anskogo pravitel'stva RSFSR, no. 47, st. 356, in Russian Historical Sources 1928 (microform collection, New York), box 15, part 1, pp. 608–11; S. Akopov, "Bor'ba s bytovymi prestupleniiami," RN, no. 4–5 (1930): 58–63.

[27] N. I. Leonov, "V nizov'iakh Amura," SS, no. 2 (1930): 96–97.

[28] Suslov, "Shamanstvo i bor'ba s nim," p. 90. See also TsGAOR, f. 3977, op. 1, d. 392, l. 105; d. 394, l. 25; and d. 650, l. 59; and V. G. Bogoraz (-Tan), "Religiia, kak tormoz sotsstroitel'stva sredi malykh narodnostei Severa," SS, no. 1–2 (1932): 144.

the shamanistic séances struck the "militant godless" as particularly blatant examples of cheating and trickery, through which the crafty shamans robbed the credulous populace of their meager possessions as well as their hope for a better life.[29] Not content with that, they deliberately distracted everybody from productive work, for "while the natives are singing half a thousand songs over each bear, no work of any kind is being done."[30]

One way of dealing with them was coercion; shamans were deprived of the vote, kicked out of meetings, stripped of their regalia, and exiled. An even better way was to outsmart and outargue them because by exposing their cheating and their false gods one could dispose of idolatry and superstition with one crushing blow. In the retelling these confrontations between a "cultural worker" and a cunning shaman acquired a striking resemblance to Russian folk tales about a worldly soldier (sluzhivyi) who fools a witch. He might shoot at the sky to prove that there were no spirits; or, like G. A. Ushakov, the head of the Vrangel' Island expedition, pretend to be the devil and then embarass the shaman (A. I. Mineev later claimed that after this incident the Eskimos "stopped believing in [the shaman] Anal'ko as an intermediary between them and the spirits"). Pursuing another popular motif, T. Z. Semushkin claimed to have used the eclipse of the moon to put a shaman to shame. In a different but related mode, the cultural worker could play the role of a fearless apostle who, in the manner of Novitskii's Filofei (and his numerous literary predecessors) engaged the pagans in an earnest disputation or a test of strength. The same Ushakov was reported to have risen from his deathbed and killed a bear in order to prove once and for all that he was stronger than the devil.[31]

Less literary accounts present a very different picture. The native northerners could not understand why their shamans were being per-

---

[29] Leonov, "Kul'tbaza v taige," p. 88; Suslov, "Shamanstvo i bor'ba s nim," pp. 92–98; I. Skachkov, "Ob antireligioznoi rabote na Severe," RN, no. 7 (1934): 53; Semushkin, Chukotka, pp. 143–44; "Kul'tura, byt i shkola na Severe," TT, no. 4 (1932): 28–42.

[30] I. Skachkov, "Ob antireligioznoi rabote," p. 53. See also E. D. Kantor, "Liudi i fakty. Staroe i novoe," SS, no. 3–4 (1935): 189.

[31] Leonov, "Kul'tbaza v taige," p. 88; Kruglov, "O revoliutsionnoi zakonnosti," p. 100; K. Sergeeva, "V Urelikskom natssovete," SS, no. 1 (1935): 96–97; G. Ul'ianov, "Nabolevshie voprosy," PN no. 1 (1929): 49; A. I. Mineev, Ostrov Vrangelia (Moscow, 1946), pp. 71–72, 65–67; Semushkin, Chukotka, pp. 167–72. When Chukchi children parodied their Russian teachers, they made speeches against shamans. See Semushkin, Chukotka, pp. 117–18, 84, 112. See also I. Mukhachev, "Ballada o tungusakh i o shamane," ORS, no. 4 (1934): 63–64; Suslov, "Shamanstvo i bor'ba s nim," pp. 139–40; and G. N. Prokof'ev, "Tri goda v samoedskoi shkole," SS, no. 7–8 (1931): 157–58.

secuted ("Maybe because they did a bad job treating diseases").[32] Those Russians who wanted to explain their motives ran into the usual linguistic problems: most of them did not speak the local languages, and those who did had to deal with the fact that, for example, the Chukchi language had the same word for "shaman," "doctor," and "priest."[33] Their actions, however, were quite straightforward and were not kindly received. As one cultural revolutionary put it, "the influence of the shamans is just as limitless and unrestrained as their impudence."[34] Time after time the native northerners refused to testify against shamans in court or to attend meetings without them. Often whole communities followed their shamans into expulsion. In more places still, shamanism became secret: the shamans retained their right to vote by surrendering their tambourines but continued to practice outside the reach of the Russian administrators. The difficulty was compounded by the official inability to distinguish between professional shamans and simply misguided laborers. As A. Kruglov explained, "The disenfranchisement of all shamans past and present leads to a situation where a significant part of the poor and middle toilers who practice shamanism for themselves and do not profit from it are also deprived of the vote." This kind of shamanism was, of course, difficult to combat because, in the words of G. N. Prokof'ev "They all shamanize at any time of day or night. For many shamanism is an addiction in the manner of tobacco."[35] Difficult but not impossible. Another teacher disciplined guilty students by making them write "Shamanism is the opium of the people" fifty times over.[36]

In those areas where Orthodox priests had become important helpers in dealing with the world of spirits, the antireligious campaign was somewhat more effective. Shamans were recruited from within native communities; priests had to be provided by the Russians. As a group of Kazym Khanty explained,

> We are not against the Soviet government, but we don't like the Polnovat

[32] A. K. L'vov, "Ekspeditsiia Pushnogostorga i Sibtorga v Eloguiskii raion Turukhanskogo kraia," SS, no. 2 (1930): 109. See also TsGAOR, f. 3977, op. 1, d. 299, l. 23.

[33] Bogoraz, "Religiia, kak tormoz," p. 146.

[34] Skachkov, "Ob antireligioznoi rabote," p. 52.

[35] TsGAOR, f. 3977, op. 1, d. 682, l. 14, and d. 841, l. 1; N. B-ov, "Budni krasnykh iurt," PN, no. 1 (1931): 62; Skachko, "Vos'moi Plenum Komiteta Severa," p. 7; A. Kruglov, "Perevybory sovetov na Severnom Urale," SS, no. 5 (1931): 99; G. Vasilevich, "Symskie tungusy," SS, no. 2 (1931): 146; Kruglov, "O revoliutsionnoi zakonnosti," p. 100; TsGAOR, f. 3977, op. 1, d. 645, l. 7; d. 646, l. 39; d. 650, ll. 59–65; and d. 651, ll. 2–10; Prokof'ev, "Tri goda," p. 148.

[36] TsGAOR, f. 3977, op. 1, d. 392, l. 116.

government because it won't allow us to have a priest. From childhood
we hunt in forests that are full of devils. Sometimes you might fall asleep
tired, and no one is watching over you because there is no cross. We can't
live without a priest because that's the kind of faith we've got. We wanted
to give the priest some money, so that he'd give us crosses, but in Polnovat
they take away whatever we give him for the church.[37]

The Khatanga Nenets tried to be diplomatic: "If Father Flafion lags
behind our new social system, then send Father Grigorii." The answer
was friendly but firm: "We can't send you the priest due to bad transport in the tundra and because we are carrying out sovietization." Several years later, V. P. Zisser met a group of the Upper-Kolyma Tungus
who were going to Nogaevo Bay, the administrative center of a large
forced labor empire. They had heard that there were priests among the
prisoners and intended to ask the authorities to lend them one.[38]
    Most theoreticians agreed that in order to defeat such cultural "im-
maturity," one needed to bring about what Bogoraz called "a forceful
destruction of the local social system under the influence of the new
Soviet factors, including the destruction of the old productive methods
by the new ones." That, of course, was a long-term program that depended on the success of industrialization. In the meantime, the brunt
of the cultural war was to be borne by the kul'tbazy and the so-called
red tents, which were a sort of traveling kul'tbazy modeled after the
mobile churches of the missionaries. The red tents were an extension
of the various "cultural detachments" that proliferated throughout
Russia during the cultural revolution and were usually manned by
young Komsomol enthusiasts. Unlike the rest of Russia, however, the
far north had very few Komsomol members and even fewer enthusiasts.
Of the eight kul'tbazy completed by 1935 none had all the facilities
and cadres required by the statutes, and the red tents were expected to
rely almost exlusively on local personnel—which meant that they
rarely had any personnel at all.[39]
    Even more troublesome and discouraging was the continuing and
seemingly implacable hostility of the local population. Most native

[37] Skachkov, "Ob antireligioznoi rabote," p. 54.
[38] I. Pervukhin, "Sredi malykh narodnostei Sibirskogo kraia," SS, no. 5 (1930): 49; V.
P. Zisser, "Sredi Verkhne-Kolymskikh tungusov," SS, no. 1 (1934): 113.
[39] Bogoraz, "Religiia, kak tormoz," p. 148; TsGAOR, f. 3977, op. 1, d. 477, ll. 14–16;
and d. 495, l. 24; I. Pervukhin. "Peredvizhnoi krasnyi chum na Turukhanskom Severe,"
SS, no. 5 (1930): 132; E. D. Kantor, "Kazymskaia kul'tbaza," SS, no. 6 (1933): 66–68; P.
E. Terletskii, "Kul'tbazy Komiteta Severa," SS, no. 1 (1935): 36–47.

northerners agreed with the Shemagir Tungus, who declared that all they wanted from the Soviet government was "to get permission to hunt all animals in all seasons, to receive material help, and to have all Russians leave their settlement."[40] They would also agree with the Synsk Khanty who were just as certain about the things they did not want: "Little by little schools and hospitals will appear; the natives will be taken to school and drafted into the army; new trading centers will be opened, and along with them the Russians will start coming, and steamers will be going up and down the Synsk River. And we don't want and don't need any of this."[41]

The Khanty vision of the apocalypse was, of course, the bright future according to the cultural revolutionaries. The encounter of these two interpretations led to numerous arguments, clashes, and misunderstandings. The kul'tbazy and the red tents—these harbingers of things to come—were not welcome. "You're wasting your time in coming here. We don't need any red tents. Our fathers and grandfathers didn't know of any red tents, and they lived better than we live now. We'll manage without them, too."[42] Accordingly, the small peoples of the North refused to help build kul'tbazy, refused to give reindeer for the red tents, did not allow the red tents into their encampments, and sometimes left particularly persistent "red tenters" to freeze in the tundra. There were some exceptions—one activist attracted the natives to the red tent by playing his balalaika and showing pictures, others fixed traps or brought radio receivers—but the overall picture was not in favor of cultural revolution.[43]

Both Bolshevik theory and experience in the field suggested that in order to overcome resistance the Russian propagandists needed allies among the local population. Here theory and experience parted ways, however. The former prescribed the creation of so-called groups of the poor and foresaw the breakup of an antiquated society through action by the exploited classes guided by conscientious instructors. Experience, however, seemed to show that the exploited classes refused to

[40] A. Shepovalova, "Sotsial'no-bytovaia sreda tungusskikh detei na Sev. Baikale," *P*, no. 2 (1930): 185.

[41] Zibarev, *Sovetskoe stroitel'stvo*, p. 112.

[42] Davydov, "Ocherednye zadachi," p. 94.

[43] TsGAOR, f. 3977, op. 1, d. 529, l. 12; d. 740, ll. 4–5; and d. 936, l. 66. Also Leonov, "Kul'tbaza v taige," 86–90; A. Putintseva, "Dva goda raboty Goriuno-Amurskoi krasnoi iurty," *SS*, no. 1–2 (1932): 168, 174, 177; I. Nesterenok, "Smotr natsional'nykh shkol na Taimyre," *SS*, no. 6 (1932): 84–85; A. Terent'ev, "Na putiakh k vseobuchu v tundre," *PN*, no. 1 (1933): 25; L. Osipova, "Ogon'ki sovetskoi kul'tury na Severe," *SS*, no. 2 (1933): 77–78; B. Shmyrev, "Iamal'skaia kul'tbaza," *SS*, no. 6 (1933): 69–70.

identify themselves as such, let alone organize and act as their station required. This was not a problem for an essentially negative campaign such as dekulakization: a person could be "neutralized" whether he considered himself an exploiter or not. In "cultural construction," on the other hand, the beneficiaries had to be ready and willing. Violence was much less effective if one's task was to make people brush their teeth, use underwear, read books, and boil the meat they ate. If the poor as a group were not interested, another group had to be found.

It did not take the cultural revolutionaries very long to find it. By 1930 it became clear that "the real and most authentic proletarians" of the north were women.[44] Ever since the eighteenth century the non-northern Russians had regarded the position of women as one of the most objectionable aspects of native societies. In the case of the "fair sex" the lack of cleanliness had seemed particularly hazardous; the never-ending hard work, unusually cruel; and the various rules of avoidance, deliberately humiliating. At the end of the nineteenth century the missionaries had decided that the combination of oppression with a special role as keepers of the hearth and protectors of children made women the ideal candidates for early conversions and successful proselytizing. Independently but for the same basic reasons, the new missionaries of Communism also arrived at this conclusion.

Women were "the mainspring through which the old way of life could be changed," "the key to a healthier domestic and social life for the natives." Teach them new skills, and the children and men will have no choice but to follow. As one appeal to Eskimo women put it, "Women, wash yourselves and wash your children three times a month. Make your men wash." Even more important, the intolerable oppression would have to stop. The emancipation of women was a prominent aspect of the Russian radical tradition and a very important motif of the cultural and social revolution of the 1920s and the early 1930s. When the new action-minded militants arrived in the north, their shock and indignation was even stronger than that of their predecessors. Comrade S. Golubev, for one, would not stand idly by while a native girl "became the slave of her husband, fed the dogs, tanned hides, sewed clothes and footwear, chopped wood, and picked berries and edible herbs; and, when the time came to have a baby, was put

---

[44] The idea was first introduced by Central Asian activists, who pointed out that the main instruments of oppression in the north (bridewealth, polygamy, and segregation) were the same as those in Muslim areas. See TsGAOR, f. 3977, op. 1, d. 391, ll. 2–7, and d. 397, ll. 61–65. Cf. Massell, *Surrogate Proletariat.*

outside in a makeshift shack, no matter if it was winter cold or a summer rain."[45]

This sentiment, coupled with a frantic search for social cleavages, produced an active and very forceful campaign. Collectivization and emancipation became one, as they were supposed to be: the same Russian was usually in charge of both campaigns; the kulak and the family despot was one and the same person; and the groups of the poor were often equivalent to women's volunteer groups. In 1930 a special Conference of Native Women from the North was held in Moscow, and at the Institute of the Peoples of the North the oppression of women ("very bad customs") became the central theme of the students' soul-searching.[46]

Back in the tundra, the easiest and most obvious first step was to attack the dirt and the perceived domestic ineptitude. This was usually done by women—teachers, doctors, and ethnographers—who were the first to be offended by the "incorrect" practices. They tried to teach their native "sisters" how to wash themselves, clean their tents, do the dishes, bake bread, and in general to do everything that a self-respecting Russian wife and mother would be able to do.[47] Direct persuasion rarely worked, so the most popular method, in tune with the spirit of the times, was to organize some kind of contest: a contest for the cleanest tent, for the best meal (as judged by a Russian palate), and so on. Here is an announcement for one such event:

Starting on March first all the women of our settlement will take part

[45] E. Kuz'mina, "Koriakskaia zhenshchina," PN, no. 7 (1932): 98; V. L'vov, "Zhenshchina Severa," PN, no. 1 (1932): 42; Sergeeva, "V Urelikskom natssovete." TsGAOR, f. 3977, op. 1, d. 397, ll. 11f; S. Golubev, "Danka iz stoibishcha Andy," SS, no. 4 (1932): 130.

[46] TsGAOR, f. 3977, op. 1, d. 397, ll. 11–95; "Pervoe soveshchanie zhenshchin-tuzemok Severa," SS, no. 1 (1930): 150–52; Afanas'ev, "Zhizn' zhenshchiny-evenki na Sakhaline," TT, no. 2 (1930): 121–24; Angin, "Rabota zhenshchin v Bol'shemikhailovskom raione Nikolaevskogo okruga," TT, no. 3 (1931); V. Egorov and E. Zakharov, "Polozhenie zhenshchin u evenkov Verkhne-Selimdzhinskogo raiona," TT, no. 2 (1930): 116–18; K. Khodzher, "Semeinye i brachnye otnosheniia u gol'dov na Amure," TT, no. 3 (1931): 97; Labazov, "Zhizn' zhenshchiny-nenki Bol'shezemel'skoi tundry," TT, no. 3 (1931): 94–96; Mashikhina, "O polozhenii zhenshchiny-koriachki Karaginskogo raiona, Kamchatskogo okruga," TT, no. 2 (1930): 118–21; Oninka, "Material po rabote sredi zhenshchin u nanaitsev Khabarovskogo okruga," TT, no. 2 (1930): 97–104; Sipin, "Trud i byt zhenshchin nani (ul'chei) Nikolaevskogo na Amure okruga Bol'she-Mikhailovskogo raiona," TT, no. 2 (1930): 105–16; Taleeva, "Polozhenie nenetskoi (samoedskoi) zhenshchiny," TT, no. 2 (1930): 127–29.

[47] TsGAOR, f. 3977, op. 1, d. 397, ll 20–21, and d. 584, l. 38; "Pervoe soveshchanie zhenshchin-tuzemok Severa," pp. 150–51; N. B-ov, "Budni krasnykh iurt," p. 62; Putintseva, "Dva goda raboty," pp. 169, 171; V. A., "U chukoch v Chaunskoi gube," SS, no. 2 (1935): 60–64.

in a competition: whose *iaranga* [tent] will be the cleanest by May
First. What should one do for the competition?
1. Wash the floor with clean water once every six days.
2. Dust and wipe off the soot with a wet rag every day.
3. Wash all the dishes with clean water and dry them with a towel.
4. Every day all the inhabitants of the iaranga should wash their face
and hands with warm water and soap and then dry them with a towel.
5. Once a month all the inhabitants of the iaranga should take a bath
in warm water with soap.
6. Twice a month all the inhabitants of the iaranga should wash their
hair with warm water and soap.
8. Wash all clothes with warm water and soap once a month.
The cleanest iaranga will receive a prize.
First prize: A big copper tea pot, a wash tub, a spoon, a fork, and
a knife.
Second prize: A big tub (enamel), a mug, and three spoons.
Women, try to win a prize![48]

To qualify for the competition, the women had to take a bath and
discard their loin cloths, "that malodorous symbol of a woman's submission and a remnant of the stone age."[49]
It is difficult to measure the success of such actions. Soap was reportedly quite popular in some communities, and tea pots, tubs, and knives
were very valuable prizes, but a bath, for example, was a much resented
ordeal, and what was a symbol of submission to some was an important
religious protection for others. In any case, many of the same contests
were still taking place several decades later.
Women's equality was a much more contentious issue. Here the war
was waged by men, most of them officials, over basic institutions of the
native societies. The majority of native men would not even hear of
women attending meetings and taking part in decision making. As the
chairman of a native executive committee from Iamal put it, "If there's
a woman in the soviet, let them elect my wife; I, for one, am not going
to have meetings with a woman." (He was fired and his statement was
characterized as anti-Soviet and pro-kulak).[50] Women had very serious
reservations, too:

If we ask to be equal to men, the men will tell us: "Today you boiled the

---

[48] Sergeeva, "V Urelikskom natssovete," p. 99.
[49] Ibid., p. 98.
[50] Kruglov, "Perevybory sovetov," p. 98; See also A. M. Khazanovich, *Krasnyi chum v Khatangskoi tundre* (Leningrad, 1939), pp. 24–26.

water and sat in the tent while I was hunting. Tomorrow I'll boil water and you'll go hunting." The man will boil the water all right, but we'll never be able to get the meat. We don't even know how to shoot.

We're used to obeying the men. Whatever they tell us is the law. We don't argue. What if they leave us—where will we go?"[51]

Not everyone agreed with these Nenets wives. The Koriak women, for example, had more political autonomy and played a greater role in decision making. The main issue, however, was not the women's participation in political life as understood by the Russians. It was the institution of marriage itself, most notably bridewealth and polygamy. As far as the cultural revolutionaries were concerned, native matrimonial practices differed little from outright slave trading and had to be reformed quickly and radically. "We need repressions," one woman activist said, "severe repressions."[52]

Unlike the formal, ex officio reports on kulak crimes, many accounts of the women's predicament reached almost lyrical intensity. Every native girl was a Cinderella waiting to be rescued:

> Her father was poor, did not have any reindeer, and sold her at the age of three to the kulak Iakunia for six head of reindeer. Since she was a child, she was made to do hard work: chop wood, carry water, skin slaughtered reindeer, fish, round up the reindeer, and so on. In addition to that, she had to get up early every morning and start the fire. She was dressed in old and wornout clothes, given the worst food, and forced to cook for herself using rotten flour and other spoilt food. Very often she was beaten—beaten for oversleeping and not starting the fire on time, for not having chopped wood, brought water, and so on.[53]

The role of the prince was played by the district executive committee. Indeed, stories of rebellious women who, guided and encouraged by the local Russian officials, left their tyrannical husbands, fathers, and, perhaps more symbolically, stepfathers, became a special genre of literature about the north.[54] It also became a fact of life. Although many

---

[51] TsGAOR, f. 3977, op. 1, d. 528, l. 35. See also Ustiugov, "Samokritika na suglanakh," pp. 54–55.

[52] N. N. Bilibin, "Zhenshchina u koriakov," SS, no. 4 (1933): 92–96; TsGAOR, f. 3977, op. 1, d. 397, l. 85.

[53] Barakhov, "V Evenkiiskom natsional'nom okruge," p. 44. See also TsGAOR, f. 3977, op. 1, d. 500, ll. 18–19.

[54] B. E. Petri, "Dun'ka-okhotnitsa," ORS, no. 10 (1929): 48–51; G. Mokshanskii, "Tygrena iz stoibishcha Akkani," SS, no. 3 (1933): 113–15; Nikolai Nikolaevich, "Sukonnaia rukavichka," ORS, no. 8 (1929): 46–55.

women resisted the officials' urgings to seek help from the red tents or courts, quite a few seem to have responded. From the time of the conquest the native northerners had been using Russian courts, Russian symbols, and Russian influence in their internal politics. Now it was the women's turn to use their new and powerful allies. Unlike the "poor laborers," they knew themselves to be a distinct group and were not averse to enlisting some outside support. Here, for instance, is a letter to the judge of the Chumsko-Taimurskii clan soviet from a Tungus widow Dzhal'gurik:

> In the winter of 1926 my husband Chiktykon Garbaul' of the Kochenil' clan passed away. I became a widow, with two small children. Living with me is my adopted daughter, orphan Tyral'dyn, recently married to Basto of the Shoniagir' clan. At present Basto is living in my tent, working off the bridewealth. After my husband died, his uncle Parchen of the Kochenil' clan demanded that I go live with him. Considering that Parchen had always disliked my late husband and has now transferred his hatred onto me, I do not want to live with him. I declare that I can live by myself because I get proper help from my adopted daughter Tyral'dyn. I ask the court to consider this case and to make Parchen abandon his claims to my children and property.
>
> Because of my illiteracy, I am hereby signing with a print of my right thumb.[55]

The court decided the case to the widow's complete satisfaction, but by the time Basto had discharged his obligations and the young couple had left, Dzhal'gurik could once again be claimed by Parchen's family (the court showed understanding and appointed Parchen's son as her official protector). Her other options were to remarry or return to her father's tent, in which case she would have to surrender her children and her property to her husband's brother—Parchen. Moreover, if she chose to return home, her father would have to return the bridewealth, something he might be unwilling to do.[56]

Thousands of northern women had to make similar choices, and if they could not support themselves but did not like their protectors, wanted to remarry but were not prepared to part with their children, or decided to return home but were not welcome, Russian courts could be very useful.[57] In extreme cases (when the Russian decision could

---

[55] N. Leonov, "Tuzemnye sovety," p. 256.
[56] Ibid., p. 257.
[57] TsGAOR, f. 3977, op. 1, d. 299, ll. 19, 47–48; d. 530, l. 12; and d. 584, l. 4.

not be enforced or when there were no eligible native protectors)
women could be adopted by the local red tent or executive committee.[58] Most of these women were orphans or outcasts, and the reports
claimed that many of them were sent off to study. That is usually the
last one hears of them. Whatever their fate, they did not return armed
with political knowledge and revolutionary values to lead groups of
activists. In other words, in spite of some initial success and great expectations, the emancipation campaign did not result in the creation
of the much needed class of native allies. Most women used the new
policies and new politicians to improve their position within their
communities, not to subvert those communities; and those who
dropped out could never return. "When I stepped ashore wearing my
Komsomol outfit, everybody walked away from me," complained one
such convert. "'You're not one of us anymore,' they said. 'Now you're
one of the bosses.'"[59]

There was another pool of potential allies: the young people. Along
with their mothers, they came to represent the exploited underclass of
native societies, and the standard formula called for the "increase of
the leading role of the poor and the hired hands, particularly women
and young people."[60] To most participants, the Stalin revolution was a
war of generations. The activists were young and quite explicitly associated youth with progress and old age with obsolescence. In the mythology of the time, "youth" was the dominant theme: the country was
young and its heroes were young; the coming of adulthood and the
building of socialism were the same process, and both presupposed
the rejection of the previous generation ("the enemy"). In the north
this dichotomy was exemplary: all kulaks were elders and all elders
were kulaks.

Education was the way to defeat the old generation, for education
was how "new cadres" were formed and "consciousness" was raised.
In the case of the taiga and tundra this meant primary schools, and in
the case of the majority of the native northerners it meant taking children away from their parents.

[58] N. I. Leonov, "V nizov'iakh Amura," pp. 94–98; Leonov, "Kul'tbaza v taige," p. 89;
N. B-ov, "Budni krasnykh iurt," p. 63; Putintseva, "Dva goda raboty," p. 173; Golubev,
"Danka," p. 132; Bilibin, "Zhenshchina u koriakov," pp. 92–96; Osipova, "Ogon'ki sovet-
skoi kul'tury," p. 78.

[59] TsGAOR, f. 3977, op. 1, d. 397, l. 50.

[60] "Tsirkuliar oblispolkomam Leningradskoi i Obsko-Irtyshskoi oblastei, kraiispolkomam Severnogo, Zapadno-Sibirskogo, Vostochno-Sibirskogo i Dal'nevostochnogo kraev
i TsK Iakutskoi i Buriat-Mongol'skoi ASSR," SS, no. 5 (1934): 112.

No other policy met with as much bitterness, hostility, and resistance. Children provided labor that was crucial for survival, and even a short absence could make a difference for the season ("Kids help a lot in our work; there's no way we can do without them".) More important, even a short absence could mean losing one's child forever, for, as all parents and some of the teachers agreed, the task of the schools was to turn out little Russians. The practical benefit of such an arrangement was dubious ("You Russians study a lot but walk around with holes in your pockets"), and its morality seemed indefensible. The new missionaries were told what the old ones had heard many a time: all peoples had their own gods, laws, customs, and—yes—children. And they were all entitled to keep them. "A Tungus child won't live with the Russians any more than a Russian child will live with the Tungus."[61] As one Khanty woman said to a young musicology student,

> Why are you Russians trying to prevent us from living our way? Why do they take our children to school and teach them to forget and to break up the Khanty ways? They'll take our children to school, and then take them to Leningrad. There they'll forget their parents and won't come back home. You like children, for example, so how would you feel if they took away your children and taught them to despise everything about the way you live? Would it make you feel good?[62]

The student answered as all her friends always did: that in school the children would learn good, useful, and necessary things. To which the usual reply invariably completed the vicious circle: "Nobody ever taught us how to read but we've managed somehow, and now our kids will learn and then refuse to live in the tundra."[63]

Russian persistence led to threats and open defiance. "You can't take our children by force; it's against the law. What if we resist, what then?" "I've got kids who are school age, but I won't let them go to school; only when they shoot me dead will they be able to take them."[64] Characteristically, the Nenets meeting at which these and similar views were expressed ended with the following resolution: "The decision of the

---

[61] Ustiugov, "Samokritika na suglanakh," p. 54; Kantorovich, Po Sovetskoi Kamchatke, p. 154; K. I. Usova, "Rebenok-tungus v shkole," P, no. 2 (1930): 192.

[62] V. Senkevich, "V Voitekhovskikh iurtakh," SS, no. 6 (1934): 101. See also TsGAOR, f. 3977, op. 1, d. 757, ll. 13–23.

[63] Ustiugov, "Samokritika na suglanakh," p. 54.

[64] TsGAOR, f. 3977, op. 1, d. 528, l. 31. See also Ustiugov, "Samokritika na suglanakh," p. 54.

provincial executive committee on compulsory education should be regarded as correct."[65] Presumably, this allowed the Russian envoy to report on the success of his mission, and the native parents, to do what they always did: express their loyalty and then leave for the tundra. Their credo was best summed up by one Koriak herdsman: "We obey the authorities but we aren't sending our kids to no schools" ("my vlasti povinuemsia, no detei uchit' ne khochem").[66]

With the nomads, violence did not help for the usual reasons of remoteness and lack of personnel. In Iamal, for example, the would-be students were constantly "visiting with their relatives" or turning deaf, mute, blind, or hysterical on the teacher's arrival.[67] The tested alternative was to collect orphans or, in settled communites, to persuade appointed native officials to surrender their children.[68] Most of these officials owed whatever prestige they had to the Russians and often had no choice but to give in. Also, some children and their parents could be attracted to schools by movies, radios, flags, and tea.[69] This was rarely a sufficient reason for enrolling, but it sometimes helped to establish the crucial first contact. The other reasons were intimidation (quite effective with settled populations) and, in relatively few cases, the desire by some parents to have their children learn certain skills. (Some trade-oriented maritime Chukchi, for example, hoped that the Russians would teach their children some of their commercial secrets.)[70] Finally, some schools offered their recruits food and clothing, and in some areas that was the most convincing argument. The students of the Iamal kul'tbaza issued the following appeal: "We have already received new shirts, pants, coats, and hats. We have meat, fish, bread, sweet rolls, and

[65] Ustiugov, "Samokritika na suglanakh," p. 54.

[66] Kantorovich, Po Sovetskoi Kamchatke, p. 154. See also TsGAOR, f. 3977, op. 1, d. 300, l. 39; d. 528, l. 32; d. 642, l. 147; d. 646, l. 21; and d. 934, l. 22. See also "Sovetskaia shkola u tuzemtsev Tobol'skogo Severa," SS, no. 1 (1931): 46; Kruglov, "Perevybory sovetov," pp. 98–99; T. Z. Semushkin, "Prosveshchenie narodnostei Krainego Severa," PN, no. 1 (1932): 31; N. Shakhov, "Rastet natsional'naia kul'tura v tundre i na ostrovakh," PN, no. 2–3 (1932): 47; Davydov, "Ocherednye zadachi," p. 94; I. Telishev, "God raboty v Ostiatskoi shkole," SS, no. 5 (1932): 125–26; Medvedev, "O rabote s bednotoi," p. 75; Terent'ev, "Na putiakh k vseobuchu," p. 25; Shmyrev, "Iamal'skaia kul'tbaza," p. 70; Ia. P. Al'kor, "Zadachi kul'turnogo stroitel'stva na Krainem Severe," SS, no. 2 (1934): 30; P. Kovalevskii, "V shkole-iurte," SS, no. 2 (1934): 103; A. G. Bazanov, "Vogul'skie deti," SS, no. 3 (1934): 93; and N. Leonov, "Tuzemnye shkoly na Severe," pp. 200–201.

[67] Shmyrev, "Iamal'skaia kul'tbaza," p. 70.

[68] TsGAOR, f. 3977, op. 1, d. 301, l. 11; "Sovetskaia shkola," p. 46; Kovalevskii, "V shkole-iurte," p. 104; Semushkin, Chukotka, p. 72.

[69] TsGAOR, f. 3977, op. 1, d. 936, l. 27; Putintseva, "Dva goda raboty," pp. 169, 174; Kovalevskii, "V shkole-iurte," p. 104; Semushkin, Chukotka, pp. 71–72.

[70] Semushkin, Chukotka, p. 30.

butter. We eat well. Native children, come study with us—it is good here. We are waiting for you."[71]

Rounding up the children was only the first step in a very long and difficult process. Teachers were for the most part just as unwilling. The pay remained low; living quarters, poor or nonexistent; the local authorities, unfriendly; and the native people, unwelcoming.[72] Women-teachers were particularly ill-received because of their "impurity."[73] Of those who stayed a few were enthusiastic cultural revolutionaries (mostly ethnographers) and the rest, hard-drinking, unlicensed, or exiled outcasts unable to teach elsewhere.[74] According to one such initially enthusiastic ethnographer, Pavel Moll, the Chukotka cultural station had "discredited Russian workers in the eyes of the natives to an extraordinary degree, because the natives witnessed everything that was going on there," including alcoholism, embezzlement, persecution, incompetence, and fierce vendettas. In addition to setting a bad example, the station "did serious damage by spreading gonorrhoea," allegedly with the "active participation" of the future writer T. Semushkin.[75] Even when teachers were willing to teach and students agreed to learn, they were lucky to have a place to meet. Buildings were few and precious, and the local officials rarely allowed potential warehouses or trade points to be used as schools, especially schools for the natives ("So you're teaching Asians instead of Russians, eh?").[76] Thus the houses where the students ended up were very far from being the temples of learning that the cultural revolutionaries had in mind.

It is very cold in the classroom. The wind enters freely through the badly caulked walls of an old chapel converted into a school. Four crumbling desks (a heritage of the priest's teaching days) have been pulled closer to the stove. But to no avail. The homemade stove generates smoke but no warmth. Fourteen students have been sqeezed behind the four desks. They are wearing fur *kukhliankas*, constantly blowing on their

[71] Shmyrev, "Iamal'skaia kul'tbaza," p. 73.

[72] Davydov, "Ocherednye zadachi," p. 99; Telishev, "God raboty," p. 127; Gilev, "Zapiski," p. 92; Bazanov and Kazanskii, *Shkola na Krainem Severe*, pp. 119–21.

[73] P. Sletov, "Ot iukoly k kartofeliu," *PN*, no. 7–8 (1931): Khazanovich, *Krasnyi chum*, p. 25.

[74] TsGAOR, f. 3977, op. 1, d. 497, ll. 4–5, and d. 990, ll. 58–59.

[75] Ibid., d. 477, ll. 15–6. See also d. 500, l. 36. For examples of sexual abuse of native students by their teachers, see TsGAOR, f. 3977, op. 1, d. 497, ll. 4–5.

[76] N. Leonov, "Tuzemnye shkoly na Severe," p. 204. See also Davydov, "Ocherednye zadachi," p. 96; Sergeeva, "V Urelikskom natssovete," pp. 97–98; and K. Sergeeva, "Shkola v bukhte Provideniia," *SS*, no. 2 (1935): 54.

hands. . . . There are three ink-wells. The homemade notebooks are made of thick dark paper. The blackboard is the back side of an icon. . . . [77]

The school might not remain in such a place for very long. Even if the local executive committee did not kick them out, the wood for the stove would probably run out or, as was sometimes the case, the building would fall apart completely. The Karaul'skaia school in Taimyr, for example, did not have a roof, "and so, when the snow began to melt, the walls became damp and the ceiling collapsed. The children ran away, and it was impossible to round them up again." Sometimes the parents took their children back home in protest over poor conditions.[78]

The only alternative was to hold classes in native tents or dugouts, and that was a test not every teacher could pass:

> The hosts were present during classes (they had no place to go), watching what was going on, drinking tea and even eating their "kopal'khen" (slightly fermented walrus or seal meat). The air . . . was very heavy because about thirty people were crammed into a small enclosure of approximately seven square meters barely lit up by seal oil lamps which filled the place with soot and gases. To this should be added the pungent ammoniac smell of the [urine-cured] walrus skins that covered the floor. . . . The children were almost naked, boys in their underwear and girls in slips specially made at the kul'tbaza. Every thirty to thirty-five minutes the lamp would, of course, go out, and we had to take a break during which the kids stuck their heads out to get some fresh air and to fill the room with oxygen. Then the lamp would start burning again and the class would resume.[79]

To most teachers, the students themselves were an even bigger problem. As one Leningrad graduate said after her first encounter with her Chukchi wards, "the children are completely savage."[80] "The teachers had a difficult and very peculiar pedagogical task ahead of them. The students needed to be taught not only how to use a pen or a pencil but also how to eat, how to sit on a chair, how to sleep in a bed, and how to

[77] S. N. Stebnitskii, "Iz opyta raboty v shkole Severa (koriakskaia shkola). Zapiski uchitelia," PN, no. 8–9 (1932): 52. See also TsGAOR, f. 3977, op. 1, d. 300, ll. 105–6; Sletov, "Ot iukoly k kartofeliu," p. 63; N. Firsov, "O nenetskikh shkolakh," TT, no. 2 (1928): 90–92.
[78] Nesterenok, "Smotr natsional'nykh shkol," pp. 83–84; Gilev, "Zapiski," p. 92.
[79] N. Komov, "Rabota v Chukotskoi shkole," SS, no. 1 (1933): 73.
[80] Semushkin, Chukotka, p. 48.

wash themselves."[81] Thus where boarding schools were available the emphasis was on "civilized behavior" understood primarily as cleanliness and a general competence in the "everyday skills" (bytovye navyki) that were expected of urban Russian children. As usual, the first and necessary step on the way to civilization was a bath, an act vested with great symbolic significance and featured very prominently in every conversion story. The purging ritual was completed by a haircut and a change of clothes.[82]

What followed was a cultural revolution of the most basic kind. The native children had to relearn how to eat, sit, sleep, talk, dress, and be sick, as well as to assimilate a totally new view of the world and their place in it. Besides the "slovenliness such as spitting on the floor, behind the stove, and under the bed," the teachers disliked what they saw as "a shopkeeper mentality," "national prejudice," religious superstitions, and a lack of discipline, among other things. As the meaning of most "superstitions" remained obscure, the struggle was waged primarily against symbols: braids, tattoos, and amulets. As K. Sergeeva wrote in her diary: "A small victory: after many fruitless attempts at persuasion, my student Aka has finally given in and today came without either of his talismans. Actually, they were very curious things, although I still haven't found out what they are supposed to represent."[83]

Along with "domestic skills," the single most important indicator of progress was "political maturity."[84] As the teachers discovered, the native northerners were equally deficient on both scores. When one trader showed his customers a portrait of Lenin,

the first question was: "Who's this bald-headed merchant?" Then another man said quite earnestly that it was not a merchant but the Soviet tsar, so that it took a lot of time and effort to explain to them that it was not a merchant and not a tsar but the great leader of all toilers. In order

[81] Ibid., p. 42

[82] T. Z. Semushkin, "Opyt raboty po organizatsii shkoly-internata chukotskoi kul t-bazy DVK," SS no. 3–4 (1931): 177–82; Shmyrev, "Iamal'skaia kul'tbaza," p. 73; Kovalevskii, "V shkole-iurte," p. 105; Sergeeva, "Shkola v bukhte Provideniia," p. 57; Bazanov and Kazanskii, Shkola na Krainem Severe, pp. 131–33; Semushkin, Chukotka, pp. 37, 43, 49, 90–99.

[83] Prokof'ev, 'Tri goda," pp. 148–50; Sergeeva, "Shkola v bukhte Provideniia," p. 57. See also P. Skorik, "Molodye pobegi Sakhalinskoi taigi," SS, no. 4 (1932): 108.

[84] Most teachers' accounts are by political activists. The "silent majority" of northern educators had nothing to do with the cultural revolution and, like the teacher Ugriumov, "did nothing but drink, so that, after one drinking orgy accompanied by a fight, one Nenets got his skull cracked open." Terent'ev, "Na putiakh k vseobuchu," p. 26.

to do that, it was necessary to tell the illiterate natives who did not even understand Russian all about the October revolution, the heroic battles of the Red Army men during the Civil War, and the peaceful reconstruction.[85]

One Chukotka teacher reported just how difficult it was:

I managed to teach the children the very beginnings of class consciousness and an understanding of the nature of the exploitation of the poor by the rich. It may sound strange but at that particular moment in time the children did not have such notions at all. Therefore the schoolteachers have to work very hard, particularly considering their poor knowledge of the Chukchi language, in order to instill in the children the feeling of hatred towards shamanism and exploitation. What makes it especially difficult is the fact that the Chukchi language still does not have words to express certain socioeconomic phenomena. For example, there is no word for "struggle" in its class meaning.[86]

There was no end to such problems. Bogoraz, the foremost authority on the subject, worked hard on an intelligible translation of "five-year plan in four years" and a new version of "the First of May," known to the Chukchi under the English word "Christmas." He also wondered if "the new boss" was a fair rendering of "the Soviet regime."[87] A satisfactory solution to these problems was crucial because of the government's resolve to offer instruction in the native languages. The Soviet education officials inherited the Il'minskii system without major revisions: for the natives to assimilate the new message, the message should be given in the native languages.[88] A group of linguists at the Institute of the Peoples of the North was to codify the grammars of northern languages and devise a Latin-based writing system for them. A few anonymous voices argued that using the Cyrillic alphabet would be cheaper and easier for students as well as providing a shield against pernicious foreign influences, but there was no serious discussion of the issue: all scholars and prominent non-Russian (mostly Turkic) politicians agreed that the Latin script signified progress, a rejection of

---

[85] V., "Neobkhodimo raskachat'sia," *ORS*, no. 6 (1929): 11.

[86] Komov, "Rabota v Chukotskoi shkole," pp. 77–78.

[87] V. G. Bogoraz (-Tan), "Chukotskii bukvar'," *SS*, no. 10 (1931): 125–28.

[88] K. Ia. Luks, "Problema pis'mennosti u tuzemnykh narodnostei Severa," *SS*, no. 1 (1930): 39–42; "Protokol sed'mogo rasshirennogo plenuma," pp. 124–25. Cf. Isabelle Kreindler, "A Neglected Source of Lenin's Nationality Policy," *SR* 36 (March 1977): 86–100.

the old Russification policies, and the possibility of an expansion of Soviet ideology abroad (in the case of the northern languages, the future beneficiaries would include the Chinese Manchus, the Finnish Saami, and the American Eskimos).[89] In December of 1930 the Institute of the Peoples of the North formally completed its work on the Unified Northern Alphabet and began publishing primers and other textbooks in the languages of the small peoples.[90]

It was new work, and most authors lacked experience in either linguistics or the conditions of the extreme north, never quite sure how to combine "local peculiarities" and the national educational requirements. Also, the northern transportation system did not work any better for textbooks than it did for food and clothes. Some materials took over a year to arrive at their destination; some never arrived at all; and some confronted the local officials with an impossible task of deciding who should be taught what language (some Nenets were to be taught in Komi, and some Evenk, in Yakut). To add to the confusion, most small peoples were given new official names putatively based on their self-appellations. On one occasion, a Nivkh, formerly Giliak, region received a shipment of textbooks in the Gypsy language.[91]

Many parents were quite unhappy with the idea. If literacy was of any value at all, it was to get to know the Russian ways and to learn the skills that could not be mastered at home. Literacy in Russian could prepare one for a career in the new world (trading agent, kolkhoz official); literacy in the native languages could not.[92] There was little reason for worry, however: the teachers did not speak those languages and could not use the new textbooks anyway. The instruction was almost universally in Russian, with every teacher trying to bridge the linguistic gap as he or she saw fit.[93]

[89] Luks, "Problema pis mennosti," p. 46; S. Tadzhiev, "Novyi latinizirovannyi alfavit—moshchnoe orudie kul'turnoi revoliutsii," RN, no. 2 (1930): 64–67; Ia. P. Al'kor, "Pis'-mennost' narodov Severa," SS, no. 10 (1931): 113–14.

[90] Al'kor, "Pis'mennost' narodov Severa"; "Vvedenie pis'mennosti na rodnom iazyke dlia narodov Severa," SS, no. 3 (1932): 133; "Raport Instituta narodov Severa," SS, no. 6 (1932): 113; Al'kor, Zadachi kul'turnogo stroitel'stva," pp. 23–24.

[91] Davydov, "Ocherednye zadachi," p. 98; M. Solomonov, "Kul'tstroitel'stvo na Severe," RN, no. 10–11 (1932): 139–40; Luks, "Problema pis'mennosti," p. 41; Zisser, "Sredi Verkhne-Kolymskikh tungusov," p. 113; Ustiugov, "Zadachi natsional'noi raboty na Krainem Severe," RN, no. 1 (1931): 44.

[92] Luks, "Problema pis'mennosti," p. 40; Kovalevskii, "V shkole-iurte," p. 106.

[93] Prokof'ev, "Tri goda, ' p. 144; Nesterenok, "Smotr natsional'nykh shkol," p. 84; Stebnitskii, "Iz opyta raboty," pp. 49–51; Al'kor, "Zadachi kul'turnogo stroitel'stva," p. 26; Kovalevskii, "V shkole-iurte," pp. 105–6; Bazanov and Kazanskii, Shkola na Krainem Severe, p. 119.

Even more controversial was the so-called principle of polytechnic education—a pedagogical innovation according to which the school's function was to prepare students for "real life" understood primarily as work in industry and agriculture ("socially useful work"). In the north it also reflected the ethnographers' determination not to expose native children to needs and ambitions that could not as yet be satisfied. During the cultural revolution the boundary between school and life-as-production all but disappeared, and the preferred method of instruction was through "projects," whereby groups of students were given specific economic tasks to perform. In the aboriginal north the projects were divided into three main categories: nomadic reindeer breeding; settled fishing; and nomadic and seminomadic hunting. It was hoped that schools would eventually become exemplary productive units spreading advanced skills and technologies.[94]

These hopes were not realized. First of all, there was a chronic shortage of technology, advanced or not; second, and much more important, the idea seemed absurd to the parents and most everybody else. Why would Russians want to take children away from their parents and teach them something that the parents knew so much more about? How could a graduate of the Herzen Pedagogical Institute be expected to teach a fisherman's son to fish? The "correct" answers to such questions (through the import of advanced technology and superior organization) made much less sense in the tundra than they did in Moscow. Polytechnic education never took root in the north. Behaviorial and political training remained the primary concerns of the tundra and taiga teachers.

The last line of resistance was the children themselves. They boycotted certain foods; refused to solve math problems with ficticious characters; secretly communicated with the spirits; suffered from depression; and, as G. N. Prokof'ev put it, continued to "spit on the floor, behind the stove, and under the bed." Following their parents' lead, they tended to regard schooling as a favor that had to be rewarded with money, food, or clothes (hence accusations of "a shopkeeper mentality"). They missed many classes because they had more important things to attend to and, for both practical and cultural reasons, did very badly by nationwide standards. Many of them were not enrolled in schools at all. The young people could not be relied on as internal allies of the cultural revolution, and the few extant reports of acute genera-

---

[94] Bazanov and Kazanskii, Shkola na Krainem Severe, pp. 78–79.

tional conflicts within native communities seem to have been isolated incidents or wishful thinking.[95]

Thus, measured against its own ambitious goals, the cultural revolution in the north was not altogether successful. Universal primary education was not achieved by 1932–33, and universal literacy was not achieved by 1935.[96] The native societies demonstrated remarkable vitality, and neither women nor children seemed willing to rise in revolt against their kinsmen. Still, the cultural revolution had not passed unnoticed. Its main policies did not end in 1932–34 when the central Party leadership put the revolution on hold and began emphasizing normalcy and stability. The native elite was still being trained, women could still take advantage of the new laws, and children were still going to school. As a result, "civilized behavior" made some inroads, although not always in ways that the cultural revolutionaries approved of. Images of new Soviet saints now hung beside icons and traditional amulets (the picture of Lenin that had given rise to a discussion of whether he was a merchant or a tsar had later become an object of veneration and was reputed to have magical qualities). New Soviet holidays had joined other fairs as occasions for contests and conviviality. Some new imports, particularly movies, radio sets, and sewing machines, had generated new demand and could be used in exchange for various concessions.[97] Even those things that had initially provoked the most resistance might go on to become important status symbols: a child's ability to read and write added to a family's prestige and in some cases promised an improved position vis-à-vis the Russians. (When a Chukchi schoolboy died, he was buried with the tools of his

[95] In the long run, the graduates of Russian boarding schools would prove to be very important agents of change, but during the revolution "the long run" did not count. Prokof'ev, "Tri goda," pp. 145, 148–49; Bazanov and Kazanskii, Shkola na Krainem Severe, pp. 98–100, 131–33 Semushkin, Chukotka, pp. 49, 62–64, 90, 102; Kantor, "Liudi i fakty," pp. 189–90; Alachev, "Novyi byt u ostiakov," TT, no. 2 (1930): 136; N. Leonov, "Tuzemnye shkoly na Severe," p. 203; TsGAOR, f. 3977, op. 1, d. 945, ll. 7–19; "Sovetskaia shkola," p. 46; Davydov, "Ocherednye zadachi," p. 98; Telishev, "God raboty," p. 127; Al'kor, "Zadachi kul'turnogo stroitel'stva," p. 27; Terletskii, "Kul'tbazy Komiteta Severa," pp. 41–42; P. Nikolaev, "Natsional'nye shkoly na Sakhaline," PN, no. 4 (1934): 45; Senkevich, "V Voitekhovskikh iurtakh," pp. 103–5; Skorik, "Molodye pobegi Sakhalinskoi taigi," p. 108.

[96] Cf. K. Koril'skii, "O zaezzhikh domakh dlia tuzemtsev," SS, no. 9–12 (1930): 160; Solomonov, "Kul'tstroitel'stvo na Severe," p. 138.

[97] V. "Neobkhodimo raskachat'sia," p. 11; I. Bulanov, "Materialy po izucheniiu povedeniia rebenka-tungusa," P, no. 2 (1930): 200; Kantor, "Liudi i fakty," pp. 190–92; Semushkin, Chukotka, pp. 28, 71–72, 127–29, 166–67; Ustiugov, "Tuzemnye sovety," pp. 25–28; B-ov, "Budni krasnykh iurt," p. 64; Semushkin, "Opyt raboty," pp. 185–86; Bogoraz, "Religiia, kak tormoz," p. 149.

trade: a sheet of paper, a pen, and a pencil.)[98] Also, once all the school-boys in a settlement had been forced to cut their hair or wash their faces, their younger brothers might feel hopelessly old-fashioned in bangs and demand towels from their mothers.[99] "Civilization" worked in mysterious ways. Some of the older ethnographers might have suggested that such results hardly justified a cultural revolution complete with violence, threats, and expulsion. They never did, however. By the time the cultural revolution was over, so was ethnography.

The War against Ethnography

The cultural revolution was not limited to providing culture to those who apparently did not have any. The Kulturträger themselves had to be purged of everything obsolete, incorrect, and un-Marxist. Bourgeois ethnographers were as dangerous as unrepentant kulaks, and errors in the theory of backwardness were as pernicious as backwardness itself. In fact, as Party leaders made clear, they were all one and the same thing or, better even, one and the same person. "The enemy" (usually in the singular) was conceived as a kind of shaman's spirit: ever present, ever treacherous, and ever pretending to be someone else. As one Stalinist ethnographer put it,

> In the desperate last struggle the class enemy keeps changing and modifying his strategy, mobilizing all forces from religion to school; from deskbound theoretician to petty thief or pacifist; from supposedly innocent researcher to arrogant wrecker; from social-fascist to downright bandit and arsonist. . . . It would be ludicrous to think that a wrecker armed with "scholarly" glasses is less dangerous than his companion armed with a gas mask or some other kind of lethal mask [sic].[1]

To draw the line between friend and foe, one needed to know the difference between a "truly scientific" and a harmful theory, but in most academic fields there was no direct guidance from either "the classics of Marxism" or the current Party leaders. The classics had of course equipped the leaders to deal with all "objective phenomena," so that in principle the keepers of sacred knowledge could issue encyc-

---

[98] Semushkin, Chukotka, p. 161.
[99] Semushkin, "Opyt raboty," p. 182, and Chukotka, pp. 77, 94, 227.
[1] B. Khotinskii, "XVI s"ezd partii i nashi zadachi," E, no. 4 (1930): 5.

licals on doctrinal problems in every field of inquiry, from pedagogy to chemistry. In the 1920s, however, they almost never did: there were limits to what the old Bolsheviks saw as politically relevant or even socially appropriate. Rather than instructing all scholars all the time, they relied on preferential college admissions to create truly scientific scholars. Healthy social roots were a guarantee of sound theoretical judgment.[2]

In one sense these hopes came true. By the beginning of the cultural revolution most professions included young, Soviet-educated practitioners bent on transforming their fields in accordance with Marxist principles. Triumphant yet defensive beneficiaries of class-based quotas, they were passionately committed to the people and the ideology that had pulled them out of the "swamp" and distrusted and often disliked their "bourgeois" professors (and eventually colleagues), who tended to be older, more experienced, and better trained professionally.[3] Politically the young Communists enjoyed a definite edge—or at least had high hopes for the future: they were trying to apply the official discourse to their disciplines and could easily claim that any opposition to their activities was tantamount to counterrevolution. It was the "theoretical front" that presented them with the greatest challenge. What did Marxism stand for in each particular case? In art and literature, was it forward-looking avant-gardism or down-to-earth forms accessible to the masses? In philosophy, was it "mechanism" or dialectics? In psychology, was it the "materialist" biological reductionism or activist social environmentalism? The intensity of the anti-establishment struggle and of the Marxist internal debate varied from one profession to another. By 1928 the Russian Association of Proletarian Writers had bullied its way to the top of the publishing world; the physiologists, reactologists, and reflexologists had all but outlawed subjective psychology despite their inability to agree on any other issue; and Marxist historians seemed united behind their leader and coexisted rather amicably with their non-Marxist colleagues.[4]

[2] See Sheila Fitzpatrick, Educational and Social Mobility in the Soviet Union 1921–1934 (Cambridge, 1979), pp. 89–112.

[3] Sheila Fitzpatrick, "Cultural Revolution as Class War," in Cultural Revolution in Russia, 1928–1931, ed. Sheila Fitzpatrick (Bloomington, 1978), pp. 28–31.

[4] On cultural revolution in various professions, see John Barber, Soviet Historians in Crisis, 1928–1932 (London, 1981); Raymond Bauer, The New Man in Soviet Psychology (Cambridge, Mass., 1952); Edward J. Brown, The Proletarian Episode in Russian Literature, 1928–1932 (New York, 1953); Fitzpatrick, Cultural Revolution in Russia; Susan Gross Solomon, The Soviet Agrarian Debate: A Controversy in Social Science, 1923–

Of all the disciplines that fell within the confines of traditional Marxism, ethnography was the most innocent of "bolshevizing"[5] tendencies. It was associated with the study of backward peoples and bizarre customs and thus did not seem very attractive to many young Communists, who thirsted for "real action" or ideological controversy. Furthermore, although the acknowledged leaders of the field, Shternberg and Bogoraz, were not Marxists, they did not easily fit into the "bourgeois scholar" category. Both were well-known martyrs to the revolutionary cause, and Shternberg had been mentioned favorably by Engels himself. The international reputation of the two men went far beyond that, and both were known at home as "the classics of Russian ethnography."

How to define ethnography, or ethnology, was a matter of lively debate. The 1920s saw a great expansion of the discipline in Western Europe and the United States. Classical evolutionism was in decline: postwar scepticism had led to doubts about global progress and the psychic unity of mankind, and a new emphasis on fieldwork seemed to confirm these doubts by producing numerous examples of apparent retrogression and simplification. Theories of universal development were out of fashion, and Morgan's, Tylor's, and Spencer's grand systems were being criticized as too abstract and based on preselected and secondhand evidence. Great stress was laid on pragmatism and scientific rigor, and the theories that seemed to meet those criteria were usually concerned with migrations and diffusion.

The Russia of the 1920s was fertile terrain for some of the new approaches. It worshiped materialism, the natural sciences, and the "limitless possibilities" of technology. Popular gurus claimed that all social sciences could be reduced to basic biological or mechanical components or at least improved through the introduction of "truly scientific" methods. Among ethnographers, Boas was often praised for his historicism and moderation, but it was German ethnology, particularly the work of Ratzel, Frobenius, and the *Kulturkreis* school of Schmidt and Graebner that received the greatest acclaim.[6] According to Bogoraz,

> Approximately twenty years ago ethnography knew only two approaches: either isolated descriptions of individual tribes or broad uni-

---

1929 (Boulder, Colo., 1977); David Joravsky, *Soviet Marxism and Natural Science* (New York, 1961); Loren R. Graham, *The Soviet Academy of Sciences and the Communist Party, 1927–1932* (Princeton, 1967).

[5] Joravsky's term.

[6] The related approach of the American "culture area" school was rarely mentioned.

versal generalizations based on superficial and uncritically selected material. At the present time broad generalizations are to be supplemented by narrower theories that encompass the natural ties of peoples and groups that live in close proximity, united (albeit not always) by a common origin and above all linked in a single geographical complex by common natural conditions and common cultural achievements produced as a result of mutual influences.[7]

Bogoraz went on to formulate—and teach—something he called ethnogeography, or rather the history of culture as a "resultant of geographical, anthropological, and economic factors." He talked about the spread of culture according to the laws of geometry; about positive and negative "alternating currents of culture;" and about the mutual repulsion of races.[8] For most of Bogoraz's colleagues this was going too far, but the spirit of daring experimentation was shared by all. Even Shternberg, who never wavered in his commitment to classical evolutionism, was greatly intrigued by some Freudian notions and incorporated them in his work.[9]

One influence that was conspicuous by its absence was Marxism In contrast to what was happening in many other fields, there were Marxist ethnographers but no serious attempt to construct a Marxist ethnography. In 1924 one militant atheist accused contemporary ethnographers of fruitless theorizing (a standard formula used by young activists), adding that Shternberg's Institute of Geography "reeked of old-fashioned populism."[10] In the summer of the same year, when all colleges were being purged of "socially alien elements," a group of radical students from the Institute of Geography complained to Moscow and asked for a new curriculum (both Shternberg and Bogoraz were abroad at the time). When classes resumed in the fall, the Institute had to offer a host of Marxist subjects and drop all of its courses deemed unrelated to the humanities.[11] There would be no more "ethnogeography" and no "universal science of culture." At the end of the school year the Institute was attached to Leningrad University and lost its administrative autonomy altogether. Still, the cause of Marxist eth-

[7] V. G. Bogoraz (-Tan), "XXI kongress amerikanistov," E, no. 1–2 (1926): 129.

[8] V. G. Bogoraz (-Tan), Rasprostranenie kul'tury na zemle; Osnovy etnogeografii (Moscow, 1928), and "K voprosu o graficheskom metode analiza elementov etnografii i etnogeografii," E, no. 1 (1928): 3–10.

[9] See his "Izbrannichestvo v religii," E, no. 1 (1927): 3–56.

[10] Quoted in N. M. Matorin, "Sovremennyi etap i zadachi sovetskoi etnografii," SE, no. 1–2 (1931): 12.

[11] Ratner-Shternberg, "L. Ia. Shternberg," pp. 144–45.

nography as a doctrine and a school was not greatly advanced. Professional publications remained undisturbed by Marxism, and professional organizations had few Marxists. Young would-be iconoclasts were lurking in the background, but in 1928 they were not organized and had no theoretical platform.

Thus when Stalin announced that the class war was on and that all non-Marxist scholars were on the wrong side of the barricade, the attack against ethnography had to come from the outside. During the very first fight "on the historical front" V. D. Aptekar', a delegate from the Academy of the History of Material Culture, fired a salvo against Bogoraz and his "hidden struggle against Marxism."[12] The alleged offense was "the attitude of the scholarly community toward the Japhetic theory of N. Ia. Marr, which is being subjected to a most disgraceful campaign of persecution—all the more disgraceful because it is taking place in Soviet Russia."[13]

N. Ia. Marr and his disciples from the Academy of the History of Material Culture had good reasons to dislike the scholarly community in general and ethnography in particular. As a young Georgian linguist, Marr had developed a strong antipathy for the Indo-Europeanist slant of mainstream academic linguistics. He felt that the other languages (including Georgian) were neglected, patronized, and colonized much as their speakers had been. The same held true for the class-based concern with "literary languages" at the expense of "living popular speech." Marr's professional task and moral duty was to triumph over linguistic imperialism in both the national and the social realm.

By the late 1920s he had come a long way. Inspired by Marxism and greatly encouraged by the postrevolutionary interest in intellectual reductionism, he had formulated his revolutionary "new theory of language," otherwise known as the "Japhetic theory," and had become something of an elder statesman among Marxist scholars. According to Marr, language belonged to the social superstructure and thus reflected the cyclical changes of the economic base. In other words, it belonged to history and, like any other institution, was part of the universal evolution toward progress. The Indo-Europeanist theory of a constantly

---

[12] Soon afterward Bogoraz became fair game in the war between "northerners" and "orientalists" at the Leningrad Institute of Oriental Languages. See Chapter 6, first section. For the historical debate, see Barber, *Soviet Historians in Crisis*, pp. 31–34; Konstantin F. Shteppa, *Russian Historians and the Soviet State* (New Brunswick, N.J., 1962), pp. 52–58.

[13] V. D. Aptekar', "Vystuplenie na obsuzhdenii knigi D. M. Petrushevskogo 'Ocherki iz ekonomicheskoi istorii srednevekovoi Evropy,'" *IM*, no. 2 (1928): 115.

fragmented protolanguage was idealistic and unnatural in that it postulated a movement toward plurality. In fact, the history of language, like that of the society it served, was a process of steady amalgamation until all speech became fused under communism. The numerous "diffuse," "mollusk-like" languages of primitive societies had given rise to the more sophisticated languages of later stages, but their four basic elements (the names of the original "totemic production units") remained the irreducible components of human speech. All the words in all languages were ultimately derived from one of these four elements. The so-called linguistic families represented different but historically related developmental stages. Chinese was a relict of ancient monosyllabic and polysemantic languages; next on the scale of evolution came the Uralo-Altaic, the Japhetic,[14] and finally the Semitic family. In a different formulation, the history of language consisted of linear, synthetic, agglutinative, and inflective stages, each corresponding to a specific socioeconomic formation and developing dialectically (that is, replacing one another via revolutionary "leaps"). This tenet implied that all languages were historically and semantically connected; all contributed to the global "glottogony"; and none—except for future communist speech—could claim superiority over others. The formalism of Indo-Europeanism had finally been overcome; the unity of human language had been restored; and linguistics had become part of history. The job of the "new linguist" was to reconstruct material evolution through language.[15]

Marr's irritation with ethnography stemmed from the intellectual and emotional core of his doctrine. As far as he was concerned, ethnography had artificially—and maliciously—divorced the history of the exploited classes and preliterate peoples from the history of mankind. With imperialistic arrogance, ethnographers were involved in a patronizing examination of whatever was discarded by bourgeois historians and linguists.[16] Another reason for the particular shrillness and enthusiasm with which Marr and his students answered the call for

[14] Georgian and other languages of the Caucasus.

[15] For example, see N. Ia. Marr, "K zadacham nauki na sovetskom Vostoke," PN, no. 2 (1930): 11–15; S. Bykhovskaia, "O bespis'mennykh iazykakh (v osveshchenii iafeticheskoi teorii)," PN, no. 3, 1930): 51–54; S. N. Bykovskii, "Iafeticheskii predok vostochnykh slavian—kimmeriitsy" IG 8, no. 8–10 (1931): 1–12; I. Kusik'ian, "N. Ia. Marr i ego uchenie o iazyke," PN, no. 6 (1933); I. I. Meshchaninov, "Nikolai Iakovlevich Marr," SE, no. 1 (1935): 8–16; M. G. Khudiakov, "Graficheskie skhemy istoricheskogo protsessa v trudakh N. Ia. Marra," SE, no. 1 (1935): 18–41.

[16] Marr, "K zadacham nauki," pp. 11–15; Bykhovskaia, "O bespis'mennykh iazykakh," pp. 51–54.

class war in the academic world was that in spite (and, as they would have it, because) of their "momentous achievements," they had not managed to break into the professional establishment. In contrast to some other Marxist groupings, such as A. A. Pokrovskii's school in history, they had seen nothing but ridicule and indifference. Marr was routinely referred to as a charlatan and his four elements as alchemy. Characteristically, a dissertation by one of Marr's closest disciples was described as "sheer fantasy" by an anonymous outside reviewer.[17] When the cultural revolution began, their desire for revenge was almost palpable.

It began in April 1929, when the Academy of the History of Material Culture organized a large conference of Moscow and Leningrad ethnographers. Speaking for the hosts, V. B. Aptekar' declared that ethnology was "a bourgeois surrogate for social sciences" that claimed a separate existence for such phenomena as "culture" and "ethnos." By looking for causal explanations within the superstructure rather than the base, it stood the problem "on its head" and contradicted the very essence of the only truly scientific approach to the study of culture—historical materialism. Marxism and ethnology were incompatible: theoretical ethnology was a class-based distortion, and practical ethnography was not (and should not be) any different from Marxist sociology.[18]

The young bolshevizing ethnographers faced a serious problem. On the one hand, they were eager to dislodge their seniors, disrupt the status quo, and generally wreak havoc on the unwelcoming "bourgeois" world of academe. On the other hand, they were now part of this world and wanted to prove the usefulness of their newly acquired expertise to true science and socialist construction. Most of them were sympathetic to various kinds of intellectual and organizational reductionism but not quite prepared to have themselves decreed out of existence. After a long debate the conference accepted Aptekar''s theses in the case of *ethnology*, which was defined as a bourgeois attempt to construct a separate science about culture, but made it clear that within historical materialism there was room for practical *ethnography*, or rather, "a historical study of temporally and spatially specific human societies and cultural phenomena."[19] In what way such a study would

[17] V. B. Aptekar' and S. N. Bykovskii, "Sovremennoe polozhenie na lingvisticheskom fronte i ocherednye zadachi marksistov–iazykovedov," *IG* 10, no. 8–9 (1931): 31–34; Bykovskii, "Iafeticheskii predok," p. 1.

[18] "Soveshchanie ethnografov Leningrada i Moskvy," *E*, no. 2 (1929): 115–16.

[19] Ibid., p. 118.

be different from Marxist historiography was not explained—presumably because the sponsors of the resolution did not know themselves. What they did know was that their work had to be useful: it had to be a part of the Party's struggle for a better future. The practical (as opposed to theoretical) goals of Soviet ethnographers were to study popular life in the light of the "Great Transformation" and to participate in the Great Transformation itself.[20]

As usual, the transformation consisted in the struggle against the enemies of the transformation. For three years after the conference, the young radicals, implicitly supported by the Party leaders (or so everybody thought), waged war on the non-Marxists and their organizations, journals, professional goals, and professional topics. Museums were closed, scholarly societies disbanded, the teaching of ethnography discontinued, and teachers of ethnography persecuted.[21] As the exhilaration of destruction grew, so did the number of enemies, taboo subjects, and "subversive activities." At the same time, the social and generational aspects of the campaign became more explicit, with the "revolutionaries" accusing the "counterrevolutionaries" of "individualistic class habits which had led . . . to caste-like isolationism and hierarchical divisions,"[22] as well as of writing books that had been "muddling the minds of the new generation of scholars."[23]

The non-Marxists put up some resistance in the early stages of the cultural revolution. P. F. Preobrazhenskii defended ethnology and the Kulturkreis school; Bogoraz valiantly fought against Marrist ethnographers, Tarantaeva and friends in the Committee of the North, and youthful (and of course Marrist) orientalists in his Northern *rabfak*. Later, when the difference between "scholarly glasses" and a "gas

[20] Ibid., pp. 118–23.

[21] See, for example, S. P. Tolstov, "K probleme akkul'turatsii," *E*, no. 1–2 (1930): 87; Matorin, "Sovremennyi etap i zadachi," p. 34; "Etnograficheskaia sektsiia obshchestva istorikov-marksistov pri leningradskom otdelenii Kommunisticheskoi akademii," *SE*, no. 1–2 (1931): 155; "Leningradskoe obshchestvo izucheniia kul'tury finno-ugorskikh narodov (LOIKFUN)," *SE*, no. 1–2 (1931): 156; M. G. Khudiakov, "Kriticheskaia prorabotka rudenkovshchiny,' *SE*, no. 1–2 (1931): 167–69; "K organizatsii muzeia istorii religii," *SE*, no. 1–2 (1931): 171–72; S. N. Bykovskii, "Etnografiia na sluzhbe klassovogo vraga," *SE*, no. 3–4 (1931): 4; S. Maizel', "Trinadtsat' let akademicheskoi arabistiki," *SE*, no. 3–4 (1931): 251–54; I. Razmanov, "Protiv idealizma professorskoi 'uchenosti' i shovinisticheskikh teorii " *PN*, no. 7–8 (1931): 94–97; Ersari, "Ob odnom uchastke nauchno-teoreticheskogo fronta," *RN*, no. 7 (1932): 95–98; N. M. Matorin, "Piatnadtsat' let oktiabr'skoi revoliutsii," *SE*, no. 5–6 (1932): 13.

[22] "Leningradskoe obshchestvo izucheniia kul'tury finno-ugorskikh narodov (LOIKFUN)," p. 156.

[23] Bykovskii, "Etnografiia na sluzhbe," p. 4.

mask" disappeared completely, most of the older professors either fell silent or, like Preobrazhenskii and Bogoraz, tried their best to become Marxists.[24]

Unfortunately for them, however, this was not much easier in 1931 than it had been in 1929. One way of being Marxist was to discover and analyze class differentiation and class conflict. This was a political requirement: collectivization was a given, and collectivization presupposed the existence of classes. On a loftier theoretical plane, all Marxist ethnographers agreed that their primary task was to define the place of a given society in the chain of sociopolitical formations and, having thus established their bearings, proceed to examine the interplay of base and superstructure and the operation of specific economic, social, and cultural phenomena. They also assumed, however, that the unique subject of ethnography (as part of history) was the study of backward, or rather, primitive communist societies. In other words, the ethnographers' usefulness to the building of socialism consisted in their ability to uncover class structures, whereas their task as scholars was to study societies that by definition had no classes. The resulting difficulty led to great terminological confusion and contributed to the painful doubts about ethnography's raison d'être.[25]

Some unexpected help came from psychology. While ethnographers were having great difficulty being Marxists, Marxist psychologists were having a field day with "primitive peoples." The ideological inspiration for the Great Transformation in general and the cultural revolution in particular was a belief in the plasticity of man and unconditional primacy of the environment. The environment bore the sole responsibility for backwardness and superstition, and a revolutionary change in the environment was expected to result in prompt and predictable changes in society and the human psyche. The theoretical foundation and the ultramodern methodology for studying such processes were provided by the new science of pedology, or applied child psychology. Using various testing techniques, the pedologists claimed to be able to measure and predict the degree and forms of psychological mutability

---

[24] V. G. Bogoraz (-Tan), "K voprosu o primenenii marksistskogo metoda k izucheniiu etnograficheskikh iavlenii," E, no. 1–2 (1930): 3–56; P. F. Preobrazhenskii, "Razlozhenie rodovogo stroia i feodalizatsionnyi protsess u turkmenov–iomudov," E, no. 4 (1930): 11–28; Bogoraz (-Tan), "Klassovoe rassloenie," pp. 93–116.

[25] See, for example, S. A. Tokarev, "Obshchestvennyi stroi melaneziitsev. K voprosu o proiskhozhdenii klassov i gosudarstva," E, no. 2 (1929): 4–46; Bogoraz (-Tan), "K voprosu o primenenii marksistskogo metoda," pp. 6–16; Preobrazhenskii, "Razlozhenie rodovogo stroia," pp. 11–28; and S. P. Tolstov, "Problemy dorodovogo obshchestva," SE, no. 3–4 (1931): 69–103.

and thus put human engineering on a "truly scientific" basis. In this connection a "primitive" child was an especially fascinating and useful object for study, "particularly if one bears in mind that such a human organism should develop and grow at an accelerated rate, skipping whole historic periods."[26] With the help of pedology, it would be possible to "speed up the adoption by various nationalities, particularly the backward ones, of Soviet technology, economy, and ideology."[27] In the words of I. Bikchentai, "We need a builder, a member of the future Communist society. We have a hunter, a pastoralist, a beekeeper, a peasant. How we can transform his psyche in the shortest time possible in such a way that he will inevitably become a member of the Communist society; which environmental changes produce more effective results in this regard—this is what interests us."[28]

All but abandoned by bewildered ethnographers, the small peoples of the north, along with other "nationals," provided the testing ground for pedologists. Scientific expeditions were sent to Siberia, and native children had their IQs measured and their attitudes evaluated—for the most part by student interns.[29] The pedologists suggested environmental reasons for various instances of backwardness and made recommendations for their speedy elimination; however, they soon ran into trouble. According to most tests, the native children were either hopelessly retarded or so different that they required a total revision of the testing techniques. At first this did not worry the researchers too much: great differences in both the social and the natural environment made such findings understandable. But as time went on, more and more pedologists found themselves saying that overcoming these differences might take more time and effort than they had anticipated. In some cases the numerous and enduring peculiarities of the "primitive mind" led the researchers away from pure environmentalism toward a study of the biological and psychological uniqueness of backward peoples.[30] This view was reinforced by a very successful exhibit of drawings by the students of the Institute of the Peoples of the North. Influential avant-garde critics were impressed by their "high formal

[26] P. V. Ventskovskii, "Pedagogicheskoe izuchenie natsmen," PN, no. 7–8 (1930): 98.
[27] Ibid.
[28] I. Bikchentai "Ocherednye zadachi natspedologii," P, no. 7–8 (1931): 32.
[29] See A. M. Shubert, "Opyt pedologo-pedagogicheskikh ekspeditsii po izucheniiu narodov dalekikh okrain," P, no. 2 (1930): 167–71.
[30] A. Frenkel', ' Protiv eklektizma v pedologii i psikhologii," PN, no. 7–8 (1930): 108–110; A. M. Shubert, "Problemy pedologii natsional'nostei," PN, no. 3 (1931): 56–59; P. P. Blonskii, "O nekotorykh tendentsiiakh pedologicheskogo izucheniia detei razlichnykh natsional'nostei," PN, no. 4 (1932): 48–50.

culture" and warned against the imposition of European conventions on the people who obviously possessed "a unique artistic worldview totally different from ours."[31]

All this was unacceptable to both the Party leaders and the majority of the new Soviet intelligentsia, who saw any suggestion of genetic ("racial") determinism as an attack on the revolution and on their own status. As Bukharin had put it in the early days of the Great Transformation, "If we were to take the point of view that racial and national characteristics were so great that it would take thousands of years to change them, then, naturally, all our work would be absurd."[32] The original sin of pedology was that no matter how optimistic the researchers were and how much they believed in psychic unity, the very formulation of their goals presupposed that there were limits to change—at least in time.[33] The pedologists owed their existence to the belief that some environmental factors were prejudicial for growth and saw their primary task as finding ways to compensate for these drawbacks. Consequently, they could not help irritating certain groups by devising separate (usually longer-term) educational strategies for women, national minorities, and the socially disadvantaged.[34]

Even more unfortunate was the fact that although the First Five-Year Plan was "changing the face of Russia," the test results did not indicate a parallel change in human minds. Given the expectation of an immediate and automatic connection between the two, pedologists had a lot of explaining to do. The speed, thoroughness, and correctness of the Great Transformation itself could not be doubted, so the obvious culprits were the tests and the people who put them together. By mid-1932 pedology had all but disintegrated under the accusations and confessions of incompetence, slander against Soviet children, and other politically harmful activities.[35] The field languished for a while longer, but in the era of consciousness, individual achievement, and cadres "deciding everything" there was no legitimate place for it.[36] All

[31] L. N., "Bol'shoe iskusstvo malykh narodov," *PN*, no. 6 (1930): 116–21; L. Mess, "Iskusstvo severnykh narodnostei," *SO*, no. 3 (1930): 115–21.

[32] Quoted in Raymond Bauer, *The New Man*, p. 81.

[33] See Ventskovskii, "Pedagogicheskoe izuchenie natsmen," p. 98.

[34] G. Gasilov, "O sisteme narodnogo obrazovaniia natsional'nykh men'shinstv RSFSR," *PN*, no. 1 (1929): 31; Blonskii, "O nekotorykh tendentsiiakh," pp. 48–51.

[35] P. Nikolaev, "Ob odnoi iz zadach marksistko-leninskoi pedagogiki," *PN*, no. 4 (1931): 34–40; "Protiv velikoderzhavnogo shovinizma v pedologii," *P*, no. 1 (1932): 46–49; I. Bikchentai, "Pis'mo v zhurnal 'Prosveshchenie natsional'nostei,'" *PN*, no. 4 (1932): 102–3.

[36] Fitzpatrick, *Educational and Social Mobility*, pp. 228–30.

peoples, including the most backward, were unconditionally change-able, and that change could be effected directly through education, without all the "environmental factors" being there. In fact, with no slanderous tests to disprove it, both the environmental and psychologi-cal change could be postulated as a given, and the work of practical training could begin in earnest.[37]

Pedology was not the only discipline that produced unacceptable evidence about the "underdeveloped peoples." The very existence of ethnography seemed to suggest that some groups took too long to be-come modern. Highly suspect to begin with, it was a prime candidate for abolition or self-destruction. In early 1932 N. M. Matorin, formerly the "populist'-bashing provincial atheist and now the uncontested leader of Soviet ethnographers, declared that practical fieldwork under the existing conditions was imperialistic in nature. At the conference of 1929 he had led the pragmatists against the abolitionists and had insisted on a special role for ethnography; now he agreed that ethnogra-phy was nothing but the first chapter in a history book. "The term 'eth-nography' may be retained for that part of history which studies the preclass society and its survivals."[38] This meant that the parts of reality that had undergone the Great Transformation could not be studied by ethnographers lest doubt be cast on the effectiveness of the transforma-tion. "It is clear to me now," wrote Matorin, "that there is nothing spe-cifically ethnographic in a study of a kolkhoz or sovkhoz equipped with modern technology."[39] And as all kolkhozes and sovkhozes were expected to be thus equipped, ethnographers had no business study-ing them.

The logical step of dropping a name that had effectively lost all meaning was taken by the All-Russian Conference on Archaeology and Ethnography in May 1932. On the basis of addresses by Matorin and chief archaeologist (and Marr's student) S. N. Bykovskii, the confer-ence formally expelled both sciences from Marxism. Archaeology was charged with separating and deifying material artifacts; ethnography, with doing the same for culture. Sciences were real (Marxist) inasmuch as they studied separate forms of the movement of matter (objective laws). Neither the excavation of artifacts nor the participant observa-tion of society was based on any separate set of laws, and therefore the distinction between Marxist ethnography and bourgeois ethnology

[37] Bauer, The New Man, pp. 83–112.
[38] Matorin, "Sovremennyi etap i zadachi sovetskoi etnografii," p. 20.
[39] Ibid., p. 21.

was in itself "a particularly harmful and disorienting activity which employed leftist jargon to conceal rightist contents and various forms of bourgeois and petit bourgeois opportunism and eclecticism."[40] Archaeology and ethnography were in fact nothing but concrete methods of historical data-gathering, and any claim to the contrary was patently anti-Marxist. Even keeping a special name for the branch of history that dealt with "primitive peoples" was a tribute to colonialism.[41] Rather than constructing nonexistent sciences, the practitioners of this kind of history should devote themselves to the study of the issues raised by Marx, Engels, and Lenin, namely,

> (1) the process of ethnogenesis and the distribution of ethnic and national groups; (2) material production in its specific variants; (3) the origins of the family; (4) the origins of classes; (5) the origins and various forms of religion, art, and other superstructures; (6) the forms of disintegration of primitive-communist feudal [sic] society in the capitalist environment; (7) the forms of transformation of precapitalist society into socialism directly, bypassing capitalism; [and] (8) the construction of culture national in form and socialist in content.[42]

The victory of Marr's men came at the wrong time. In October 1931 Stalin's letter to *Proletarskaia revoliutsiia* signaled the beginning of the end of the cultural revolution.[43] Radical experimentation, utopianism, professor-bashing, and professional abolitionism were counterproductive at a time of "consolidation of achievements"—all the more so because the new breed of Party leaders obviously found cultural and academic iconoclasm in poor taste. Teachers, rote memorization, and discipline were returning to schools; romantic heroes to literature; "middle-class values" to family life; and punishment to the legal system. Equality was proclaimed to have been a confused petit-bourgeois invention, and the institutions that had been destined to "wither away" were reasserting themselves. The "cultural heritage" and its embattled representatives were coming back to replace their former prosecutors, now "left deviationists."

In this context the decisions of the conference struck a false note. Shortly after Matorin and Bykovskii had erased the last reminder of

---

[40] "Rezoliutsiia Vserossiiskogo Arkheologo-etnograficheskogo soveshchaniia 7–11 maia 1932 goda," *SE*, no. 3 (1932): 13.

[41] Ibid., pp. 12–13.

[42] Ibid., p. 14.

[43] I. V. Stalin, *Sochineniia*, 13 vols. (Moscow, 1946–51), 13: 84–102.

different approaches to "historic" and "nonhistoric" peoples, the Party's Central Committee issued a decree against northern collectivizers, declaring such leveling to be the root of all evil and demanding an immediate stop to the "mechanical and crude application of the experience of the advanced regions of the Union to backward native regions."[44] In relation to the new Party line, ethnography was in danger of moving toward an extreme that was opposite to that of pedology. When the conference resolution was finally published, it was accompanied by a disclaimer stating that the "burial" of ethnography and archaeology was the result of "simplistic leftist attitudes" and led to a "nihilistic negation of the role of the old heritage in science."[45] More "self-criticism" followed, and Soviet ethnography continued to exist. Still, the Party did not intervene directly, and Matorin, Bykovskii, and their comrades retained their position at the head of Soviet ethnography and even succeeded in carrying out their ideological agenda. (In this they were helped by the fact that most scholars were not certain what to do under the new conditions and thus adhered by default to the Marrist minimalist platform.) Fieldwork and the study of specific contemporary societies disappeared almost completely, to be replaced by an exegesis of Marr's Japhetic writings and Engels's *Origins of the Family*. Ethnography had been effectively reduced to the theory of the "primitive communist formation," and the debate revolved around the genesis of class institutions, the problem of the internal contradictions of preclass societies, and the role of survivals in subsequent evolution.[46]

Thus, the small peoples of the north had become one big survival. As the present was assumed to be socialist, nonsocialist reality became past. Almost overnight the peoples without history were summarily consigned to history—and in the process acquired a history of their own. In an indirect rebuke to those who still thought (or thought it their duty to say) that there was no life without class struggle, Stalin's letter to *Proletarskaia revoliutsiia* had asserted that an alliance with "oppressed peoples and colonies"—and not with the oppressed classes among those peoples—had always been the cornerstone of Bolshevik ideology.[47] A consequence of this statement was the appearance

[44] "O rabote v natsional'nykh raionakh Krainego Severa," p. 53.

[45] "Itogi Vserossiiskogo arkheologo-etnograficheskogo soveshchaniia," SE, no. 3 (1932): 3.

[46] The journal SE is consistent in this regard from 1933 through 1936.

[47] Stalin, *Sochineniia*, 13:91–92. See also M. Arzhanov, "Protiv liuksemburgskikh ustanovok," RN, no. 2 (1932): 88–98. The journal *Revoliutsiia i natsional'nosti* withdrew as

of numerous works on the struggle of native Siberians against tsarist colonialism,[48] a trend greatly reinforced by a special exhortation from *Pravda* in 1936.[49]

The traditional (primitive) subjects of ethnography were not to be reduced to mere episodes in the history of Russian imperialism, however. First and foremost, they represented stages in the development of mankind. In accordance with the new goals of ethnography/history, the researcher's most important task was to determine a particular group's stage of development and decide what to do about it. This remained a dangerous undertaking, with most of the participants in the discussion struggling against logic and exposing themselves to accusations of being non-Marxist. The old leaders of the Committee of the North had had to accept the political imperative of finding exploiters in societies they considered classless, and the radicals continued to claim that hunting and gathering peoples had somehow progressed to the feudal or even capitalist stage without changing their economies. The latter view was mostly held by the practitioners of collectivization and those cultural revolutionaries for whom class struggle was a way of life. The legitimacy of their position was derived from the posited reality of the Great Transformation and from Engels's definition of the "childlike simplicity" of preclass society: "No soldiers, no gendarmes or police, no nobles, kings, regents, prefects, or judges, no prisons, no lawsuits—and everything takes its orderly course. . . . There cannot be any poor or needy—the communal household and the gens know their responsibilities towards the old, the sick, and those disabled in war. All are equal and free—the women included."[50]

Could this be said about any group in the USSR? No, it could not. Therefore primitive communism (preclass society, the clan system) no longer existed; anything that looked like it was actually a survival of

"erroneous" its favorable review (No. 1, 1930) of E. Ia. Drabkina's popular *Natsional'nyi i kolonial'nyi vopros v tsarskoi Rossii* (Moscow, 1930).

[48] V. Kornienko, "Vosstanie Vaulia," *SE*, no. 5–6 (1932): 112–19; A. Terent'ev, "Pogromy nentsami iasachnoi kazny v 1641 i 1642 gg.," *SE*, no. 5–6 (1933): 67–76; M. P. Alekseev, "Skazaniia inostrantsev o Rossii i nenetskii epos," *SE*, no. 4–5 (1935): 153–59; Al'kor and Drezen, eds., *Kolonial'naia politika tsarizma*; Ia. P. Al'kor and B. D. Grekov, eds., *Kolonial'naia politika moskovskogo gosudarstva v Iakutii Sbornik dokumentov* (Leningrad, 1935–36); Bakhrushin, *Nauchnye trudy*; Miller, *Istoriia Sibiri*; Kartsov, *Ocherk istorii narodov Severo-zapadnoi Sibiri*; Okun', *Ocherki*.

[49] *Pravda*, 27 January 1936. See also O.K., "Rabota po istorii narodov SSSR," *RN*, no. 5 (1936): 79–83.

[50] Friedrich Engels, *The Origin of the Family, Private Property, and the State* (New York, 1970), pp. 86–87. For an analysis of this passage, see P. T. Khaptaev, "O nekotorykh osobennostiakh klassovoi bor'by v natsional'noi derevne," *RN*, no. 2 (1933): 47–55.

the previous stage of development. The notion of survivals was central to all arguments: it provided an almost limitless flexibility of analysis by allowing the researcher to dismiss any fact that did not fit the adopted definition. Moreover, in the eyes of the professional discoverers of exploitation the survivals were nothing but cynical kulak mystification, artificially maintained under the "slogan of clan solidarity and blood relationship."[51] Traditional "production units" such as *parma* and *baidara* were seen as hotbeds of militant backwardness, "an obstacle to socialist construction and a tool of the class enemy."[52] The implication was that northern kulaks were equal to Russian kulaks were equal to capitalists (or at least feudal lords), but the actual assignment of a given group to a particular socioeconomic formation usually got lost in the survivals. The important thing was the struggle—the struggle against the kulaks and the struggle against the "neopopulists" ("right opportunists") who were myopic or malicious enough to regard the survivals as genuinely collective social and economic communities.[53]

For their part, the leaders of the Committee of the North and other alleged neopopulists accused the radicals of theoretical ignorance and occasionally of Trotskyism. Obviously encouraged by the official campaign against "leftist simplifications," Skachko and friends insisted that the northern societies did not know capital, surplus value, or an agricultural proletariat; that the idyllic picture of primitive communism was an example of the "vulgar egalitarianism" so derided now by

[51] Anisimov, "O sotsial'no-ekonomicheskikh otnosheniiakh," p. 47.

[52] A. G. Danilin, "Sektsiia etnografii Vsesoiuznogo geograficheskogo s"ezda," SE, no. 2 (1933): 115.

[53] TsGAOR, f. 3977, op. 1, d. 991, ll. 37–41; Medvedev, "O rabote s bednotoi," p. 76; Khaptaev, "O nekotorykh osobennostiakh," pp. 47–55; Danilin, "Sektsiia etnografii," p. 115; Anisimov, "O sotsial'no-ekonomicheskikh otnosheniiakh," pp. 38–49; Maslov, "Kochevye ob"edineniia," pp. 27–34; P. T. Khaptaev, "Ob izvrashcheniiakh v voprosakh istorii Buriato-Mongolii," RN no. 7 (1935): 52–56; Anatolii Skachko, "Teoriia i praktika v rabote sredi narodov Severa," SS, no. 6 (1934): 6–7, 9. All Soviet scholars faced the same basic challenge: the Great Transformation was a class phenomenon, hence all societies that had undergone the Great Transformation used to be class societies. Accordingly, following collectivization and forced settlement, experts on Central Asia ended up with the concept of "nomadic feudalism"; after the last word had been said on the "antifeudal" revolution in China, Sinologists rejected the "Asiatic mode of production"; and in the wake of the reinterpretation of the term "socialism" ("in one country"), historians had to reconsider the nature of Russia's own feudalism and capitalism. See Barber, *Soviet Historians in Crisis*, pp. 46–79; A. N. Bernshtam, "Problema raspada rodovykh otnoshenii u kochevnikov Azii," SE, no. 6 (1934): 86–115; Ernest Gellner, *State and Society in Soviet Thought* (Oxford, 1988), pp. 39–68, 92–114; Preobrazhenskii, "Razlozhenie rodovogo stroia," pp. 11–28; Shteppa, *Russian Historians*, pp. 71–90; B. Ia. Vladimirtsov, *Obshchestvennyi stroi mongolov: Mongol'skii kochevoi feodalizm* (Leningrad, 1934).

comrade Stalin; and that traditional collective institutions could and should be used as a basis for kolkhozy.[54] After 1932 the political climate in Moscow seemed right for this message, but attempts to develop the argument ran into severe conceptual problems. One still could not deny the existence of class struggle, and not even the broadest definition of primitive communism could be stretched that far. Just as in the eighteenth century, native societies had to be defined in terms of what they were not—except that now the picture was not static and the small peoples were seen as constantly moving from one point to another, never quite arriving. According to Skachko, they were "in transition from barter to commodity production and from preclass to class society," whereas N. N. Bilibin, another Committee theoretician, suggested that they represented a "system of underdeveloped serf relations."[55] Even the direction of evolution seemed problematic. Why were the "preclan" Chukchi so much more developed than the clan Yukagir? Why was it that the farther away one got from the Russian market, the greater was the social differentiation and the economic development? Why did commodity fur production produce less wealth and fewer exploiters than primitive reindeer breeding? Skachko tried to tackle these questions by suggesting that northern exploitation was produced by trade rather than hired labor and that Russian colonization had had a leveling effect on the native societies, but he remained vulnerable to radical attacks: If there were no full-fledged classes among the native northerners, what was the antagonistic contradiction that propelled their historic development? And why had two hundred years of "Russian serf-owning capitalism" failed to produce classes if, in the accepted view of the time, it "acted in Siberia with all the cynicism of the primary accumulation"?[56] Finally, the newly developed scorn for "vulgar egalitarianism" proved to be as much an enemy as an ally, for although collective work was a good thing, collective distribution was not. As a result, the Committee's policy of using the survivals to create socialist kolkhozy was once again in doubt, this time because the na-

[54] TsGAOR, f. 3977, op. 1, d. 990, ll. 175–81; N. N. Bilibin, "Rabota koriakskogo kraevedcheskogo punkta," SS, no. 6 (1932): 102–6, and "Batratskii trud v kochevom khoziaistve koriakov," SS, no. 1 (1933): 36–46; Anatolii Skachko, "O sotsial'noi strukture malykh narodov Severa," SS, no. 2 (1933): 39–51; Terletskii, "K voprosu" pp. 35–44; Krylov, V Penzhinskom raione," p. 93; Skachko, "Teoriia i praktika," pp. 5–15.

[55] Skachko, "O sotsial'noi strukture," p. 51; Bilibin, "Batratskii trud," p. 46.

[56] Anatolii Skachko, "Pis'mo v redaktsiiu," SS, no. 3–4 (1935): 224–26. The quotation is from Drabkina, Natsional'nyi i kolonial'nyi vopros, p. 60.

tives exhibited too much equality. As one Evenk put it, "I am against vulgar egalitarianism, but surely the food should be divided equally."[57]

The debate was still unresolved when in 1936 the last debaters departed the scene. The "neopopulists" lost their institutional base and publication outlet after the Committee of the North was quietly disbanded as useless;[58] the radicals were accused of heresy and effectively banned along with their science of Soviet ethnography and their journal *Sovetskaia etnografiia*. Matorin and Bykovskii were arrested as terrorists and enemies of the people who had deliberately sabotaged the sciences that were entrusted to them. In the words of the editorial staff of *Sovetskaia etnografiia*, "Instead of studying specific facts on the basis of the methodology of Marxism-Leninsm, they engaged in pseudo-sociological scholasticism and demanded the same from others, disorienting a number of scholars and distracting them from their direct responsibilities."[59] Thus disoriented, the young ethnographers had embarked on "an abstract formal-logical search for the law of contradiction and development of preclass society" while replacing real scholarship with "pompous but totally meaningless talk about stages."[60]

The wording of the indictment seemed to suggest that the old ethnography was back, but the uncertainty, the fear, and the disarray were so great that the surviving ethnographers were rendered almost completely speechless. Fieldwork was largely ignored, and some of the old professors followed their former persecutors into prison (including Preobrazhenskii, Matorin's most vocal "bourgeois" opponent). At about the same time, pedology was delivered the *coup de grace* when all its "pseudoscientific experiments" and "meaningless and harmful tests" were outlawed by a Central Committee decree.[61] The circumpolar peoples were protected from slander and from all scholars in general. Backwardness had been conquered. The small peoples had grown up.

---

[57] Nikul'shin, *Pervobytnye proizvodstvennye ob"edineniia*, p. 130.

[58] See Chapter 8.

[59] "Ot redaktsii," *SE*, no. 6 (1936): 3.

[60] Ibid., pp. 4–5.

[61] See A. M. Valitov, "Pedologicheskie izvrashcheniia v izuchenii detei-natsionalov," *RN*, no. 10 (1936): 44.

"A kolkhoz hydroelectric station," from M. G. Levin and L. P. Potapov, eds., *Narody Sibiri* (Moscow, 1956)

8

The Uncertain Proletarians

"The classics of Marxism," he said uncertainly, "say there is
no great profit to be gained from slave labor. But to tell you
the truth, Vanya, we're in no position to turn up our noses at
even a little profit."
—Vladimir Voinovich, *The Life and Extraordinary
Adventures of Private Ivan Chonkin*

The Native Northerners as Industrial Laborers

Collectivization and cultural revolution were regarded as
necessary for the successful construction of socialism and great
achievements in their own right, but for most activists socialism meant
the future, and the future meant industrialization. The Great Transformation was seen as a leap from the age of wood (or stone) into the
age of heavy machinery, and the revolutionaries, assembled in huge
collectives at huge industrial projects, were "tempering" themselves
and their country under the guidance of the man of steel in the Kremlin. In the iconography of the time, collectivizing "somnolent" peasants or backward non-Russians was a heroic sacrifice; toiling in
industry was an honor and a privilege.

Industrialization had two dimensions. It was to bring socialism to
Russia and take Russia into Asia. The economic structure of the country was to become fair and rational, with the eastern borderlands no
longer colonies of the center. Dreams of a developed socialist union of
republics included plowing the virgin tundra and breaking the ice of
the northern passage. No wonder, therefore, that the bourgeois engi-
neers accused of wrecking and sabotage were also found guilty of try-

ing to stop the eastward movement of industry "under the pretext" of realism, practicality, and cost-effectiveness.[1]

During the First Five-Year Plan this movement was, indeed, relatively limited, but there was enough new activity to make an impression on the local inhabitants.[2] The year 1928 saw the creation of Komseveroput', a state joint-stock company for the economic development of the Arctic Ocean littoral. It mined for graphite on the Kureika and for graphite and coal on the Nizhniaia Tunguska, but its main task was to obtain hard currency by transporting northern lumber from the Ob' and Enisei to Western Europe. By the end of the First Five-Year Plan Komseveroput' had approximately 40,000 employees.[3] In Kamchatka, a large fishing concern (AKO) settled 3,166 families as permanent colonists and brought in about 3,000 additional workers each season.[4] On the Upper Kolyma and the Okhotsk coast the growing gold and lumber industries employed numerous volunteers, exiles, fugitives from collectivization, and eventually almost exclusively labor camp inmates.[5] In the Narym region, 47,000 exiled peasant households (about 196,000 people) were put to work felling trees, fishing, breeding horses, and growing grain and potatoes.[6] All in all, about a million new people arrived in the north between 1926 and 1932.[7]

The small peoples were not included in the plans but were apparently expected to welcome the newcomers and volunteer their help. The ideal scenario was described by an Evenk delegate to a regional Congress of Soviets:

> We the toiling natives must and will procure more furs. We must learn how to fish so that we will not only satisfy our own needs but also export fish from our region. The natives should get used to working in the mines of Komseveroput' and thus help in the construction of this country. . . .

[1] P. Rysakov, "Otgoloski vreditel'stva v natsional'nykh raionakh," RN, no. 6 (1931): 40–41.

[2] V. L. Popov, "Istoricheskaia piatiletka Severnoi Azii," SA, no. 4 (1929): 5–24.

[3] S. V. Slavin, Promyshlennoe i transportnoe osvoenie severa SSSR (Moscow, 1961), pp. 115–16; L. E. Kiselev, Sever raskryvaet bogatstva (Iz istorii promyshlennogo razvitiia sovetskogo Krainego Severa) (Moscow, 1964), pp. 11–12.

[4] Kiselev, Sever raskryvaet bogatstva, pp. 13–14.

[5] Popova, Eveny, pp. 231–36; David Dallin and Boris Nicolaevsky, Forced Labor in Soviet Russia (New Haven, 1947), pp. 113–14.

[6] N. A. Ivnitskii, Klassovaia bor'ba v derevne i likvidatsiia kulachestva kak klassa (1929–1932) (Moscow, 1972), pp. 304, 319–21.

[7] P. G. Smidovich, "Sotsialisticheskaia rekonstruktsiia Krainego Severa," SS, no. 1–2 (1932): 44; P. N. Orlovskii, "Territoriia i naselenie Krainego Severa," SS, no. 1–2 (1932): 69–83.

The Soviet government was right to start mining and to begin a project which the natives cannot accomplish by themselves but which will be both useful for the state and provide a new source of income for the natives.[8]

Overall, the new industrial enterprises held little attraction for the hunting and gathering population. As one Russian-educated Tofalar put it, "the Tofalar do not take part in the mining of gold either as miners or as prospectors. They are not interested in the bowels of the earth."[9] The Russians who were interested were not always welcome. The Korkodon Evenk repeatedly refused to serve as guides for a group of geologists, saying, "The mountains are ours, the rocks are ours, and the river is ours—you've no business going there and looking."[10]

The geologists went and looked anyway, and so did many other surveyors, miners, and settlers. Around the large gold-mining center of Nogaevo the newcomers hunted down the Even reindeer, looted their food stocks, and burned down the taiga, forcing the nomads to leave the area and the local kul'tbaza to be permanently closed.[11] On the important Dudinka-Khatanga route the local Dolgan, Nenets, Evenk, and Nganasan were forced to transport numerous state officials as well as commercial cargo. A round trip took from three and a half to four months during the winter hunting season, and between 1930 and 1932 the number of men involved in transportation grew from 41 to 71 percent. In the same period the number of reindeer dropped by about 46 percent.[12]

Elsewhere, the Evenk of Nizhniaia Tunguska had their reindeer taken away from them, and the population of Kamchatka was deprived of fish by the wholesale operations of AKO.[13] On the Ob' 14 percent of commercial fishermen were exiles, and 70 percent, peasant recruits from the southern provinces.[14] In the gold mines of the Vitimo-Olekma

[8] I. Pervukhin, "Ob organizatsii Evenkiiskogo natsional'nogo okruga," SS, no. 10 (1931): 23–24.

[9] Tobolaev, "V Tofalarskom raione," p. 95. See also Galkin, V zemle polunochnogo solntsa, p. 113.

[10] S. V. Obruchev, Kolymskaia zemlitsa. Dva goda skitanii (Moscow, 1933), p. 99.

[11] TsGAOR, f. 3977, op 1, d. 925, ll. 1–62; Popova, Eveny, pp. 231–36; Terletskii, "Kul'tbazy Komiteta Severa," p. 38; Skachko, "Vos'moi plenum Komiteta Severa," p. 16.

[12] A. A. Popov, "Poezdka k dolganam." SE, no. 3–4 (1931): 211; A. Smesov, "Khatangskaia ekspeditsiia Akademii nauk," SS, no. 6 (1933): 43–44; "V Taimyrskom okruge," p. 84.

[13] Skachko, "Ocherednye zadachi," pp. 8–11.

[14] E. D. Kantor, "Khoziaistvo Iamal'skogo (Nenetskogo) natsional'nogo okruga," SS, no. 6 (1933): 47.

district exiles constituted 50 percent of the labor force.[15] The natives were forced to make room for the industrializers—sometimes literally in their own homes. Of the 196,000 "kulaks" banished to the Tobol'sk north, 33,000 ended up in the Berezov and Surgut districts. "They were put wherever a fishing company official decided to start a fishery or a lumber company official fancied putting a sawmill."[16] Some of them were housed in Khanty winter dugouts during the summer and then transferred to Khanty summer tents when winter arrived—"without any consideration for the interests of the natives" (let alone the lives of the exiles).[17] According to one account, "The special settlers[18] not only oppress the natives by taking away their land and their homes but also infect them with various contagious diseases such as typhus, dysentery, scarlet fever, etc. As the high percentages of the sickness and mortality rates demonstrate, the native population is very vulnerable to these diseases."[19]

The gradual change brought about by the proximity of a gold mine is described by the Tofalar student I. Tobolaev:

We have had some bad cases here. For example, one Komsomol member, a young fellow, went to town and contracted a venereal disease. First got it himself and then infected a number of young girls. When we discovered it, we started treating the sick, and as for this Komsomol member, we are going to treat him the hard way, with a show trial. This is the first time that the Tofalar people have had a venereal disease.

Last fall there was another unheard of event. During the pine-cone picking, one fellow raped a girl. This was the first time it had ever happened. This case shocked both the young and the old people. Once again, we have decided on a show trial, in order to expose and eradicate this evil.

Then there was another unpleasant incident. We live quietly around here—wine is forbidden, and fighting and stealing are unknown. But we had a Russian policeman in our native soviet—more as a formality than because we needed him. So he himself would get vodka at the gold mine

---

[15] TsGAOR, f. 3977, op. 1, d. 737, l. 116.

[16] Anatolii Skachko, "Zemlia Iugorskaia i Obdorskaia v leto 1930," SS, no. 2 (1931): 109.

[17] Ibid.

[18] The euphemism for exiled peasants.

[19] P. K. Ustiugov, Puti sotsialisticheskoi rekonstruktsii khoziaistva malykh narodnostei Severa (Moscow, 1931), p. 41. The actual percentages are not cited.

or some place else and then get drunk and start carousing. For this we took him to court and had a show trial.[20]

The show trials did not seem to help. On another occasion fourteen (out of 439) Tofalar died of alcohol poisoning.[21]

The Committee of the North was in a very difficult position. By all accounts, the small peoples needed protection, and needed it more than ever before. In a restatement of the traditional Committee policy, Skachko warned that mass colonization and rapid economic development "may lead to the destruction of the peoples of the north, these best exploiters of northern nature."[22] Yet mass colonization and rapid economic development were the official articles of faith and had to be taken as a given. "There could, of course, be no 'North for the Northerners' doctrine."[23]

One was left, therefore, with what the Communists liked to call a dialectical contradiction: on the one hand, "the breakneck speed of development of the productive forces of the Extreme North," and on the other, "the extremely backward peoples whom we have inherited from the former regime still in the late Neolithic period and who, by virtue of their extreme backwardness, cannot keep up either economically or culturally with the furious speed of the emerging socialist society."[24] In a key pronouncement on the Great Transformation, Stalin addressed one side of the equation. "Sometimes we are asked if it would be possible to slow down a bit, to reduce the speed. No, comrades, it would not! We cannot reduce the speed! On the contrary, it should be increased as much as possible."[25]

Did this mean that if the small peoples of the north "could not be included in this process, they would have to be cast aside"?[26] Skachko and his comrades at the Committee did not think so. Their solution was an urgent application of the policy of natsional'noe raionirovanie (demarcation of ethnic boundaries), an old project constantly frustrated by immigration and a lack of surveyors.[27] The renewed interest

[20] Tobolaev, "V Tofalarskom raione," pp. 95–96. See also TsGAOR, f. 3977, op. 1, d. 300, ll. 99, 105, 128–29, and d. 647, ll. 38–42.

[21] Murnik, "V Tofalarskom raione," pp. 95–98.

[22] Skachko, "Problemy Severa," p. 33. See also TsGAOR, f. 3977, op. 1, d. 628, l. 1.

[23] Skachko, "Problemy Severa," p. 23.

[24] Skachko, "Ocherednye zadachi," p. 18.

[25] Stalin, Sochineniia, 13:38.

[26] Anatolii Skachko, "Natsional'naia politika i malye narody Severa," RN, no. 6 (1931): 33.

[27] "Protokol zasedaniia VI rasshirennogo plenuma," pp. 4, 7–8; TsGAOR, f. 3977, op. 1, d. 496, l. 59, and d. 645, ll. 1–5.

in *raionirovanie* was both a concession to the inevitability of industrial development and an attempt to set limits to it. First of all, it meant the end of a special central administration for the native northerners. The formation of "national regions" would put them on a par with the other officially recognized minorities and assign them a standard place in the federal structure. In traditional Narkomnats terms, the problem of backwardness would be solved by promoting the northerners to the status of full-fledged nationalities. According to Skachko, who was equally eloquent on both sides of the issue,

> The Soviet government does not intend to preserve the peoples of the north in a primitive state, as rare ethnographic specimens, or to keep them as helpless charges of the state in special areas reserved for them and isolated from the rest of the world like zoological gardens. On the contrary, the government's goal is their all-around cultural and national development and their participation as equal (not just in principle but also de facto) and active partners in the socialist economy.[28]

The formation of the national districts would reassure the Soviet government that no one was asking for any special consideration or a reduction in the "furious speed." It would, Smidovich promised, "undermine the separation of the small peoples of the North from the rest of the northern population, which we have inherited from the past, and unite these peoples with all the other peoples of the USSR in the cause of the construction of socialism."[29]

At the same time, the Committee leaders clearly hoped that the new autonomous districts would offer some degree of protection or at least planning. The *raionirovanie* was to be accompanied by a land survey and an apportionment of all hunting and fishing grounds on the basis of ethnicity. Natives were to be segregated from non-natives, and "where needed," the new arrivals were to be forcibly removed.[30] (These measures were to be an affirmation of Leninist nationality policies, not a relapse into antidevelopment "populism.") Inside the districts, the small peoples were to be included in economic development: cautiously, gradually, and in an orderly fashion. Skachko's main concern was not industrialization per se but rather the growing use of non-

---

[28] Skachko, "Problemy Severa," p. 23.

[29] Smidovich, "Sotsial'naia rekonstruktsiia," p. 46; TsGAOR, f. 3977, op. 1, d. 738, ll. 3–9.

[30] "Protokol zasedaniia VI rasshirennogo plenuma," pp. 15–18; Skachko, "Problemy Severa," p. 33.

native labor. In his view, mastering new skills was a challenge; being left out was certain death. "The development of industry and agriculture in backward borderlands without drawing the local population into the process is a capitalist, not a socialist, method of colonization."[31] For the socialist method to be successful, the small peoples would have to learn to like mines, sawmills, and factories, but most of all they would have to become more efficient food producers. Skachko obviously believed that because most early industrial workers would have to be imported in any case, the only realistic way to prevent large-scale permanent settlement was for the native population to provide these workers with food. To achieve this goal, the local reindeer-breeding economy would have to become "rational," and this—as so many times before—meant learning from the "cultured nomads" of Sweden and Finland.[32]

No one claimed that the "extremely backward peoples" could accomplish all this by themselves. Once again, the cadres were the key to success—eventually native cadres but for the time being well-trained and conscientious Russians. "The absence of an organized native proletariat and the weakness of Party and soviet organizations requires good leaders who know the principles of Leninist nationality policy and have experience working in national regions."[33] Finding such people was an old problem, but the Committee of the North did not know of any other way of dealing with the situation. The small peoples needed to be guided, and one had no choice but to go on looking for good guides.

Finally, for *raionirovanie* to work, the new national districts would need independent funding.[34] This requirement lay at the heart of the Committee plan: there could be no protection from the settlers, no "cultured nomadism," no trained personnel, and no escape from "corrupt" local officials unless the districts were subsidized directly (and generously) by Moscow. In the final analysis, the success of the whole enterprise hinged on whether the new administrative units would have enough money to represent the native interests as the Committee understood them. To make sure of that, the Committee asked the State

---

[31] Skachko, "Ocherednye zadachi," p. 12; TsGAOR, f. 3977, op. 1, d. 645, l. 14.

[32] Skachko, "Problemy Severa," p. 27; TsGAOR, f. 3977, op. 1, d. 738, l. 11. Another model for emulation was Alaska. See Ustiugov, "Zadachi natsional'noi raboty," p. 43.

[33] Skachko, "Natsional'naia politika," p. 35. See also Skachko, "Ocherednye zadachi," p. 22.

[34] "Protokol zasedaniia VI rasshirennogo plenuma," p. 4; A. Chebotarevskii, "Sed'moi rasshirennyi plenum Komiteta Severa," SA, no. 3–4 (1930): 339–40.

Planning Commission (Gosplan) and all the ministries active in the north to form special northern departments.[35] Even if the new administrative structure led to the closure of the Committee of the North, the planning system would presumably not be affected. The small peoples of the north would still have protectors in high places—hopefully much more powerful and influential ones than Skachko and Smidovich.

The demarcation was carried out quickly and without much preparation. In the face of continuing immigration and development, the motto was "now or never," and by the end of 1930 the extreme north had nine national regions (okrug) and eight national districts (raion).[36] (Several groups, such as the Sel'kup, Ket, Saami, and some indigenous inhabitants of the lower Amur were left out "due to insufficient knowledge of their areas of settlement and economic activities.")[37] The clan soviets, obviously incompatible with both the new territorial arrangement and the collectivization drive, were quietly dropped with a few words of apology and replaced by settled and "nomadic" versions of standard all-union soviets.[38] The new statutes were not approved until 1933, but there is no indication that their introduction was followed by any change in how the native administrative units were actually formed. In legal terms, however, the change was of the greatest import. Far ahead of the Committee's original schedule, the small peoples of the north joined the brotherly family of Soviet nationalities "as equal partners in the socialist economy." There was one difference, of course. The Committee was still there, and the Committee leaders were trying their best to make the partnership in the socialist economy as easy on the northerners as was politically possible.

The odds were against them, however. According to Smidovich, the borders of the newly autonomous units "were drawn on a map that often had nothing to do with reality. . . . Because the land had never been properly assigned to the old inhabitants, the new enterprises and population groups often settled in previously occupied areas thereby

[35] Skachko, "Piat' let," p. 10, and "Problemy Severa," p. 32.

[36] "Protokol zasedaniia VI rasshirennogo plenuma," pp. 7–8; P. E. Terletskii, "Natsional'noe raionirovanie Krainego Severa," SS, no. 7–8 (1930): 5–29; "Postanovlenie Prezidiuma VTsIK 'Ob organizatsii natsional'nykh ob"edinenii v raionakh rasseleniia malykh narodov Severa'," SS, no. 1 (1931): 230–33.

[37] Terletskii, "Nastional'noe raionirovanie," p. 15.

[38] Skachko, "Piat' let," p. 15; Chebotarevskii, "Sed'moi rasshirennyi plenum," p. 337; Skachko, "Vos'moi plenum," p. 19; Smidovich, "Nashi zadachi," pp. 14–15; "Polozhenie o kochevykh sovetakh v natsional'nykh okrugakh i raionakh severnykh okrain RSFSR," SS, no. 5 (1933): 125–28.

disrupting the economic life of the old inhabitants. The situation of the natives was often tragic."[39]

The Committee continued to lobby against the unplanned movement of people and industries into native areas and issued urgent appeals "to limit the exile of socially dangerous elements into the national regions" and "to allow the alienation of land held in tenure by the working population only in exceptional cases of special importance to the state."[40] The problem was that in the heat of industrialization everything remotely resembling economic development was of special importance to the state. As far as industrial planners and provincial officials could tell, the state was not overly concerned about the natives as long as the targets of the Five-Year Plan were met. And the Five-Year Plan had nothing to say about the natives. In Skachko's impassioned words, "The 'men of figures' who are used to dealing with hundreds of millions of humans and billions of rubles find it difficult to understand the great political significance of the measures directed at such an insignificant group of the population, and for this reason there is rarely any funding left for this group."[41] Gosplan and the ministries refused to form special northern departments, arguing that their mode of operation was not territorial; the Commissariat of Agriculture never had the time or the means to survey native lands and claimed that hunting was not part of its responsibilities; the Commissariat of Finance ignored the government decree to raise the salaries of the local Committee agents; and Gosplan officials did not know about the formation of national districts until Skachko told them about it a year after the event.[42]

In the absence of central funding, the national districts and nomadic soviets had to rely on provincial budgets. The results were painfully familiar to the Committee of the North. In Nikolaevsk-on-Amur the native peoples constituted 48 percent of the population but received 12

[39] Smidovich, "Nashi zadachi," p. 17.

[40] Skachko, "Vos'moi plenum," p. 20; "Vos'moi rasshirennyi plenum," p. 139; Firsov and Petrova, "Organy iustitsii," p. 85; Ustiugov, Puti sotsialisticheskoi rekonstruktsii, p. 41.

[41] Anatolii Skachko, "K voprosu prakticheskogo provedeniia leninskoi natsional'noi politiki," SS, no. 1 (1931): 8.

[42] Skachko, "Piat' let," p. 9; Ustiugov, "Zadachi natsional'noi raboty," p. 44; Skachko, "K voprosu prakticheskogo provedeniia," pp. 6–7; P. K. Ustiugov, "Podgotovka piatiletnego plana severnogo khoziaistva," SS, no. 2 (1931): 31; Skachko, "Vos'moi plenum," p. 14; "Vos'moi rasshirennyi plenum," pp. 142, 152–54; Skachko, "Natsional'naia politika," pp. 34, 36, and "Natsional'nyi vopros i rekonstruktsiia khoziaistva narodov Severa," SS, no. 3 (1932): 28–29.

percent of the budget, and in the mostly native Berezov and Obdorsk districts not a single native soviet had a paid secretary (for lack of both money and personnel). As a result, native-level state organs either did not exist at all or were run for purposes of procurement by the Russian district executive committees (and not by the national regions). When pressed about native affairs, local administrators tended to point to the Committee of the North as the sole responsible agent. The vicious circle was complete. Defeated, the Committee announced that the only source of revenue for the native administration were the native (kulak) taxes.[43]

The economic managers had even less reason to take the Committee's advice. Their main responsibility was to their commissariat, and the commissariats wanted immediate results. Accordingly,

> the local employees of a number of economic enterprises not only do not assist in the consolidation of the national organs of the Soviet state but do what they can to avoid the control and supervision of the national executive committees, and sometimes ignore them completely. Carrying out their work outside the supervision of soviet organs, such employees of economic enterprises occasionally commit the most outrageous violations of the nationalities policy of the Party.[44]

In other words, they found the northern nationalities unwilling, unskilled, and inefficient as either industrial laborers or large-scale food-producers, and felt that they had no choice but to "consider all land vacant and unused and take it for sovkhozy or exile settlements without proper regard for the interests of the peoples of the north."[45] More and more fishermen were being brought from the south; the reindeer sovkhozy were given priority over kolkhozy; and even the fur industry tried to rely on improvised "game reserves" and hired volunteers.[46] The well-trained cadres that could prevent all this from happening were slow in coming. There was little financial or institutional incen-

---

[43] Skachko, "Piat' let," p. 10; Chebotarevskii, "Sed'moi rasshirennyi plenum," p. 340; Skachko, "Ocherednye zadachi," p. 14, and "Vos'moi plenum," p. 7; "Vos'moi rasshirennyi plenum," pp. 131, 142; Medvedev, "Za podgotovku kadrov," pp. 12–13; "Rezoliutsii Deviatogo rasshirennogo plenuma," pp. 3–4; Kantor, "Sever zovet," p. 133.

[44] "Rezoliutsii Deviatogo rasshirennogo plenuma," p. 4.

[45] Skachko, "Natsional'nyi vopros," p. 34.

[46] Kozin, "Dal'nevostochnaia kompleksnaia ekspeditsiia," p. 208; Skachko, "Vos'moi plenum," p. 13; "Rezoliutsii Deviatogo rasshirennogo plenuma," p. 15; Ispravnikov, "Kolkhoznoe stroitel'stvo," p. 90; Sergeev, "Zadachi vtoroi piatiletki na Severe," p. 47; Skachko, "Osnovnye voprosy," p. 10; A. Balandin, "Rybozagotovki na Sos've," SS, no. 5 (1934): 93–96.

tive, and even the selfless enthusiasts of industrialization felt that there was "'nothing interesting there'—no huge enterprises, no large Party organizations, etc."[47]

Thus, Skachko's plan never went beyond the first step. What was to be a formal concession became the death sentence for the Committee and, many thought, for the natives. The promotion of the small peoples to full nationality and administrative equality meant that, in legal terms, they were not "extremely backward" any more. The Committee had no choice but to represent "the whole mass of the population" of the new territorial units, including their old enemies who lived off the natives and their new enemies who were trying to drive the natives away.[48] According to Smidovich's cheerful admission of defeat, "Soviet life has transformed the Committee of the North into a committee for the assistance to the economic and socio-cultural construction in the northern borderlands."[49]

The North without the Native Northerners

The Committee's role became particularly hard to define in 1932, after the Seventeenth Party Conference unveiled the Second Five-Year Plan. The industrialization of the north was now a major priority, and considerable sums were being invested in exploration and development. Countless geological parties set out for the remotest corners of the new national regions, and within a short period of time new mines were launched in Amderma (fluorite), Vorkuta (coal), Noril'sk (coal and iron ore), and Yakutia (gold). Large river ports were built to accommodate the expanding lumber industry, and an increasing number of labor camps followed the new projects into the taiga and the tundra.[1]

As the planners saw it, the future of these undertakings depended on successful navigation in the Arctic Ocean. In late 1932–early 1933 Komseveroput' was dissolved and replaced by a state agency attached directly to the Council of Peoples' Commissars—the Main Administration of the Northern Sea Route (GUSMP).[2] GUSMP was responsible for

[47] Skachko, "Natsional'naia politika," p. 35.
[48] Skachko, "Vos'moi plenum," p. 18.
[49] Smidovich, "Nashi zadachi," p. 16.
[1] M. I. Belov, *Nauchnoe i khoziaistvennoe osvoenie sovetskogo severa, 1933–1945* (Leningrad, 1969), pp. 16–93; Dallin and Nicolaevsky, *Forced Labor*, pp. 115, 199.
[2] "Organizatsiia Glavnogo upravleniia Severnogo morskogo puti," SS, no. 1 (1933): 123; "V Komitete Severa pri Prezidiume VTsIK," pp. 99–102; Belov, *Nauchnoe i kho-*

both sea exploration and industrial projects on the mainland, and was encouraged to "involve the local population in socialist construction."[3] The potential institutional conflict was easily resolved: in 1934 a decree of the Council of Peoples' Commissars and the Central Committee of the Party made GUSMP the absolute ruler of the whole of northern Asia above the sixty-second parallel (parallel of Yakutsk).[4] The only important exception was the giant mining and lumber trust Dal'stroi, formally controlled by the Council of Labor and Defense but run by the NKVD (the secret police). Dal'stroi had begun its operations in Nogaevo Bay (future Magadan) in 1932 and soon took over the "organization of all social and political life" in the vast area east of the Lena and north of the Aldan.[5]

Thus most native northerners became part of two quasi-independent fiefdoms bent on industrial development. The national regions and the Committee of the North remained in existence, but there was no doubt who held the real power—political, economic, and, indeed, military. Far less definite were the GUSMP and Dal'stroi plans for the small peoples. It was clear at the outset that there was no role for them in the actual industrial operations as both organizations used almost exclusively convict labor (the first commercial use of the great sea route was to transport Dal'stroi prisoners from Arkhangel'sk to Ambarchik).[6] There were hopes, however, that they might help overcome the greatest obstacle to northern industrialization: the lack of a reliable agricultural base. Thus one author suggested that the native inhabitants of the Kolyma basin should switch to agriculture in order to feed the growing population of the Dal'stroi labor camps. Not only would it be a contribution to "the development of gold mining in the area"—it would also provide a useful occupation in the summertime: "Because at present the only productive industry is the procurement of fur, which takes place in the winter; fishing on the upper Kolyma is not very efficient and therefore needs to be replaced by more productive work such as

---

ziaistvennoe osvoenie, pp. 94–98. The president of GUSMP was the scientist/administrator Otto Shmidt, the director of the Arctic Institute, a former member of the Presidium of the Communist Academy and of various commissariats, and a former director of the state publishing company.

[3] "V Komitete Severa pri Prezidiume VTsIK," p. 99.

[4] "O razvitii Severnogo Morskogo Puti i severnogo khoziaistva," SS, no. 5 (1934): 110–11.

[5] Popova, Eveny, pp. 242–46; Robert Conquest, Kolyma: The Arctic Death Camps (London, 1978), pp. 39–40; Kiselev, Sever raskryvaet bogatstva, pp. 28–29.

[6] Dallin and Nicolaevsky, Forced Labor, pp. 127–28.

agriculture.'"[7] In similar vein, M. A. Sergeev argued that while the industrial laborers needed to be fed, the tundra reindeer herders were suffering from an exceedingly monotonous and unhealthy diet. The solution was "an urgent reduction in the consumption of meat by the local population." The Russians were to get the meat, and the small peoples were to improve their eating habits by switching to bread, grains, and vegetables.[8]

Much more common were the suggestions to have the natives produce grains and vegetables for the Russians.[9] And this could mean only one thing—the end of nomadism. In fact, in Central Asia, Kazakhstan, and southern Siberia settlement was seen as a prerequisite for collectivization. It was supposed to allow for "mechanization"; promote exportable grain production at the expense of cattle breeding; put an end to "economic and cultural inequality among nations"; and, of course, eradicate backwardness and exploitation. According to one programmatic statement, "the preservation of the nomadic economy prolongs the life of semifeudal and clan survivals, which are skillfully manipulated by the kulaks who try to increase their influence on the masses and step up their struggle against socialist reconstruction."[10] Thousands of people—particularly in Kazakhstan—were forcibly settled, and those who argued that nomadism was a "natural" adaptive pattern were accused of opportunism and wrecking.[11]

The Committee's first pronouncement after the Seventeenth Party Conference seemed to suggest that it had decided to give up the fight. Its official tasks for the next five years included the struggle against left and right deviationists, mass colonization, industrial planning, and the study of natural resources—but no mention of any "assistance to the peoples of the northern borderlands."[12] Before long, however, the danger of forced settlement induced Skachko and friends to rise up for what was to be the Committee's last campaign on behalf of the small peoples. They had always opposed settlement as an unrealistic and theoretically misguided policy;[13] now, with one-third of the reindeer

---

[7] I. M., "K voprosu o zemledelii v basseine r. Kolymy," SS, no. 1–2 (1932): 223–26.

[8] Sergeev, "Rekonstruktsiia byta narodov Severa," pp. 90–91.

[9] See SS, no. 4 (1933): 31–83.

[10] I. Kosokov, "Ob osedanii kochevogo i polukochevogo naseleniia sovetskogo Vostoka," RN, no. 5 (1932): 50

[11] Ibid., pp. 52–55; U. D. Kulumbetov, "Perekhod na osedlost' v Kazakhstane," RN, no. 5 (1932): 59–65; P. T. Khaptaev, "Osedanie Buriat-Aiginskogo aimaka," RN, no. 5 (1932): 65–73; Kh. Shorukhov, "Osedanie v Kirgizii," RN, no. 5 (1932): 73–76.

[12] SS, no. 1–2 (1932): 3–4.

[13] Skachko, "Problemy Severa," pp. 24–28; TsGAOR, f. 3977, op. 1, d. 652, l. 58.

gone, it was a matter of life and death for the natives and of political survival for Skachko.

> These days settlement is often featured in bureaucratic projects as an end in itself, not tied to any other economic measures and representing neither their cause nor consequence. People who come up with such projects must think that nomadism is simply a bad habit and a survival of a primitive barbaric way of life; and that this vestige of the ancient past, inappropriate in a socialist system, can be eradicated with the help of purely administrative measures.

> One should simply tell the nomads, "Enough of this wandering around; it's time to get settled . . ." and the nomads will stop wandering, start to develop at a record pace both economically and culturally, and in a year or two will tearfully thank their thoughtful masters for showing them the right way. . . .

> Of course, there is no need to prove the anti-Marxist nature of such an attitude toward settlement. Anyone remotely familiar with Marxism should know that nomadic and settled lifestyles represent the economic *form*, which is wholly determined by the economic *content*. . . . Therefore, the nomads can be settled only if we change the nature of their economy, reduce the importance of those activities that require nomadism, and introduce new activities that would tie workers to one particular place.[14]

Thus, Skachko argued that the government should first achieve industrialization and true agricultural development and then offer the small peoples a viable economic alternative. He also felt that "it does not make any sense to replace the northern specialties of fur production and reindeer breeding with stock-raising and market gardening because it is obviously not profitable from the point of view of the state."[15] In other words, the viable alternative was not really viable anyway, and grain production was not worth mentioning because it was unthinkable in the extreme north.

Similar views were expressed in the spring and summer of 1932 after the government's crackdown against the "excesses" in the north and left deviationism in ideology,[16] but by 1933 collectivization was pro-

---

[14] Skachko, "Resheniia XVII partkonferentsii," pp. 10–11. See also Smidovich, "Sotsialisticheskaia rekonstruktsiia," p. 50.

[15] Skachko, "Resheniia," p. 11.

[16] Smidovich, "Nashi zadachi," p. 18; Skachko, "Natsional'nyi vopros," p. 35, and "Deviatyi plenum," p. 19.

ceeding undisturbed, and Central Asian opponents of forced settlement were once again being accused of wrecking.[17] The Committee of
the North joined the discussion on the necessity of developing agriculture and market gardening,[18] and the case of the Tofalar (the only northern group that had been subjected to wholesale forced settlement) was
presented as an outstanding success story. The Russians were reportedly teaching the natives how to milk cows, fish properly, and wash
themselves—in other words, how "not to be lazy" ("They're like little
kids, you've got to watch them all the time").[19] At about the same time,
GUSMP announced its plan to change the face of the north by launching the widely publicized *Cheliuskin* expedition; Dal'stroi did away
with the short-lived Okhotsk-Even national region; and the local authorities on Sakhalin promised to resettle the Nivkh in larger Russian-
style villages in order to guarantee the "planned exploitation of river
resources and the rational utilization of the thinly spread manpower
of the small peoples.' [20] It seemed that the native northerners had a lot
of settling to look forward to.

Before the year was over, however, a new campaign against abuses in
Central Asia largely discredited the idea of immediate settlement. It
turned out that the replacement of animal husbandry by grain production had been a leftist deviation and that in effect much of the traditional economy had been destroyed in vain.[21] The Committee of the
North came alive again, and two of its spokesmen announced that although in general terms settlement was a very good idea, the native
northerners were not quite ready for it yet: there was no alternative to
reindeer pastoralism, and reindeer pastoralists had no alternative to
being nomads; there were no building materials for projected permanent settlements; and there was no doubt that "administrative fervor"
of the Central Asian variety could only lead to catastrophe.[22] It was also
revealed that the northern nomads had always seen settlement as the

[17] I. Kosokov, "Itogi planovogo osedaniia i prakticheskie zadachi," RN, no. 5–6 (1933):
70; I. Batrakov, "Plan osedaniia v Srednei Azii," RN, no. 5–6 (1933): 75–79.

[18] SS, no. 3 (1933): 83–85; no. 4 (1933): 31–83.

[19] Al. Smirnov-Sibirskii, "V Saianskoi taige," SS, no. 5 (1933): 91–93.

[20] TsGAOR, f. 3977, op. 1, d. 946, ll. 3–4; Belov, *Nauchnoe i khoziaistvennoe osvoenie*
pp. 106–7; Popova, *Eveny,* pp. 242–43; Walter Kolarz, *The Peoples of the Soviet Far East*
(New York, 1954), p. 88.

[21] D. Mukhardzhi and N. Nazar'evskii, "Osedanie kochevnikov Kirgizii," RN, no. 12
(1933): 16–25; N. Iushunev, "Osedanie kochevnikov Buriato-Mongolii," RN, no. 12
(1933): 25–28.

[22] Sergeev, "Rekonstruktsiia byta narodov Severa," pp. 93–94; E. D. Kantor, "Problema
osedaniia malykh narodov Severa," SS, no. 5 (1934): 3–10.

last resort of the poor and the miserable; that the settlement of the Tofa-lar had been an unmitigated disaster; and that the few other cases of administrative settlement had been even worse.[23] In the Bauntovskii district of northern Buriatia the authorities claimed to have spent 30,000 rubles on three shacks without roofs and windows that the local Tungus refused to occupy; and on the Aian the planners had first built permanent houses for an Even fishing kolkhoz and then discovered that "there were no good pastures for reindeer, no squirrels, and that market fishing was absolutely impossible."[24] This time the Committee of the North was on the right side: the government had obviously de-cided that Central Asian stock-raising needed to be rehabilitated. In 1935 settlement of the Aian kind was officially declared to have been sabotage, and the new secretary of the Council of Nationalities at the Central Executive Committee demanded patience and sensitivity in dealing with the nomads because "they are not vagabonds who aim-lessly roam around; they are people who suffer from the most profound historic and social deprivation, extraordinary abuse, and back-wardness."[25]

The victory had been won, but the Committee was not there to cele-brate. After the summer 1934 decision to transfer the entire northern economy to GUSMP, its position had become increasingly uncertain and politically awkward. There was nothing left to "coordinate," no numerous commissariats to lobby, and no stalling bureaucrats to com-plain about. Any suggestion of defending the small peoples from the Northern Sea Route Administration was unthinkable at a time when the regime was having a love affair with industrialization in general and polar exploration in particular. The Committee's new role of repre-senting the entire north contradicted the official doctrine of GUSMP's infallibility as well as the notion of the newly formulated equality of the small peoples—after all, the other national regions did not have special committees representing them in Moscow. Meanwhile, the de-mise of ethnography had put an end to the Committee's oldest and fondest hope—to produce scientifically trained cadres for the north. It

[23] Murnik, "V Tofalarskom raione," pp. 95–98; Sergeev, "Rekonstruktsiia byta narodov Severa," p. 93; Bagmut, "Kochevoi sovet," p. 17; Kantor, "Problema osedaniia," p. 6; Gilev, "Zapiski o Bauntovskom raione," p. 91; Andreev, "Iz opyta kollektivizatsii," p. 98; "Nam pishut," p. 105.

[24] Gilev, "Zapiski o Bauntovskom raione," p. 91; Andreev, "Iz opyta kollektivizatsii," p. 98.

[25] "Soveshchanie po voprosam osedaniia kochevykh khoziaistv i zemleustroistva kol-khozov natsional'nykh respublik i oblastei," RN, no. 10 (1935): 85; A. Khatskevich, "Ob osedanii kochevogo i polukochevogo naseleniia," RN, no. 12 (1935): 15.

had also drawn its leaders into what the government would soon call "pseudosociological scholasticism."

Everyone seemed to agree that under the circumstances there was no point in carrying on. At its 1934 plenum the Committee decided to dissolve itself—but "on one condition:" the Council of Peoples' Commissariats was to form "a special organization responsible for the socialist exploration and reconstruction of the economy of the northern borderlands."[26] The former defenders of the native northerners claimed that "the goals set by the Party with respect to the small peoples of the north could not be considered fully achieved," and wanted to be replaced by a financially independent agency that would deal with the present rather than the future and thus counterbalance GUSMP, whose activities, in Skachko's cautious words, were "not yet connected with the local economy."[27]

Their last wish was not granted. In the summer of 1935 the Committee for the Assistance to the Peoples of the Northern Borderlands was quietly disbanded, and the administration of the small peoples was formally transferred to GUSMP.[28] In an optimistically worded obituary Skachko implied that the Party's goals with respect to the small peoples had, in fact, been achieved.[29]

Meanwhile, the Main Administration of the Northern Sea Route had become the primary symbol of the speed, scale, and daring of Soviet industrialization. The all-powerful ruler of one-third of the territory of the USSR, it represented the ultimate proof that even the harshest of conditions were nothing in the face of Soviet resolve and, increasingly, competence. This was the heroic age of the country's evolution: armies of selfless toilers had been replaced by larger-than-life heroes; environment had given way to consciousness; and "cadres" had triumphed over technology.[30] As part of the change, the huge anthills of the First Five-Year Plan construction sites had yielded the stage to the Northern Sea Route, and the uneasy alliance of proletarian directors and bourgois experts had been supplanted by wholesome expert directors symbolized by the tall and bearded figure of the GUSMP president—the

[26] "V Komitete Severa," SS, no. 1 (1935): 106.

[27] Ibid; Anatolii Skachko "Novye organizatsionnye formy raboty na Severe," SS, no. 3–4 (1935): 30.

[28] Anatolii Skachko, "Narody Severa na novom etape," RN, no. 8 (1935): 31; Belov, Nauchnoe i khoziaistvennoe osvoenie, p. 100.

[29] Skachko, "Narody Severa na novom etape," p. 31.

[30] See Katerina Clark, "Utopian Anthropology as a Context for Stalinist Literature," in Stalinism: Essays in Historical Interpretation, ed. Robert Tucker (New York, 1977), pp. 180–99.

ubiquitous and ever optimistic "scientific genius" Otto Iul'evich Shmidt. Under his tutelage the new breed of giants could defy cold, great distances, and gravity and conquer the universe for Russia as they were conquering Russia for socialism.

In August of 1933 the ship Cheliuskin set out from the port of Murmansk to the Pacific. A special commission had pronounced her unfit for the voyage, and two captains had refused to lead the doomed enterprise, but Shmidt insisted on the necessity to "dispel all doubt about the Northern passage as a commercial route."[31] Unprepared, ill-equipped, and behind schedule, the Cheliuskin squeaked through to the Bering Straits but was stopped by the ice, pushed back, and crushed in the Chukchi Sea in February 1934, leaving the crew stranded on a drifting ice floe.[32] What followed was one of the central public events in Soviet history and the beginning of a polar epic that would provide the regime with a powerful metaphor and a patriotic rallying cry. As "the entire Soviet people" looked on, the highest Party officials personally directed rescue operations; daredevil pilots cheerfully performed amazing feats of heroism; and the "Cheliuskin men" converted their drifting ice floe into a model "piece of Soviet land." One of the aviators reported that when he finally succeeded in establishing radio contact with the camp, Shmidt refused to talk to him because he was giving one of his regular lectures on dialectical materialism. And when the first plane finally landed on the ice floe, the stranded seamen immediately demanded a report on the Seventeenth Party Congress and listened for two and a half hours with rapt attention.[33] The drama ended with the successful rescue of the Cheliuskin men and their triumphal arrival in the Kremlin amid parades and enormous demonstrations. As the special government commission phrased it, "Soviet aviation has won."[34]

From then on, the symbolic function of the Northern Sea Route was to test the true grit of the new Soviet man by providing an awesome icy stage for his ever-more-daring exploits. The country's great leaders had been "tempered" by Arctic exile; now it was the turn of their "sons" and disciples.[35] Every year new victories were won and new records set as planes flew closer to the North Pole and ships sailed faster and

[31] Belov, Nauchnoe i khoziaistvennoe osvoenie, p. 112.
[32] Ibid., pp. 114–28; G. N. Gurari, "GUSMP," SS, no. 6 (1934): 25–32.
[33] G. Ushakov, "V lagere Shmidta," SS, no. 4 (1934): 72.
[34] Belov, Nauchnoe i khoziaistvennoe osvoenie, p. 139.
[35] Katerina Clark, The Soviet Novel: History as Ritual (Chicago, 1981), pp. 103, 124–25.

traveled farther. Undeterred by the elements, GUSMP was not going to be slowed down by the natives. Nothing was impossible, and no special policy would be needed or, indeed, tolerated. The small peoples were not any different from other peoples, except in size: to underscore this fact, the new masters of the north were to refer to them as "nationals" (natsionaly) and not natives (tuzemtsy). Whatever backwardness still existed was due to the lack of material prerequisites and, by implication, the incorrect policies of the previous administration that had led to these shortages.

GUSMP officials were appalled at the state of the northern economy and the services that they inherited. They had not realized that most nomadic soviets were out of reach most of the time, that reindeer sovkhozy had become transport terminals, that there was no cash economy, that the supply system did not work, and that cadres were few and unreliable. Of the officially existing 466 schools only 125 had buildings; the teachers and doctors did not speak the local languages, were badly paid, had no place to live, and were forever trying to flee. The kul'tbazy buildings, whatever their original purpose, served mostly as dormitories.[36] The solution was to put an end to the misguided policies of protection and exclusion and extend to the "nationals" the tested Soviet methods of overcoming the "contradiction" between the productive potential and the "development of the forces of production": "By implementing Leninist nationality policy, the GUSMP organizations, together with territorial Party and soviet organs, can correct this discrepancy in a short period of time and quickly raise the economic and cultural level of the northern peoples to the level of the more advanced districts and provinces of the USSR."[37]

Kul'tbazy, those most obvious survivals of the era of special treatment, would have to go. "This strategy has outlived its usefulness," declared Shmidt. "Of course, it does not mean that we should close down the existing kul'tbazy, but now we must already follow the normal path of developing education and health care separately." The "normal" way was to ask for a lot of money, and GUSMP felt that it had the muscle: in the first three years 19 million rubles were to be invested in school construction alone. More important, "the question of north-

[36] S. Ia. Babakhan, "Sozdadim sobstvennuiu prodovol'stvennuiu bazu na Krainem Severe," SAr, no. 3 (1935): 46; O. Iu. Shmidt, "O zadachakh khoziaistvenno-kul'turnogo stroitel'stva sredi malykh narodov Severa," RN, no. 1 (1936): 35–40; I. Samigullin, "Taimyrskii natsional'nyi okrug," RN, no. 8 (1936): 27–31.

[37] I. O. Serkin, "Kolkhoznoe stroitel'stvo v Taimyrskom natsional'nom okruge," SAr, no. 6 (1936): 4.

ern culture cannot be separated from the question of the development of the northern economy." That meant that health care and education would improve as a result of better supplies, control, and communications. Similarly, the native economy would benefit from an inclusion (real, and not just *de jure*) in the national financial market. There would be no more barter, "even if it reduces the procurement of furs," and eventually "people will understand what money is, and that with it they can buy what they want and not what some contract, sometimes badly drawn up, imposes on them." The special commercial administration of native kolkhozy ("integral cooperation") would have to be scrapped, and all trade conducted directly by the state—that is, by GUSMP officials.[38]

As usual, the implementation of the reforms was seen to depend on successful personnel policies, only this time the emphasis was on the immediate nativization of all economic activities. The new Party policy stated that whereas the period of the First Five-Year Plan had been the time for "mastering technology," the present era of "consolidation" was largely concerned with the *quality* of the people in charge ("cadres decide everything"). The small peoples had missed out on most of the First Five-year Plan, and Shmidt wanted them to be educated and promoted at the same time.[39] In early 1936 N. N. Evgen'ev, assistant head of the GUSMP transport department, and S. A. Bergavinov, the head of the GUSMP political department, published a letter to the head of the Obdorsk political department of GUSMP, A. P. Mikhailov, with copies for all heads of political departments of the Northern Sea Route. The authors expressed their concern over the fact that in a whole year the Obdorsk department had not promoted "a single national from among the local population." They also pointed out that the "political workers" still had not learned any of the northern languages—"even though it is not difficult at all: the Nenets language has only 600 to 700 everyday words." The way to correct these mistakes was to memorize these words and draw the native northerners into production and administration by organizing reindeer races, meetings of shock-workers, and conferences of the wives of polar explorers.[40] A few months later Mikhailov wrote a reply in which he reported on the early accom-

[38] Shmidt, "O zadachakh khoziaistvenno-kul'turnogo stroitel'stva," pp. 35–40. See also "Postanovlenie Prezidiuma Soveta natsional'nostei TsIK SSSR," *RN*, no. 2 (1936): 75–76; O. Iu. Shmidt, "Nashi zadachi v 1936 godu," *SAr*, no. 3 (1936): 41–42.

[39] Shmidt, "Nashi zadachi v 1936 godu," p. 42.

[40] N. N. Evgen'ev and S. A. Bergavinov, "Nachal'niku Obdorskogo politotdela Glavsevmorputi t. Mikhailovu," *SAr*, no. 4 (1936): 65–67.

plishments of his department. In record time, the trading points had employed twenty-one Nenets, ten Khanty, and one Altaian; the reindeer sovkhozy had recruited some Nenets and Komi; and various reindeer races, women's conferences, and local Olympics had taken place.[41] Along with promotion came education/Russification:

> Khariuchi An, the head of the Komsomol brigade of the Nyda reindeer sovkhoz, was encouraged by the sovkhoz Party organization to join the Komsomol. Thanks to the systematic work of the primary Party organization, he liquidated his illiteracy, and now his understanding of political matters is not bad, and his cultural growth is obvious. When he leaves his herd and comes to the district center, he always puts on a European suit and tie, and shaves carefully.[42]

Thus the concept of "cultural growth" had not changed very much (Mikhailov's Olympians had to bathe and get haircuts), but these days much greater importance was attached to "political matters." V. P. Ostroumova, a former stenographer at Party congresses and now the head of the Igarka political department of GUSMP (and hence the supreme ruler of most of the Enisei basin), saw her tasks among the "national population" as follows: "(1) the profound study of the Constitution; (2) the explanation . . . of the most important Party decisions, Party slogans, and government decrees, as well as the explanation of issues of Soviet domestic life and international affairs; [and] (3) the questions of the Stakhanov movement."[43] In other words, GUSMP political tasks among the "national population" were not any different from those among the Russians—and that, of course, was the whole point. One red-tent worker who spent the winter of 1936–37 among the Nganasan knew her primary responsibility to be the explanation of the Constitution through an interpreter. The library that she brought for the enjoyment of the reindeer herders contained a *History of the Party*, *The Origin of the Family* by Engels, *State and Revolution* by Lenin, *Problems of Leninism* by Stalin, *Popular Astronomy* by Flammarion, *Le Feu*

[41] A. P. Mikhailov, "Pervye itogi raboty s natsional'nym naseleniem," SAr, no. 9 (1936): 31–9.

[42] Ibid., p. 32.

[43] V. P. Ostroumova, "Zadachi massovoi politicheskoi raboty sredi natsional'nogo naseleniia," SAr, nc. 3 (1937): 11. This does not mean that Ostroumova approved of the policies she was formally advocating. In the summer of 1938 she and her friend E. I. Kalinina (the wife of the Soviet president) were arrested for saying (to each other) that Stalin was "a tyrant and a sadist who destroyed the Leninist guard and millions of innocent people." See A. M. Larina, "Nezabyvaemoe," Znamia, no. 11 (1988): 99.

and *Stalin* by Henri Barbusse, *Solitude* by Nikolai Virta, *In the East* by Petr Pavlenko, *L'île des Pingouins* by Anatole France, "and a number of other books by Soviet and foreign authors."[44]

The small peoples were not simply encouraged to be like everybody else—they were *assumed* to be like everybody else. And that meant that their promotion by administrative appointment was not quite good enough. They were supposed to actively desire to take part in socialist construction, take baths, study the Constitution, and read Stalin and Anatole France. Every state-sponsored initiative invariably found enthusiastic supporters among hunters and gatherers, and when in late 1935 the country was shaken by the Stakhanov movement, the small peoples were out there volunteering to join.[45] In the jurisdiction of the Obdorsk political department—and presumably in the other GUSMP districts—this activism was ensured by the local Russian agents who received their orders from the territorial center and then reported back on the results. In the case of the Stakhanov movement they, "not having any newspapers and other literature and not knowing anything about the nature and significance of the Stakhanov movement, took it for just another campaign which they promised to carry out and complete by a certain date."[46]

To those who knew, Stakhanovites were workers who pushed the limits of the possible by repeatedly overfulfilling the plan and constantly demonstrating the triumph of the "cadres" over both nature and technology. Paradoxically, their motives were assumed to be mostly material. In the era of restoration of "real culture" and old values much of the former self-sacrifice and asceticism went the way of "vulgar equality" and other leftist deviations. Every normal person was expected to aspire to a comfortable, prosperous, and "cultured" existence—and that is what the Stakhanovites got for their hard work.[47] The small peoples were, of course, not any different. They, too, were presumed to have normal human desires:

> We in the tundra want to have pretty clothes. We want nice, big shawls with tassels. We need colored ribbons. For holiday dress we need large Persian beads. We also need beads and small necklaces for our children and silver rings for our girls. . . .

[44] Khazanovich, *Krasnyi chum*, p. 14.

[45] B. I. Grinshpan, "Stakhanovskoe dvizhenie v pushnom khoziaistve," *SAr*, no. 3 (1936): 69–70; Mikhailov, "Pervye itogi," p. 33; B. I. Grinshpan, "Na pushnom uchastke," *SAr*, no. 11 (1936): 73–74.

[46] N. N. Begichev, "Posle proverki partdokumentov (na Iamale)," *SAr*, no. 6 (1936): 18.

[47] See, for example, *Geroini sotsialisticheskogo truda* (Moscow, 1936).

We need small tea cups, with pretty colorful designs. Also good table-cloths. For lining the tent we need colored material—bright with flowers.[48]

This was the kind of home that a tired reindeer herdsman would want to sing about:

> The northern lights are flashing cheerfully,
> My heart is filled with joy.
> When I get back, I'll start listening to the radio.[49]

Even though the folkloric authenticity of this song is questionable, there is little doubt that these wishes would be considered reasonable by most northerners. It is just as certain, however, that they could almost never be fulfilled. The supply system continued to malfunction, and instead of tea cups and colored shawls the native trading points kept selling rusty sinks and canvas shoes.[50] If only for this reason, the reports of widespread Stakhanovism among the small peoples seem less than convincing—particularly because the sources of such reports were being repeatedly accused of cheating and incompetence.

The other side of the concern for the quality of the cadres was an attempt to get rid of those whose quality was demonstrably low. According to the official explanation, during the years of great speed and great enthusiasm the Party had become infested with all sorts of cynical hangers-on. The purge of 1935–36 was intended to get rid of these people wherever they might be—and quite a few of them turned out to be hiding in the tundra. It was discovered that a great many Russians who were closest to the natives—sovkhoz officials, clerks, and trading agents—were drunks, thieves, scoundrels, and former kulaks. High on the list of crimes were rudeness to the natives, cheating on them, and taking advantage of their weakness for alcohol (almost all of the offenders were accused of having the same weakness themselves).[51]

[48] Al. Vol'skii, "Na Taimyre," SAr, no. 11 (1936): 28. See also R. B. Kaufman, "Delegaty Taimyra," SAr, no. 11 (1936): 59–63; P. S. Bolin, "Chto dala nam sovetskaia vlast'," SAr, no. 11 (1936): 63–64.

[49] V. Tonkov, "Iz nenetskogo fol'klora," SAr, no. 11 (1936): 65.

[50] V. F. Tabelev, "Na Iamal'skom Severe," SAr, no. 7 (1936): 21; Samigullin, "Taimyrskii natsional'nyi okrug," p. 30; "Svet i teni v rabote Glavsevmorputi," SAr, no. 1 (1937): 10–11; S. A. Bergavinov, "O razvertyvanii sovetskoi torgovli na Krainem Severe," SAr, no. 2 (1937): 5–8.

[51] R. L. Iakubovich, "Ochishchaia riady," SAr, no. 4 (1936): 68–73; Begichev, "Posle proverki partdokumentov," pp. 17–19; "Uroki Semenchukovshchiny," SAr, no. 7 (1936): 3–7; Tabelev, "Na Iamal'skom Severe," pp. 11–23.

The campaign peaked during the May 1936 Moscow trial of the head of the Vrangel' Island polar station Semenchuk and his sled driver Startsev. The two men were accused of murdering another member of the expedition, but state prosecutor A. Ia. Vyshinskii, the main theoretician of Stalin's jurisprudence and the future star of the Moscow show trials, turned the case into a chilling demonstration of how not to conduct "Leninist-Stalinist nationality policy."[52] The GUSMP station on the island was supported by a few dozen Eskimo hunters brought there in 1926 to back the Soviet territorial claims in the area.[53] According to Vyshinskii, friendship with these people was the number-one requirement for successful polar exploration. The GUSMP's greatest challenge and sacred duty was to "show the fundamental difference between the Bolsheviks who have come to the island and the old traders, trappers, and colonists who used to come to the island in order to rob and to exploit the population."[54] Before 1926 the island had been uninhabited, but this was immaterial: the task of every political trial was to tie the crime to a prerevolutionary or counterrevolutionary source. This time the court proceedings revealed that Semenchuk and Startsev (himself an old settler) had been robbing and exploiting the "natives" just like the old traders, trappers, and colonists. Semenchuk had allegedly forced them to work for the station at the expense of hunting, refused them credit, refused them medical help, and eventually starved twelve people to death.[55] Both men were executed, and the most publicized result of the trial was the joy of the liberated Eskimos whose cultural needs had finally been met: "We hunt better and we live better. Now we go to the bathhouse, consult only doctors, wash our dishes clean, and know how to bake bread. We have gotten to like underwear, and we wash it. We have European clothes, and we wear them when it is not cold. . . . We have all decided to stay on the island; it is our Soviet island now."[56]

Thus everything turned out fine, but the implications for GUSMP leadership were quite serious. True to the Party line, Vyshinskii left no doubt that the crimes of the "class enemy" had been made possible by bad personnel policies, and GUSMP quickly agreed that the island's Party secretary was a "windbag, coward, and careerist," and that the other station employees, most notably Party members, were "human

---

[52] A. Ia. Vyshinskii, Sudebnye rechi (Moscow, 1948), p. 225.
[53] Mineev, Ostrov Vrangelia, p. 50.
[54] Vyshinskii, Sudebnye rechi, p. 244.
[55] Ibid., pp. 250–55; Mineev, Ostrov Vrangelia, pp. 172–81.
[56] Pravda, 27 May 1936.

waste."[57] The recruitment of such people to a frontline post and the appointment of a "degenerate," "class enemy," and former thief to lead them was not a good recommendation for the organizers of the expedition. GUSMP was never blamed directly but its image was tarnished: at least some of the fearless polar explorers had turned out to be human waste.

Several months after the Semenchuk trial the campaign against incompetence and corruption among low-level Party officials gave way to the war against high-level wrecking and espionage in most Soviet professions and institutions. The obviously unnerved GUSMP leaders staged a large show of vigilance and preventive "self-criticism." It was revealed among other things that all branches of the native economy were in sharp decline; that collectivization was largely formal; and that the kul'tbazy were "in a sorry state." There was no denying the fact that the local GUSMP administrators had made some mistakes, but it was the other organizations that had really messed things up. The Commissariats of Health and Enlightenment had wreaked havoc with GUSMP's ambitious plans to develop the culture of the small peoples: there were not enough doctors, teachers, textbooks, and students, and the construction of ten hospitals and twenty-one schools had been "bungled." Even worse were various supply agencies that kept sending their unwanted merchandise to the north. As much as 90 percent of the fall 1936 shipment of footwear had consisted of canvas shoes, and most food items had never made it to the consumers—at least not in edible form.[58]

None of these organizations escaped the vigilance of the secret police—and neither did GUSMP. The first terrorists were found at the Belogorsk sawmill, in the territory of the always path-breaking Obdorsk political department. Not only had they arranged for the mill and the living quarters to be regularly flooded and for the workers to be underpaid and underfed—it was also discovered that the report about twenty Khanty and Mansi employees had been "pure invention."[59]

This was only the beginning. In late 1937 the overextended and, according to some, "totally impractical"[60] operations of the Main Administration of the Northern Sea Route came to a grinding halt as twenty-

---

[57] "Uroki semenchukovshchiny," p. 4.

[58] "Svet i teni v rabote Glavsevmorputi," pp. 8–12; Bergavinov, "O razvertyvanii sovetski torgovli."

[59] I. O. Serkin, "Ob oshibkakh Obdorskogo politotdela," SAr, no. 10 (1937): 9–15.

[60] See N. T. Zhdanova, "Vrednaia vylazka B. V. Lavrova v Moskovskom Dome uchenykh," SAr, no. 9 (1937): 9.

six ships, including all of GUSMP's icebreakers, spent a disastrous winter frozen in the Arctic Ocean.[61] In the current climate this could mean only one thing—sabotage. As arrests were made and numerous instances of "deliberate wrecking" uncovered, the native northerners were repeatedly depicted as victims. The "Great Terror" was frequently presented in terms of defending the little man from evil officials, and no one fit the role of the little man better than the "small peoples." The result was a hair-raising picture of abuse, neglect, and incompetence. Almost all traders and administrators were kulaks, bandits, former White officers, or terrorists; the publishers of books in native languages had deliberately sabotaged production; suppliers had deliberately produced shortages; and the situation with schools and hospitals was worse than previously reported.[62] Even the authors of native primers (the first-generation students of Shternberg and Bogoraz) had distorted their material to please the "bourgeois nationalist wreckers." Chernetsova and Vasilevich (Mansi and Tungus) were not "precise enough" about the revolution; Prokof'ev (Nenets) did not say enough about Lenin; Sunik (Nanai) said nothing about the kolkhozy; and Stebnitskii (Koriak) dispensed with political material almost completely.[63]

Not all natives were represented as victims, however; some turned out to be wreckers, terrorists, and spies, who had done their best to exacerbate the suffering of their fellows. According to the script enacted elsewhere in the country, most of these enemies of (their own) people were the beneficiaries of the Great Transformation (Leningrad graduates, kolkhoz chairmen, first teachers); the surviving victims of the Great Transformation (elders, shamans, and kulaks); and all those who had had contact with foreigners (and perhaps betrayed their continuing disloyalty by wearing Chinese silk or Japanese glasses).[64] On

[61] "O rabote Glavsevmorputi za 1937 god," SAr, no. 5 (1938): 21; Belov, Nauchnoe i khoziaistvennoe osvoenie, p. 102; Slavin, Promyshlennoe i transportnoe osvoenie, p. 119.

[62] E. Ubriatova, "Neuklonno provodit' leninsko-stalinskuiu natsional'nuiu politiku," SAr, no. 12 (1937): 33–40; "Likvidirovat' posledstviia vreditel'stva," SAr, no. 1 (1938): 10–12; F. P. Trofimov, "Pushnozagotovki bez rukovodstva," SAr, no. 2 (1938): 15–18; V. F. Tabelev, "Posledstviia sluchainogo podbora liudei," SAr, no. 2 (1938): 22–25; S. A. Volodarskii, "Likvidirovat' negramotnost' sredi narodov Severa," SAr, no. 2 (1938): 29–30; S. P. Ivanov, "Udovletvorit' spros naseleniia Chukotki," SAr, no. 3 (1938): 66; F. L. Leont'ev, "Zdravookhranenie na Chukotke trebuet pomoshchi," SAr, no. 3 (1938): 118; S. Arkhangel'skii, "Narkompros ne rukovodit shkolami Severa," SAr, no. 5 (1938): 59–61.

[63] K. D. Egorov, "Protiv izvrashchenii i uproshchenstva," SAr, no. 2 (1938): 30–32.

[64] See Bruce Grant's path-breaking article, "Siberia Hot and Cold: Reconstructing the Image of Siberian Indigenous Peoples," in Diment and Slezkine, Between Heaven and Hell, pp. 235–37.

Sakhalin, this meant arresting a significant proportion of the population and taking them away in five-ton trucks, "the kind they used on the kolkhoz for transporting the fishing nets."[65] In the words of an NKVD official,

> As a result of repressive measures undertaken against counterrevolutionary and rebel elements among peoples of the North in 1937–38, approximately 36 percent of the adult population was removed [iz"iat], composed mainly of Nivkhi and Evenki from forty to sixty years of age, whereas the remaining 64 percent expressed their understanding and support for the measures undertaken by the Soviet government.[66]

In the final analysis, the native northerners were not primarily victims because they were no longer seen as essentially different. In August 1938 the Council of Peoples' Commissars demanded that GUSMP concentrate on its job of exploring the Northern Sea Passage, not waste its time and resources on less urgent things, and transfer the local population to the jurisdiction of local organizations.[67] The small peoples of the north had lost the last vestige of the special legal status that they had been granted by Speranskii and then again by the Committee of the North.

In symbolic fashion, the event was preceded by the abolition of the newly created northern writing system and its replacement by the Cyrillic alphabet.[68] Many linguists who had devised the system were arrested, as were several northern ethnographers and other friends of the natives in the capitals. The same fate befell the GUSMP leaders (except for Shmidt, who was at the North Pole); the management of the fur procurement agency; the rulers of Dal'stroi, and the Party bosses of the Komi, Buriat, and Yakut republics and the Far Eastern territory.[69] If the "backward tribes of the northern borderlands" were no longer backward, then the experts on northern backwardness belonged in the northern borderlands. And those native people who were not them-

[65] From a recollection by a Nivkh informant as cited by Bruce Grant in "Siberia Hot and Cold," p. 236

[66] Quoted in ibid., p. 237.

[67] "Po-bol'shevistski vypolnim reshenie Sovnarkoma SSSR ob uluchshenii raboty Glavsevmorputi," SAr, no. 9 (1938): 3–4.

[68] "Postanovlenie Prezidiuma TsIK SSSR," SAr, no. 6 (1937): 109–10.

[69] "Likvidirovat' posledstviia vreditel'stva," pp. 10–12; "Likvidirovat' posledstviia Auerbakhovshchiny v Soiuzzagotpushnine," OS, no. 8 (1937): 7; Vladimir Petrov, Soviet Gold: My Life as a Slave Laborer in the Siberian Mines (New York, 1949), pp. 237–46; Kolarz, The Peoples of the Soviet Far East, pp. 4–10, 108, 120–24, Roy Medvedev, Let History Judge (New York, 1972), pp. 203–4.

selves arrested were offered special rewards for catching them if they tried to escape.[70]

The Long Journey of the Small Peoples

No sooner had the northern nomads lost their special legal status and become last among equals in the "fraternal family of peoples" than their literary image improved rapidly and dramatically. The triumph of Stalin's "paradise found" was asserted by the newly formulated canon of socialist realism, in which every story was a parable of revolutionary ascent from primeval chaos to the resolution of life's contradictions under communism. A man of the people—spontaneous, immature, and inherently good—was subjected to various tests of strength and political apprenticeship until he came to a full realization of revealed truth ("consciousness") and joined the ranks as a disciplined fighter for the Cause. In the process he always won his personal revolution, achieved the serenity of higher knowledge, and reasserted the correctness of the Marxist-Leninist-Stalinist view of the world as well as the legitimacy of their succession.[1]

The master plot of socialist realism was thus the ultimate story of conquered backwardness, and as far as many iconographers were concerned, the greater the backwardness the sharper the focus. Indians, savages, children of nature, and all sorts of former aliens emerged from the wilderness to stand beside the workers and peasants. The "wandering" kind were particularly appropriate: the most spontaneous, immature, and artless dwellers in the Russian imagination, they were the quintessential young proletarians—nomads in search of homes.[2] They were also the closest one could get to primitive communism, which meant that their path to scientific communism would be particularly well rounded, truly dialectical, and universal in its significance.

Few people appeared as well qualified to build the bridge between noble savages and fighters for communism as Aleksandr Fadeev, a lead-

---

[70] A. I. Solzhenitsyn, *Arkhipelag Gulag* (Paris, 1974), 3–4:388; Petrov, *Soviet Gold*, pp. 373, 401.

[1] Clark, *The Soviet Novel*, pp. 10–17.

[2] "The long journey" was the usual metaphor for the northern peoples' path to consciousness: compare the titles of A. Koptelov's *Velikoe kochev'e*, M. I. Osharov's *Bol'shoi argish*, Gol'dberg's "Bol'shaia nul'ga Barkaulia" and "Kak Iukhartsa poshel po novym tropam, in *Izbrannye proizvedeniia*, and R. I. Fraerman's "Puteshestvie v nastoiashchee," in *Nikichen (Izbrannoe)*.

ing "proletarian writer" and Gor'kii's official replacement as the dean of Soviet literature. His *Last of the Udege*, published in installments between 1929 and 1940, was conceived as a grandiose epic of the revolutionary Far East, with dozens of characters from all walks of life moving toward self-realization in the new world or self-betrayal under the weight of the old. One of the key figures is an Udege named Sarl, a slightly retouched Dersu Uzala whose road to understanding is the longest but also the easiest—for, as Fadeev stated in one of the introductions to his novel, Engels has taught us that the primitive communism was economically backward but morally admirable ("no soldiers, no gendarmes, no police").[3] Accordingly, Sarl is pure, honest, and childlike; he looks like Dersu, talks like Dersu, and makes his spectacular appearance in the same way as Dersu.[4] Yet he is no longer a lone man of the forest—he represents a culture in crisis and is surrounded by people who are at the same time bronze-skinned Mohicans with impenetrable faces and foul-smelling have-nots in the populist tradition. In a dramatic reversal of roles it is the Russian Red commander who sees beyond the surface of things and shares his knowledge about the world's deeper secrets. Sarl follows him beyond the confines of the dark forest but he is not destroyed as Dersu was—he receives the true light and is anointed as the prophet of his people. "He felt in himself that invisible, indomitable, and that most human of all forces—the force of talent, only he considered it divine."[5] Sarl saw the future and he liked what he saw. The Udege should abandon the old ways, take up agriculture, and follow the Bolsheviks into a society much better than their own but just as pure and equitable.

Fadeev never finished the novel, and the reader never sees the death and the ultimate rebirth of the "last of the Udege," but the Great Transformation of Dersu Uzala had been accomplished. The natives had made the transition to socialist realism and proved themselves useful as travelers in time.

Their "long journeys" usually began with the appearance of one or more Russians: a Red partisan detachment, a teacher, a doctor, or a Party instructor. They came and they made speeches—"about big houses, about big men from big cities, about big theaters, about girls who jump with parachutes," and about schools "where even grownups come to study and where children laugh and sing, happy and well-

[3] A. A. Fadeev, *Sobranie sochinenii* (Moscow, 1970), 2:562–64.
[4] For a detailed comparison, see Nichols, "Stereotyping," pp. 198–200.
[5] Fadeev, *Sobranie sochinenii*, 2:199.

fed."[6] The natives could not always understand the meaning of the words but they always sensed their sincerity and the greater truth that they revealed. One word—"Lenin"—had a particularly powerful effect. It stood for all the beautiful things that the natives had been denied for so long, and the long polar night and the darkness of ignorance retreated before the sound of Lenin's name and the voices of his emissaries. "It seemed that the river, the forest, and the sky were singing together with these fairhaired and blue-eyed men."[7] They were always men, very tall and not very young, tempered by privation, fire, and discipline. Their manner was rough and their faces were stern, but their eyes never failed to suggest a "teasing but good-natured smile."[8] As one of them told his Nivkh friends, "You are human beings, and those who live in the cities in big warm houses are also human beings. The difference between you is small—about ten thousand years or more. . . . Now we need to think how you can catch up with the other peoples of our country."[9] They did not just talk and think. They protected their charges from bad people, built houses for them, treated their diseases, taught them right from wrong, and brought "many goods, tasty and indispensable."[10]

The light brought by the Russians illuminated all the tension, exploitation, inequality, and abuse that lay dormant in every settlement and encampment: "The entire tribe was there, but people were not sitting in their usual places. New groups were being formed—social differentiation had begun, as if the mere sound of Lenin's name had called forth new forces that would shake loose this petrified and lethargic tribal structure."[11] On one side were all the women and children, "the most exploited group"; a short distance away were the men, young and old; and apart from everybody sat the elder and the shaman, "the representatives of social and spiritual power."[12] The poor and the downtrodden knew very well whose side they were on: "The Reds respect the

---

[6] Gennadii Gor, Nesi menia, reka, in Bol'shie pikhtovye lesa (Leningrad, 1968), p. 186; Ivan Kratt, "Kaiur," in Moia zemlia. Kolymskie rasskazy (Moscow, 1938), p. 51.

[7] Trofim Borisov, Syn orla (Khabarovsk, 1939), p. 156; see also V. Itin, "V chume," SO, no. 3 (1930), 62.

[8] Ivan Kratt, "Ulakhan poslednii," in Moia zemlia, p. 31, and "Tin'ka," in Dal'niaia bukhta (Leningrad, 1945), p. 158; Gennadii Gor, Nesi menia, reka, in Bol'shie pikhtovye lesa, p. 264.

[9] Gor, Lanzhero, in Bol'shie pikhtovye lesa, p. 279.

[10] Kratt, "Ulakhan poslednii," p. 35.

[11] Bogoraz, Voskresshee plemia, p. 93. Cf. Gor, "U bol'shoi reki," in Bol'shie pikhtovye lesa, pp. 26–27.

[12] Ibid., p. 95.

poor and persecute the rich. And what about me, Vas'ka the Giliak, aren't I poor and aren't I mad at the rich?"[13] More important, the dirt in the native tents was so disgusting; the social arrangement so unfair; and the customs so patently absurd that the unbiased and "the talented" among the natives needed but a mild rebuke to make them rub their eyes and see the light. If not for the shaman's intrigues, would a normal person—no matter how backward—want to kill his own father? Or live in an unhealthy environment? Or carry out blood vengeance against someone he liked personally? Or marry his late brother's old wife?[14] Of course not. And so one after another the good natives realized the full extent of the "malice, hunger, and ignorance" in which the bad natives had kept them. As Bogoraz's Yukagir boy says to the formerly terrifying spirits, "It turns out that you don't even exist; it's all lies, deceit, and old fairy tales. . . . I'm going to see Lenin."[15]

Unlike their Russian literary counterparts, most of the northern rebels were young women: independent-minded, strong-willed, free-spirited, and with a poor but proud father (no mother is ever mentioned).[16] The actual experience of the cultural revolution in the north was clearly not the only reason for such a choice, however. The defiant warrior girls from the far north had memorable literary predecessors in I. T. Kalashnikov's *Kamchadalka* and in the voluminous romantic fiction set in the Caucasus. Only now instead of being a captive and an admiring lover the Russian was a father-figure and the self-assured master of the situation, while his ally the girl did not have to choose between him and her freedom-loving people: her role was to bring the rest of the tribe under Russian protection (given the new filial nature of the relationship, this role was sometimes played by a child).[17]

[13] R. I. Fraerman, *Vas'ka-giliak*, in *Izbrannoe* (Moscow, 1958), p. 136.

[14] Borisov, *Syn orla*, p. 122; Fraerman, *Vas'ka-giliak*, in *Izbrannoe*, pp. 163, 180; A. L. Koptelov, *Velikoe kochev'e* (Moscow, 1937), p. 231; Nikolai Nikolaevich, "Sukonnaia rukavichka," pp. 46–55; Il'ia Sel'vinskii, *Umka belyi medved'*, in *Sobranie sochinenii v shesti tomakh* (Moscow, 1973), 4:49–50; I. Voblov, "Eskimosskaia byl'," *SAr*, no. 9 (1937): 56–61.

[15] Bogoraz (-Tan), *Voskresshee plemia*, pp. 79, 87.

[16] See Kratt, "Ulakhan poslednii," and "Moia zemlia," in *Moia zemlia*; Fraerman, *Nikichen*, in *Izbrannoe*; Gor, *Nesi menia, reka*, in *Bol'shie pikhtovye lesa*; Koptelov, *Velikoe kochev'e*; Mokshanskii, "Tygrena iz stoibishcha Akkani," pp. 113–15; P. Kuchiiak, "Arbachi," *SO*, no. 2 (1935): 107–12; Nikolai Nikolaevich, "Sukonnaia rukavichka," pp. 46–55; Petri, "Dun'ka-okhotnitsa," pp. 48–51.

[17] Bogoraz (-Tan), *Voskresshee plemia*; Gor, "U bol'shoi reki," *Nesi menia, reka*, and *Lanzhero*, in *Bol'shie pikhtovye lesa*; Kratt, "Tin'ka," in *Dal'niaia bukhta*; G. F. Kungurov, *Topka* (Irkutsk, 1964); Semushkin, *Chukotka*.

The final break with the old family and the acceptance of the new one was usually marked with a bath or a haircut, whereupon the novice left the tribe and went to town to study, work, or simply see the larger world of the "big people."[18] On her return, the fully conscious activist embarked on a series of reforms designed to turn natives into Russians ("We'll be like the Russians . . . , and let nobody say that the Oroch are lazy").[19] This was no easy task. For the activists, elected at birth and marked with special qualities, the Russian truth was absolutely self-evident and transparent, but the others demanded proof and tangible advantages, so that much of the plot revolved around the hero's economic projects, which, in the interests of suspense, usually took some time to succeed. More important, these projects always depended on Russian cooperation, and the real issue was whether the Russians would deliver on the promises that the native activists had made on their behalf.

In this they were obstructed by the tribe's villains ("the enemy"). Old, filled with hatred, and with their faces usually contorted by a "scornful smile," the kulaks and the shamans would do anything in their power to stop progress and embarrass the Russians, for they stood to lose their privileges, their influence, and the whole dark world of "medieval savagery" that they had been been able to maintain for so long.[20] Their struggle was against the future, and they "could not forgive [the activists] their youth, freshness, and laughter" (the enemy never had any children of their own).[21] For all their cunning and desperation, however, they could not offer their kinsmen anything but the long-discredited slogans of the past: independence, pride, sacred customs, and the honor of the ancestors. In other words, the frequently evoked Mohicans were now standing firmly on their heads. Only the villains preached romantic freedom and dignity, and the eponymous antihero of Ivan Kratt's *Ulakhan the Last* was last because he had led the doomed attempt to escape the Russians: no Russians meant no food, no future, and consequently no freedom and dignity. As Ulakhan's wise opponent (and the father of the strong-willed young girl) put it, "For many winters I have waited for just people. And they have

[18] Fraerman, *Vas'ka-giliak* and *Nikichen*, in *Izbrannoe*; Bogoraz (-Tan), *Voskresshee plemia*; S. Leonov, "Stoibishche Udomi-Darakhta," *SO*, no. 8 (1930): 3–19; Gol'dberg, "Bol'shaia nul'ga Barkaulia," in *Izbrannye proizvedeniia*, pp. 117–31; Gor, *Lanzhero*, and *Nesi menia, reka*, in *Bol'shie pikhtovye lesa*; Kungurov, *Topka*.

[19] Kratt, "Rybaki," in *Moia zemlia*.

[20] Voblov, "Eskimosskaia byl'," p. 61.

[21] Gor, *Lanzhero*, in *Bol'shie pikhtovye lesa*.

come. They have driven out the merchants, brought cheap goods, and given reindeer to poor people." Later, when a spy catcher *ex machina* came to Magadan to flash a "teasing but good-natured smile" and to deliver the final judgment, the wise man gave him the highest praise that a proud native could give a Russian official: "Looks like he's going to be a good master [*khoziain*]."[22]

The kulaks and the shamans could not be reformed or reasoned with. Defeated, they left their kinsmen and went back to the wilderness where they belonged—to the forest, tundra, or, like Ulakhan, "back to the distant and forbidding mountains . . . , useless and alien to everything."[23] Sometimes—particularly in the works written after 1936—they returned for one last battle, this time as spies or terrorists.[24] Gor's kulak, for example, who started off as a rather amusing windbag and buffoon, turned progressively more sinister with every new story until he became a murderous Japanese agent bent on senseless destruction.[25] What had started as nostalgic demagoguery inevitably led to bourgeois nationalism ("Chukotka for the Chukchi")[26] and eventual betrayal to the Japanese and Americans, whose foreignness always stood for evil, and to the false Russians, conveniently marked as impostors by their shifty eyes, false teeth, or glasses.[27]

All of them, whoever they might be, were always crushed in the end. Youth, life, and progress prevailed, and "the resurrected tribe" could march on toward cultural and economic development. As Gor'kii said about Sel'vinskii's Umka, "He quit walking on all fours and stood upright."[28] The only challenge left to the writers was to test the firmness of the newly established union between the real Russians and the reformed natives. That posed no problem at all: of the standard procedures available for this purpose the most popular were trials by Arctic cold, and Jack London remained the public's favorite and the principal

[22] Kratt, *Ulakhan poslednii*, p. 35.

[23] Ibid., p. 41.

[24] See Gor, "U bol'shoi reki," and *Lanzhero*, in *Bol'shie pikhtovye lesa*, pp. 345–46; Kratt, "Pastukh" and "Moia zemlia"; Kungurov, *Topka*; Semushkin, *Chukotka*, pp. 310–11; Koptelov, *Velikoe kochev'e*; Sel'vinskii, *Umka belyi medved'*.

[25] Cf. "U bol'shoi reki," "Ivt odnoglazyi," "Starik Tevka," *Nesi menia, reka*, and *Lanzhero*.

[26] Sel'vinskii, *Umka belyi medved'*, 4:80.

[27] Cf. Kratt's Dudiuk, Koptelov's Govorukhin, and Gor's Samovarov.

[28] Sel'vinskii, *Sobranie sochinenii*, 4:411. Actually, Sel'vinskii overdid the "all fours" part, and the play was canceled in 1935 after a group of Chukchi complained that it was "slanderous," "insulting," and full of "disgusting details." See *Pravda*, 18 April 1937, and "Vrednaia p'esa iz zhizni luoravetlanov," *SE*, no. 4 (1937): 153–54.

source of characters, imagery, and decorations.[29] Chukchi women chose to starve in the snowy desert rather than touch the food left by border guards for a polar expedition, and injured geologists crawled for miles to get help for their native guides.[30] The long journey had worked; the native had become part of the family. And when a Tungus Rip Van Winkle emerged from the forest, he found that there were no more bribes or vodka, that people were friendly, debts had been abolished, and furs fetched good prices.[31]

Here, at the threshold of paradise, literature became speechless and folklore—reinterpreted as "people's literature" and wrested from ethnography—took over.[32]

> My tundra, my beloved tundra;
> I'm walking along, joyous and happy.
> Our kolkhoz, our reindeer.
> I feel good, I feel happy.
> I said: "Let me help the Party."[33]

Such lyrical introspection was not frequent, however. The greatest demand was for epic folklore, and most published material presented variations on the general theme of the long journey—except that, seen "from within," it was not a journey but a gift of light received by the people from the giants. The dominant metaphor was the sun: personified by Stalin or offered by Stalin, it not only drove away the forces of darkness but also melted the fetters of ice and brought a cozy glow into the native tents.

> Happiness came into the tundra
> And brought warmth.
> A Russian visited our tent
> And spoke about Moscow.
> In our tent we read books all by ourselves.
> Who gave us such good life?
> —Our dear,
> Our best friend,

[29] Clark, The Soviet Novel, pp. 102–3.
[30] M. E. Zinger, "Ukunaut," in Severnye rasskazy (Moscow, 1938); Kratt, "Zolotoiskateli," in Moia zemlia.
[31] Gol'dberg, "Evseikina pesnia," in Izbrannye proizvedeniia.
[32] See Frank J. Miller, Folklore for Stalin: Russian Folklore and Pseudofolklore in the Stalin Era (Armonk, NY, 1990), esp. pp. 6–15.
[33] Tonkov, "Iz nenetskogo fol'klora," p. 65.

Our sun—
Stalin![34]

By far the most common vehicle for this theme was a kind of parable referred to as a folktale (though usually written by an identifiable author and reworked by a professional folklorist).[35] In it Stalin-sun could act directly, and the whole process of cure or resurrection could unfold from beginning to end.

> One morning a Khanty got up, went outside, and started looking at the sunrise. Then he looked toward the south. The sun was above the tops of the tall trees. The rays of the bright sun were reaching the North. That sun was Stalin. He told us: "The people who live in the North are very poor and blind. These people need help. These people need eyes."
>
> Stalin gave us eyes and gave us strength. The poor Khanty understood everything and learned about everything. Many warm rays came to our taiga from Stalin-sun. And we all said to him: "Dear Stalin, you were brought by a kind mother, and you gave us happy days on the edge of a faraway land, in the virgin taiga."
>
> Our forests are full of valuable sables and silver foxes. Many many different birds sing and chirp in our rich forests. Like a stone that falls from a mountain into a stream, so the tsar's laws have fallen. Khanty life is easy now. Stalin-sun is always shining over the taiga. We, the people of the northern land, have received happiness, and there is joy in our kolkhozy.[36]

Whether the native northerners had any part in creating this kind of folklore, it—along with the "long journey" literature—was the only source of information about their life that the Soviet reading public had access to. With no ethnography, no special legal status, and no more backwardness, the history of the native northerners seemed to have ended. The future had become present.

---

[34] V. V. Senkevich, "Sovremennost' v fol'klore narodov Severa," *SAr*, no. 11 (1937): 105.

[35] Miller, *Folklore for Stalin*, pp. 75–94.

[36] *Skazki narodov Severa* (Moscow, 1951), p. 83.

IV

LAST AMONG EQUALS

"Enjoying a Russian-style house in the I. V. Stalin kolkhoz, Anadyr' district," from M. G. Levin and L. P. Potapov, eds., *Narody Sibiri* (Moscow, 1956)

9

The Socialist Nationalities

To make a happy fireside clime
To weans and wife,
That's the true pathos and sublime
Of human life.

—Robert Burns, "To Dr. Blacklock"

Socialist Realism in the Social Sciences

Being an equal member of the family of Soviet peoples entailed an equal responsibility to the Soviet state. In 1939 the first northerners were drafted into the army, and in 1941 large numbers of males were encouraged to volunteer "to defend the great achievements of October to their last drop of blood." Those staying behind were expected to work overtime, donate their personal reindeer, contribute large sums of money, subscribe to various state bonds, and generally do their best to support—and hopefully understand—the war effort.[1]

By the war's end, however, it was clear that the members of the family were no longer considered equal. The Russians, who in 1941 had emerged as the "older brother," had reemerged as the powerful patriarch or had left the family altogether to become a teacher or group leader.[2] The Koriak youth who had promised to defend the great achievements of October had found himself fighting "for the Mother-

[1] Sergeev, *Nekapitalisticheskii put'*, pp. 411–20; V. G. Balitskii and A. S. Kislichko, *Malye narody Dal'nego Vostoka v Velikoi Otechestvennoi Voine* (Vladivostok, 1985); V. I. Osmolovskaia, "Zhizn' na Iamale v gody voiny" (unpublished); Vladimir Sangi, *V tsarstve vladyk* (Moscow, 1973), pp. 6–8.
[2] Lowell Tillett, *The Great Friendship: Soviet Historians on the Non-Russian Nationalities* (Chapel Hill, 1969), pp. 61–86.

land, for Stalin," both representing the Russian state as inherited from
Ancient Rus', Muscovy, and St. Petersburg—the same Russian state
that until quite recently had been depicted as the ruthless colonizer of
the northern peoples and whose destruction had been regarded as the
great achievement of October. The names most frequently invoked for
the inspiration of the troops had been those of the old princes and
generals who had distinguished themselves in the defense of "the
Faith, the Tsar, and the Fatherland," not those of the revolutionary heroes who had claimed to have created a common family in which a
Koriak could feel at home. The war had been fought for Russia, and, as
Stalin announced at the victory celebration for Red Army commanders, it had been won by the Russians, "the most outstanding of all nations comprising the Soviet Union," the "leading nation" endowed
with a "clear mind, a firm character, and patience," the "great people"
that "guaranteed the defeat of Germany" by having infinite "trust in
the Soviet Government."[3]

During the next ten years the theme of the chosen people and Russia's manifest destiny became central in official discourse—scholarly,
literary, and political. If in the early 1930s the concept of socialism had
been reinterpreted to mean "state-led modernization," then in the late
1940s it came to designate a special attribute of Russians as a nation.
Being inherently superior to all other peoples, the Russians had provided the focus for world history, the articulation of mankind's eternal
yearnings, and the location for an earthly paradise that would eventually embrace everyone. M. V. Lomonosov had laid the foundation of
modern natural sciences, I. I. Polzunov had invented the steam engine,
A. S. Popov had invented radio, A. F. Mozhaiskii had built the first
airplane, and P. N. Iablochkov and A. N. Lodygin had created the first
electric lightbulbs. It turned out, in fact, that Russia had always been
known in the West as "the birthplace of light."[4] "The great Russian
nation gave to the world the greatest genius, the leader and teacher of
the international proletariat and all the working people of the world,
Vladimir Il'ich Lenin," under whose guidance it redeemed the world
in the fire of the October Revolution.[5] Russian science had always been
the most scientific; Russian art had always been the closest to the people; and Russian soldiers had always been the bravest.

[3] I. V. Stalin, Sochineniia (Stanford, Calif., 1967), 2:204.
[4] A. I. Zakharov, "Russkii narod—vydaiushchaiasia natsiia," in Vedushchaia rol' russkogo naroda v razvitii narodov Iakutii (Iakutsk, 1955), p. 35.
[5] Ibid., pp. 39–40.

But it was the state that had been the true source of light, and it was patriotism—or trust in the government, as Stalin called it—that was the greatest trait of the Russian people. "In the defense of their Father-land, the Russian people always showed courage, firmness, heroism, and patience in overcoming difficulties and dangers, foresight in esti-mating any situation."[6] The history of the Russian state was the true manifestation of the history of the Russian people and hence the true history of universal progress toward socialism. And what gave Russian state history its meaning and inner logic was the story of growing cen-tralization and territorial expansion (with territorial expansion often defined as a prerequisite for greater centralization).

In the history of discovery and exploration, the Russian people justifi-ably occupy the number-one spot. They have given the world the largest number of outstanding travelers and geographers. This is not an accident. The Russian nation has always been a nation of discoverers. Courage, perseverance in pursuing their goals, endurance, and an indestructible desire for discovery have been characteristic of its sons throughout the centuries-long history of Russia.[7]

If not for their "remarkable modesty" and "profound respect for the native peoples," not to mention the shameless cheating on the part of Western travelers and academics, the map of the world would contain hundreds of Russian place-names.[8] If not for the imbecility and cow-ardly cosmopolitanism of mostly German tsarist bureaucrats, much of the world would have been contained within the map of Russia. Ethnic Russians (Chirikov rather than Bering, Lazarev rather than Bellings-gauzen, Lisianskii rather than Kruzenshtern) had discovered Antarc-tica, Central Asia, large portions of Ethiopia and much of the Pacific. But the grandest and most successful of them all was the conquest of the enormous expanses of Northern Asia (and, as the Cold War pro-gressed, Alaska and the Far East).[9] Thus, less than a decade after

[6] A. M. Pankratova, Velikii russkii narod (Moscow, 1948), p. 19.
[7] A. G. Adamov, Pervye russkie issledovateli Aliaski (Moscow, 1950), p. 3.
[8] Ibid., pp. 3–5.
[9] See also A. G. Adamov, Pravda o russkikh otkrytiiakh v Amerike (Moscow, 1952) idem, G. I. Shelikhov—zamechatel'nyi russkii moreplavatel' i issledovatel' (Moscow Pravda, 1951); idem, G. I. Shelikhov (Moscow, 1952); M. I. Belov, Semen Dezhnev (Mos-cow, 1955); V. A. Divin, A. I Chirikov—zamechatel'nyi russkii moreplavatel' i uchenyi (Moscow, 1950); S. N. Markov, Liudi velikoi tseli (Moscow, 1944); idem, Letopis' Aliaski [1946–1948], in Iukonskii voron (Moscow, 1970); idem, Tamo-Rus Maklai (Moscow, 1975); B. P. Polevoi, Pervootkryvateli Sakhalina (Iuzhno-Sakhalinsk, 1959), and I. Vino-kurov and F. Florich, Podvig admirala Nevel'skogo (Moscow, 1951).

achieving formal equality in the Union, the indigenous inhabitants of those regions were called on to provide a setting for Russian imperial exploits.

There was no debate on the causes of the great eastward expansion. According to L. I. Potapov,

> The Russian state, which was growing economically and getting stronger politically, needed to expand its territory and protect its frontiers. The annexation of Siberia, discovered by the Russian people, was in full accord with that aim. In Siberia, which was a natural extension of the territory of the Russian state beyond the Urals, rich in natural resources and almost uninhabited, the Moscow government saw an important source of Russia's territorial and economic growth.[10]

In other words, the annexation was legitimate because it was needed by the Russian state. And the annexation by the Russian state was legitimate because of the natives. Or rather, (1) because there were practically no natives on the "large, unsettled territories" that "no one claimed and no one defended"; (2) because the natives were too badly armed and badly organized to offer any serious resistance;[11] (3) because the natives agreed to pay tribute, and "in those days the payment of iasak served to signal the subjugation of a given nationality to the state";[12] (4) because the natives welcomed the newcomers on account of the useful items and protection that they offered;[13] and (5) because the natives were too backward to improve themselves or make good use of their environment. The Russians opened up the new lands for science: they mapped large territories, mined for minerals, classified plants and animals, and studied the indigenous peoples. Most significant, they launched the indigenous peoples on the path of progress by introducing new tools and new weapons, destroying obsolete primitive-communist institutions, spreading agriculture, improving trade, preventing internecine warfare, and contributing to the early stages of nation-building. The imposition of fur tribute led to greater political stability and (male) equality. Even Christianization was an important step in the right direction.[14]

[10] Levin and Potapov, eds., Narody Sibiri, p. 118.

[11] Ibid., p. 119.

[12] Polevoi, Pervootkryvateli Sakhalina, p. 61.

[13] Levin and Potapov, eds., Narody Sibiri, pp. 120–21, 124–25.

[14] V. N. Skalon, Russkie zemleprokhodtsy XVII v. v Sibiri (Moscow, 1951); I. S. Gurvich, "Izmeneniia v kul'ture i byte naseleniia Krainego Severa Iakutii pod vliianiem kul'tury russkogo naroda," in Vedushchaia rol', pp. 160–64; S. V. Bakhrushin, "Polozhitel'nye

Could not the same arguments be made to justify all types of colonialism? No, they could not. The works published in the 1920s and 1930s, which claimed that Russian imperialism had been at least as bad as its Western counterpart, were now out of print, thoroughly rewritten,[15] or as in the case of Bakhrushin's posthumous collection, rendered inoffensive by numerous editorial corrections.[16] There was, however, no sign of anyone arguing that Western colonialism was essentially as beneficial as the Russian "Great Discoveries." The whole point, and perhaps the greatest discovery (or rather a rediscovery of a hundred-year-old nationalist formula),[17] was that Russian expansion was truly unique in its efficacy and benevolence—"as opposed to the parasitic colonization of the New World by the Anglo-Saxons and Spaniards, who had used for the purpose bands of adventurers, vagabonds, and criminals."[18]

First of all, that was because the Russians had always been more Western than the Westerners—that is, more developed culturally and technologically. At the time of the conquest of Siberia, for example, most Russians had been "rationally thinking," or even "enlightened" people, whereas "a century later in Germany, . . . the life of the people was still full of all kinds of superstitions."[19] As a result, Western imperialism, in contrast to the Russian version, "led to economic and cultural stagnation" or even "threw very far back" the development of the affected peoples.[20] Second, and most important, the Russians were simply much better people. "The industrious, humane, and magnanimous Russian nation" respected the natives, helped them, intermar-

---

rezul'taty russkoi kolonizatsii v sviazi s prisoedineniem Iakutii k Russkomu gosudarstvu," in *Vedushchaia rol'*, pp. 49–69. Bakhrushin's article was published posthumously, with a reminder from the editors that by "colonization" Bakhrushin actually meant "settlement" *(zaselenie)* and "development of resources" *(osvoenie)*.

[15] See, for example, P. T. Khaptaev, *Kratkii ocherk istorii Buriat-Mongol'skogo naroda* (Ulan-Ude, 1936); P. T. Khaptaev, ed., *Istoriia Buriat-Mongol'skoi ASSR* (Ulan-Ude, 1954); and Tillett, *The Great Friendship*, pp. 343–50.

[16] Bakhrushin, *Nauchnye trudy*.

[17] See Nebol'sin, *Pokorenie Sibiri*, p. 113.

[18] Adamov, *G. I. Shelikhov*, p. 39.

[19] Skalon, *Russkie zemleprokhodtsy*, pp. 180–81; Adamov, *G. I. Shelikhov—zamechatel'nyi*, p. 12. Skalon took great pains to avoid using standard Russian words for various sciences, most of which are of non-Russian origin. Instead, he exhumed archaic terms or coined quaint-sounding Slavic-based neologisms such as "zemlevedy" (for "geographers") "zverovedy" (for "zoologists"), and "znatoki pernatykh" (for "ornithologists"). Ironically, the title of the crucial chapter on "culture-carriers" *(nositeli kul'tury)* is a transparent calque from German.

[20] Belov, *Semen Dezhnev*, p. 6.

ried with them, and joined hands with them in their common struggle against injustice.[21] As far as the natives themselves were concerned, it meant that although they were no longer regarded as equal to the Russians, their truly progressive development had started about three hundred years before the October Revolution.

In other words, it meant that, historically, the indigenous "past" (the primitive, prerevelation existence) had shrunk considerably. Even if the full-fledged "present" was not traced back beyond the Revolution, there was now a long "Old Testament" period prefiguring the Age of the Gospel, a kind of transition from darkness to light, from past to present, from chaos to order. The first, primitive-communist and basically static period, was to be studied by ethnographers; the second, colonial and inherently dynamic period, was to be studied by historians (of Russia). But what of the present? Could the native northerners be considered separately from other sections of the Soviet population? Even with the Russians singled out as the elect, was there any way to distinguish among the various non-Russian toilers other than along vestigial class lines? Were the equal peoples still national in form, and if so, what did it mean and who would be able to tell the difference—especially since the ehnographers had taken refuge in prehistory (or preclass history, which came down to the same thing)? Or was the refuge temporary?

After the banning and unbanning of ethnography in 1932 and the disappearance of its revolutionary leaders in 1936, the "disoriented" survivors had received a new lease on life when the Party issued an appeal for the integration of the history of the non-Russian peoples into Russian history.[22] In 1939 a chair of ethnography was formed within the Department of History of Moscow University, and in 1942 wartime enthusiasm for nationality issues resulted in the resurrection of the moribund Institute of Ethnography.[23] By the end of the war the Institute's Moscow branch had forty-two graduate students, many of whom were professional ethnographers trained before the Cultural

[21] Zakharov, "Russkii narod," in *Vedushchaia rol'*, p. 32; Bakhrushin, "Polozhitel'nye rezul'taty," in *Vedushchaia rol'*, p. 61; Gurvich, "Izmeneniia v kul'ture," p. 164; Levin and Potapov, eds., *Narody Sibiri*, p. 127.

[22] *Pravda*, 27 January 1936.

[23] Kozlova and Cheboksarov, "Etnografiia v Moskovskom universitete," pp. 110–11; S. P. Tolstov, "Sorok let sovetskoi etnografii," *SE*, no. 5 (1957): 39.

Revolution and now returning from scholarly exile.[24] The director of
the institute and the man in charge of reinventing Soviet ethnography
was S. P. Tolstov, who had made his name during the academic wars of
1928–1934 as a close collaborator of Matorin and an implacable foe of
all non-Marxist (non-Marrist) professors. Although Matorin's name
was now taboo (it was never mentioned even in criticizing the sins of
the past), Marr remained the only safe authority (and Tolstov remained
Marr's disciple), so that the new Soviet ethnography represented a
mild revision of the 1935 edition. The subject was the primitive
communist society, and the method was Morgan's, as refined by Engels
and then Marr. Consequently, the native peoples of the north remained relevant as prehistoric survivals, as denizens of ethnographic—not historic—time, and as mostly "low barbarians" (one step
above "savages").[25]

They were also, however, victors in the Great Patriotic War, or at least
loyal and conscientious allies of the true victors. Every day and every
hour, in every classroom and at every meeting, the Soviet people, ethnographers among them, were told that the war had been won by the
Russians and their friends; that the Russians had won the war because
they were a great nation; that they had been a great nation for as long
as Russian had been spoken; that the rest of the world consisted of
friends and enemies also constituted as nationalities; that to deny any
of the above was to be a cosmopolitan; and that to be a cosmopolitan
meant to fawn before foreigners who were led by the Anglo-American
imperialists. In other words, the ethnographers—many of them former
fieldworkers with thousands of unpublished materials—were getting
the same message as the historians, except that in the ethnographers'
case it seemed to suggest a total rejection of an orthodoxy that had
never been explicitly challenged by the Party. Moreover, whereas the
historians of the north were all historians of Russia, most ethnographers had specialized in other peoples. That the Russians were to have
a national present as well as a past did not necessarily mean that
others, particularly barbarians, were entitled to the same treatment.

For a while caution prevailed, and in April 1947 when Tolstov suggested that ethnography should study ethnic communities, he made

[24] M. G. Rabinovich and S. A. Tokarev, "Institut etnografii v period Velikoi Otechestvennoi Voiny i pervye poslevoennye gody," SE, no. 4 (1975): 7–17.

[25] V. I. Ravdonikas, Istoriia pervobytnogo obshchestva (Leningrad, 1947), 2:30–32;
S. P. Tolstov, "K voprosu o periodizatsii istorii pervobytnogo obshchestva," SE, no. 1
(1946): 29.

sure to confine his remarks to "ethnogenesis," or national origins.[26] Finally, however, the long-awaited authorization came—not an explicit program of action, perhaps, but eminently quotable as such. On April 7, 1948, speaking at a dinner in honor of a Finnish government delegation, Stalin declared:

> Every nation, whether large or small, has its own specific qualities and its own peculiarities, which are unique to it and which other nations do not have. These peculiarities form a contribution that each nation makes to the common treasury of world culture, adding to it and enriching it. In this sense all nations, both small and large, are in the same position, and each nation is equal to any other nation.[27]

Thus, ethnicity was seen as universal and irreducible. All culture was still national in form, and perhaps even in content. All nations had an ethnographic present. Ethnography could once again study ethnicity.

Such, at any rate, were the conclusions (and possibly the instructions) of Soviet ethnographic administrators. The concentration on primitive communism was immediately proclaimed to have been a "pernicious tendency," which, unforgivably, had led to the cessation of meaningful research, the flight of many good scholars, and the existence of certified ethnographers who had never been in the field.[28] It was time to move away from "abstract sociology" and realize that "the people [narod] and their national or ethnic specificity [were] the alpha and omega of ethnographic science, its beginning and its end."[29] In other words, ethnography was to study "the ethnic peculiarities of given peoples," or "the ethnic manifestations of human culture in given peoples."[30] This seemed to suggest that some elements of culture were not ethnic, that they should be studied by other disciplines, and that therefore no one was guilty of reviving Shternberg's universal "science of culture." The other, and potentially very disturbing, implications were that not all culture was national even "in form" and that

---

[26] S. P. Tolstov, "Sovetskaia shkola v etnografii," SE, no. 4 (1947): 19–22.

[27] Stalin, Sochineniia (Stanford), 3:100.

[28] "Obsuzhdenie nauchno-issledovatel'skoi raboty Instituta etnografii AN SSSR," SE, no. 1 (1949): 163–66, 170.

[29] I. I. Potekhin, "Zadachi bor'by s kosmopolitizmom v etnografii," SE, no. 2 (1949): 8, 24.

[30] S. A. Tokarev, "K postanovke problem etnogeneza," SE, no. 3 (1949): 36; P. I. Kushner (Knyshev), "Uchenie Stalina o natsii i natsional'noi kul'ture i ego znachenie dlia etnografii," SE, no. 4 (1949): 4.

ethnography was essentially a method of participant observation.[31] Those, however, were worries for future scholars and politicians: what mattered now was that ethnography was primarily a science of the present.[32]

Whose science? With *Zhdanovshchina* raging outside, the "ethnicization" of ethnography went even further. Not only was it supposed to study nationality it was to be recognized as an important manifestation of nationality. According to I. I. Potekhin, ethnography was created by emerging nation states to provide them with past roots and present legitimacy. As a result, "every scientific discovery belongs to a certain nation, and every new theory is put forward by a scholar belonging to a certain nation."[33] The Russian case was unique, however, for Russian ethnography reflected the interests of the Russian state, which reflected the interests of the Russian people, which reflected the interests of all progressive people on Earth. Hence anyone who denied the preeminence of Russian ethnography (state, nation) was an enemy of progress, or a "cosmopolitan."[34]

Who were the most dangerous enemies? First and foremost, all non-Communist foreigners, in as much as they inevitably expressed the interests of their states—"a whole gang of pseudoscholars selling science, people without honor who muddle the water to make it easier for Anglo-Saxon imperialists to fish in it." Particularly devious were those "learned lackeys of Wall Street" who questioned the ontological reality of nations, thereby claiming superiority for the ostensibly nonethnic nationalism of the United States.[35] The second detachment of cosmopolitans were those Russians/Soviets who, intentionally or not, served the interests of foreigners (usually by doubting Russian superiority in a certain sphere). In 1948 Soviet folklore studies were purged of V. Ia. Propp and P. G. Bogatyrev because of their alleged reliance on Lévy-Bruhl and Malinowski, and of Veselovskii's "traveling-motifs school," because most of their motifs had traveled from places other than Rus-

[31] Tokarev's "K postanovke" is clearly open to such an interpretation: a "culture" can be studied on the basis of written sources (history), material artifacts (archaeology), and linguistic analysis, as well as ethnographic fieldwork.
[32] "Obsuzhdenie nauchno-issledovatel'skoi raboty," p. 166; "Rabota Instituta etnografii AN SSSR v 1949 g.," SE, no. 2 (1950), 182–85.
[33] Potekhin, "Zadachi bor'by," pp. 9, 20.
[34] Ibid., pp. 18–23; "Obsuzhdenie nauchno-issledovatel'skoi raboty," pp. 163, 166; "Obsuzhdenie doklada I. I Potekhina," SE, no. 2 (1949): 171.
[35] Potekhin, "Zadachi bor'by," pp. 11–13.

sia.[36] Ethnography in its new incarnation was still young and feeble, so that in 1949 when ethnographers were called on to purge the cosmopolitans in their midst, the accusers had to dredge up the deceased classics who had already proved their usefulness as targets—L. Ia. Shternberg and V. G. Bogoraz. The new leaders of ethnography were themselves surviving cultural revolutionaries who had been responsible for the "pernicious" turn toward "abstract sociology" and primitive-communist studies: in order to avoid being branded as cosmopolitans themselves, they thought it wise to once again attack their former victims.

Thus, in a truly remarkable development, the same scholars who twenty years earlier had been reviled as Russian populists lacking in internationalist vision or as sentimental defenders of backwardness were now accused of "fawning before the bourgeois west." The influence of Shternberg and Bogoraz was judged to have been "extremely harmful" because they had falsified the history of the northern peoples by ignoring "the friendly relations between the Russians and the local population" (M. A. Sergeev); because they had smuggled into Russia "pernicious bourgeois theories . . . of a cosmopolitan nature" (S. M. Abramzon, D. A. Ol'derogge, L. P. Potapov); because Shternberg had dared compare Malinowski "with the pride of Russian science Miklukho-Maklai" (L. P. Potapov); and—most extravagant—because both men had been responsible for ethnography's current "divorce from social reality" (M. S. Dolgonosova).[37] The choice was made easier by the fact that both Shternberg and Bogoraz had been Jewish: anti-Semitism was an integral part of the anticosmopolitanism campaign. In fact, S. M. Abramzon, who had initiated the attack, soon found himself apologizing for his own errors. In 1952 he replaced his former victims as the number-one falsifier of Russian achievements.[38]

Another important requirement was to remember what was meant

<hr>

[36] "Zadachi etnografov v sviazi s polozheniem na muzeinom fronte," SE, no. 2 (1948): 6; "Diskussii po voprosam fol'kloristiki na zasedaniiakh sektora fol'klora Instituta etnografii," SE, no. 3 (1948): 139–46; "Obsuzhdenie nauchno-issledovatel'skoi raboty," p. 167; "Obsuzhdenie doklada I. I. Potekhina," p. 171.

[37] "Obsuzhdenie doklada I. I. Potekhina," pp. 174–77. One of the victims of the 1949 campaign was D. K. Zelenin, an influential old ethnographer and philologist. In 1930 Tolstov had accused him of "providing a 'scientific' justification for those groups inside and outside the Soviet Union that were interested in the growth of Russian chauvinism." "K probleme akkul'turatsii," p. 87. In 1949 Tolstov presided over a campaign that found Zelenin guilty of minimizing the cultural accomplishments of the Russian people. Potekhin, "Zadachi bor'by," p. 24; "Obsuzhdenie doklada I. I. Potekhina," p. 171.

[38] "Obsuzhdenie doklada I. I. Potekhina," p. 174; "Obsuzhdenie rabot S. M. Abramzona," SE, no. 4 (1952): 184–87.

by the "present," or "modernity." No one—and least of all the aging cultural revolutionaries—doubted that

> The task of Soviet science [was] to struggle for a strictly Party-based, strictly discriminating approach to the cultural heritage of each nationality, an ability to differentiate between progressive phenomena that [would] . . . enter the treasury of the national socialist culture of each nationality, and those phenomena that reflected the old, backward, stagnant way of life, exploded by the Great October Revolution and subject to the speediest elimination.[39]

Every ethnographic work on non-Russian peoples would have to consist of two parts: a sketch of the backward and stagnant life as it used to be followed by descriptions of the radical changes of which Soviet scholars were "happy contemporaries."[40] A possible alternative was to describe modern communities "in the context of the intense development of socialist industry and large-scale mechanized socialist agriculture, the gradual liquidation of existing differences between town and country, and the quick rise in the material welfare of the people and in the satisfaction of their spiritual needs," while being on the lookout for all possible survivals of the past that might interfere with progress (life as it is minus survivals equals life as it should be).[41] A failure to distinguish between the old and the new or "a total impartiality or equal partiality" amounted, at best, to formalism (of which two of the best known northern fieldworkers, Popov and Vasilevich, were found guilty).[42] A total blindness toward the new was tantamount to nationalism or slander, and an inability to find the old reduced the ethnographer to the status of "a happy contemporary," whereas his real task was "not to just register facts but to fight against survivals in people's lives and minds," as well as to "unmask the malicious slander of imperialist propaganda about the lives of the peoples of the USSR."[43]

Before one could begin producing "modern ethnography," however,

[39] S. P. Tolstov, "V. I. Lenin i aktual'nye problemy etnografii," SE, no. 1 (1949): 6.

[40] "Obsuzhdenie nauchno-issledovatel'skoi raboty," p. 172.

[41] "Koordinatsionnoe soveshchanie po etnograficheskomu izucheniiu sotsialisticheskoi kul'tury i byta narodov SSSR," SE, no. 1 (1953): 179–80.

[42] "Obsuzhdenie nauchno-issledovatel'skoi raboty," p. 168; Tolstov, "V. I. Lenin i aktual'nye problemy," p. 6.

[43] "Sessiia nauchno-issledovatel'skogo instituta kraevedcheskoi i muzeinoi raboty," SE, no. 2 (1949): 182; "K novym uspekham sovetskoi etnografii," SE, no. 2 (1951): 3–6; "Obsuzhdenie nauchno-issledovatel'skoi raboty," p. 175; Potekhin, "Zadachi bor'by," pp. 18–19.

one had to swear allegiance to a general concept of man that would make the new science possible. In the official view, the success of the revolution in general and the Great Transformation in particular was predicated on a belief in the final and absolute victory of nurture over nature. After the war, it was biology's turn to make the strongest claim in that direction, as "the bourgeois pseudoscience of genetics" was being exorcized from all spheres of Soviet life and the Lysenko-Michurin theory on the transmission of acquired characteristics was being introduced as a kind of Leninism in the natural sciences. There was no limit to directed change, and there was no problem in making that change irreversible.[44] As the ethnographers understood it, not only was the human psyche not determined by heredity, but "conditions of life" actually "[influenced] the formation of a person's physical type and [produced] changes in his inheritable nature."[45] Anything else was racism, which, paradoxically, was a version of cosmopolitanism. "It is well known that ethnographers and travelers in Africa have pointed out the great giftedness of Negro children in their natural surroundings. They observed, for example, how three and four-year-old Negro children could handle a canoe, set traps for birds, catch foxes, etc."[46] In other words, in good hands they could grow up to become good Soviets and, if Michurin was right, perhaps even physically different. V. V. Bunak, the head of the Soviet school of physical anthropology and the newly demoted chair of the Physical Anthropology Section at the Institute of Ethnography, protested that "if a person eats an extra kilo of sugar, it does not mean that his skull shape will change or any other such thing."[47] A short time later he had to recant and admit "the unconditional correctness of the principles of Soviet Darwinism as formulated by the academician T. D. Lysenko."[48]

Finally, the newly reborn Soviet ethnography was formally baptized in the summer of 1950, when Stalin published his "Marxism and Problems of Linguistics."[49] In it he dethroned the ghost of Marr, the last of the Great Transformation's radical gurus whose theories and students had somehow escaped the fate of the other "simplifiers and vulgarizers

[44] David Joravsky, The Lysenko Affair (Cambridge, Mass., 1970).
[45] M. Levin, Ia. Roginskii, and N. Cheboksarov, "Anglo-amerikanskii rasizm," SE, no. 1 (1949): 25; "Itogi sessii VASKhNIL i sovetskaia antropologiia," SE, no. 1 (1949): 176. See also Gennadii Gor, Iunosha s dalekoi reki (Leningrad, 1953), pp. 254–55.
[46] Levin, Roginskii and Cheboksarov, "Anglo-amerikanskii rasizm," p. 27.
[47] "Itogi sessii VASKhNIL," p. 183.
[48] V. V. Bunak, "Pis'mo v redaktsiiu," SE, no. 1 (1949).
[49] Stalin, Sochineniia (Stanford), 3:114–71.

of Marxism, such as the RAPPists and Proletkul'tists."[50] According to Stalin, languages were not part of the superstructure; they were not class-based; they did not change their nature with changes in socioeconomic formations; they could certainly be studied by the historic-comparative method (particularly the Slavic languages); and they never emerged as a result of any "explosive crossing" of two different parent tongues (Russian, for example, "always came out victorious" in its contacts with other languages).[51] Language, as Stalin claimed over and over again, "belonged to the whole nation" and was "common to the whole society" across social classes and throughout history.[52] In fact, the term "society" as used by Stalin invariably referred to ethnic communities, especially "nations." Classes might have their own cultures (which were definitely elements of the superstructure attached to a given base), but peoples had languages—and presumably also cultures—whose "essence" did not change as long as those peoples existed, that is, "incomparably longer than any base or any superstructure."[53]

There was no doubt what this meant for Soviet ethnography. Its subject was definitely back, indeed it was "big." The switch toward ethnicity and modernity had been correct. Marr's shadow, and hence ethnography's greatest identity crisis, had disappeared. And Marr's students, who had not disappeared, had to renounce their past (Tolstov administered the last kick to his purged comrades by referring to them as "'activists' from Marr's immediate circle who had never had anything to do with science and who [had fallen] into oblivion a long time ago.").[54]

For a while there was a scare that the science of ethnogenesis might have to follow its creators into oblivion, and perhaps even drag its current champions with it, but no one went quite that far, and Tolstov's rule remained firm. If ethnicity was an ontological reality, so were its origins; and if ethnicity was sacred, then its origins were doubly so.[55]

[50] Ibid., p. 146.
[51] Ibid., pp. 143–47
[52] Ibid., p. 117.
[53] Ibid., pp. 119, 138.
[54] S. P. Tolstov, "Itogi perestroiki raboty Instituta etnografii AN SSSR v svete truda I. V. Stalina 'Marksizm i voprosy iazykoznaniia,'" SE, no. 3 (1951): 5.
[55] S. P. Tolstov, "Znachenie trudov I. V. Stalina po voprosam iazykoznaniia dlia razvitiia sovetskoi etnografii," SE, no. 4 (1950): 5, and "Itogi perestoiki," pp. 7–8; "Soveshchanie po metodologii etnogeneticheskikh issledovanii v svete stalinskogo ucheniia o natsii i iazyke," SE, no. 4 (1951): 3–6; S. A. Tokarev and N. N. Cheboksarov, "Metodologiia etnogeneticheskikh issledovanii na materiale etnografii v svete rabot I. V. Stalina po vo-

Another side effect of Stalin's intervention was the attempt to label all "magic and cosmological" explanations as Marrism and thus liberate Soviet ethnography from "idealism" in a way that Marr himself would have approved of. A programmatic article to that effect appeared prominently in *Sovetskaia etnografiia's* editorial space and claimed, among other things, that the female Slav's loincloth was used for reasons of warmth rather than religious protection, and that the Australian aborigines wore belts "to squeeze their stomachs in order to minimize the pangs of hunger."[56] The swift and crushing rebuttal came from *Pravda* itself, and the editorial board duly apologized and promised never to do it again.[57]

Finally, Stalin's article contained one passage that seemed to be a very serious long-term challenge. It referred to the "development from clan languages to tribal languages, from tribal languages to nationality [*narodnost'*] languages, and from nationality languages to national languages."[58] The implications were clear and inescapable. As Tokarev and Cheboksarov put it, "If language emerges and develops with the emergence and development of society, then it is obvious that stages in the history of society should correspond to these stages [that is, from clan to national] in the history of language."[59] In other words, one had to construct a historical hierarchy of ethnicity based on a single set of criteria—a truly daunting task considering that Stalin's linguistic scheme did not correspond to the Marxist social scheme, and that both were obligatory. Clans and tribes both belonged in primitive communism, and nations belonged in both capitalism and socialism. And if that was not bad enough, what was *narodnost'*? It might be the ethnicity of feudalism, but Stalin insisted that the French Revolution had not led to any significant change in the French language. Or were the old formations to be abandoned altogether? Closer to home—and of great consequence for the native northerners—what had happened to clans and tribes after the socialist revolution? Had they automatically become nations, or was there no equality in the Soviet family even with the Russians left out?

---

prosam iazykoznaniia," *SE*, no. 4 (1951): 13; "Rabota Instituta etnografii AN SSSR v 1951 g.," pp. 172–77.

[56] V. Belitser and G. Maslova, "Protiv antimarksistskikh izvrashchenii v izuchenii odezhdy," *SE*, no. 3 (1954): 5–6.

[57] "Vul'garizatory v poze marksistov," *Pravda*, 9 December 1954; "Obsuzhdenie korrespondentsii, opublikovannoi v gazete 'Pravda,'" *SE*, no. 1 (1955): 172–73.

[58] Stalin, *Sochineniia*, (Stanford), 3:122.

[59] Tokarev and Cheboksarov, "Metodologiia etnogeneticheskikh issledovanii," p. 7.

These questions would haunt Soviet ethnography for the next thirty years, but in the meantime (by the mid-1950s) the most immediate tasks were clear. Ethnography was to study ethnic communities and, in the case of the USSR, it was to show them in transition from the past to the future, with the future being prepared by the whole history of Russia but truly occurring only after the October Revolution. In other words, ethnography was to adopt the Long Journey paradigm that had emerged in fiction twenty years before. The past was associated with darkness, backwardness, and spontaneity; the future, with light, progress, and consciousness. The future was already present, but there remained some traces of the past that needed to be identified in order to be overcome. The ethnic communities of ethnographic texts were to resemble the "positive heroes" of fictional texts.

The first experiments in new research among the native northerners took the form of articles describing specific kolkhozes, with particular emphasis on successful plan-fulfillment, new social structure, and improved dwellings and garments. The basic argument is best illustrated by the conclusion to one such article:

> The main changes that have occurred in the lives of the Enets and Nenets members of the Kirov kolkhoz are the transition from a semisubsistence patriarchal economy to a Soviet kolkhoz economy with the accompanying liquidation of the kulaks as a class; the transformation of the whole population into workers in a socialist society; the increase in commodity production; the steady growth of the members' material well-being and cultural level; and the incorporation of the formerly backward "Samoeds" into the Soviet culture, the culture of the great Russian nation.[60]

Within a decade, the monograph summarizing the transformation of an entire ethnic group emerged as the dominant genre in northern ethnography and as an important career goal for most professional ethnographers.[61] All such monographs consisted of two sections: life before the Revolution and life after the Revolution. Within each section "life" was broken down into three basic categories: "material culture"

[60] B. O. Dolgikh, "Kolkhoz imeni Kirova Taimyrskogo natsional'nogo okruga," SE, no. 4 (1949): 93. See also M. M. Brodnev, "Ot rodovogo stroia k sotsializmu (po materialam Iamalo-Nenetskogo natsional'nogo okruga)," SE, no. 1 (1950): 92–106.

[61] See, for example, Alekseenko, Kety; Antropova, Kul'tura i byt koriakov; Khomich, Nentsy; Kiselev and Kiseleva, Sovetskie saamy; Lar'kin, Orochi, and Levin and Potapov, Narody Sibiri; Liapunova, Ocherki po etnografii aleutov; Menovshchikov, Eskimosy; Novaia zhizn' narodov Severa (Moscow: 1967); Smoliak, Ul'chi; Taksami, Nivkhi.

(economic activities, tools, dwellings, food, clothing, transportation); "social organization" (kinship structure, kinship terminology, status of women and children, marriage and burial rituals); and "spiritual culture" (religious/Communist consciousness, folklore). Theoretically, the first category belonged to the base, and the other two, to the super-structure, but only the first and last were "cultures," thus reflecting the strict matter-spirit (being-consciousness) dualism of Soviet Marxism. Social analysis was wedged uneasily between the two and usually re-ceived very little attention—remarkably little, in fact, considering the ferocity of the recent battles over "stratification."

What was supposed to have changed? What were the greatest benefits of socialism? What, in other words, was progress? In contrast to the Great Transformation texts, the postwar Long Journey ethnographies pointed unanimously to the material sphere. The revolution was over, and the new (formerly proletarian) elite were busy looking for comfort and stability, providing for their distinctly nonproletarian children, and furnishing their apartments with what used to be called the sym-bols of philistine contentment. The change had been inaugurated in the first half of the 1930s and expressed in the north by the natives from newspaper accounts cheerfully demanding "nice shawls with tassels," "colored ribbons," "small tea cups with pretty, colorful designs," and "brightly colored flowered materal."[62] Now, with the Great Transforma-tion, the Great Terror, and the Great War behind them, Party bosses, scholars, and artists (many of them young war veterans educated in the late 1930s), were doubly anxious to restore the socialism of upward mobility, the socialism of private happiness, the socialism of nice shawls with tassels.[63]

Accordingly, in the new accounts of native life the most dramatic improvements were to be found in people's dwellings, formerly smoke-filled tents and currently "Russian-style" houses: "Tables, chairs, beds, china and kitchenware, curtains on the windows, brightly colored bed-spreads and tablecloths have all become common household items. In many houses there are record players and sewing machines. . . . There

---

[62] Vol'skii, "Na Taimyre," p. 28. See Chapter 8, section b.

[63] Cf. Vera S. Dunham, *In Stalin's Time: Middle-Class Values in Soviet Fiction* (Cam-bridge, 1976). Dunham concentrates on fiction and thus leaves out the prewar glorifica-tion of "middle-class values" present mostly in periodicals and inspirational autobiographies.

is great new demand for watches, bicycles, motorcycles, radios, musi-
cal instruments, or sporting goods."[64]

Reportedly, the inhabitants of the new houses were wearing Russian
clothing (with particular emphasis on underwear) and eating Russian
food, which was said to be healthier and more varied than the traditional kind. Changes in social organizations were usually limited to
membership in the kolkhoz, the enhanced role of women, and the diminishing importance of clan divisions. Even "spiritual" accomplishments tended to be "material" in nature, measured as they were by the
number of school graduates, white-collar professionals, books in native
languages, clubs, and folkloric groups. If the long journey was a trip
from savagery to civilization, then civilization meant upward mobility
and unpretentious bodily pleasures.

But what about the trip itself? Static by nature, the ethnographic accounts stopped the clock twice—at some point before the revolution
and in the present—with very little to say about the actual movement
from point A to point B. This, of course, was where native history came
in. Or rather, another Russian chapter in native history, for true history
was political, and only states could have political histories. The natives, who had ethnographies instead, could join the world-historical
time frame only if they got a ride from the Russians. Before the mid-
1950s, their history had been a history of Russian colonization, Russian colonial administration, anti-Russian struggle, or pro-Russian
sentiment. Now, for the first time, they were to have their own, totally
unique story of change over time, albeit initiated by the Russians, carried out under the Russians, and eventually leading to Russification
(in content). The plot included various Party and government initiatives and their successful implementation in the course of collectivization, industrialization, and the cultural revolution. The starting point
and the results were known from ethnographic texts, and the story's
significance consisted in the remarkable achievement of having bypassed most of Marx's developmental stages. In fact, these histories,
usually titled *From a Patriarchal Society to Socialism*, became particularly popular in the late 1960s and 1970s, when the USSR's new
allies in the "Third World" were expected to benefit from the experience of Soviet hunters gatherers, and reindeer breeders.

---

[64] E. V. Iakovleva, *Malye narodnosti Priamur'ia posle sotsialisticheskoi revoliutsii*
(Khabarovsk, 1957), p. 66.

There are countries and peoples that did not pass through certain stages of social development. The Slavic and Northern European peoples, as well as the nomadic peoples of Asia and Africa skipped the slaveholding phase; the peoples of North America bypassed feudalism; and the peoples of North Caucasus, Central Asia, and Kazakhstan avoided capitalism. And only the peoples of the North skipped all three stages one after another.[65]

There remained one aspect of the newly rediscovered indigenous life that was not covered by the Long Journey paradigm, either ethnographic or historic. This was the elusive ethnicity, or what Stalin called national peculiarities. Material, social, and spiritual changes were said to have occurred in similar ways and to have led to similar results all over the north. But would a newly settled Chukchi be more likely to marry a Koriak? Would they speak Koriak or Chukchi under their "brightly-colored bedspread"? Would their Russian-educated children be Russians? And how did the Chukchi and Koriak become different in the first place? These questions became paramount after 1961, when the new Party Program took a closer look at the fate of ethnicity under socialism, but they were first raised and formulated in the early 1950s, when ethnicity became fully legitimate.[66] The usual heading was "Ethnic Processes," and the main purpose was to establish a given group's ethnic identity (in the sense of objective "national belonging"), and perhaps to follow its fate from "ethnogenesis" to the present through the vagaries of intermarriage, migration, and bilingualism.[67]

[65] V. A. Zibarev, Bol'shaia sud'ba malykh narodov (Novosibirsk, 1972), p. 6. See also V. G. Balitskii, Ot patriarkhal'no-obshchinnogo stroia k sotsializmu (O perekhode k sotsializmu malykh narodov severo-vostoka RSFSR) (Moscow, 1969); M. E. Budarin, Put' malykh narodov severa k kommunizmu (Omsk, 1968); L. E. Kiselev, Ot patriarkhal'shchiny k sotsializmu (Sverdlovsk, 1974); Kleshchenok, Narody Severa; I. P. Kleshchenok, Istoricheskii opyt KPSS po osushchestvleniiu leninskoi natsional'noi politiki sredi malykh narodov Severa (1917–1935) (Moscow, 1972); V. S. Lukovtsev, Minuia tysiacheletiia (Moscow, 1982); G. L. Sanzhiev, Perekhod narodov Sibiri k sotsializmu, minuia kapitalizm (Novosibirsk,1980); Sergeev, Nekapitalisticheskii put'; and V. N. Uvachan, Perekhod k sotsializmu malykh narodov Severa: Po materialam Evenkiiskogo i Taimyrskogo natsional'nykh okrugov (Moscow, 1958), and Put' narodov Severa k sotsializmu.

[66] For the earliest examples, see B. O. Dolgikh, "O nekotorykh etnogeneticheskikh protsessakh (pereseleniiakh narodov i rasprostranenii iazykov) v Severnoi Sibiri," SE, no. 1 (1952): 51–59; I. M. Suslov, "O natsional'noi prinadlezhnosti sovremennogo naseleniia severo-zapada Iakutskoi ASSR," SE, no. 2 (1952): 68–72; I. S. Gurvich, "Po povodu opredeleniia etnicheskoi prinadlezhnosti naseleniia basseinov rek Oleneka i Anabary," SE, no. 2 (1952): 73–85; and B. O. Dolgikh, "O naselenii basseinov rek Oleneka i Anabary," SE, no. 2 (1952): 86–91.

[67] Not all "ethnic history" was written in response to hints, orders, and challenges from the government. A remarkable example of a work deliberately—and apparently

From the very beginning, the new academic ways of looking at the native northerners ran into serious conceptual problems. The appeals for an "ethnography of the present" and a movement away from "abstract sociology" seemed to fall on deaf ears. According to critics, "the lives of the people" was still nowhere to be found, and the descriptions of kolkhozes were bland, "schematic, and "skeletal."[68] As P. I. Kushner (Knyshev) put it, "Ethnographic science is the study of the ethnic or national specificity of peoples," which meant that economic plan fulfillment, not being ethnically specific, was not to be studied by ethnographers. Ethnicity, in his view, was about *byt*, or "private everyday life." To study ethnicity, scholars must follow—who else?—Shternberg and Bogoraz in learning the native languages, spending years in the field, and "touching on all aspects of *byt*."[69] This they did not do. The support that Kushner received seemed to indicate widespread frustration but his pleas would not be heeded for another quarter of a century. A lengthy description of private everyday life by a participant observer might put into question the Long Journey model, and that clearly could not be done yet. Moreover, if ethnography were to study the everyday lives of "real people,"[70] there would be no reason for it to concentrate on the rural population. Or, to use a more orthodox argument, if ethnography were to study "ethnic specificity," it should certainly study the working class, "the leading force of socialist nations."[71] The working class, however, was supposed to be internationalist by its very nature—Soviet rather than ethnically Russian or Nanai. And that meant that urban ethnography would also have to wait.

Historical narratives were in a similar predicament, which they had

---

inoffensively—divorced from the Party line is B. O. Dolgikh's classic *Rodovoi i plemennoi sostav*. (Some aspects of Dolgikh's work would be continued by his students Iu. B. Simchenko, A. V. Smoliak, Z. P. Sokolova, V. A. Tugolukov, and V. I. Vasil'ev, among others.) Another outstanding effort is Gurvich's *Etnicheskaia istoriia*.

[68] P. I. Kushner (Knyshev), "Ob etnograficheskom izuchenii kolkhoznogo krest'ianstva," *SE*, no. 1 (1952): 136–38; N. I. Vorob'ev, "K voprosu ob etnograficheskom izuchenii kolkhoznogo krest'ianstva," *SE*, no. 1 (1952): 142–46; N. A. Kisliakov, "K voprosu ob etnograficheskom izuchenii kolkhozov," *SE*, no. 1 (1952): 146–49; S. M. Abramzon, "Ob etnograficheskom izuchenii kolkhoznogo krest'ianstva," *SE*, no. 3 (1952): 145–50; I. I. Potekhin, "Novye zadachi etnografii v svete truda I. V. Stalina 'Ekonomicheskie problemy sotsializma v SSSR,'" *SE*, no. 2 (1953): 14.

[69] Kushner, "Ob etnograficheskom izuchenii kolkhoznogo krest'ianstva," pp. 135–41.

[70] Abramzon, "Ob etnograficheskom izuchenii," p. 148.

[71] "Deviatnadtsatyi s"ezd Kommunisticheskoi partii Sovetskogo Soiuza i voprosy etnografii," *SE*, no. 4 (1952): 7; P. I. Kushner (Knyshev), "Ob etnograficheskom izuchenii sotsialisticheskoi kul'tury i byta narodov SSSR," *SE*, no. 1 (1953): 15; "Za tesnoe sotrudnichestvo etnografov i istorikov," *SE*, no. 3 (1953): 3–8; "K itogam etnograficheskogo soveshchaniia 1956 goda," *SE*, no. 3 (1956): 3–4.

inherited from the Great Transformation theoreticians. Everyone agreed that before the Revolution the native northerners did not have classes as defined by Marx. This was the starting point for the Long Journey, the raison d'être of a given text, and the precondition for the claim of northern uniqueness (bypassing almost the whole of world history). Yet no one failed to describe the transition "from patriarchy to socialism" in terms of the class struggle, "which had affected the interests of all the indigenous inhabitants of the north and was therefore universal, implacable, and acute, posing as it did a question of life or death, of who conquers whom."[72] Where did these class antagonists come from? It could not be feudalism; it surely could not be capitalism; and only I. P. Kleshchenok offered the eccentric view that the Chukchi and Koriak economies had been founded on slaveholding.[73] There were two possibilities left: the prerevolutionary northerners had been at the stage of primitive (clan) communism, or they had been in a constant "precapitalist" transitiia, and thus not at any stage in particular. M. A. Sergeev, an early proponent of the more popular second view, had defined the native societies as "a peculiar combination of elements from different socioeconomic formations, starting with the archaic heritage of the most ancient clan society and ending with the seeds of capitalist relations" (hence the frequent use of the term "patriarchy," which has no precise meaning in traditional historical materialism).[74] In other words, this approach, which effectively dispensed with the Marxist scheme of social evolution while building the whole "skipped-stages" narrative upon it, dealt with the question by looking the other way. If Stalin could define language as neither base nor superstructure, yet not an "in-between" entity either ("because no such 'in-between' entities exist"),[75] then Stalinist historians could define the northern societies as neither clan nor capitalist nor anything in the middle. One thing remained certain: true native exploiters did not exist at the beginning of the story and did not exist at the end. They had appeared during collectivization for the express purpose of engaging in the class struggle and had then disappeared forever.

Finally, the "ethnic processes" genre suffered from the related problem of having to classify the "small peoples" as tribes (the ethnicity of primitive communism), nations (the ethnicity of capitalism and social-

[72] Lukovtsev, Minuia tysiacheletiia, pp. 140–41.

[73] Kleshchenok, Narody Severa, pp. 37–38. For broader implications of Soviet debates on the nature of primitive society, see Gellner, State and Society, pp. 12–15, 18–38.

[74] Sergeev, Nekapitalisticheskii put', p. 129.

[75] Stalin, Sochineniia (Stanford), 3:150.

ism), or narodnosti (the ethnicity of everything in between). The pre-Soviet correlation of national and socioeconomic stages was inconsistent but generally intelligible. The difficulty that the change from slaveholding to feudalism did not affect ethnicity was rendered harmless by ignoring slaveholding; the same difficulty for capitalism and socialism was resolved by distinguishing between capitalist and socialist nations without dwelling on the nature of the difference. But what was happening under socialism? There could clearly be no tribes, but did that mean that all ethnic communities in the USSR were nations? Apparently it did not, because most scholars referred to the native northerners as narodnosti; no one called them nations; and quite a few evaded the issue by always using the generic term narod (people). This was extremely significant because it meant that not only were the "small peoples" now inferior to the Russians (a special case)—they were also inferior to a large number of other Soviet peoples who were recognized as nations. What was the reason for such inequality, given that everyone shared the same (socialist) mode of production? Perhaps their "small numbers, intensive processes of cultural interaction, and so on," or possibly the "degree of development of general forms of national culture "[76] No one knew for sure, but one thing was obvious: in at least this particular case, the Long Journey seemed to have failed.

Fiction as History

While the social sciences were striving toward socialist realism, fiction was doing its best to accommodate the new scientific discoveries. The wartime disclosure of Russia's uniqueness and the introduction of the Imperial Age of Prophets presaging the Socialist Revolution resulted in a new version of the Long Journey, in which "the native's education" commenced with the arrival of the first Russian pioneer. It was a tale of adventure set in the exotic locale of the Far Eastern frontier and built around the struggle between righteous Russians and felonious foreigners, with the natives serving as witnesses for the prosecution and as legitimizers of Russian territorial claims.

Unlike the Bolshevik fathers from the standard Long Journey texts,

[76] "Deviatnadtsatyi s"ezd Kommunisticheskoi partii Sovetskogo Soiuza i voprosy etnografii," p 8; "Teoreticheskie problemy stroitel'stva kommunizma v SSSR i zadachi sovetskikh etnografov," SE, no. 5 (1958): 10.

the Russian frontiersmen proved their elect status and impressed their native Fridays by exhibiting a superhuman physical strength.

> Once armed Indians came to see Lukin. They obviously wanted to do away with the Creole. But Lukin did not lose his presence of mind. He chose the biggest Indian . . . , grabbed him by the shoulders, turned him around, and threw him out the door. The embarrassed Indian took a long time checking his bones to see if any were broken. But he made peace with Lukin right away and has been his best friend ever since.[1]

How could a timid and diminutive native not admire such people? "Locha [Russians] are big people. Oh, they are so very-very tall, such great shots, good fighters, and fast skiers."[2] Even the Americans from Alaska, in their usual Captain Blood accents, admitted as much: "Russians are devilishly energetic. . . . They reached this land almost a century before we did and settled it all the way down to California, that true gem of the Pacific."[3] When push came to shove, even a Russian woman—the hardy and hefty pioneer kind—could "[seize] two Tlinkits and [bump] their foreheads together so hard that both fell down unconscious."[4] But it was not energy and physical prowess alone that made the Russians special. Like the Bolsheviks, the Russian peasant explorers were the messengers of light (true faith), and to any unbiased observer, that light was always reflected in their eyes. Except that now the fatherly "teasing twinkle" had given way to the pristine color of the sky or the sea, which suggested the purity of the Russians' intentions and perhaps hinted at their racial superiority.

The reason for the "blue-eyed giants'"[5] presence in the forbidding northern wilderness was their unbounded patriotism and their desire to seek "the true destiny of the Fatherland."[6] Unlike "Motherland" (Rodina), which referred to the native soil and the socialist paradise, the term Fatherland (Otechestvo) stood for the empire (derzhava). Its destiny was to expand and thus to acquire "glory," the Otechestvo's most precious attribute.

In their patriotic endeavor the Russians were opposed by the Ameri-

---

[1] Markov, Iukonskii voron, p. 60. See also Ivan Kratt, Velikii okean [1941–1949], in Izbrannoe (Leningrad, 1951), p. 245; Nikolai Zadornov, Amur-Batiushka [1937–1940], in Sobranie sochinenii (Moscow, 1978), 1:211–16; Gor, Iunosha s dalekoi reki pp. 247–48.

[2] Nikolai Zadornov, Dalekii krai [1938–1948], in Sobranie sochinenii, 3:22.

[3] Nikolai Maksimov, Poiski schast'ia [1946–1952] (Blagoveshchensk, 1962), p. 12.

[4] Kratt, Velikii okean, in Izbrannoe, p. 252.

[5] Zadornov, Dalekii krai, in Sobranie sochinenii, 1:29, 33, 150.

[6] Kratt, Velikii okean, in Izbrannoe, p. 385.

cans, the Chinese, and the Japanese, whose sole purpose in being there was to pillage, rape, and murder. The devious and physically unimpressive Chinese and Japanese ("fat and looking like old women")[7] specialized in the former, whereas the more formidable Americans excelled at all three. They were depicted as pirates: romantic predators with no roots and no conscience. "In the boat stood a blackbearded Yankee. The tops of his high boots were fastened to his leather pants. He had a pistol in his belt and a cigar in his mouth."[8] He and others like him had respect for nothing but strength and affection for nothing but rum and dollars. They turned Chukotka into their own Treasure Island and made the icy shores resonate with hoarse shouts of "you dog," "you devil," and "Goddamn" (goddem).

> The pirates had to support Kotlean and other chiefs in their struggle against the Russians in order to keep their bandits' havens. Roberts was running too big an operation: his ships provided loot for the gambling dens of Macao and the markets of Hong-Kong; they circled Cape Horn on numerous occasions. The Indians could not be allowed to realize that the Russians were doing a better job protecting them from plunder than they would ever be able to manage on their own. The Russians showed too much concern for the savages.[9]

In this genre the natives' role was to test the heroes' true worth. Needless to say, the foreigners, especially the Americans who called the Chukchi savages when they were not calling them "niggers" (chernomazye),[10] never failed to flunk the test. Their ring-in-the-nose and patch-over-one-eye villainy brought back the most powerful images from the exotic and transparent world of adolescent mythology—as when one gang of bearded Americans is caught transporting chained Chukchi "for the Argentine planters"[11] and another is eventually prevented by the Russians from slaughtering and raping the whole population of a peaceful Nivkh settlement: "Their hearts were so cruel and merciless that, while committing injustice, they would not hear the wailing of old women, the complaining of old men, or the crying of young girls. As they were taking a wife away from her husband, a

---

[7] Gor, Iunosha s dalekoi reki, pp. 211–16; Zadornov, Dalekii krai, in Sobranie sochinenii, 1:39 (quotation).

[8] Maksimov, Poiski schast'ia, pp. 289–90.

[9] Kratt, Velikii okean, in Izbrannoe, p. 234.

[10] Maksimov, Poiski schast'ia, p. 288.

[11] Ibid., p. 347.

mother away from her children, or a daughter away from her father, they would laugh heartily."[12]

The Russian settlers and seamen, on the other hand, did all those things that their fictional Bolshevik predecessors (and chronological descendants) had been so good at: they protected the natives from foreigners, taught them useful skills, brought desirable goods, and generally treated them in a spirit of comradeship and benevolence.[13] Even Christianity (in its Orthodox version) was a worthy precursor of Communism, with the icons of St. Nicholas playing the role of Lenin's portraits.[14]

In this way, the natives had their own test to pass, faced as they all were with the inevitable choice between "good white people and bad white people," or rather between real and false ones.[15] After class, age, religion, and gender had done their jobs, the indigenous community would be unevenly split between those who chose falsehood (the wealthy old shamans and patriarchs) and those who opted for truth (everyone else). The alliance between the aboriginal majority and the Russians would result in the incorporation of native lands into the Fatherland and would be firmly cemented by a love union between a native Amazon and a Russian pioneer (or his native representative). In Markov's *Iukonskii voron*, for example, the girl proceeds to perish in the best "Caucasian Captive" tradition but not before she breaks the rules of the genre by producing a child—a living proof of Russian rights in the area.

Why then were the Amur and Sakhalin lost for so long, and Alaska lost forever? Because of the tsarist bureaucrats of German extraction, who spoke Russian with heavy accents and whose cosmopolitanism invariably led to treason (the loss of territory acquired by patriots). "A grimace of irritation distorted the baron's face.—'Motherlant, tearest, is where you live, and not where your kreat krantfather was porn. The

[12] Gor, *Iunosha s dalekoi reki*, p. 247. Zhores Troshev's *Bol'shoi Oshar* (Krasnoiarsk, 1987) is set in western Siberia, thus the "pirates" are White Russians. They do have foreign masters, however, and are functionally indistinguishable from Americans. "You've called the gold valley the Treasure Island," said the main villain to himself, "Now you are Flint! A typical pirate . . ." (p. 344).

[13] Markov, *Iukonskii voron*, p. 153; Maksimov, *Poiski schast'ia*, pp. 16, 156, 300, 318; Kratt, *Velikii okean*, in *Izbrannoe*, p. 389; Gor, *Iunosha s dalekoi reki*, pp. 27, 186, 228–29; Zadornov, *Dalekii krai*, in *Sobranie sochinenii*.

[14] Zadornov, *Dalekii krai*, in *Sobranie sochinenii*, 1:33; Markov, *Iukonskii voron*, p. 55; Maksimov, *Poiski schast'ia*, pp. 248, 297.

[15] Maksimov, *Poiski schast'ia*, pp. 300, 398, 432.

whole Earth is our Motherland.'"[16] Still, the patriots' cause was just, and in the end it had to prevail. "They were, after all, the first Russian border guards there,"[17] and as one such guard says in mid-1850 America: "The Russians have been prevented from extending their hand to the black and yellow peoples. But in one hundred years we'll settle the score!"[18] For the time being, it was the job of the natives to carry the flame and preserve the memory of their blue-eyed friends. In Nikolai Zadornov's Dalekii krai, one Nanai hero is in love with a fair-haired descendant of Russian Cossacks, and another inherits from his father an old Russian gun, which, in a prophetic dream, becomes as big as the whole of the ancient Amur. Even Alaska, Russia's "by right of discovery and settlement" and now a veritable hell for the indigenous peoples, might some day be retrieved. One of Markov's characters, a fugitive from across the Bering Straits, brings a handful of Alaskan soil with her. 'Let it mix with Russian earth, they are the same . . .' says the woman simply."[19]

Meanwhile, in the postwar Soviet Union, the Long Journey continued. Indeed, it picked up speed with the emergence (graduation) of the first generation of fully Soviet-educated native intellectuals trained as teachers and, in the most promising cases, promoted as authors of fiction. They wrote chiefly in Russian and for the Russian public, and became full-fledged (and, for the time being, eager) members of the Soviet "creative intelligentsia." Their works contributed significantly to the development of the Long Journey paradigm without introducing any important elements that had not been present in the oeuvre of their non-native teachers and friends. The Chukchi Iurii Rytkheu inherited Semushkin's plots and characters and the Nanai Grigorii Khodzher faithfully continued the ambitious epic begun by Fadeev and Zadornov. In this sense, the government's nationality policy was a resounding success: the socialist-realist fiction of the 1940s and 1950s reflected the official reality by not exhibiting any ethnic-based differences "in content."[20]

This does not mean, of course, that the content itself had not

---

[16] Ibid., p. 310. Cf. Zadornov, Dalekii krai, in Sobranie sochinerii, 236; Markov, Iukonskii voron, p. 153; and Kratt, Velikii okean, in Izbrannoe, pp. 383–85.

[17] Gor, Iunosha s dalekoi reki, p. 247.

[18] Markov, Iukonskii voron, p. 153.

[19] Gor, Iunosha s dalekoi reki, p. 247; Markov, Iukonskii voron, See also Maksimov, Poiski schast'ia, p. 16.

[20] I include in this section a number of later works that reproduce the master plot as formulated in the first postwar decade.

changed. Although the theme of a giant yet relatively painless leap forward from the remotest past continued to be central, some very important changes had taken place. First of all, with the leap definitely
accomplished by the mid-1930s, the Long Journey became a historical
theme, which could be introduced as a series of flashbacks by a triumphant but now serene protagonist.[21] It could be rescued from the past
by the discovery of a forgotten tribe presenting all the usual challenges[22] or recreated by the war, which temporarily resurrected the de-
funct creatures of darkness and thus provided new opportunities for
the heralds of light.[23] More important, the new certainties of ethnic
messianism and the Cold War, as well as the successful artistic discoveries of the novels set on the pre-Bolshevik frontier combined to affect
the nature of the journey itself.

In the literature of the 1930s the native subjects had been presented
with a single alternative to the status quo: the Bolshevik way to communism. In the 1940s and 1950s they almost always began their journey at the crossroads, with the foreigners providing the alternative. In
other words, the standard Long Journey texts had incorporated the perfect structural symmetry of the pioneer narratives (having moved to
Chukotka and the Amur for that purpose). On the one side there were
the Bolsheviks, all of them ethnic Slavs, and on the other, the foreigners, all of them villains.[24] Neither side had arrived unannounced:
the Bolsheviks were "the descendants of Ermak and Poiarkov" returning to "the historically Russian [iskonno russkie] lands," whereas
the Americans were "the descendants of ancient pirates" bent on "getting devilishly rich or starving to death like a hungry old wolf."[25] Once
again, the eyes were the mirror of the soul, and once again, the new
Bolsheviks resembled the Cossacks more than their fellow communists
from the 1930s: they all had eyes the color of "the blue sky on a long
clear day," "the blue sea water in still weather when the sea seems to
be asleep, with not even the tiniest wave moving," and sometimes like

[21] R. K. Agishev, Syn taigi (1947; Moscow, 1968); S M. Bytovoi, Poezd prishel na Tumnin (Leningrad, 1951), and Sady u okeana (Leningrad, 1957).

[22] Iurii Rytkheu, V doline malen'kikh zaichikov (Leningrad, 1972).

[23] N. E. Shundik, Bystronogii olen' [1947–1951], in Sobranie sochinenii v chetyrekh
tomakh (Moscow, 1983), vol. 1; V. N. Azhaev, Daleko ot Moskvy (Moscow, 1949). Azhaev's
novel is primarily concerned with other matters, but the native Long Journey is an important subplot.

[24] Azhaev's Zalkind was one of the last Jewish Bolsheviks.

[25] Azhaev, Daleko ot Moskvy, p. 30; T. Z Semushkin, Alitet ukhodit v gory (Moscow,
1974), pp. 127, 40.

both the sky and the sea plus "the radiant, warm little sun."[26] This was an ethnic-specific peculiarity, so that a reference to the Party secretary's "simple Russian face" might be enough to conjure up images of friendly elements.[27] Indeed, the Russian role of protecting the natives from foreigners became so important that on at least one occasion a fatherly Party secretary is replaced by a local chief of the KGB concerned with border violations (his face is "of the ordinary Russian type").[28] In another instance, the Long Journey is a transfer of a group of Eskimos from Chukotka to Vrangel' Island with the sole purpose of asserting Soviet territorial claims in the area. Thus the attainment of consciousness coincided with the realization of the sacred nature of national defense. Consciousness (civilization) was fully covered by patriotism, and patriotism was wholly built on the trust placed in one "tall, fair-haired Russian lad."[29]

The Americans' true character was also revealed in their eyes. Their dress (top boots and belts with pistols) had "predator" written all over it; their words ("goddem!") never failed to announce their plans; and their actions (rape and murder) spoke louder than words; but it was their eyes—colorless and "clouded"—that showed them for what they really were: dead souls and ghosts whose true place was not under the Jolly Roger but on the Flying Dutchman, condemned by a terrible curse to be eternal ambassadors of evil. In a less sinister vein and to make sure there was no mistake about their character, most foreigners had the usual stamp of falsehood in the shape of false teeth, glasses, grotesquely big noses, or extraordinary amounts of facial and body hair.[30] They represented Hell. "The accursed land" (usually Alaska) whence they came and whither they vanished unless apprehended by Soviet border guards or the secret police was a place where all human values were deliberately trampled on: parents abused their children; sons spat in their mothers' faces; friendship did not exist; and freedom meant

---

[26] Semushkin, Alitet ukhodit v gory, p. 122; N. Shundik, Belyi shaman, in Sobranie sochinenii, 3:68, 123. See also Bytovoi, Poezd prishel na Tumnin, p. 25; and Sady u okeana, p. 18; N. E. Shundik, Na Severe Dal'nem (Moscow, 1952), p. 9; Vladimir Sangi, Izgin (Moscow, 1969), pp. 105–6; and Anna Nerkagi, Severnye povesti (Moscow, 1983), p. 37.

[27] Rytkheu, V doline malen'kikh zaichikov, p. 36, and Ostrov nadezhdy (Moscow, 1987), p. 14; Iuvan Shestalov, Izbrannoe (Leningrad, 1976), p. 190.

[28] Iurii Rytkheu, Povesti (Leningrad, 1972), p. 228.

[29] Rytkheu, Ostrov nadezhdy, p. 14. After the creation of a nature reserve on the island in 1976 most of the settlers were moved back to the mainland.

[30] Semushkin, Alitet ukhodit v gory, pp. 40–49, 104, 118, 143–68, 187; Shundik, Na Severe Dal'nem, pp. 33, 37; Rytkheu, Ostrov nadezhdy, p. 27.

robbery. Most significant, all whites there were racists and all non-whites were persecuted, ridiculed, starved, and sometimes lynched (in the case of the Chinese, racism was replaced by cultural imperialism). If not for the "happy shore" across the water, there would be no hope of salvation.[31]

The happy shore, meanwhile, stood firm in spite of all attempts to penetrate it with spies and to contaminate it with U.S. canned food that caused diarrhea or with special germs prepared by Japanese doctors and tested by the FBI on the Alaskan natives.[32] In the Manichaean world of the postwar opposition of "the two systems," the USSR represented paradise, a place where dreams came true. Later, after Chingiz Aitmatov's "White Steamer" had become a common metaphor for lost innocence and elusive happiness, Iurii Rytkheu published a story about a Chukchi woman who is seduced by an American captain and then spends the rest of her life vainly waiting for the return of the "beautiful ship." Her last words sum up the wisdom of the only world she knows: "The most beautiful ships always pass by." But that is before the Long Journey. When the woman's daughter grows up and becomes subject to some of the same yearnings, she sees a large Soviet ship led by a newly trained Chukchi captain drop anchor opposite her settlement.[33] The wait was over—for her and for all the native peoples of the USSR. As Iuvan Shestalov put it,

> My shore is rich with people,
> Like a green meadow with flowers.
> The flock of white steamers
> Is thicker than a flock of swans.[34]

But what exactly was happiness? As elsewhere in postwar Soviet utopias (including field ethnography), the image of an urban paradise with tall buildings and gigantic construction sites had given way to a private bliss with cozy interiors and young mothers wearing "nice shawls with tassels."[35] When the ship finally arrived, it brought mar-

---

[31] See, in particular, Shundik, *Na Severe Dal'nem*; also Semushkin, *Alitet ukhodit v gory*; Shundik, *Bystronogii olen'*; in *Sobranie Sochinenii*, vol. 1; Grigorii Khodzher, *Belaia tishina* (Moscow, 1970), pp. 70–84; Iurii Rytkheu, *Inei na poroge* (Moscow, 1971), pp. 66–67, 151–58 and *Povesti*, pp. 133, 208–10.

[32] Shundik, *Na Severe Dal'nem*, pp. 336–41; Rytkheu, *Povesti*, p. 84.

[33] Rytkheu, *Povesti*, pp. 13–106.

[34] Iuvan Shestalov, *Shag cherez tysiacheletiia* (Moscow, 1974), p. 19.

[35] Cf. Dunham, In *Stalin's Time*, and Clark, *The Soviet Novel*, pp. 189–209.

riage and motherhood, and—one hoped—a TV set as well.[36] But some things had not changed. Most significant, paradise still meant an escape from freedom, understood as freedom for evil spirits, "freedom for wild beasts."[37] In a short story by Iu. I. Shamshurin, a domesticated reindeer escapes to the tundra only to be attacked and almost killed by a pack of wolves. Saved by its former master, the chastened animal "obediently follows him" home. "Live with the humans, recommends his savior, it's safer that way."[38] Lest one miss the analogy, Rytkheu has his Eskimos obediently follow the youthful Bolshevik to Vrangel' Island, that Soviet version of Avalon where "the main dreams of the inhabitants . . . come true" because all the important decisions are made for them by the "tall, fair-haired Russian lad."[39]

Once the choice between the worlds of light and darkness had been made, the tactics and the personality of the Russian lad became the center of the plot. The shamans and elders as American agents had a much harder time swaying their kinsmen than had the shamans and elders as agents of the past. In fact, they rarely tried, limiting themselves to single acts of terrorism and, when defeated, to piercing, "ratlike" squealing.[40] As a result, in the postwar Long Journeys the question of the allegiance of the undecided lost some of its importance because of the obvious unattractiveness of evil. The choice was not so much between "our way" and "the right way" but between the right (Russian) way and the wrong (non-Russian) way, with the unacceptability of the status quo apparent at the outset. In the novels set during the war the problem of choice was very marginal indeed (most protagonists had already attained the state of consciousness), and by the late 1950s the representations of the hell lying beyond the border had lost much of their prominence. Thus, with the question of whether to launch the expedition safely out of the way, the new generation of Long Journey texts concentrated on the best and fastest ways of reaching the final destination. Given that the Party emissary was in charge of all aspects of the project, the real challenge was to find the right man and provide him with the correct guidelines.

There were usually two main candidates who disagreed considerably, though amicably on how to deal with the natives. One was a burly,

[36] Rytkheu, *Povesti,* pp. 13–106; Roman Rugin, *Solntse nad snegami* (Sverdlovsk, 1986), pp. 35–36.

[37] Nerkagi, *Severnye povesti,* p. 60; Pavel Kile, *Idti vechno* (Novosibirsk, 1972), p. 24.

[38] Iu. I. Shamshurin, *U studenogo moria* (Moscow, 1952), p. 88.

[39] Rytkheu, *Ostrov nadezhdy,* p. 111 and passim.

[40] Azhaev, *Daleko ot Moskvy,* p. 279.

impulsive, gregarious, rough, naive, and lovable proletarian bully who wore a trenchcoat, brandished a revolver, relied on his class instincts, and defiantly disregarded "the objective conditions" as he herded the masses down the road to progress. He was, in other words, the hero of the Great Transformation, at his best when exposing enemies and storming fortresses but not altogether comfortable around nice shawls with tassels. He represented the heroic public past and was regarded with nostalgic respect and friendly condescension by those who possessed full consciousness, which was now called "culture." It was precisely that culture, understood as a formal education and proper manners, that distinguished Communist Number 2. He was solid, reserved, dignified, sensitive, and tactful. He had a college degree and exhibited inexhaustible attention to detail. Most important, he specialized in individuals rather than the "masses," skillfully playing on personal strengths and weaknesses and not forgetting his own private happiness, which was an important test of his ability as a leader.[41] Significantly, in novels set during or even after the war (as in the case of a discovery of a forgotten tribe), both could be ethnic natives, though clearly Russian "in content." They were, in fact, the erstwhile rebellious girls who had acquired culture, risen to leadership positions, and become men in the process (Party bosses were still fathers to their natives, which made the sex change obligatory).[42] In this version the outmoded "heroic" behavior could be attributed to youthful belligerence or insufficient education.[43]

The essence of the conflict is well expressed in the following exchange:

COMMUNIST NO. 1: But why, why are they the way they are, these people? You pull them with your hands and your teeth toward the light, toward clean air, but they drag their feet like a lassoed reindeer!

[41] Cf. Dunham, In Stalin's Time, pp. 22, 59–86, 188–90; Clark, The Soviet Novel, pp. 199–204. For examples, see Semushkin, Alitet ukhodit v gory; Shundik, Bystronogii olen', in Sobranie sochinenii, vol. 1; Azhaev, Daleko ot Moskvy; Khodzher, Belaia tishina; Rytkheu, Inei na poroge, and V doline malen'kikh zaichikov; Grigorii Khodzher, Amur shirokii (Moscow, 1973); Shundik, Belyi shaman, in Sobranie sochinenii, vol. 3; and Troshev, Bol'shoi Oshar.

[42] In socialist-realist novels set in ethnic Russia, the spontaneous hero of the 1930s was always a young man, whereas the mature and family-oriented leader could be a woman. The frequent reversal of this sequence in northern texts is due to the persistence of the noble savage paradigm: the best "unspoilt" natives were Amazons and wise elders, but the kindly missionary had to be male.

[43] Shundik, Bystronogii olen', in Sobranie sochinenii, vol. 1; Rytkheu, V doline malen'kikh zaichikov.

COMMUNIST NO. 2: Why pull them? We should reach out to them, reach out with our hearts, so that they will believe us and go by themselves. That is how we should convince them. When a person is being pulled, he will always drag his feet.[44]

"Reaching out" meant verbal persuasion, and skillful verbal persuasion always worked because the native northerners were essentially reasonable and thus ultimately open to the message, although in some difficult cases one still had to perform a few miracles (usually cure the sick). The true key was tact: if you burned idols, the idol-worshipers would rally and remonstrate; but if you chose the right words and guaranteed a plentiful harvest, they—and certainly their schooled children—would burn their idols themselves. As Pavel Glotov, a tactful Bolshevik, says: "I don't believe in the Russian God or in the Nanai *enduri*, or in any other gods. . . . But I respect people, respect you, and cannot allow anybody to offend you and your faith in my presence. You still believe in your shamans—well, go ahead and believe in them, but your children are not going to believe in them, just like I don't."[45]

In later novels, Communist Number 1 could be reinterpreted as a dry unimaginative bureaucrat who was not able to see the real people behind the forms and circulars, or even as an official of the secret police who thoughtlessly enforced all instructions even though some of them may have issued from "false" Russians.[46] The basic point, however, remained the same. The Party emissary among the indigenous peoples was not a fiery crusader but a respected village priest (a Russian Orthodox one, for he had to be married to do a good job).

The correctness of the new approach was testified to by the natives themselves, who were obviously "grateful to the Russian for not openly ridiculing their customs."[47] According to Khodzher's fishermen, "the Russians [unlike the Japanese] do not take the Nanai encampments away from them and do not kick them out into the forest."[48] A much more serious endorsement of the change in policy came from the Party higher-ups. In the fiction of the 1930s the Bolshevik usually acted alone, supported only by the name, and sometimes the image, of Lenin. In the postwar novels he always had a superior in the district Party

[44] Shundik, *Bystronogii olen'*, in *Sobranie sochinenii*, 1:61.

[45] Khodzher, *Belaia tishina*, p. 259.

[46] Khodzher, *Amur shirokii*; Shundik, *Belyi shaman*, in *Sobranie sochinenii*, vol. 3.

[47] Rytkheu, *Ostrov nadezhdy*, p. 247.

[48] Khodzher, *Belaia tishina*, p. 240.

headquarters whose job it was to appear at crucial moments and legitimize the politics of personal touch. This was particularly important if the junior Communist was a native, in which case the Russian mentor was a surrogate father and life-long sponsor. In terms of plot development, however, the most important test of the "native disciples" was their amorous and professional success. In almost all the postwar Long Journey texts the central characters—both the Spontaneous Native Disciple and the Native Local Leader (both male and sometimes one and the same person)—faced serious challenges on two fronts. One was the usual task of overcoming backwardness and getting the rank-and-file natives to follow suit, the other, a determined effort to be united with a beautiful woman kept away and usually abused by her traditionalist husband or father. The dramatic denouement would involve the creation of a kolkhoz (fulfillment of a plan) and the capture of the love interest. The hero would be rewarded by being married and promoted at the same time.[49]

This scheme accorded well with the dominant master plot of the socialist-realist literature of the first postwar decade.[50] Indeed, in its basic form the Long Journey paradigm survived into the 1980s, reenacting the unprecedented leap "from patriarchy to socialism" over and over again for as long as it remained the officially accepted view of the past. This was precisely the problem, however. The journey having been formally completed, this kind of narrative had no choice but to remain "historical" at a time when academic indigenous studies and Party ideologues were demanding more representations of the socialist present. Fictional representations of the socialist present might bring about the demise of the fictional native: ethnographers could define their field as the study of phenomena "national in form," but the writers were supposed to deal with content, or "human souls," which were now free from ethnicity. Or were they? Even within the framework of the existing Long Journey narratives, some elements were problematic. The attainment of consciousness meant Russification in content and increasingly in form, as enlightened natives moved into Russian-type houses and bought bedspreads and bicycles (potentially a serious threat to ethnography). It also meant skilled jobs and marriage, just as the success of the Russian missionary was marked by promotion and marriage. The equality was seemingly achieved—except that for some

---

[49] Shundik's *Bystronogii olen'*, in particular, has an almost Dickensian ending with wedding bells all around.

[50] Clark, *The Soviet Novel*, pp. 204–9.

reason the Russian missionary never married a native woman. Was it because she was not enlightened (Russian) enough and an affair with her would turn him into another "Caucasian Captive"? Soviet fiction of the 1960s and 1970s would address itself to this issue. Now the time had come for it to catch up with the present.

"Protesting oil development in the tundra," from *Severnye prostory*, no. 39 (March 1991). Courtesy of Vladimir Zharov.

10

The Endangered Species

They call—wild voices call thee o'er the main
Back to thy free and boundless woods again.
      —Felicia Dorothea Hemans, "The Child of the Forests"

Planners' Problems and Scholars' Scruples

While the fictional natives continued to live mostly in the past and the ethnographers' small peoples were concentrating on their newly transformed "everyday lives," the native northerners themselves were witnessing the unabated growth of industrial development. During the war the circumpolar mines worked by convict labor had grown in importance and in size, with the Kolyma road network expanding tenfold and the Noril'sk mining region emerging as a major nickel-producing center. In 1944 the inmates of Noril'sk defeated the inmates of Dal'stroi in "socialist competition" to become the best industrial enterprise of the Peoples' Commissariat of Internal Affairs (secret police).[1] In the next two decades the rate of industrial expansion continued to accelerate, and by the late 1960s the traditional hunting grounds and reindeer pastures of the far north had become the major source of Soviet phosphates, nickel, gold, tin, mica, and tungsten, as well as timber. At the same time, northwestern Siberia emerged as the largest oil- and gas-producing center in the USSR and thus the focus of a new nation-wide development strategy.[2]

[1] Kiselev, *Sever raskryvaet bogatstva*, pp. 42–47.
[2] Ibid., pp. 70–84; A. P. Tiurdenev and V. P. Andreev, "Osnovnye napravleniia v razvitii sel'skogo i promyslovogo khoziaistva Severa SSSR," *Problemy Severa*, no. 13 (1968): 9; I. S. Gurvich, "Printsipy leninskoi natsional'noi politiki i primenenie ikh na Krainem Severe," in *Osushchestvlenie leninskoi natsional'noi politiki u narodov Krainego*

As far as the indigenous inhabitants of these areas were concerned, the crucial change came after Stalin's death in 1953, when the labor-camp system ceased to be the basis for industrial growth and Dal'-stroi—the largest concentration of convict labor and the last vestige of special-status territory anywhere in the north—was transformed into a regular province. From then on, the problem of northern manpower would become extremely acute and the future of the local residents would depend on the manner of its solution. The solution was never in doubt, however: even if one disregarded the GUSMP experience and assumed that the native northerners would make willing and efficient proletarians, their numbers were totally inadequate for the purpose. As early as 1956 the Central Committee of the Party and the USSR Council of Ministers appealed to the nation's young people to go to the north and take up the jobs vacated by their convict parents.[3] To ensure large-scale migration, special northern bonuses and vacation privileges were greatly expanded, and as the native foragers were still unable to feed the new arrivals, central supply agencies were to increase their (highly unprofitable) activities in the area. By 1959, the population of the seven remaining autonomous (formerly national) districts was 349,510, including 70,049 native northerners. Twenty years later the numbers were respectively 997,556 and 81,012. The immigrant population had doubled in the Iamalo-Nenets district, tripled in Chukotka, and increased by the factor of 4.6 in the Khanty-Mansi autonomous district. The proportion of the indigenous population had dropped from 27.7 to 22.6 percent in the relatively undeveloped Koriak district, from 25.8 to 9.0 percent in Chukotka, and from 14.5 to 3.2 percent in the oil-rich Khanty-Mansi district.[4]

Having become irrelevant to the industrialization effort (and thus to the all-powerful central ministries) as sources of labor or food supply, the native settlements and encampments became economically "unviable" and thus useless. The ministries in charge of the economic development of the north were not responsible to the local administrators, and the local administrators, whose performance was measured by plan fulfillment, were not responsive to native demands, which had little to do with production quotas. Something needed to be done, and in 1957 the Central Committee of the Party and the Council of Ministers issued a joint decree urging all developers big and small to involve

---

Severa, ed. I. S. Gurvich (Moscow, 1971), pp. 35–36; S. V. Slavin, *Osvoenie Severa Sovetskogo Soiuza* (Moscow, 1982).

[3] Kiselev, *Sever raskryvaet bogatstva*, p. 63.

[4] I. S. Gurvich, ed., *Etnicheskoe razvitie narodnostei Severa v Sovetskii period* (Moscow, 1987), pp. 104–5.

the aboriginal peoples in their industrial and large-scale agricultural projects—mostly through affirmative action (preferential recruitment and promotion) but also through the intensification of the traditional reindeer-breeding, hunting, and fishing economies.[5]

To oversee this process, a special Group (later redesignated a "section," *otdel*) for the Economic and Cultural Development of the Peoples of the Extreme North was created in 1962 at the Council of Ministers of the Russian Federation. Similar sections were formed in several northern provinces and eventually in almost half the ministries.[6] Thus the watchdogs belonged to the same ministerial structure as the people they were supposed to supervise. Moreover, given the unequal importance attached to industrial growth and aboriginal development, the new defenders of the native interests were actually subordinate to those who, in the words of the Party decree, "[did] not pay sufficient attention to the customs and traditions of the local population."[7] According to S. I. Balabanov, who headed the Moscow Section in the 1980s, the system "was not totally efficient" because of ministerial and local preoccupation with the plan at the expense of everything else.[8] Theoretically the aboriginal sections answered to the provincial officials as well as to the central section, but they drew their salaries from the local executive committees. It was perhaps no surprise, therefore, that the "*oblispolkom* heads did not always show respect for the sections' activities."[9] Meanwhile, the Council of Ministers of the Russian Federation did not always show respect for its own northern section, which, in the words of its long-time chief, consisted mostly of failed ministerial and provincial bureaucrats overseeing their more successful former colleagues.

But even if the Section for the Economic and Cultural Development of the Peoples of the Extreme North had consisted of passionate crusaders with a large budget of their own, the crucial problem remained that they had no clear task and no standards. The only formal criteria of the section's work (and of the natives' welfare) were the plans put together by the provincial executive committees themselves. In other words, the section could only check to see if northern officials were

[5] "Postanovlenie TsK KPSS i Soveta Ministrov SSSR 16 marta 1957 'O merakh po dal'neishemu razvitiiu ekonomiki i kul'tury narodnostei Severa,'" in *Resheniia partii i pravitel'stva po khoziaistvennym voprosam* (Moscow, 1968), 4:331–36.

[6] S. I. Balabanov, personal interview, 18 June 1990. See also I. S. Gurvich, "Printsipy leninskoi natsional'noi politiki i primenenie ikh na Krainem severe," in *Osushchestvlenie*, pp. 34–35.

[7] "Postanovlenie TsK KPSS," p. 333.

[8] Balabanov, personal interview, 18 June 1990.

[9] Ibid.

fulfilling their own plans—because the "small peoples" were not included in any other. According to Balabanov, the section never tired of asking Gosplan to mention the northerners as a separate category. If nothing else, that would have justified the section's existence and given them something to work with. It was not to be, however, and the fate of the circumpolar peoples continued to depend on the imperatives of industrial development and the needs of the growing non-native majority.

In light of these needs and imperatives, most aboriginal groups were an irritating distraction and a financial drain, all the more exasperating because their "inefficiency" seemed to be the result of sheer obstinacy. Even while fishermen appeared to be idle in the winter and reindeer-breeders' wives appeared to be underemployed (and exploited) throughout the year, larger market-oriented enterprises, which often subsidized native schools and hospitals, desperately needed labor. In the 1950s most local officials, unchecked by effective outside agencies, had arrived at the only solution that seemed to make sense under the circumstances: forced resettlement and "consolidation" (ukrupnenie). Small cooperatives based on traditional social units and regarded as both hopeless producers of planned goods and wasteful recipients of subsidies were to be replaced by large state-run enterprises capable of purchasing modern technology and subject to immediate supervision by provincial administrators. By the 1980s, most native kolkhozy had been liquidated or transformed into sovkhozy, and many native northerners had been moved to large prefab settlements where they were expected to earn their pay by working rationally in productive branches of the economy. In the Khanty-Mansi autonomous district, the number of aboriginal settlements had dropped from 650 to 126; in Chukotka, almost all kolkhozy had become sovkhozy; on Sakhalin, all eleven traditional Nivkh settlements in the Nogliki district had disappeared; and on the Kola Peninsula, only one Saami village had remained officially "national" (although it was 86 percent non-native).[10]

"Rational and productive" work meant that in their new places of

---

[10] Z. P. Sokolova, ed., *Etnokul'turnoe razvitie narodnostei Severa v usloviiakh nauchno-tekhnicheskogo progressa na perspektivu do 2005 g.* (Moscow, 1989), pp. 39–40 (at least twenty Khanty settlements were closed between 1979 and 1987); Kiselev, *Sever raskryvaet bogatstva*, pp. 38–39; Fondahl, 'Native Economy,' pp. 262–69; Gurvich, ed., *Etnicheskoe razvitie*, pp. 92–94; Gurvich, "Printsipy," in *Oshushchestvlenie*, p. 36; E. E. Selitrennik, "Nekotorye voprosy kolkhoznogo stroitel'stva v Chukotskom natsional'nom okruge," *SE*, no. 1 (1965): 13–27; Antonova, "Pis'mo predsedateliu Soveta Ministrov RSFSR tov Vlasovu A. V., 11 November 1988 (unpublished), p. 1. For a remarkable treatment of resettlements on Sakhalin, see Grant, "Siberia Hot and Cold." See also "Chaut nad Paren'iu," *SP*, no. 2 (1988): 9–10; Vladimir Sangi, "Chtoby krona ne ogoli-

residence the indigenous northerners were either to abandon their traditional pursuits altogether or to transform them in order to maximize
their output. Thus, reindeer breeders were to adopt "nomadism as production" (*proizvodstvennoe kochevanie*) as opposed to "nomadism as
a way of life" (*bytovoe kochevanie*). Specialized brigades consisting of
five to ten professional male herders assisted by one or two female
"tent-employees" (*chum-rabotnitsy*) would work shifts in the tundra
and their wives would find full-time employment on dairy farms, fox-
breeding farms, and in other new enterprises. In the meantime, their
elderly parents would enjoy their newfound leisure with the help of
radio, television, and "houses of culture," and the children would continue to attend boarding schools where they would learn skills that
were relevant in an industrial society.[11]

It did not quite work out that way, at least not according to the new
cohort of Soviet ethnographers—educated in the postwar atmosphere
of personal touch, forever changed by the experience of the "Thaw,"
secure in the increasingly stable world of the academic establishment,
and hostile to the utopianism, violence, and enforced equality of the
Cultural Revolution as well as to the "overly bureaucratic" and "un-
intelligentsia-like" high-handedness of the newly cultured administrators. By the mid-1960s these young scholars (fated to remain young for
a quarter of a century until Gorbachev restored the flow of time as they
understood it) were reaching professional prominence and witnessing
without regret the slow departure of their teachers, most of them cultural revolutionaries turned bureaucrats. Trained in the age of fieldwork and "national peculiarities," the 1960s generation tended to
identify themselves with their subjects (a particular native community) and their subject (ethnicity). Thus even as they engaged in the
obligatory discourse on leaps into socialism and ethnic fusion, they
had begun questioning the means to these ends and ultimately the
meaning and morality of both socialism and ethnic fusion.

First of all, it turned out that not everybody agreed that the new modern settlements were centers of productive labor, unpretentious afflu-
ence, and cultured entertainment. Russian-type houses were often too
cold, their doors faced the main street and were exposed to the winds,
and their rectangular shape contributed to the formation of large snow-
drifts. Due to melting permafrost, some new houses tilted southward

---

las'," *Literaturnaia gazeta*, 15 February 1989, and "Posleslovie k sudu i sledstviiu," SP
no. 2 (1988): 6–9; A. I. Pika "Paren'—poselok morskikh okhotnikov i kuznetsov," 1987
(unpublished); and Mikhail Chlenov and Igor Krupnik, "Aziatskie eskimosy: Istoriia
akkul'turatsii na beregu Beringova proliva," 1990 (unpublished), chap. 4, pp. 4–7.

[11] Sokolova, ed., *Etnokul'turnoe razvitie*, pp. 20–22.

and had to be constantly propped up. Such widely advertised ameni-
ties as plumbing, sewage, and central heating were either nonexistent
or did not function properly. The more enterprising tenants had added
storehouses, smokehouses, and other necessities of northern living,
whereas others had pitched tents in the courtyard and converted the
new dwellings to nonresidential use. Some "consolidated" settlements
were miles away from the nearest hunting or fishing sites, which meant
that many males were never "at home"; whereas most fox-breeding
farms had proved unprofitable, which meant that many females were
unemployed. Consequently, married couples had the option of staying
unemployed at home, busy (and, in the wife's case, unpaid) at a remote
site, or living separately for long periods of time.

The situation of the nomadic herders was even more difficult. As it
was obviously impossible to settle reindeer, the settlement of reindeer
breeders became synonymous with "nomadism as production," or nomadism by husbands without wives or parents (children were in
boarding schools and thus not subject to discussion). One proposed
solution was to separate the herds and the herders by fencing off large
areas for "free pasture," but it was very expensive, probably inefficient,
and generally amounted to a return to hunting. Another possibility was
to reverse the equation completely and, rather than settling nomads,
make settlements nomadic by pulling Russian-type houses around by
tractors. This did not seem to be practicable, either: the costs were high
and the damage to the fragile tundra pastures, irreversible. The solution preferred by most experts was to have the herders take turns with
the herd, working relatively short shifts and spending much of the time
in the settlement with their families. Given the distances covered by
reindeer in the course of the year, however, it appeared that the implementation of this plan would have to wait for the time when each native
settlement could afford a helicopter.

In the meantime, the reindeer breeders would have to live separately
from their wives or even without wives altogether as more and more
young women refused to enter into long-distance relationships with
low-status nomads. The number of single mothers was growing precipi-
tously; in many cases the fathers were immigrant contract laborers, and
in all cases there was no economic price to pay since the state assumed
full responsibility for all indigenous children from a very early age.
To complete the vicious circle, the products of the state-run boarding-
schools were completely unprepared for the chores that Russian teachers knew nothing about and the Russo-centered education system ignored as backward. Successive generations of native graduates (and
dropouts) found themselves unwilling and unable to rejoin their elders

or even communicate with them in their mother tongue, and the modern equipment that was supposed to render traditional skills obsolete was either not in evidence or manned by better-prepared immigrants.[12]

This picture was usually framed by cheerful accounts of growing production, clean clothes, cozy interiors, and rising consciousness, as well as practical suggestions on how to correct a given "flaw" (nedostatok), but its wider implications were very disturbing indeed. Most scholars agreed that the indigenous northerners were adopting a version of the "Soviet culture," but some seemed to suggest that they had not been very successful in terms of that culture and thus were becoming Soviet but not equal. Moreover, there could be no doubt that the absolute superiority of Soviet culture was no longer taken for granted. Indeed, some authors claimed that certain indigenous traditions represented "accumulated experience" and thus were actually better than their "formal" (that is, bureaucratic) Soviet substitutes, and that in any event culture change was a complex and painful process that could result in social and psychological dislocations.[13] I. S. Gurvich even suggested that "the rapid dissolution of the Upper Kolyma Yukagir [was] hardly a positive phenomenon" because "unfortunately, the rapid and drastic destruction of a way of life often results in the disappearance of cultural values created by various ethnic groups."[14] In other words, ethnic diversity was to be preserved—apparently because of its intrinsic value and possibly because it was ethnography's only raison d'être.

This was going too far. In 1963 the official guardian of theoretical purity, the journal Kommunist, published an article denouncing Soviet

[12] V. A. Tugolukov, review of Perekhod k sotsializmu malykh narodnostei Severa, by V. P. Uvachan, SE, no. 4 (1959): 143–44; I. S. Gurvich, "Sovremennye etnicheskie protsessy, protekaiushchie na severe Iakutii," SE, no. 5 (1960): 3–11, and "O putiakh dal'neishego pereustroistva ekonomiki i kul'tury narodov Severa," SE, no. 4 (1961): 45–57; V. I. Vasil'ev, Iu. B. Simchenko and Z. P. Sokolova, "Problemy rekonstruktsii byta malykh narodov Severa," SE, no. 3 (1966): 9–22; Iu. B. Strakach, Narodnye traditsii i podgotovka sovremennykh promyslovo-sel'skokhoziaistvennykh kadrov. Taezhnye i tundrovye raiony Sibiri (Novosibirsk, 1966); V. A. Tugolukov, review of Narodnye traditsii, by Iu. B. Strakach, SE, no. 3 (1968): 50–53; I. S. Gurvich, "Desiat' let deiatel'nosti sektora severa Instituta etnografii SSSR," Problemy Severa 11 (1967): 258–61; Z. P. Sokolova, "Preobrazovaniia v khoziaistve, kul'ture i byte Obskikh ugrov," SE, no. 5 (1968): 25–39; V. V. Leont'ev, Khoziaistvo i kul'tura narodov Chukotki (Novosibirsk, 1973); I. S. Gurvich and Ch. M. Taksami, "Vklad sovetskikh etnografov v osushchestvlenie leninskoi natsional'noi politiki na Severe," in Leninizm i problemy etnografii, ed. Iu. V. Bromlei and R. F. Its (Leningrad, 1987), p. 191. For Western analyses, see Ethel Dunn, "Educating the Small Peoples of the Soviet North: The Limits of Cultural Change," ArA 5, no. 1 (1970): 1–31 and "Education and the Native Intelligentsia in the Soviet North: Further Thoughts on the Limits of Cultural Change," ArA 6, no. 2 (1970).
[13] See, especially, Strakach, Narodnye traditsii, and Leont'ev, Khoziaistvo i kul'tura.
[14] Gurvich, "Sovremennye etnicheskie protsessy," p. 10.

ethnography for insufficient attention to Party directives relating to nationalities policy. In a special mention Gurvich was told not to worry about the so-called cultural values because the developments that he had described "were all positive."[15] The comment was not altogether fair, given that Gurvich's article had appeared before the Twenty-Second Congress made clear the Party's views on the subject. In any case, the ethnographers duly apologized[16] and embarked on the study of what the new Program of the Communist Party of the Soviet Union called "a new stage in the development of national relations in the USSR in which the nations will draw still closer together until complete unity is achieved."[17] For the next two decades, the northern ethnographers led by Gurvich concentrated primarily on how ethnic "merging" *(sblizhenie)* was occurring in practice. Ethnographic Long Journeys remained prominent ("upon entering any house one will find that the people who live there do not lack anything at all: good furniture, carpets in many houses, radios, cameras, and record players"),[18] but it was the study of "ethnic processes" that came to dominate the field. The chief assignment was to study "various forms of interrelationships among ethnic groups," with particular emphasis on the factors that "stimulate the emergence of common elements in the life of nations and *narodnosti*."[19] As theory developed, "merging" (leading to eventual *sliianie*, or "fusion") was broken down into "consolidation" (for instance, of various Evenk groups into one ethnicity), "assimilation" (for instance, of other Evenk groups by the Russians or the Yakuts), and "integration" or "merging" proper (for instance, of the Evenk, Yakut, and Russians into one Soviet nation).[20] All of these "eth-

---

[15] A. Artsikhovskii, N. Vorob'ev, D. Gusev, and S. Smirnov, "Zhurnal sovetskikh etnografov," *Kommunist*, no. 5 (1963): 124–27. See Boris Chichlo, "Trente années d'anthropologie *(etnografija)* soviétique," *Revue des études slaves* 57, no. 2 (1985): 312–13.

[16] A. G. Podol'skii, "Rasshirennoe zasedanie redaktsionnoi kollegii zhurnala 'Sovetskaia etnografiia,' posviashchennoe obsuzhdeniiu retsenzii 'Zhurnal sovetskikh etnografov,'" *SE*, no. 5 (1963): 122–23.

[17] Jan F. Triska, ed., *Soviet Communism: Programs and Rules* (San Francisco, 1962), p. 107.

[18] A. V. Smoliak, "Iuzhnye oroki," *SE*, no. 1 (1965): 34.

[19] I. S. Gurvich, "Nekotorye problemy etnicheskogo razvitiia narodov SSSR," *SE*, no. 5 (1967): 63; Iu. V. Arutiunian and L. M. Drobizheva, "Sovetskii obraz zhizni: Obshchee i natsional'no-osobennoe," *SE*, no. 3 (1976): 11.

[20] There could be variations. For the debate on the nature of "ethnic processes," see V. N. Gardanov, B. O. Dolgikh, and T. A. Zhdanko, "Osnovnye napravleniia etnicheskikh protsessov u narodov SSSR," *SE*, no. 4 (1961): 9–29; T. A. Zhdanko, "Etnograficheskoe izuchenie protsessov razvitiia i sblizheniia sotsialisticheskikh natsii v SSSR," *SE*, no. 6 (1964): 16–24; Gurvich, "Nekotorye problemy etnicheskogo razvitiia"; V. I. Kozlov, "Sovremennye etnicheskie protsessy v SSSR," *SE*, no. 2 (1969): 60–72; Iu. V. Bromlei

nic processes" could be observed and predicted by studying the functioning of language (particularly bilinguism), intermarriage, self-identification, and, to a much lesser extent, such traditional Long Journey ingredients as changes in clothing, diet, and house interiors.[21] The consensus was that the circumpolar peoples, like all Soviet peoples with the apparent exception of the Russians, were quickly consolidating only to be assimilated or merged in the end. On the one hand, their national existence was characterized by "the overcoming of the former isolation of ethnographic and local groups, the leveling of dialectal differences, the obliteration of tribal distinctions, the formation of modern literature and professional forms of art, and the consolidation of a national consciousness."[22] On the other hand, it demonstrated their gradual but irreversible merging with other ethnic groups "on the basis of the commonality of the socialist content of their culture."[23] This tension is reminiscent of contemporary Western discussions on the relationship between nationalism and the spread of "cultural uniformity" in the wake of growing consumerism—except that in the USSR the cause-effect sequence was reversed and the tension was expected to disappear "dialectically" in the same way as the state would grow ever stronger until it withered away.

Even as these "ethnic processes" were being catalogued by occasionally agonizing ethnographers, the underlying theoretical principles remained shaky. First of all, no amount of "consolidating" seemed sufficient for the native northerners to become nations. Equal or not, they remained Socialist narodnosti through the mid-1980s even though no one seemed to know what that meant or even cared to define the term. One thing was certain: the ethnicity of the circumpolar peoples seemed qualitatively different from that of the Russians or the Georgians in spite of the presumably common economic basis that

---

and V. I. Kozlov, "Leninizm i osnovnye tendentsii etnicheskikh protsessov v SSSR," SE no. 1 (1970): 3–14; I. S. Gurvich, "Sovremennoe napravlenie etnicheskikh protsessov v SSSR," SE, no. 4 (1972): 16–33; idem, "Etnokul'turnoe sblizhenie narodov SSSR," SE, no. 5 (1977): 23–35; and idem, "Osobennosti sovremennogo etapa etnokul'turnogo razvitiia narodov Sovetskogo Soiuza," SE, no. 6 (1982): 15–27.

[21] Along with numerous articles in Sovetskaia etnografiia during the 1960s, 1970s, and early 1980s, see Preobrazovaniia v khoziaistve i kul'ture i etnicheskie protsessy u narodov Severa (Moscow, 1970); I. S. Gurvich, ed., Etnogenez i etnicheskaia istoriia narodov Severa (Moscow, 1975); idem, ed., Etnogenez narodov Severa (Moscow, 1980); and idem, ed., Etnokul'turnye protsessy u narodov Sibiri i Severa (Moscow, 1985).

[22] Gurvich, "Sovremennye napravleniia etnicheskikh protsessov," p. 25.

[23] L. P. Potapov, "Etnograficheskoe izuchenie sotsialisticheskoi kul'tury i byta narodov SSSR," SE, no. 2 (1962): 16.

everyone in the USSR shared. Were there other ways to distinguish among different kinds of ethnicity? What did ethnicity mean, anyway?

After Tolstov's departure in 1967 these questions came to the fore as the new director of the Institute of Ethnography Iu. V. Bromlei led his colleagues on a long search for their elusive subject. During the next two decades Soviet ethnographers, surrounded by the conflicting claims of the newly legalized fields of sociology, psychology, and genetics wrestled with the concept of ethnos. It was not an easy task: ethnos was claimed to be an ontological reality, yet none of its traditional elements (language, territory, and so on) were essential—except for self-designation, that is—which seemed to take one away from the ontological reality. With Lysenko and "Soviet Darwinism" out of the way, Bromlei suggested "endogamy broadly defined" as "the objective mechanism of ethnic integration." In the final analysis, each ethnos strove for genetic homogeneity; any significant violation of endogamy led to the destruction of the ethnos.[24] The potentially very disturbing implications of this thesis became apparent soon enough, and only one scholar (L. N. Gumilev) went all the way and proclaimed ethnos to be a biological category. Bromlei stepped back and was supported by most other ethnographers in saying that ethnoses tended to overlap with genetic populations but ought not to be deduced from them. Ethnic consciousness resulted in endogamy that could result in the creation of a race (the Japanese were cited as an example), but not the other way around.[25]

Complicating matters further was the change that had taken place in the meaning of ethnicity. Stalin may have been wrong with his tribe–narodnost'–nation paradigm, but certainly ethnicity had signified different things under "primitive communism" and socialism, as well as for the modern Ul'ch and the Estonians as described by Soviet ethnographers. Accordingly, Bromlei devoted a great deal of time to building complex hierarchies of ethnic communities, always with the same general result: the higher up on the evolutionary ladder the ethnic community found itself, the less "ethnic" it was. Tribal units were totally "permeated" with ethnicity; later feudal communities had lost some of it (especially in the social sphere); whereas developed nations had retained it only in their "spiritual culture," most things material having been leveled. Once again, therefore, ethnic reality eluded those who sought it: in the USSR, at least, it was mostly in people's heads.[26]

[24] Iu. V. Bromlei, "Etnos i endogamiia," SE, no. 6 (1969): 84–91.

[25] "Obsuzhdenie stat'i Iu. V. Bromleia 'Etnos i endogamiia,'" SE, no. 3 (1970): 86–103.

[26] Iu. V. Bromlei and O. I. Shkaratan, "O sootnoshenii istorii, etnografii i sotsiologii," SE, no. 3 (1969): 6; Iu. V. Bromlei, "Opyt tipologizatsii etnicheskikh obshchnostei," SE,

Also, as it turned out, ethnicity varied according to class, gender, geographical area, and even individual personality. By the mid-1980s the territory over which Tolstov's ethnography had ruled uncontested was being carved up by ethnosociology, ethnopsychology, ethnohistory, ethnoecology, ethnogeography, and ethnodemography—and not everyone bothered with the "ethno" part.[27] Some of these trends were pioneered by members of the Thaw generation but the greatest impetus came from a new cohort of young scholars who had read neither Marr nor Stalin but had studied a lot of English and were generally as interested in Western scholarship as they were skeptical about what they saw as Soviet reductionism.[28] The search for ontological ethnicity came to an almost complete halt: whatever was left of "ethnography proper" was now increasingly being defined as the study of "culture," or "the culture of everyday life" (bytovaia kul'tura).[29] By the 1990s

---

no. 5 (1972): 61–81; Iu. V. Bromlei and V. N. Basilov, "Sovetskaia etnograficheskaia nauka v deviatoi piatiletke," SE no. 1 (1976): 8; Iu. V. Bromlei, "K voprosu ob osobennostiakh etnograficheskogo izucheniia sovremennosti," SE, no. 1 (1977): 8. For Western critiques, see Tamara Dragadze, "The Place of 'Ethnos' Theory in Soviet Anthropology," in Soviet and Western Anthropology, ed. Ernest Gellner (New York, 1980), pp. 161–70, and "Some Changes in Perspectives on Ethnicity Theory in the 1980s: A Brief Sketch," Cahiers du monde russe et soviétique 35, no. 2–3 (1990): 205–12; Stephen P. Dunn, "New Departures in Soviet Theory and Practice of Ethnicity," Dialectical Anthropology 1 (1975): 64–69; Gellner, State and Society, pp. 115–36; and Debra L. Schindler, "The Political Economy of Ethnic Discourse in the Soviet Union" (Ph.D. diss., University of Massachussetts, Amherst, 1990), esp. pp. 18–77.

[27] See, for example, Iu. V. Arutiunian, "Opyt sotsial'no-etnicheskogo issledovaniia (po materialam Tatarskoi ASSR)," SE, no. 4 (1986): 3–13; V. I. Kozlov and V. V. Pokshishevskii, "Etnografiia i geografiia," SE, no. 1 (1973): 3–13; V. I. Kozlov and G. V. Shelepov, "'Natsional'nyi kharakter' i problemy ego issledovaniia," SE, no. 2 (1973): 69–82; L. M. Drobizheva, "Ob izuchenii sotsial'no-psikhologicheskikh aspektov natsional'nykh otnoshenii," SE no. 4 (1974): 15–25; G. V. Starovoitova, "K issledovaniiu etnopsikhologii gorodskikh zhitelei," SE, no. 3 (1976): 45–56; I. I. Krupnik, "Stanovlenie krupnotabunnogo olenevodstva u tundrovykh nentsev," SE, no. 2 (1976): 57–69; V. I. Kozlov, "Osnovnye problemy etnicheskoi ekologii," SE, no. 1 (1983): 3–15; N. G. Volkova, "Etnicheskaia istoriia: Soderzhanie poniatiia," SE, no. 5 (1985): 16–25; and A. I. Pika, "Gomeostaz v demograficheskoi istorii narodov Severa [XVII–XIX]: Real'nost' ili illiuziia," SE, no. 2 (1986): 36–46. For an interesting—though early and isolated—foray of structuralist philology into circumpolar studies, see Ivanov et al., Ketskii sbornik.

[28] For pioneering work by Western anthropologists in the Soviet north, see Marjorie Mandelstam Balzer, "Ethnicity without Power: The Siberian Khanty in Soviet Society," SR 42 (Winter 1983): 633–48; idem, "Rituals of Gender Identity: Markers of Siberian Khanty Ethnicity, Status, and Belief," AA 83, no. 4 (1981): 850–67; idem, "The Route to Ethnicity: Cultural Persistence and Change in Siberian Khanty Burial Ritual," ArA 17, no. 1 (1980): 77–90; and Caroline Humphrey, Karl Marx Collective: Economy, Society and Religion in a Siberian Collective Farm (Cambridge, 1983).

[29] "Simpozium po tipologii iavlenii kul'tury," SE, no. 2 (1979): 155–60; "Simpozium 'Metodologicheskie problemy issledovaniia etnicheskikh kul'tur,'" SE, no. 6 (1979): 145–48; E. S. Markarian, "Uzlovye problemy teorii kul'turnoi traditsii," SE, no. 2 (1981):

most young ethnographers who had not become sociologists, psychologists, or demographers were calling themselves "culturologists."

Thus the science founded in Russia by Lev Shternberg had come full circle. But what did it mean for the native northerners, the people who had moved Shternberg to embark on his quest in the first place? As far as ethnography was concerned, there were at least two possibilities. On the one hand, given the decline of ethnic "material culture," one might agree with Bromlei and Basilov that what was needed was more descriptive ethnography: "It is absolutely clear that in the very near future a number of traditional cultures will vanish completely, so that while there is still time for ethnographic fieldwork, it is necessary to describe those elements of the unique culture of various peoples that have not yet become objects of detailed study."[30] On the other hand, with ethnicity only one element among many in the puzzle of culture, one might be tempted to explore the ethnographic virgin land of Soviet cities, families, or children.[31] On the eve of perestroika, this latter tendency was by far the stronger of the two. The aboriginal northerners, as the "small peoples" were increasingly being called for reasons of tact, had once again left the limelight of Soviet ethnography.

Ethnography's loss was a gain for the disciplines that had intruded on its traditional territory. An interest on the part of some historians in the "culture of everyday life" led to the invention of Soviet social history—with striking results for the Siberian peasants[32] and, in one case, for the native Siberians as well.[33] For the first time in the history of their representation the indigenous peoples of the north shared a historical narrative with the Russians. The mode of such cohabitation presented some difficulties, but the fact itself was a remarkable, though largely ignored, innovation.

Later, ecology, demography, and psychology would also suggest new ways of studying the indigenous northerners,[34] but it was sociology, the Soviet social science of the 1970s and 1980s, that was the most

---

78–115; M. G. Rabinovich and M. N. Shmeleva, "K etnograficheskomu izucheniiu goroda," *SE*, no. 3 (1981): 23–34.

[30] Bromlei and Basilov, "Sovetskaia etnograficheskaia nauka," p. 10.

[31] O. A. Gantskaia, "Etnos i sem'ia v SSSR," *SE*, no. 3 (1974): 20–30; Rabinovich and Shmeleva, "K etnograficheskomu izucheniiu goroda," pp. 23–34; I. S. Kon, "Etnografiia detstva," *SE*, no. 5 (1981): 3–14.

[32] N. A. Minenko, *Russkaia krest'ianskaia sem'ia v Zapadnoi Sibiri* (Novosibirsk, 1979); M. M. Gromyko, *Iz istorii sem'i i byta sibirskogo krest'ianstva v XVI-nachale XX veka* (Novosibirsk, 1975).

[33] Minenko, *Severo-zapadnaia Sibir'*.

[34] Krupnik, "Stanovlenie," pp. 57–69; *Narodnosti Severa: Problemy i perspektivy ekonomicheskogo i sotsial'nogo razvitiia* (Novosibirsk, 1983), pp. 23–24, 68–93; Pika, "Gomeostaz," pp. 36–46; A. M. Karelov and A. V. Dragan, "Sotsial'no-psikhologicheskie

noticeable new presence. It was considered a pragmatic discipline that dealt with specific social and economic problems and offered solutions based on objective scientific data. As the "inefficient" and heavily subsidized circumpolar peoples were perceived as a problem, it was only a matter of time before a group of Novosibirsk sociologists headed by V. I. Boiko addressed itself to a search for solutions. The problems were essentially those that the ethnographers had identified in the 1960s: the displacement of the traditional economy by industry and its destruction by pollution, the aging of competent hunters and herders and the inability of school graduates to replace them, the unprofitability of some alternative activities (such as fox-breeding) and the growing unemployment, the breakup of families, and the continuing reliance on non-native technical and managerial personnel. According to some new revelations, the fish in the Amur had all but disappeared and the claims of a total settlement of the nomads (in Kamchatka, Chita, and Amur provinces) apparently meant that herders had houses and wives that they never saw (about 40 percent of all reindeer breeders were officially single).[35]

The task of the sociologists was to find out, through questionnaires, how the native northerners were reacting to these developments, why they were reacting the way they were, and what was to be expected in the future. The main subjects were the eastern aboriginal communities directly affected by industrial development: the Evenk and Even of northern Yakutia, the Nivkh of northern Sakhalin, and, most urgently, the Evenk, Nanai, and Ul'ch groups whose traditional territories were to be traversed by the BAM (Baikal-Amur Mainline), the Brezhnev era equivalent of the Northern Sea Route. Government planners (if they were so inclined) could then use the results to find the appropriate economic role for the communities in question and to maximize the rationality and efficiency of indigenous labor at the lowest possible cost to everyone involved.

When the news came, it could be interpreted as both encouraging and disconcerting. According to the sociologists, the school-educated northerners did not simply lack the skills to succeed their parents in

faktory v zhiznedeiatel'nosti olenevodcheskoi brigady," in *Sotsial'nye problemy truda u narodnostei Severa*, ed. V. I. Boiko (Novosibirsk, 1986), pp. 114–19.

[35] *BAM i narody Severa* (Novosibirsk, 1979), pp. 71–77; V. I. Boiko, *Sotsial'noe razvitie narodov Nizhnego Amura* (Novosibirsk, 1977), pp. 52–62; *Narodnosti Severa*; Boiko, ed., *Sotsial'nye problemy truda*, pp. 8, 16–19, 42; V. I. Boiko and Iu. V. Popkov, *Razvitie otnosheniia k trudu u narodnostei Severa pri sotsializme* (Novosibirsk, 1987), pp. 102–11, 146–49; *Problemy sovremennogo sotsial'nogo razvitiia narodnostei Severa* (Novosibirsk, 1987), pp. 147–49.

the taiga or tundra—they had, in fact, made a deliberate and apparently irreversible decision to stay away from most aspects of the traditional economy. One half of all Nanai living in small settlements (under fifty households) expressed a desire to move to a larger settlement. In the 14–19 age group 90 percent of all potential migrants said they would prefer a city to a rural settlement of any size; 81 percent of the Magadan province reindeer breeders under twenty said that they did not consider either traditional or commercially produced tents appropriate places to live, and 59 percent of the BAM-area Evenk said that they would not chose to work in reindeer breeding under any circumstances (the reasons given were the tedium, excessive physical demands, isolation, and low wages). Indeed, 86 percent of the Evenk expected improvements from various BAM-related changes, although they acknowledged that it would be detrimental to reindeer-breeding. Fifty percent of them hoped to find new jobs as a result of the BAM activities. Of those actually engaged in reindeer breeding and hunting 26 percent considered the consequences of industrial intrusion "completely negative," and 23 percent, "completely positive." One half of them had already tried to change occupations. Education had become a crucial status symbol for a great majority of the surveyed population: most young people who continued their studies beyond high school knew that they might not be able to find a job that would correspond to their training, yet only 1 percent of the Evenk eighth and tenth graders in the BAM area pictured themselves in anything other than skilled occupations of "high and medium" skill level. Out of 100 rural Nanai parents none wanted their children to become hunters, and the three who recommended that their children take up fishing wanted them to acquire special skills at professional schools. In most areas included in the study the children and their parents seemed to agree that the boys should become white-collar professionals or skilled industrial workers (such as drivers and mechanics), and the girls should grow up to become doctors and teachers. Those who had gone on to fulfill their ambitions did not seem to regret it: among the indigenous peoples of northern Sakhalin 80 percent of college-educated professionals and 90 percent of skilled workers expressed satisfaction with their work. The corresponding figure for fishermen was 3.4 percent.[36]

Thus although the young ethnographers of the 1960s had suggested

[36] V. I. Boiko, Opyt sotsiologicheskogo issledovaniia problem razvitiia narodov Nizhnego Amura (Novosibirsk, 1973), pp. 179–88; N. V. Vasil'ev, "Kharakter i tendentsii sotsial'no-professional'nykh peremeshchenii evenskoi i evenkiiskoi molodezhi," in Sel'skaia molodezh' Iakutii: Sotsial'naia mobil'nost', otnoshenie k trudu, professional'naia orientatsiia, ed. V. I. Boiko (Iakutsk, 1977), pp. 37–48; BAM, pp. 86–108; Boiko,

that the state may have gotten in over its head and had hinted, however obliquely, that the solution lay in preserving and supporting the more useful aspects of traditional life, the sociologists were saying that the native northerners had successfully internalized the dominant Soviet values and that the state needed to live up to the expectations that it had deliberately created. In other words, the unemployment and the breakdown of the family were not the unforeseen consequences of ignorant intervention by plan-driven bureaucrats but rather the temporary result of insufficient or unbalanced (not scientifically calculated) technological development. If 90 percent of all northern Sakhalin natives employed as skilled workers were happy with their jobs and about 22.9 percent of those trained to do such work were unhappily employed as fishermen and menial laborers, then the creation of proper jobs for the latter group (through economic development and perhaps some special quotas) would result in total satisfaction for everyone. Likewise, as a total elimination of the traditional economy was not possible for economic and psychological reasons, the key was to make it more attractive through the importation of modern technology, the satisfaction of the consumers' growing needs, and the introduction of some traditional skills into the school curriculum.

These recommendations were, of course, a concession. V. I. Boiko and his colleagues invariably pointed out that the incorporation of the circumpolar peoples into the mainstream of Soviet society must be as painless as possible and that allowances should be made for lingering cultural and economic peculiarities. Reindeer breeding, in particular, presented the usual challenges: nomadism seemed incompatible with development; settlement seemed incompatible with reindeer breeding; and all attempts to square the circle could result in severe social dislocations that Boiko, for one, was not prepared to countenance.[37] Moreover, there were indications that the growing unemployment among indigenous peoples could not be attributed solely to the state's failure to create attractive jobs. Some scholars, for example, claimed that even educated northerners could not successfully compete with immigrant workers due to their unique psychological makeup as well

---

Sotsial'noe razvitie, pp. 111–13, 212–23; B. V. Lashov and O. P. Litovka, Sotsial'no-ekonomicheskie problemy razvitiia narodnostei Krainego Severa (Leningrad, 1982); Sotsial'noe razvitie sel'skogo naseleniia Iakutskoi ASSR (Iakutsk, 1984); Boiko, ed., Sotsial'nye problemy truda, pp. 10, 43, 76, 90; Boiko and Popkov, Razvitie otnoshenii k trudu, pp. 111–17; Problemy sovremennogo sotsial'nogo razvitiia narodnostei Severa, pp. 147–49.

[37] Boiko, ed., Sotsial'nye problemy truda, p. 19; Boiko and Popkov, Razvitie otnosheniia k trudu, p. 149. Cf. a more uncompromising position in Lashov and Litovka, Sotsial'no-ekonomicheskie problemy, p. 121.

as their newly developed reliance on constant state sponsorship in the form of quotas and subsidies.[38]

Accordingly, psychologists and "ethnopedagogues" who had revived pedology but avoided the term were beginning to enter the debate and to question—mostly by implication—assumptions that had not been questioned since the Cultural Revolution.[39] In spite of all this, however, most sociologists continued to proceed from the same basic premises. Before contact indigenous communities had been governed by "customs and traditions" that had "forced human beings to act blindly, . . . limited the social role of individuals, and in the final analysis stilted the development of the community."[40] Presented with an alternative lifestyle based on the emancipation of the individual and the active transformation of the environment, most northerners had opted for freedom from traditional constraints. It was the function of the state to provide them with a real opportunity for self-fulfillment by promoting massive but carefully planned development. Most humans, however, were culturally conservative, and "the overcoming of this inertia in the name of the earliest possible realization of the power of creative consciousness, and thus of true human nature, would ivevitably be accompanied by certain side effects [izderzhki]."[41] It was the task of the scholar to minimize these costs and help the state and the native peoples in their common endeavor.

The Return of Dersu Uzala

The fictional Long Journeys were much more ambitious than the academic discussions: they dealt with the grand metaphor of universal evolution and Soviet history leading to a state of mechanized—and increasingly personalized—perfection. Accordingly, as each passing year took one farther away from the "last and decisive battle," each representation of the present faced the monumental challenge of portraying perfection. The ethnography of paradise ran into serious problems in the 1960s; its fictional image, which could not afford to be entirely static, was in an even graver predicament.

All evil had become temporary: its agents were smuggled in from hell (overseas) and expelled immediately upon detection, whereas

---

[38] Boiko and Popkov, *Razvitie otnosheniia k trudu*, pp. 121–22.
[39] *Narodnosti Severa*, pp. 23–24, 94–130.
[40] Boiko, *Sotsial'noe razvitie*, p. 20.
[41] Ibid., p. 26.

homegrown deviations from total goodness could be caused only by a relapse into the past or a temperamental maladjustment. The new life of the native peoples consisted of material proofs of their well-being: there were the Russian-type houses, boarding-schools, hospitals, and clubs; there were the usual interiors with bright curtains, typewriters, sewing machines, and well-salted Russian meals on "neatly ironed tablecloths"; there were the well-educated and contented people proud of their kolkhoz's productivity, their Russian haircuts, and their imported furniture.[1] If anyone still argued, it was "in a good-natured kind of way: they [did] not know what to do with all the money they were making."[2] S. M. Bytovoi in his *Poezd prishel na Tumnin* offered a marvelous metaphor for the native peoples' literary transformation. If in the past most adult Oroch had acted like children, now it was the old folks' home that served as the symbolic center of the settlement and "the pride of the inhabitants of the former encampment": "The elders and consequently the most respected people from all clans live in this light, spacious building provided with all the necessities. The state feeds them, clothes them, looks after their health, and makes sure that nothing cast a shadow over their old age."[3]

In their leisure the elders take reading courses, work as volunteers, sew warm traditional shoes for comrade Stalin, and sign appeals for international peace. Even the shaman, who used to scare the village children, gives up his pranks and lets his granddaughters send his robe and sacred bones to the local museum.[4]

If this was the beginning of the narrative, what could be the end? Where could one go from paradise? One possibility was to find refuge in 1930s-style folklore,[5] but there was no escaping the writer's primary official responsibility—"to portray life as it is" (*pravdivo otrazhat' zhizn'*). Thus in the 1960s and 1970s the "legends" and the historical Long Journeys had to take a back seat to what could only be termed the "Short Journeys"—usually short stories dealing with one last survival or one particular case of untamed spontaneity, with the conflict between very good and very good indeed. The basic proposition is well illustrated by a dialogue from Semen Kurilov's "Uvidimsia v tundre"

[1] For an early description of paradise as the heroes' present state, see Azhaev, *Daleko ot Moskvy*, pp. 258–79. Cf. *Ot Moskvy do taigi odna nochevka. Sbornik* (Moscow, 1961), pp. 108, 137, 463; Rytkheu *Povesti*, pp. 118–19; Iuvan Shestalov, *Sibirskoe uskorenie* (Moscow, 1977), pp. 22–31, and *Shag cherez tysiacheletiia*, pp. 7–8.

[2] *Ot Moskvy do taigi odna nochevka*, p. 457.

[3] Bytovoi, *Poezd prishel na Tumnin*, p. 187.

[4] Ibid., pp. 156–65.

[5] Ivan Istomin, "Legenda," in *Radost'* (Moscow, 1961); *Ot Moskvy do taigi odna nochevka*, p. 204; Shestalov, *Shag cherez tysiacheletiia*, p. 12.

("See you in the tundra"). "The Yukagir have gotten to live really well," exclaims a young man back in his native land after two years in the Army. "'Yes, but they've got to live even better,' says the secretary of the district Party committee."[6]

Each story represented a small and final step toward consciousness, culture, and Russianness. In the absence of villains, it was essentially an inner journey for one hero, as he (almost never she) purged himself of one last trace of backwardness. A former shaman throws his wooden idols under a tractor to help the Russian driver get out of a ditch; an old patriarch turns into a housewife to support his daughter's record-breaking productivity; a dying hunter ignores an ancient prediction to lead his geologist son to a rich mineral deposit in the tundra; an old kolkhoznik fishes in a taboo spot and comes back with a spectacular catch; an elderly couple find happiness after they are finally persuaded to move into a Russian-type house; a young man sees the light when a Russian doctor saves his wife and newborn child who were almost killed by traditional practices; and two young lovers get married although both belong to the same exogamous clan. Interspersed with these were stories that assumed total national equality "in content" and dealt with the usual last wrinkles of the "neatly ironed table cloth" of Soviet life without any reference to the indigenous origins of the heroes. The heroes' job was to pass a dramatic test "at work and in personal life" and thus clear themselves of all suspicion of puerile impetuosity or doddering complacency.[7]

Meanwhile, having been relegated to the "historical novel" category, the Long Journey paradigm was losing its inner wholeness along with its dominance. If the 1930s twinkle-in-the-eye Bolshevik had had no problem being a father to the natives, his blue-eyed postwar successor was supposed to retain this role even as everyone around him began combining business with pleasure and he himself started getting more personally involved in the intimate lives of his charges. By the 1970s his youth and virility had caught up with him, and he began showing signs of strain. Istomin's Bolshevik, for example, broods and agonizes until he is almost seduced by an alluring kulak's daughter.[8] He does

[6] Ot Moskvy do taigi odna nochevka, p. 95.

[7] Shamshurin, U studenogo moria, and Severnaia shirota (Moscow, 1956); Istomin, Radost'; Ot Moskvy do taigi odna nochevka; Ivan Istomin, Tsvety v snegakh (Moscow, 1966); Rytkheu, Povesti; Iu. I. Shamshurin, Shli dvoe po tundre (Moscow, 1972); Grigorii Khodzher, Pustoe ruzh'e (Moscow, 1982); Aleksei Valdiu, Svet v okne (Khabarovsk, 1984); Rugin, Solntse nad snegami.

[8] Ivan Istomin, Zhivun (Moscow, 1974).

pull back at the last moment ("We're of different faiths! . . I'm a Bolshevik from the working people! And she's a rich girl, the daughter of an enemy of the people's power"), but some of the mystique and the inner conviction is lost forever. No matter how firm the Bolshevik is, there is nothing he can do about his effect on the native women. Increasingly, the willful and determined Amazon's decision to mobilize the population in support of the Russian is due to her romantic interest in him: "Wherever you go, I'll go with you. I want to walk by your side."[9] Even Rytkheu's Ushakov, impeccably ascetic and asexual in the traditional mold, cannot help noticing the peculiar electricity that one of his very first appearances among the Eskimos produces: "'My dear friends and comrades,' Ushakov began and looked over the audience. It seemed to him that Nanekhak was suddenly shaken by a kind of strange tremor and a fleeting smile appeared on her round face with its still childish features."[10]

What follows represents a considerable challenge in terms of plot development. Nanekhak, married to a colorless but virtuous fellow, is Ushakov's best disciple, but her devotion is obviously based on physical attraction and is thus potentially subversive. The model of the Russian-native relationship consecrated and reproduced by the Long Journey narratives required that the Russian be godlike and that the natives achieve a state of total happiness. In The Island of Hope, however, the two conditions cannot be reconciled: he will have to surrender his aura of mystery, or she—and hence the people she represents—will have to remain unsatisfied.

The solution is suggested by Christianity, an old ally of Soviet mythmakers. During a sea hunt Ushakov falls into the icy water and is saved from death by hypothermia by Nanekhak who (in her husband's presence) takes off her clothes and warms him with her body. Shortly afterward she becomes pregnant and declares that the child is Ushakov's. The reader, the husband, and Ushakov himself know that it is not true ("Nothing really happened between us," he protests), but Nanekhak will have none of that. She goes on to produce a son and names him after Ushakov, whom she has officiate at the ceremony of "Soviet baptism." The Bolshevik remains divine and the Amazon is totally fulfilled. The first fruit of the Russian-Eskimo alliance issues from an immaculate conception.

Such plot resolutions were precarious balancing acts at a time when

[9] N. D. Kuzakov, Liubov' shamanki (Moscow, 1975), p. 89.
[10] Rytkheu, Ostrov nadezhdy, p. 40.

most scholars and writers were questioning—no matter how obliquely—the infallibility of the Bolshevik mentor. He may have been too dogmatic or he may have "broken too many eggs"—in any case he was overcome by doubt and reflection.[11] In at least two Long Journey novels the Russian hero breaks down, falls in love, and finally consummates his relationship with the native girl.[12] Before this can happen, however, she has to cease being a loyal student and an empty vessel: if he is to fall, she has to provide a truly powerful temptation; if he is to be demoted from fatherhood, she has to move out of her filial status by acquiring an autonomous value and mystery of her own. In a dramatic reversal of the fictional native hierarchy—and with the rest of the Long Journey structure intact—she becomes a shaman. Rather than being a rebel against the oppressive obsolescence of her tribe, she becomes its guardian and main representative, "the mistress of the taiga." And a brilliant representative she is, too: strikingly beautiful, graceful, proud. "There is fire in her black eyes; her braids tremble on her breast with a tinkling of coins, her gestures are energetic and imperious."[13]

It is, of course, no accident that she looks like a fictional Gypsy or a Circassian, but neither novel breaks with the Long Journey paradigm in favor of an updated version of the "Caucasian Captive." There is no doubt about the Russian way (progress) being superior, and the Bolshevik, although fascinated by the magnificence of her "art," never considers defection. She, not he, is a tragic figure, "a knight of woeful countenance."[14] He loses his chastity but keeps his faith; she has to discard her whole identity if she is to find love. In the end, she makes the right choice and, in Kuzakov's *Shaman's Love*, quite literally surrenders the image of the clan's founder along with her own vestments to the museum. For obvious reasons, we are not shown the conjugal bliss that follows: he loves her mysterious poetry but agrees to marry her only on condition that she forsake it. The proud mistress of the taiga could not survive in front of a TV set and a sewing machine.

A subspecies of the Long Journey literature—the education of a young northerner in a big city—was also undergoing important changes. In the 1930s the young northerner's personal quest had resulted in the discovery of social justice (along with high technology and human warmth); in the first postwar years he had been struck by

---

[11] For early examples in mainstream literature set in Russia, see V. V. Ovechkin's "Raionnye budni," in *Gosti v Stukachakh* (Moscow, 1972). Cf. Clark, *The Soviet Novel*, pp. 213–14.

[12] Kuzakov, *Liubov' shamanki*; Troshev, *Bol'shoi Oshar*.

[13] Kuzakov, *Liubov' shamanki*, p. 163. Cf. Troshev, *Bol'shoi Oshar*, pp. 108, 110.

[14] Troshev, *Bol'shoi Oshar*, pp. 113, 301.

the unique qualities of the simple Russian people; by the 1970s he was writing his own memoirs and talking almost exclusively about "culture." Living in Moscow and Leningrad and looking back on their pilgrimage, college-educated northern writers told a story of physical and spiritual liberation. Their origins were painful and grim, as all Long Journey origins had to be: "A cramped and dark dwelling with an earthen floor, with rows of beds from one wall to another, with smoke flues under the beds, with the dirty rags of the shaman's children, never seeing light in the winter and always scorched by the sun in the summer—did we really live like that at the turn of the century and for a thousand years?"[15]

It was no longer the image of Lenin, however, that opened a boy's eyes to a new world of light and freedom. It was Pushkin. Or Lermontov. Or Tolstoy. "The Russian book. It took me very far away from the usual howling of a blizzard outside, from the frosty tinkling of the high Siberian stars."[16] Rytkheu's young hero quite explicitly models himself on Gor'kii's *Childhood* as he devours book after book in his dark hiding place: the books themselves "were the little rays that lit up the world hidden from Rintyn."[17] Thus, the traditional light/darkness opposition takes on a new, more "elemental" meaning as it pits the poles of "nature" and "culture" against each other: "Nature is the fur of the bearskin and my fears. The blizzards. The world of beauty is schools, books, and Russian speech. Nature enslaved me; culture liberated. I wanted to get away from nature and move into the world of culture."[18]

As a guide into the world of culture thus defined, a Bolshevik would not do. Only a true member of the Russian *intelligentsia*, a priest at the altar of Pushkin and Gogol, could introduce the novice to the mysteries of spiritual freedom. Both Rytkheu's and Kile's heroes are orphans, and as they look for Russian surrogate fathers, they look for erudition and book learning. Petr Kile, in his remarkably fresh memoir, evokes unmistakably Bulgakovian images of the heavy dignity of the tradition-bound aristocracy of the spirit: "Some doors, according to the ancient custom, have brass plaques: 'Professor So-and-so'. And I like that."[19] In a crucial scene, Kile's narrator is taking an entrance exam from a college history professor, a benevolent old *intelligent*, when he realizes that their mentor-disciple relationship extends far beyond the class-

---

[15] Kile, *Idti vechno*, p. 22.

[16] Shestalov, *Shag cherez tysiacheletia*, p. 24. Also Iuvan Shestalov, *Zemlia Iugoriia* (Moscow, 1985), 16.

[17] Iurii Rytkheu, *Vremia taianiia snegov* (Moscow, 1981), p. 113. See also pp. 84, 122.

[18] Kile, *Idti vechno*, p. 57.

[19] Ibid., p. 88.

room: "It was always like this in my life when I met real Russian *intelligenty.* I had realized it early on, and my dream of a great life was often associated with my adoption by such an old man and his old wife, who had to live in Leningrad"[20]—not in the city of Lenin's revolution, that is, or Peter's empire, but in the city still haunted by Pushkin and Dostoyevsky. The equality attained through membership in the intelligentsia is cemented by friendship with a Russian. "It was uncanny how, one thousand miles apart—I in the taiga wilderness and he in Leningrad—we had thought about basically the same things and discovered the same writers. And it was pleasant to realize that we were equal, that I liked him and he liked me."[21]

At the end of the journey the pilgrim usually acquires a Russian wife and becomes a Russian writer or teacher.[22] The child of their marriage (a "gift from Russia")[23] will grow up entirely in the world of culture (in Russia), and the fruits of his creative labors are clearly destined for his new and true peers, the Russian intelligentsia.

> There is no point in writing in my native language because out of eight thousand Nanai living in this world, if anybody reads poetry, they read it in Russian. There is no need to translate Pushkin into Nanai. I love Pushkin in the element of Russian speech and I cannot reject it. In any case, writing poetry in any other language strikes me as strange. And who knows to what extent Russian has become my native language?[24]

By 1972, when Kile's book came out, the nature-culture dichotomy had become a popular theme. A growing number of people, however, disagreed with Kile concerning the relative value of the two categories. Ever since the Twentieth Party Congress writers had been sending their young heroes away from the big cities in search of fulfillment elsewhere. The Emperor, as his heirs proclaimed to the people, did not have a full set of clothes, and to the eyes of some members of the cheated generation, neither did the heirs themselves. The reassertion of family values after the Great Transformation and the spread of bureaucratic sensitivity after the war had already softened Soviet revolutionary urbanism; now there was a whole cohort of authors who rejected "culture" as represented by Moscow and Leningrad in favor of

---

[20] Ibid., p. 65.

[21] Ibid., p. 83.

[22] Cf. Iuvan Shestalov, "Iazycheskaia poema," in *Izbrannoe*; Rytkheu, *Vremia taianiia snegov*; Khodzher, *Pustoe ruzh'e*, pp. 3–54; and Val'diu, *Svet v okne*, p. 52.

[23] Shestalov, *Izbrannoe*, p. 210.

[24] Kile, *Idti vechno*, p. 154.

"nature" as represented by faraway wooded places. The Mecca of young northerners was increasingly seen by its native inhabitants as a world of *poshlost'*, as a world of triviality, vulgarity, and falsehood. The Thaw had questioned the past and hence obscured the future, with the present still dominated by the productive and occasionally adulterous little family eating borscht in their cozy little apartment. Where, asked the stifled and jaded young hero, was the place for true feelings, time-tested certainties, true love, and eternal friendship? The farther from "nice tassels" the better, was the answer, as dozens of fictional youngsters streamed out of the capitals to hunt, hike, or join geological expeditions.[25]

Once again, the extreme north emerged as a dangerous and harsh (*surovaia*) wilderness, a perfect place to separate "worthy people" (*dostoinye liudi*) from "dudes" (*pizhony*).[26] "The tundra does not like the weak," proclaimed a typical book on the subject.[27] But if the snowbound desert of Stalin's romantic explorers was an enemy to be defeated and chained once and for all, the north of the 1960s was a stern mentor, a repository of true values forgotten by the decadent, effeminate urbanites. "The tundra helps a person understand himself and find his place in the world," and it can do so because "the harsh [*surovaia*] life forces one to break with all things meaningless and futile."[28] The old north was largely uninhabited—there was no place for the indigenous foragers in the world of polar exploration and technological advances; the new north, as it turned out, was populated by people who had had the benefit of this harsh, meaningful life for many generations. Just as refugees to other areas rediscovered the beauty and purity of remote Russian villages, the polar travelers found that unspoiled nature produced unspoiled natural people: "The North does not coddle people. It demands from them a total emotional and physical commitment. It was probably the harsh [*surovaia*] northern nature that tempered small peoples of a very special kind. Their character and customs are just as simple, laconic, and beautiful as nature itself."[29]

Thus, for the first time since the 1920s the native northerners returned to Russian literature as artless, unaffected, and noble children

[25] Clark, *The Soviet Novel*, pp. 228–31, 242.

[26] Oleg Kuvaev, *Izbrannoe* (Moscow, 1988), 1:5. I am grateful to Igor Krupnik for drawing my attention to his work.

[27] Vladimir Litbovtsev and Iu. V. Simchenko, *Tundra ne liubit slabykh* (Moscow, 1968). See also Kuvaev, *Izbrannoe*, 1:157.

[28] Linboutsev and Simchenko, *Tundra*, p. 75; Iu. V. Simchenko, *Liudi vysokikh shirot* (Moscow, 1972), p. 7.

[29] V. A. Tugolukov, *Sledopyty verkhom na oleniakh* (Moscow, 1969), p. 5.

of nature always willing to instruct the misguided representative of "culture." An unbiased city dweller who spent some time in their midst would eventually stop looking for "politely indifferent smiles concealing ill will" and realize that "here in the tundra there was no distinction between yours and mine; grief and joy were divided equally among all."[30] Even professional ethnographers, who in their Institute-sponsored publications wrote about ethnic merging and rising living standards, put quotation marks around "civilization" when they addressed a popular audience. In the 1960s and 1970s many young authors and their young readers agreed that it was time to embark on a long journey in the opposite direction. "Their settlements may have electric light and radio, but even today the life of the Evenk is full of adventure and danger, of the joys and disappointments of people who live within nature and not outside of it."[31]

What were these natural people like at close range? The socialist-realist tradition had defined "spontaneity" as a lack of "consciousness" (and later culture), as a world of darkness from which to escape. If one wished to reverse the equation, one had to look elsewhere. The obvious choices were the Amazons of early Russian romanticism and the redskins of Fenimore Cooper. Both were well-known companions of Soviet adolescence, and as early as 1951 a young Chukchi Party secretary could gain prestige by posing as a Mohican: "His aquiline nose and tightly pressed lips gave a stern expression to his face. His proud posture and the dignity apparent in his every gesture and each glance made him look like an Indian chief."[32] Both models were fairly productive, but neither was quite right in the USSR of the 1960s because of their unavoidably tragic finale: the Indians derived their nobility from being doomed, and the Circassian girl had to die or disappear to remain attractive. This clashed with the essential optimism of the new Soviet romanticism, which assumed that the fugitive from culture would be accepted by nature. What was needed was a noble savage who could repeatedly enlighten the urbanite without losing his nobility. What was needed was a Dersu Uzala.

In fact, the death of Dersu had been totally accidental. Arsen'ev's

[30] Liubovtsev and Simchenko, Tundra ne liubit slabykh, pp. 65, 67.

[31] Tugolukov, Sledopyty, p. 209. See also V. A. Tugolukov, Idushchie poperek khrebtov (Krasnoiarsk, 1980), which is a slight revision of Sledopyty, and Kto vy, iukagiry? (Moscow, 1979); Iurii Simchenko, Zimniaia doroga (Moscow, 1985). A special case is V. V. Leont'ev, a Magadan-based writer and ethnographer who grew up among the Chukchi. See his V Chukotskom more (Magadan, 1961); his Okhotniki proliva Beringa (Magadan, 1969); and his Po zemle drevnikh kerekov (Magadan, 1976).

[32] Shundik, Sobranie sochinenii, 1:31.

narrative did not necessarily require a direct confrontation between the wise old man and the corrupt world of false civilization. To be himself, all Dersu Uzala needed was his native environment and a will-ing disciple eager to shed the blinkers of civilization and be instructed in the art of living. Arsen'ev could have killed his hero after the very first expedition or not at all: Dersu's only function was to serve as a guide—physical and spiritual.

Hence, when a new generation of Russian romantics arrived in the taiga, the old pathfinder was brought back to do his job. His most popu-lar reincarnation was G. A. Fedoseev's Ulukitkan, a wise Evenk hunter and the loyal friend of Siberian geodesists. In the intervening years he had aged and mellowed a great deal: Ulukitkan is over eighty, "tiny, frail, and always meek," "almost transparent." His coat is old and worn out; his fur boots are old and barely patched up, his gun is old and unwieldy. "His hands do not have their former nimbleness, his old back does not bend too well, and when his feet fall through the snow, he can get up only with my assistance, like a helpless child."[33] All the more remarkable, therefore, that he should have preserved intact his wisdom, his tenacity, his "imperturbable calmness," his ability to "comprehend the nature of things" as well as all things in nature, "his total ignorance of the meaning of lies, hypocrisy, and weakness!"[34] In a key episode, Ulukitkan loses his eyesight, yet even blind he can see more than his vigorous Russian friend and employer. Always the guide, he can lead the narrator to safety because his strength and knowledge are of a different kind: he is at one with the mystery of nature. Curi-ously—and invariably—he is also one on one with nature. According to Fedoseev, the "law of the taiga" (jungle) required that a lone individ-ual learn its ways the hard way—on his own.[35] City dwellers were flee-ing from frantic crowds, false intimacy, and enforced collectivism. Understandably, and presumably to the dismay of students of primitive communism, they found the natural man to be a Byronic loner and a committed individualist. When the narrator suggests that Ulukitkan sing along with him, the old Evenk snaps: "Even if two men live in the same tent, eat out of the same pot, and walk on the same trail, they

[33] G. A. Fedoseev, Glukhoi, nevedomoi taigoiu (Krasnoiarsk, 1960), pp. 17, 41, Tropoiu ispytanii, in Izbrannye proizvedeniia (Moscow, 1976), 1:33, 61–62, 262, and Poslednii koster, in ibid., 2: 284.

[34] Fedoseev, Tropoiu, in Izbrannye proizvedeniia, 1:33, 196; Fedoseev, Poslednii kos-ter, in ibid., 2:282

[35] See, in particular, G. A. Fedoseev, Zloi dukh Iambuia, in Izbrannye proizvedeniia, 2:39–45.

think differently. How is it possible to sing together?! . . . No, you sing your song, and I'll sing mine."[36]

This, however, did not mean that light and darkness should switch places completely and that the Long Journey had to be reversed. When Fedoseev, himself a geodesist and an explorer, moved from travelogue to more structured and more "novelistic" forms, he had young Ulukitkan suffer under the old regime and sacrifice his own family in order to lead a giant Bolshevik to a rich mineral deposit in the mountains.[37] How could this be reconciled? Outside of censorship requirements, was there anything that Soviet power could bring to the already wise native northerners? Apparently so. In an ironic twist, one role of the Russian disciple is to force his guide to be more consistent in his philosophy. If being natural involves understanding nature, and if "to understand it means to know how to fight it," then most traditional beliefs are superstitions obscuring the great truth of the law of the taiga.[38] "I know perfectly well," says Fedoseev's narrator, "that all this stuff [Ulukitkan's belief in spirits] is but an echo of the past. In fact, he believes only in his own strength and his knowledge of nature."[39] Thus, in a typical Short Journey mode, Russian disciples challenged their misguided mentors to disregard the taboo, to go to an "enchanted" spot and realize once and for all that the gods stood for weakness while true knowledge stood for self-reliance. One of Ulukitkan's doubles, a deaf and mute old hunter more eloquent than most mortals, ends up killing an evil spirit (in fact a man-eating bear) to save his Russian friend. "The old man understood that man was stronger than the spirit. And everything that he had inherited from his ancestors suddenly collapsed."[40]

"Everything" was obviously an exaggeration, but most authors still agreed that some elements of tradition owed their existence to true backwardness and had to go. "Today you aren't going to obtain fire the way your grandfather did—you've got matches. It's been a long time since you last hunted with a crossbow. And what about radio in the tent? Your grandmother couldn't even have dreamed of that!"[41] Another narrator, who waxes nostalgic about the quaint little settlements of his childhood, interrupts himself with the question: "Would you really

---

[36] Fedoseev, Tropoiu, in Izbrannye proizvedeniia, 1:242.

[37] Fedoseev, Poslednii koster in Izbrannye proizvedeniia.

[38] Fedoseev, Tropoiu, in Izbrannye proizvedeniia, 1:196.

[39] Fedoseev, Glukhoi, p. 148.

[40] Fedoseev, Zloi, in Izbrannye proizvedeniia, 2:250. Cf. Nikolai Kuzakov, Taiga—moi dom (Moscow, 1977), esp. pp. 51–52.

[41] Fedoseev, Zloi, in Izbrannye proizvedeniia, 2:40.

want your children to grow up in this godforsaken hole, not knowing what television, theater, and the Palace of Young Pioneers are? Of course not. It's not for nothing that I have betrayed the taiga myself."[42] His guide, an old Evenk woman, shares his feelings as she ridicules a romantic writer who has bemoaned the disappearance of this earthly paradise: "Let him come and live in the taiga all by himself, and then tell us all about paradise."[43]

Thus, the Soviet state was to abolish the backwardness, dirt, and isolation while preserving the ancient wisdom, purity, and "imperturbable calmness." The true task of the Long Journey was to combine the best of nature and culture, to ensure a harmonious merging of town and country. In a sense, the Russian state was to become the true heir to the best of the indigenous traditions, building on them and weaving them into the modern world. In symbolic recognition of this fact, Vladimir Kornakov's old Cheglok, "the Last of the Falcon Tribe," passes his "baton" to the geologists he has served for many years. They have learned true wisdom; they understand that people should not destroy the house in which they live.[44] Similarly, R. K. Agishev's Aianka works as a professional forest ranger, urging his geologist friends to "look after the green house."[45] The indigenous tradition and the state interest had become one and the same thing.

This fusion called for further plot readjustments. Nikolai Shundik, the first to dress up Party secretaries as Indians, constructed a traditional Long Journey sequence in which the native convert is a "white" (good) shaman, a wise old man with an Indian profile who can communicate with all living things.[46] A peculiar Dersu-meets-Komsomol-girl character, he enthusiastically accepts boarding-schools, hospitals, and collectivization even as he introduces his fascinated teachers to the anthropomorphic world of his forebears. The Bolsheviks need the white shaman because they realize that true social justice is but an element of a larger natural harmony. In the USSR, as in the West, the new romantics had discovered environmentalism, and their noble savages had no choice but to do likewise.

> How many people like that are still left on this planet, people who understand the animal soul as if it were their own, understand their language

[42] Kuzakov, Taiga—moi dom, p. 34.
[43] Ibid., pp. 77–78. See Nichols, "Stereotyping," pp. 204–6.
[44] Vladimir Kornakov, "Cheglok," SO, no. 12 (1972): 69–81.
[45] R. K. Agishev, Lunc v ushchel'iakh (Moscow, 1967), pp. 9, 45–46.
[46] Shundik, Belyi shaman, in Sobranie sochinenii, vol. 3.

and behavior and, most important, understand how much man needs a
natural link with his little brothers, and not only with them, but with
every leaf, every blade of grass, everything that comprises the great concept of life?[47]

Even Iurii Rytkheu, the creator of Long Journeys par excellence,
joined the fold by putting quotation marks around "the civilized
world" and by arguing that the circumpolar peoples had created a
unique civilization of their own, had "discovered" their environment
long before European explorers, and had generally acquired "truthful
information about nature and man that had allowed these people not
only to exist in extreme climatic conditions but also to create an amazing material culture, a moral code, and popular medicine."[48] (Much of
this culture, it turned out, had been transmitted by shamans—not the
"scarecrow" that Rytkheu and others had been "guilty" of depicting
but "the most knowledgeable and experienced person of the tribe.")[49]
Yet this subtle and fragile civilization would probably have perished
under the onslaught of the predatory whites had it not been for that
very special brand of whites—"the true knights of the idea of social
transformation"—who had understood the real but inarticulate aspirations of the indigenous peoples.

> The new ideology corresponded fully to the innermost dreams of the
> inhabitants of the northeastern tip of Asia. . . . The ideas of social equal-
> ity based on a just attitude toward work as the true measure of everything
> real and human—these were the very things that constituted the founda-
> tion of the philosophy of the Chukchi-Eskimo working community, never
> formulated but practiced for centuries.[50]

Thus, the revived dichotomy of native (nature) versus Russian (culture) was overcome by the discovery that natives had a high (communistic) culture of their own and that Russians were sensitive to the
environment. Moreover, as a growing number of writers were discovering purity and true values in Russia's rural present and remote
past, this unique consonance was once again extended to the pre-Soviet

---

[47] Ibid., pp. 522–23.
[48] Iurii Rytkheu, *Sovremennye legendy* (Leningrad, 1980), pp. 182, 193–94, 212, 215,
218, 269–70. See Adele Barker, "The Divided Self: Yuri Rytkheu and Contemporary
Chukchi Literature," in Diment and Slezkine, eds., *Between Heaven and Hell,*
pp. 218–26.
[49] Rytkheu, *Sovremennye legendy*, pp. 214–15.
[50] Ibid., p. 213.

period. Except that now, amid the growing popularity of folkish roman-ticism and retrospective environmentalism, the unifying force was not the Russian state but an alliance of like-minded and tradition-bound peasants and foragers. In a bizarre elaboration on this theme, Aleksandr Sheludiakov populated northwestern Siberia with the animist de-scendants of Novgorodian refugees from Christianity who "worshiped the beauty and spirit of nature" in the same way as their indigenous brothers and sisters.[51] In similar customs and rituals, both celebrated "the fabulous kingdom of birds and animals, the amazing sea of flowers in the meadows, . . . the mysterious sky and that wonder of wonders of the Universe—the immortal sun."[52] Indeed, it turned out that "the conservation of nature and ancient graves had become law in Russia in the ninth century: at that time Russian princes and communes were already limiting wood-cutting and protecting certain rare animals."[53] They were not mindless preservationists, however. For centuries the native northerners and the "glorious descendants of the Novgorodian divines" had been extracting petroleum for their own use. No wonder, therefore, that they greeted the new oil and gas industry with open arms: laying pipelines through their forests indicated respect for their ancient traditions.[54] In the end, Sheludiakov's wise old Evenk woman and the district Party secretary (the grandson of a Civil War hero) agree on the need for both continuity and oil exploration. The traditional representatives of nature and culture had nothing left to quarrel about.[55]

This resolution was precariously balanced. Every once in a while even the most serene of Dersu's sons could complain that young school graduates could "not tell a dog's tracks from a wolf's," could not find their way in the taiga, and could not speak the language of their el-ders.[56] Was it possible that TV sets and pipelines could not, after all, be reconciled with nature—and if nature and native culture were syn-onymous, was it possible that they were inimical to native life? In an age when Russian authors were looking for unspoiled rural sources of a nonbureaucratic Russian identity, it could only be a matter of time before a similar opposition was formulated by a northern writer.

[51] Aleksandr Sheludiakov, *Iugana* (Moscow, 1982), p. 203.
[52] Ibid.
[53] Ibid., p. 264.
[54] Ibid., pp. 126–27, 254.
[55] Cf. Nichols, "Stereotyping," pp. 206–9.
[56] Fedoseev, *Zloi*, in *Izbrannye proizvedeniia*, 2:40, 52–53; Fedoseev, *Tropoiu is-pytanii*, in ibid., 1:199; Kuzakov, *Taiga—moi dom*, pp. 33–34.

In fact, it did not take any time at all. By the late 1960s Vladimir Sangi, a Nivkh folklorist and fiction writer, had essentially rejected the idea of Russia as social paradise, brother-protector, guide to world culture, or even fellow guardian of traditional values. Sangi's heroes were wise old tribesmen who not only epitomized tradition and continuity but refused to serve as guides to curious Europeans. Their tradition was for their people only and was supposed to stay that way. They were the only mentors, and their Russian-educated grandchildren were the only students. Indeed, the youngster might have a college degree or a fancy job; he might have taken many an exam from Russian school teachers, Party secretaries, or university professors, but his one true test, his real rite of passage was the traditional test of the taiga. In the course of the ordeal (usually a hunt) the elder proved his continuing wisdom and relevance, while the youth proved that he was "not a youth but a man"—a real Nivkh.[57] In the short novel *Lozhnyi gon* Sangi dots the "i" by introducing a third character—a "rootless" shock worker in his prime, a man of uncertain lineage but of superior kolkhoz and newspaper credentials. As events unfold, with the old hunter asserting his nobility and the young apprentice demonstrating his courage, the shock worker is exposed as a cheat and a ruthless predator. Moreover, it turns out that he is a former kolkhoz chairman who had distinguished himself by forcibly settling his people, ruining them in the process, and having at least one of them arrested and executed for insubordination. For the first time, the Long Journey had been attacked directly and unequivocally. Heroes and villains had switched places.

Having undermined the dominant paradigm, Sangi proceeded to reverse the standard images of prerevolutionary Russo-northern cooperation as well. In *Zhenit'ba Kevongov* (The marriage of the Kevongs), the first Russians to present themselves before the Nivkh are runaway prisoners—hairy monsters who rape, pillage, and murder as only the Americans and Japanese had done before.[58] This first encounter is prophetic: the story that follows describes the slow disintegration of a Nivkh clan after the arrival of Russian and Yakut traders. What rape and murder had not done was accomplished by money, liquor, and enslavement. Far from bringing light into the lives of the northern peoples, let alone supporting them in their environmentalism, Russian

---

[57] See "Izgin," "U istoka," "Pervui vystrel," and *Lozhnyi gon* in *V tsarstve vladyk* (Moscow, 1973). "Pervyi vystrel" and "Izgin" are also to be found in *Izgin* (Moscow, 1969).

[58] Vladimir Sangi, *Zhenit'ba Kevongov* (Moscow, 1975), pp. 59–60.

culture brought nothing but death and corruption. As far as Sangi was concerned, the Long Journey had been a trail of tears.

Thus when the new generation of future native poets, teachers, and librarians arrived in the federal or provincial capitals in the 1960s and 1970s, they found "the world of the future" in a state of self-doubt and cynicism. As all new elites rescued from "the world of the past," they had to define their position with regard to their new peers (in this case the Russian intelligentsia) and their old ones ("the people")—a task made more urgent by the collapse of the official relationship between the two. Some remained "westernizers"—which meant that the national elite would be equal to the dominant one and that the "people" would eventually join the club through education, but an increasing number of intellectuals attempted to construct a separate, yet commonly northern, identity defined in opposition to Russia. The difficulty of the "westernizing" position, in addition to the doubts voiced by the "westerners" themselves, consisted in the fact that one was expected to try to become Russian while remaining a representative of one's own people—for such representation was, in Soviet and traditional Russian terms, the principal goal of any national intelligentsia. Indeed, one needed to receive a Russian education to truly represent the circumpolar peoples. Moreover, equality—to the extent that one could be non-Russian but equal in the USSR—was not forthcoming. During the "stagnant" 1970s, when most official values were subject to carnivalesque debunking through popular humor, the Chukchi emerged as the most popular butt of jokes that parodied Soviet claims of rapid development and spectacular cultural advances by the formerly backward. Thus the native northerners were taken up by the folk mythmakers for the same reason they had been used by the creators of socialist realism: seen as an extreme case, they provided maximum edification in the heroic genre and the most striking implausibility in the comic. Meanwhile, professional scholars refused to consider the native peoples as full-fledged nations, occasionally hiding their refusal behind the never-defined concept of *narodnost'*. Could a spokesman for a *narodnost'* be equal to a spokesman for a (great) nation, particularly if the latter expressed his disgust for Soviet egalitarianism by laughing at Chukchi jokes?

One could try to escape guilt by association by ceasing to be a spokesman for anyone and insisting on total cultural assimilation or total individualism. This option, however, frequently brought moral censure as a betrayal of one's parents (and thus, to some, oneself) as well as being impracticable due to the increasing association of Russianness with racial "whiteness." Consequently, as was the case with German Romantics, Russian populists, and Negritude poets, among others, the solution seemed to lie in national self-assertion, in reinterpreting backwardness as purity and progress as corruption. This meant that rather than enlightening "the people," the *intelligent* was to learn from them, to partake of their ancient wisdom.

Accordingly, translations and interpretations of northern folklore (that "most life-giving and inexhaustible" source of "poetic imagery, national character, and spirit")[59] became an important scholarly/political activity, and "my land" and "my people" became the dominant lyrical motif as young authors celebrated their roots, their belonging to the simple and dignified world of their ancestors.

> My father is a Nanai maple—
> I have his loyalty.
> My mother is a Nanai birch—
> I have her eyes and braids.
> My grandfather is the Amur,
> Majestic, strong, and wise.
> The precious gifts I got from him
> Are countless songs and tales.
> My grandmother, the stern taigá,
> Albeit harsh and strict,
> Taught me how to be agile,
> Courageous, firm, and tough.
> Would I be able to forget
> The wooded Amur banks?
> Could I stop loving for one day
> The width of the Amur?
> The birds and animals and fish—
> They all belong to me.
> And every door of every house
> Is open to me.
> I sing the strength of the Amur,
> The beauty of my land.
> I am a Nanai through and through,
> The Nanai house is mine.[60]

---

[59] Vladimir Sangi, ed., *Antologiia fol'klora narodnostei Sibiri, Severa i Dal'nego Vostoka* (Krasnoiarsk, 1989), p. 12. See also Vladimir Sangi, *Legendy Ykh-Mifa* (Moscow, 1967) and *Pesn' o nivkhakh* (Moscow, 1989). For other examples, see Anna Khodzher, Prokopii Lonki, Georgii Porotov, and Valentina Kialundziuga, in *Blizok krainii Sever* (Moscow, 1982).

[60] Anna Khodzher, "Ia—zemli nanaiskoi doch'," in *Blizok krainii Sever*, p. 118.

This celebration of "roots" meant that one needed to preserve one's native tongue, observe old customs, and respect the elders who had kept them alive.[61] It also meant that whoever was responsible for their destruction was the enemy and had to be exposed as such. In the short story "The Morning Star" the Khanty writer Eremei Aipin makes ample use of the language and imagery of nineteenth-century antiserf-dom literature as he describes a disastrous encounter between a trusting native hunter and a pair of ruthless, rootless mercenaries from the ever-expanding oil fields. The story ends with an apology from a high-ranking official, but a bitter aftertaste remains: the hunter's favorite reindeer that has been killed for its antlers cannot be resurrected, and a part of his dignity that he has lost in a drunken stupor cannot be retrieved.[62]

Like Westernism, "Volk" romanticism had its own contradictions to resolve. Most odes to tradition were written in Russian, and almost all were aimed at the Russian public. The activity of writing itself was nontraditional and had to rely on images, plots, and tropes taken from Russian literature. The authors, no matter how unique their voices, inhabited the same world of literary associations as their readers—after all, they had gone to school together. Could—and would—these people shed their Russianness? And what did it mean if the protest against modernity was itself a part of modern discourse? Was the northern intelligentsia destined to suffer from the same unfulfilled nostalgia and the same unrequited love for "the people" as their Russian colleagues? In what way was one to claim "the Nanai house"?

An interesting attempt to probe these issues can be found in Anna Nerkagi's short story "Aniko from the Nogo Clan" (written in Russian).[63] A young Nenets woman who lives in a big city and studies geology in college receives a letter from her father, Seberui, informing her that her mother and little sister have been killed by a wolf and that she is needed at home. Filled with guilt and apprehension, the young woman decides to go for a short stay and, several airplane and helicopter flights later, arrives in her native tundra.

[61] See poems by Dmitrii Aprosimov, Oktiabrina Voronova, Vasilii Keimetinov, Askol'd Bazhanov, Nikolai Kurilov, Andrei Krivoshapkin, Nikolai Oegir, Zoia Nenliumkina, and Nikolai Kalitin in *Blizok krainii Sever.* Also Antonina Kymytval', *Moi liubimyi tsvetok* (Magadan, 1982). For an interesting interpretation, see Barker, "The Divided Self."
[62] Eremei Aipin, "Zvezda utrennei zari," in *Blizok krainii Sever.*
[63] *Blizok krainii Sever,* pp. 11–106.

Aniko jumped off the sled. Turning toward the tents, she saw a little man. He was approaching with hurried, awkward steps.

"Father!", she suddenly realized, and was immediately struck with fear and confusion. Could this completely unknown and pathetic old man really be her father? Did she have to hug him, pick up the pieces of the feelings that she had once had, get to love him and consider him the person closest to her? She panicked, and for some reason grabbed her briefcase and placed it before her, as if trying to protect herself or push away the person who was in such a hurry to approach her. When her father came up close, she instinctively stepped back: the old man reeked of smoke, tobacco, and an unwashed body. Seberui did not notice anything. He rubbed the palm of his hand twice against his dirty robe, as if to clean it, and reached out for her.

But Aniko did not return his greeting. She looked with fear at her father's black robe, his tangled and greasy hair, his wrinkled face, and felt the nausea well up inside of her.[64]

After the initial ordeal, compounded by the forgotten taste of raw meat and the smell of "dog sweat, mouldy leather, and dampness," the young woman is presented with a number of claims on her future. Her father needs help and comfort in his old age; her orphaned clan needs an heir; and her people need her education and experience in order to improve their lives. These are serious responsibilities, and Aniko knows she cannot shrug them off no matter how defensive and victimized she may feel. And still, what about her own life, her education, her dreams?

How could she abandon it all: college, the theater, movies, dances, discussions with friends about art, about their interesting and bright future? How could she forget the hot and noisy city streets, the favorite spots where she had thought and dreamed so much—and surrender voluntarily to the frozen silence, get lost in the white snowy spaces, put on a leather robe, live by the light of a kerosene lamp and . . . get old?![65]

Little by little, however, she realizes that the choice is not just between duty and freedom, between martyrdom and self-fulfillment. She begins to feel that there may be some real truth in the life that her kinsmen have inherited from their ancestors: "Now Aniko was struck . . . by the general expression of serenity and dignity on the faces of the Nenets and their stone gods. Perhaps these people sitting in front of

[64] Ibid., pp. 48–49.
[65] Ibid., p. 65.

her knew something important and basic about life that she did not know—otherwise they would not behave with such calm and confidence."[66]

Finally, still undecided but not confused anymore, she receives from her father the ancestral images of her clan: "Aniko . . . took the Idol and stood motionless for several minutes, realizing that she had just received the soul of her father, mother, grandfather, and everybody who had lived before her. It was not the Idol that her father had given her, it was the right, the sacred duty to live on one's native land and be human."[67]

Does this mean that she should stay in the tundra? And if so, should she stay in order to dissolve herself in tradition, to discover what was "important and basic about life"—and thus erase her fourteen years of education and discovery? Or should she stay and use her education "to help the Nenets make tundra living just as prosperous and fulfilling as life on the mainland"—for instance, as one character suggests, by preventing them from spending all their money on liquor?[68] And if so, what will happen to the mystery of the ancient Idol? And would this mean that her children would have to face the same dilemma?

Aniko has not yet thought these things through. At the end of the story she leaves for the city, still not knowing whether to come back.[69]

Perestroika and the Numerically Small Peoples of the North

With the advent of perestroika and the collapse of censorship in 1986–88, the discussion of indigenous affairs in the Soviet Union grew in intensity and changed in focus. The northern intellectuals were free to articulate their frustration with the continuing state-sponsored destruction of the way of life that presumably represented their roots, the core of their identity, and the reason for their existence as a group. The 1960s generation of ethnographers were free to say "we told you so" as they pointed to the acute social and economic problems resulting from the settlements and resettlements that they had quietly

---

[66] Ibid., p. 57.
[67] Ibid., p. 68.
[68] Ibid., pp. 72, 80–81, 83–84.
[69] The author, Anna Nerkagi, did return to the tundra with the intention of staying there. See SP, no. 2 (1990) 32. For a literary version of a successful homecoming, see Liubov' Neniang, "Zvon olen'ikh rogov," in Blizok krainii Sever.

opposed. They could also, for the first time in their careers, explicitly associate themselves with the welfare of "their peoples" in opposition to state interests and in support of the indigenous intelligentsia. Young demographers, ecologists, and psychologists were free to apply their new methodologies in the remotest corners of the extreme north and use the results to prove the bankruptcy of the old moral and political order. Finally, mass media were now eager to air these views as well as send their own reporters in search of new revelations.[1]

Almost overnight the reading public discovered that the indigenous economy as a whole was a mess, that resettlement had been a disaster, that the elimination of nomadism had been a sham, and that reindeer breeding was steadily declining.[2] It also turned out that most Arctic *sovkhozy* were permanently and hopelessly in debt (the polar-fox pelt for which the state paid 65 rubles 13 kopeks cost about 150 rubles to produce) and that the emphasis on plan-fulfillment had led to a dramatic decrease in traditional forms of consumption.[3] Most guns and boats were controlled by state enterprises; all hunting and fishing for personal needs was severely restricted; and most traditional meals in boarding schools were banned for sanitary reasons (often with canned food as the only substitute). In Chukotka, between 1970 and 1987 the annual per capita fish allowance was cut by half (from 80 to 40 kilos); on the lower Ob' the native northerners were forbidden to fish for salmon and sturgeon or to hunt moose and bear; and the Tiumen' provincial executive committee had outlawed all spring hunting. It was now revealed, in other words, that many circumpolar peoples had become poachers on their own traditional hunting grounds, and that the promised consumer items from the south were scarce, expensive, and frequently unwanted, aimed as they were at the immigrant population.[4]

Most of these were but the latest (if unusually well-advertised) addi-

---

[1] Perhaps the earliest of such exposés to reach a wide audience was V. Sharov's article, "Mala li zemlia dlia malykh narodov?" *Literaturnaia gazeta*, 17 August 1988, written after a trip to Chukotka with the ethnographers Mikhail Chlenov and Igor Krupnik and published after several months of delays.

[2] See in particular, A. I. Pika and B. B. Prokhorov, "Bol'shie problemy malykh narodov," *Kommunist*, no. 16 (1988); A. I. Pika and D. D. Bogoiavlenskii, *Sovremennye problemy razvitiia narodnostei Severa* (Moscow, 1989); Z. P. Sokolova, "Perestroika i sud'by malochislennykh narodov Severa," *Istoriia SSSR*, no. 1 (1990); Sokolova, ed., *Etnokul'turnoe razvitie*; "Chaut nad Paren'iu," pp. 9–10; and Sangi, "Chtoby krona ne ogolilas'," and "Posleslovie k sudu i sledstviiu."

[3] Pika and Prokhorov, "Bol'shie problemy," p. 78; Pika and Bogoiavlenskii, *Sovremennye problemy*, pp. 11–12; Sokolova, "Perestroika," pp. 160.

[4] Sokolova, ed., *Etnokul'turnoe razvitie*, pp. 51–53; Sokolova, "Perestroika," p. 159.

tions to traditional concerns, but now these concerns were rearranged and redefined to form a fragile and ultimately redeemable whole known as "the environment." A favorite cause of the village romantics and an important chip in regional politics, it had never figured very prominently in the discussion of northern indigenous affairs: the Iamal tundra and the Khanty-Mansi taiga could not stir the imagination of government planners or Russian intellectuals the way Lake Baikal could. With the emergence of "northern interests" in the press and eventually in elected bodies, however, "ecology" emerged as a potent metaphor for the monumental—indeed elemental—evil of unchecked state power. It was revealed, among other things, that between the early 1960s and late 1980s the northern reindeer herds had been depleted by 25 percent; the Amur basin fish resources, by 95 percent; and the total fishable waters (measured in terms of surface area) in the Khanty-Mansi district, by 96 percent. During the years 1976–77 1.2 million hectares of reindeer pastures had been destroyed in the Iamalo-Nenets autonomous district; in 1986, 900 tons of oil had been spilled in the Harutei-iaga river; and in 1987, 6 tons of copper, 10 tons of arsenic, and 27 tons of zinc had been dumped into two Amur tributaries. Every year, the Amur paper mill poured 50 million cubic meters of waste into the river, and the Nenets autonomous district had already lost 25 percent of its reindeer pastures.[5] According to the writer Eremei Aipin, who had transferred his concerns from fiction to politics, a growing number of native groups were moving from place to place, "running from oil rigs, pipelines, winter barracks, and highways."[6]

As a result of the unrestrained industrial expansion between 1959 and 1979 the share of the aboriginal population engaged in the traditional economy dropped from 70 to 43 percent.[7] At the same time, it was now claimed that the new modern settlements that were supposed to provide a tempting alternative had failed to live up to the early promises, let alone to the Long Journey descriptions. In the late 1980s, the average living area was approximately four square meters per person.

[5] Pika and Prokhorov, "Bol'shie problemy," p. 78; Sokolova, "Perestroika," pp. 158–59; A. Filin, "Kal'ma prosit zashchity," Sovetskaia kul'tura, 27 October 1988; Pika and Bogoiavlenskii, Sovremennye problemy, p. 18; Igor' Duel', "Stena," SP, no. 2 (1987): 12–13, and no. 3 (1988): 14–15; B. B. Prokhorov, "Kak sberech' Iamal," Znanie-sila, no. 7 (1988].

[6] E. D. Aipin, "Ne neft'iu edinoi," Moskovskie novosti, 8 January 1989. See also Alitet Nemtushkin, "Na chashu vesov," SP, no. 3 (1988): 2–3; Sokolova, "Perestroika," pp. 158–59; "Na perelome," Sovetskaia kul'tura, 11 February 1989; V. Vakhnina, "Komu nuzhny sanktsii?" SP, no. 4 (1987): 4; and E. D. Aipin, "Chum na doroge razdora," Moskovskie novosti, 14 October 1990, pp. 8–9.

[7] Pika and Bogoiavlenskii, Sovremennye problemy, p. 13.

Three percent of the houses had gas; 0.4 percent had running water; and 0.1 percent had central heating.[8] The buildings themselves had been criticized as unsuitable for Arctic conditions when they were first built in the late 1950s–early 1960s. Most of them had never been repaired or modified in the interim.[9] Perhaps most alarming, the native northerners who had been squeezed out of their traditional environment had by and large been unable to compete for new opportunities. The problems that sociologists had first tackled in the 1970s were now described as man-made catastrophes—enormous in scale and perhaps irreversible. In Aipin's words, the circumpolar peoples "have not accomplished the 'great leap from antiquity into socialism' that social scientists prophesied; they have not grown up to become oilmen, geologists, and builders."[10] Instead, according to one group of ethnographers, "for over twenty years northern schools have been producing people who are not prepared for any form of productive work."[11] Between 1959 and 1979 the share of native northerners employed in low-status menial jobs (cleaners, loaders, guards) rose from 13 to 30 percent, and in the oil-rich Khanty-Mansi and Iamalo-Nenets districts, to 30–60 (in some sovkhozy up to 90) percent.[12] According to the ethnogropher Z. P. Sokolova, a typical native settlement could offer jobs to about a third of its residents (the others were enrolled as administrative and auxiliary personnel with very little to do). The local administration seemed to regard this as a natural state of affairs: if native women were entitled to longer stays in maternity wards (up to 30 days); native children grew up in boarding schools at full government expense; and native college students received free round-trip tickets to their places of study in addition to free room, board, and clothing, then there was nothing extraordinary in the fact that the adult natives (who, it was widely believed, never really grew up) were treated as eternal wards of the state.[13]

If the state of the environment—including the traditional econ-

---

[8] Pika and Prokhorov, "Bol'shie problemy," p. 77.

[9] Ibid.; Sokolova, ed., Etnokul'turnoe razvitie, pp. 47–48; Aipin, "Ne neft'iu edinoi."

[10] Aipin, "Ne neft'iu edinoi."

[11] Sokolova, ed., Etnokul'turnoe razvitie, p. 59. See also Kontseptsiia razvitiia Taimyrskogo avtonomnogo okruga (Dudinka, 1990), p. 13; Kontseptsiia ekonomicheskogo i sotsial'nogo razvitiia narodnostei Severa na period 1991–2005 gg. (Iakutsk, 1988), p. 27; "Komu doverit' detstvo?" SP, no 3 (1988): 24–26; E. Kuzakova, "Uroki dobra i oshibok," SP, no. 6 (1986): 32–33.

[12] Pika and Prokhorov, "Bol'shie problemy," p. 80; Pika and Bogoiavlenskii, Sovremennye problemy, p. 13; Kontseptsiia ekonomicheskogo i sotsial'nogo razvitiia, p. 6.

[13] Sharov, "Mala li zemlia."

omy—was the most widely publicized and politically important concern of the early perestroika years, the demographic situation in the north was the newest and, in the eyes of some, the most pressing. It was revealed that in some areas (particularly those with a large immigrant population) up to 30 percent of all native households were headed by single mothers, and in some reindeer-breeding communities up to 30 percent of the herders were bachelors.[14] In spite of a dramatic drop in the infant mortality rate (40 percent in the mid-1980s), the overall population growth between 1970 and 1979 fell by 80 percent (seven "nationalities" actually suffered an absolute decrease in population). The reason cited by most scholars was the rapidly growing adult mortality rate. Between the 1960s and 1980s the average life expectancy among circumpolar peoples dropped twenty years, to age 45 for men and 55 for women. And although the number of tuberculosis-related deaths exceeded the national average by over 500 percent, lung diseases were no longer the leading cause of death in the Arctic. In the late 1980s every other native northerner died as a result of injury, murder, or suicide. Most of these deaths were alcohol-related. In the 20 to 34 age group the northern mortality rate was six times higher than the all-Union average.[15]

Even before the Gorbachev reforms, the realization that not all was well in the Far North had led to the publication of the 1980 Party and government decree urging both local officials and central ministries to improve the native economy, health care, food supplies, housing, and communications. Two academies and two ministries were to battle with reindeer gnats; one ministry was to turn out more boots with fur lining; and all "ministries concerned" were to receive precise quotas with regard to the number of indigenous northerners to be admitted to colleges free of charge.[16] However, given the administrative structure in the north and the unchanged priorities of "all the ministries concerned," it is perhaps not surprising that the decree was diluted even before it reached the pages of Izvestiia: the "measures aimed at further social and economic development" referred to the "territories inhab-

[14] Sokolova, ed., Etnokul'turnoe razvitie, p. 54, and "Perestroika," p. 161.

[15] Sokolova, "Perestroika," p. 161; Pika and Prokhorov, "Bol'shie problemy," p. 80; Pika and Bogoiavlenskii, Sovremennye problemy, p. 26; A. I. Pika, "Demograficheskaia politika v raionakh prozhivaniia narodov Severa: Problemy i perspektivy," in Regional'nye problemy sotsial'no-demograficheskogo razvitiia (Moscow, 1987); O. M. Zdravomyslova and V. B. Kozlov, "O metodakh izucheniia obraza zhizni korennykh narodnoste: Severa," in Regional'nye problemy, pp. 116–17.

[16] Izvestiia, 26 February 1980.

ited by the peoples of the north"—not the peoples of the north themselves. Accordingly, most of the new funds were invested in industrial
centers and their temporary immigrant employees.[17]

With the advent of perestroika, the economic situation of the indigenous northerners deteriorated even further. In the summer of 1988 the
Council of Ministers of the USSR announced the abolition of centralized consumer-good deliveries and proclaimed a new era of free *khoz-
raschet*-based agreements among regions and enterprises. This meant
the end of the so-called Special Conditions for the Shipment of Goods
to the Areas of the Far North, which had forced trading organizations to
undertake unprofitable deliveries to the Arctic territories where prices
were artificially low and transportation losses unusually high. Given
that the northern districts had almost no manufactured goods and did
not own the raw materials they produced, the newly liberated trading
organizations promptly discontinued their relations with them, selling
their wares to the highest bidder and willingly paying relatively low
fines for breaking old treaties.[18]

One way to deal with the situation was to bring back the old "command methods" and restore the Special Conditions, as requested by
twelve northern deputies at the Supreme Soviet of the USSR.[19] Or one
could strike a deal with the rich ministries active in the north, as did
the people's deputy from Iamal, Roman Rugin, who surprised his antidevelopment colleagues by writing a letter to Prime Minister Ryzhkov
urging a speedy increase in gas exploration in exchange for new housing, services, and guaranteed jobs for the natives.[20] Meanwhile, the Novosibirsk sociologists continued to insist that in the long run, given the
"objective inevitability" of technological progress and its social and
economic side effects, the only viable solution was to increase direct
government subsidies in order to make the aboriginal economy more
"rational" and thus more competitive and self-sufficient.[21]

These were new times, however, and most of the new spokesmen for

[17] Vladimir Sangi, "Otchuzhdenie," *Sovetskaia Rossiia*, 11 September 1988, and
"Posleslovie k sudu i sledstviiu," p. 7; "Na perelome"; Ch. M. Taksami, "O politicheskom
i ekonomicheskom polozhenii malochislennykh narodov Severa i putiakh ikh razvitiia,"
in *Materialy s"ezda malochislennykh narodov severa* (Moscow, 1990), pp. 11–12; Sokolova, "Perestroika," p. 158.

[18] V. Gendlin, "Iarmarka pokupatelei," *SP*, no. 1 (1990): 4–6, and no. 2 (1991): 12.

[19] "Deputatskii zapros," *SP*, no. 1 (1990): 4.

[20] Roman Rugin, "Deputatskii zapros," *SP*, no. 6 (1989): 6–8.

[21] *Kontseptsiia ekonomicheskogo i sotsial'nogo razvitiia*, pp. 11, 14–15, 22, 26, 33;
*Predlozheniia k kontseptsii sotsial'nogo i ekonomicheskogo razvitiia narodnostei
Severa v usloviiakh nauchno-tekhnicheskogo progressa* (Novosibirsk, 1988), p. 43.

the northern peoples (Russian ethnographers and native intellectuals) favored new solutions. One such solution, which swept the country and seemed to embrace all others, was the "proclamation of sovereignty," or rather, the "restoration of sovereignty" (usurped by the Party/State) to its legitimate source, the People. Just who constituted the People and in what bodies their sovereignty could be vested was a matter open to discussion. Municipalities, local soviets, autonomous districts, and ethnic groups might all claim to be the true embodiment of popular sovereignty, whereas the Russian Federation as a whole might belong either to the Russians (Rossiia dlia russkikh) or to the "people of Russia" (Rossiia dlia rossiian). Whatever hierarchies of representation one tried to construct, however, most early pro-perestroika intellectuals agreed that ethnic differences were primary and, indeed, sacred, and that there were at least as many "Peoples" in the Soviet Union as there were nationalities. National (ethnic) governments might be asked to transfer some of their powers elsewhere, but no one seemed to doubt that they should have those powers in the first place.

In other words, all sovereign nationalities (that is, all nationalities) were entitled to their own governments. Hence the first demand with regard to the former small peoples was the (re)creation of autonomous districts, or at least national soviets or villages, for the nineteen narodnosti who did not possess any.[22] In this way the native northerners would join the other nationalities of the USSR, but they would not become equal members of the federation. As Russia's parliamentarians heard repeatedly in the Supreme Soviet, if there were no second-class ethnic groups, why were there second-class administrative units? As the writer Vladimir Sangi put it,

> I do not quite understand why in a democratic state which proclaims the equality of all peoples, fifteen of them, which gave their names to federal republics, have special rights that set them apart from the peoples that have autonomous republics, and even farther apart from those peoples that have been granted only autonomous provinces or autonomous districts. Not to mention those that still have no state structures of their

[22] Sangi, "Chtoby krona ne ogolilas'"; Sokolova, "Perestroika," p. 164; Sokolova, ed. Etnokul'turnoe razvitie, p. 10; Vladimir Sangi, Iuvan Shestalov, V. Ledkov, Roman Rugin, E. D. Aipin, V. Koianto, G. Varlamova, "Letter to M. S. Gorbachev," 20 April 1988 (unpublished); Taksami, "O politicheskom i ekonomicheskom polozhenii," p. 13; I. Pika and Bogoiavlenskii, Sovremennye problemy, p. 9; B. B. Prokhorov, I. I. Krupnik, G. V. Starovoitova, and A. I. Pika, "Reshenie i rekomendatsii ob"edinennogo zasedaniia gruppy 'Trevozhnyi Sever,'" 22 February 1989 (unpublished), pp. 3, 6; Iu. Samar, "Nashi popravki k konstitutsii," SP (February 1991): 12.

own . . . I am convinced that we must have a commonwealth [*sodruzhest-vo*] of equal peoples, irrespective of their numbers.[23]

Any upgrading of administrative status to republic level had to involve the creation of a legislature. To quote Sangi again, "the Tatars and the Estonians have their own supreme soviets. Why don't we?"[24] Accordingly, the various national societies formed by the local intelligentsia to promote traditional culture, language study, and environmental protection[25] were regarded by the activists as embryonic parliaments, and in March 1990 an all-Union congress of circumpolar peoples created the Association of the Numerically Small Peoples of the North.[26] The congress was convened with the encouragement of the Party leadership[27] and organized by the Northern Section of the RSFSR Council of Ministers, but the candidate supported by the sponsors (the Nivkh ethnographer Ch. M. Taksami) was defeated by the writer Vladimir Sangi, who vowed to turn the Association into a Northern Supreme Soviet with its own budget.[28] A year later, in May 1991, the native-northern members of the USSR and the Russian Federation Supreme Soviets formed their own caucus known as the Deputies' Assembly of the Numerically Small Peoples of the North. The purpose of the Assembly was to promote and coordinate legislative and public-relations activities at all levels of representation, from the Union and republic parliaments to local soviets.[29]

The problem remained, however, that none of these levels of representation were run along ethnic lines. All autonomous units had been formed as national homelands, and all of them were named after the "primary" ("titular") nationality, but as far as citizenship was concerned, no legal distinction was drawn between "natives" and "non-

---

[23] Vladimir Sangi, "Vernut' prava khoziaevam zemli," *Izvestiia*, 12 July 1990.

[24] Vladimir Sangi, personal interview, 27 June 1990. See also E. D. Aipin, "Idet bezzas-tenchivyi grabezh," SP (January 1991): 3.

[25] Such as the Association of the Kola Saami, the Society of Ket Culture, and the Association "Iamal for Our Descendants!"

[26] The former official designation *malye narody Severa* ("small peoples of the North") was seen as demeaning and was therefore replaced by the term *malochislennye narody Severa* ("numerically small peoples of the North"). Sometimes the modifier was dropped altogether.

[27] See *Pravda*, 24 September 1989.

[28] Thus, curiously, the native northerners would have a "federal parliament" before each ethnic group had established a legislature of its own.

[29] See "Status Deputatskoi Assamblei malochislennykh narodov Severa, 7 May 1991" (unpublished); "Ustav Deputatskoi Assamblei malochislennykh narodov Severa, 7 May 1991" (unpublished); "Programma Deputatskoi Assamblei malochislennykh narodov Severa, 7 May 1991" (unpublished).

natives." In the north more than anywhere else, the indigenous nationalities as defined by the state remained "numerically small," that is,
tiny minorities in their home districts. If democracy meant "one per-
son-one vote," and if citizenship remained ethnicity-blind, then democracy would spell the end of the circumpolar peoples as sovereign
nationalities.[30]
One way to deal with the problem was to extend ethnic quotas to all
elective and nonelective managerial positions. Another familiar remedy was to create a special chamber of nationalities, this time at the
district level. Finally the individuals belonging to a particular ethnic
group could be granted veto power over all decisions concerning their
welfare.[31] This way, it was hoped, they would become true masters of
their land and all its resources. After all, this is what sovereignty was
all about and this is what all the peoples of the Soviet Union were
aspiring to. In the words of one Nenets journalist,

> The capitals of Arab states have used their petrodollars to build marble
> palaces. Envy is not a nice sentiment. But what is a Nenets supposed to
> feel if he knows that every year, every month, every day millions of tons
> of oil and billions of cubic meters of gas are being pumped out of his
> native soil? What is a Khanty supposed to think, if he knows that under
> different circumstances this oil and this gas could drastically change the
> life of his people?[32]

To most reformers, however, there was much more to northern sovereignty than getting a fair share of the industrial spoils. The idea was to
preserve a *way of life*, and like so many perestroika-related ideas, it led
one to the West or back to the 1920s—that is to say, to reservations,
otherwise known as ethnic territories, reserves, zones for the preferential development of traditional economies, nature and culture parks,
and even "ethnoecopolises," and defined as special areas set aside for
exclusive or privileged aboriginal use, with non-native participation

[30] V. Golubchikova, "Kuda pereselilis' ikh dushi?" SP (January 1991): 20–21.
[31] "Programma Deputatskoi Assamblei," p. 3; Predlozheniia k kontseptsii, p. 12; "Proekt Programmy i Ustava Assotsiatsii 'Iamal—potomkam!'" Krasnyi sever, no. 37 (September 1989); Taksami, "O politicheskom i ekonomicheskom polozhenii," p. 13; Iu.
Ivanchuk, "Iamal: Chem velik i chem mal," Sovetskaia kul'tura, 7 October 1989; Pika
and Bogoiavlenskii, Sovremennye problemy, p. 16; Kontseptsiia razvitiia Taimyrskogo
avtonomnogo okruga, pp. 14, 20, 21; V. P. Pervushin, "Politicheskii aspekt avtonomii,"
Dialog, no. 8 (1989): 30.
[32] Quoted in Ivanchuk, "Iamal." See also Aipin, "Idet bezzastenchivyi grabezh," p. 3;
Prokhorov, "Kak sberech' Iamal," p. 2.

(and immigration) restricted or forbidden.[33] In this context, the indigenous peoples of the north were not usually seen as equal members of
the federation. They did not differ from the Estonians simply because
they did not have a majority in their districts or a national legislature.
They were regarded as culturally unique and therefore entitled to special status. In the opinion of most authors, therefore, the only fully applicable legal model for the northerners was not a nation-state
constitution but the *Convention Concerning Indigenous and Tribal
Peoples in Independent Countries,* which singled out certain ethnic
groups as sufficiently distinct from the surrounding "national community" to require special protection.[34] In this context, the model for
northern sovereignty would be found in Alaska and Scandinavia, not
in the newly emancipated nation states of the former Soviet Union.[35]

Since the mid-1930s it had been assumed that all nationalities, no
matter how different, were "socialist in content." They might have
started out at different levels, but they shared the same interests and
aspirations. A Russian oilman and an Evenk trapper were equally committed to the onward march of industrialization, except that, in order
for them to reach the finish line at the same time, the northerner would
have to march a bit faster. The official purpose of "affirmative action"
had been to overcome his temporary "cultural backwardness," not to
preserve his inherent cultural distinctiveness. Half a century later,
most northern scholars (and a good number of Soviets) regarded these
assumptions as unacceptable. As far as they were concerned, human-
kind consisted of individuals and "ethnoses," which were the only
fully legitimate subjects of rights, autonomy, and morality. Emphasizing class identity and universal brotherhood at the expense of ethnic
diversity and individual uniqueness was regarded as both politically
unrealistic and morally perverse.

[33] "Proekt Programmy"; Sangi, "Chtoby krona ne ogolilas'"; "Na perelome"; Sharov,
"Mala li zemlia?"; Sangi et al., "Letter," p. 3; Taksami, "O politicheskom i ekonomicheskom polozhenii," p. 14; "S"ezd korennykh narodnostei Iamalo-Nenetskogo avtonomnogo okruga" (unpublished), pp. 1–2; *Osvoenie bez otchuzhdeniia: Materialy
ekspertnogo oprosa* (Tiumen', 1989), pp. 6–9, 15–17, 20–21; A. I. Pika, "Samoustranenie—ne luchshii sposob," *Dialog,* no. 8 (1989): 31–34; Iuvan Shestalov, "O tom, chto
nravstvenno i chto beznravstvenno," *Dialog,* no. 8 (1989): 41–43. See also other articles
in *Dialog,* no. 8 (1989).
[34] Convention 169, adopted by the International Labor Organization at its Seventy-
Sixth Session, Geneva, 27 June 1989.
[35] A. I. Pika, "Severnye pripoliarnye strany: Problemy i perspektivy primeneniia konventsii MOT no. 169 (1989) 'O korennykh i vedushchikh plemennoi obraz zhizni narodakh v nezavisimykh stranakh," in *Mezhdunarodnyi simpozium "pravo i etnos."
Materialy dlia obsuzhdeniia, Golitsyno 1–5 oktiabria 1991 g.* (Moscow, 1991), pp. 54–

Nevertheless, some students of northern affairs believed (and had plenty of perestroika-generated evidence to show) that human rights and national rights were not necessarily compatible. Consequently, they stressed that reservations ought to be regarded as an opportunity, as one choice among many. In the words of I. A. Nikolaeva and E. A. Khelimskii, total isolation would be "not only unrealistic but also essentially undemocratic, because it would put the interests of national and cultural ecology above the interests of individuals."[36] E. L. Dubko (a philosopher from Moscow State University) went even further by suggesting that "one should worry not about 'saving an ethnos' or a primitive uniqueness but about the people who must not be swept away by this 'catastrophe' [meaning progress], which was, of course, historically predetermined."[37]

This was a minority view. According to the general consensus, in the case of small peoples in general and the small peoples of the north in particular, equality had been a sham and human rights, a fiction. "In conditions of equality the strongest always prevails and the expert at the "rules of the game" always wins. Unfortunately, the northern peoples are not yet in this position."[38] Individualism and competition were thus immoral if one of the participants was unable to compete. The state should practice "reasonable interference"[39] and support "not just the people who live in the cold and remote northern lands, but the nations who strive to survive and preserve their ethnic uniqueness."[40] Hence most of those who emphasized choice talked about collective choice (through an election or referendum) and a collective national future, assuming that this choice would involve some form of protection and separation.[41]

Given the generally accepted belief in the absolute and inherent importance of national identity (understood in cultural and biological terms), it seemed natural that all forms of "ethnic uniqueness" be protected. In Taksami's words, "Each nation, irrespective of its size, is unique, and the loss of any one of them is an irreplaceable loss for

---

66; "Konventsiia 26 (Assotsiatsii malochislennykh narodov Severa Sovetskogo Soiuza 16 October 1990" (unpublished).

[36] Predlozheniia k kontseptsii, pp. 27–28. See also Osvoenie bez otchuzhdeniia, pp. 8–9, 13–15, and V. N. Sagatovskii, "Garantii vybora," Dialog, no. 8 (1989): 35–36.

[37] Osvoenie bez otchuzhdeniia, p. 30. Cf. p. 34.

[38] Pika and Prokhorov, "Bol'shie problemy," p. 82.

[39] Osvoenie bez otchuzhdeniia, p. 7.

[40] Pika and Prokhorov, "Bol'shie problemy," p. 81.

[41] Osvoenie bez otchuzhdeniia, pp. 11, 15–17, 23–24, 42–44; A. K. Omel'chuk, "U 'nas' net prava reshat' za 'nikh,'" Dialog, no. 8 (1989): 26–28.

world culture, the world community as a whole."[42] But this was not all. According to most northern scholars and activists, the circumpolar peoples might be more unique and more irreplaceable than others.

> The ethnographers who study the culture of these peoples are amazed by its singularity and its capacity to adapt to local conditions and to adhere to the principle of ecological balance in nature . . . ; by the principles of collectivism . . . , by the simplicity bordering on genius as well as the elegance of their abodes, clothing, and footwear; by the vividness and expressiveness of their thinking.[43]

This "fragile civilization" is contrasted with the "aggressive, self-righteous, technocratic"[44] culture of industrial society, which, "like a tank, rolls over the body of northern culture which it finds alien and incomprehensible."[45] Once again, political and scholarly discourse had caught up with fiction—partly because novelists (most notably Sangi, Aipin, and Nerkagi) had become politically active and partly because many scholars were now acting primarily in their capacity as Russian *intelligenty*, that is, as defenders of true morality and the true interests of the "people." In the discussions about indigenous life, Dersu Uzala reigned supreme as many intellectuals saw a kind of spontaneous environmentalism as the most precious feature of traditional societies. "There is no doubt that the culture of the indigenous peoples of the North, particularly their ecological culture, is more complete and organic than the culture of the migrant population because it reflects a centuries-old homeostasis between man and northern nature."[46]

As Sangi explained, "It so happened in history that during many centuries Europeans were forced to wage wars, seize something, enslave someone. . . . During the same period, the aboriginal northerners were perfecting their relationship with their environment."[47] In other words, reservations or ethnic territories were needed not only to en-

---

[42] Taksami, "O politicheskom i ekonomicheskom polozhenii," p. 7. Cf. Stalin, *Sochineniia* (Stanford), 3:100. For a dissenting opinion based on a constructionist theory of ethnicity and a dim view of non-Russian nationalism, see Valery A. Tishkov, "The Crisis in Soviet Ethnography," *Current Anthropology* 33, no. 4 (1992): 371–82.

[43] Sokolova, ed., *Etnokul'turnoe razvitie*, p. 16.

[44] Pika and Prokhorov, "Bol'shie problemy," p. 79.

[45] Sangi, "Vernut'."

[46] Iu. M. Fedorov, "Kul'turnaia integratsiia," *Dialog*, no. 8 (1989): 38. This thesis is questioned by I. I. Krupnik in his *Arkticheskaia etnoekologiia*.

[47] Sangi, "Vernut'."

sure meaningful sovereignty, not only to guarantee autonomous utilization (or nonutilization) of resources, or even to preserve ethnic
differences for their own sake, but first and foremost to preserve cultures that were both morally superior and industrially noncompetitive.
These two traits were, of course, but two sides of the same coin.

> The European view of the world and the view of the world of the indige-
> nous population are qualitatively different. Their attitude toward nature
> is also completely different. If a European regards nature as a partner
> from whom he can get "more" "at a cheaper price," the indigenous popu-
> lation lives in nature and alongside nature, and sees itself as a continu-
> ation of nature.[48]

Thus, the point of the reservation was to provide a place where the
native northerners would be allowed and encouraged to "be themselves": live in traditional settlements, engage in traditional economic
activities, eat traditional food, wear traditional clothes, practice traditional values and speak the language of their forefathers.[49]

The reservation solution had one large and obvious problem. Thousands of young northerners were said to have lost their ethnic identity
along with their mother tongue and traditional skills. Who was to help
them and their children recover their former selves (as defined by the
ethnographers and fiction writers)? Who was to convince them that
their former selves were worth recovering? The answer was clear although not always spelled out: the Russian state and the Russian-
educated national intelligentsia were the only viable agents of positive
change. As Vladimir Sangi, Iuvan Shestalov, V. Ledkov, Roman Rugin,
E. D. Aipin, V. Koianto, and G. Varlamova phrased it in their letter to
Gorbachev,

> With regard to deputies to the Supreme Soviets of the USSR and RSFSR
> from the territories inhabited by the peoples of the north, it would be
> desirable to elect persons who would be educated, politically literate,
> nonparochial in their outlook [s gosudarstvennym myshleniem], fluent

---

[48] Osvoenie bez otchuzhdeniia, p. 16. Cf. "Proekt Programmy".
[49] See, especially, Sokolova, ed, Etnokul'turnoe razvitie; Sokolova, "Peretsroika";
"Proekt Programmy"; Ustav Assotsiatsii Kol'skikh Saamov; Ustav Obshchestva Ketskoi
kul'tury; and Osvoenie bez otchuzhdeniia, pp. 20–21. Some authors wished to see traditional economies modernized, but most agreed that the economies to be "reserved" and
rationalized should be traditional. See, in particular, Prokhorov et al., "Reshenie i rekomendatsii," pp. 6–7; Pika and Bogoiavlenskii, Sovremennye problemy, p. 14; and
Sangi, "Vernut'."

in their native languages, and capable of solving the crucial problems of economic and cultural development in today's North at the appropriate level.[50]

Supported by sympathetic Russian *intelligenty*, these people ("the cultural core of the nation"[51] and themselves *intelligenty* in the Russian tradition) would work through the parliaments, the Association of Northern Peoples, and the local cultural organizations in order to "take [the northern peoples] back to their origins, to their traditional way of life, to their habitual occupations."[52] According to the Statutes of the Society of Ket Culture, for example, the members' main task was "to teach the Ket people and other peoples to respect the language, history, culture, and economic traditions of the Ket, and to engage in the propaganda of the historical, cultural, and linguistic heritage of the Ket people."[53] This meant that throughout the north there would be a great need for museums, books, clubs, colleges, teachers, textbooks, and publishing houses; that a centralized Institute of the Peoples of the North for the training of the native elite would have to be reopened; and—most important—that large boarding schools would have to be replaced by small, perhaps "semi-nomadic" or half-time schools where indigenous children would be taught the skills needed in the traditional economy.[54]

In other words, most northern reformers expected the state to contribute significantly to the protection and revival of the aboriginal peoples—partly for financial reasons, partly because the aboriginal peoples were regarded as incapable of defending themselves, and partly because nobody wanted the reservations (or sovereign republics) to preserve the status quo: going back, just like marching forward, would require a lot of effort. Hence the Association's attempts to become a branch of the Russian government (its Russian-trained leaders would thus provide a bridge between their people and the state machinery, educating the former and directing the "reasonable interference" of the latter). Hence, also, the efforts by some activists, including the leaders of the Association and prominent northern parliamentari-

[50] Sangi et al., "Letter," p. 4.
[51] Sagatovskii, "Garantii vybora," p. 34.
[52] Sangi, "Vernut'."
[53] *Ustav Obshchestva Ketskoi kul'tury,* p. 2.
[54] Taksami, "O politicheskom i ekonomicheskom polozhenii," pp. 16–20; "S"ezd korennykh narodnostei Iamalo-Nenetskogo avtonomnogo okruga," pp. 6–7; Prokhorov et al, *Reshenie i rekomendatsii,* p. 8; Pika and Bogoiavlenskii, *Sovremennye problemy,* pp. 24–25; Sangi et al., "Letter," p. 4; Sokolova, ed., *Etnokul'turnoe razvitie,* pp. 57–65.

ans, to revive the old Committee of the North, closed half a century before when aboriginal cultural uniqueness (defined as backwardness) had been "finally overcome."[55]

Whatever forms state-directed assistance might take, the exact nature of the relationship between Moscow and the various local organizations remained unclear. The indigenous peoples of the north were sovereign nations, but they seemed to need the Russian state to assert their sovereignty, perhaps even to maintain it. This, in fact, is the dilemma at the heart of the reformist discourse. If diversity is preferable to commonality; if true diversity is based on ethnicity; if all ethnic groups are equal; and if all equal nations are sovereign; then the native northerners are entitled to a nation-state, or at least an autonomous administrative structure equal to that of other republics. This version of emancipation might be impossible, however, because the native northerners are a tiny minority wherever they live and because there might be something about their culture that makes them noncompetitive in an industrial society. Yet if the aboriginal culture is "qualitatively different" from most others, and if that difference manifests itself in a weaker adaptability to the postindustrial social (as opposed to preindustrial natural) environment, then formal equality will lead to the destruction of that culture, which means that if that culture is worth preserving, this preservation has to be done by someone outside the traditional community—be it the Russian state, the Russian-educated native intelligentsia, or (most likely) a combination of the two. This, however, contradicts the commonly accepted principles of national sovereignty and democracy from below.

Different authors tackled these problems differently, but the great majority of them shared the same general assumptions. Whatever the outcome, therefore, the war against backwardness and ethnic diversity "in content" was definitely over. The future of the circumpolar peoples seemed to lie in the past.

[55] Taksami, "O politicheskom i ekonomicheskom polozhenii," p. 21; Sangi et al., "Letter," p. 3; Appeal by Vladimir Sangi and A. V. Krivoshapkin to Yeltsin, Sovetskaia Rossiia, 14 June 1990.

"Multiple mirrors of representation: A Nanai artist and the Bronze Horseman," from M. G. Levin and L. P. Potapov, eds., *Narody Sibiri* (Moscow, 1956)

Conclusion

Now, if you'll only attend, Kitty, and not talk so much, I'll tell
you all my ideas about Looking-glass House.
                              —Lewis Carroll, *Through the Looking-Glass*

This book has been a story of otherness. For as long as Russians have known the circumpolar peoples, they have considered them
essentially different from themselves. Foreigners, aliens, pagans,
brutes, children of nature, primitive communists, national minorities,
or endangered indigenous populations, the native northerners have always been outsiders. Even after the Soviet state formally abolished all
differences "in content," official novelists, theoreticians, and administrators continued to treat the "survivals" of past otherness as an important, albeit transient, reality to be reckoned with—until the
"national form" and "socialist content" finally changed places and difference vigorously reasserted itself under the banner of sovereignty.
The circumpolar *inozemtsy* had come full circle; indeed, it turned out
that they had never really ceased to be *inozemtsy*.

As definitions, explanations, and proposed solutions changed, one
thing remained permanent: difference implied hierarchy. Backward
tribes or wise environmentalists, the circumpolar peoples had always
been better or worse, above or below, more or less; otherness had always
implied a moral judgment. An apparent alternative to this approach
was proposed by the native northerners themselves, as they argued repeatedly with their would-be Russian mentors. To repeat the words of
a Chukchi shaman,

You are Russian people; God gave you the Russian faith and horses;
therefore you have the Russian faith and use horses, while God is in the
sky. We are the Chukchi people; God gave us the Chukchi faith and rein-

deer; therefore we have the Chukchi faith and use reindeer, while God is in the sky. And so you Russians worship the Russian way and keep your horses, while we Chukchi will worship the Chukchi way and keep our reindeer.[1]

It is clear, however, that this ostensible symmetry is but another version of the "separate therefore unequal" approach. In the world of the "Chukchi faith" full humanity was reserved for the members of one's own community; "Chukchi" and "human" signified one and the same thing; and the meaning of a given action depended on whether the actor was friend (kinsman) or foe (foreigner).[2] Customs and spirits were "true" only insofar as they were one's own; there were as many truths as there were peoples.

The Russian peasants and Cossacks who settled in the north lived in a similar world. Common law and common morality were not fully applicable outside one's own community; in fact, the "community of believers" bonded by mutual obligations was generally coterminous with the peasant commune or the Cossack settlement. What was cheating at home was diplomacy when dealing with a state agent, trade when dealing with a native trapper. By the same token, the "Asians" were entitled to their customs and beliefs because it was "their heathen way." They were different, and they were expected to stay that way.

But there were other, "Western" Russians who believed in universal values and equality, and thus had a problem with diversity and with the moral double standard that it implied. Eighteenth-century scholars from Germany and their Russian disciples saw the world as one harmonious whole and equated difference with inadequacy. The Church—not always eagerly—applied the same measure to all of God's children. In both cases toleration of "the Chukchi faith" was a sin—against progress or against divine revelation. When absolute moral consistency (identification of self with other) proved impossible to maintain, however, both the scholars and the missionaries rationalized their concessions to diversity by relegating the natives to permanent childhood. Thus they were fully human (not really aliens), yet not quite ready to be judged and treated like "the rest of us."

Once placed in this category, the small peoples could join the large and variegated group of innocents that had always formed links in the "great chain of being." Growth, progress, and development could repre-

---

[1] Argentov, *Putevye zametki*, p. 41.
[2] Status was subject to change: for certain crimes a kinsman could be expelled from the group and cease to be a "real person," whereas a foreigner could be adopted through a variety of friendship arrangements.

sent corruption as well as perfection, and after the romantic exiles' Siberian sojourn the frozen "infants of mankind" became children of nature, taking their place alongside the denizens of the Golden Age, Avalon, El Dorado, Utopia, Ethiopia, America, and other terrestrial paradises.[3] They remained "other," but their place in the hierarchy had changed. They were superior by virtue of being inadequate, civilized because they were uncorrupted by civilization, truer to "our" values than "we" ourselves.[4] This was a hegemonic discourse—infants are purer than adults as long as they remain infantile, and their perfection is by its very nature incomplete (as that of Marx's primitive communists, Nietzsche's barbarians, and Freud's primal hordes)[5]—but if taken seriously, the noble savage paradigm could have very important implications for administrative practice. One's own return to erstwile innocence might not be practicable, but a policy of protection for those still unspoiled might seem both realistic and vicariously ennobling.

A belief in linear progress and a profound ambivalence about its moral implications lay at the center of nineteenth-century intellectual debate, so that the native question as posed by the regionalists, populists, and other "progressive" intellectuals was generally an attempt to reconcile conflicting rationalist and romantic impulses. On the one hand, progress and human equality demanded that the natives grow up and be treated with the respect and dignity that adults deserve, and this (given the presumed constancy of "human nature") meant that they ought to be measured by a universal moral standard. On the other hand, the application of this same standard revealed a purity and innocence that were worth defending from both progress and equality. The Bolsheviks tried to resolve the dilemma: in their theory nothing was worth defending from progress and equality, and nobody was to be exempt from either progress or (eventually) equality. Some of the Old Guard intellectuals with deep populist roots objected to the universal application of this approach, but when Stalin and his cultural revolutionaries brought the matter to a head, the "native tribes of the northern borderlands" were obliged to join the modern (adult) world without delay. The perception of difference survived the cultural revolution,

[3] See Baudet, *Paradise on Earth*; Boas and Lovejoy, eds. *A Documentary History of Primitivism*; Gilbert Chinard *L'Amérique et le rêve exotique dans la littérature française au XVIIe et au XVIIIe siecle* (Paris, 1934); Fairchild, *The Noble Savage*; G. S. Rousseau and Roy Porter, eds., *Exoticism in the Enlightenment* (Manchester, 1990), esp. pp. 1–22; and White, "The Forms of Wildness."

[4] Roy Harvey Pearce, *The Savages of America: A Study of the Indian and the Idea of Civilization* (Baltimore, Md., 1965), p. 138.

[5] White, "The Forms of Wildness," pp. 35–36.

however, and when noble savages returned in the 1960s, they found their family tradition unbroken. Nobility had come and gone and come again, but difference as a form of incompleteness remained.

There is little doubt that whatever changes in representation did occur were largely a function of Russia's view of itself. For as long as Russian identity was defined in terms of Orthodox Christianity the circumpolar peoples were generally seen as inferiors redeemable through baptism. After the introduction of the cultured/backward dichotomy, however, the Russian intelligentsia (itself the creature of this dichotomy) invariably measured the country, "the people," and sundry Asians and Europeans in evolutionary terms. The circumpolar peoples could be admired or despised, pitied or respected depending on what one thought of progress and development, but the constant was that one always thought of progress and development. This is not to say, however, that all Russian representations of the native northerners—indeed all colonial representations—were "self-contained fantasies that are entirely indifferent to reality" (except the basic "realities of domination").[6] In some cases perceptions clearly changed because the policies based on earlier perceptions had not led to expected outcomes, as when the natives refused to play their parts and failed to demonstrate that they had proper priests, princes, or proletarians. Nor is it fair to assume that all colonial representations are ultimately determined by the "gross political fact" of colonial domination.[7] Even the all-pervasive image of northern inferiority (including superiority by virtue of simplicity) was not the inevitable result of imperial hegemony. The changes that had taken place in circumpolar societies proved largely irrelevant to certain Russian perceptions because they did not affect the principles on which those perceptions were based. If all societies are classified relative to their degree of "westernization"—and they have been so classified in Russia since at least the eighteenth century—then a truly "meaningful" change has to result in the West's being "outwested," that is, in certain economic, social, and cultural expectations being fulfilled. That this goal has never been achieved in subarctic Eurasia, sub-Saharan Africa, or indeed Central Russia does not mean that it cannot happen at all, for better or worse. The Estonians, for example, who in nineteenth-century Russia tended to be portrayed as "sullen Finns" and inarticulate rural barbarians

---

[6] Abdul R. JanMohamed, *Manichean Aesthetics: The Politics of Literature in Colonial Africa* (Amherst, 1983), p. 3; Edward W. Said, *Orientalism* (New York, 1979), p. 21.

[7] Said, *Orientalism*, pp. 15, 21.

(*chukhontsy*), came to represent the epitome of Western development and sophistication after their reincorporation into the empire in 1940. This "test by development" can of course be challenged, but it seems fairly clear that it has never been abandoned. In other words, the small peoples of the north possess a certain reality that has not been questioned since the early eighteenth century and that imposes rigid constraints on the variability of discourse about them. Guests from remoter realms can be all things to all people, from the Abominable Snowman to E.T., from the Houyhnhnms to Mr. Spock, but the taiga and tundra foragers have to be primitives—noble or ignoble—for as long as they remain foragers.

The relationship between these images and actual native administration operated on multiple levels and in both directions. On the one hand, the perceived consequences of certain colonial practices led to changes in representation and the formulation of new colonial practices, as when the failure to find sufficient class cleavages resulted in the discovery of female "proletarians." On the other hand, concepts articulated in a totally different context—primarily that of the Russia-West opposition—were frequently applied to the circumpolar societies and translated into specific imperial policies, as when the northerners were forced to follow the Russians in building socialism (and ended up by modifying the theory of transition). On at least two occasions—under Speranskii and Smidovich/Skachko—German romanticism and its descendant Russian populism reached the pinnacle of the imperial structure and brought the noble savage to a position of legislative prominence. If Russians were the primary agents of corruption and the northerners were worthy of admiration insofar as they were not like Russians, the best colonial government was the least intrusive colonial government—even if the result was that more colonial government was necessary to ensure "protection." Both the 1822 and the 1926 statutes of indigenous administration included some thoroughly unromantic practical concerns: Speranskii and Skachko harbored strong evolutionary commitments, and in both cases local frontiersmen continued to pursue their own interventionist activities. Still, it is obvious that the state policy of unhurried paternalism "made a difference" to the extent that it limited ideological proselytizing, economic development, Army conscription, and tax collection. Most of the time, however, the Russian government proceeded from a far less benevolent view, so that the real question was not how much of the native culture was worth preserving but whether to bother saving the people whose culture was assumed to be worthless. The times when the state answered in the affirmative were as infrequent as they were dramatic. It took Peter the Great's modernizing, Alexander III's Russification, and Stalin's combination of the two for the imperial goverment to identify itself fully with its own universalist claims (ultimately egalitarian and hence intolerant of difference).

These were but brief interludes, however. As in the circumpolar areas of Fennoscandia, Greenland, and North America, the natural and man-made conditions in the Russian Arctic were not conducive to interventionism. Agriculture was largely unfeasible; most industries were unprofitable; and prior to the twentieth century the region's strategic importance was deemed minimal. As a result, long-term immigration was limited and attempts at intensive cultural and economic change were of relatively short duration. The fur trade, the most important and often the only link between the northerners and the world economy, did not require the alienation of land or the recruitment of unfree labor. In Siberia as in Canada, it relied on a continuation of the hunting and trapping economy, discouraged incursions by non-natives (other than as trading intermediaries), and usually demanded a greater adaptive effort from southern settlers than from northern trappers. Ironically, when the perceived economic role of the circumpolar territories changed decisively in the middle of the twentieth century, the primitivist canon was back in vogue, disproving the notion of an essential connection between the economic "base" of imperialism and its rhetorical justifications. The interventionist discourse had spent itself before the actual economic intervention, and the government had reverted to its traditional policy of accepting de facto inequality while continuing to predict the imminent death of all difference.

But does difference really have to be sacrificed to equality? Is otherness always hierarchical? Is sameness the only alternative to inequality? These are the central questions of most studies of representation, the questions which the majority of authors answer with a resounding "no" and which they consequently present as moral challenges to their readers. According to Johannes Fabian, who is particularly interested in temporal otherness, "the absence of the Other from our Time has been his mode of presence in our discourse—as an object and victim. That is what needs to be overcome."[8] (In this particular discourse "the Other" stands for non-Western humanity, and "our" refers to the West in general and anthropology—as Western science of the Other—in particular.) In Edward Said's characteristically clear formulation, "per-

[8] Fabian, *Time and the Other* (New York), p. 154.

haps the most important task of all would be . . . to ask how one can study other cultures and peoples from a libertarian, or a nonrepressive and nonmanipulative, perspective."[9] The real question is thus not "whether" but "how," even though the "knowledge-is-power" assumption held by the same authors would seem to make the whole endeavor quixotic.[10]

The most determined effort to construct difference-cum-equality has come from postmodernist anthropologists who experiment with polyphony, dialog, and "coevalness" in an interesting but ultimately unsuccessful attempt to author texts without assuming authority over them.[11] Stephen A. Tyler goes further than most in his rejection of a modernity "where others are only ghosts out of a romanticized past, summoned like natives from far off places to justify and legitimize alienation by their outlandish otherness"—only to conjure up ghosts of a romanticized future in which "orality implicates participation, common action, common sense, reciprocity, communication, and the *communis* as key concepts in place of our 'letterized' epistemology of being, knowing, and representation founded on the distanced, alienated, and impersonal observation of a transcendental, panoptic ego."[12] The postmodern paradise has met the premodern Gemeinschaft.

Similarly, Joan Wallach Scott argues that equality "means the ignoring of differences between individuals for a particular purpose or in a particular context," but refuses either to subsume women into a general "human" category (because it leads to the loss of experiences that are uniquely women's) or to accept the binary construction of sexual difference (because it results in the destruction of diversity within each category). The solution, according to Scott, "is to refuse to oppose

[9] Said, *Orientalism*, p. 24.

[10] Cf. Said, *Orientalism*, pp. 10, 13–14, and 24; Fabian, *Time and the Other*, pp. 144 and 154; Marianna Torgovnick, *Gone Primitive: Savage Intellects, Modern Lives* (Chicago, 1990), pp. 17 and 70–72.

[11] For an introduction, see James Clifford, *The Predicament of Culture* (Cambridge, Mass., 1988); James Clifford and George E. Marcus, eds., *Writing Culture: The Poetics and Politics of Ethnography* (Berkeley, Calif., 1986); Clifford Geertz, *Works and Lives: The Anthropologist as Author* (Stanford, Calif., 1988); Marc Manganaro, ed., *Modernist Anthropology: From Fieldwork to Text* (Princeton, N. J. 1990); George E. Marcus and Michael M.J. Fisher, *Anthropology as Cultural Critique: An Experimental Moment in the Human Sciences* (Chicago, 1986); and Stephen P. Sangren, "Rhetoric and the Authority of Ethnography," *Current Anthopology*, no. 29 (1988): 405–35.

[12] Stephen Tyler, "On Being Out of Words," *Cultural Anthropology* 1, no. 1 (1986): 131, 136. For an interesting critique, see Thomas de Zengotita, "Speakers of Being: Romantic Refusion and Cultural Anthropy," in *Romantic Motives: Essays on Anthropological Sensibility*, ed. George W. Stocking, Jr. (Madison, Wis., 1989), pp. 74–123.

equality to difference and insist continually on differences: differences as the condition of individual and collective identities, differences as the constant challenge to the fixing of those identities, history as the repeated illustration of the play of differences, differences as the very meaning of equality itself."[13] Thus equality implies the suppression of differences, but the celebration of differences leads back to equality and the eventual disappearance of differences. When all identities and all concepts have been subjected to this procedure, one ends up in a world with no power and hence—given Scott's own assumptions—no knowledge, no communication, no being.

Like most Romantic paradigms, this one discerns the seeds (vestiges) of perfection on our side of the looking glass. If "ours" is the "expansive, aggressive, and oppressive" culture of "blood, death, and horror," "in which social and cultural continuities appear to be fractured and individuals, abruptly wrenched from their human and spiritual contexts, are no longer able to recognize or realize themselves"[14] (let alone respect differences), then our salvation lies in our others, who are by definition the opposite of death and alienation. Depending on who "we" are, this group may include peasants, women, or proletarians, but towering over them all are the remote "natives" who have the longest history of nobility and exoticism. They are natural beings who exist "beyond chronological time" as true "participant-observers of Nature" (as opposed to Western "voyeurs"): "undogmatic, experiential, integrated into a whole way of life, including environment and kinship relations."[15] *Mutatis mutandis*, they are also the ultimate deconstructionists, with the shamans mobilizing colonial otherness in

> creative deployments of improvised building and rebuilding neocolonial healing ritual wherein fate is wrested from the hands of God and transcribed into a domain of chance and perhapsness. In place of the order of God and the steadfastness of his signifiers/signatures where the divine and the natural fuse, the domain of chance foregrounds the epistemic murk of sorcery where contradiction and ambiguity in social relations

[13] Joan Wallach Scott, *Gender and the Politics of History* (New York, 1988), pp. 172–75.

[14] Fabian, *Time and the Other*, p. 144; Fredric Jameson, "Postmodernism, or the Cultural Logic of Capital," *New Left Review*, no. 146 (1984): 57; Jean Comaroff, *Body of Power, Spirit of Resistance: The Culture and History of a South African People* (Chicago, 1985), p. 2.

[15] Calvin Martin, Introduction to *The American Indian and the Problem of History*, ed. Martin (Oxford, 1987), pp. 16–18, and "The Metaphysics of Writing Indian-White History," in ibid., p. 28; Christopher Vecsey, "Envision Ourselves Darkly, Imagine Ourselves Richly," in ibid., p. 123.

undermine his steadfastness in a weltering of signs cracking the divine and the natural apart from one another and into images from which what Barthes called the third or obtuse meaning erupts into play.[16]

If "knowledge and power are one," the native knew about it long before Foucault; if "the dogma of investigator neutrality" is "naive, unnecessary, and improbable," he does not want anything to do with it; and if the ultimate human value is the promotion of diversity and "affirmation of the Other," the native is sure to be its most passionate and consistent champion.[17] As Marianna Torgovnick puts it, "The Tarzan I like best is the doubt-filled Tarzan, willing to learn from blacks and women, willing to ask and examine the question What does a man do? . . . He believes apes worthy of respect, love, fear, and consideration (as we all believe 'our kind' worthy)."[18]

Do all attempts to rescue the native from otherness-as-inferiority have to result in the triumphant return of the noble savage? Perhaps so. Perhaps this is an "eternal moment in human culture."[19] Perhaps as long as we are not fully whole—and hence a little savage—someone else will always have to bear the burden of our backwardness.

[16] Taussig, Shamanism, Colonialism, and the Wild Man: A Study in Terror and Healing (Chicago, 1980), p. 465.

[17] Robin Ridington, "Fox and Chickadee," in The American Indian and the Problem of History, ed. Martin, p. 134; Joanna Overing, ed., Reason and Morality (London, 1985) p. 11; Robert Jaulin, La paix blanche: Introduction à l'ethnocide (Paris, 1974), 2:280.

[18] Torgovnick, Gone Primitive, pp. 70–71.

[19] White, "The Forms of Wildness," p. 25. See also Michael Herzfeld, Anthropology through the Looking Glass. Critical Ethnography in the Margins of Europe (Cambridge 1987), p. 18.

Bibliography

Abramov, N. A. "Materialy dlia istorii khristianskogo prosveshcheniia Sibiri."
ZhMNP 81, no. 5 (1854): 15–53.
———. "Opisanie Berezovskogo kraia." Zapiski IRGO, no. 12 (1857): 329–448.
Abramzon, S. M. "Ob etnograficheskom izuchenii kolkhoznogo krest'ianstva."
SE, no. 3 (1952): 145–50.
———. "Sovetskaia etnografiia v nachale 30kh godov (iz vospominanii etno-
grafa)." SE, no. 4 (1976): 90–92.
Adamov, A. G. G. I. Shelikhov. Moscow: Geofrafgiz, 1952.
———. G. I. Shelikhov—zamechatel'nyi russkii moreplavatel' i issledovatel'.
Moscow: Pravda, 1951.
———. Pervye russkie issledovateli Aliaski. Moscow: Uchpedgiz, 1950.
———. Pravda o russkikh otkrytiiakh v Amerike. Moscow: Znanie, 1952.
Adler, Bruno. "Eniseiskie ostiaki." ZhN, no. 31, (1921).
Afanas'ev, G. "Zaniatiia i zhizn' Sakhalinskikh Evenkov." TT, no. 1 (1928):
38–42.
———. "Zhizn' zhenshchiny-evenki na Sakhaline." TT, no. 2 (1930): 121–24.
Agishev, R. K. Luna v ushchel'iakh. Moscow: Sovetskaia Rossiia, 1967.
———. Syn taigi. 1947. Reprint. Moscow: Detskaia literatura, 1968.
Aipin, E. D. "Chum na doroge razdora." Moskovskie novosti, 14 October
1990, pp. 8–9.
———. "Idet bezzastenchivyi grabezh." SP (January 1991): 3.
———. "Ne neft'iu edinoi." Moskovskie novosti, 8 January 1989.
Akimova, T. "Poezdka na Aldanzoloto." SA, no. 2 (1927): 99–106.
Akopov, S. "Bor'ba s bytovymi prestupleniiami." RN, no. 4–5 (1930): 58–69.
Alachev. "Novyi byt u ostiakov." TT, no. 2 (1930): 134–39.
Aleksandrov, M. "Vozdushnyi tarantas ili vospominaniia o poezdkakh po Vos-
tochnoi Sibiri." In Gurevich, ed., Vostochnaia Sibr', pp. 69–110.
Aleksandrov, V. A. Rossiia na dal'nevostochnykh rubezhakh (vtoraia polovina
XVII v.). Moscow: Nauka, 1969.
———. Russkoe naselenie Sibiri XVII–nachala XVIII v. AN SSSR. Trudy Insti-
tuta etnografii im. N. N. Miklukho-Maklaia. Novaia seriia, vol. 87. Moscow:
Nauka, 1964.

Alekseenko, E. A. *Kety: Istoriko-etnograficheskie ocherki.* Leningrad: Nauka, 1967.

———. "Khristianizatsiia na Turukhanskom Severe i ee vliianie na mirovozz-renie i religioznye kul'ty ketov." In Vdovin, ed., *Khristianstvo i lamaizm*, pp. 55–71.

Alekseev, M. P. *Sibir' v izvestiiakh zapadno-evropeiskikh puteshestvennikov i pisatelei, XIII–XVII vv.* Irkutsk: Irkutskoe oblastnoe izdatel'stvo, 1941.

———. "Skazaniia inostrantsev o Rossii i nenetskii epos." *SE*, no. 4–5 (1935): 153–59.

Aliev, I. "Novyi ugolovnyi kodeks RSFSR i ego primenenie k bytovym uslovi-iam respublik i oblastei." *ZhN*, no. 16 (1922): 151.

Al'kor [Koshkin], Ia. P. "Pis'mennost' narodov Severa." *SS*, no. 10 (1931): 102–21.

———. "V. G. Bogoraz-Tan." *SE*, no. 4–5 (1935): 5–29.

———. "Zadachi kul'turnogo stroitel'stva na Krainem Severe." *SS*, no. 2 (1934): 22–35; no. 3 (1934): 45–50.

Al'kor, Ia. P., and A. K. Drezen, eds. *Kolonial'naia politika tsarizma na Kam-chatke i Chukotke: Sbornik arkhivnykh materialov.* Leningrad: Izdatel'stvo Instituta narodov Severa, 1935.

Al'kor, Ia. P., and B. D. Grekov, eds. *Kolonial'naia politika moskovskogo gosu-darstva v Iakutii.* Leningrad: Institut narodov Severa 1935–36.

Amosov, M., "Problema natskadrov v period sotsialisticheskoi rekonstruktsii." *RN*, no. 1 (1930): 20–28.

"Amurskie inorodtsy i religiozno-nravstvennoe sostoianie ikh." *PB*, no. 8 (1896): 358.

Amyl'skii, N. "Kogda zatsvetaiut zharkie tsvety." *SA*, no. 3 (1928): 54–62.

Andreev, A. "Iz opyta kollektivizatsii." *SS*, no. 4 (1934): 96–98.

Andreev, A. I. *Ocherki po istochnikovedeniiu Sibiri, XVII v.* Moscow and Leningrad: AN SSSR, 1960.

———, ed. "Opisaniia o zhizni i uprazhnenii obitaiushchikh v Turukhanskoi i Berezovskoi okrugakh raznogo roda iasachnykh inovertsev." *SE*, no. 1 (1947): 84–103.

Andrievich, V. K. *Istoricheskii ocherk Sibiri po dannym predstavliaemym pol-nym sobraniem zakonov.* 6 vols. St. Petersburg, 1886–1889.

Angin. "Rabota zhenshin v Bol'shemikhailovskom raione Nikolaevskogo ok-ruga." *TT*, no. 3 (1931).

Anisimov, A. F. "O sotsial'nykh otnosheniiakh v okhotkhoziaistve evenkov," *SS*, no. 5 (1933): 38–49.

Antonova, "Pis'mo predsedateliu Soveta Ministrov RSFSR tov. Vlasovu A. V., 11 November 1988. Unpublished.

Antropova, V. V. *Kul'tura i byt koriakov.* Leningrad: Nauka, 1971.

———. "Uchastie etnografov v prakticheskom osushchestvlenii leninskoi natsio-nal'noi politiki na Krainem Severe (1920–1930 gg.)." *SE*, no. 6 (1972): 19–27.

———. "Voprosy voennoi organizatsii i voennogo dela u narodov krainego Severo-Vostoka Sibiri." In *Sibirskii etnograficheskii sbornik*, vol. 2. AN SSSR, Trudy instituta etnografii im N. N. Miklukho-Maklaia. Novaia seriia, vol. 35. Moscow and Leningrad: AN SSSR, 1957.

Anuchin, D. N. "K istorii oznakomleniia s Sibir'iu do Ermaka." *Trudy Impera-torskago moskovskago arkheologicheskago obshchestva* 14 (1890): 227–313.

Aptekar', V. B. "Vystuplenie na obsuzhdenii knigi D. M. Petrushevskogo

'Ocherki iz ekonomicheskoi istorii srednevekovoi Evropy.'" *IM*, no. 2 (1928): 115.

Aptekar', V. B., and S. N. Bykovskii. "Sovremennoe polozhenie na lingvisticheskom fronte i ocherednye zadachi marksistov-iazykovedov." *IG* 10, no. 8–9 (1931): 9–34.

Argentov, Andrei. *Putevye zamietki sviashchennika missionera Andreia Argentova*. *Vostochnaia Sibir'*. Nizhnii Novgorod, 1886.

Arkhangel'skii, S., "Narkompros ne rukovodit shkolami Severa." *SAr*, no. 5 (1938): 59–61.

Armstrong, Terence. "The Administration of Northern Peoples: The USSR." In *The Arctic Frontier*, ed. R. St. J. MacDonald. Toronto: University of Toronto Press, 1966.

———. *Russian Settlement in the North*. Cambridge: Cambridge University Press, 1965.

Aronshtam, G. "K chistke natsional'nykh partorganizatsii," *RN*, 5–6 (1933): 7–18.

Arsen'ev, V. K. *Izbrannye proizvedeniia v 2kh tomakh*. Moscow, Sovetskaia Rossiia, 1986.

———. *Po Ussuriiskomu kraiu*. Moscow: Gosudarstvennoe izdatel'stvo geografischeskoi literatury, 1955.

Artsikhovskii, A., N. Vorob'ev, D. Gusev, and S. Smirnov. "Zhurnal sovetskikh etnografov." *Kommunist*, no. 5 (1963): 124–27.

Arutiunian, Iu. V. "Opyt sotsial'no-etnicheskogo issledovaniia (po materialam Tatarskoi ASSR)." *SE* no. 4 (1986): 3–13.

Arutiunian Iu. V., and L. M. Drobizheva. "Sovetskii obraz zhizni: Obshchee i natsional'no-osobennoe." *SE*, no. 3 (1976): 10–22.

Arzhanov, M. "Protiv liuksemburgskikh ustanovok." *RN*, no. 2 (1932): 88–98

Atkinson, Thomas William. *Travels in the Regions of the Upper and Lower Amoor and the Russian Acquisitions on the Confines of India and China*. (New York: Harper & Brothers, 1860.

Avvakum, *Zhitie protopopa Avvakuma, im samim napisannoe*. Moscow: Khudozhestvennaia literatura, 1960.

Azhaev, V. N. *Daleko ot Moskvy*. Moscow: Khudozhestvennaia literatura, 1949.

Aziatskaia Rossiia. 3 vols. St. Petersburg, 1914.

B-ov, N. "Budni krasnykh iurt." *PN*, no. 1 (1931): 60–64.

B. Z. "Sredi tuzemtsev DVR." *ZhN*, no. 15 (1922): 12–13.

Babakhan, S. Ia. "Sozdadim sobstvennuiu prodovol'stvennuiu bazu na Krainem Severe." *SAr*, no. 3 (1935): 41–46.

Baddeley, John F. ed. *Russia, Mongolia, China*. 2 vols. 1919. Reprint. New York: Burt Franklin, 1964.

Bagmut, Ivan. "Kochevoi sovet na Okhotskom poberezh'e." *SS*, no. 4 (1934): 11–23.

Bakhrushin, S. V. *Nauchnye trudy* Moscow: AN SSSR, 1955.

———. "Polozhitel'nye resul'taty russkoi kolonizatsii v sviazi s prisoedineniem Iakutii k russkomu gosudarstvu." In *Vedushchaia rol'*.

———. "Sibirskie tuzemtsy pod russkoi vlast'iu do revoliutsii 1917 goda." In *Sovetskii Sever: Pervyi sboornik statei*, pp. 66–97.

Balandin, A. "Rybozagotovki na Sos've." *SS*, no. 5 (1934): 93–96.

Balitskii, V. G. *Ot patriarkhal'no-obshchinnogo stroia k sotsializmu (O perekhode k sotsializmu malykh narodov severo-vostoka RSFSR)*. Moscow: Mysl', 1969.

Balitskii, V. G., and A. S. Kislichko. *Malye narody Dal'nego Vostoka v Velikoi Otechestvennoi voine*. Vladivostok: Izdatel'stvo Dal'nevostochnogo universiteta, 1985.

Balzer, Marjorie Mandelstam. "Ethnicity without Power: The Siberian Khanty in Soviet Society." *SR* (Winter 1983): 633–48.

——. "Rituals of Gender Identity: Marking of Siberian Khanty Ethnicity, Status, and Belief." *AA* 83, no. 4 (1981): 850–67.

——. "The Route to Ethnicity: Cultural Persistence and Change in Siberian Khanty Burial Ritual." *ArA* 17, no. 1 (1980): 77–90.

Balzer, Marjorie Mandelstam, ed. *Shamanism: Soviet Studies of Traditional Religion in Siberia and Central Asia*. Armonk, N.Y.: M.E. Sharpe, 1990.

BAM i narody Severa. Novosibirsk: Nauka, 1979.

Barakhov, I. "V Evenkiiskom natsional'nom okruge Vostsibkraia." *SS*, no. 3 (1933): 44–52.

Barber, John. *Soviet Historians in Crisis, 1928–1932*. London: Macmillan, 1981.

Barker, Adele. "The Divided Self: Yuri Rytkheu and Contemporary Chukchi Literature." In Diment and Slezkine, eds., *Between Heaven and Hell*, pp. 215–26.

Barker, Francis, et al., eds. *Europe and Its Others*. 2 vols. Colchester: University of Essex, 1985.

Barsukov, I. P. *Graf Nikolai Nikolaevich Murav'ev-Amurskii po ego pis'mam, offitsial'nym dokumentam, rasskazam sovremennikov i pechatnym istochnikam: Materialy dlia biografii*. Moscow, 1891.

Basargin, N. V. *Zapiski*. Petrograd, 1917.

Basharin, G. P. *Istoriia agrarnykh otnoshenii v Iakutii: 60e gody XVIII-seredina XIX v.* Moscow: An SSSR, 1956.

Baskakov, N. A. *Vvedenie v izuchenie tiurkskikh iazykov*. Mosow: Vysshaia shkola, 1969.

Bassin, Mark. "Expansion and Colonialism on the Eastern Frontier: Views of Siberia and the Far East in Pre-Petrine Russia." *Journal of Historical Geography* (January 1988): 3–21.

——. "Inventing Siberia: Visions of the Russian East in the Early Nineteenth Century." *American Historical Review* 96, no. 3 (1991): 763–94.

——. "Russia between Europe and Asia: The Ideological Construction of Geographical Space." *SR* 50 (Spring 1991): 1–17.

——. "The Russian Geographical Society, the 'Amur Epoch,' and the Great Siberian Expedition 1855–1963." *Annals of the Association of American Geographers* 73, no. 2 (1983): 240–56.

——. "A Russian Mississippi? A Political-Geographical Inquiry into the Vision of Russia on the Pacific, 1840–1865." Ph.D. diss., University of California, Berkeley, 1983.

Baten'kov, G. S. "Dannye: Povest' o sobstvennoi zhizni." *RA*, no. 2 (1881): 251–77.

Batotsyrenov, V. B. *Natsional'nye raiony Sibiri v sovetskoi istoricheskoi literature. Bibliograficheskii ukazatel'*. Ulan Ude: Buriatskoe khizhnoe izdatel'stvo, 1984.

Batrakov, I. "Plan osedaniia v Srednei Azii." *RN*, no. 5–6 (1933): 75–79.

Baudet, Henri. *Paradise on Earth: Some Thoughts on European Images of Non-European Man*. New Heaven: Yale University Press, 1965.

Bauer, Raymond. *The New Man in Soviet Psychology.* Cambridge: Harvard University Press, 1952.

Bazanov, A. G. *Ocherki po istorii missionerskikh shkol na Krainem Severe.* Leningrad: Izdatel'stvo Instituta narodov Severa, 1936.

——. "Vogul'skie deti." *SS*, no. 3 (1934): 93–96.

Bazanov, A. G. and N. G. Kazanskii. *Shkola na Krainem Severe.* Leningrad: Narkompros RSFSR, 1939.

Beazley, C. Raymond, *The Texts and Versions of John de Plano Carpini and William de Rubruquis.* London: Hakluyt Society, 1903.

Becker, Seymour. "Contributions to a Nationalist Ideology: Histories of Russia in the First Half of the Nineteenth Century." *Russian History/Histoire russe* 13, no. 4 (1986): 331–53.

Begichev, N. N. "Posle proverki partdokumentov (na Iamale)." *SAr,* no. 6 (1936): 17–19.

Beliavskii, F. I. *Poezdka k Ledovitomu moriu.* Moscow: Institut vostochnykh iazykov, 1833.

Belitser, V., and G. Maslova. "Protiv antimarksistkikh izvrashchenii v izuchenii odezhdy." *SE,* no. 3 (1954): 3–11.

Belov, M. I. *Mangazeia.* Moscow: Gidrometeoizdat, 1969.

——. *Nauchnoe i khoziaistvennoe osvoenie sovetskogo severa, 1933–1945.* Leningrad: Gidrometeorologicheskoe izdatel'stvo, 1969.

——. *Semen Dezhev.* Moscow: Morskoi transport, 1955.

——, ed. *Russkie morekhody v Ledovitom i Tikhom okeanakh. Sbornik dokumentov.* Moscow and Leningrad: Glavsevmorput', 1952.

Bergavinov, S. A. "O razvertyvanii sovetskoi torgovli na Krainem Severe." *SAr* no. 2 (1937): 3–13.

Bergman, Sten *Through Kamchatka by Dog-sled and Skis.* London: Seeley Service, 1927.

Berkhofer, Robert F. Jr. *The White Man's Indian: Images of the American Indian from Columbus to the Present.* New York: Alfred A. Knopf, 1978.

Bernheimer, Richard. *Wild Men in the Middle Ages: A Study in Art, Sentiment and Demonology.* New York: Octagon, 1970.

Bernshtam, A. N. 'Problema raspada rodovykh otnoshenii u kochevnikov Azii." *SE,* no. 6 (1934): 86–115.

Beskorsyi, P. "Integral'naia kooperatsiia v novykh usloviiakh." *SS,* no. 6 (1933): 7–11.

——. "Nekotorye itogi (Materialy o sostoianii kollektivizatsii na Krainem Severe)." *SS,* no. 2 (1934): 57–61.

Bestuzhev-Marlinskii, A. A. *Sochineniia v dvukh tomakh.* Moscow: Khudozhestvennia literatura, 1958.

Bikchentai, I. "Ocherednye zadachi natspedologii." *P,* no. 7–8 (1931): 31–36.

——. "Pis'mo v zhurnal 'Prosveshchenie natsional'nostei'." *PN,* no. 4 (1932): 102–3.

Bilibin, N. N. "Batratskii trud v kochevom khoziaistve koriakov." *SS,* no. 1 (1933): 36–46.

——. "Rabota koriakskogo kraevedcheskogo punkta." *SS,* no. 6 (1932): 102–6

——. "Sredi koriakov." *SS,* no. 3 (1933): 91–97.

——. "U zapadnykh koriakov." *SS,* no. 1–2 (1932): 196–218.

——. "Zhenshchina u koriakov," *SS,* no. 4 (1933): 92–96.

Billington, James H. *Mikhailovsky and Russian Populism.* Oxford: Clarendon Press, 1958.

Billington, Ray Allen. *Land of Savagery, Land of Promise: The European Image of the American Frontier in the 19th Century.* New York: Norton, 1981.

Bitterli, Urs. *Los "salvajes" y los "civilizados": El encuentro de Europa y Ultramar.* Mexico City: Fondo de cultura económica, 1981. Originally published in German as *Die "Wilden" und die "Zivilisierten."* Munich: C. H. Beck, 1976.

Black, J. Lawrence. *G.-F. Miller and the Imperial Russian Academy.* Kingston: McGill-Queen's University Press, 1986.

——. "Opening up Siberia: Russia's 'Window on the East.'" In Wood, ed., *The History of Siberia,* pp. 57–68.

Black, Lydia. "The Nivkh (Gilyak) of Sakhalin and the Lower Amur." *ArA,* no. 10 (1973): 1–110.

Blizok Krainii Sever. Moscow: Sovremennik, 1982.

Blonskii, P. P. "O nekotorykh tendentsiiakh pedologicheskogo izucheniia detei razlichnykh natsional'nostei." *PN,* no. 4 (1932): 48–51.

Boas, George, and Arthur O. Lovejoy, eds. *A Documentary History of Primitivism and Related Ideas in Antiquity.* Baltimore: Johns Hopkins University Press, 1935.

Bogdanov, A. "Kolkhoznoe stroitel'stvo v natsional'nykh raionakh." *RN,* no. 3 (1930): 39–46.

Bogoras, Waldemar G. [V. G. Bogoraz (-Tan)], *The Chukchee.* Memoirs of the American Museum of Natural History, vol. 11. New York: The American Museum of Natural History, 1904.

——. *The Eskimo of Siberia.* Memoirs of the American Museum of Natural History, vol. 12. New York: The American Museum of Natural History, 1913.

Bogoraz (-Tan), V. G. "Chukotskii bukvar'." *SS,* no. 10 (1931): 122–32.

——. "Etnograficheskaia belletristika." *SE,* no. 3–4 (1931): 136–55.

——. "K voprosu o graficheskom metode analiza elementov etnografii i etnogeografii." *E,* no. 1 (1928): 3–10.

——. "K voprosu o primenenii marksistskogo metoda k izucheniiu etnograficheskikh iavlenii." *E,* no. 1–2 (1930): 3–56.

——. "Klassovoe rassloenie u chukoch-olenevodov." *SE,* no. 1–2 (1931): 93–116.

——. "Ob izuchenii i okhrane okrainnykh narodov." *ZhN,* no. 3–4 (1923): 168–77.

——. "O pervobytnykh plemenakh," *ZhN,* no. 1 (1922): 130.

——. "Predlozheniia k voprosu ob izuchenii i okhrane okrainnykh narodov." *ZhN,* no. 3–4 (1923): 178–80.

——. "Podgotovitel'nye mery k organizatsii malykh narodnostei." *SA,* no. 3 (1925): 40–50.

——. *Rasprostranenie kul'tury na zemle: Osnovy etnogeografii.* Moscow: Gosizdat, 1928.

——. "Religiia, kak tormoz sootsstroitel'stva sredi malykh narodnostei Severa." *SS,* no. 1–2 (1932): 142–57.

——. "Severnyi rabfak (Severnoe otdelenie rabfaka Leningradskogo universiteta zhivykh vostochnykh iazykov)." *SA,* no. 2 (1927): 52–63.

——. "Shternberg kak etnograf." In *Pamiati L'va Iakovlevicha Shternberga,* pp. 4–28.

——. *Sochineniia.* 4 vols. Moscow: Zemlia i fabrika, 1929.

——. *Vosem' plemen. Chukotskie rasskazy.* Moscow: Gosudarstvennoe izdatel'stvo khudozhestvennoi literatury, 1962.

——. *Voskresshee plemia.* Moscow: Khudozhestvennaia literatura, 1935.

——. "XXI kongress amerikanistov." *E*, no. 1–2 (1926): 125–31.

Boiko, V. I. *Opyt sotsiologicheskogo issledovaniia problem razvitiia narodov Nizhnego Amura.* Novosibirsk: Nauka, 1973.

——. *Sotsial'noe razvitie narodov Nizhnego Amura.* Novosibirsk: Nauka, 1977.

——. *Sotsial'nye problemy truda u narodnostei Severa.* Novosibirsk: Nauka, 1986.

——, ed. *Sel'skaia molodezh' Iakutii: Sotsial'naia mobil'nost', otnoshenie k trudu, professional'naia orientatsiia.* Iakutsk: Iakutskoe knizhnoe izdatel'- stvo, 1977.

Boiko, V. I., and Iu. V. Popkov. *Razvitie otnosheniia k trudu u narodnostei Severa pri sotsializme.* Novosibirsk: Nauka, 1987.

Bolin, P. S. "Chto dala nam sovetskaia vlast'." *SAr*, no. 11 (1936): 63–64.

Bol'shakov, M. A. "Naselenie Kamchatki i ego khoziaistvo." *SS*, no. 11–12 (1931): 51–98.

——. "Problema osedaniia kochevogo naseleniia (na Iamale)." *SAr*, no. 5 (1936): 14–24.

Bol'shakov, O. G., and A. L. Mongait, eds. *Puteshestvie Abu-Khamida Al-Gar- nati v Vostochnuiu i Tsentral'nuiu Evropu (1131–1153).* Moscow: Glavnaia redaktsiia vostochnoi literatury, 1971.

Boltin, Ivan. *Primechaniia na Istoriiu drevniia i nyneshniia Rossii g. Leklerka.* 2 vols. St. Petersburg, 1788.

Bonch-Osmolovskii, A. "Kamchatsko-Chukotskii krai." *SA*, no. 1–2 (1925): 77.

Borisov, Trofim *Syn orla.* Khabarovsk: Dal'giz, 1939.

Brailovskii, S. N. "Tazy ili udikhe." *ZhS*, no. 2 (1901): 129–216; no. 3–4 (1901): 323–423.

Brazhnikov, V. K. *Rybnye promysly Dal'nego Vostoka.* Vol. 1, *Osennii promysel v nizov'iakh r Amura.* St. Petersburg, 1900.

Brodnev, M. M. "Ot rodovogo stroia k sotsializmu (po materialam Iamalo- Nenetskogo natsional'nogo okruga)." *SE*, no. 1 (1950): 92–106.

Bromlei, Iu. V. "Etnos i endogamiia." *SE*, no. 6 (1969): 84–91.

——. *Etnos i etnografiia.* Moscow: Nauka, 1973.

——. "K voprosu ob osobennostiakh etnograficheskogo izucheniia sovremen- nosti." *SE*, no. 1 (1977): 3–18.

——. *Ocherki teorii etnosa.* Moscow: Nauka, 1983.

——. "Opyt tipologizatsii etnicheskikh obshchnostei." *SE*, no. 5 (1972): 61–81.

Bromlei, Iu. V., and V. N. Basilov, "Sovetskaia etnograficheskaia nauka v devia- toi piateletke." *SE*, no. 1 (1976): 3–22.

Bromlei, Iu. V., and V. I. Kozlov. "Leninizm i osnovnye tendentsii etnicheskikh protsessov v SSSR." *SE*, no. 1 (1970): 3–14.

Bromlei, Iu. V., and O. I. Shkaratan. "O sootnoshenii istorii, etnografii i sotsio- logii." *SE*, no. 3 (1969): 3–19.

Brown, Edward J. *The Proletarian Episode in Russian Literature, 1928–1932.* New York: Octagon, 1953.

Bruyn, Cornelis de. *Travels into Muscovy, Persia, and Part of the East-Indies.* London, 1737.

Budarin, M. E. *Proshloe i nastoiashchee narodov Severo-Zapadnoi Sibiri.* Omsk: Omskoe oblastnoe knizhnoe izdatel'stvo, 1952.

——. *Put' malykh narodov Severa k kommunizmu.* Omsk: Zapadno-Sibirskoe khizhnoe izdatel'stvo, 1968.

Bulanov, I. "Materialy po izucheniiu povedeniia rebenka-tungusa." *P*, no. 2 (1930): 194–207.

Bulychev, Ivan *Puteshestvie po Vostochnoi Sibiri. Chast' 1: Iakutskaia oblast', Okhotskii krai.* St. Petersburg, 1856.

Bunak, V. V. "Pis'mo v redaktsiiu." *SE*, no. 1 (1947): n. p.

Burke, John G. "The Wild Man's Pedigree: Scientific Method and Racial Anthropology." In Dudley and Novak, *The Wild Man Within*, pp. 259–80.

Bush, Richard J. *Reindeer, Dogs, and Snow-Shoes: A Journal of Siberian Travel and Exploration Made in the Years 1865, 1866, and 1867.* New York, 1871.

Butsinskii, P. N. *Mangazeia i Mangazeiskii uezd, 1601–1645.* Khar'kov, 1893.

———. *Zaselenie Sibiri i byt pervykh ee nasel'nikov.* Khar'kov, 1889.

Buturlin, S. A. "Polozhenie tuzemtsev Chukotsko-Anadyrskogo kraia." *SA*, no. 2 (1926): 90–92.

Bykhovskaia, S. "O bespis'mennykh iazykakh (v osveshchenii iafeticheskoi teorii)." *PN*, no. 3, (1930): 51–54.

Bykovskii, S. N. "Etnografiia na sluzhbe klassovogo vraga." *SE*, no. 3–4 (1931): 3–13.

———. "Iafeticheskii predok vostochnykh slavian—kimmeriitsy." *IG* 8, no. 8–10 (1931).

Bytovoi, S. M. *Poezd prishel na Tumnin.* Leningrad: Sovetskii pisatel', 1951.

———. *Sady u okeana.* Leningrad: Sovetskii Pisatel', 1957.

Carrère-D'Encausse, Hélène. *Decline of an Empire: The Soviet Socialist Republics in Revolt.* New York: Newsweek Books, 1980.

———. *The Great Challenge: Nationalities and the Bolshevik State, 1917–1930.* New York: Holmes & Meier, 1992.

Chard, Chester S. "Kamchadal Culture and Its Relationships in the Old and New Worlds." In *Archives of Archaeology*, no. 15. Madison: University of Wisconsin Press, 1961.

"Chaut nad Paren'iu." *SP*, no. 2 (1988): 9–10.

Chebotarevskii, A., "Itogi VIII rasshirennogo plenuma Komiteta Severa." *SS*, no. 3–4 (1931): 246–48.

———. "Kul'tbazy Komiteta Severa." *SS*, no. 1 (1930): 117–24.

———. "Sed'moi rasshirennyi plenum Komiteta Severa." *SA*, no. 3–4 (1930): 336–42.

Checherov, V. P. "O porochnykh vzgliadakh N. Ia. Marra i ego posledovatelei v oblasti fol'kloristiki." *SE*, no. 3 (1952): 3–15.

Chekhov, A. P. *Polnoe sobranie sochinenii i pisem.* Moscow: Nauka, 1978.

Chekin, Leonid S. "The Godless Ishmaelites: Image of the Steppe in Pre-Muscovite Rus." Paper delivered at the International Conference on the Role of the Frontier in Rus/Russian History, 800–1800, University of Chicago, May 1992.

Chernetsov, V. "N. A. Kotovshchikova." *E*, no. 1–2 (1930): 158–59.

"Chetyre goda raboty sredi estontsev Sovetskoi Rossii." *ZhN*, no. 24 (1921).

Chichlo, Boris. "L'Anthropologie soviétique à l'heure de la perestroika." *Cahiers du monde russe et soviétique*, no. 31 (1990): 223–32.

———. "L'Anthropologie soviétique et les problèmes de la culture sibérienne." *Revue des études slaves* 57, no. 4 (1985): 675–81.

———. "L'Ethnographie soviétique est-elle une anthropologie?" In *Histoires de l'anthropologie: XVI-XIX siècles*, ed. Britta Rupp Eisenreich, pp. 247–58. Paris: Klincksieck, 1984.

——. "La Tchoukotka: Une autre civilisation obligatoire." *Objets et mondes* 25, no. 3–4 (n.d.): 149–58.

——. "Trente années d'anthropologie (etnografija) soviétique." *Revue des études slaves* 57, no. 2 (1985): 309–24.

Chinard, Gilbert. *L'Amérique et le rêve exotique dans la littérature française au XVIIe et au XVIIIe siècle.* Paris: E. Droz, 1934.

Chlenov, Mikhail, and Igor Krupnik. "Aziatskie eskimosy: Istoriia akkul'turatsii na beregu Beringova proliva." 1990. Unpublished.

Chudinov, D. "V Tomponskom raione." *SS*, no. 1 (1934): 107–11.

Clark, Katerina. "Utopian Anthropology as a Context for Stalinist Literature." In *Stalinism: Essays in Historical Interpretation*, ed. Robert Tucker. New York: Norton, 1977.

——. *The Soviet Novel: History as Ritual.* Chicago: University of Chicago Press, 1981.

Clifford, James. *The Predicament of Culture.* Cambridge: Harvard University Press, 1988.

Clifford, James, and George E. Marcus, eds. *Writing Culture: The Poetics and Politics of Ethnography.* Berkeley and Los Angeles: University of California Press, 1986.

Cochrane, John Dundas. *A Pedestrian Journey through Russia and Siberian Tartary from the Frontiers of China to the Frozen Sea and Kamchatka, performed during the years 1820, 1821, 1822, and 1823.* London: John Murray, 1824.

Collins, David N. "Russia's Conquest of Siberia: Evolving Russian and Soviet Interpretations." *European Studies Review* 12, no. 1 (1982): 17–44.

——. "Subjugation and Settlement in Seventeenth and Eighteenth Century Siberia." In Wood, ed., *The History of Siberia*, pp. 37–56.

Collins, Perry McDonough. *Siberian Journey down the Amur to the Pacific, 1856–1857.* Madison: University of Wisconsin Press, 1962.

Comaroff, Jean. *Body of Power, Spirit of Resistance: The Culture and History of a South African People.* Chicago: University of Chicago Press, 1985.

Comry, Bernard. *The Languages of the Soviet Union.* Cambridge: Cambridge University Press, 1981.

Connor, Walker. *The National Question in Marxist-Leninist Theory and Strategy.* Princeton: Princeton University Press, 1984.

Conolly, Violet. *Siberia Today and Tomorrow: A Study of Economic Resources, Problems, and Achievements.* New York: Taplinger, 1975.

Conquest, Robert. *Kolyma: The Arctic Death Camps.* London: Macmillan, 1978.

Coquin, François-Xavier. "Aperçus sur le peuplement de la Sibérie au XIX siècle." *Cahiers du monde russe et soviétique* 7, no. 4 (1966): 564–81.

Curtin, Philip D. *The Image of Africa: British Ideas and Action, 1780-1850.* Madison: University of Wisconsin Press, 1964.

Czaplicka, M. A. *Aboriginal Siberia.* Oxford: Clarendon Press, 1914.

——. *My Siberian Year.* London: Mills & Boon, n. d.

D. "Iz doklada o deiatel'nosti Tomskogo gubnatsa." *ZhN*, no. 9 (1922): 144.

Dallin, David, and Boris Nicolaevsky. *Forced Labor in Soviet Russia.* New Haven: Yale University Press, 1947.

Danilin, A., G. "Etnograficheskaia rabota v Iakutskoi ASSR." *E*, no. 1 (1927): 185–92.

——. "Sektsiia etnografii Vsesoiuznogo geograficheskogo s"ezda." *SE*, no. 2 (1933): 113–17.

Dal'revkom. Pervyi etap mirnogo stroitel'stva na Dal'nem Vostoke, 1922–1926. Sbornik dokumentov. Khabarovsk: Khabarovskoe knizhnoe izdatel'stvo, 1957.

D'Amov, "Grammofon i varshavskaia krovat' (Narymskie ocherki)." *ORS*, no. 6 (1930): 55–56.

Davydov, "Ocherednye zadachi kul'turnogo stroitel'stva na Krainem Severe." *SS*, no. 4 (1932): 92–102.

Dekrety sovetskoi vlasti. Vol. 1. Moscow: Gospolitizdat, 1957.

"Deputatskii zapros." *SP*, no. 1 (1990): 4.

"A Description of the Countries of Siberia, Samoieda, and Tingoesia." In Samuel Purchas, *Hakluytus Posthumus or Purchas His Pilgrimes*, vol. 13 Glasgow: James MacLehose & Sons, 1906.

Desiatyi s"ezd Rossiiskoi Kommunisticheskoi partii. Stenograficheskii otchet. Moscow: Gosudarstvennoe izdatel'stvo, 1921.

"Deviatnadtsatyi s"ezd Kommunisticheskoi partii Sovetskogo Soiuza i voprosy etnografii." *SE*, no. 4 (1952): 3–10.

de Zengotita, Thomas. "Speakers of Being: Romantic Refusion and Cultural Anthropy." In Stocking, Jr., ed., *Romantic Motives*, pp. 74–123.

Dimanshtein, S. M. "Natsional'nye momenty na XVI s"ezde." *RN*, no. 3 (1930): 3–13.

——. "Predvaritel'nyi otvet tov. Tobolovu." *RN*, no. 4–5 (1930): 140–41.

——. "Rekonstruktivnyi period i rabota sredi natsional'nostei SSSR." *RN*, no. 1 (1930): 9–28.

——. *Revoliutsiia i natsional'nyi vopros.* Vol. 3. Moscow: Izdatel'stvo Kommunisticheskoi akademii, 1930.

——. "Sovetskaia vlast' i melkie natsional'nosti." *ZhN*, no. 46 (1919): 17.

Diment, Galya. "Exiled from Siberia: The Construction of Siberian Experience by Early Nineteenth-Century Irkutsk Writers." In Diment and Slezkine, eds., *Between Heaven and Hell*, pp. 47–66.

Diment, Galya, and Yuri Slezkine, eds. *Between Heaven and Hell: The Myth of Siberia in Russian Culture.* New York: St. Martin's Press, 1993.

"Direktivy Gosplana RSFSR po sostoianiiu perspektivnogo piatiletnego plana po sotsialisticheskoi rekonstruktsii i razvitiiu narodnogo khoziaistva Krainego Severa RSFSR." *SS*, no. 1 (1930): 183–191.

"Diskussii po voprosam fol'kloristiki na zasedaniiakh sektora fol'klora Instituta etnografii." *SE*, no. 3 (1948): 139–146.

Ditmar, Karl. *Poezdki i prebyvanie v Kamchatke v 1851–1855.* St. Petersburg, 1901.

Divin, V. A. *A. N. Chirikov—zamechatel'nyi russkii moreplavatel' i uchenyi.* Moscow: Pravda, 1950.

——. *Russkie moreplavaniia na Tikhom okeane v XVIII v.* Moscow: Mysl', 1971.

——., ed. *Russkaia tikhookeanskia epopeia.* Khabarovsk: Khabarovskoe knizhnoe izdatel'stvo, 1979.

Dmitriev, D. "Severnoe olenevodstvo i ego ekonomika." *SA*, no. 5–6 (1925): 105–14.

Dmytryshin, Basil. "The Administrative Apparatus of the Russian Colony in Siberia and Nothern Asia, 1581–1700." In Wood, ed., *The History of Siberia*, pp. 14–36.

Dobell, Peter. *Travels in Kamchatka and Siberia.* 2 vols. London, 1830.

Dobrova-Iadrintseva, L. "Puti k novomu bytu." *OPS*, no. 9 (1928):46-50.

———. "Sovetskaia vlast' na tuzemnykh okrainakh Sibirskogo severa." *SO*, no. 6 (1927): 140.

Dolgikh, B. O. *Kety.* Irkutsk, 1934.

———. "Kolkhoz im. Kirova Taimyrskogo natsional'nogo okruga." *SE*, no. 4 (1949): 75–93.

———. "Naselenie p-va Taimyra i prilegaiushchego k nemu raiona." *SA*, no. 2 (1929): 49–76.

———. "O naselenii Basseinov rek Oleneka i Anabary." *SE*, no. 2 (1952): 86–91.

———. "O nekotorykh etnogeneticheskikh protsessakh (pereseleniiakh narodov i rasprostranenii iazykov) v Severnoi Sibiri." *SE*, no. 1 (1952): 51–59.

———. "Obrazovanie sovremennykh narodnostei severa SSSR." *SE*, no. 3 (1967): 3–15.

———. *Rodovoi i plemennoi sostav narodov Sibiri v XVII veke.* AN SSSR, Trudy Instituta etnografii im. N. N. Miklukho-Maklaia. Novaia seriia, vol. 55. Moscow: AN SSSR, 1960.

———, ed. *Bytovye rasskazy entsev.* AN SSR. Trudy Instituta etnografii im. N. N. Miklukho-Maklaia. Novaia seriia, tom 75. Moscow: AN SSR, 1962.

———, ed. *Mifologicheskie skazki i istoricheskie predaniia entsev.* AN SSSR. Trudy Instituta etnografii im. N. N. Miklukho-Maklaia. Novaia seriia, vol. 66. Moscow: AN SSSR, 1961.

Donnelly, Alton S. *The Russian Conquest of Bashkiria, 1552–1740: A Case Study in Imperialism.* New Haven: Yale University Press, 1968.

Donner, Kai. *Among the Samoyed in Siberia.* New Haven: HRAF, 1954.

Drabkina, E. Ia. *Natsional'nyi i kolonial'nyi vopros v tsarskoi Rossii.* Moscow: Kommunisticheskaia akademiia, 1930.

Dragadze, Tamara. The Place of 'Ethnos' Theory in Soviet Anthropology. In Gellner, ed., *Soviet and Western Anthropology* pp. 161–70.

———. "Some Changes in Perspectives on Ethnicity Theory in the 1980s: A Brief Sketch." *Cahiers du monde russe et soviétique* 31, nos. 2–3 (1990): 205–12.

Drobizheva, L. M. "Ob izuchenii sotsial'no-psikhologicheskikh aspektov natsional'nykh otnoshenii." *SE*, no. 4 (1974): 15–25.

Dudley, Edward, and Maximilian E. Novak., eds. *The Wild Man Within: An Image in Western Thought from the Renaissance to Romanticism.* Pittsburgh: University of Pittsburgh Press, 1972.

Duel', Igor. "Stena." *SP.* no. 2 (1987): 12–13; no. 3 (1987): 14–15.

Dunbar, Moira. "The Arctic Setting." In *The Arctic Frontier,* ed. R. St. J. MacDonald, pp. 3–25. Toronto: University of Toronto Press, 1966.

Dunham, Vera S. *In Stalin's Time: Middle-Class Values in Soviet Fiction.* Cambridge: Cambridge University Press, 1976.

Dunin-Gorkavich, A. A. *Tobol'skii sever: Geograficheskoe i statistiko-ekonomicheskoe opisanie strany po otdel'nym geograficheskim raionam.* Vol. 2. Tobol'sk, 1910.

Dunn, Ethel. "Educating the Small Peoples of the Soviet North: The Limits of Cultural Change." *ArA* 5, no. 1 (1968): 1–31.

———. "Education and the Native Intelligentsia in the Soviet North: Further Thoughts on the Limits of Cultural Change." *ArA* 6, no. 2 (1970): 112–122.

Dunn, Stephen P. "New Departures in Soviet Theory and Practice of Ethnicity." *Dialectical Anthropology* 1 (1975): 61–70.

Dunn, Stephen P., and Ethel Dunn. "Directed Culture Change in the Soviet Union: Some Soviet Studies." *AA* 64, no. 2 (1962): 328–39.

———. "The Peoples of Siberia and the Far East." In Vucinich, ed., *Russia and Asia*.

———. "The Transformation of the Economy and Culture in the Soviet North." *ArA* 1, no. 2 (1963): 1–28.

E. K. "V Iamal'skom (Nenetskom) natsional'nom okruge Ob'-Irtyshskoi oblasti." *SS*, no. 5 (1934): 76–78.

Efimov, A. V. *Iz istorii velikikh russkikh geograficheskikh otkrytii*. Moscow: Uchpedgiz, 1949.

Egorov, K. D. "O 'severovedakh,' izvrashchaiushchikh deistvitel'nost'." *SAr*, no. 11 (1937): 136–39.

———. "Protiv izvrashchenii i uproshchenstva." *SAr*, no. 2 (1938): 30–32.

Egorov, V. "Bol'nye storony olenevodstva v Turukhanskom krae." *OPS*, no. 10 (1928): 46–48.

Egorov, V., and E. Zakharov. "Polozhenie zhenshchin u evenkov Verkhne-Selimdzhinskogo raiona." *TT*, no. 2 (1930): 116–18.

Elliott, J. H. *The Old World and the New, 1492–1650*. Cambridge: Cambridge University Press, 1970.

El'mets, R. "K voprosu o vydelenii chuvash v osobuiu administrativnuiu edinitsu." *ZhN*, no. 2 (1920).

Elpat'evskii, S. Ia. *Ocherki Sibiri*. Moscow, 1893.

Engelhardt, Alexander Platonovich. *A Russian Province of the North*. Westminster, 1899.

Engels, Friedrich. *The Origin of the Family, Private Property, and the State*. New York: International Publishers, 1970.

Ergis, G. U., ed. *Istoricheskie predaniia i rasskazy iakutov*. Moscow and Leningrad: AN SSSR, 1960.

Erman, Georg Adolf. *Travels in Siberia*. 2 vols. 1848. Reprint. New York: Arno Press and the New York Times, 1970.

Ersari. "Ob odnom uchastke nauchno-teoreticheskogo fronta." *RN*, no. 7 (1932): 95–98.

Etnicheskaia istoriia narodov Severa. Moscow: Nauka, 1982.

"Etnograficheskaia sektsiia obshchestva istorikov-marksistov pri leningradskom otdelenii Kommunisticheskoi akademii." *SE*, no. 1–2 (1931): 155.

"Etnograficheskie raboty Komiteta Severa." *SA*, no. 2 (1926): 96–100.

"Etnograficheskoe soveshchanie 1956 goda." *SE*, no. 3 (1956): 123-41.

Evgen'ev, N. N., and S. A. Bergavinov. "Nachal'niku Obdorskogo politotdela Glavsevmorputi t. Mikhailovu." *SAr*, no. 4 (1936): 65–67.

Evsenin, Ivan. "K voprosu o sokhranenii sibirskikh tuzemtsev." *SO*, no. 4 (1922): 89–98.

———. "Karagassy." *ZhN*, no. 6 (1922): 135.

Ezerskii, Milii. *Samoiad' (Zakon Numa)*. Moscow: Federatsiia, 1930.

F. Ia. "K voprosu of agitatsii sredi kochevnikov." *ZhN*, no. 48, (1919): 56.

Fabian, Johannes. *Time and the Other*. New York: Columbia University Press, 1983.

Fadeev, A. A. *Sobranie sochinenii*. Moscow: Khudozhestvennaia literatura, 1970.

Fainberg, L. A. "Khoziaistvo i kul'tura taimyrskikh nganasan." *SE*, no. 2 (1959): 47–60.

Fairchild, Hoxie N. *The Noble Savage: A Study in Romantic Naturalism.* New York: Columbia University Press, 1928.

Fedorov, Iu. M. "Kul'turnaia integratsiia." *Dialog,* no. 8 (1989): 38.

Fedorov [Omulevskii], I. V. *Polnoe sobranie sochinenii Omulevskogo* (I. V. Fedorova), St. Petersburg, 1906.

Fedorov, M. M. *Pravovoe polozhenie narodov Vostochnoi Sibiri, XVII–nachalo XIX v.* Iakutsk: Iakutskoe knizhnoe izdatel'stvo, 1978.

Fedoseev, G. A. *Glukhoi, nevedomoi taigoiu.* Krasnodar: Krasnodarskoe knizhnoe izdatel'stvo 1960.

——. *Izbrannye proizvedeniia.* 2 vols. Moscow: Khudozhestvennaia literatura, 1976.

Filin, A. "Kal'ma prosit zashchity." *Sovetskaia kul'tura,* 27 October 1988.

Firsov, N. "O nenetskikh shkolakh." *TT,* no. 2 (1928): 90–92.

——. "O severnom assortimente tovarov." *SS,* no. 3 (1932): 89–93.

——. "Rabota sredi malykh narodov Severa v Iakutskoi ASSR." *SS,* no. 11–12 (1931): 18–27.

Firsov, N., and Petrova. "Organy iustitsii v otdel'nykh raionakh Krainego Severa." *SS,* no. 2 (1934): 84–89.

Firsov, N. A. *Polozhenie inorodtsev severo-vostochnoi Rossii v Moskovskom gosudarstve.* Kazan', Universitetskaia tipografiia, 1866.

Fischer, Johann Eberhard. *Sibirskaia istoriia s samago otkrytiia Sibiri do zavoevaniia sei zemli Rossiiskim oruzhiem.* St. Petersburg, 1774.

Fisher, Raymond H. *The Russian Fur Trade, 1550–1700.* University of California Publications in History, vol. 31. Berkeley and Los Angeles: University of California Press, 1943.

Fitzpatrick, Sheila. "Cultural Revolution as Class War." In Fitzpatrick, ed., *Cultural Revolution in Russia,* pp. 3–38.

——. *Educational and Social Mobility in the Soviet Union 1921–1934.* Cambridge: Cambridge University Press, 1979.

——., ed. *Cultural Revolution in Russia, 1928–1931.* Bloomington: Indiana University Press, 1978.

Fondahl, Gail A. "Native Economy and Northern Development: Reindeer Husbandry in Transbaykalia." Ph.D. diss., University of California, Berkeley, 1989.

Forsyth, James. *A History of the Peoples of Siberia: Russia's North Asian Colony, 1581–1990.* Cambridge: Cambridge University Press, 1992.

——. "The Indigenous Peoples of Siberia in the Twentieth Century." In Wood and French, eds., *The Development of Siberia,* pp. 72–95.

——. "The Siberian Native Peoples Before and After the Russian Conquest." In Wood, ed., *The History of Siberia,* pp. 69-91.

Foster, G. M. *Applied Anthropology.* Boston: Little, Brown, 1969.

Foucault, Michel. *The Order of Things: An Archaeology of the Human Sciences.* New York: Vintage Books, 1973.

Fraerman, R. I. *Izbrannoe.* Moscow: Sovetskii pisatel', 1958.

Frenkel', A. "Protiv eklektizma v pedologii i psikhologii." *PN,* no. 7–8 (1930): 108–10.

Gagen-Torn, N. I. "Leningradskaia etnograficheskaia shkola v dvadtsatye gody. (U istokov sovetskoi etnografii)." *SE,* no. 2 (1971): 134–45.

——. *Lev Iakovlevich Shternberg.* Moscow: Nauka, 1975.

Gaisin, Z. "Karagasskoe bol'shoe zimnee sobranie." *ORS,* no. 4 (1929): 10–11.

Galkin, N. V zemle polunochnogo solntsa. Moscow and Leningrad: Molodaia gvardiia, 1929.

Gantskaia, O. A. "Etnos i sem'ia v SSSR." SE, no. 3 (1974): 20–30.

Gapanovich, I. I. Rossiia v Severo-vostochnoi Azii. Beijing, 1933.

Gardanov, V. N., B. O. Dolgikh, and T. A. Zhdanko. "Osnovnye napravleniia etnicheskikh protsessov u narodov SSSR." SE, no. 4 (1961): 9–29.

Gasilov, G. "O sisteme narodnogo obrazovaniia natsional'nykh men'shinstv RSFSR." PN, no. 1 (1929): 29–46.

Gedenshtrom, M. M. Otryvki o Sibiri. St. Petersburg, 1830.

Geertz, Clifford. Works and Lives: The Anthropologist as Author. Stanford: Stanford University Press, 1988.

Gellner, Ernest. "The Soviet and the Savage." Current Anthropology 10, no. 4 (1975): 595–617.

——. Soviet and Western Anthropology. New York: Columbia University Press, 1980.

——. State and Society in Soviet Thought. Oxford: Basil Blackwell, 1988.

Gendlin, V. "Iarmarka pokupatelei." SP, no. 1 (1990): 4–6; no. 2 (1991): 12.

Genest, Otto. "Kapitän Jakobsen's Reisen im Gebiete der Giljaken und auf der Insel Sachalin." Globus, no. 52 (1887). [HRAF RX2, no. 19]

Georgi, Iogann Gottlib [Iohann Gottlieb]. Opisanie vsekh obitaiushchikh v Rossiiskom gosudarstve narodov. St. Petersburg, 1799.

Gerasimovich, N. "V Taimyrskom okruge." SS, no. 6 (1933): 60–65.

Geroini sotsialisticheskogo truda. Moscow: Partizdat TsK VKP(b), 1936.

Gersevanov, "Zamechaniia o torgovykh otnosheniiakh Sibiri i Rossii." Otechestvenyia zapiski 14, no. 2 (1841), otd. 4, 23–34.

Gertsen, A. I. Sobranie sochinenii v 30 tomakh. Vol. 1 Moscow: AN SSSR, 1954.

Geyer, Dietrich. Russian Imperialism: The Interaction of Domestic and Foreign Policy, 1860–1914. New Haven: Yale University Press, 1987.

Gibson, James R. Feeding the Russian Fur Trade: Provisionment of the Okhotsk Seaboard and the Kamchatka Peninsula, 1639–1856. Madison: University of Wisconsin Press, 1969.

——. "Paradoxical Perceptions of Siberia: Patrician and Plebian Images up to the Mid-1800s." In Diment and Slezkine, eds., Between Heaven and Hell, pp. 67–94.

——. "Russia on the Pacific: The Role of the Amur." Canadian Geographer 12, no. 1 (1968): 15–27.

——. "Sables to Sea Otters: Russia Enters the Pacific." Alaska Review 111 (Fall/Winter 1968): 203–17.

——. "The Significance of Siberia to Tsarist Russia." Canadian Slavonic Papers 14, no. 3 (1972): 442–53.

Gilev, A. "Zapiski o Bauntovskom raione." SS, no. 4 (1934): 87–93.

Gleason, Abbott. Young Russia: The Genesis of Russian Radicalism in the 1860s. New York: The Viking Press, 1980.

Gol'dberg, I. G. Izbrannye proizvedeniia. Moscow: Khudozhestvennaia literatura, 1972.

Gol'denberg, L. A. Semen Ul'ianovich Remezov: Sibirskii kartograf i geograf. Moscow: Nauka, 1965.

Golovachev, P. M. Sibir': Priroda, Liudi, Zhizn'. Moscow, 1905.

——. Sibir' v Ekaterininskoi kommissii: Etiud po istorii Sibiri XVIII veka. Moscow, 1889.

Golovnin, V. M. *Sochineniia*. Moscow and Leningrad: Glavsevmorput', 1949.
Golubev, S. "Danka iz stoibishcha Andy." *SS*, no. 4 (1932): 130–33.
Gor, Gennadii. *Bol'shie pikhtovye lesa*. Leningrad: Sovetskii pisatel', 1968.
——. *Iunosha s dalekoi reki*. Leningrad: Sovetskii pisatel', 1953.
"Gotovim spetsialistov-natsionalov." *SAr*, no. 5 (1935): 56–59.
Graburn, Nelson H.H., and B. Stephen Strong. *Circumpolar Peoples: An Anthropological Perspective*. Pacific Palisades, Calif.: Goodyear, 1973.
Gracheva, G. N. "K voprosu o vliianii khristianizatsii na religioznye predstavleniia nganasan." In Vdovin, ed., *Khristianstvo i lamaizm*, pp. 29–47.
Graham, Loren R. *The Soviet Academy of Sciences and the Communist Party, 1927–1932*. Princeton: Princeton University Press, 1967.
Grande, B. "N. Ia. Marr i novoe uchenie o iazyke." *RN*, no. 2 (1935): 6-53.
Grant, Bruce. "Siberia Hot and Cold: Reconstructing the Image of Siberian Indigenous Peoples." In Diment and Slezkine, eds., *Between Heaven and Hell*, pp. 227–53.
Grazhdanskaia voina na Dal'nem Vostoke (1918–1922). Vospominaniia veteranov. Moscow: Nauka, 1978.
Greenblatt, Stephen. *Marvelous Possessions: The Wonder of the New World*. Chicago: University of Chicago Press, 1991.
Grigor'ev, A. "Nizhnee techenie Amura v kolonizatsionnom otnoshenii." *VK*, no. 5 (1909): 314–50.
Grinshpan, B. I. "Na pushnom uchastke" *SAr*, no. 11 (1936): 73–79.
——. "Stakhanovskoe dvizhenie v pushnom khoziaistve." *SAr*, no. 3 (1936): 69–70.
Gromyko, M. M. *Iz istorii sem'i i byta sibirskogo krest'ianstva v XVI-nachale XX veka*. Novosibirsk: Novosibirskii gos. universitet, 1975.
——. *Zapadnaia Sibir' v XVIII veke*. Novosibirsk: Nauka, 1965.
Gruzdev, S. "Kochevaia shkola dlia narodnostei Severa." *SA*, no. 5–6 (1925): 101–4.
Gurari, G. N. "GUSMP." *SS*, no. 6 (1934): 25–32.
Gurevich, A. V., ed. *Vostochnaia Sibir' v rannei khudozhestvennoi proze*. Irkutsk: Irkutskoe oblastnoe izdatel'stvo, 1938.
Gurvich, I. S. "Desiat' let deiatel'nosti sektora severa Instituta etnografii SSSR." *Problemy Severa*, 11 (1967): 258–61.
——. *Etnicheskaia istoriia Severo-Vostoka Sibiri*. AN SSSR, Trudy instituta etnografii im. N. N. Miklukho-Maklaia. Novaia seriia, vol. 89. Moscow: AN SSSR, 1966.
——. "Etnokul'turnoe sblizhenie narodov SSSR." *SE*, no. 5 (1977): 23–35.
——. "Izmeneniia v kul'ture i byte naseleniia Krainego Severa Iakutii pod vliianiem kul'tury russkogo naroda." In *Vedushchaia rol'*.
——. "Nekotorye problemy etnicheskogo razvitiia narodov SSSR." *SE*, no. 5 (1967): 62–77.
——. "O putiakh dal'neishego pereustroistva ekonomiki i kul'tury narodov Severa." *SE*, no. 4 (1961): 45–57.
——. "Osobennosti sovremennogo etapa etnokul'turnogo razvitiia narodov Sovetskogo Soiuza." *SE*, no. 6 (1982): 15–27.
——. "Osushchestvlenie leninskoi natsional'noi politiki u narodov Krainego Severa." *SE*, no. 1 (1970): 15–58.
——. "Polveka avtonomii narodnostei Severa SSSR." *SE*, no. 6 (1980): 3–17.
——. "Po povodu opredeleniia etnicheskoi prinadlezhnosti naseleniia bassei-nov rek Oleneka i Anabary." *SE*, no. 2 (1952): 73–85.

——. "Sovremennoe napravlenie etnicheskikh protsessov v SSSR." *SE*, no. 4 (1972): 16–33.

——. "Sovremennye etnicheskie protsessy, protekaiushchie na severe Iakutii." *SE*, no. 5 (1960): 3–11.

——, ed. *Etnicheskoe razvitie narodnostei Severa v Sovetskii period.* Moscow: Nauka, 1987.

——, ed. *Etnogenez i etnicheskaia istoriia narodov Severa.* Moscow: Nauka, 1975.

——, ed. *Etnogenez narodov Severa.* Moscow, 1980).

——, ed. *Etnokul'turnye protsessy u narodov Sibiri i severa.* Moscow: Nauka, 1985.

——, ed. *Osushchestvlenie leninskoi natsional'noi politiki u narodov Krainego Severa.* Moscow: Nauka, 1971.

Gurvich, I. S., and B. O. Dolgikh, eds. *Obshchestvennyi stroi u narodov severnoi Sibiri XVII–nachala XX v.* Moscow: Nauka, 1970.

Gurvich, I. S., and Ch. M. Taksami. "Sotsial'nye funktsii iazykov narodnostei Severa i dal'nego Vostoka SSSR v sovetskii period." *SE*, no. 2 (1985): 54–63.

——. "Vklad sovetskikh etnografov v osushchestvlenie leninskoi natsional'noi politiki na Severe." In *Leninizm i problemy etnografii,* ed. Iu. V. Bromlei and R. F. Its. Leningrad: Nauka, 1987.

Hajdu, Peter. *Finno-Ugrian Languages and Peoples.* London: André Deutsch, 1975.

——. *The Samoed Peoples and Languages.* Indiana University Publications. Uralic and Altaic Series, vol. 14. Bloomington: Indiana University Press, 1963.

Hakluyt, Richard. *The Principal Navigations Voyages Traffiques and Discoveries of the English Nation.* Glasgow: James MacLehose & Sons, 1903.

Hanson, Gary. "Grigory Potanin, Siberian Regionalism and the Russian Revolution of 1905." Paper delivered at the Nineteenth National Convention of the American Association for the Advancement of Slavic Studies, Boston, November 1987.

Harris, John. *A Complete Collection of Voyages and Travels.* London, 1705.

Hawes, Charles H. *In the Uttermost East.* New York: Harper & Brothers, 1903. [HRAF, RX2, no. 9].

Hecht, David. *Russian Radicals Look to America, 1825–1894.* Cambridge: Harvard University Press, 1947.

Herberstein, Sigismund. *Zapiski o moskovitskikh dielakh.* St. Petersburg, 1908.

Herzen [Gertsen], Alexander. *Sobranie sochinenii v tridtsati tomakh.* Moscow: AN SSSR, 1957.

Herzfeld, Michael. *Anthropology through the Looking Glass: Critical Ethnography in the Margins of Europe.* Cambridge: Cambridge University Press, 1988.

Hill, S. S. *Travels in Siberia.* 2 vols. 1854. Reprint. New York: Arno Press & the New York Times, 1970.

Hobsbawm, E. J. *Nations and Nationalism since 1780: Programme, Myth, Reality.* Cambridge: Cambridge University Press, 1990.

Hodgen, Margaret T. *Early Anthropology in the Sixteenth and Seventeenth Centuries.* Philadelphia: University of Pennsylvania Press, 1971.

Hooper, William Hulme. *Ten Months among the Tents of the Tuski, with Inci-*

dents of an Arctic Boat Expedition in Search of Sir John Franklin, as Far as the Mackenzie River and Cape Bathurst. London, 1853. [HRAF RY2, no. 6]

Humphrey, Caroline. Karl Marx Collective: Economy, Society, and Religion in a Siberian Collective Farm. Cambridge: Cambridge University Press, 1983.

I. M. "K voprosu o zemledelii v basseine r. Kolymy." SS, no. 1–2 (1932): 223–26.

Iadrintsev, N. M. "K moei avtobiografii." Russkaia mysl' (June 1904): 152–70.

———. "Osuzhdennye na smert' plemena." SSb, no. 1 (1904): 1–32.

———. Sibirskie inorodtsy, ikh byt i sovremennoe polozhenie. St. Petersburg, 1891.

———. Sibir' kak koloniia. St. Petersburg, 1882.

Iakimova, L. P. Mnogonatsional'naia Sibir' v russkoi literature. Novosibirsk: Nauka, 1982

Iakobii, A. I. O missionerskom stane v strane Nadyma i o vozmozhnoi postanovke khristianskoi missii v strankakh russkogo inorodcheskogo Severa. Tobol'sk, 1895.

———. "Ugasanie inorodcheskikh plemen Tobol'skogo Severa." ZhS, no. 3–4 (1896): 267–72.

Iakovleva, E. V. Malye narodnosti Priamur'ia posle sotsialisticheskoi revoliutsii. Khabarovsk: Khabarovskoe knizhnoe izdatel'stvo, 1957.

———. "Ob osobennostiakh ustanovleniia Sovetskoi vlasti u narodov Priamur'ia." In Sbornik statei po istorii Dal'nego Vostoka. Moscow: AN SSSR, 1958.

Iakubovich, R. L. "Ochishchaia riady." SAr, no. 4 (1936): 68–73.

Ianovich, Daniel. "Severnye tuzemtsy." ZhN, no. 1 (1923): 251–54.

———. "Zapovedniki dlia gibnushchikh tuzemnykh plemen." ZhN, no. 4 (1922): 18.

Iastrebov, I. "Vopros ob ustroistve i organizatsii obrazovatel'nykh zavedenii dlia prigotovleniia pravoslavnykh blagovestnikov (missionerov)." PB, no. 22–23 (1894); no. 3–8, 16 (1895).

Ingold, Tim. Hunters, Pastoralists, and Ranchers: Reindeer Economies and Their Transformations. Cambridge: Cambridge University Press, 1980.

Islavin, Vladimir. Samoiedy v domashnem i obshchestvennom bytu. St. Petersburg, 1847.

Ispravnikov. "Kolkhoznoe stroitel'stvo na Iamale." SS, no. 2 (1933) 89–93.

Istomin, Ivan. Radost'. Moscow: Sovetskaia Rossiia, 1961.

———. Tsvety v snegakh. Moscow: n.p., 1966.

———. Zhivun. Moscow: Sovremennik, 1974.

Istoriia Iakutskoi ASSR. 3 vols. Moscow: AN SSSR, 1957.

Istoriia i kul'tura itel'menov. Leningrad: Nauka, 1990.

Itin, V. "V chume." SO, no. 3 (1930): 62.

"Itogi raboty Komiteta sodeistviia narodnostiam severnykh okrain pri Prezidiume VTsIK." SA, no. 3 (1926): 80–85.

"Itogi sessii VASKhNIL i sovetskaia antropologiia." SE, no. 1 (1949): 176–83.

Iushunev, N. "Osedanie kochevnikov Buriato-Mongolii." RN, no. 12 (1933): 25–28.

Ivanchuk, Iu. "Iamal: Chem velik i chem mal." Sovetskaia kul'tura, 7 October 1989.

Ivanov, P. N. "Pervye meropriiatiia partiinykh i sovetskikh organizatsii Sibiri po likvidatsii ekonomicheskoi otstalosti nerusskikh narodov (1920–1925)." In Sibir' v period stroitel'stva sotsializma i perekhoda k kommunizmu, pp. 5–15.

Ivanov, S. P. "Udovletvorit' spros naseleniia Chukotki." *SAr,* no. 3 (1938): 66.

Ivanov, V. N. *Istoricheskaia mysl' v Rossii XVIII—serediny XIX v. o narodakh severo-vostoka Azii.* Moscow: Nauka, 1989.

——. *Russkie uchenye o narodakh Severo-vostoka Azii (XVII-nachalo XX v.).* Iakutsk: Iakutskoe knizhnoe izdatel'stvo, 1978.

Ivanov, V. Vs., V. N. Toporov, and B. A. Uspenskii, eds. *Ketskii sbornik.* 2 vols. Moscow: Nauka, 1969.

Ivnitskii, N. A. *Klassovaia bor'ba v derevne i likvidatsiia kulachestva kak klassa (1929–1932).* Moscow: Nauka, 1972.

"Iz deiatel'nosti predstavitel'stva Narkomnatsa v Sibiri." *ZhN,* no. 14 (1922): 11.

"Iz dnevnika (za 1895 g.) gol'dskogo missionera Kamchatskoi missii." *PB,* nos. 18, 19, 20 (1896).

"Iz nedavnego proshlogo sibirskikh missii." *PB,* no. 17 (1893): 24–33.

Jackson, Frederick George. *The Great Frozen Land (Bolshaia Zemelskija Tundra): Narrative of a Winter Journey across the Tundras and a Sojourn among the Samoyads.* London: 1895.

Jameson, Fredric. "Postmodernism, or the Cultural Logic of Capital." *New Left Review,* no. 146 (1984): 57.

JanMohammed, Abdul R. *Manichean Aesthetics: The Politics of Literature in Colonial Africa.* Amherst: University of Massachusetts Press, 1983.

Jaulin, Robert. *Le Paix blanche: Introduction à l'ethnocide.* 2 vols. Paris: 10/18, 1974.

Jochelson, Waldemar [V. Iokhel'son]. *The Koryak.* Memoirs of the American Museum of Natural History, vol. 10, parts 1 and 2. New York: The American Museum of Natural History, 1913.

——. *Peoples of Asiatic Russia.* New York: The American Museum of Natural History, 1928.

——. *The Yukaghir and the Yukaghirized Tungus.* Memoirs of the American Museum of Natural History, vol. 13. New York: The American Museum of Natural History, 1910.

Johnson, Henry. *The Life and Voyages of Joseph Wiggins, F.R.G.S., Modern Discoverer of the Kara Sea Route to Siberia, Based on His Journals and Letters.* New York: E. P. Dutton, 1907.

Joravsky, David. "The Construction of the Stalinist Psyche." In Fitzpatrick, ed., *Cultural Revolution in Russia,* pp. 105–28.

——. *The Lysenko Affair.* Cambridge: Harvard University Press, 1970.

——. *Soviet Marxism and Natural Science.* New York: Columbia University Press, 1961.

"K itogam etnograficheskogo soveshchaniia 1956g." *SE.* no. 3 (1956): 3–4.

"K novym uspekham sovetskoi etnografii." *SE,* no. 2 (1951): 3–6.

"K organizatsii muzeia istorii religii." *SE,* no. 1–2 (1931): 171–72.

"K organizatsii pervykh tuzemnykh shkol na severnom poberezh'e Chukotskogo poluostrova." *SS,* no. 1 (1931).

K—ev, Ia. "Po olenevodcheskim sovkhozam Severnogo kraia." *SS,* no. 5 (1933), 12.

K. E. "Kolkhoznye zametki." *SS,* no. 3–4 (1935): 184–88.

Kabuzan, V. M. *Dal'nevostochnyi krai v XVII–nachale XX vv., 1640–1917: Istoriko-demograficheskii ocherk.* Moscow; Nauka, 1985.

Kabuzan, V. M., and S. M. Troitskii. "Chislennost' i sostav naseleniia Sibiri v pervoi polovine XIX veka." In Okladnikov, ed., *Russkoe naselenie Pomor'ia i Sibiri* pp. 261–78.

——. "Chislennost' i sostav gorodskogo naseleniia Sibiri v 40–80-kh godakh XVIIIv." In Shunkov, ed., *Osvoenie Sibiri* pp. 165–74.

Kagarov, E. G. "Predely etnografii." *E*, no. 1 (1928): 11–21.

Kalashnikov, I. T. *Doch' kuptsa Zholobova*. St. Petersburg, 1831.

——. "Izgnanniki." In Gurevich, ed., *Vostochnaia Sibir'*, pp. 1–39.

——. *Kamchadalka*. St. Petersburg, 1831.

Kantor, E. D. "Kadry na Krainem Severe." *SAr*, no. 2 (1935): 27–29.

——. "Kazymskaia kul'tbaza." *SS*, no. 6 (1933): 66–68.

——. "Khoziaistvo Iamal'skogo (Nenetskogo) natsional'nogo okruga." *SS*, no. 6 (1933): 46–53.

——. "Liudi i fakty. Staroe i novoe." *SS*, no. 3–4 (1935): 189–93.

——. "Problema osedaniia malykh narodov Severa." *SS*, no. 5 (1934): 3–10.

——. "Sever zovet." *RN*, no. 10–11 (1932): 133–38.

——. "Sostoianie severnogo olenevodstva i puti ego razvitiia." *SS*, no. 3 (1934): 19–25.

Kantorovich, V. I. *Po Sovetskoi Kamchatke: Kniga putevykh ocherkov*. Moscow: Molodaia gvardiia, 1931.

Kappeler, Andreas. *Ruisslands erste Nationalitäten: Das Zarenreich und die Völker der Mittleren Wolga vom 16. bis 19. Jahrhundert*. Cologne: Böhlau 1982.

Karamzin, N. M. *Istoriia gosudarstva Rossiiskogo*. Moscow: Kniga, 1989.

Karger, N. K. "Ocherednye zadachi etnografii na Severe." *SA*, no. 3–4 (1931) 232–43.

Kartsov, V. G. *Dekabrist G. S. Baten'kov*. Novosibirsk: Nauka, 1965.

——. *Ocherk istorii narodov severo-zapadnoi Sibiri*. Moscow and Leningrad Gosudarstvennoe sotsial'no-ekonomicheskoe izdatel'stvo, 1937.

Kastelianskii, A. I., ed. *Formy natsional'nogo dvizheniia v sovremennykh gosudarstvakh*. St. Petersburg, 1910.

Kastren [Castrén], M. A. "Puteshestvie Aleksandra Kastrena po Laplandii, severnoi Rossii i Sibiri," *Magazin zemlevedeniia i puteshestvii* 6, no. 2 (1860).

Kaufman, R. B. "Delegaty Taimyra." *SAr*, no. 11 (1936): 59–63.

Kavelin, E. "Kolymskii krai." *SS*, no. 2 (1931): 152–72.

Kennan, George. *Tent Life in Siberia and Adventures among the Koraks and Other Tribes in Kamchatka and Northern Asia*. New York: G. P. Putnam, 1872.

Kerner, Robert J. *The Urge to the Sea: The Course of Russian History. The Role of Rivers, Portages, Ostrogs, Monasteries, and Furs*. Berkeley and Los Angeles: University of California Press, 1946.

Kertselli, S. "Goszaimy i nash Sever." *SS*, no. 7–8 (1931): 61–62.

——. "Olenevodstvo SSSR i ego perspektivy." *SA*, no. 1–2 (1931): 27–34.

Khaptaev, P. T. *Kratkii ocherk istorii buriat-mongol'skogo naroda*. Ulan Ude: Burgosizdat, 1936.

——. "O nekotorykh osobennostiakh klassovoi bor'by v natsional'noi derevne." *RN*, no. 2 (1933): 47–55.

——. "Ob izvrashcheniiakh v voprosakh istorii Buriato-Mongolii." *RN*, no. 7 (1935): 52–56.

——. "Osedanie Buriat-Aiginskogo aimaka." *RN*, no. 5 (1932): 65–73.

——, ed. *Istoriia Buriat-Mongol'skoi ASSR.* Ulan Ude: Buriat-Mongol'skoe knizhnoe izdatel'stvo, 1954.

Kharlampovich, K. V. *Malorossiiskoe vliianie na velikorusskuiu tserkovnuiu zhizn'.* Vol. 1. Kazan', 1914.

——. "O khristianskom prosveshchenii inorodtsev. Iz perepiski arkhiepiskopa Veniamina Irkutskogo s N. I. Il'minskim." *PB,* July–August 1905, pp. 1–38.

Khatskevich, A. "Ob osedanii kochevogo i polukochevogo naseleniia." *RN,* no. 12 (1935): 15–25.

Khazanovich, A. M. *Krasnyi chum v Khatangskoi tundre.* Leningrad: Izdatel'-stvo Glavsevmorputi, 1939.

Khodam., Ia. "O deiatel'nosti organov Narkomnatsa na mestakh." *ZhN,* no. 15 (1922): 150.

Khodzher, Bogdan. "Kak ia partizanil." *TT,* no. 2 (1930): 140–148.

Khodzher, Grigorii, *Amur shirokii.* Moscow: Izvestiia, 1973.

——. *Belaia tishina.* Moscow: Sovetskaia Rossiia, 1970.

——. *Konets bol'shogo doma.* Khabarovsk: Khabarovskoe knizhnoe izdatel'-stvo, 1964.

——. *Pustoe ruzh'e.* Moscow: Sovetskaia Rossiia, 1982.

Khodzher, K. "Semeinye i brachnye otnosheniia u gol'dov na Amure." *TT,* no. 3 (1931): 97.

Khomiakov, A. S. *Stikhotvoreniia i dramy.* Leningrad: Sovetskii pisatel', 1969.

Khomich, L. V. *Nentsy: Istoriko-etnograficheskie ocherki.* Leningrad: Nauka, 1966.

Khotinskii, B. "XVI s"ezd partii i nashi zadachi." *E,* no. 4 (1930): 3–10.

Khudiakov, I. A. *Kratkoe opisanie Verkhoianskogo okruga.* Leningrad: Nauka, 1969.

Khudiakov, M. G. "Graficheskie skhemy istoricheskogo protsessa v trudakh N. Ia. Marra." *SE,* no. 1 (1935): 18–41.

——. "Kriticheskaia prorabotka rudenkovshchiny." *SE* no. 1–2 (1931): 167–69.

Kile, Pavel. *Idti vechno.* Novosibirsk: Zapadno-Sibirskoe knizhnoe izdatel'-stvo, 1972.

——. *Svoistva dushi.* Moscow: Sovremennik, 1979.

Kiselev, A. A., and T. A. Kiseleva. *Sovetskie Saamy: Istoriia, ekonomika, kul'-tura.* Murmansk: Murmanskoe knizhnoe izdatel'stvo, 1987.

Kiselev, A. S. "Ocherednye zadachi sovetov na Krainem Severe." *SS,* no. 4 (1932): 13–14.

Kiselev, L. E. *Ot patriarkhal'shchiny k sotsializmu.* Sverdlovsk: Sredne-Ural'skoe knizhnoe izdatel'stvo, 1974.

——. *Sever raskryvaet bogatstva (Iz istorii promyshlennogo razvitiia sovet-skogo Krainego Severa).* Moscow: Mysl', 1964.

Kisliakov, N. A. "K voprosu ob etnograficheskom izuchenii kolkhozov." *SE,* no. 1 (1952): 146–49.

Kleshchenok, I. P. *Istoricheskii opyt KPSS po osushchestvleniiu leninskoi nat-sional'noi politiki sredi malykh narodov Severa (1917–1935).* Moscow: Vys-shaia shkola, 1972.

——. *Narody Severa i leninskaia natsional'naia politika v deistvii.* Moscow: Vysshaia shkola, 1968.

Klimushev, Ia. "Tselevoe naznachenie v tovarosnabzhenii Krainego Severa." *SS,* no. 6 (1933): 23–31.

Knox, Thomas W. *Overland through Asia: Pictures of Siberian, Chinese, and Tartar Life.* Hartford, Conn., 1873.

Kolarz, Walter. *The Peoples of the Soviet Far East.* New York: Praeger, 1954.
——. *Russia and Her Colonies.* London: G. Philip, 1952.
Kolesov, G. G., and S. G. Potapov, eds. *Sovetskaia Iakutiia.* Moscow: Sotsegiz, 1937.
Kolin, N. K. "Inostrantsy v Sibiri: Chukotskii krai." *RV* 252 (December 1897): 419–22.
——. "Zheltyi vopros na russkom Vostoke." *RV,* 252 (January 1898): 310–20.
Komanovskii, B. L. *Puti razvitiia literatur narodov Krainego Severa i Dal'nego Vostoka SSSR.* Magadan: Magadanskoe knizhnoe izdatel'stvo, 1977.
Komarov, N. "Ocherki verovanii inorodtsev, sredi kotorykh deistvuiut nashi missii." *PB,* no. 2 (1893): 19–25.
"Komitet sodeistviia narodnostiam severnykh okrain pri Prezidiume VTsIK." *SA,* no. 1–2 (1925): 136–38.
Komov, N. "Rabota v Chukotskoi shkole." *SS,* no. 1 (1933): 72–79.
Kon, F. I. "Novye zadachi," *ZhN,* no. 1 (1920): 58.
——. "Pervostepennoi vazhnosti vopros," *ZhN,* no. 49 (1919): 157.
Kon, I. S. "Etnografiia detstra." *SE,* no. 5 (1981): 3–14.
Konrad, Helmut. "Between 'Little International' and Great Power Politics: Austro-Marxism and Stalinism on the National Question." In *Nationalism and Empire: The Habsburg Empire and the Soviet Union,* ed. Richard L. Rudolph and David F. Good. New York: St. Martin's Press, 1992.
Kontseptsiia ekonomicheskogo i sotsial'nogo razvitiia narodnostei Severa na period 1991–2005 gg. Iakutsk: Iakutskii filial So AN SSSR.
Kontseptsiia razvitiia Taimyrskogo avtonomnogo okruga. Dudinka: Taimyrskii OK KPSS, 1990.
"Konventsiia 26 (Assotsiatsii malochislennykh narodov Severa Sovetskogo Soiuza) 16 October 1990." Unpublished.
"Koordinatsionnoe soveshchanie po etnograficheskomu izucheniiu sotsialisticheskoi kul'tury i byta narodov SSSR." *SE,* no. 1 (1953): 173–82.
Koptelov, A. L. *Velikoe kochev'e.* Moscow: Sovetskii pisatel', 1937.
Kopylov, A. N. "K voprosu o printsipe iasachnogo oblozheniia i poriadke sbora iasaka v Sibiri." *Izvestiia Sibirskogo otdeleniia AN SSSR: Seriia obshchestvennykh nauk,* no. 1 (1969): 58–72.
Korf, Modest A. *Zhizn' grafa Speranskogo.* 2 vols. St. Petersburg, 1861.
Koril'skii, K. "O zaezzhikh domakh dlia tuzemtsev." *SS,* no. 9–12 (1930): 160–65.
Kornakov, Vladimir. "Cheglok." *Sibirskie ogni,* no. 12 (1972): 19–81.
Kornienko, V. "Vosstanie Vaulia." *SE,* no. 5–6 (1932): 112–119.
Kornilov, A. M. *Zamechaniia o Sibiri senatora Kornilova.* St. Petersburg, 1828.
Korolenko, V. G. *Ocherki i razskazy.* Petrograd, 1915.
Koshelev, Ia. "Severnoe olenevodstvo vo vtorom piatiletnem plane." *SS,* no. 3 (1933): 10–17.
Koshelev, Ia. "V Iamal'skikh tundrakh." *SS,* no. 5 (1934): 79–84.
Kosokov, I. "Itogi planovogo osedaniia i prakticheskie zadachi." *RN,* no. 5–6 (1933): 67–73
——. "Ob osedanii kochevogo i polukochevogo naseleniia sovetskogo Vostoka." *RN,* no. 5 (1932): 49–58.
Kovalevskii, P. "V shkole-iurte." *SS,* no. 2 (1934): 103–07.
Kozin, S. "Dal'nevostochnaia kompleksnaia ekspeditsiia." *SE,* no. 3–4 (1931): 201–7.
Kozlov, V. I. "O poniatii etnicheskoi obshchnosti." *SE,* no. 2 (1967): 100–111.

——. "Osnovnye problemy etnicheskoi ekologii." *SE*, no. 1 (1983): 3–15.

——. "Sovremennye etnicheskie protsessy v SSSR." *SE*, no. 2 (1969): 60–72.

Kozlov, V. I., and V. V. Pokshishevskii. "Etnografiia i geografiia." *SE*, no. 1 (1973): 3–13.

Kozlov, V. I., and G. V. Shelepov. "Natsional'nyi kharakter i problemy ego issledovaniia." *SE*, no. 2 (1973): 69–82.

Kozlova, K. I., and N. N. Cheboksarov. "Etnografiia v Moskovskom universitete." *SE*, no. 2 (1955): 100–111.

KPSS v rezoliutsiiakh i resheniiakh s"ezdov, konferentsii i plenumov TsK. Moscow: Izdatel'stvo politicheskoi literatury, 1983.

Krasheninnikov, S. P. *Opisanie zemli Kamchatki. S prilozheniem raportov, donesenii i drugikh neopublikovannykh materialov.* Moscow and Leningrad: Izdatel'stvo Glavsevmorputi, 1949.

"Kratkii obzor deiatel'nosti Eniseiskogo komiteta Pravoslavnogo missionerskogo obshchestva za poslednee 25-letie." *PB*, no. 16 (1896): 351–60.

"Kratkii ocherk missionerstva v Tobol'skoi eparkhii." *PB*, no. 15 (1893): 12–14.

Kratt, Ivan. *Dal'niaia bukhta.* Leningrad: Molodaia gvardiia, 1945.

——. *Izbrannoe.* Leningrad: Sovetskii pisatel', 1951.

——. *Moia zemlia. Kolymskie rasskazy.* Moscow: Sovetskii pisatel', 1938.

Krauss, Michael E. "Many Tongues—Ancient Tales." In William W. Fitzhugh and Aron Crowell, eds., *Crossroads of Continents: Cultures of Siberia and Alaska.* Washington, D.C.: Smithsonian Institution, 1988, pp. 145–50.

Kreindler, Isabelle Teitz. "Educational Policies toward the Eastern Nationalities in Tsarist Russia: A Study of the Il'minskii System. Columbia University, Ph.D. diss., 1969.

——. "A Neglected Source of Lenin's Nationality Policy." *SR* 36 (March 1977): 86–100.

——. *Nivkhgu: Zagadochnye obitateli Sakhalina i Amura.* Moscow, Nauka, 1973.

Kriuchkov, Fedor. "O krashenakh." *ZhN*, no. 27 (1920).

Krivoshapkin, M. F. *Eniseiskii okrug i ego zhizn'. 2 vols.* St. Petersburg, 1865.

Krizhanich [Križanić], Iurii. "Historia de Sibiria." In Titov, ed., Sibir' v XVII v. 115–216.

Kruglov, A. "Karagassiia i ee khoziaistvo." *SS*, no. 9–12 (1930): 147–59.

——. "O revoliutsionnoi zakonnosti na mestakh." *SS*, no. 1 (1933): 97–102.

——. "Perevybory sovetov na Severnom Urale." *SS*, no. 5 (1931): 93–100.

Krupnik, I. I. *Arkticheskaia etnoekologiia.* Moscow: Nauka, 1989.

——. "Stanovlenie krupnotabunnogo olenevodstva u tundrovykh nentsev." *SE*, no. 2 (1976): 57–69.

Krupnik, I. I., and M. A. Chlenov. "Dinamika etnolingvisticheskoi situatsii u aziatskikh eskimosov (konets XIX v.—1970ye gg.)." *SE*, no. 2 (1979): 19–29.

Kruzenshtern, Ivan F. *Voyage round the World in the Years 1803, 1804, 1805, and 1806 by Order of His Imperial Majesty Alexander the First on Board the Ships Nadeshda and Neva.* London, 1813.

Krylov, V. "Administrativnaia perepiska Innokentiia, mitropolita moskovskogo za vremia ego upravleniia Kamchatskoiu eparkhieiu." *Pravoslavnyi sobesednik*, October 1904.

Krylov, V. "V Penzhinskom raione." *SS*, no. 1 (1935): 93–95.

Kudriavtsev, Iu. A. "Na putiakh rekonstruktsii olenevodstva v sovetskoi Azii." *SA*, no. 1–2 (1931): 35–41.

Kuchiiak, P. "Arbachi." *SO*, no. 2 (1935): 107–12.

Kuleshov, V. A., ed. *Nakazy sibirskim voevodam v XVII veke. Istoricheskii ocherk.* Bolgrad, 1894.

"Kul'tura, byt i shkola na Severe." *TT,* no. 4 (1932): 28–42.

Kulumbetov, U. D. "Perekhod na osedlost' v Kazakhstane." *RN,* no. 5 (1932): 59–65.

Kungurov, G. F. *Topka.* Irkutsk: Vostochno-sibirskoe knizhnoe izdatel'stvo, 1964.

Kuoljok, Kerstin Eidlitz. *The Revolution in the North: Soviet Ethnography and Nationality Policy.* Uppsala: Almquist & Wiksell, 1985.

Kushner, [Knyshev] P. I. "Ob etnograficheskom izuchenii kolkhoznogo krest'ianstva." *SE,* no. 1 (1952): 135–41.

——. "Ob etnograficheskom izuchenii sotsialisticheskoi kul'tury i byta narodov SSSR." *SE,* no. 1 (1953): 10–26.

——. "Uchenie Stalina o natsii i natsional'noi kul'ture i ego znachenie dlia etnografii." *SE,* no. 4 (1949): 4–19.

Kusik'ian, I. "N. Ia. Marr i ego uchenie o iazyke." *PN,* no. 6 (1933): 5.

Kuvaev, Oleg. *Izbrannoe.* 2 vols. Moscow: Molodaia gvardiia, 1988.

Kuzakov, Nikolai. *Liubov shamanki.* Moscow: Sovremennik, 1975.

——. *Taiga—moi dom.* Moscow: Mysl', 1977.

Kuzakova, E. "Uroki dobra i oshibok." *SP,* no. 6 (1986): 32–33.

Kuz'mina, E. "Koriakskaia zhenshchina." *PN,* no. 7 (1932): 93–99.

Kuznetsov-Krasnoiarskii, I. P., ed. *Istoricheskie akty XVII stoletiia, 1633–1699. Materialy dlia istorii Sibiri.* 2 vols. Tomsk, 1890.

Kymytval', Antonina. *Moi liubimyi tsvetok.* Magadan: Magadanskoe knizhnoe izdatel'stvo, 1982.

Kytmanov, D. "Tuzemtsy Turukhanskogo kraia." *SA,* no. 2 (1927): 37–51; no. 3 (1927): 51–67.

L. N. "Bol'shoe iskusstvo malykh narodov." *PN,* no. 6 (1930): 116–21.

Labazov, "Zhizn' zhenshchiny-nenki Bol'shezemel'skoi tundry." *TT,* no. 3 (1931): 94–96.

Lantzeff, George V. *Siberia in the Seventeenth Century: A Study of the Colonial Administration.* University of California Publications in History, vol. 30. Berkeley and Los Angeles: University of California Press, 1943.

Lantzeff, George V., and Richard A. Pierce. *Eastward to Empire: Exploration and Conquest on the Russian Open Frontier to 1750.* Montreal: McGill-Queen's University Press, 1973.

Lapin, B. M. *Tikhookeanskii dnevnik.* Moscow: Federatsiia, 1933.

Larina, A. M. "Nezabyvaemoe." *Znamia,* nos. 10 and 11 (1988).

Lar'kin, V. G. *Orochi: Istoriko-etnograficheskii ocherk s serediny XIX v. do nashikh dnei.* Moscow; Nauka, 1964.

Lashov, B. V. and O. P Litovka. *Sotsial'no-ekonomicheskie problemy razvitiia narodnostei Krainego Severa.* Leningrad: Nauka, 1982.

Latkin, N. V. *Eniseiskaia guberniia, ee proshloe i nastoiashchee.* (St. Petersburg, 1892.

Lavrov, P. L. "Tsivilizatsiia i dikie plemena." *Otechestvenyia zapiski* 184, no. 5 (1869): 107–69; no. 6, pp. 359–414; no. 8, pp. 253–311; no. 9, pp. 93–128.

Layton, Susan. "The Creation of an Imaginative Caucasian Geography." *SR,* no. 3 (1986): 470–85.

Lebedev, D. M. *Geografiia v Rossii XVII veka.* Moscow and Leningrad: AN SSSR, 1949.

——. *Ocherki po istorii geografii v Rossii XVIII v. (1725–1800).* Moscow: AN SSSR, 1957.

Lebedev, G. "Vymiraiushchie brat'ia." *ZhN*, no. 19 (1920): 76.

——. "Iakutskaia avtonomnaia respublika." *ZhN*, no. 1 (1923): 134–39.

Lebedev, P. "Na perelome." *SS*, no. 5 (1934): 19–22.

Lebedev, V. V., and Iu. B. Simchenko. *Achaivaiamskaia vesna.* Moscow: Mysl', 1983.

Leclerc, Gérard. *Anthropologie et colonialisme: Essai sur l'histoire de l'africanisme.* Paris: Fayard, 1972.

Lemke, M. K. *Nikolai Mikhailovich Iadrintsev: Biograficheskii ocherk.* St. Petersburg, 1904.

Lenin, V. I. *Polnoe sobranie sochinenii.* Moscow: Politizdat, 1958–1965.

——. *Voprosy natsional'noi politiki i proletarskogo internatsionalizma.* Moscow: Politizdat, 1965.

"Leningradskoe obshchestvo izucheniia kul'tury finno-ugorskikh narodov (LOIKFUN)." *SE*, no. 1–2 (1931): 156.

Leonov, N. I. "Kul'tbaza v taige." *PN*, no. 9–10 (1930): 86–91.

——. "Na fronte Krainego Severa." *SA*, no. 3 (1928): 92–103.

——. "Tuzemnye shkoly na Severe." In *Sovetskii sever. Pervyi sbornik statei,* pp. 219–58.

——. "Tuzemnye sovety v taige i tundrakh." In *Sovetskii Sever. Pervyi sbornik statei,* pp. 219–58.

——. "V debriakh Severa." *PN*, no. 6 (1930): 88–93.

——. "V nizov'iakh Amura." *SS*, no. 2 (1930): 94–98.

Leonov, S. "Stoibishche Udomi-Darakhta." *SO*, no. 8 (1930): 3–19.

Leont'ev, F. L. "Zdravookhranenie na Chukotke trebuet pomoshchi." *SAr*, no. 3 (1938): 18.

Leont'ev, V. V. *Antymavle—torgovyi chelovek.* Magadan: Magadanskoe knizhnoe izdatel'stvo, 1963.

——. *Khoziaistvo i kul'tura narodov Chukotki.* Leningrad: Nauka, 1973.

——. *Okhotniki proliva Beringa.* Magadan: Magadanskoe knizhnoe izdatel'stvo, 1969.

——. *Po zemle drevnikh kerekov.* Magadan: Magadanskoe knizhnoe izdatel'stvo, 1976.

——. *V Chukotskom more.* Magadan: Magadanskoe knizhnoe izdatel'stvo, 1961.

Levin, Iu. D. "Angliiskaia prosvetitel'skaia zhurnalistika v russkoi literature XVIII veka." In *Epokha Prosveshcheniia. Iz istorii mezhdunarodnykh sviazei russkoi literatury.* Leningrad: Nauka, 1967.

Levin, M., Ia. Roginskii, and N. Cheboksarov. "Anglo-Amerikanskii rasizm." *SE*, no. 1 (1949): 18–39.

Levin, M. G., and L. P. Potapov, eds. *Narody Sibiri.* Moscow-Leningrad: AN SSSR, 1956.

Liakhotskii, P. "Iz dnevnika gol'dskogo missionera Kamchatskoi missii." *PB*, no. 18–20 (1896).

——. "Iz dnevnika missionera Dole-Troitskogo stana Kamchatskoi missii." *PB*, no. 19 (1897): 120–124.

Liapunova, R. G. *Ocherki po etnografii aleutov.* Leningrad: Nauka, 1975.

Liely, Helmut. "Shepherds and Reindeer Nomads in the Soviet Union." *Soviet Studies* 31, no. 3 (1979): 401–16.

"Likvidirovat' posledstviia Auerbakhovshchiny v Soiuzzagotpushnine." OS, no. 8 (1937): 7.

"Likvidirovat' posledstviia vreditel'stva." SAr, no. 1 (1938): 10–12.

Lin, T. C. "The Amur Frontier Question between China and Russia, 1850–1860." Pacific Historical Review 3, no. 1 (1934): 1–27.

Lindgren, Ethel John. "An Example of Culture Contact without Conflict: Reindeer Tungus and Cossacks of Northwestern Manchuria." AA 40, no. 4 (October–December 1938): 605–21.

Litvinov, A., and M. Polianovskii. Skachok cherez stoletiia. Dnevnik Kamchatskoi kinoekspeditsii. Moscow: Molodaia gvardiia, 1931.

Liubovtsev, Vladimir, and Iu. V. Simchenko. Tundra ne liubit slabykh. Moscow: Mysl', 1968.

Lomonosov, M. V. Polnoe sobranie sochinenii. 11 vols. Moscow-Leningrad: AN SSSR, 1950–83.

Lotman, Iu. M. "The Decembrist in Everyday Life: Everyday Behavior as a Historical-Psychological Category." In The Semiotics of Russian Culture, ed. Ann Shukman, pp. 71–123. Ann Arbor: Michigan Slavic Contributions, 1984.

———. "Russo i russkaia kul'tura XVIII veka." In Epokha prosveshcheniia. Iz istorii mezhdunarodnykh sviazei russkoi literatury. Leningrad: Nauka, 1967.

Lukovtsev, V. S. Mintia tysiacheletiia. Moscow: Mysl', 1982.

Luks, K. Ia. "Institut narodov Severa, ego mesto i zadachi." SS, no. 1 (1930): 130–36.

———. "Problema pis'mennosti u tuzemnykh narodnostei Severa." SS, no. 1 (1930): 38–47.

Lunacharskii, A. V. "Zadachi Narkomprosa na Dal'nem Severe." SA, no. 3 (1927): 18–22.

———. "Problemy obrazovaniia v avtonomnykh respublikakh i oblastiakh." ZhN, no. 1 (1924): 32.

L'vov, A. K. "Ekspeditsiia Pushnogostorga i Sibtorga v Eloguiskii raion Turukhanskogo kraia." SS, no. 2 (1930): 102–10.

———. "Kul'turnye bazy na Severe." SA, no. 3 (1926): 28–38.

M. A. "Sibirskie inorodtsy i Kolchak." ZhN, no. 24 (1919): 32.

Maak, R. [Richard Maack]. Puteshestvie na Amur, sovershennoe po rasporiazheniiu Sibirskogo otdela Imperatorskogo russkogo geograficheskogo obshchestva, v 1855 godu. St. Petersburg, 1859.

McCarthy, Frank T. "The Kazan' Missionary Congress." Cahiers du monde russe et soviétique 14, no. 3 (1973): 308–33.

McGrane, Bernard. Beyond Anthropology: Society and the Other. New York: Columbia University Press, 1989.

McReynolds, Louise. The News under Russia's Old Regime: The Development of a Mass-Circulation Press. Princeton: Princeton University Press, 1991.

Mainov, I. I. "Naselenie Iakutii." In Iakutiia. Sbornik statei, ed. P. V. Vittenburg. Leningrad: AN SSSR, 1927.

Maizel', S. "Trinadtsat' let akademicheskoi arabistiki." SE, no. 3–4 (1931): 251–54.

Maksimov, Nikolai. Poiski schast'ia. Blagoveshchensk: Amurskoe knizhnoe izdatel'stvo, 1962.

Maksimov, Sergei. Na vostoke. Poezdka na Amur v 1860–1861 godakh. St. Petersburg, 1864.

Malozemoff, Andrew. *Russian Far Eastern Policy, 1881–1904.* Berkeley and Los Angeles: University of California Press, 1958.

Mamin-Sibiriak, D. N. *Sobranie sochinenii v 10 tomakh.* Moscow: Pravda, 1958.

Manganaro, Marc, ed. *Modernist Anthropology: From Fieldwork to Text.* Princeton: Princeton University Press, 1990.

Marcus, George E., and Michael M.J. Fisher. *Anthropology as Cultural Critique: An Experimental Moment in the Human Sciences.* Chicago: University of Chicago Press, 1986.

Marin, T. "O sklokakh i travle spetsialistov na Severe." *SS,* no. 1 (1931): 52–63.

Markarian, E. S. "Uzlovye problemy teorii kul'turnoi traditsii." *SE,* no. 2 (1981): 78–115.

Markov, Il'ia. "Kul'tpokhod v deistvii." *SS,* no. 4 (1933): 88–91.

Markov, S. N. *Iukonskii voron.* Moscow: Sovetskaia Rossiia, 1970.

——. *Liudi velikoi tseli.* Moscow: Sovetskii pisatel', 1944.

——. *Tamo-rus Maklai.* Moscow: Sovetskii pisatel', 1975.

Marks, Steven G. *Road to Power: The Trans-Siberian Railroad and the Colonization of Asian Russia, 1850–1917.* Ithaca: Cornell University Press, 1991.

Marr, N. Ia., "K zadacham nauki na sovetskom Vostoke." *PN,* no. 2 (1930): 11–15.

Martin, Calvin, ed. *The American Indian and the Problem of History.* Oxford: Oxford University Press, 1987.

Martin, Janet. "Muscovy's Northeastern Expansion: The Context and a Cause." *Cahiers du monde russe et soviétique* 24, no. 4 (1983): 459–70.

——. "Russian Expansion in the Far North." In Rywkin, ed., *Russian Colonial Expansion to 1917,* pp. 23–43.

——. *Treasure of the Land of Darkness: The Fur Trade and Its Significance for Medieval Russia.* Cambridge: Cambridge University Press, 1986.

Martos, A. I. *Pis'ma o Vostochnoi Sibiri.* Moscow, 1827.

Mashanov, M. *Obzor deiatel'nosti Bratstva Sv. Guriia za 25 let ego sushchestvovaniia.* Kazan', 1892.

Mashikhina, "O polozhenii zhenshchiny-koriachki Karaginskogo raiona, Kamchatskogo okruga." *TT,* no. 2 (1930): 118–21.

Maslov, Pavel. "Kochevye ob"edineniia edinolichnykh khoziaistv v tundre Severnogo kraia." *SS,* no. 5 (1934): 27–34.

Massa, Isaac. "A Short Account of the Roads and Rivers from Muscovy, Eastward and North-East by Land, as Already Daily Travelled Over by the Muscovites." In Baddeley, ed., *Russia,* 2: 3–12.

Massell, Gregory J. *The Surrogate Proletariat: Moslem Women and Revolutionary Strategies in Soviet Central Asia, 1919–1929.* Princeton: Princeton University Press, 1974.

Matorin, N. M. "Piatnadtsat' let oktiabr'skoi revoliutsii." *SE,* no. 5–6 (1932): 4–14.

——. "Pod znamenem marksizma." *SE,* no. 3–4 (1933): 3–8.

——. "Sovremennyi etap i zadachi sovetskoi etnografii." *SE,* no. 1–2 (1931): 3–38.

Medvedev, D. F. "Itogi perevybornoi kampanii na Krainem Severe." *SS,* no. 1–2 (1932): 128.

——. "K proektu polozheniia o kochevykh sovetakh." *SS* no. 4 (1932): 73–79.

——. "O rabote s bednotoi i batrachestvom na Krainem Severe." *SS,* no. 6 (1932): 74–81.

——. "O rabote sredi tuzemnoi bednoty i batrachestva na Tobol'skom severe." *SS*, no. 1 (1931): 47–49.

——. "Ukrepim sovety na Krainem Severe i ozhivim ikh rabotu." *SS*, no. 1 (1933): 5–12.

——. "Za podgotovku kadrov i vydvizhenie tuzemnykh sovetskikh rabotnikov." *SS*, no. 10 (1931): 12–17.

Medvedev, Roy. *Let History Judge.* New York: Alfred A. Knopf, 1972.

Mel'nik, I. S., ed. *Sibir', eia sovremennoe sostoianie i nuzhdy.* St. Petersburg 1908.

Mel'nikov, Vl. I. "K voprosu o pomoshchi brodiachim i kochevym narodnostiam." *SA*, no. 5–6 (1925): 160–64.

Melville, George W. *In the Lena Delta: A Narrative of the Search for Lieut.-Commander DeLong and His Companions.* Boston; Houghton Mifflin, 1892.

Menovshchikov, G. A. *Eskimosy.* Magadan: Magadanskoe knizhnoe izdatel'stvo, 1959.

Meshchaninov, I. I. "Nikolai Iakovlevich Marr." *SE*, no. 1 (1935): 8–16.

Mess, L. "Iskusstvo severnykh narodnostei." *SO*, no. 3 (1930): 115–21.

Middendorf, A. F. *Puteshestvie na sever i vostok Sibiri.* St. Petersburg, 1860.

Mikhailov, A. F. "Pervye itogi raboty s natsional'nym naseleniem." *SAr*, no. 9 (1936): 31–39.

Mikhailovskii [Garin-Mikhailovskii], N. G. *Sobranie sochinenii v 5 tomakh.* Vols. 3 and 5. Moscow: Khudozhestvennaia literatura, 1957.

Mikhailovskii, N. K. *Poslednie sochineniia.* Vol. 1. St. Petersburg, 1905.

——. *Sochineniia.* St. Petersburg, 1896.

Mikhalev, A. "Grimasy snabzheniia i torgovli na Krainem Severe." *SS*, no. 2 (1934): 46–56.

——. "Sovetskaia torgovlia na Krainem Severe." *SS*, no. 6 (1933): 12–22.

——. "Uspekhi i tormozy kolkhoznogo stroitel'stva." *SS*, no. 3–4 (1931): 168–70.

Mikheev, V. M. *Pesni o Sibiri.* Moscow, 1884.

Milescu Spafarii, Nikolai. *Sibir' i Kitai.* Kishinev: Kartia Moldoveniaske, 1960.

Miliukov, P. N. *Glavnye techeniia russkoi istoricheskoi mysli.* St. Petersburg, 1913.

Miller, Frank J. *Folklore for Stalin: Russian Folklore and Pseudofolklore in the Stalin Era.* Armonk, N.Y.: M. E. Sharpe 1990.

Miller, G. F. [Gerhard F. Müller]. *Istoriia Sibiri.* 2 vols. Moscow: AN SSSR, 1937), 1941.

——. *Opisanie sibirskago tsarstva i vsekh proisshedshikh v nem del, ot nachala, a osoblivo ot pokoreniia ego Rossiiskoi derzhavie po sii vremena.* St. Petersburg, 1750.

Mineev, A. I. *Ostrov Vrangelia.* Moscow-Leningrad: Izdatel'stvo Glavsevmorputi, 1946.

——. "Piat' let na o-ve Vrangelia." *SS*, no. 2 (1935): 70–85.

Minenko, N. A. *Russkaia krest'ianskaia sem'ia v Zapadnoi Sibiri.* Novosibirsk: Nauka, 1979.

——. *Severo-zapadnaia Sibir' v XVIII–pervoi polovine XIX v.* Novosibirsk: Nauka, 1975.

Miropiev, M. A. *O polozhenii russkikh inorodtsev.* St. Petersburg, 1901.

Mirzoev, V. G. *Istoriografiia Sibiri: Domarksistskii period.* Moscow: Mysl', 1970.

Mokshanskii, G. "Tygrena iz stoibishcha Akkani." *SS*, no. 3 (1933): 113–15.

Mostovaia, E. "Sovety v natsional'nykh respublikakh i oblastiakh." *RN*, no. 4–5 (1930): 47–57.
Mukhachev, B. I. *Bortsy za vlast' sovetov na Kamchatke.* Petropavlovsk-Kamchatskii: Dal'nevostochnoe knizhnoe izdatel'stvo, 1977.
——. *Bor'ba za vlast' sovetov na Chukotke (1919–1923).* Sbornik dokumentov i materialov. Magadan: Magadanskoe knizhnoe izdatel'stvo, 1967.
Mukhachev, I. "Ballada o tungusakh i o shamane." *ORS*, no. 4 (1934).
Mukhardzhi, D., and N. Nazar'evskii. "Osedanie kochevnikov Kirgizii." *RN*, no. 12 (1933): 16–25.
Murav, Harriet. "'Vo glubine Sibirskikh rud': Siberia and the Myth of Exile." In Diment and Slezkine, eds., *Between Heaven and Hell*, pp. 95–112.
Murav'ev, A. N. *Russkaia Fivaida na Severe.* St. Petersburg, 1894.
Murnik. "V Tofalarskom raione." *SS*, no. 2 (1934): 95–98.
My—liudi Severa. Leningrad: Molodaia gvardiia, 1949.
Na novom puti: zhizn' i khoziaistvo Dal'nevostochnoi oblasti v 1923–1924 gg. Vladivostok: Knizhnoe delo, 1925.
"Na perelome." *Sovetskaia kul'tura*, 11 February 1989.
"Nam pishut." *SS*, no. 1 (1935): 104–5.
Narodnosti Severa: Problemy i perspektivy ekonomicheskogo i sotsial'nogo razvitiia. Novosibirsk: AN SSSR, 1983.
Naumov, N. I. *Sobranie sochinenii.* 3 vols. Novosibirsk: Novosibirskoe oblastnoe gosudarstvennoe izdatel'stvo, 1940.
——. *Rasskazy o staroi Sibiri.* Tomsk: Tomskoe knizhnoe izdatel'stvo, 1960.
"Neblagopriiatnye usloviia dlia missionerskoi deiatel'nosti v Sibiri i ee rezul'taty." *PB*, no. 17 (1896): 30.
Nebol'sin, P. I. *Pokorenie Sibiri: Istoricheskoe issledovanie.* St. Petersburg, 1849.
Nechkina, M. V., ed. *"Russkaia Pravda" P. I. Pestelia i sochineniia, ei predshestvuiushchie.* Glavnoe arkhivnoe upravlenie. Moscow: Gosudarstvennoe izdatel'stvo politicheskoi literatury, 1958.
Nepriakhin, M. "Sotsial'naia podpochva pushnogo i rybnogo promyslov Tobol'skogo Severa." *SA*, no. 2 (1926): 40–50.
Nerkagi, Anna. *Severnye povesti.* Moscow: Sovremennik, 1983.
Nesterenok, I. "Smotr natsional'nykh shkol na Taimyre." *SS*, no. 6 (1932): 82–87.
Neuhäuser, Rudolf. *Towards the Romantic Age: Essays on Sentimental and Preromantic Literature in Russia.* The Hague: Martinus Nijhoff, 1974.
Nevel'skoi, G. I. *Podvigi russkikh morskikh ofitserov na krainem vostoke Rossii, 1849–1855.* St. Petersburg, 1878. Reprint. Moscow: Ogiz, 1947.
Nichols, Johanna. "Stereotyping Interethnic Communication: The Siberian Native in Soviet Literature." In Diment and Slezkine, eds. *Between Heaven and Hell*, pp. 185–214.
Nik. Nikolaevich. "Samoedskaia iarmarka." *ORS*, no. 3 (1929): 45–48.
——. "Sukonnaia rukavichka." *ORS*, no. 8 (1929): 46–55.
Nikiforov, V. V. "Sever Iakutii." *SA*, no. 1–2 (1925): 90–98.
Nikolaev, P. "Natsional'nye shkoly na Sakhaline." *PN*, no. 4 (1934): 43–46.
——. "Ob odnoi iz zadach marksistsko-leninskoi pedagogiki." *PN*, no. 4 (1931): 34–40.
Nikul'shin, N. P. *Pervobytnye proizvodstvennye ob"edineniia i sotsialisticheskoe stroitel'stvo u evenkov.* Leningrad: Izdatel'stvo Glavsevmorputi, 1939.

Noianov, N. "S Kamchatki v Leningrad." *TT*, no. 4 (1932).

Nordenskiöld, A. E. *The Voyage of the Vega round Asia and Europe, with a Historical Review of Previous Journeys along the North Coast of the Old World*. New York, 1882.

Nosilov, K. D. "K proektu luchshei postanovki Obdorskoi missii." *PB*, no. 9 (1895): 27–37.

———. "Moi zapiski o zhizni, obychaiakh i verovaniiakh samoedov." *PB*, no. 1 (1895): 38–46.

———. "Voguly desiat' let nazad i teper'." *PB*, no. 19 (1897) 130–36.

Notkin, A. I. "Severnyi morskoi put'." *SA*, no. 1–2 (1925): 28–43 no. 4 (1925): 53–75.

Novitskii, Grigorii. "Kratkoe opisanie o narode ostiatskom, sochinennoe Grigoriem Novitskim v 1715 godu." In *Pamiatniki drevnei pis'mennosti i iskusstva*, vol. 21, no. 53. St. Petersburg, 1884.

Novitskii, V. M. "Tuzemtsy Tobol'skogo Severa i ocherednye voprosy po ustroeniiu ikh zhizni." *SA*, no. 5–6 (1928): 68–83.

"Novye polozheniia o kochevykh sovetakh i kochevykh obshchestvennykh sudakh." *SS*, no. 6 (1933): 3–6.

O. K. "Rabota po istorii narodov SSSR." *RN*, no. 5 (1936): 79–83.

"O merakh po dal'neishemu ekonomicheskomu i sotsial'nomu razvitiiu raionov prozhivaniia narodnostei Severa." *Izvestiia*, 26 February 1980.

"O merakh po dal'neishemu razvitiiu ekonomiki i kul'tury narodnostei Severa." In *Resheniia partii i pravitel'stva po khoziaistvennym voprosam*, 4:331–36. Moscow: Izdatel'stvo politicheskoi literatury, 1968.

"O nalogovykh l'gotakh plemenam, naseliaiushchim severnye okrainy SSSR." *SA*, no. 2 (1926): 86.

"O rabote Glavsevmorputi za 1937 god." *SAr*, no. 5 (1938): 21.

"O rabote v natsional'nykh raionakh Krainego Severa." *PS*, no. 13 (1932).

"O razvitii Severnogo Morskogo Puti i severnogo khoziaistva." *SS*, no. 5 (1934): 110–11.

"O sibirskikh tuzemtsakh." *ZhN*, no. 14 (1921): 112.

"O sostoianii korenizatsii apparata po Iamal'skomu (Nenetskomu) okrugu." *SS*, no. 2 (1933): 112–14.

"Ob odnom neobosnovannom i nedobrosovestnom obvinenii." *SS*, no. 2 (1931): 182–93.

"Obrashchenie ko vsem malochislennym narodam Severa Sovetskogo Soiuza." *Severnye prostory*, no. 1 (1990): 2–8.

Obruchev, S. V. *Kolymskaia zemlitsa. Dva goda skitanii*. Moscow: Sovetskaia Aziia, 1933.

"Obsuzhdenie doklada I. I. Potekhina." *SE*, no. 2 (1949): 170–177.

"Obsuzhdenie korrespondentsii, opublikovannoi v gazete 'Pravda,'" *SE*, no. 1 (1955): 172–73.

"Obsuzhdenie nauchno-issledovatel'skoi raboty Instituta etnografii AN SSSR." *SE*, no. 1 (1947): 163–75.

"Obsuzhdenie rabot S. M. Abramzona." *SE*, no. 4 (1952): 184–87.

"Obsuzhdenie stat'i Iu. V. Bromleia 'Etnos i endogamiia.'" *SE*, no. 3 (1970): 86–103.

Ocherki literatury i kritiki Sibiri. Novosibirsk: Nauka, 1976.

Ogloblin, N. N. "'Zhenskii vopros' v Sibiri v XVII veke." *IV* 41 (1890): 195–207.

Ogorodnikov, V. I. *Ocherk Istorii Sibiri do nachala XIX stol*. Vol. 1. Irkutsk: Tipografiia Shtaba voennogo okruga, 1920.

Ogryzko, I. I. *Khristianizatsiia narodov Tobol'skogo Severa v XVIII v.* Leningrad: Uchpedgiz, 1941.

Okladnikov, A. P. "Kureiskie tungusy v XVIII v." In Shunkov, ed., *Osvoenie Sibiri v epokhu feodalizma.*

——, ed. *Ocherki russkoi literatury Sibiri.* 2 vols. Novosibirsk: Nauka, 1982.

——, ed. *Russkoe naselenie Pomor'ia i Sibiri (Period feodalizma).* Moscow: Nauka, 1973.

——, ed. *Voprosy istorii Sibiri dosovetskogo perioda.* Novosibirsk: Nauka, 1973.

Okladnikov, A. P., et al., eds. *Istoriia Sibiri s drevneishikh vremen do nashikh dnei.* 5 vols. Leningrad: Nauka, 1968.

Oksenov, A. V. "Ermak Timofeevich v istoricheskikh pesniakh russkogo naroda." *SSb*, no. 1–2 (1886).

——. *Ermak v bylinakh russkago naroda.* St. Petersburg, 1892.

——. "Politicheskiia otnosheniia Moskovskogo gosudarstva k Iugorskoi zemle." *ZhMNP* 273 (1891): 245–72.

——. "Slukhi i vesti o Sibiri do Ermaka." *SSb*, no. 4 (1887).

——. "Snosheniia Novgoroda Velikago s Iugorskoi zemlei (istoriko-geograficheskii ocherk po drevneishei istorii Sibiri)." In *Literaturnyi sbornik "Vostochnago Obozreniia,"* ed. N. M. Iadrintsev St. Petersburg, 1885.

Okun', S. B. *Ocherki po istorii kolonial'noi politiki tsarizma v Kamchatskom krae.* Leningrad: Sotsekgiz, 1935.

Omel'chuk, A. K. "U 'nas' net prava reshat' za 'nikh,'" *Dialog*, no. 8 (1989): 26–28.

Oninka, A. "Material po rabote sredi zhenshchin u nanaitsev Khabarovskogo okruga." *TT*, no. 2 (1930): 97–104.

"Ordenanzas de Su Magestad hechas para los nuevos descubrimientos, conquistas y pacificaciones, Julio de 1573." In *Coleccion de documentos inéditos relativos al descubrimiento, conquista y organizacion de las antiguas posesiones españolas de América y Oceania sacados de los archivos del Reino*, vol. 16. Madrid: Imprenta del Hospicio, 1871.

"Organizatsiia Glavnogo upravleniia Severnogo morskogo puti." *SS*, no. 1 (1933): 123.

Orlov, Vladimir, ed. *Dekabristy.* Moscow and Leningrad: Khudozhestvennaia literatura, 1951.

Orlova, E. P. "Khoziastvennyi byt lamutov Kamchatki." *SA*, no. 5–6 (1928): 84–99.

——. "Koriaki poluostrova Kamchatki." *SA*, no. 3 (1929); 83–113.

Orlova, N. S., ed. *Otkrytiia russkikh zemleprokhodtsev i poliarnykh morekhodov XVII veka na severo-vostoke Azii: Sbornik dokumentov.* Moscow: Geografgiz, 1951.

Orlovskii, P. N. "Beseda s predsedatelem PNOKa." *SS*, no. 5 (1931): 134–37.

——. "God Anadyrsko-Chukotskogo olenevoda." *SA*, no. 2 (1928): 61–70.

——. "Kollektivizatsiia na severe." *SS*, no. 1 (1930): 48–58.

——. "Territoriia i naselenie Krainego Severa." *SS*, no. 1–2 (1932): 69–83.

Orosin, R. "O brodiachikh tuzemtsakh Sibiri." *ZhN*, no. 1 (1922): 130.

Osharov, M. I. "Bol'shoi argish." *SO*, no. 2 (1934): 1–87.

Oshirov, A. "Korenizatsiia v sovetskom stroitel'stve." *RN*, no. 4–5 (1930): 110–15.

Osipova, L. "Ogon'ki sovetskoi kul'tury na Severe." *SS*, no. 2 (1933): 77–79.

Osmolovskaia, V. I. "Zhizn' na Iamale v gody voiny." Unpublished.

Ostroumov, N. "Sposobny li kochevye narody Azii k usvoeniiu khristianskoi very i khristianskoi kul'tury?" *PB*, no. 22 (1895): 239–246.

Ostroumova, V. P. "Zadachi massovoi politicheskoi raboty sredi natsional'nogo naseleniia." *SAr*, no. 3 [1937]: 9–18.

Ostrovskikh, P. E. "K sanitarnomu polozheniiu severnykh tuzemtsev." *ZhN*, no. 3 (1922): 9–138.

——. "Okhrana pervobytnykh plemen v sviazi s podniatiem ekonomicheskoi zhizni okrain." *ZhN*, no. 6 (1922): 135.

——. "Sredi tuzemtsev Sibiri." *ZhN*, no. 18 (1922): 153.

Osvoenie bez otchuzhdeniia: Materialy ekspertnogo oprosa. Tiumen', 1989.

Ot Moskvy do taigi odna nochevka, Sbornik. Moscow: Molodaia gvardiia, 1961.

"Ot redaktsii." *SE*, no. 6 [1936]: 3–5.

"Otchet iakutskogo Eparkhial'nogo komiteta Pravoslavnogo missionerskogo obshchestva za 1892 g.' *PB*, no. 24 (1893): 119–123.

"Otchet o deiatel'nosti Komiteta Severa pri Prezidiume VTsIK za aprel'-oktiabr' 1926 g." *SA*, no. 1 (1927): 118–23.

"Otchet o sostoianii missii i missionerskoi deiatel'nosti v Eniseiskoi eparkhii." *PB*, nos. 12–13 (1894).

"Otchet Zabaikal'skoi dukhovnoi missii." *PB*, no. 6 (1893): 98.

Ovechkin, V. V. *Gosti v Stukachakh*. Moscow: Sovetskaia Rossiia, 1972.

Overing, Joanna, ed. *Reason and Morality*. London: Tavistock, 1985.

Pagden, Anthony. *The Fall of Natural Man: The American Indian and the Origins of Comparative Ethnology*. Cambridge: Cambridge University Press, 1982.

Pakin. "Kolkhoz 'Krasnaia zvezda' Ostiako-Vogul'skogo okruga." *SS* no. 1 (1933): 106–7.

Pallas, Peter Simon. *Puteshestvie po raznym mestam Rossiiskago gosudarstva po poveleniiu sanktpeterburgskoi imperatorskoi Akademii nauk*. 3 vols. St. Petersburg, 1786.

Pamiati L'va Iakovlevicha Shternberga. Leningrad: AN SSSR, 1928.

Pamiati V. G. Bogoraza. Sbornik statei. Moscow and Leningrad: AN SSSR, 1937.

Pankratova, A. M. *Velikii russkii narod*. Moscow: Gospolitizdat, 1948.

Panov, A. "Zheltyi vopros v Priamur'e." *VK*, no. 7 (1910): 53–117.

Parshin, V. P. *Poezdka v Zabaikal'skii krai*. 2 vols. Moscow, 1844.

Patkanov, S. K. *Statisticheskie dannye, pokazyvaiushchie plemennoi sostav naseleniia Sibiri, iazyk i rody inorodtsev*. St. Petersburg, 1911.

Pearce, Roy Harvey. *The Savages of America: A Study of the Indian and the Idea of Civilization*. Baltimore: Johns Hopkins University Press, 1965.

Peredol'skii, V. V. *Po Eniseiu. Byt eniseiskikh ostiakov*. St. Petersburg, 1908.

"Perevodcheskaia Kommissiia pri Bratstve Sv. Guriia v Kazani i eia deiatel'nost'." *PB*, no. 12 (1893): 18–35.

"Pervoe soveshchanie zhenshchin-tuzemok Severa." *SS*, no. 1 (1930): 150–52.

Pervukhin, I. "Karagassy" *SS*, no. 2 (1930): 82–93.

——. "Na bor'bu s tundrovym kulachestvom." *ORS*, no. 2 (1930): 25–26.

——. "Na Tobol'skom Severe." *SS*, no. 1 (1930): 75–83.

——. "Ob organizatsii Evenkiiskogo natsional'nogo okruga." *SS*, no. 10 (1931): 18–27.

——. "Peredvizhnoi krasnyi chum na Turukhanskom Severe." *SS*, no. 5 (1930).

——. "Sredi malykh narodnostei Sibirskogo kraia." *SS*, no. 5 (1930): 132–33.

Pervushin, V. P. "Politicheskii aspekt avtonomii." *Dialog*, no. 8 (1989): 30.

Pestkovskii, S. "Natsional'naia kul'tura." *ZhN*, no. 21 (1919): 29.

———. "Partiinaia agitatsiia sredi kochevnikov." *ZhN*, no. 47 (1919): 55.

Pestov, I. S. *Zapiski ob Eniseiskoi gubernii Vostochnoi Sibiri*. Moscow, 1833.

Petri, B. E. "Karagasiia stroitsia." *ORS*, no. 6 (1929): 8–10.

———. "Dun'ka-okhotnitsa." *ORS*, no. 10 (1929): 48–51.

Petrov, Vladimir. *Soviet Gold: My Life as a Slave Laborer in the Siberian Mines*. New York; Farrar, Straus, 1949.

"Piatidesiatiletie Imperatorskogo russkogo geograficheskogo obshchestva." In *IV*, 63 (1896): 278–90.

Pika, A. I. "Demograficheskaia politika v raionakh prozhivaniia narodov Severa: Problemy i perspektivy." In *Regional'nye problemy sotsial'no-demograficheskogo razvitiia*, pp. 43–55. Moscow: Institut sotsiologicheskikh issldovanii, 1987.

———. "Gomeostaz v demograficheskoi istorii narodov Severa [XVII–XIX]: Real'-nost' ili illiuziia?" *SE*, no. 2 (1986): 36–46.

———. "Malye narody Severa: Iz pervobytnogo kommunizma v 'real'nyi sotsia-lizm'." In *V chelovecheskom izmerenii*, ed. A. G. Vishevskii, pp. 306–24. Moscow: Progress, 1989.

———. "Samoustranenie—ne luchshii sposob," Dialog, no. 8 (1989): 31–34.

———. "Severnye pripoliarnye strany: Problemy i perspektivy primeneniia konventsii MOT no. 169 (1989) 'O korennykh i vedushchikh plemennoi obraz zhizni narodakh v nezavisimykh stranakh." In *Mezhdunarodnyi simpozium "pravo i etnos." Materialy dlia obsuzhdeniia*, Golitsyno 1–5 oktiabria 1991 g. pp. 54–66. Moscow: Ekologiia cheloveka, 1991.

Pika, A. I., and D. D. Bogoiavlenskii. *Sovremennye problemy razvitiia narod-nostei Severa*. Moscow: An SSSR, Goskomtrud SSSR, Institut sotsial'no-ekonomicheskikh problem narodonaseleniia, 1989.

Pika, A. I., and B. B. Prokhorov. "Bol'shie problemy malykh narodov." *Kommu-nist*, no. 16 (1988): 76–83.

Pilsudskii, B. O. "Aborigeny O-va Sakhalina." *ZhS*, no. 2–3 (1909): 3–16.

Pipes, Richard. *The Formation of the Soviet Union: Communism and Nation-alism 1917–1923*. Cambridge: Harvard University Press, 1964.

"Plenum [3d] Komiteta Severa." *SA*, no. 3 (1926): 85–94.

Pliguzov, A. I. "Skazanie o chelovetsekh neznaemykh v Vostochnoi strane." In *Russian History/Histoire russe*. Forthcoming.

Plotnikov, M. V. *Iangal-Maa. Vogul'skaia poema*. Moscow and Leningrad: Aka-demia, 1933.

———. "Poslerusskii vogul'skii epos." *SO*, no. 3 (1924): 122–59.

"Po-bol'shevistski vypolnim reshenie Sovnarkoma SSSR ob uluchshenii raboty Glavsevmorputi." *SAr*, no. 9 (1938): 3–4.

Podol'skii, A. G. "Rasshirennoe zasedanie redaktsionnoi kollegii zhurnala 'Sovetskaia etnografiia,' posviashchennoe obsuzhdeniiu retsenzii 'Zhurnal sovetskikh etnografov.'" *SE*, no. 5 (1963): 122–23.

Pokrovskii, A. A., ed. *Ekspeditsiia Beringa: Sbornik dokumentov*. Moscow: Glavnoe arkhivnoe upravlenie NKVD SSSR, 1941.

Polevoi, B. P. *Pervootkryvateli Sakhalina*. Iuzhno-Sakhalinsk: Sakhalinskoe knizhnoe izdatel'stvo, 1959.

Polevoi, N. A. *Ermak Timofeich, ili Volga i Sibir'*. St. Petersburg, 1845.

———. *Istoriia russkogo naroda*. Moscow, 1830.

"Polevye etnograficheskie raboty Antropologicheskogo NII pri Pervom MGU v 1926." *E*, no. 1 (1927): 201–2.

Poliakov, I. S. *Pis'ma i otchety o puteshestviiakh v dolinu reki Obi.* St. Petersburg, 1877.

Polo, Marco. *The Travels of Marco Polo.* Harmondsworth, U.K.: Penguin Books, 1988.

"Polozhenie o Glavsevmorputi SNK SSSR." *SAr*, no. 9 (1936): 27–30.

"Polozhenie o kochevykh sovetakh v natsional'nykh okrugakh i raionakh severnykh okrain RSFSR." *SS*, no. 5 (1933): 125–28.

"Polozhenie o Komitete sodeistviia narodnostiam severnykh okrain pri Prezidiume VTsIK." *SA*, no. 1–2 (1925): 136–38.

"Polozhenie o kul'tbazakh Komiteta Severa pri Prezidiume VTsIK." *SS*, no. 5 (1932): 32.

"Polozhenie o pozemel'nom ustroistve krest'ian i inorodtsev na kazennykh zemliakh sibirskikh gubernii i oblastei." *VK*, no. 8 (1910): 458–61.

Popov, A. A. *The Nganasan: The Material Culture of the Tavgi Samoeds.* Indiana University Publications. Uralic and Altaic Series, vol. 56. Bloomington: Indiana University Press, 1966.

——. *Nganasany: Sotsial'noe ustroistvo i verovaniia.* Leningrad: Nauka, 1984.

——. "Poezdka k dolganam." *SE*, no. 3–4 (1931): 210–12.

Popov, V. L. "Istoricheskaia piatiletka Severnoi Azii." *SA*, no. 4 (1929): 5–24.

Popov-Kokoulin, N. "Inorodtsy na o-ve Sakhaline." *PB*, no. 10. (1896): 76–84.

Popova, U. G. *Eveny Magadanskoi oblasti: Ocherki istorii, khoziaistva i kul'tury evenov Okhotskogo poberezh'ia, 1917–1977.* Moscow: Nauka, 1981.

"Poseshchenie preosviashchennym Makariem, episkopom Tomskim, sela Ketnago i Borkinykh iurt, naselennykh ostiakami." *PB*, no. 8 (1893): 38–42.

"Postanovlenie biuro redaktsii zhurnala 'Revoliutsiia i natsional'nosti.'" *RN*, no. 8–9 (1930): 3.

"Postanovlenie Kommissii ispolneniia pri SNK SSSR." *SS*, no. 5 (1932): 149–50.

"Postanovlenie Prezidiuma Soveta natsional'nostei TsIK SSSR." *RN*, no. 2 (1936): 75–76.

"Postanovlenie Prezidiuma TsIK SSSR." *SAr*, no. 6 (1937): 109–10.

"Postanovlenie Prezidiuma VTsIK 'Ob organizatsii natsional'nykh ob"edinenii v raionakh rasseleniia malykh narodov Severa'." *SS*, no. 1 (1931): 230–33.

"Postanovlenie SNK RSFSR o khoziaiastvennom razvitii narodov Krainego Severa." *SS*, no. 10 (1931): 188–92.

"Postanovlenie Soveta Ministra Narodnogo Prosveshcheniia." *ZhMNP*, 148 (April 1870): "Pravitel'stvennye rasporiazheniia" 47–63.

"Postanovlenie TsK KPSS i Soveta Ministrov SSSR 16 marta 1957 'O merakh po dal'neishemu razvitiiu ekonomiki i kul'tury narodnostei Severa.'" In *Resheniia partii i pravitel'stva po khoziaistvennym voprosam* 4:331–36. Moscow, 1968.

"Postanovlenie TsK VKP(b) ot 22 iunia 1932 goda." *PS*, no. 13 (1932): 53–54.

"Postanovlenie VTsIK i SNK RSFSR o merakh protiv khishchnicheskogo uboia olenei." *SS*, no. 5 (1931): 146.

"Postanovlenie VTsIK i SNK RSFSR o vypolnenii sudebnykh funktsii organami tuzemnogo upravleniia narodnostei i plemen severnykh okrain RSFSR." *SA*, no. 1 (1928): 79–81.

"Postanovleniia Soveta Ministra Narodnogo Prosveshcheniia." *ZhMNP*, 148 (April 1870): 47–63.

Postnov, Iu. S. "Literatura Sibiri v russkoi kritike pervoi poloviny XIX veka." In *Ocherki literatury i kritiki Sibiri.*

——. "Poeziia romantizma v literature Sibiri." In *Voprosy russkoi i sovetskoi literatury Sibiri.* Novosibirsk: Nauka, 1971.

——. *Russkaia literatura Sibiri pervoi poloviny XIX v.* Novosibirsk: Nauka, 1970.

Potanin, G. N. "Nuzhdy Sibiri." In Mel'nik, ed., *Sibir', eia sovremennoe sostoianie i nuzhdy.*

——. *Oblastnicheskaia tendentsiia v Sibiri.* Tomsk, 1907.

——. *Zametki o Zapadnoi Sibiri.* N.p., n.d.

Potapov, L. P. "Etnograficheskoe izuchenie sotsialisticheskoi kul'tury i byta narodov SSSR." *SE*, no. 2 (1962): 3–19.

Potekhin I. I. "Novye zadachi etnografii v svete truda I. V. Stalina 'Ekonomicheskie problemy sotsializma v SSSR.'" *SE*, no. 2 (1953): 10–20.

——. "Zadachi bor'by s kosmopolitizmom v etnografii." *SE*, no. 2 (1949): 7–26.

Pradt, Dominique de. *Des colonies, et de la révolution actuelle de l'Amérique.* 2 vols. Paris, 1817.

Prager, P. K. "K postanovke voprosa o nekapitalisticheskom puti razvitiia otstalykh stran." *Proletarskaia revoliutsiia*, nos. 5 and 6 (1930).

"Pravoslavnoe missionerskoe obshchestvo." *PB*, no. 1 (1893): 10–12; no. 2 (1893): 12–19.

Pravoslavnoe missionerskoe obshchestvo. Sbornik svedenii o pravoslavnykh missiiakh i deiatel'nosti Pravoslavnogo missionerskogo obshchestva. Moscow, 1872.

Predlozheniia k kontseptsii sotsial'nogo i ekonomicheskogo razvitiia narodnostei Severa v usloviiakh nauchno-tekhnicheskogo progressa. Novosibirsk, 1988.

Preobrazhenskii, P. F. "Razlozhenie rodovogo stroia i feodalizatsionnyi protsess u turkmenov–iomudov." *E*, no. 4 (1930): 11–28.

Preobrazovaniia v khoziaistve i kul'ture i etnicheskie protsessy u narodov Severa. Moscow: Nauka, 1970.

Problemy sovremennogo sotsial'nogo razvitiia narodnostei Severa. Moscow: Nauka, 1970.

"Proekt Programmy i Ustava Assotsiatsii 'Iamal—potomkam!'" *Krasnyi Sever*, no. 37 (September 1989).

"Programma Deputatskoi Assamblei malochislennykh narodov Severa." 7 May 1991. Unpublished.

Prokhorov, B. B. "Kak sberech' Iamal." *Zhanie-sila*, no. 7 (1988): 1–7.

Prokhorov, B. B., I. I. Krupnik, G. V. Starovoitova, and A. I. Pika. "Reshenie i rekomendatsii ob"edinennogo zasedaniia gruppy "Trevozhnyi Sever.'" 22 February 1989. Unpublished.

Prokof'ev, G. N. "Kul'turnyi ochag dalekogo Severa." *SA*, no. 5–6 (1927): 76–78.

——. "Ostiako-samoedy Turukhanskogo kraia." *E*, no. 2 (1928): 96–103.

——. "Tri goda v samoedskoi shkole." *SS*, no. 7–8 (1931): 143–60.

"Protiv velikoderzhavnogo shovinizma v pedologii." *P*, no. 1 (1932): 46–49.

"Protokol sed'mogo rasshirennogo plenuma Komiteta Severa." *SS*, no. 4 (1930): 116–162.

"Protokol zasedaniia [5th] rasshirennogo plenuma Komiteta sodeistviia narodnostiam severnykh okrain pri Prezidiume VTsIK." *SA*, no. 4 (1928): 109–23.

"Protokol zasedaniia VI rasshirennogo plenuma Komiteta Severa." *SA*, no. 3 (1929): 1–26, annex.

Prucha, Francis Paul. *The Great Father: The United States Government and the American Indians*. Lincoln: University of Nebraska Press, 1984.

Prutchenko, S. *Sibirskie okrainy*. St. Petersburg, 1899.

Przheval'skii, N. M. *Puteshestviia v Ussuriiskom krae, 1867–1869*. St. Petersburg, 1870.

"Puteshestvie ital'iantsa Som'e po Sibiri." *SSb*, no. 1 (1886).

Putintseva, A. "Dva goda raboty Goriuno-Amurskoi krasnoi iurty." *SS*, no. 1–2 (1932): 168–76.

Pypin, A. N. *Istoriia russkoi etnografii*. 4 vols. St. Petersburg, 1892.

——. *Religioznye dvizheniia pri Aleksandre I*. Vol. 1. Petrograd, 1916.

Rabinkov, L. "Za vnimatel'noe otnoshenie k zhalobam trudiashchikhsia." *RN*, no. 8 (1934): 20–27.

Rabinovich, M. G., and M. N. Shmeleva. "K etnograficheskomu izucheniiu goroda." *SE*, no. 3 (1981): 23–34.

Rabinovich, M. G., and S. A. Tokarev. "Institut etnografii v period Velikoi Otechestvennoi Voiny i pervye poslevoennye gody," *SE*, no. 4 (1975): 7–17.

"Rabota Instituta etnografii AN SSSR v 1949g." *SE*, no. 2 (1950), 182–85.

Rabtsevich, V. V., "K voprusu ob upravlenii aborigennym naseleniem Sibiri v 80-kh godakh XVIII–pervykh desiatiletiiakh XIX stoletiia." In Okladnikov, ed., *Voprosy istorii Sibiri dosovetskogo perioda*, pp. 232–40.

Radishchev, A. N. *Polnoe sobranie sochinenii*. Moscow and Leningrad: AN SSSR, 1959.

Rae, Edward. *The Land of the North Wind, or Travels among the Laplanders and the Samoyeds*. London, 1875.

Raeff, Marc. *Michael Speranskii: Statesman of Imperial Russia, 1772–1839*. The Hague: Martinus Nijhoff, 1957.

——. "The Philosophical Views of M. Speransky." *SEER* 30 (June 1953): 437–51.

——. *Siberia and the Reforms of 1822*. Seattle: University of Washington Press, 1956.

Rafienko L. S. "Politika rossiiskogo absoliutizma po unifikatsii upravleniia Sibir'iu vo vtoroi polovine XVIII v." In Okladnikov, ed., *Voprosy istorii Sibiri*, pp. 135–65.

——. "Sledstvennye komissii v Sibiri v 30kh–60kh godakh XVIII veka." In Shunkov, ed., *Osvoenie Sibiri*.

"Raport Instituta narodov Severa." *SS*, no. 6 (1932): 113.

"Rasshirennyi [2d] plenum Komiteta Severa." *SA*, no. 3 (1925): 109–22.

"Rasshirennyi [4th] plenum Komiteta Severa pri Prezidiume VTsIK." *SA*, no. 3 (1927): 76–91.

Rastvorov, T. "Dva suglana," *OPS*, no. 10 (1928): 50–51.

Ratner-Shternberg, S. A. "L. Ia. Shternberg i leningradskaia etnograficheskaia shkola 1904–1927 gg.' *SE*, no. 2 (1935): 134–54.

Ravdonikas, V. I. *Istoriia pervobytnogo obshchestva*. Vol. 2. Leningrad: LGU, 1947.

Ravenstein, Ernest G. *The Russians on the Amur; Its Discovery, Conquest, and Colonization*. London, 1861.

Razmanov, I. "Protiv idealizma professorskoi 'uchenosti' i shovinisticheskikh teorii." *PN*, no. 7–8 (1931): 94–97.

Reed, Eugene E. "The Ignoble Savage." *Modern Language Review* 59 (1964).

Revkomy Severo-vostoka SSSR (1922–1928 gg.). Sbornik dokumentov i materialov. Magadan: Magadanskoe knizhnoe izdatel'stvo, 1973.

"Rezoliutsii Desiatogo rasshirennogo plenuma Komiteta Severa." *SS*, no. 3 (1934): 138–156.

"Rezoliutsii Deviatogo rasshirennogo plenuma Komiteta Severa pri Prezidiume VTsIK." *SS*, no. 4 (1932): annex.

"Rezoliutsiia Pervogo Vserossiiskogo s"ezda integral'noi kooperatsii o rabote na Krainem Severe." *SS*, no. 5 (1934): 68–72.

"Rezoliutsiia Uchenogo soveta Instituta etnografii AN SSR o rabote zhurnala 'Sovetskaia etnografiia.'" *SE*, no. 4 (1951): 215–16.

"Rezoliutsiia Vserossiiskogo Arkheologo-etnograficheskogo soveshchaniia 7–11 maia 1932 goda." *SE*, no. 3 (1932): 4–14.

Riabkov, P. "Poliarnye strany Sibiri." *SSb*, no. 1 (1887).

Riasanovsky, Nicholas V. "Asia through Russian Eyes." In Wayne S. Vucinich, ed., *Russia and Asia.*

———. *Nicholas I and Official Nationality in Russia, 1825–1855.* Berkeley and Los Angeles: University of California Press, 1959.

———. "Russia and Asia: Two Nineteenth-Century Russian Views." *California Slavic Studies*, no. 1 (1960): 170–81.

Riazanovsky, Valentin A. *Customary Law of the Nomadic Tribes of Siberia.* Uralic and Altaic Series, no. 48. Bloomington: Indiana University Press, 1965.

Rinchenko, E. D., "Inorodcheskii vopros v Sibiri." *ZhN*, no. 6 (1921): 104.

Rousseau, G. S., and Roy Porter, eds. *Exoticism in the Enlightenment.* Manchester: Manchester University Press, 1990.

Rubinskii, V. I. "Pereselenie v Sibiri i na Dal'nem Vostoke." *SA*, no. 1 (1928): 13–26.

———. "Perspektivy kolonizatsii Sibiri." *SA*, no. 1–2 (1925): 132–133.

———. "Sovremennaia postanovka pereselencheskogo dela v Sibiri." *SA*, no. 3 (1927): 43–50.

Rugin, Roman. "Deputatskii zapros." *SP*, no. 6 (1989): 6–8.

———. *Solntse nad snegami.* Sverdlovsk: Sredne-Ural'skoe knizhnoe izdatel'stvo, 1986.

Russkie ekspeditsii po izucheniiu severnoi chasti Tikhogo okeana v pervoi polovine XVIII v. Sbornik dokumentov. Moscow: Nauka, 1984.

Russkie ekspeditsii po izucheniiu severnoi chasti Tikhogo okeana vo vtoroi polovine XVIII v. Sbornik dokumentov. Moscow: Nauka, 1989.

Rysakov, P. "Otgoloski vreditel'stva v natsional'nykh raionakh." *RN* no. 6 (1931): 37–46.

Rytkheu, Iurii. *Golubye pestsy.* Moscow: Sovetskaia Rossiia, 1976.

———. *Inei na poroge.* Moscow, Sovetskaia Rossiia, 1971.

———. *Konets vechnoi merzloty.* Moscow: Sovetskaia Rossiia, 1984.

———. *Ostrov nadezhdy.* Moscow: Sovremennik, 1987.

———. *Povesti.* Leningrad: Khudozhestvennaia literatura, 1972.

———. *Sovremennye legendy.* Leningrad: Sovetskii pisatel', 1980.

———. *V doline malen'kikh zaichikov.* Leningrad: Sovetskii pisatel', 1972.

———. *Vremia taianiia snegov.* Moscow: Molodaia gvardiia, 1981.

Rywkin, Michael, ed. *Russian Colonial Expansion to 1917.* London: Mansell, 1980.

Safronov, F. G. *Russkie na severo-vostoke Azii v XVII-seredine XIX v: Uprav-*

lenie, sluzhilye liuc⁣, krest'iane, gorodskoe naselenie. Moscow: Nauka, 1978.

———. "Zapiski Genrikha Fika o iakutakh i tungusakh pervoi poloviny XVIII v." In Istochnikovedenie i istoriografiia Sibiri, ed. A. M. Pokrovskii and E. K. Romodanovskaia, pp 235–51. Novosibirsk: Nauka, 1977.

Sagatovskii, V. N. "Garantii vybora." Dialog, no. 8 (1989): 35–36.

Said, Edward W. Orientalism. New York: Vintage, 1979.

———. "Representing the Colonized: Anthropology's Interlocutors." Critical Inquiry 15, no. 2 (1989): 205–25.

Samar, Ia. "Vpechatlenie o demonstratsii." TT, no. 4 (1932): 49.

Samar, Iu. "Nashi p000pravki k konstitutsii." SP, (February 1991): 12.

Samigullin, I. "Taimyrskii natsional'nyi okrug." RN, no. 8 (1936): 27–31.

Samokvasov, D. Ia. Sbornik obychnogo prava sibirskikh inorodtsev. Warsaw, 1876.

Sangi, Vladimir. "Chtoby krona ne ogolilas'." Literaturnaia gazeta, 15 February 1989.

———. Izgin. Moscow: Detskaia literatura, 1969.

———. Legendy Ykh-mifa Moscow: Sovetskaia Rossiia, 1967.

———. Mudraia nerpa. Moscow: Sovetskaia Rossiia, 1971.

———. "Otchuzhdenie." Sovetskaia Rossiia, 11 September 1988.

———. Pesn' o nivkhakh. Moscow: Sovremennik, 1989.

———. "Posleslovie k sudu i sledstviiu." SP, no. 2 (1988): 6–9.

———. V tsarstve vladyk. Moscow: Sovremennik, 1973.

———. "Vernut' prava khoziqevam zemli." Izvestiia, 12 July 1990.

———. Zhenit'ba Kevongov Moscow: Sovetskii pisatel', 1975.

———, ed. Antologiia fol'klora narodnostei Sibiri, Severa i Dal'nego Vostoka Krasnoiarsk: Krasnoiarskoe knizhnoe izdatel'stvo, 1989.

Sangi, Vladimir, Iuvan Shestalov, V. Ledkov, Roman Rugin, E. D. Aipin, V. Koianto, G. Varlamova. "Letter to M. S. Gorbachev." 20 April 1988. Unpublished.

Sangren, Stephen P. "Rhetoric and the Authority of Ethnography." Current Anthropology, no. 29 (1988): 405–35.

Sanzhiev, G. L. Perekhod narodov Sibiri k sotsializmu, minuia kapitalizm. Novosibirsk: Nauka, 1980.

Saprygin, N. "Olenevodcheskii sovkhoz i olenkolkhozy v Nenetskom okruge." SS, no. 9 (1931): 21–4⁣.

Sarkisyantz, Emanuel. Geschichte der orientalischen Völker Russlands bis 1917. Munich: Oldenbourg, 1961.

———. "Russian Attitudes towards Asia." Russian Review, no. 13 (1954): 245–54.

Sarychev, G. A. Puteshestvie po severo-vostochnoi chasti Sibiri i Ledovitomu moriu i Vostochnomu okeanu. Moscow: Izdatel'stvo geograficheskoi literatury, 1952.

Sauer, Martin. An Account of a Geographical and Astronomical Expedition to the Northern Parts of Russia. London, 1802. Reprint. Richmond, England: Richmond Publishing Company, 1972.

Schindler, Debra L. "The Political Economy of Ethnic Discourse in the Soviet Union." Ph. D. diss., University of Massachusetts, Amherst, 1990.

Schrenk, Alexander Gustav. Reise nach dem Nordosten des europäischen Russlands, durch die Tundren der Samojeden, zum arktischen Uralgebirge. Dorpat: Heinrich Laakmann, 1854. [HRAF RU4, no. 16]

Scott, Joan Wallach. *Gender and the Politics of History.* New York: Columbia University Press, 1988.

Selitrennik, E. E. "Nekotorye voprosy kolkhoznogo stroitel'stva v Chukotskom natsional'nom okruge." *SE*, no. 1 (1965): 13–27.

Sel'vinskii, I. *Sobranie sochinenii v shesti tomakh.* Moscow: Khudozhestvennaia literatura, 1973.

———. *Umka belyi medved'.* Moscow and Leningrad: Iskusstvo, 1936.

Sem, Iu. A. "Khristianizatsiia nanaitsev, ee metody i resul'taty." In Vdovin, ed., *Khristianstvo i lamaizm.*

Semushkin, T. Z. *Alitet ukhodit v gory.* Moscow: Izvestiia, 1974.

———. *Chukotka.* Moscow: Sovetskii pisatel', 1941.

———. "Opyt raboty po organizatsii shkoly-internata chukotskoi kul'tbazy DVK." *SS*, no. 3–4 (1931): 171–92.

———. "Prosveshchenie narodnostei Krainego Severa." *PN*, no. 1 (1932): 31–38.

Semyonov, Yuri, *Siberia: Its Conquest and Development.* Baltimore: Helicon Press, 1963.

Senkevich, V. V. "Sovremennost' v fol'klore narodov Severa." *SAr*, no. 11 (1937): 103–8.

———. "V Voitekhovskikh iurtakh." *SS*, no. 6 (1934): 98–105.

Sergeev, M. A. *Nekapitalisticheskii put' razvitiia malykh narodov Severa.* AN SSSR. Trudy instituta etnografii im. N. N. Miklukho-Maklaia. Novaia seriia, vol. 27. Moscow and Leningrad: AN SSSR, 1955.

———. "Rekonstruktsiia byta narodov Severa." *RN*, no. 3 (1934): 90–95.

———. "Zadachi vtoroi piatiletki na Severe," *RN*, no. 7 (1934): 42–50.

Sergeev, O. I. *Kazachestvo na russkom Dal'nem Vostoke v 17–19 vv.* Moscow: Nauka, 1983.

Sergeeva, K. "Shkola v bukhte Provideniia." *SS*, no. 2 (1935): 54–59.

———. "V Urelikskom natssovete." *SS*, no. 1 (1935): 95–101.

Serkin, I. O. "Kolkhoznoe stroitel'stvo v Taimyrskom natsional'nom okruge." *SAr*, no. 6 (1936): 3–12.

———. "Ob oshibkakh Obdorskogo politotdela." *SAr*, no. 10 (1937): 9–15.

"Sessiia nauchno-issledovatel'skogo instituta kraevedcheskoi i muzeinoi raboty." *SE*, no. 2 (1949): 179–83.

Sever poet. Leningrad: Goslitizdat, 1939.

Sevrunov, A. "O nekotorykh nedochetakh v rybozagotovitel'noi rabote." *SS*, no. 3 (1934): 26–29.

"S"ezd korennykh narodnostei Iamalo-Nenetskogo avtonomnogo okruga." Unpublished.

Sgibnev, A. "Istoricheskii sbornik glavneishikh sobytii v Kamchatke." *Morskoi sbornik*, nos. 1 and 4 through 8 (1869).

Shakhnovich, M. "Etnografiia na sluzhbe klassovogo vraga." *SE*, no. 3–4 (1934): 131–35.

Shakhov, N. "Rastet natsional'naia kul'tura v tundre i na ostrovakh." *PN*, no. 2–3 (1932): 46–51.

Shamshurin, Iu. I. *Severnaia shirota.* Moscow: Molodaia gvardiia, 1956.

———. *Shli dvoe po tundre.* Moscow: Molodaia gvardiia, 1972.

———. *U studenogo moria.* Moscow: Molodaia gvardiia, 1952.

Sharov, V. "Mala li zemlia dlia malykh narodov?" *Literaturnaia gazeta*, 17 August 1988.

Shashkov, S. S. *Istoricheskie etiudy.* St. Petersburg, 1872.

Shchapov, A. P. *Sochineniia.* Vols. 1–3. St. Petersburg, 1905–08. Vol. 4. Irkutsk: Vostochnos-birskoe oblastnoe izdatel'stvo, 1935.

Shchukin, N. S. *Poezdka v Iakutsk.* St. Petersburg, 1844.

Shelikhov, G. I. *Rossiiskogo kuptsa Grigoriia Shelikhova stranstvovaniia iz Okhotska po Vostochnomu okeanu k Amerikanskim beregam.* Khabarovsk: Khabarovskoe knizhnoe izdatel'stvo, 1971.

Sheludiakov, Aleksandr. *Iugana.* Moscow: Sovremennik, 1982.

——. *Iz plemeni kedra* Moscow: Sovremennik, 1972.

Shemelin, Fedor. *Zhurnal pervogo puteshestviia rossiian vokrug zemnogo shara.* St. Petersburg, 1816.

Shepovalova, A. "Sotsial'no-bytovaia sreda tungusskikh detei na Sev. Baikale." *P,* no. 2 (1930): 172–86.

Shestalov, Iuvan. *Izbrannoe.* Leningrad: Khudozhestvennaia literatura, 1976.

——. "O tom, chto nravstvenno i chto beznravstvenno," *Dialog,* no. 8 (1989): 41–43.

——. *Pesnia poslednego lebedia.* Moscow: Sovetskii pisatel', 1969.

——. *Shag cherez tysiacheletiia.* Moscow: Politizdat, 1974.

——. *Sibirskoe uskorenie.* Moscow: Sovetskaia Rossiia, 1977.

——. *Zemlia Iugoriia.* Moscow: Sovetskaia Rossiia, 1985.

Shipikhin, V. "K sozdaniiu natsional'nykh tuzemnykh okrugov." *SA,* no. 5–6 (1929): 107–26.

Shirokogoroff, S. M. *Psychomental Complex of the Tungus.* London: Kegan Paul, Trench, Trubner, 1935.

——. *Social Organization of the Northern Tungus.* Shanghai: The Commercial Press, 1933.

Shishkov, V. Ia. *Sobranie sochinenii.* vol. 1 Moscow: Khudozhestvennaia literatura, 1960.

Shklovsky, Izaak V. *In Far North-East Siberia.* London: Macmillan, 1916. [HRAF RY2, no. 11]

Shmidt, O. Iu. "Nashi zadachi v 1936 godu." *SAr,* no. 3 (1936): 28–43.

——. "O zadachakh khoziaistvenno-kul'turnogo stroitel'stva sredi malykh narodov Severa." *RN* no. 1 (1936): 35–40.

Shmyrev, B. "Iamal'skaia kul'tbaza." *SS,* no. 6 (1933): 69–74.

Shorukhov, Kh. "Osedanie v Kirgizii." *RN,* no. 5 (1932): 73–76.

Shrenk, L. I. [Leopold von Schrenck]. *Ob inorodtsakh Amurskogo kraia.* 3 vols. St. Petersburg, 1883–1903.

Shteppa, Konstantin F. *Russian Historians and the Soviet State.* New Brunswick: Rutgers University Press, 1962.

Shternberg, L. Ia. *Giliaki, orochi, gol'dy, negidal'tsy, ainy.* Khabarovsk: Dal'-giz, 1933.

——. "Inorodtsy." In Kastelianskii, ed., *Formy natsional'nogo dvizheniia.*

——. "Izbrannichestvo v religii." in *E,* no. 1 (1927): 3–56.

——. "Sovremennaia etnologiia. Noveishie uspekhi, nauchnye techeniia i metody." *E,* no. 1–2 (1926): 15–43.

Shubert, A. M. "Opyt pedologo-pedagogicheskikh ekspeditsii po izucheniiu narodov dalekikh okrain." *P,* no. 2 (1930): 167–171.

——. "Problemy pedologii natsional'nostei." *PN,* no. 3 (1931): 56–59.

Shumakher, P. V. "K istorii priobreteniia Amura." *RA,* vol. 3 (1878): 257–340.

——. "Oborona Kamchatki i Vostochnoi Sibiri protiv anglo-frantsuzov v 1854–1855 gg." *RA,* 2 (1878): 395–425.

Shundik, Nikolai. *Na Severe Dal'nem.* Moscow and Leningrad: Detgiz, 1952.

——. *Sobranie sochinenii v chetyrekh tomakh*. Moscow: Sovetskaia Rossiia, 1984.

Shunkov, V. I. *Ocherki po istorii kolonizatsii Sibiri v XVII-nachale XVIII vekov*. Moscow and Leningrad: AN SSSR, 1946.

——, ed. *Ekonomika, upravlenie i kul'tura Sibiri XVI-XIX vv*. AN SSSR. Sibirskoe otdelenie. Materialy po istorii Sibiri. Sibir' perioda feodalizma, no. 2. Novosibirsk: Nauka, 1965.

——, ed. *Osvoenie Sibiri v epokhu feodalizma*. Novosibirsk: Nauka, 1968.

Sibir' v period stroitel'stva sotsializma i perekhoda k kommunizmu. Vyp. 6 Novosibirsk: Nauka, 1966.

Sibirskiia lietopisi. Russia. Arkheograficheskaia kommissiia. St. Petersburg, 1907.

Sieroszewski, Waclaw. *Sochineniia*. Vol. 1. St. Petersburg: Znanie, 1908–09.

Sil'nitskii, A. "14 mesiatsev sluzhby na Kamchatke," *IV*, 11 (1909): 507–41.

Simchenko, Iu. V. *Liudi vysokikh shirot*. Moscow: Mysl', 1972.

——. *Zimniaia doroga*. Moscow: Sovetskii pisatel', 1985.

Simon, Gerhard. *Nationalism and Policy toward the Nationalities in the Soviet Union: From Totalitarian Dictatorship to Post-Stalinist Society*. Boulder; Westview Press, 1991.

"Simpozium 'Metodologicheskie problemy issledovaniia etnicheskikh kul'-tur.'" *SE*, no. 6 (1979): 145–48.

"Simpozium po tipologii iavlenii kul'tury." *SE*, no. 2 (1979): 155–60.

Sinitsyn, T. *Pod voi purgi. Zapiski o shkole za poliarnym krugom*. Moscow and Leningrad: Gosizdat, 1929.

Sipin. "Trud i byt zhenshchin nani (ul'chei) Nikolaevskogo na Amure okruga Bol'she-Mikhailovskogo raiona." *TT*, no. 2 (1930): 105–16.

Skachko, Anatolii. "Desiat' let raboty Komiteta Severa." *SS*, no. 2 (1934): 9–21.

——. "Deviatyi Plenum Komiteta Severa." *SS*, no. 5 (1932): 14–22.

——. "Imushchestvennye pokazateli sotsial'nykh grupp u malykh narodnostei Severa." *SS*, no. 3 (1930): 5–28.

——. "K voprosu prakticheskogo provedeniia leninskoi natsional'noi politiki." *SS*, no. 1 (1931): 5–11.

——. "Klassovoe rassloenie, mery bor'by s kulachestvom i kollektivizatsiia." *SS*, no. 2 (1930): 38–49.

——. *Narody Krainego Severa i rekonstruktsiia severnogo khoziaistva*. Leningrad: Institut narodov Severa, 1934.

——. "Narody Severa na novom etape." *RN*, no. 8 (1935): 31–33.

——. "Natsional'naia politika i malye narody Severa." *RN*, no. 6 (1931): 29–36.

——. "Natsional'nyi vopros i rekonstruktsiia khoziaistva narodov Severa." *SS*, no. 3 (1932): 28–40.

——. "Novye organizatsionnye formy raboty na Severe." *SS*, no. 3–4 (1935): 27–35.

——. "O sotsial'noi strukture malykh narodov Severa." *SS*, no. 2 (1933): 39–51 and no. 3 (1933): 35–43.

——. "Ocherednye zadachi sovetskoi raboty sredi malykh narodov Severa." *SS*, no. 2 (1931): 5–29.

——. "Osnovnye voprosy sotsialisticheskogo stroitel'stva na Krainem Severe." *SS*, no. 3 (1934): 3–18.

——. "Piat' let raboty Komiteta Severa." *SS*, no. 2 (1930): 5–38.

——. "Pis'mo v redaktsiiu." *SS*, no. 3–4 (1935): 224–26.

——. "Postanovleniia TsK partii i SNK v ikh primenenii v Severu." *SS*, no. 3 (1932): 3–13.

——. "Problemy Severa." *SS*, no. 1 (1930): 15–37.

——. "Resheniia XVII partkonferentsii v ikh primenenii k Severu." *SS*, no. 1–2 (1932): 5–17.

——. "Sotsial'no-proizvodstvennye otnosheniia v okhotnich'em khoziaistve severa." *SS*, no. 11–12 (1931): 28–33.

——. "Teoriia i praktika v rabote sredi narodov Severa." *SS*, no. 6 (1934): 5–15.

——. "Vos'moi plenum Komiteta Severa." *SS*, no. 5 (1931): 5–28.

——. "Zemlia Iugorskaia i Obdorskaia v leto 1930." *SS*, no. 2 (1931): 58–113

Skachkov, I., "Ob antireligioznoi rabote na Severe." *RN*, no. 7 (1934): 50–54.

Skal'kovskii, K. A. *Russkaia torgovlia v Tikhom okeane.* St. Petersburg, 1883.

Skalon, V. N. "Magnaty Severa," *ORS*, no. 2 (1929): 57–62.

——. *Russkie zemleprokhodtsy XVII v. v Sibiri.* Moscow: Moskovskoe obshchestvo ispytatelei prirody, 1951.

——. "V tundre Verkhnego Taza." *SS*, no. 3 (1930): 129–139.

Skazki narodov Severa. Moscow and Leningrad: Khudozhestvennaia literatura, 1951.

Skorik, P., "Kul'turnyi shturm taigi i tundry." *PN*, no. 10 (1932): 32–39.

——. "Kul'turnyi shturm taigi i tundry." *SS*, no. 1–2 (1932): 158–167.

——. "Molodye pobegi Sakhalinskoi taigi." *SS*, no. 4 (1932): 106–14.

Skrynnikov, R. G. *Sibirskaia ekspeditsiia Ermaka.* Novosibirsk: Nauka, 1982.

Slavin, S. V. *Osvoenie Severa Sovetskogo Soiuza.* Moscow: Nauka, 1982.

——. *Promyshlennoe i transportnoe osvoenie severa SSSR.* Moscow: Ekonomgiz, 1961.

Sletov, P. "Ot iukoly k kartofeliu." *PN*, no. 7–8 (1931): 63–69.

Slezkine, Yuri. "Savage Christians or Unorthodox Russians? The Missionary Dilemma in Siberia." In Diment and Slezkine, eds., *Between Heaven and Hell,* pp. 15–31.

Sliunin, N. V. *Okhotsko-Kamchatskii krai: Estestvenno-istoricheskoe opisanie.* 2 vols. St. Petersburg 1900.

Slovtsov, P. A. *Istoricheskoe obozrenie Sibiri.* 1839. Reprint. St. Petersburg, 1886.

Smesov, A. "Khatangskaia ekspeditsiia Akademii nauk." *SS*, no. 6 (1933): 40–45.

Smidovich, P. G. "Nashi zadachi na Severnykh okrainakh." *SS*, no. 3 (1932): 14–27.

——. "Soprovoditel'noe pis'mo mestnym komitetam severa." *SA*, no. 1–2 (1925): 130.

——. "Sotsialisticheskaia rekonstruktsiia Krainego Severa." *SS*, no. 1–2 (1932): 43–60.

——. "Sovetizatsiia Severa." *SS*, no. 1 (1930): 5–14.

Smirnoff, Eugene. *A Short Account of the Historical Development and Present Position of Russian Orthodox Missions.* London: Rivingtons, 1903.

Smoliak, A. V. "Ekspeditsiia Nevel'skogo 1850–1854 gg. i pervye etnograficheskie issledovaniia XIX v. v Priamur'e, Primor'e i na Sakhaline." *SE*, no. 3 (1954): 77–82.

——. *Etnicheskie protsessy u narodov Nizhnego Amura i Sakhalina: Seredina XIX-nachalo XX v.* Moscow: Nauka, 1975.

——. "Iuzhnye oroki." *SE*, no. 1 (1965): 28–42.

——. *Traditsionnoe khoziaistvo i material'naia kul'tura narodov Nizhnego Amura i Sakhalina: Etnograficheskii aspekt.* Moscow: Nauka, 1984.

——. *Ul'chi: Khoziaistvo, kul'tura i byt v proshlom i nastoiashchem.* Moscow: Nauka, 1966.

Sobranie uzakonenii i rasporiazhenii raboche-krest'ianskogo pravitel'stva RSFSR. In Russian Historical Sources 1928. Box 15, part 1. Microform collection. New York: Readex Microprint Corp., n.d.

Sokolova, Z. P. "Perestroika i sud'by malochislennykh narodov. Severa." *Istoriia SSSR,* no. 1 (1990): 155–66.

——. "Preobrazovaniia v khoziaistve, kul'ture i byte Obskikh ugrov." *SE,* no. 5 (1968): 25–39.

——, ed. *Etnokul'turnoe razvitie narodnostei Severa v usloviiakh nauchno-tekhnicheskogo progressa na perspektivu do 2005 g.* Moscow: Institut etnografii AN SSSR, 1989.

Solomon, Susan Gross. *The Soviet Agrarian Debate: A Controversy in Social Science, 1923–1929.* Boulder: Westview, 1977.

Solomonov, M. "Kul'tstroitel'stvo na Severe," *RN,* no. 10–11 (1932): 138–42.

Solzhenitsyn, A. I. *Arkhipelag Gulag.* Paris: YMCA Press, 1974.

"Sostoianie kolkhoznogo stroitel'stva v Iamal'skom okruge Uraloblasti." *SS,* no. 3 (1933): 107–8.

Sosunov, P. I. "Tobol'skii Sever." *SA,* no. 4 (1925): 76–83.

Sotsial'noe razvitie sel'skogo naseleniia Iakutskoi ASSR. Iakutsk: Iakutskoe knizhnoe izdatel'stvo, 1984.

"Soveshchanie ethnografov Leningrada i Moskvy." *E,* no. 2 (1929): 110–44.

"Soveshchanie po metodologii etnogeneticheskikh issledovanii v svete stalinskogo ucheniia o natsii i iazyke." *SE,* no. 4 (1951): 3–6.

"Soveshchanie po voprosam osedaniia kochevykh khoziaistv i zemleustroistva kolkhozov natsional'nykh respublik i oblastei." *RN,* no. 10 (1935): 83–89.

"Soveshchanie sibirskikh komitetov sodeistviia malym narodnostiam." *SA,* no. 4 (1925): 87–94.

"Sovetskaia shkola u tuzemtsev Tobol'skogo Severa." *SS,* no. 1 (1931): 45–46.

Sovetskii sever. Pervyi sbornik statei. Moscow: Komitet Severa, 1929.

Speranskii, M. M. "Pis'ma k docheri." *RA,* vol. 6 (1868): 1103–1212, 1681–1811.

"Sredi sibirskikh tuzemtsev." *ZhN,* no. 6 (1921): 104.

Stalin, I. V. *Marksizm i natsional'nyi vopros.* Moscow: Politizdat, 1950.

——. *Sochineniia.* 13 vols. Moscow: Politizdat, 1946–51. 3 vols. Stanford, Calif.: Hoover Institution, 1967.

Starovoitova, G. V. "K issledovaniiu etnopsikhologii gorodskikh zhitelei." *SE,* no. 3 (1976): 45–56.

Startsev, G. A. *Ostiaki: Sotsial'no-etnograficheskii ocherk.* Leningrad: Priboi, 1928.

"Status Deputatskoi Assamblei malochislennykh narodov Severa." Unpublished.

Stebakova, L. N., ed. *Tvorchestvo narodov Dal'nego Severa.* Magadan: Magadanskoe knizhnoe izdatel'stvo, 1958.

Stebnitskii, S. N. "Iz opyta raboty v shkole Severa (koriakskaia shkola). Zapiski uchitelia." *PN,* no. 8–9 (1932): 49–54.

Stepanov, A. P. *Eniseiskaia guberniia.* 2 vols. St. Petersburg, 1835.

Stepanov, N. N. "'Peshie Tungusy' Okhotskogo poberezh'ia v XVI–XIX vv." In Shunkov, ed., *Ekonomika.*

——. "Prisoedinenie Vostochnoi Sibiri v XVII v. i tungusskie plemena." In Okladnikov, ed., Russkoe naselenie Pomor'ia i Sibiri.

Stephan, John J. The Kuril Islands: Russo-Japanese Frontier in the Pacific. Oxford: Clarendon Press, 1974.

——. Sakhalin: A History. Oxford: Clarendon Press, 1971.

Stocking, George W., Jr. Race, Culture, and Evolution: Essays in the History of Anthropology. New York: Free Press, 1968.

——, ed., Romantic Motives: Essays on Anthropological Sensibility. Vol. 6 of History of Anthropology. Madison, University of Wisconsin Press, 1989.

Strakach, Iu. B. Narodnye traditsii i podgotovka sovremennykh promyslovo-sel'skokhoziaistvennykh kadrov. Taezhnye i tundrovye raiony Sibiri. Novosibirsk: Nauka, 1966.

Stralenberg, Philip Johan Tabbert von. Russia, Siberia, and Great Tartary. 1738. Reprint. New York: Arno.

Stukov, F. "Iz perepiski N. I. Il'minskogo s missionerami Vostochnoi Sibiri " PB, no. 18 (1895): 67–73.

Sushilin, N. "K voprosu o novoi granitse mezhdu Priangarskim kraem Kanskogo okruga i raionom Podkamennoi Tunguski." SA, no. 3 (1929): 114–25.

Suslov, Iv. M. "O natsional'noi prinadlezhnosti sovremennogo naseleniia severo-zapada Iakutskoi ASSR." SE, no. 2 (1952): 68–72.

——. "Raschet minimal'nogo kolichestva olenei, potrebnykh dlia tuzemnogo khoziaistva." SS, no. 3 (1930): 29–35.

——. "Shamanstvo i bor'ba s nim." SS, no. 3–4 (1931): 89–152.

——. "Sotsial'naia kul'tura u tungusov basseina Podkamennoi Tunguski i verkhov'ev r. Taimury." SA, no. 1 (1928): 55–64.

Svatikov, S. G. Rossiia i Sibir' (K istorii sibirskogo oblastnichestva v XIX v.). Prague: Izdatel'stvo Obshchestva sibiriakov v ChSR, 1929.

"Svet i teni v rabote Glavsevmorputi." SAr, no. 1 (1937): 8–12.

Szporluk, Roman. Communism and Nationalism: Karl Marx versus Friedrich List. New York: Oxford University Press, 1988.

Tabelev, V. F. "Na Iamal'skom Severe." SAr, no. 7 (1936): 11–23.

——. "Posledstviia sluchainogo podbora liudei." SAr, no. 2 (1938): 22–25.

Tadzhiev, S. "Novyi latinizirovanyi alfavit—moshchnoe orudie kul'turnoi revoliutsii." RN, no. 2 (1930): 64–67.

Takho-Godi, A. A. "Podgotovka vuzovskikh kadrov natsmen." RN, no. 6 (1930): 80–88.

Taksami, Ch. M. Nivkhi: Sovremennoe khoziastvo, kul'tura i byt. Leningrad: Nauka, 1967.

——. "O politicheskom i ekonomicheskom polozhenii malochislennykh narodov Severa i putiakh ikh razvitiia." In Materialy s"ezda malochislennykh narodov severa, pp. 7–22. Moscow: n.p., 1990.

——. Ot taezhnykh trop do Nevy. Leningrad: Leninizdat, 1976:

——. "Ustanovlenie sovetskoi vlasti i organizatsiia sovetov sredi nivkhov." In Velikii Oktiabr' i malye narody Krainego Severa, pp. 29–49.

——. "Vliianie khristianstva na traditsionnye verovaniia nivkhov." In Vdovin, ed., Khristianstvo i lamaizm.

Taleeva, "Polozhenie nenetskoi (samoedskoi) zhenshchiny." TT, no. 2 (1930): 127–29.

Taracouzio, Timothy A. Soviets in the Arctic. New York: Macmillan, 1938.

Tatishchev, A. "Amurskaia oblast' v kolonizatsionnom otnoshenii." VK, no. 5 (1909): 179–215.

Tatishchev, V. N. *Izbrannye proizvedeniia.* Leningrad: Nauka, 1979.
——. *Izbrannye trudy po geografii Rossii.* Moscow: Geografgiz, 1950.
——. "Razgovor dvu priiatelei o pol′ze nauki i uchilishchakh." In *Izbrannye proizvedeniia*, pp. 51–133. Leningrad: Nauka, 1979.
Taussig, Michael. *Shamanism, Colonialism, and the Wild Man: A Study in Terror and Healing.* Chicago: University of Chicago Press, 1980.
Telishev, I. "God raboty v Ostiatskoi shkole." *SS*, no. 5 (1932): 125–30.
——. "Teoreticheskie problemy stroitel′stva kommunizma v SSSR i zadachi sovetskikh etnografov." *SE*, no. 5 (1958): 8–16.
Terent′ev, A. "Na putiakh k vseobuchu v tundre." *PN*, no. 1 (1933): 24–30.
——. "Pogromy nentsami iasachnoi kazny v 1641 i 1642 gg." *SE*, no. 5–6 (1933): 67–75.
Terletskii, P. E. "Kul′tbazy Komiteta Severa." *SS*, no. 1 (1935): 36–47.
——. "K voprosu o parmakh Nenetskogo okruga." *SS*, no. 5 (1934): 35–44.
——. "K voprosu o stroitel′stve olenevodcheskikh kollektivnykh khoziaistv." *SS*, no. 11–12 (1931): 45–50.
——. *Naselenie Krainego Severa.* Leningrad: Institut narodov Severa, 1932.
——. "Natsional′noe raionirovanie Krainego Severa." *SS*, no. 7–8 (1930): 5–29.
——. "Osnovnye cherty khoziaistva Severa." *SS*, no. 9–12 (1930): 42–85.
Tillett, Lowell. *The Great Friendship: Soviet Historians on the Non-Russian Nationalities.* Chapel Hill: University of North Carolina Press, 1969.
Tishkov, Valery A. "The Crisis in Soviet Ethnography." *Current Anthropology* 33, no. 4 (1992): 371–82.
Titov, A. A., ed. *Sibir′ v XVII veke. Sbornik starinnykh russkikh statei o Sibiri i prilezhashchikh k nei zemliakh.* Moscow, 1890.
Tiurdenev, A. P. and V. P. Andreev. "Osnovnye napravleniia v razvitii sel′skogo i promyslovogo khoziaistva Severa SSSR." *Problemy Severa*, no. 13 (1968): 9–10.
Tobolaev, I. "V Tofalarskom raione." *SS*, no. 2 (1933): 94–96.
Todorov, Tzvetan. *The Conquest of America: The Question of the Other.* New York: Harper & Row, 1984.
Tokarev, S. A. *Istoriia russkoi etnografii. Dooktiabr′skii period.* Moscow: Nauka, 1966.
——. "K postanovke problem etnogeneza." *SE*, no. 3 (1949): 12–36.
——. "Obshchestvennyi stroi melaneziitsev. K voprosu o proiskhozhdenii klassov i gosudarstva." *E*, no. 2 (1929): 4–46.
Tokarev, S. A., and N. N. Cheboksarov. "Metodologiia etnogeneticheskikh issledovanii na materiale etnografii v svete rabot I. V. Stalina po voprosam iazykoznaniia." *SE*, no. 4 (1951): 7–26.
Tolmacheff, Innokenty P. *Siberian Passage: An Explorer's Search into the Russian Arctic.* New Brunswick: Rutgers University Press, 1949.
Tolstov, S. P. "Itogi perestroiki raboty Instituta etnografii AN SSSR v svete truda I. V. Stalina 'Marksizm i voprosy iazykoznaniia.'" *SE*, no. 3 (1951): 3–14.
——. "K probleme akkul′turatsii." *E*, no. 1–2 (1930): 63–87.
——. "K voprosu o periodizatsii istorii pervobytnogo obshchestva." *SE*, no. 1 (1946): 29.
——. "Problemy dorodovogo obshchestva." *SE*, no. 3–4 (1931): 69–103.
——. "Sorok let sovetskoi etnografii." *SE*, no. 5 (1957): 31–55.
——. "Sovetskai shkola v etnografii." *SE*, no. 4 (1947): 14–22.
——. "V. I. Lenin i aktual′nye problemy etnografii." *SE*, no. 1 (1949): 3–17.

———. "Znachenie trudov I. V. Stalina po voprosam iazykoznaniia dlia razvitiia sovetskoi etnografii." SE, no. 4 (1950): 3–23.

Tonkov, V. "Iz nenetskogo fol'klora." SAr, no. 11 (1936): 64–71.

Torgovnick, Marianna. Gone Primitive: Savage Intellects, Modern Lives. Chicago: University of Chicago Press, 1990.

Trainin, I."O plemennoi avtonomii." ZhN, no. 2 (1923): 19–26.

Treadgold, Donald W. The Great Siberian Migration: Government and Peasant in Resettlement from Emancipation to the First World War. Princeton; Princeton University Press, 1957.

Tret'iakov, P. "Turukhanskii krai." Zapiski IRGO po obshchei geografii 2 (1869): 215–531.

Triska, Jan F., ed. Soviet Communism: Programs and Rules. San Francisco, Chandler, 1962.

Trofimov, F. P. "Pushnozagotovki bez rukovodstva." SAr, no. 2 (1938): 15–18.

Troshev, Zhores. Bol'shoi Oshar. Krasnoiarsk: Krasnoiarskoe knizhnoe izdatel'stvo, 1987.

Trudy pravoslavnykh missii Vostochnoi Sibiri. 2 vols. 1883.

"Tsirkuliar oblispolkomam Leningradskoi i Obsko-Irtyshskoi oblastei, kraiispolkomam Severnogo, Zapadno-Sibirskogo, Vostochno-Sibirskogo i Dal'nevostochnogo kraev i TsIK Iakutskoi i Buriat-Mongol'skoi ASSR." SS, no. 5 (1934): 111–12.

Tugolukov, V. A. Idushchie poperek khrebtov. Krasnoiarsk: Krasnoiarskoe knizhnoe izdatel'stvo 1980.

———. Kto vy, iukagiry? Moscow: Nauka, 1979.

———. "Poezdka k okhotskim evenkam i evenam." SE, no. 3 (1956): 142–46.

———. Review of Naiodyre traditsii, by Iu. B. Strakach. SE, no. 3 (1968): 150–53.

———. Review of Perekhod k sotsializmu malykh narodnostei Severa, by V. P. Uvachan. SE, no. 4 (1959): 143–44.

———. Sledopyty verkhom na oleniakh. Moscow: Nauka, 1969.

Tyler, Stephen. "On Being Out of Words." Cultural Anthropology 1, no. 1 (1986): 131–37.

Tyvlianto, P. "Rabota kochevykh sovetov v Chukotskom natsional'nom okruge." TT, no. 4 (1932).

Ubriatova, E. "Neuklonno provodit' leninsko-stalinskuiu natsional'nuiu politiku." SAr, no. 12 (1937): 33–40.

Ul'ianov, G. "Nabolevshie voprosy." PN, no. 1 (1929): 46–52.

Unterberger, P. F. Priamurskii krai, 1906–1910. St. Petersburg, 1912.

———. Primorskaia oblast' 1856–1898. St. Petersburg, 1900.

"Uroki Semenchukovshchiny." SAr, no. 7 (1936): 3–7.

Ushakov, G. "V lagere Shmidta." SS, no. 4 (1934): 66–78.

Usova, K. I. "Rebenok-tungus v shkole." P, no. 2 (1930): 187–94.

"Ustav Deputatskoi Assamblei malochislennykh narodov Severa," 7 May 1991. Unpublished.

"Ustav ob upravlenii inorodtsev (1822)." In PSZ, 38, no. 29.126.

"Ustav Pravoslavnogo missionerskogo obshchestva." PB, no. 1 (1893): 12–20.

Ustiugov, P. K., "Podgotovka piatiletnego plana severnogo khoziaistva." SS, no. 2 (1931): 30–44.

———. Puti sotsialisticheskoi rekonstruktsii khoziaistva malykh narodnostei Severa. Moscow: Vlast' sovetov, 1931.

———. "Samokritika na suglanakh." SS, no. 7–8 (1930): 33–59.

———. "Tuzemnye sovety i zadachi ikh ukrepleniia." SS, no. 9–12 (1930): 5–41

——. "Zadachi natsional'noi raboty na Krainem Severe." *RN*, no. 1 (1931): 40–49.

Uvachan, V. N. *Perekhod k sotsializmu malykh narodov Severa: Po materialam Evenkiiskogo i Taimyrskogo natsional'nykh okrugov.* Moscow: Gospolitizdat, 1958.

——. *Put' narodov Severa k sotsializmu: Opyt sotsialisticheskogo stroitel'stva na Eniseiskom Severe.* Moscow: Mysl', 1971.

"V Institute narodov Severa." *SS*, no. 1 (1931): 130–34.

"V Komitete Severa pri Prezidiume VTsIK." *SS*, no. 1 (1933): 125–27; no. 2 (1933): 99–102.

"V Komitete Severa." *SS*, no. 1 (1935): 106–10.

"V natsional'nykh okrugakh i raionakh." *SS*, no. 1 (1933): 127–31.

"V natsional'nykh okrugakh." *SS*, no. 6 (1933): 78–80.

"V Taimyrskom okruge." *SS*, no. 3 (1934): 84.

V. "Neobkhodimo raskachat'sia." *ORS*, no. 6 (1929): 10–12.

V. A. "U chukoch v Chaunskoi gube." *SS*, no. 2 (1935): 60–64.

V. B.-T [Bogoraz (-Tan), V. G.], "Severnyi rabfak (Severnoe otdelenie rabfaka Leningradskogo instituta zhivykh vostochnykh iazykov)." *SA*, no. 2 (1927): 52–63.

Vagin, V. I. *Istoricheskie svedeniia o deiatel'nosti grafa M. M. Speranskogo v Sibiri s 1819 po 1822 god.* 2 vols. St. Petersburg, 1872.

Vagner, Nikolai. *Izbrannye prizvedeniia v 2kh tomakh.* Leningrad: Khudozhestvennaia literatura, 1973.

Vakhnina, V. "Komu nuzhny sanktsii?" *SP*, no. 4 (1987): 4.

Vakhrusheva, M. "Na beregu Maloi Iukondy." In *My—liudi Severa.*

Val'diu, Aleksei. *Svet v okne.* Khabarovsk: Khabarovskoe knizhnoe izdatel'stvo, 1984.

Valitov, A. M. "Pedologicheskie izvrashcheniia v izuchenii detei-natsionalov." *RN*, no. 10 (1936): 44–49.

Vasil'ev, B. A. "Osnovnye cherty etnografii orokov." *E*, no. 1 (1929): 3–22.

Vasil'ev, N. V. "Kharakter i tendentsii sotsial'no-professional'nykh peremeshchenii evenskoi i evenkiiskoi molodezhi." In Boiko, ed. *Sel'skaia molodezh'.*

Vasil'ev, V. I., Iu. B. Simchenko, and Z. P. Sokolova. "Problemy rekonstruktsii byta malykh narodov krainego Severa." *SE*, no. 3 (1966): 9–22.

Vasilevich, G. M. *Evenki. Istoriko-etnograficheskie ocherki (XVIII–nachalo XX).* Leningrad: Nauka, 1969.

——. "Evenki-poety i perevodchiki." *SE*, no. 1 (1950): 124–36.

——. "Na Nizhnei Tunguske." *SA*, no. 5–6 (1926): 150–57.

——. "Symskie tungusy." *SS*, no. 2 (1931): 132–47.

——, ed. *Istoricheskii fol'klor evenkov: Skazaniia i predaniia.* Moscow and Leningrad: Nauka, 1966.

Vdovin, I. S. *Istoriia izucheniia paleoaziatskikh iazykov.* Moscow: AN SSSR, 1954.

——. *Ocherki etnicheskoi istorii koriakov.* Leningrad: Nauka, 1973.

——. *Ocherki istorii i etnografii chukchei.* Moscow and Leningrad: Nauka, 1965.

——. "Vliianie khristianstva na religiozne verovaniia chukchei i koriakov." In Vdovin, ed., *Khristianstvo i lamaizm.*

——, ed. *Khristianstvo i lamaizm u korennogo naseleniia Sibiri.* Leningrad: Nauka, 1979.

Vedushchaia rol' russkogo naroda v razvitii narodov Iakutii. Iakutsk: Ia-kutskoe knizhnoe izdatel'stvo, 1955.

Velikii Oktiabr' i malye narody Krainego Severa. Leningradskii gosudarstvennyi pedagogicheskii institut im. A. I. Gertsena. Uchenye zapiski, vol. 353. 1967.

Venedikt, Ieromonakh. "U chukchei." *PB*, no. 5 (1895): 248–54.

Veniamin, Arkhiepiskop Irkutskii i Nerchinskii. *Zhiznennye voprosy pravoslavnoi missii v Sibiri.* St. Petersburg, 1885.

Veniamin, Arkhmandrit. "Samoiedy mezenskie." In *Vestnik IRGO*, part 14 (1855). [HRAF RU4, no. 5].

Veniukov, M. I. *Puteshestviia po okrainam russkoi Azii i zapiski o nikh.* St. Petersburg, 1868.

———. *Rossiia i Vostok. Sobranie geograficheskikh i politicheskikh statei M. Veniukova.* St. Petersburg, 1877.

Ventskovskii, P. V. "Pedagogicheskoe izuchenie natsmen." *PN*, no. 7–8 (1930): 98–100.

Vesin, L. P. *Istoricheskii obzor uchebnikov obshchei i russkoi geografii, izdannykh so vremeni Petra Velikogo po 1876 g.* St. Petersburg, 1877.

Vesnovskii. "Mashel-Pel'tesh." *ORS*, no. 6 (1929): 24–27.

Vilenskii-Sibiriakov, V. D. "Inorodcheskii vopros v Sibiri." *ZhN*, no. 30 (1920): 87.

———. "Samoopredelenie iakutov." *ZhN*, no. 3 (1921).

———. "Zadachi izucheniia malykh narodnostei Severa." *E*, no. 1 (1926): 55–60.

———. "Zadachi izucheniia Severnoi Azii." *SA*, no. 1–2 (1925): 7–19.

Vinokurov I., and F. Florich. *Podvig admirala Nevel'skogo.* Moscow: Goskul'-prosvetizdat, 1951.

Vladimirtsov, B. Ia. *Obshchestvennyi stroi mongolov: Mongol'skii kochevoi feodalizm.* Leningrad: AN SSSR, 1934.

Vlasova, V. F. "Eskimosy o-va Vrangelia." *SAr*, no. 5 (1935): 60–65.

Voblov, I. "Eskimosskaia byl'." *SAr*, no. 9 (1937): 56–61.

Volkova, N. G. "Etnicheskaii istoriia: Soderzhanie poniatiia." *SE*, no. 5 (1985): 16–25.

Volodarskii, S. A. "Likvidirovat' negramotnost' sredi narodov Severa." *SAr*, no. 2 (1938): 29–30.

Vol'skii, Al. "Na Taimyre." *SAr*, no. 11 (1936): 27–30.

———. "Po Khatangskoi trope." *SAr*, no. 9 (1937): 40–48.

Vorob'ev, N. I. "K voprosu ob etnograficheskom izuchenii kolkhoznogo krest'-ianstva." *SE*, no. 1 (1952): 142–46.

Voronin, A. "Nasha rabota letom." *TT*, no. 1 (1928): 4–5.

———. "Zhizn' evenkov-murchenov." *TT*, no. 1 (1928): 23–27.

Voskoboinikov, M. G. "Narody Sovetskogo Krainego severa o Lenine i Staline." *SE*, no. 4 (1949): 95–101.

"Vos'moi rasshirennyi plenum Komiteta Severa." *SS*, no. 6 (1931): 128–63.

Vrangel', F. P. *Puteshestvie po Severnym beregam Sibiri i Ledovitomu moriu.* Moscow: Glavsevmorput', 1948.

"Vrednaia p'esa iz zhizni luoravetlanov." *SE*, no. 4 (1937).

"Vremennoe polozhenie ob upravlenii tuzemnykh plemen, prozhivaiushchikh na territorii Dal'nevostochnoi oblasti." In *Dal'revkom. Pervyi etap.*

"Vremennoe polozhenie ob upravlenii tuzemnykh narodnostei i plemen Severnykh okrain RSFSR." *SA*, no. 2 (1927): 85–91.

"Vseobuch na Krainem Severe." *SS*, no. 5 (1933): 94–96.

Vucinich, Alexander. "Soviet Ethnographic Studies of Cultural Change." *AA*, 62, no. 5 (1960).

Vucinich, W. S., ed. *Russia and Asia: Essays of the Influence of Russia on the Asian Peoples*. Stanford: Hoover Institution Press, 1972.

"Vul'garizatory v poze marksistov," *Pravda*, 9 December 1954.

"Vvedenie pis'mennosti na rodnom iazyke dlia narodov Severa." *SS*, no. 3 (1932): 133.

Vvedenskii, A. A. *Dom Stroganovykh v XVI–XVII vekakh*. Moscow: Izdatel'stvo sotsial'no-ekonomicheskoi literatury, 1962.

Vyshinskii, A. Ia. *Sudebnye rechi*. Moscow: Izdatel'stvo iuridicheskoi literatury, 1948.

Vyucheiskii, I. "Slet udarnikov olenevodstva." *SS*, no. 2 (1934): 90–94.

Watrous, Stephen D. "The Regionalist Conception of Siberia, 1860 to 1920." In Diment and Slezkine, eds., *Between Heaven and Hell*, pp. 113–32.

———. "Russia's 'Land of the Future': Regionalism and the Awakening of Siberia, 1819–1894." Ph.D. diss., University of Washington, 1970.

———. ed. *John Ledyard's Journey through Russia and Siberia, 1787–1788. The Journal and Selected Letters*. Madison: University of Wisconsin Press, 1966.

White, David Gordon. *Myths of the Dog-Man*. Chicago: University of Chicago Press, 1991.

White, Hayden. "The Forms of Wildness: Archaeology of an Idea." In Dudley and Novak, eds., *The Wild Man Within*, pp. 3–38.

Wood, Alan, ed. *The History of Siberia from Russian Conquest to Revolution*. London: Routledge, 1991.

Wood, Alan, and R. A. French, eds. *The Development of Siberia: People and Resources*. London: Macmillan, 1989.

Wrangell [Vrangel'], Ferdinand von. *Narrative of an Expedition to the Polar Sea in the Years 1820, 1821, 1822, and 1823*. London, 1844.

"Za leninskuiu natsional'nuiu politiku (po materialam KK RKI Tobol'skogo okruga)." *SS*, no. 9 (1931).

"Za liniiu partii v kolkhoznom stroitel'stve na Krainem Severe." *SS*, no. 4 (1933): 3–8.

"Za tesnoe sotrudnichestvo etnografov i istorikov." *SE*, no. 3 (1953): 3–8.

"Zadachi etnografov v sviazi s polozheniem na muzeinom fronte." *SE*, no. 2 (1948): 3–7.

Zadornov, Nikolai. *Sobranie sochinenii*. 6 vols. Moscow: Khudozhestvennaia literatura, 1977.

Zaitsev, V. A. "Otvet moim obviniteliam po povodu moego mneniia o tsvetnykh plemenakh." *Russkoe slovo*, no. 12 (1964): 20–24, 81–82.

Zalkind, E. M. "Iasachnaia politika tsarizma v Buriatii v XVIII–pervoi polovine XIX vv." In Shunkov, ed., *Ekonomika, upravlenie*, pp. 236–48.

"Zapiska Predsedatelia Soveta ministrov i glavnoupravliaiushchego zemleustroistvom i zemledeliem o poezdke v Sibir' v 1910 g." *VK*, no. 8 (1911): 277–335.

Zavalishin, A. Iu. "Ob istokakh sovremennykh problem narodov Sibiri i Dal'nego Vostoka." *Istoriia SSSR*, no. 3 (1991): 50–63.

Zavalishin, Dmitrii. "Kaliforniia v 1824 godu." In *RV* 60 (November 1865): 322–68.

Zdravomyslova, O. M., and V. B. Kozlov. "O metodakh izucheniia obraza zhizni korennykh narodnostei Severa." In *Regional'nye problemy sotsial'no-demograficheskogo razvitiia, pp. 114–17. Moscow: Institut sotsiologicheskikh issledovanii AN SSSR, 1987.

Zelenin, D. K. "V. G. Bogoraz—etnograf i fol'klorist." In Pamiati Bogoraza (1865–1936). Sbornik statei. Moscow and Leningrad: AN SSSR, 1937.

Zenzinov, Vladimir, with Isaac Don Levine. The Road to Oblivion. New York: Robert M. McBride, 1933.

Zhdanova, N. T. "Vrednaia vylazka B. V. Lavrova v Moskovskom Dome uchenykh." SAr, no. 9 (1937): 9.

Zibarev, V. A. Bol'shaia sud'ba malykh narodov. Novosibirsk: Zapadno-Sibirskoe knizhnoe izdatel'stvo, 1972.

——. "Izmeneniia sotsial'noi struktury malykh narodov severa." In Leninskaia natsional'naia politika KPSS i malye narody Severa, vol. 2. Tomsk: Izdatel'stvo Tomskogo universiteta, 1984.

——. Sovetskoe stroitel'stvo u malykh narodnostei Severa, 1917–1932. Tomsk: TGU, 1969.

——. "Sovetskoe stroitel'stvo u malykh narodnostei Severa (1927–1930)." In Sibir' v period stroitel'stva sotsializma i perekhoda k kommunizmu, vol. 6.

Zinger, M. E. Osnovnye zakony po Krainemu Severu. Leningrad: GUSMP, 1935.

——. Severnye rasskazy. Moscow: Sovetskii pisatel', 1938.

Zisser, V. P. "Brodiachie tungusy Charinskogo nagor'ia." ORS, no. 3 (1929): 50–52.

——. "Sredi Verkhne-Kolymskikh tungusov." SS, no. 1 (1934): 112–14.

Zolotarev, A. "Perezhitki rodovogo stroia u giliakov raiona Chome." SS, no. 2 (1933): 52–69.

——. "Propaganda idealizma pod markoi Akademii nayk." IM, no. 5–6 (1937): 201–2.

Zuev, V. F. Materialy po etnografii Sibiri XVIII veka (1771–1772). AN SSSR. Trudy Instituta etnografii im. N. N. Miklukho-Maklaia. Novaia seriia, vol. 5. Moscow-Leningrad: AN SSSR, 1947.

Index

Abramzon, S. M., 312
Academy of the History of Material Culture, 250, 252
Acosta, José de, 36
Addison, Joseph, 57
Agishev, R. K., 363
Agriculture, native labor in, 24, 276–77
Aian, 280
Ainu, 78n, 139
Aipin, Eremei D., 369 373–74, 382–83
Aitmatov, Chingiz, 330
Alachev, Dmitrii, 18
Alaska, 97, 106, 168, 324, 326–27, 329, 380
Alazeia, 48
Aldan, 164
Aleksandriia, 33
Aleut, 1, 3
Alexander I, 81
Alexander III, 120, 392
Alexander the Great, 11
All-Russian Conference on Archaeology and Ethnography, May 1932, 257–58. See also Anthropologists
Ambarchik, 276
Amderma, 275
America, 54, 114, 168 329–30; Americans, 107, 133, 328–29
Amur, 2–3, 7, 14, 38n, 76, 95–97, 100–102, 108, 132, 326–28, 349, 368, 373; Amur peoples, 5, 96–97, 173, 272
Anadyr' (Anadyrsk), 17, 28n, 48, 62n
Andaman islands, 33
"Aniko from the Nogo Clan" (Nerkagi), 369–71
Anthropologists: and the concept of sur-

vivals, 259–61; and "cosmopolitanism," 311–12; Cossacks as, 38–40, 62–63; Cultural Revolution among, 252–63; on ethnicity, 310–11, 315–16, 320, 322–23, 346–48; and evolutionism, 124, 248; and folkloric studies, 123–24, 311; and Lysenkoism, 314; and Marxism, 249–50, 254, 257–58; as "missionaries of socialism," 159–60, 167–68, 172; and the Narkomnats, 147; and Perestroika, 371–72, 376–85; purges of, 253, 263, 290–91; and Siberian exile, 124–26; as Soviet officials, 149–50; training of, 160–63, 197
Anuchin, D. N., 160
Aptekar', V. D., 250, 252
Arakcheev, A. A., 81
Argentov, Andrei, 90
Argippaei, 33
Arimaspi, 33
Arkhangel'sk, 12, 173, 276
Arkticheskaia etnoekologiia (Krupnik), 382n
Arsen'ev, V. K., 127, 360–61. See also *Dersu Uzala*
Association of the Numerically Small Peoples of the North, 379, 384
Astrakhan', 12
Atlasov (Otlasov), Vladimir, 50
Autonomization, 143, 146, 221
Aventures de Télémaque (Fénelon), 66
Azhaev, V. N., 328n
Aztecs, 35, 40

Bagmut, Ivan, 204
Baikal, 373

447